*International Human Rights Law*

PENNSYLVANIA STUDIES IN HUMAN RIGHTS
Bert B. Lockwood, Jr., Series Editor

A complete list of books in the series is available from the publisher.

# *International Human Rights Law*

## An Introduction

DAVID WEISSBRODT AND
CONNIE DE LA VEGA

**PENN**

University of Pennsylvania Press

Philadelphia

Copyright © 2007 David Weissbrodt and Constance de la Vega

All rights reserved. Except for brief quotations used for purposes of review or scholarly citation, none of this book may be reproduced in any form by any means without written permission from the publisher.

Published by
University of Pennsylvania Press
Philadelphia, Pennsylvania 19104-4112

10  9  8  7  6  5  4  3  2  1

A Cataloging-in-Publication Record is available from the Library of Congress

ISBN: 978-0-8122-2120-6

# Contents

Preface    ix


I. BASIC INTRODUCTION TO INTERNATIONAL HUMAN RIGHTS    1

A. **Introduction to Human Rights as Part of International Law**    3
   1. Sources of Law and Enforcement    4
   2. Why Have Nations Agreed to Grant Human Rights?    6
   3. The Role of Other Organizations and Individuals    8
   4. Criminal Sanctions for Perpetrators of Human Rights Abuses    9

B. **Overview and History of International Human Rights**    14
   1. Early Development—From the Ten Commandments to the Treaty of Westphalia    14
      a. *Protection of Aliens*    16
      b. *Protection of Minorities*    16
      c. *Human Rights Guarantees in National Laws*    16
      d. *Abolition of Slavery and Women's Rights*    17
      e. *Protection of Victims of Armed Conflict*    17
   2. World War I, the League of Nations, and Self-Determination    18
   3. The Interwar Years    19
   4. World War II and the Beginning of the Modern Human Rights Movement    20
      a. *The Nuremberg and Tokyo Tribunals, and Control Council Law No. 10*    23
      b. *The Creation of the United Nations: Dumbarton Oaks and San Francisco*    23
   5. The United Nations and Multilateral Protection of Human Rights    24

II. HUMAN RIGHTS CATEGORIZED BY PARTICULAR
RIGHTS, RESPONSIBILITIES, AND GROUPS   27

A. **Categorized by Particular Rights and Responsibilities**   29
   1. Self-Determination (Covenants, Art. 1)   29
   2. Equality and Nondiscrimination (Universal Declaration, Arts. 1, 2, 6, 7)   34
   3. Life (Universal Declaration, Art. 3)   38
   4. Slavery and Forced Labor (Universal Declaration, Art. 4)   42
      a. *Violations of Other Fundamental Rights Associated with Slavery*   45
      b. *Forced Labor*   47
      c. *Application of Prohibitions Against Slavery and Forced Labor*   49
   5. Torture and Ill-Treatment (Universal Declaration, Art. 5)   53
   6. Procedural Fairness in the Criminal Process and the Administration of Justice (Universal Declaration, Arts. 8, 9, 10, 11)   59
   7. Detention and Imprisonment (Universal Declaration, Art. 9)   63
   8. Privacy (Universal Declaration, Art. 12)   67
   9. Freedom of Movement—Travel (Universal Declaration, Art. 13)   70
      a. *The Right to Movement and Residence Within National Borders*   70
      b. *The Right to Leave*   71
      c. *The Right to Return to One's Country*   72
   10. Asylum and Refugee Status (Universal Declaration, Art. 14)   74
   11. Nationality (Universal Declaration, Art. 15)   82
   12. Protection of the Family (Universal Declaration, Art. 16)   87
   13. Property (Universal Declaration, Art. 17)   91
   14. Freedom of Religion and Belief (Universal Declaration, Art. 18)   97
   15. Freedom of Expression (Universal Declaration, Art. 19)   102
   16. Freedom of Association and Assembly (Universal Declaration, Art. 20)   109
   17. Political Participation and Voting (Universal Declaration, Art. 21)   113
   18. Economic, Social, and Cultural Rights (Universal Declaration, Art. 4, 22–27)   120
      a. *Work-Related Rights (Universal Declaration, Art. 23) and Rest (Art. 24)*   124
      b. *Social Security (Universal Declaration, Arts. 22, 25)*   129
      c. *Health (Universal Declaration, Art. 25)*   136

        d. *Food (Universal Declaration, Art. 25)*   144
        e. *Clothing (Universal Declaration, Art. 25)*   150
        f. *Housing (Universal Declaration, Art. 25)*   156
        g. *Water*   163
        h. *Education (Universal Declaration, Art. 26)*   169
        i. *Culture (Universal Declaration, Art. 27)*   177
    19. Healthy Environment   189
    20. Sustainable Development   197
    21. Peace   203
    22. Humanitarian Law   212
        a. *Four Categories of Armed Conflicts*   212
        b. *Summary of Humanitarian Law Protections Under Different Kinds of Armed Conflict*   214
    23. Genocide, War Crimes, Crimes Against Humanity, and Crimes Against Peace   222
        a. *Genocide*   222
        b. *War Crimes*   225
        c. *Crimes Against Humanity*   227
        d. *Crimes Against Peace*   229
        e. *Criminal Tribunals*   229
        f. *Sample of Jurisprudence*   231
    24. Security/Terrorism and Human Rights   234

B. **Groups at Risk**   244


III. PROCEDURES FOR IMPLEMENTATION OF HUMAN RIGHTS   247

A. **International Procedures**   251
    1. UN Charter-Based Procedures   252
        a. *General Assembly*   252
        b. *Security Council*   254
        c. *Commission on Human Rights and Its Sub-Commission*   255
        d. *Human Rights Council*   263
        e. *Commission on the Status of Women*   266
        f. *Commission on Crime Prevention and Criminal Justice*   266
        g. *Secretary-General*   267
        h. *High Commissioner for Human Rights*   267
        i. *International Court of Justice*   268
    2. Human Rights Treaty-Based Procedures   271
    3. Specialized and Other Agencies   279
        a. *International Labor Organization*   279
        b. *UN Educational, Scientific and Cultural Organization*   284
        c. *UN High Commissioner for Refugees*   285

viii    Contents

        d. *International Financial Institutions—International Monetary Fund, World Bank, and World Trade Organization*    286
        e. *Other Specialized Agencies*    291
    4. World Conferences    293
    5. International Criminal Procedures    296
        a. *Nuremberg, Tokyo, and Other Post-World War II Developments*    296
        b. *Former Yugoslavia and Rwanda*    297
        c. *International Criminal Court*    301
        d. *Mixed (International and National) Tribunals*    303

**B.  Regional Institutions and Procedures**    311
    1. European Mechanisms    311
        a. *Council of Europe*    312
        b. *European Union*    321
        c. *Organization for Security and Cooperation in Europe*    323
    2. Mechanisms for the Americas    325
        a. *Inter-American Commission on Human Rights*    327
        b. *Inter-American Court of Human Rights*    331
        c. *Other OAS Procedures*    333
    3. African Mechanisms    334
        a. *African Commission on Human and Peoples' Rights*    334
        b. *African Court on Human and Peoples' Rights*    336
    4. Other Regional Mechanisms    338

**C.  National Institutions and Procedures**    342
    1. Constitutional Protections for Human Rights    342
    2. Role of Courts and Legislatures in Applying International Human Rights Law    343
    3. National Human Rights Institutions    346

**D.  Truth and Reconciliation Commissions**    352

**E.  Nongovernmental Organizations**    359


IV. CONCLUSION    363


Notes    371

Index of Subjects and Sources    415

Acknowledgments    433

# Preface

Nelson Mandela was released after twenty-six years of imprisonment for his opposition to apartheid in South Africa. Aung San Suu Kyi has been held in house arrest because the government of Burma refused to acknowledge that her political party won the last fair election in that country. Archbishop Oscar Romero was assassinated as he was saying mass in El Salvador. Young women of Kosovo were systematically raped at a Serb army camp. U.S. soldiers exchanged photographs of detainees they had tortured and degraded in Iraq. A child is compelled to leave primary school and work long hours in a brick factory. A union leader is killed because of her efforts to organize at a factory. A refugee is forced to return to his country of origin despite his well-founded fear of political persecution. A woman with AIDS is deprived of medical treatment that will prevent transmission of her illness to her infant. An indigenous leader is not permitted to worship in his holy place. A group of people left the appalling conditions in which they were living and occupied someone else's land, but were then evicted and left homeless.

How should we think about these events? What can we do to prevent such suffering? Are there any remedies or other recourse?

International human rights is the first worldview which has attained universal acceptance. Religious, political, philosophical, and economic ideas have adherents in parts of the globe, but human rights represents an idea that has attained general acceptance. The idea of human rights permits us to understand the difficulties we must face and join with others in campaigning to stop abuses. Human rights law helps prevent violations, punish violators, and afford some relief to victims.

This book provides an introduction to human rights. It is intended for people who want to consider how they can improve situations in which their rights might be endangered or how to respond when others are placed at risk. As Elie Wiesel said when he accepted the Nobel Peace Prize in 1986, it is sometimes necessary "to speak truth to power."

The book first provides a basic history and places human rights in the context of international law. It then discusses the most important human rights and responsibilities. Next, it looks briefly at the various groups that may be at risk. And third, it discusses the institutions and procedures for protecting against or remedying violations.

Because the format is intended for a wide audience, the book generally contains citations only to quotations, cases, and other principal sources, not to secondary sources—even where such citations clearly exist. The end of each chapter, however, identifies the most useful print and Web references. Web links cited in the book were active as of 2007. Several portions of the book rely heavily upon updates of the authors' writings elsewhere.

# Part I
# Basic Introduction to International Human Rights

# A. Introduction to Human Rights as Part of International Law

Many observers regard the formation of the United Nations in 1945 and the promulgation of the Universal Declaration of Human Rights in 1948[1] as the beginning of the modern struggle to protect human rights. One can, however, trace the origins of human rights back to early philosophical and religious ideas as well as legal theories of the "natural law"—a law higher than the "positive law" of states (such as legislation). According to those theories, positive laws must either be derived from or reflect "natural law" because individuals have certain immutable rights as human beings. Whether human rights and the corresponding duties find their source in positive laws or in some underlying moral imperative, human rights precepts and procedures can still help answer such basic questions as: How can one identify or understand an injustice? What can one do about the injustices that are experienced in one's own life or that others are suffering? Can something be done to understand, prevent, and remedy these events?

For more than half a century the world community has codified a series of fundamental precepts that are intended to prevent such grave abuses as arbitrary killing, torture, discrimination, starvation, and forced eviction. Standards have also been developed for positive rights such that governments can provide the means for assuring, for example, fair trials, education, and health care. Gradually over the same period the United Nations, other international organizations, regional institutions, and governments have developed various procedures for protecting against and providing remedies for human rights abuses.

To comprehend, prevent, and remedy injustice we need to understand human rights and how they can be vindicated. Accordingly, after introducing the basic rights, part II of this book contains a series of short chapters that summarize the applicable law and identify some of the most important issues that have arisen. The book does not attempt a comprehensive and exhaustive treatment of each subject because many subjects would require an entire book on their own, but at minimum it is meant to provide a point of departure in understanding many important aspects of human rights.

4   Introduction

Once relevant principles have, for example, been set forth in a treaty, it is still necessary to determine how to apply those principles to a concrete problem or situation. Part III covers procedures for implementation at the international, regional, and national level. Human rights are a domain of international law, so it is necessary to have a basic understanding of international law and its relationship to national and local laws which may apply in a particular case.

## 1. Sources of Law and Enforcement

The principal sources of international law are treaties and custom. As the most important source of international law, treaties are agreements between nations that are intended to have binding legal effect between the governments that have formally agreed to them. The most important treaty in the world is the United Nations Charter,[2] which established the United Nations. Nearly every nation in the world (except for example, the Vatican) has ratified the Charter, and it prevails over any conflicting treaty. The UN Charter is a multilateral treaty among all the UN member nations, as distinguished from a bilateral treaty between two nations. Among the most important human rights treaties drafted by the United Nations are the International Covenant on Economic, Social and Cultural Rights[3] and the International Covenant on Civil and Political Rights.[4] Those two human rights covenants have been ratified by 155 and 160 nations respectively. The covenants with the Universal Declaration of Human Rights comprise the International Bill of Human Rights. International law can also be formed by the customary practices of nations widely accepted as a matter of legal obligation.

The most effective mechanism for enforcing international law is for each ratifying government to incorporate its treaties and customary obligations into national laws. For example, the Constitution of the Netherlands states that any ratified treaty is part of the national law and prevails even over the constitution.[5] Other nations consider treaties to have the same status as statutes, such that they may be asserted in any court and must be followed by the governmental administration unless there is a more recent statute or treaty. Countries that automatically make international law a part of their national laws have been characterized as taking a "monist" approach to international law. Most monist countries follow the civil law tradition derived from Roman law and include such nations as: Austria, Belgium, Luxembourg, France, and Germany.

Many other nations, particularly those countries that follow the common law tradition begun in the United Kingdom and spread later to most former British colonies, such as Australia, Canada, India, New Zealand, and Sri Lanka, generally follow a "dualist" approach to international law. Although those nations ordinarily consider international law as binding between governments, it may not be asserted by individual residents of the country in national courts unless the legislature or other branch of government makes it national law or regulation.

Even the United Kingdom, however, is not entirely dualist in its approach, since it has accepted all of European Union law as part of its national law which may be directly applied by the courts and administration. European Union law contains quite a number of human rights principles that may be directly enforced in British courts. As to other aspects of human rights law, however, the British Parliament adopted the Human Rights Act 1998,[6] which legislated almost all of the European Convention on Human Rights[7] into UK law that may be asserted in any court. While the United Kingdom has also ratified a number of other human rights treaties, such as the International Covenant on Civil and Political Rights, it has not legislated most of those treaties into national law. Hence, if the United Kingdom violates one of those other treaties, it would not ordinarily be subject to national legal action.

Violations of international law by dualist nations remain violations of international law, but they can only be asserted at the international level. The different individuals and groups briefly identified in Part II B of this book may assert violations of human rights treaties by means of the procedures discussed later in Part III.

In addition to nations that are principally monist or dualist, there are also some countries, such as Japan and the United States, that take a compromise position in which they pursue some aspects of each approach. The U.S. Constitution provides that treaties are the "supreme Law of the Land."[8] Courts will generally not give effect to a treaty ratified by the U.S. government unless the treaty has been implemented by legislation (that is, the dualist approach) or unless the courts find that the particular provision of the treaty is self-executing (that is, the monist approach).

Whether one lives in a dualist or a monist nation, the existence of a law does not assure that there will be 100 percent compliance. After all, people do not always obey commonplace national laws, and failures to comply are not always the subject of prosecution or other methods of enforcement. In some respects, international law does have weaker methods of implementation than are ordinarily associated with the enforcement of national law. The lack of adequate enforcement may be one reason for serious human rights violations.

Does that mean we should not care about international human rights law? Human rights law provides a set of globally agreed norms, which, even if not always enforced, can and do still declare certain conduct to be abhorrent. The ability to identify standards and violations of those standards constitutes a powerful weapon of deterrence. By declaring that certain activities violate agreed principles of international human rights law, we can persuade governmental authorities to (1) establish national law to accord with those principles, (2) interpret national law along the same lines, and (3) enforce those laws in a way that will avoid national and international criticism. Human rights law provides us with important tools for norm setting, persuasion, threats of embarrassment, embarrassment, and possibly punishment.

Treaties and other human rights instruments help to identify those norms and establish standards that will protect our rights. As a matter of terminology, multilateral treaties are the most visible sort of standard-setting "instrument" in the human rights field. The United Nations and other international organizations also adopt other international instruments or norm-creating standards called declarations, rules, principles, or resolutions, as well as other documents, which interpret treaties or may begin the process of creating international customary law.

## 2. Why Have Nations Agreed to Grant Human Rights?

It is rather remarkable, even counterintuitive, that governments have agreed among themselves to establish a vast array of international human rights principles that have the impact of limiting their capacity to deal with their own residents. Why have governments been so willing to establish norms and comply with them—at least some of the time? There are some political theorists who believe that governments follow *realpolitik* principles in which they act only out of their own rational self-interest. If that view were entirely correct, governments would never draft, promulgate, or ratify human rights law unless they gain some benefit. But governments do, indeed, benefit from joining the preparation and ratification of human rights treaties because they gain positive publicity and even economic advantages. Governments are motivated to show that they are fulfilling the expectation of the international community, so they draft and ratify human rights treaties at the same time as they join other countries in agreeing to trade, security, and other accords reflecting international cooperation. In contrast to the *realpolitik* analysis, some theorists have argued that governments agree to ratify and implement human rights law, because providing for human rights is a requisite condition on legitimacy of a government. Those governments that acknowledge this condition might take part in the drafting, promulgation and ratification of human rights law not simply out of the need to appear legitimate and decent, but out of a genuine concern over legitimacy. Whatever the case may be, governments evidently do feel the need to subscribe to human rights principles. A government can demonstrate that it is partly fulfilling its purpose by creating and adhering to human rights norms. If, however, there is a clear conflict between national interest and treaty provisions, a government may not want to comply with its obligations.

Some governments, including most prominently the United States, seek to compromise between accepting human rights treaties and avoiding some of the human rights responsibilities pronounced in those treaties. They ratify human rights treaties, but at the same time they interpose reservations or other understandings, declarations, or other conditions that limit various provisions. The International Court of Justice in an Advisory Opinion of 1951 on reservations to the Genocide Convention authoritatively declared that such limitations are acceptable only if they do not defeat the "object and purpose" of the treaty.[9]

Once a government has agreed, however, to a particular standard, it can ordinarily be persuaded to fulfill its promise. The credibility of the government and its standing in the world community are at stake. To use a mundane analogy, we follow the law that establishes on which side of the road we should drive our automobiles not principally because there is something inherently right or wrong about driving on one side or because we are worried about ever-vigilant police who may take us to jail if we drive on the wrong side. We generally drive on the same side as everyone else because we can get where we want to go more easily, and a cooperative law-abiding approach is the most suitable way of achieving our mutual objectives. Similarly, governments can be expected to fulfill their promises formalized in treaties and follow international custom.

Some governments and scholars refer to national customs or practices to diminish the impact of human rights norms. For example, the European Court of Human Rights sometimes interprets European Convention provisions with a "margin of appreciation" in such a way so as to allow nations the capacity to vary their application in light of varying national practices. Claims of cultural relativism and religious belief, particularly as to women's rights, have also been asserted by some nations to avoid positive treaty obligations.

Some scholars have argued that governments often ratify treaties because they are engaging in a public relations exercise without necessarily intending to comply with their obligations. Governments do, in part, ratify treaties because they are motivated by peer pressure and by a desire for inclusion in regional or international communities. Take, for example, Turkey; a country that aspires to join the European Union. Hence, it has ratified the [European] Convention for the Protection of Human Rights and Fundamental Freedoms and the European Convention for the Prevention of Torture and Inhuman or Degrading Treatment or Punishment.[10] It is unclear whether Turkey intended to comply with its obligations in regard to these treaties, but it ratified the two treaties because it knew it had an endemic problem with torture and was trying to show that it cared about this problem. Nonetheless, torture has been a continuing problem for Turkey. The ratification of a treaty does not bring about immediate compliance any more than the adoption of a statute ensures universal obedience. Over time, however, Turkey has begun to take practical measures, including decreasing the period of incommunicado detention and ensuring the right to counsel at an early stage. As a result, Turkey has experienced a decline in instances of torture.

One aspect of persuasion to fulfill human rights obligations is the implicit threat that failure to comply will be accompanied by embarrassment. Many international human rights procedures that will be discussed in greater detail in Part III of this book have the objective of persuasion, threat of embarrassment, or actual embarrassment. Indeed, the clearer the message sent by the international procedure, the more likely will be the improvement in the human rights situation. Often the threat of embarrassment is more effective than the embarrassment itself. The government has a harder time calculating the impact of embarrassment before it occurs and is more likely to amend its conduct before being confronted in public with the embarrassment of an accusation that it violated human rights. After the government has been publicly confronted regarding its human rights abuses, it may resist international pressures by face-saving measures other than amending its violative conduct.

## 3. The Role of Other Organizations and Individuals

States are considered to be the principal subjects of international law in that they have the authority to enter into treaties and conduct themselves in such a way as to develop international customary law. The roles of intergovernmental organizations, nongovernmental organizations (NGOs), and individuals in international human rights law have grown in the past fifty years. Intergovernmental organizations, like the United Nations, convene state representatives to draft and promulgate treaties and other instruments of international law. As discussed in Part III, the United Nations and other intergovernmental organizations also have many functions in human rights.

Some NGOs, such as the International Committee of the Red Cross,[11] have similarly developed a role in convening state representatives to draft the Geneva Conventions and Protocols and to implement those treaties.[12] Many other NGOs provide ideas and factual input for the human rights procedures of the UN and other intergovernmental organizations. As discussed in Part III, NGOs have increasingly developed a function in the procedures of intergovernmental organizations in submitting complaints or otherwise invoking or contributing to human rights procedures. In the context of humanitarian law applicable to armed conflict situations, both states and armed opposition groups have been given responsibilities. For example, under Common Article III of the Geneva Conventions, both States parties and armed opposition groups in non-international armed conflicts are bound to protect civilians, wounded soldiers, and others taking no active part in the conflict from inhumane treatment, violence to life and person, hostage taking, unfair judicial proceedings, and being left on the battlefield without medical care.

Individuals have also been given an increasing role in international human rights procedures. Several human rights treaties permit individuals to submit complaints. For example, under the Optional Protocol to the Civil and Political Covenant,[13] individuals in the 109 nations that have ratified the protocol may submit communications claiming they are victims of a violation of the Covenant and may have their cases decided. Importantly, many non-treaty procedures also allow individuals to initiate and submit complaints to various UN bodies.

## 4. Criminal Sanctions for Perpetrators of Human Rights Abuses

Part III will also discuss criminal procedures for addressing individual responsibility for human rights abuses. Under the four Geneva Conventions and two Protocols, States parties are obligated to establish effective penal sanctions for persons committing, or ordering to be committed, any grave breaches of humanitarian law, such as killing or torturing civilians or wounded soldiers who are no longer taking an active part in hostilities. Hence, humanitarian law authorizes states to establish individual criminal responsibility for soldiers who commit violations. The Nuremberg and Tokyo tribunals established after World War II tried and sentenced the major war criminals and there were also thousands of trials of minor war criminals in Germany. There followed a nearly fifty year hiatus in the use of international criminal procedures to protect human rights. During that period, however, a few governments did subject their own soldiers to military courts martial for violations of humanitarian law, as required by the Geneva Conventions. For example, the United States court-martialed Lt. William Calley for committing war crimes in killing civilians during the Viet Nam Conflict in 1969.

In 1984 the UN General Assembly adopted the Convention Against Torture and Other Cruel, Inhuman or Degrading Treatment or Punishment,[14] which not only contained precepts as to how governments should prohibit, prevent, investigate, punish, and remedy instances of torture, but also called for universal jurisdiction over and extradition of suspected torturers. Pursuant to the Convention Against Torture and the Geneva Conventions, several governments adopted statutes establishing universal jurisdiction over war crimes, torture, and other crimes against humanity. For example, in 1987 Canada amended the Canadian criminal code[15] to grant national courts jurisdiction to prosecute crimes against humanity and war crimes committed abroad. After the United Kingdom ratified the Convention Against Torture, the UK Parliament adopted the Criminal Justice Act 1988, providing for universal jurisdiction over the crime of torture committed any place in the world.[16]

In 1993–94 the UN Security Council established ad hoc tribunals for trying the crimes of genocide, crimes against humanity, and war crimes committed by individuals in the former Yugoslavia[17] and Rwanda.[18] Those ad hoc tribunals reignited interest in using international criminal law to protect the most fundamental principles of human rights and to hold individuals criminally responsible for violations. On July 17, 1998, the UN Diplomatic Conference in Rome adopted the Rome Statute for the International Criminal Court (ICC),[19] which came into force in 2002, has been ratified by 104 nations, and begun to pursue its first criminal prosecutions as to the most responsible for crimes against humanity and war crimes in the Democratic Republic of the Congo, Northern Uganda, and Sudan.

National courts have during this same period become more interested in prosecuting perpetrators of human rights abuses under the principle of universal jurisdiction. For example, in 1994, a Danish court convicted and sentenced a Bosnian Serb residing in Denmark for murdering and torturing inmates of a concentration camp in Bosnia.[20] In 1997, the Supreme Court of the Netherlands decided that a Bosnian Serb could be tried by a Dutch Court for war crimes against Muslims in Bosnia under the principle of universal jurisdiction.[21] The most visible of such cases arose in 1998 when a trial judge in Spain sought to have Augusto Pinochet, the former leader of Chile, extradited from his temporary visit in the United Kingdom to stand trial for torture and other crimes against humanity.[22] Pinochet eventually was sent back to Chile, and the Chilean courts have initiated criminal proceedings against him there. Pinochet was under house arrest when he died at the age of ninety-one. There have also been efforts to develop mixed national-international criminal tribunals in countries where the national legal systems are not sufficiently robust to permit prosecutions of grave human rights abuses, for example, in Sierra Leone.[23]

While criminal prosecutions and punishment for the perpetrators of human rights abuses certainly represent a significant potential strengthening of the international human rights system, there have been so few offenders actually brought to justice, and the capacities of the ICC, mixed tribunals, ad hoc tribunals, and the like are so limited that it would be far too early to disregard the traditional mechanisms for human rights implementation and focus solely on criminal procedures. Even in national systems where apprehension, trial, and punishment are fairly predictable, it is difficult to demonstrate that criminal law actually deters offenders. The likelihood of being subjected to international criminal punishment for grave human rights abuses is far smaller and thus the deterrent impact of international procedures is even less certain. Since national courts in many countries are more efficient and reliable, the use of national criminal procedures to exercise universal jurisdiction over human rights abuses committed abroad—as well as to try domestic human rights abuses—are more likely to constitute an effective mechanism for human rights enforcement. In any case, criminal procedures for implementing human rights deserve attention along with the other mechanisms discussed in Part III.

The development of international human rights and humanitarian law in which individuals are subjected to criminal responsibility and universal jurisdiction, the increasing role of individuals and NGOs as participants in international human rights proceedings, and the imposition of international legal responsibility on armed opposition groups have evolved because the traditional, state-oriented model of international human rights did not adequately address the range of abuses. There are many human rights abuses committed by private actors in diverse contexts, such as the following: sexual exploitation of children, trafficking in children and human organs, baby selling for transnational adoption, female infanticide, rape and honor killings of women, sweatshops run by subcontractors of multinational corporations, business repression of labor organizers, refusal by pharmaceutical companies to make HIV-AIDS medicines available, war crimes and slavery by German industrialists during World War II, refusal by Swiss and other banks and insurance companies to acknowledge responsibility to victims of the Holocaust or for hiding the assets of dictators, environmental damage and complicity in repression by oil companies, and trade in diamonds that have been used to finance bloody civil wars. States parties to human rights and humanitarian law conventions have an obligation to assure that no individual, company, or other organ of society within their respective jurisdictions may commit such abuses, but there is a trend in human rights law to place responsibility directly upon the private actors themselves.

12    Introduction

*Further Reading for All Chapters:*

Charter of the United Nations, June 26, 1945, 59 Stat. 1031, T.S. NO. 993, 3 Bevans 1153, *entered into force* Oct. 24, 1945.

Convention Against Torture and Other Cruel, Inhuman or Degrading Treatment or Punishment, G.A. res. 39/46, [annex, 39 U.N. GAOR Supp. (No. 51) at 197, U.N. Doc. A/39/51 (1984)], *entered into force* June 26, 1987.

Convention on the Elimination of All Forms of Discrimination Against Women, G.A. res. 34/180, U.N. GAOR Supp. (No. 46) at 193, U.N. Doc. A/34/180, *entered into force* Sept. 3, 1981.

Convention on the Prevention of the Crime of Genocide, 78 U.N.T.S. 277, *entered into force* Dec. 9, 1948.

Convention on the Rights of the Child, G.A. res. 44/25, annex, 44 U.N. GAOR Supp. (No. 49) at 167, U.N. Doc. A/44/49 (1989), *entered into force* Sept. 2, 1990.

Oona A. Hathaway, *Do Human Rights Treaties Make a Difference?* 111 Yale L.J. 1935 (2002).

Human Rights Committee, General Comment 24 (52), General comment on issues relating to reservations made upon ratification or accession to the Covenant or the Optional Protocols thereto, or in relation to declarations under article 41 of the Covenant, U.N. Doc. CCPR/C/21/Rev.1/Add.6 (1994).

International Convention on the Elimination of All Forms of Racial Discrimination, G.A. res. 2106 (XX), Annex, 20 U.N. GAOR Supp. (No. 14) at 47, U.N. Doc. A/6014 (1966), 660 U.N.T.S. 195, *entered into force* Jan. 4, 1969.

International Convention on the Rights of Migrant Workers and Members of Their Families, G.A. res. 45/158, annex, 45 U.N. GAOR Supp. (No. 49A) at 262, U.N. Doc. A/45/49 (1990), *entered into force* July 1, 2003.

International Covenant on Civil and Political Rights, G.A. res. 2200A (XXI), 21 U.N. GAOR Supp. (No. 16) at 52, U.N. Doc. A/6316 (1966), 999 U.N.T.S. 171, *entered into force* Mar. 23, 1976.

The International Covenant on Civil and Political Rights: Cases, Materials, and Commentary, (Sarah Joseph, Jenny Schultz, & Melissa Castan eds., 2d ed. 2004).

International Covenant on Economic, Social and Cultural Rights, G.A. res. 2200A (XXI), 21 U.N. GAOR Supp. (No. 16) at 49, U.N. Doc. A/6316 (1966), 993 U.N.T.S. 3, *entered into force* Jan. 3, 1976.

Yuji Iwasawa, International Law, Human Rights, and Japanese Law: The Impact of International Law on Japanese Law (1998).

John H. Jackson, *The Status of Treaties in Domestic Legal Systems: A Policy Analysis*, 86 AJIL 310 (1992).

Susan Marks and Andrew Clapham, International Human Rights Lexicon (2005).

*Reservations to the Convention on the Prevention and Punishment of the Crime of Genocide, Advisory Opinion of 28 May 1951,* 1951 ICJ Reports 15.

*United States v. Calley,* 46 C.M.R. 1131 (1973).

Universal Declaration of Human Rights, G.A. res. 217A (III), U.N. Doc A/810 at 71 (1948).

Vienna Convention on the Law of Treaties, 1155 U.N.T.S. 331, *entered into force* Jan. 27, 1980.

David Weissbrodt, Joan Fitzpatrick, and Frank Newman, International Human Rights: Law, Policy, and Process (3d ed. 2001).

*Links to Consult for All Chapters:*

http://www1.umn.edu/humanrts/education/historical.html
http://www1.umn.edu/humanrts/instree/aunchart.htm
http://www1.umn.edu/humanrts/instree/auob.htm
http://www1.umn.edu/humanrts/instree/auoy.htm
http://www1.umn.edu/humanrts/instree/h2catoc.htm

# B. Overview and History of International Human Rights

This chapter first places human rights in historical context by looking at the early development of human rights law prior to World War I. It then looks at developments surrounding World War I and the advent of the League of Nations and the International Labor Organization. Third, it traces developments during the period between World War I and World War II. Fourth, it identifies the Holocaust and World War II as the events that prompted the modern movement to protect human rights—principally through the United Nations. Fifth, it shows how human rights have become a subject of international legislation through the UN Charter and multilateral treaties. Later chapters provide not only an overview of the United Nations and its various structures, but also address other sources of human rights law. For example, human rights are protected through humanitarian law including the Geneva Conventions and Protocols as well as international criminal law. Later chapters also focus on several regional human rights systems—particularly in Africa, Europe, and the Western Hemisphere—as well as national human rights institutions and nongovernmental organizations.

## 1. Early Development—From the Ten Commandments to the Treaty of Westphalia

The idea of human rights can be traced to antiquity—for example, the Ten Commandments, the Code of Hammurabi,[24] and the Rights of Athenian Citizens. Early efforts to identify and defend human rights often came in response to atrocities of war and refugee problems. Religious, moral, and philosophical origins can be identified not only in biblical and classical history, but also in Buddhism, Christianity, Confucianism, Hinduism, Islam, Judaism, Shinto, and other faiths.[25]

For example, the Golden Rule ("Do onto others as you would wish them to do onto you") is a fundamental human rights principle found in many religious traditions. In the Old Testament (Leviticus) it is said, "thou shalt love thy neighbor as thyself." An ancient teaching of Buddhism is "Hurt not others in ways that you yourself would find hurtful." Christ declared, "Therefore all things whatsoever ye would that men should do to you, do ye even so to them." A teaching of Confucius was "Do not do to others what you do not want them to do to you." In Islam it is said, "None of you believes until he wishes for his brother what he wishes for himself."

Rights concepts later began to appear in national documents such as the Magna Carta of 1215.[26] Also in the thirteenth century, St. Thomas Aquinas used the theory of natural rights to argue that unjust laws are not laws in the fullest sense and that state sovereignty should not be respected when a government is systematically mistreating its subjects. One can trace women's human rights back to the fifteenth century when early efforts were made in Italy to assert women's rights to education, employment, and later to vote. Following the revolution of 1688 in England, Parliament enacted the Declaration of the Rights of Man (1689) to protect citizens from violations by the monarchy.[27]

Starting with the Protestant Reformation and the religious wars of the sixteenth and seventeenth centuries, peace treaties began to include clauses aimed at protecting religious minorities. A state's ill-treatment of minorities could provoke intervention by another state. Via its own military, a state might punish or replace an abusive government. Intrusion on sovereignty was believed permissible when a government's treatment of its own subjects "shocked the conscience of humankind."

With the rise of nation-states in the seventeenth century, however, classical international law rejected the notion of human rights and favored state sovereignty, in part because sovereignty was seen not simply as an instrument for the protection and promotion of the welfare of its citizens, but as a good in itself. Beginning in 1648, with the Treaty of Westphalia, states occasionally agreed to protect some individual rights. Still, such agreements typically reflected the view that individuals were objects of international law only insofar as their rights existed as derivative of states' sovereignty.

During the eighteenth and nineteenth centuries the nation-state dominated the development of international law as the sole subject of international law, but a number of precursors to the modern protection of human rights began focusing attention on the role of individuals as at least objects of international law. Those precursors began to intrude upon the state-oriented fabric of international law in such previously isolated fields as the protection of aliens, the protection of minorities, human rights guarantees in national constitutions and laws, the abolition of slavery, women's rights, the protection of victims of armed conflict, self-determination, and labor rights.

16   Overview and History

A. Protection of Aliens

Developments in the eighteenth and nineteenth centuries reflect incremental steps to recognize individual rights and diminish the centrality of the notion of sovereignty. They included, for example, diplomatic efforts to protect rights of aliens abroad. Early enforcement of aliens' rights took the form of reprisals, including seizures of property. Reprisals in the nineteenth century were gradually replaced by negotiations between governments of aggrieved individuals and of the territory where the wrongs occurred. A state's right to intervene on citizens' behalf rested on two principles—the rights of aliens to be treated in accordance with "international standards of justice" and to be treated equally with nationals of the country wherein they resided.

B. Protection of Minorities

Minimum international standards of justice also developed through early efforts to protect religious minorities. As mentioned above, peace treaties in the sixteenth and seventeenth centuries began to include provisions protecting religious minorities. A state's treatment of its minorities also could provoke humanitarian interventions by other states. Some governments have invoked humanitarian purposes as reasons for their military interventions and other governments have made diplomatic interventions on humanitarian grounds.

In a military intervention the intervening state sought to replace or punish the state found to be abusing its minorities. Great Britain, France, and Russia explained their military intervention against the Ottoman Empire in 1827 as necessary to stop Turkish abuse of its Greek population.

Diplomatic intervention presented a less intrusive means for a state to express its concern for another state's treatment of its minorities. For example, the United States and six European nations sent a collective diplomatic note to the government of Romania in 1872 protesting Romanian mistreatment of Jews. The United States also appealed on behalf of Russian Jews at the beginning of the twentieth century.

C. Human Rights Guarantees in National Laws

During the eighteenth and early nineteenth centuries, governments took further measures to recognize inherent rights of the individual under national laws. The 1776 American Declaration of Independence proclaimed, "as self evident," the "unalienable rights" of all men to "life, liberty and the pursuit of happiness."[28] Those rights were based on eighteenth-century theories of natural law philosophers like John Locke and Jean-Jacques Rousseau, who argued that fundamental rights were beyond state control and that individuals were inherently autonomous in nature. Following this logic, upon entering society each individual's autonomy combined to form the people's sovereignty, but each individual also retained some personal autonomy in the form of inviolable rights. The resulting people's sovereignty, in turn, gave rise to other inalienable rights, like the right of self-government, including the right to choose and change the government.

Belief in such rights produced the French Declaration of the Rights of Man and of the Citizen in 1789[29] and led federated states to insist on adding the Bill of Rights to the U.S. Constitution between 1789 and 1791.[30] A number of nations followed the French and U.S. examples in their constitutions: the Netherlands (1798), Sweden (1809), Spain (1812), Norway (1814), Belgium (1831), Liberia (1847), Sardinia (1848), Denmark (1849), and Prussia (1850).

D. ABOLITION OF SLAVERY AND WOMEN'S RIGHTS

In addition, nineteenth-century efforts to abolish the slave trade and protect workers' rights evidenced a growing international concern for human rights. The slave trade was first condemned by treaty in the Additional Articles to the Paris Peace Treaty of 1814 between France and Britain. In 1823, several British campaigners against the slave trade (including Clarkson Wilberforce) established the first NGO concerned with human rights, the Anti-Slavery Society.[31] In 1885, the General Act of the Berlin Conference on Central Africa affirmed that "trading in slaves is forbidden in conformity with the principles of international law."

Efforts to abolish slavery in the nineteenth century awoke concern for women's rights. In 1840, at an anti-slavery conference in London, two prominent abolitionists—Elizabeth Cady Stanton and Lucretia Mott—were forced to remain behind a closed balcony curtain during discussions. They began the international struggle for women's rights that led to the Seneca Falls (New York) Convention in 1848 and the formation of the International Women Suffrage Alliance in 1904. The alliance focused on issues such as trafficking of women, education and literacy of women, and labor laws that were sensitive to the needs of women.

E. PROTECTION OF VICTIMS OF ARMED CONFLICT

In 1859 Henri Dunant, a Swiss businessman, witnessed the aftermath of the bloody battle of Solferino in Northern Italy during the Franco-

18   Overview and History

Austrian War and the suffering of the wounded soldiers. As a result of that experience he helped to convene the 1863 Geneva Conference, which founded the International Committee of the Red Cross (ICRC).[32] The ICRC was instrumental in preparing initial drafts of what became the first multilateral treaty protecting victims of armed conflict—the 1864 Geneva Convention for the Amelioration of the Condition of the Wounded and Sick in Armies in the Field, which aimed to protect military hospitals and provided for equal medical treatment for combatants on both sides of a conflict.[33] The fifteen Hague Conventions of 1899 and 1907 emphasized limits on methods and means of warfare.[34] For example, they banned poisonous gases and other weapons calculated to induce unnecessary suffering.

## 2. World War I, the League of Nations, and Self-Determination

Further concern for human rights developed after World War I. In 1918, President Woodrow Wilson presented Congress with his "Fourteen Points," a program designed to end war and create a world dedicated to fair dealing and justice.[35] He called, inter alia, for rights to self-determination through newly drawn national borders and statehood for nationalities seeking autonomy. The Senate, however, repudiated the program, and Secretary of State Lansing criticized the principle of national self-determination. Other countries also withheld support.

The war ended after the Paris Peace Conference in 1919 produced the Versailles Treaty.[36] The treaty created the League of Nations and the International Labor Organization (ILO).[37] During the Paris Peace Conference, President Wilson proposed a provision for the League's Covenant that called upon governments to refrain from religious discrimination; the Japanese delegate proposed a prohibition of discrimination for reasons of race or nationality; and the British delegate proposed a more forceful provision calling for intervention when states disturb world peace by engaging in a policy of religious intolerance. None of those proposals were adopted.

Even though human rights were not explicitly mentioned in the League's Covenant, they were not ignored by the League of Nations. "Self-determination" became a basic component of agreements that the League administered in countries and regions including Austria, Bulgaria, Czechoslovakia, Greece, Hungary, Poland, Romania, Turkey, and Yugoslavia. These treaties protected groups of individuals who share certain national, ethnic, religious, or linguistic characteristics that are different from those of the majority population. They purported to guarantee protection of life and liberty for all inhabitants of the countries or regions party to the treaties, as well as nationals' equality before the law and in the enjoyment of civil and political rights. The League also required Albania, Estonia, Finland, Latvia, and Lithuania to pledge protection of minority rights before becoming members. These treaties are significant, not only for their codification of important norms such as nondiscrimination, freedom of religion, and language rights, but also for establishing the legitimacy in international relations of other states taking an interest in the treatment of the nationals of the obligated states.

League protection, however, extended only to nationals of countries and regions who were party to the treaties. In 1922, the Assembly of the League expressed hope that countries and regions not party to the treaties would extend the same protection to their nationals. Thrice, however, the Assembly rejected proposals to draft a new treaty applicable to all members prescribing each member's obligations toward minorities.

The League also created a mandate system to regulate colonies or non-self-governing territories with a view to achieving self-determination for those colonies/territories. The League's mandate system also protected the human rights of the inhabitants of those colonies/territories that were awaiting independence. For example, the mandate system of the League protected freedom of conscience and religion in former colonial territories of Germany and Turkey. Governments controlling non-self-governing mandated territory promised to promote the material and moral well-being, as well as the social progress, of inhabitants. The goal was to prepare the colonies for independent statehood. They would be ready for autonomy when they could guarantee protection of religious, linguistic, and ethnic minorities, as well as rights of aliens and freedom of conscience. The territories included Palestine and Transjordan administered by Britain, Syria and Lebanon administered by France, the Cameroons and Togoland administered by Britain and France, and Rwanda administered by Belgium. The mandate system subsequently evolved into the UN trusteeship system.

## 3. The Interwar Years

Scholarly internationalists were responsible for much of the human rights development prior to and during the interwar years. Alejandro Álvarez of Chile, for example, was among the first to advocate international rights for individuals. Cofounder of the American Institute of International Law, he submitted a 1917 draft declaration on future international law that included a section on individual rights.

Another noted scholar, Russian jurist Andre Nicolayevitch Mandelstam, emigrated to Paris after the Bolsheviks came to power. In 1921, he persuaded the International Law Institute to establish a commission to study protection of minorities and human rights generally. He served as rapporteur and, in 1929, persuaded the commission to adopt a Declaration of the International Rights of Man. It included a preamble and six articles. The first three articles defined a state's duty to recognize the equal rights of each person within its territory to life, liberty, property, and religious freedom. The remaining articles defined states' duties toward their citizens.

In an October 1939 letter to the *Times*, British novelist H. G. Wells spoke of rights to food, medical care, education, as well as access to information, freedom of discussion, association, and worship. He also discussed rights to work, freedom of movement, and protection from violence, compulsion, and intimidation. Wells and colleagues eventually wrote a document known as the Sankey Declaration. Throughout 1940 and 1941 he promoted the Declaration at meetings and in various publications. In 1940 he published *The Rights of Man, or What Are We Fighting For?* which contained the Declaration and his commentary. Reportedly 30,000 copies were circulated in Britain and it was translated into ten languages and offered for world syndication. He received reactions from numerous human rights pioneers, including Mahatma Gandhi and Jawaharlal Nehru, as well as Jan Masaryk, Chaim Weizmann, and Jan Christian Smuts (who in 1945 drafted Articles 55 and 56 of the UN Charter).

While scholars and others were promoting human rights, events in Europe undermined their work. Most notorious was the rise of Adolf Hitler. He and the Nazis took control of Germany in 1933 and quickly began implementing their agenda of anti-Semitism. In May 1933, the League of Nations heard a complaint from a German who claimed he had been fired from his job because of an April 1933 decree to discharge all Jewish civil servants, to exclude Jewish lawyers from legal practice and Jewish doctors from practice for health insurance funds, and to limit admission of Jewish students to German schools. Germany assured the League that it would protect the life and liberty of its citizens without discrimination, and apparently led the League to close the case. The League reconsidered Germany's anti-Semitic policies at the end of 1933, and Germany responded by withdrawing from the League.

## 4. World War II and the Beginning of the Modern Human Rights Movement

The modern human rights movement began during World War II. The war represented the ultimate extension of state sovereignty concepts that had dominated international relations for three centuries. The Nazis, seeking international preeminence, acted with unprecedented brutality and demonstrated that previous attempts to protect individuals

## World War II and the Human Rights Movement 21

from ravages of war were hopelessly inadequate. The war demonstrated that unfettered national sovereignty could not continue to exist without untold hardships and, ultimately, the danger of total destruction of human society. It was out of the trauma of World War II with fifty million killed, many more injured, and such great suffering that the modern human rights movement was born. Human rights became a rallying cry of the allies struggling against the wartime brutality of Germany, Italy, and Japan.

Germany's tactics were based on speed, surprise, and terror. In the Battle of Britain, the German air force bombarded English population centers and sought to destroy British cities. During the heaviest bombing, from July to October 1940, more than 23,000 civilians were killed and 32,000 were injured. The German assault on the Soviet Union was even more brutal. That conflict raged for nearly four years and resulted in Soviet military casualties of six and one-half million. Including civilians, an estimated twenty million Soviets were killed during the attempted German conquest of the Soviet Union. The industrial cities of Germany and Italy were also the subject of intensive bombing by England and the United States. The most visible bombing by the British air force was of the city of Dresden where tens of thousands were killed in February 1945.

The most infamous brutality during the war was the Holocaust. The extermination of Jews began in the summer of 1941, when Reichsfuhrer Himmler gave the order for the liquidation of Russian Jews encountered during the invasion of the Soviet Union. In the course of the first year, the German army killed an estimated 90,000 Jews. Massive deportations of Jews to death camps began in 1942. From all over Europe they were brought by train; when the trains arrived, Germans unloaded the prisoners—primarily Jews but also gypsies, homosexuals, and assorted political dissidents—and stood them in lines for inspection by SS doctors. From trainloads of 1,500 people the doctors generally selected 1,200–1,300 for immediate extermination by firing squads or gas chambers. By the end of the war the Germans in the death camps had exterminated an estimated 6,000,000 Jews and nearly that many non-Jews. Another two million died outside the camps as a result of the German policy of extermination. This total amounted to nearly two-thirds of the population of prewar European Jewry.

The war in Asia and the Pacific was also brutal. The Japanese occupation of China, for instance, proved to be as vicious as Germany's conquest and control of Eastern Europe. Among the worst atrocities of the Sino-Japanese war was the occupation commonly known as the "Rape of Nanking." When the Japanese conquered the city in 1937, an estimated 500,000 civilians resided there. During the first few months, when acts of brutality were at their highest, the army killed at least 43,000 civilians and soldiers raped countless women. One observer of the Japanese occupation of Nanking estimated that at least 1,000 rapes took place each night.

The Japanese Army also established camps for forced prostitution of women from China, Korea, the Philippines, and elsewhere.

In response to those and other horrors, world leaders spoke out in defense of peace and protection of human rights. On January 6, 1941, President Roosevelt, in his State of the Union address to Congress, outlined his vision of the future based on the "four essential human freedoms":

The first is freedom of speech and expression everywhere in the world.
The second is freedom of every person to worship God in his own way everywhere in the world.
The third is freedom from want, which, translated into world terms, means economic understandings which will secure to every nation a healthy peacetime life for its inhabitants everywhere in the world.
The fourth is freedom from fear, which, translated into world terms, means a world-wide reduction of armaments to such a point and in such a thorough fashion that no nation will be in a position to commit an act of physical aggression against any neighbor-anywhere in the world.[38]

His speech was one of many strong statements on the crucial importance of human rights in the international community. In addition, on August 14, 1941, Roosevelt and Prime Minister Churchill set forth aims of the allied war effort in a joint declaration known as the Atlantic Charter. It stated general principles regarding the structure of the postwar world. Among those principles, Article 6 stressed the importance of human rights:

After the final destruction of Nazi tyranny they hope to see established a peace which will afford to all nations the means of dwelling in safety within their own boundaries, and which will afford assurance that all men in all the lands may live out their lives in freedom from fear and want.[39]

During 1941 the Atlantic Charter received endorsements from all the European allies, which were followed by the Declaration of the United Nations on January 1, 1942, in which twenty-six nations pledged alliance in the war against the German/Italian/Japanese axis.[40]

After the war, political leaders and scholars continued to look to the protection of human rights as both an end and a means of helping to ensure international peace and security. The victors responded to the war and the Holocaust by forming the United Nations, which had the dual purpose of preserving the peace and protecting human rights. Soon thereafter, intergovernmental organizations in Europe and the

Americas also established their standards for the protection and promotion of human rights.

A. THE NUREMBERG AND TOKYO TRIBUNALS AND CONTROL COUNCIL LAW NO. 10

During the war and the immediate postwar period, most human rights advocates focused on the prosecution of perpetrators of wartime abuses. The allied governments had received innumerable reports of German and Japanese atrocities and, in response, the allies vowed to punish the individuals responsible. The International Military Tribunal, which sat at Nuremberg, was created by the London Agreement of August 8, 1945.[41] The International Military Tribunal for the Far East was established in Tokyo on January 19, 1946.[42] Both tribunals served the immediate function of punishing the leading war criminals. The Control Council for Germany (composed of Britain, France, the Soviet Union, and the United States) issued Control Council Law No. 10 in 1946 to expand the London Agreement and authorize the trial of thousands of cases not pursued by the International Tribunal at Nuremberg.[43]

B. THE CREATION OF THE UNITED NATIONS: DUMBARTON OAKS AND SAN FRANCISCO

In 1944, Britain and the United States. met with the Soviet Union (and later with China) at Dumbarton Oaks in Washington, D.C., to formulate a "proposal for the establishment of a general international organization." The initial plan proposed by the U.S. State Department included an international bill of rights that member governments of the organization would agree to accept. The proposal envisioned that the organization's structure would include means to help ensure protection of human rights.

By the time U.S. delegates reached Dumbarton Oaks, however, they had decided to include only a general statement on human rights. Even that approach met with resistance from the British and Soviet delegations. Eventually the U.S. persuaded Britain and the Soviets to include a brief statement demonstrating support for human rights in a draft UN Charter issued by the Conference on October 7, 1944. It mentioned human rights only once, stating that "the Organization should facilitate solutions of international economic, social and other humanitarian problems and promote respect for human rights and fundamental freedoms."[44]

After the Dumbarton Oaks Conference, various nongovernmental organizations (NGOs) lobbied for a stronger and more specific statement on human rights. A proposal made by several Jewish groups advocated explicit reference in the Charter to protection of human rights. They proposed also that either the Security Council or the Economic and Social Council be empowered to establish human rights guidelines and take action to enforce compliance with the guidelines. A coalition of twenty-two NGOs, including the National Council of Women, the National Board of the Young Women's Christian Association (YWCA), the American Federation of Labor-Congress of Industrial Organizations (AFL-CIO), and the National Association for the Advancement of Colored People (NAACP), similarly pressed for an active UN role to counter human rights abuses. They proposed that each member nation pledge to secure progressively, for its inhabitants, rights including life, liberty, and freedom of religion. In a strong statement on duties of a state with respect to its own citizens, the American Jewish Committee (AJC) declared:

no plea of sovereignty shall ever again be allowed to permit any nation to deprive those within its borders of fundamental rights on the claim that they are matters of internal concern. It is now a matter of international concern to stamp out infractions of basic human rights.[45]

In spite of the early difficulties, government representatives—particularly those from North and South America—sought at the UN Conference in San Francisco in Spring 1945 to fulfill President Roosevelt's vision of the future and to incorporate human rights clauses in the UN Charter.

## 5. The United Nations and Multilateral Protection of Human Rights

The UN Charter established human rights as a matter of international concern. The UN set forth these rights in the International Bill of Human Rights, and began the process of codifying human rights.

The Charter's preamble states that the "Peoples of the United Nations" are determined "to reaffirm faith in fundamental human rights, in the dignity and worth of the human person, in the equal rights of men and women and of nations large and small."[46] The Charter was promulgated in 1945 to maintain international peace and security; to develop friendly relations among nations based on respect for the principle of equal rights and self-determination; and to achieve international cooperation in solving international problems of an economic, social, cultural, or humanitarian character. According to Article 1 of the Charter, the UN seeks "To achieve international cooperation . . . in promoting and encouraging respect for human rights and for fundamental freedoms for all without distinction as to race, sex, language, or religion." Article 55 of the Charter requires that the United Nations shall promote "conditions of economic and social progress and development; solutions of international economic, social, health, and related problems; and international cultural and educational cooperation; and universal respect for . . . human rights . . . without discrimination. . . ." In accordance with Article 56, members pledge "joint and separate action . . . for the achievement of the purposes set forth in Article 55."

Article 68 called for the establishment of a Commission on Human Rights.[47] Its first task was to draft the Universal Declaration of Human Rights and thus provide an authoritative definition of the broad human rights obligations of member states under Articles 1, 55, and 56.

In 1948, the UN General Assembly adopted the Universal Declaration of Human Rights, articulating the importance of rights that were placed at risk during the 1940s: the rights to life, liberty, and security of person; freedoms of expression, peaceful assembly, association, religious belief, and movement; and protections from slavery, arbitrary arrest, imprisonment without fair trial, and invasion of privacy. The Universal Declaration also contains provisions for economic, social, and cultural rights. The Declaration's force, however, is unfortunately limited by very broad exclusions and the omission of monitoring and enforcement provisions. Nonetheless, it sets forth the core principles of international human rights law and many of its provisions are now considered to constitute customary international law.

Following adoption of the Universal Declaration, the UN Commission on Human Rights drafted the remainder of the International Bill of Human Rights, which contains the Covenant on Economic, Social and Cultural Rights, the Covenant on Civil and Political Rights, and an Optional Protocol to the Civil and Political Covenant. The three instruments were adopted by the General Assembly in 1966 and entered into force in 1976. The International Bill of Human Rights comprises the most authoritative and comprehensive prescription of human rights obligations that governments undertake in joining the UN.

The two Covenants distinguish between implementation of civil and political rights on the one hand and economic, social, and cultural rights on the other. Civil and political rights, such as freedom of expression and the right to be free from torture or arbitrary arrest, are immediately enforceable. Economic, social, and cultural rights are to be implemented "to the maximum of available resources, with a view to achieving progressively the full realization of the rights . . . by all appropriate means, including particularly the adoption of legislative measures."[48] In other words, governments that ratify the Covenants must immediately cease torturing their citizens and must stop any discrimination in regard to civil, political, economic, social, and cultural rights, but they are not immediately required to feed, clothe, and house them. These latter obligations are generally to be accomplished progressively as resources permit.

In addition to the International Bill of Human Rights, the United Nations has drafted, promulgated, and now helps implement more than eighty human rights treaties, declarations, and other instruments dealing with genocide, racial discrimination, discrimination against women, religious intolerance, the rights of disabled persons, the right to development, and the rights of the child. Human rights law has thus become the most codified domain of international law. As discussed in much greater detail in Part III of this book, the United Nations has established many political institutions, expert bodies, and other procedures to promote and protect human rights.

One early focus of the United Nations emphasized self-determination through the elimination of colonial domination of the developing world. The constitutions of most nations that have become established since the formation of the UN include reference to the rights that are protected by the Universal Declaration of Human Rights and the remainder of the International Bill of Human Rights.

*See also: Genocide, War Crimes, Crimes Against Humanity, Crimes Against Peace; Humanitarian Law; Self-Determination*

*Further Reading for All Chapters:*

Carol Anderson, Eyes Off the Prize (2005).
Robert F. Drinan, Cry of the Oppressed: The History and Hope of the Human Rights Revolution (1987).
Mary Ann Glendon, A World Made New: Eleanor Roosevelt and the Universal Declaration of Human Rights (2001).
Human Rights in Western Civilization: 1600 to the Present (John A. Maxwell & James J. Friedberg eds., 2d ed. 1994).
Micheline R. Ishay, The History of Human Rights: From Ancient Times to the Globalization Era (2004).
M. Glen Johnson & Janusz Symonides, The Universal Declaration of Human Rights: A History of Its Creation and Implementation, 1948–1998 (1998).
Jon E. Lewis, A Documentary History of Human Rights: A Record of the Events, Documents, and Speeches That Shaped Our World (2003).
Johannes Morsink, The Universal Declaration of Human Rights: Origins, Drafting, and Intent (1999).
The Wilson Chronology of Human Rights (David Levinson ed., 2003).

# Part II
# Human Rights Categorized by Particular Rights, Responsibilities, and Groups

# A. Categorized by Particular Rights and Responsibilities

In order to prevent human rights violations there need to be norms that separate what is permissible from what is forbidden. There are many human rights treaties—mostly adopted under the aegis of the United Nations—that codify the substance of human rights law. There are also some nontreaty UN pronouncements that interpret and elaborate on the substance of human rights law. Several UN and regional human rights treaties establish courts and other institutions to focus on particular situations and decide cases. Their decisions and views further interpret and elaborate on the substance of human rights law.

Using those sources of law and interpretation, this part focuses on the most important substantive norms of international human rights law. The chapters in this part generally follow the structure of the Universal Declaration of Human Rights,[1] but add other rights (such as the right to self-determination, which does not appear in the Universal Declaration but is guaranteed by both the UN Charter[2] and the two Human Rights Covenants).[3] Each chapter identifies the operative language from the UN Charter, Universal Declaration, Covenants, and other UN and regional instruments. Most chapters also reflect some of the authoritative interpretations that have been issued by the Human Rights Committee[4] for the Civil and Political Covenant; the Committee on Economic, Social and Cultural Rights;[5] and other human rights bodies. Most chapters describe principal efforts at implementation of the respective rights at the international, regional, and national levels. Further, many chapters identify important issues or situations that have arisen in applying each right. Every chapter contains references to further readings and relevant links that support the text or would afford the reader an opportunity to delve further into the subject.

## 1. Self-Determination (Covenants, Art. 1)

U.S. President Woodrow Wilson was one of the earliest and most visible advocates of self-determination, which he defined as the "aspiration to rule one's self and not be ruled by others."[6] Self-determination was initially a rallying cry for achieving self-rule for the peoples inhabiting colonies under the political and economic domination of European governments. The UN Charter, which is the most important treaty in international law, calls in Articles 1(ii) and 55 for "respect for the principle of equal rights and self-determination of peoples," but does not set forth the meaning of self-determination.[7]

Self-determination and decolonization represented a very important part of the UN agenda when the Covenant on Civil and Political Rights and the Covenant on Economic, Social and Cultural Rights were being drafted (1946–66). Hence, the contours of self-determination are set forth prominently in Article 1 of both Covenants:

1. All peoples have the right of self-determination. By virtue of that right they freely determine their political status and freely pursue their economic, social and cultural development.
2. All peoples may, for their own ends, freely dispose of their natural wealth and resources without prejudice to any obligations arising out of international economic co-operation, based upon the principle of mutual benefit, and international law. In no case may a people be deprived of its own means of subsistence.
3. The States Parties to the present Covenant, including those having responsibility for the administration of Non-Self-Governing and Trust Territories, shall promote the realization of the right of self-determination, and shall respect that right, in conformity with the provisions of the Charter of the United Nations.

In 1945, when the United Nations was established, about 750 million people were living in colonies or similar non-self-governing territories and had thus not achieved self-determination. With the assistance of the United Nations Trusteeship Council and its Special Committee on Decolonization, more than eighty former colonies have gained national independence, that is, political separation from foreign domination by such historical colonial powers as Belgium, England, France, the Netherlands, Portugal, and Spain. The UN has identified only sixteen remaining non-self-governing territories with about two million inhabitants, including the British Virgin Islands, Guam, New Caledonia, the U.S. Virgin Islands, and Western Sahara.

The right to self-determination was very prominent during the aftermath of the Cold War era, when the Soviet Union, Czechoslovakia, and Yugoslavia broke apart and several new nations were established, including Estonia (1991), Latvia (1991), Lithuania (1991), Bosnia and Herzegovina (1992), Croatia (1992), Georgia (1992), Kazakhstan (1992), Kyrgyzstan (1992), Slovenia (1992), Tajikistan (1992), Uzbekistan

(1992), the Czech Republic (1993), Slovakia (1993), Serbia and Montenegro (2000), Montenegro (2006), and Serbia (2006). In 1993, Eritrea obtained its independence from Ethiopia. Another recent situation in which a people exercised their right of self-determination occurred in 2002, when the former Portuguese colony of East Timor obtained its independence from Indonesia and became Timor-Leste.

In 2004, the International Court of Justice issued an advisory opinion in which it concluded that Israel has an "obligation to cease forthwith the works of construction of the wall being built by it in the Occupied Palestinian Territory" because "Israel is bound to comply with its obligation to respect the right of the Palestinian people to self-determination and its obligations under international humanitarian law and international human rights law."[8]

While there is clearly a right of peoples to independence from colonial or foreign domination, it is less clear whether there exists a right of secession. Political, military, and economic separation from a contiguous country would undermine the national unity and territorial integrity of an existing nation. With so many newly independent nations established in the 1990s, several governments began to express concern that if the full logic of the right to self-determination were pursued there might be 3,000 or more communities claiming independence.

The Committee on the Elimination of Racial Discrimination in a General Recommendation of 1996 responded to these concerns by declaring that

none of Committee's actions shall be construed as authorizing or encouraging any action which would dismember or impair, totally or in part, the territorial integrity or political unity of sovereign and independent states conducting themselves in compliance with the principle of equal rights and self-determination of peoples and possessing a government representing the whole people belonging to the territory without distinction as to race, creed or colour. In view of the Committee international law has not recognized a general right of peoples to unilaterally declare secession from a state. In this respect, theCommittee follows the views . . . that a fragmentation of States may be detrimental to the protection of human rights as well as to the preservation of peace and security.[9]

For purposes of determining claims of self-determination a people should have significant ties of a racial, linguistic, religious, cultural, economic, and/or historical nature as well as common institutions or organs and a common economic base within a defined territory or geographical location. The people should also be comprised of a sufficient number of individuals. It is rather difficult to distinguish between a "people" and a "minority," although it is clear that only the former is entitled to self-determination. Minorities are entitled to certain cultural, religious, and linguistic rights.

Indigenous communities have campaigned for their right of self-determination. Canada has acknowledged indigenous claims for autonomy and self-government for its Inuit people by establishing the Nunavut territory. Similarly, Denmark afforded "home rule" to its Inuit residents in Greenland. Other indigenous communities have referred to the UN Draft Declaration on the Rights of Indigenous Peoples, which states in Article 3, "Indigenous peoples have the right of self-determination."[10] That right of self-determination may involve a degree of autonomy as well as control over natural resources rather than complete secession and independence. As the draft Declaration's Article 31 explains more fully:

> Indigenous peoples, as a specific form of exercising their right to self-determination, have the right to autonomy or self-government in matters relating to their internal and local affairs, including culture, religion, education, information, media, health, housing, employment, social welfare, economic activities, land and resources management, environment and entry by non-members, as well as ways and means for financing these autonomous functions.[11]

The reaction of the world community to claims of self-determination—particularly involving the dismemberment of existing nations—is more likely to be affected by political and strategic considerations than legal definitions. Hence, for example, the campaign to achieve some degree of autonomy or even independence for Abkhazians, African Americans, Basques, Chechens, Karens, Kashmiris, Kosovars, Karabakh, Kurds, Ossetians, Québécois, Palestinians, Saharawis, Taiwanese, Tamils, and Tibetans have both a human rights and a political dimension.

*Further Reading:*

*Advisory Opinion on Greco-Bulgarian Communities,* 1930 P.C.I.J. (ser. B.) No. 17, at 22–30 (July 31).
Committee on the Elimination of Racial Discrimination, General Recommendation 21, The Right to Self-Determination (Forty-eighth session, 1996), U.N. Doc. A/51/18, annex VIII at 125 (1996).
Jamar Crawford, *The Right of Self-Determination in International Law: Its Development and Future* in People's Rights (Philip Alston ed., 2001), chap. 7.
Declaration on Principles of International Law Concerning Friendly Relations and Co-operation Among States in Accordance with the Charter of the United Nations, G.A. res. 2625, Annex, 25 U.N. GAOR, Supp. (No. 28), U.N. Doc. A/5217 at 121 (1970).
Draft Declaration on the Rights of Indigenous Peoples, U.N. Doc. A/HRC/1/L.10 (2006).
Hector Gros Espiell, The Right to Self-Determination, Implementation of United Nations Resolutions, U.N. Doc. E/CN.4/Sub.2/405/Rev.1 (1980).
Hurst Hannum, Autonomy, Sovereignty, and Self-Determination (1992).
*Western Sahara* [Advisory Opinion], 1975 I.C.J. 12 (Oct.16).

*Links to Consult:*

http://www.icj-cij.org/
http://www.lexum.umontreal.ca/csc-scc/en/pub/1998/vol2/index.html
http://www.un.org/Depts/dpi/decolonization/main.htm
http://www1.umn.edu/humanrts/gencomm/genrexxi.htm
http://www1.umn.edu/humanrts/instree/declra.htm

## 2. Equality and Nondiscrimination (Universal Declaration, Articles 1, 2, 6, 7)

Equality and its correlative norm of nondiscrimination are two of the most important precepts of human rights. While the UN Charter is generally quite vague as to human rights principles, Article 55 is much more specific in stating that the United Nations shall promote "universal respect for, and observance of, human rights and fundamental freedoms for all without distinction as to race, sex, language, or religion."[12]

Of the original 51 members of the UN, only 30 allowed women equal voting rights. Of the 160 individuals who signed the Charter in San Francisco and were involved in the drafting, only four were women. Hence, it is quite remarkable that the UN Charter was one of the first international statements assuring gender equality.

The Charter's protection against nondiscrimination was elaborated further by the Universal Declaration of Human Rights that broadened the categories of forbidden discrimination:

> Everyone is entitled to all the rights and freedoms set forth in this Declaration, without distinction of any kind, such as race, colour, sex, language, religion, political or other opinion, national or social origin, property, birth or other status.[13]

The same categories of discrimination—race, color, sex, language, religion, political or other opinion, national or social origin, property, birth, or other status—were codified in the twin Covenants on Civil and Political Rights and on Economic, Social and Cultural Rights.[14]

All the major regional human rights treaties also contain nondiscrimination provisions. The African [Banjul] Charter on Human and Peoples' Rights in the Preamble refers to the duty to eliminate "all forms of discrimination, particularly those based on race, ethnic group, color, sex, language, religion or political opinions" and in Article 2 recognizes more specifically that all the rights and freedoms of the Charter are to be enjoyed "without distinction of any kind such as race, ethnic group, color, sex, language, religion, political or any other opinion, national and social origin, fortune, birth or other status."[15] The American Convention on Human Rights in Article 1 prohibits discrimination on the basis of "race, color, sex, language, religion, political or other opinion, national or social origin, economic status, birth, or any other social conditions."[16] The American Declaration of the Rights and Duties of Man in Article II provides for equality before the law without distinction as to "race, sex, language, creed or any other factor."[17] The European Convention for the Protection of Human Rights and Fundamental Freedoms in Article 14 provides that the "rights and freedoms in this

Convention" shall be "secured without discrimination on any ground such as sex, race, colour, language, religion, political or other opinion, national or social origin, association with a national minority, birth or other status."[18] Protocol No. 12 of the European Convention widened the prohibition against discrimination from the "rights and freedoms set forth in this Convention" to "any right set forth by law" and any act of a public authority.[19]

It should be noted that the last category "other status" is open-ended in the various treaties and has been applied to such additional forms of discrimination as age, capacity to bear children, caste, descent, disability, dwarfism, employed and unemployed persons, health status (including HIV/AIDS), indigenous status, individuals serving military and nonmilitary national service, marital status, nationality, natural and foster children, non-citizen status, place of residence, pregnancy, public and private school residents of a house who are close relatives or not close relatives, students, sexual orientation, and so on.

Not every distinction of treatment between groups of individuals will, however, constitute discrimination. If a distinction is to be made between groups, that difference in treatment must serve a legitimate state objective and must be proportional to the achievement of that objective. For example, a conscientious objector to military service who was performing alternative civilian service in The Netherlands complained that he was a victim of discrimination because he received a smaller living allowance than ordinary civilians. The Human Rights Committee rejected the claim because a person performing compulsory national service or military service is not entitled to be paid as if he or she were still in private civilian life.[20]

To fortify the general prohibitions against nondiscrimination in the Charter, Universal Declaration, and Covenants, more detailed human rights treaties have been promulgated with regard to discrimination on the basis of race and discrimination against women. Article 5 of the International Convention on the Elimination of All Forms of Racial Discrimination requires the 173 nations that have ratified the treaty to "to prohibit and to eliminate racial discrimination in all its forms" and to provide under Article 2 for affirmative action so long as such special measures are required.[21] The Convention forbids discrimination in regard to treatment before tribunals; security of person and protection against violence or bodily harm, whether inflicted by government officials or by any individual group or institution; political rights; and equal access to public service. The Convention also forbids discrimination in regard to other "civil rights, in particular:

(i) The right to freedom of movement and residence within the border of the State;

36  Particular Rights and Responsibilities

(ii) The right to leave any country, including one's own, and to return to one's country;
(iii) The right to nationality;
(iv) The right to marriage and choice of spouse;
(v) The right to own property alone as well as in association with others;
(vi) The right to inherit;
(vii) The right to freedom of thought, conscience and religion;
(viii) The right to freedom of opinion and expression; [and]
(ix) The right to freedom of peaceful assembly and association. . . .²²

Furthermore, the Convention gives protections against racial discrimination as to economic, social and cultural rights, in particular,

(i) The rights to work, to free choice of employment, to just and favourable conditions of work, to protection against unemployment, to equal pay for equal work, to just and favourable remuneration;
(ii) The right to form and join trade unions;
(iii) The right to housing;
(iv) The right to public health, medical care, social security and social services;
(v) The right to education and training;
(vi) The right to equal participation in cultural activities; as well as . . . [t]he right of access to any place or service intended for use by the general public, such as transport, hotels, restaurants, cafés, theatres and parks.²³

Both the Race Convention and the Convention on the Elimination of All Forms of Discrimination Against Women provide for affirmative action, that is, for example, "special and concrete measures to ensure the adequate development and protection of certain racial groups or individuals belonging to them, for the purpose of guaranteeing them the full and equal enjoyment of human rights and fundamental freedoms."²⁴ There are, however, time limits to affirmative action measures that "shall in no case entail as a consequence the maintenance of unequal or separate rights for different racial groups after the objectives for which they were taken have been achieved."²⁵

When the U.S. Supreme Court in 2003 considered whether white students had been subjected to discrimination on the basis of their race in being denied admission to the University of Michigan²⁶ and its law school,²⁷ the Supreme Court sustained the validity of the law school's affirmative action program in admissions under the Fourteenth Amendment to the U.S. Constitution's guarantee of equal protection, because diversity was a sufficiently compelling interest that permitted the use of race in admissions programs of the type used by the law school. At the same time, the Supreme Court found that the undergraduate admissions program was not narrowly tailored to the compelling interest in diversity and therefore violated the Fourteenth Amendment's guarantee of equal protection. Justice Ginsburg in her individual opinions in those two cases cited the affirmative action provisions of the Race and Women's Conventions for guidance in interpreting the U.S. Constitution.

*See also*: Groups at Risk

*Further Reading:*

Marc Bossuyt, The Concept and Practice of Affirmative Action, U.N. Doc. E/CN.4/Sub.2/2002/21 (2002).
Committee on Economic, Social and Cultural Rights, General Comment 18, Article 6: The Equal Right of Men and Women to the Enjoyment of All Economic, Social and Cultural Rights (Thirty-fifth session, 2006), U.N. Doc. E/C.12/GC/18 (2006).
Convention on the Elimination of All Forms of Discrimination Against Women, G.A. res. 34/180, 34 U.N. GAOR Supp. (No. 46) at 193, U.N. Doc. A/34/46, *entered into force* Sept. 3, 1981.
Gratz v. Bollinger, 123 S.Ct. 2411 (2003).
Grutter v. Gratz, 123 S.Ct. 2325 (2003).
H. A. E. d. J. [name deleted] v. The Netherlands, Communication No. 297/1988, U.N. Doc. CCPR/C/37/D/297/1988 (1989).

### 3. Life (Universal Declaration, Art. 3)

The Universal Declaration of Human Rights (1948) provides that "Everyone has the right to life, liberty and the security of person."[28] The Universal Declaration contains the most widely accepted definition of human rights and is considered to be an authoritative explication of the human rights obligations of all 191 UN members (including the U.S.). The Covenant on Civil and Political Rights (1966) expanded on this right in Article 6.[29] The first mandate was that the right shall be protected by law and that no one shall be arbitrarily deprived of his life. Second, in countries where the death penalty has not been abolished, such a sentence may be imposed only for the most serious crimes in accordance with the law in force at the time of the commission of the crime and must be carried out pursuant to final judgment by a competent court. Also, it must be in compliance with other provisions of the Covenant and the Convention on the Prevention and Punishment of the Crime of Genocide, which is deemed to be non-derogable, that is, not subject to exceptions or limitations in times of emergency.[30] Persons sentenced to death shall have the right to seek pardon or commutation of the sentence. The sentence of death cannot be imposed on persons who were under eighteen years of age at the time of the commission of the crime and on pregnant women. Further, the Covenant specifically provides that its provisions shall not be used to "delay or prevent the abolition of capital punishment by any State Party."[31]

The Human Rights Committee was established by the Civil and Political Covenant to interpret and apply the Covenant's provisions.[32] The Committee further defined the obligations under Article 6. The Committee in 1982 viewed the right broadly and noted that it includes duties to prevent loss of life in a number of contexts, such as war (especially thermonuclear war), genocide, and other acts of mass violence causing arbitrary loss of life.[33] The right to life also includes positive obligations to reduce infant mortality and increase life expectancy, as well as to prevent arbitrary killings by government security forces and to prevent disappearances of individuals. The Committee also observed that while States parties are not obligated to abolish the death penalty, they are required to limit its use and to abolish it for other than the "most serious crimes." Abolition of the death penalty is also considered as progress in enjoyment of the right to life.

The Second Optional Protocol to the International Covenant on Civil and Political Rights, Aiming at Abolition of the Death Penalty (1989), provides for the abolition of the death penalty.[34] It provides for no reservation except for the application of the death penalty for military crimes in time of war. While the Civil and Political Covenant has been ratified by 160 nations, the Second Optional Protocol has 60 States parties. The Convention on the Rights of the Child (1989) prohibits the death penalty for persons who were under eighteen at the time of the commission of a crime.[35] This treaty has been ratified by all countries (193) except the United States and Somalia, and the prohibition against juvenile executions has been obeyed by all except for a handful of countries, which through 2004 included the United States. The International Convention on the Protection of the Rights of All Migrant Workers and Members of their Families (1990) provides for the right to life of all migrant workers regardless of their status.[36]

The UN Commission on Human Rights, its successor Human Rights Council, and its Sub-Commission have since 1997 worked toward abolition of the death penalty.[37] Due to the number of countries that still have the death penalty, there are a number of dissents on resolutions calling for the abolition. The Commission has been more successful getting agreement on the principle that persons under eighteen at the time of the commission of their crime should not be subject to the death penalty. The Sub-Commission on Promotion and Protection of Human Rights has also passed resolutions calling for an end to juvenile executions. In March 2005 the U.S. Supreme Court decided that the Eighth Amendment of the U.S. Constitution forbids the execution of juvenile offenders, citing international sources.[38]

The UN Commission on Human Rights in 1982 also established a thematic mechanism to protect the right to life by authorizing its chairperson to select the Special Rapporteur on extrajudicial, summary, or arbitrary executions.[39] The Special Rapporteur receives information about political killings, impending executions in which there had been no trial or a trial without fair procedures, juvenile executions, and other matters within the rapporteur's remit. The Special Rapporteur responds to these urgent appeals by communicating concerns to governments and undertaking visits to particular countries. For example, during the period 1998–2003 the Special Rapporteur visited Albania (in connection with the Kosovo conflict), Brazil, the Democratic Republic of Congo, East Timor, Honduras, Jamaica, the former Yugoslav Republic of Macedonia, Mexico, Nepal, and Turkey. In 2004 the Special Rapporteur expressed concerns—together with several other special rapporteurs—about violence and loss of life during peaceful demonstrations in the Rafah refugee camp of the Gaza Strip.[40] The Special Rapporteur also annually reports on extrajudicial, summary, or arbitrary executions throughout the world to the UN Human Rights Council (formerly Commission on Human Rights) and the General Assembly.

All the regional human rights bodies protect the right to life. The African [Banjul] Charter on Human and Peoples' Rights provides that every human being is entitled to respect for life and the integrity of person and that the deprivation of the right cannot be arbitrary.[41] The American Declaration of the Rights and Duties of Man (1948) provides that every human being has the right to life, liberty and security of his person.[42] The American Convention on Human Rights (1969) expands on the right and provides that the right to life cannot be arbitrarily deprived.[43] Further, in countries that have not abolished the death penalty, it may be imposed only for the most serious crimes pursuant to final judgment issued by a competent court and to a law that was in effect at the time of the crime. Once abolished, the death penalty may not be reestablished. Capital punishment cannot be imposed for political offenses or related common crimes and cannot be imposed on persons who were under eighteen or over seventy at the time of the commission of the crime. It cannot be applied to pregnant women. Every person shall have the right to apply for amnesty, pardon, or commutation of sentence. Most of the countries that are party to the Organization of American States have abolished the death penalty.

The European Convention for the Protection of Human Rights and Fundamental Freedoms (1950) also protects the right to life.[44] While it allowed for the death penalty with certain protections, Protocol No. 6 (1985) provides for the abolition of the death penalty.[45] Adoption of the Protocol is required for membership in the European Union and as a result the death penalty has been abolished throughout Europe.

*See also*: Torture and Ill-Treatment

*Further Reading*:

Amnesty International, Political Killings by Governments (1983).
Amnesty International, Getting Away with Murder, Political Killings and 'Disappearances' in the 1990s (1993).
Connie de la Vega, *Amici Curiae Urge the U.S. Supreme Court to Consider International Human Rights Law in Juvenile Death Penalty Claim*, 42 Santa Clara L. Rev. 1041 (2002).
Human Rights Committee, General Comment 6, Article 6 (Sixteenth session, 1982), Compilation of General Comments and General Recommendations Adopted by Human Rights Treaty Bodies, U.N. Doc. HRI/GEN/1/Rev.1 at 6 (1994).
Jude Ibegbu, Rights of the Unborn Child in International Law (2000).
Principles on the Effective Prevention and Investigation of Extra-Legal, Arbitrary and Summary Executions, E.S.C. res. 1989/65, annex, 1989 U.N. ESCOR Supp. (No. 1) at 52, U.N. Doc. E/1989/89 (1989).
The Right to Life in International Law (Bertie G. Ramcharan ed., 1985).
William A. Schabas, The Abolition of the Death Penalty in International Law (3rd ed. 2002).
Second Optional Protocol to the International Covenant on Civil and Political

Rights, aiming at the abolition of the death penalty, G.A. res. 44/128, annex, 44 U.N. GAOR Supp. (No. 49) at 207, U.N. Doc. A/44/49 (1989).

Pieter Willem Smits, The Right to Life of the Unborn Child in International Documents, Decisions and Opinions (1992).

*Links to Consult:*

http://www.amnesty.org
http://www.ohchr.org/english/issues/executions/index.htm
http://www1.umn.edu/humanrts/gencomm/hrcom6.htm
http://www1.umn.edu/humanrts/instree/i7pepi.htm
http://www1.umn.edu/humanrts/links/deathpenalty.html

## 4. Slavery and Forced Labor (Universal Declaration, Art. 4)

Slavery has existed since ancient times, but in the modern world slavery may appear to be a historical problem overcome by an enlightened and expanding civil society governed by the rule of law. Unfortunately, this perception is far from true: although it is widely believed that slavery has been abolished, various forms of slavery remain at the beginning of the twenty-first century.

The abolitionist movement in the early nineteenth century was led by the Anti-Slavery Society, the first international human rights NGO, and began as an effort to stop the Atlantic slave trade and to free slaves in the colonies of European countries and in the United States.[46] The first victory of the abolitionist movement was the 1815 Declaration Relative to the Universal Abolition of the Slave Trade (the "1815 Declaration").[47] A large number of agreements dating from the early nineteenth century, both multilateral and bilateral, contain provisions prohibiting the slave trade and slavery in times of war and peace. It has been estimated that between 1815 and 1957 some 300 international agreements were implemented to suppress slavery. None have been totally effective.

The predecessor of the United Nations, the League of Nations, was very active in its work to eliminate slavery after World War I. After World War II, the UN continued working toward the elimination of slavery, and as a result it is now well established that customary international law prohibits slavery and slavery-like practices. Indeed, the International Court of Justice has identified the protection from slavery as one of very few examples of "obligations *erga omnes* arising out of human rights law," that is, obligations owed by a state to the international community as a whole.[48] The practice of slavery has also been universally accepted as a crime against humanity.[49]

In order for the UN or any other international body to carry out a mandate concerned with slavery, it is necessary to develop an international consensus on what practices are included within the concept of slavery. If the term is interpreted in such a manner as to include all of the social injustices or human rights violations that may occur, it becomes so broad as to be meaningless. This overly broad approach in turn would lead to a dilution of the work against slavery and reduce its effectiveness in achieving its objective of eliminating slavery. Slavery as defined in the international instruments must, therefore, be reviewed in an effort to identify the practices included within its scope.

A definition of slavery first appeared in an international agreement in the League of Nations Slavery, Servitude, Forced Labour and Similar Institutions and Practices Convention of 1926 ("Slavery Convention of

1926").[50] It defined slavery as "the status or condition of a person over whom any or all of the powers attaching to the right of ownership are exercised." It further defined the slave trade as "all acts involved in the capture, acquisition or disposal of a person with intent to reduce him to slavery; all acts involved in the acquisition of a slave with a view to selling or exchanging him; all acts of disposal by sale or exchange of a slave acquired with a view to being sold or exchanged, and, in general, every act of trade or transport in slaves." The convention also provided that "forced labour may only be exacted for public purposes" and required States parties "to prevent compulsory or forced labour from developing into conditions analogous to slavery."

Although the Slavery Convention outlawed slavery and associated practices, it not only failed to establish procedures for reviewing the incidence of slavery in States parties, but also neglected to create an international body that could evaluate and pursue allegations of violations. Despite these drawbacks, the League of Nations was able, through publicity and pressure on governments, to encourage the implementation of legislation abolishing slavery in countries such as Burma (1928) and Nepal (1926).

The period before World War II also saw the adoption of a series of international conventions concerning the traffic of women for prostitution. These abuses were not mentioned in the Slavery Convention or addressed by the various committees of experts on slavery, although the first of the international conventions on traffic in women referred in its title to the "white slave trade." That 1904 convention focused on cases in which women and girls were moved across international frontiers without their consent for the purposes of prostitution.[51] The Suppression of the White Slave Trade Convention in 1910 imposed an obligation on the parties to punish anyone who recruits a woman below the age of majority into prostitution, even with her consent.[52] In 1933, Article 1 of the Suppression of the Traffic of Women of Full Age Convention established a duty to prohibit, prevent, and punish the trafficking of women even when done with their consent.[53] This 1933 Convention specifically relates to the international traffic in consenting women of full age, but only in situations where there is traffic from one country to another.

This trend toward criminalizing the recruitment of women in one country to work as prostitutes in another continued after World War II with the adoption of the 1949 Convention for the Suppression of the Traffic in Persons and of the Exploitation of the Prostitution of Others ("Suppression of Traffic Convention" or "1949 Convention").[54] The 1949 Convention consolidated the earlier instruments relating to the "white slave trade" and traffic in women and children. The Suppression of Traffic Convention makes it an offense to procure, entice, or lead away a person for the purposes of prostitution even with the consent of that person. The notion of trafficking was inextricably linked to prostitution as in the earlier conventions, resulting in a narrow interpretation of trafficking as it does not include the procurement of individuals for any other purpose than sexual exploitation. The reality today is that people are trafficked not only for use in the sex industry but for many other reasons. Accordingly, Article 35 of the Convention on the Rights of the Child prohibits the abduction, sale, or traffic in children for any reason, for example, begging.[55]

The Supplementary Convention on the Abolition of Slavery, the Slave Trade and Institutions and Practices Similar to Slavery of 1956 ("Supplementary Convention") expanded the definition of slavery found in the 1926 Convention in order abolish institutions and practices, identified collectively as "servile status," including (a) debt bondage, (b) serfdom, and

(c) Any institution or practice whereby:
(i) A woman, without the right to refuse, is promised or given in marriage on payment of a consideration in money or in kind to her parents, guardian, family or any person or group; or
(ii) The husband of a woman, his family, or his clan, has the right to transfer her to another person for value received or otherwise; or
(iii) A woman on the death of her husband is liable to be inherited by another person;
(d) Any institution or practice whereby a child or young person under the age of 18 years, is delivered by either or both of his natural parents or by his guardian to another person, whether for reward or not, with a view to the exploitation of the child or young person or of his labour.[56]

Although there have been subsequent appeals to redefine slavery in the context of today's world, the combined definition of slavery set forth in the Convention of 1926 and the Supplementary Convention of 1956 has remained unchanged. For example, the Rome Statute of the International Criminal Court defines "enslavement" which is an aspect of a crime against humanity as "the exercise of any or all of the powers attaching to the right of ownership over a person . . . includ[ing] the exercise of such power in the course of trafficking in persons, in particular women and children."[57] This definition is essentially the same as the original definition adopted by the League of Nations about eighty years ago, adding only a specific reference to trafficking.

The prohibitions set out in the Slavery Convention of 1926 and its 1956 Supplement were given significant legal support by the International Bill of Human Rights. The Universal Declaration of Human Rights states that "No one shall be held in slavery or servitude; slavery and the slave trade shall be prohibited in all their forms."[58] The Civil and Political Covenant contains a similar prohibition against slavery and servitude in Article 8.[59] The importance accorded by the Covenant to the slavery provision is emphasized by its status as a non-derogable right under Article 4(2), that is, a right that cannot be suspended even in times of public emergency. Article 8 also contains a provision that prohibits the use of forced or compulsory labor subject to certain limited exceptions. The Economic, Social and Cultural Rights Covenant recognizes the right to work "which includes the right of everyone to the opportunity to gain his living by work which he freely chooses or accepts."[60] In Article 7 and 8 the Covenant further sets certain conditions and rights that help to prevent slavery and forced labor, such as the right to fair wages and equal remuneration for work of equal value, and the right to form and join trade unions.

In 2000 the UN General Assembly elaborated on existing instruments addressing trafficking in women and children and the illegal trafficking in and transporting of migrants through two protocols to the International Convention Against Transnational Organized Crime.[61] The Protocol to Prevent, Suppress and Punish Trafficking in Persons, especially Women and Children, Supplementing the United Nations Convention Against Transnational Organized Crime criminalizes "trafficking in persons," which it defines as "recruitment, transportation, transfer, harbouring or receipt of persons, by means of the threat or use of force or other forms of coercion, of abduction, of fraud, of deception, of the abuse of power or of a position of vulnerability or of the giving or receiving of payments or benefits to achieve the consent of a person having control over another person, for the purpose of exploitation."[62]

A. VIOLATIONS OF OTHER FUNDAMENTAL RIGHTS ASSOCIATED WITH SLAVERY

Ownership is the common theme existing in all of the conventions concerning the abolition of slavery and slavery-like practices. Traditional slavery was referred to as "chattel slavery" on the grounds that the owners of such slaves were able to treat them as if they were possessions, like livestock or furniture, and to sell or transfer them to others. Today, such practices are extremely rare and the criterion of ownership may obscure some of the other characteristics of slavery.

The circumstances of the enslaved person are crucial to identifying what practices constitute slavery, including (1) the degree of restriction of the individual's inherent right to freedom of movement; (2) the degree of control of the individual's personal belongings; and (3) the existence of informed consent and a full understanding of the nature of the relationship between the parties. These elements of control and ownership, often accompanied by the threat of violence, are central to identifying the existence of slavery. The migrant worker whose passport has been confiscated by his or her employer, the child sold into prostitution, or the "comfort woman" forced into sexual slavery—all have the element of choice and control of their lives taken from them and passed to a third party, either an individual or a state. Sexual slavery received considerable international attention due to publicity about the systematic rape of women prisoners during the 1992 conflict in the former Yugoslavia and concerning the efforts of "comfort women" from Korea, the Philippines, China, and other Asian countries to seek compensation for the abduction and forced prostitution they suffered during World War II in or near Japanese military camps.

The process of enslavement, as well as, in many cases, the treatment of victims of slavery, servile status, and forced labor, is often accompanied by other violations of human rights. For example, the classic process of enslavement, involving either abduction or recruitment through false promises or duplicity, involves a violation of the individual's right to liberty and security of person, as guaranteed by Article 9 of the Civil and Political Covenant, together in many cases with a violation of the right of a person deprived of their liberty to be treated with humanity and of the right not to be subjected to cruel, inhuman, or degrading treatment. Historical images of slavery, again based on the Atlantic slave trade and treatment of African slaves in the Americas, focus on the ill-treatment of slaves, particularly branding or mutilation of individuals to facilitate their identification. The Supplementary Convention of 1956 explicitly prohibits "the act of mutilating, branding or otherwise marking a slave or a person of servile status in order to indicate his status, or as a punishment, or for any other reason. . . ."[63] Other forms of ill-treatment, including beatings and other corporal punishment, are a violation of the right not to be subjected to torture or to cruel, inhuman, or degrading treatment or punishment.

Victims of slavery, servile status, and forced labor are, almost by definition, deprived of their rights under Article 12 of the Civil and Political Covenant to liberty of movement and freedom to choose their residence. Almost invariably they are deprived of or prevented from exercising their right to access to the courts and to a fair trial by their owners, controllers, employers, or by the authorities themselves.

The list of aggravating circumstances, of abuses of fundamental rights that accompany slavery and related abuses, is almost endless. In the harshest cases it includes depriving individuals of their identity (by giving them a new name, often one associated with a different religion or ethnic identity), obliging them to speak a new language, and forcing them to change their religion. Some extreme cases also involve preventing individuals from exercising their right to marry and to establish a family, notably when the victims are women who are forced to act as mistresses or concubines of the men who control them, or are forced to remain in prostitution. Virtually all cases involve violations of the victims' freedom of expression, their right to receive and impart information, their right of peaceful assembly, and their freedom of association.

In some societies slaves have been prevented from owning or inheriting property. One of the legacies of slavery still affecting people categorized as "slaves" in Mauritania where slavery has been formally abolished on several occasions is that, on the death of former slaves, the families of their former owners still intervene to take possession of their property—sometimes with the authority of the courts—thus preventing the heirs of former slaves from inheriting.

B. FORCED LABOR

The International Labor Organization (ILO) has adopted 187 conventions ranging from maternity protection to protection of the most vulnerable and poverty stricken laborers.[64] The ILO aims to achieve through these conventions the following four fundamental principles:

(1) the elimination of forced labor;
(2) freedom of association, including the right to a trade union;
(3) the effective abolition of child labor; and
(4) the ending of discrimination in employment.

The Forced Labour Convention of 1930 (ILO Convention No. 29) provides for the abolition of forced labor.[65] It defines forced or compulsory labor in Article 2(1) as "all work or service which is exacted from any person under the menace of any penalty and for which the said person has not offered himself voluntarily." This definition distinguishes forced labor from slavery in that it does not include a concept of ownership. Yet forced labor imposes a similar degree of restriction on the individual's freedom—often through violent means—making forced labor similar to slavery in its effect on the individual.

ILO Convention No. 29 obliged States parties to "suppress the use of forced or compulsory labour *within the shortest possible time.*"[66] The lack of an absolute prohibition, along with the existence of such an ambiguous timeline for eradicating forced labor may be explained by the fact that it was still routine for colonial authorities to rely on forced labor for public works. In its 1998 report on forced labor in Myanmar (Burma), the ILO noted, however, that a country may no longer rely on this timeline to justify inadequate national protections against forced labor.[67]

Finding that the use of forced labor as a means of political coercion violated Articles 2 (political discrimination), 9 (arbitrary arrest), 10 (fair hearing), 11 (presumption of innocence), and 19 (freedom of expression) of the Universal Declaration of Human Rights, the ILO created the Abolition of Forced Labour Convention (No. 105) of 1957, which, in Article 1, imposes an obligation on States parties to suppress the use of forced labor for political purposes, for purposes of economic development, as a means of labor discipline or punishment for strike action, and as a means of discrimination.[68] This convention, together with ILO Convention No. 29 (collectively referred to as the "ILO forced labor conventions")[69] are the most basic and important instruments concerning freedom of labor. The ILO forced labor conventions apply to work or service exacted by governments or public authorities, as well as to forced labor exacted by private bodies and individuals, including slavery, bonded labor, and certain forms of child labor.

The Civil and Political Covenant provides in Article 8 that "No one shall be required to perform forced or compulsory labour," subject to certain exceptions concerning prisoners, military service, emergencies, and normal civil obligations.[70] Regional agreements also address forced labor. The European Convention for the Protection of Human Rights, for example, prohibits forced or compulsory labor in Article 4.[71] Although the convention does not define forced labor, the European Commission of Human Rights identified as the two factors characterizing forced or compulsory labor "that the work [be] performed against the complainant's will and secondly, that the work entail unavoidable hardship to the complainant."[72]

Not all forms of forced labor are prohibited under the ILO forced labor conventions and the Civil and Political Covenant. Article 2(2) of ILO Convention No. 29 and Article 8 of the Covenant set out certain specific exemptions that otherwise would have fallen under the definition of forced or compulsory labor. For example, Article 2(2) of Convention No. 29 exempts "any work or service which forms part of the normal civic obligations of the citizens of a fully self-governing country," including compulsory military service, work provided in emergency situations, and minor communal service.[73] The ILO forced labor conventions do not prohibit prison labor, but they do place restrictions on its use.

Extremely low wages are a cause of forced labor and debt bondage. The ILO has therefore encouraged national authorities to set minimum wages to prevent the payment of extremely low wages that are insufficient to maintain the workers and their families. ILO Convention No.

131 concerning Minimum Wage Fixing with Special Reference to Developing Countries and its accompanying Recommendation No. 135 seek to give wage earners the necessary social protection in terms of minimum permissible levels of wages.[74] ILO Convention No. 117 concerning Basic Aims and Standards of Social Policy of 1962 also states that "wages shall normally be paid in legal tender only,"regularly, "at such intervals as will lessen the likelihood of indebtedness among the wage earners."[75]

Debt bondage or bonded labor still exists today, affecting millions of adults and children in their own countries and migrant workers throughout the world. In Convention No. 182 of 2000 concerning the Prohibition and Immediate Action for the Elimination of the Worst Forms of Child Labour, the ILO included debt bondage among the "worst forms" prohibited by Article 3.[76]

In view of the prevalence of bonded labor among the landless in rural areas, governments may in some instances be forced to reform the existing land tenure systems in order to prevent debt bondage and thereby comply with their obligations under the Supplementary Convention. In addition to passing legislation to abolish debt bondage, to extinguish debts that have been incurred, and to take preventive action, rehabilitation is a crucial element governments must undertake to fulfill their obligations under ILO Conventions No. 95 and 117.[77] They must ensure that once bonded workers are freed they must not be drawn back into bonded status by promptly assuming another loan. In India and Pakistan the governments make payments to individuals identified as bonded laborers, seeking to prevent the process of bonded labor from starting again.

C. APPLICATION OF PROHIBITIONS AGAINST SLAVERY AND FORCED LABOR

National authorities possess the primary obligation to protect the human rights of residents, including, of course, the prohibition of slavery and slavery-like practices. For example, in *United States v. Sanga* a man forced a woman to work as a domestic maid for more than two years and forced her to have sex with him.[78] The U.S. Court of Appeals for the 9th Circuit unanimously held that she was a "virtual slave" contrary to the provision of the Thirteenth Amendment to the U.S. Constitution, which prohibits slavery and involuntary servitude. The efforts of national authorities are augmented, however, by international human rights norms and procedures for implementing and ensuring compliance with international human rights treaties. There are therefore important links between national and international monitoring methods that cannot be overlooked although the focus of this chapter is on international mechanisms.

Under the Slavery Convention of 1926 and the Supplementary Convention, States parties agree, but are not obliged to send information on measures implemented in accordance with the slavery conventions to the Secretary-General, who in turn communicates such information to the Economic and Social Council for discussion "with a view to making further recommendations for the abolition of slavery."[79] The Economic and Social Council has not pursued this role actively. Instead, in 1975 it established the Working Group on Contemporary Forms of Slavery of the UN Sub-Commission on the Promotion and Protection of Human Rights to monitor the existence of "slavery and the slave trade in all their practices and manifestation. The Working Group operates with a large degree of flexibility and receives information from member States and nongovernmental organizations (NGOs) relating to slavery, servitude, forced labor, and other slavery-like practices."[80] Ordinarily at each session the Working Group receives information from NGOs and then promptly informs the relevant governments that they have been mentioned and may wish to submit further information. Since governments are rarely given more than a couple of days notice, their responses are often spontaneous and they often offer to submit further information when it can be obtained.

The ILO has established a monitoring method for the Forced Labour Convention of 1930 (No. 29),[81] the Abolition of Forced Labour Convention of 1957 (No. 105),[82] and other relevant labor conventions that is based on reports received from governments and is exercised by the Committee of Experts on the Application of Conventions and Recommendations. These state reporting procedures of the ILO are described below in the chapter relating to Specialized and Other Agencies.

The second type of supervision exercised by the ILO involves investigation into allegations that a state has failed to comply with its obligation under a convention it has ratified. This mechanism can be invoked by a state, any employers' or workers' organization, or the ILO Governing Body alleging that a state is in breach of its obligation under Article 26 of the ILO Constitution to observe the provisions of a ratified treaty.[83] Under Article 26 of the ILO Constitution, a Commission of Inquiry examined the compliance of Burma (Myanmar) with the forced labor conventions and issued a report of its findings and recommendations in 1998. The report clearly set out "an international labour standard that protects a fundamental human right—the right not to be reduced to a state of slavery of forced labour, whichever form this may take." The Commission of Inquiry confirmed that international law prohibits absolutely any recourse to forced or compulsory labor and that any person who "violates this peremptory norm is guilty of a crime."[84] The government of Myanmar in its response to the report agreed to try to complete the reform process within the allocated time-frame, but has not achieved that objective.

*See also*: Genocide, War Crimes, Crimes Against Humanity, and Crimes Against Peace; Specialized and Other Agencies; Torture and Ill-Treatment; Work-Related Rights and Rest

*Further Reading:*

Abolition of Forced Labour Convention (ILO No. 105), 320 U.N.T.S. 291, *entered into force* Jan. 17, 1959.
*Barcelona Traction, Light and Power Co. (Belgium v. Spain)*, 1970 ICJ 3.
Kathleen Barry, Female Sexual Slavery (1984).
M. Cherif Bassiouni, *Enslavement as an International Crime*, 23 N.Y.U.J. of Law & Politics 445 (1991).
Convention Concerning Basic Aims and Standards of Social Policy (ILO No. 117), 1 International Labour Conventions and Recommendations 1919–1991 at 746 (1992), *entered into force* Apr. 23, 1964.
Convention Concerning Forced or Compulsory Labour (ILO No. 29), 39 U.N.T.S. 55, *entered into force* May 1, 1932.
Convention Concerning Minimum Wage Fixing with Special Reference to Developing Countries (ILO No. 131), 1 International Labour Conventions and Recommendations 1919–1991 at 949 (1992), *entered into force* Apr. 29, 1972.
Convention Concerning the Prohibition and Immediate Action for the Elimination of the Worst Forms of Child Labour (ILO No. 182), 38 I.L.M. 1207 (1999), *entered into force* Nov. 19, 2000.
Convention Concerning the Protection of Wages (ILO No. 95), 1 International Labour Conventions and Recommendations 1919–1991 at 482 (1992), *entered into force* Sept. 24, 1952.
Convention for the Suppression of the Traffic in Persons and of the Exploitation of the Prostitution of Others, 96 U.N.T.S. 271, *entered into force* July 25, 1951.
Declaration Relative to the Universal Abolition of the Slave Trade, Feb. 8, 1815, (Annex XV of the Treaty of Vienna), 63 Consol. T. S. 473.
Michael Dottridge & David Weissbrodt, *Review of the Implementation of and Follow-up to the Conventions on Slavery*, 42 German Yearbook of International Law 242 (1999).
E.S.C. Resolution of Dec. 16, 1974, 56 U.N. ESCOR, Supp. 1, 25, U.N. Doc E/5544 (establishing the Working Group on Contemporary Forms of Slavery).
Human Rights Committee, General Comment No. 24, U.N. Doc. CCPR/C/21/Rev.1/Add. 6 (1994).
Inter-American Convention on International Traffic in Minors, Mar. 18, 1994, OEA/Ser.K/XXI.5, CIDIP-V/doc.36/94 rev. 5, 79 O.A.S.T.S., 33 I.L.M. 721 (1994).
International Agreement for the Suppression of the "White Slave Traffic," May 18, 1904, 35 Stat. 1979, 1 L.N.T.S. 83.
International Convention for the Suppression of the Traffic in Women and Children, Sept. 30, 1921, 9 L.N.T.S. 415.

International Convention for the Suppression of the Traffic in Women of Full Age, Oct. 11, 1933, 150 L.N.T.S. 431.
International Convention for the Suppression of the White Slave Traffic, May 4, 1910, 211 Consol. T.S. 45, 103 B.F.S.P. 244.
International Labor Organization, Declaration on Fundamental Principles and Rights at Work and its Follow-up, 137 International Labour Review 253 (1998).
International Labor Organization, Report of the Commission of Inquiry Appointed under Article 26 to Examine the Observance of Myanmar of the Forced Labour Convention 1930 (No. 29) (1998).
Ved Nanda and Cherif Bassiouni, *Slavery and the Slave Trade: Steps Toward Eradication*, 12 Santa Clara Lawyer 424 (1972).
A. Yasmine Rassam, *Contemporary Forms of Slavery and the Evolution of the Prohibition of Slavery and the Slave Trade Under Customary International Law*, 39 Virginia Journal of International Law 303 (1999).
Renee Colette Redman, *The League of Nations and the Right to be Free from Enslavement: the First Human Right to be Recognized as Customary International Law*, 70 Chicago-Kent Law Review 759 (1994).
Rome Statute of the International Criminal Court, 2187 U.N.T.S. 3, *entered into force* July 1, 2002.
Klaus Samson, *The Standard-Setting and Supervisory System of the ILO* in An Introduction to the International Protection of Human Rights 170 (Raija Hanski and Markku Suksi eds., 1997).
Slavery, Servitude, Forced Labour and Similar Institutions and Practices Convention of 1926 (Slavery Convention of 1926), 60 L.N.T.S. 253, *entered into force* Mar. 9, 1927.
Supplementary Convention on the Abolition of Slavery, the Slave Trade, and Institutions and Practices Similar to Slavery, 226 U.N.T.S. 3, *entered into force* Apr. 30, 1957.
Temporary Slavery Commission Report to the Council, LN Doc. A.17.1924.VI.B (1924).
U.O. Umozurike, *The African Slave Trade and the Attitude of International Law Towards It*, 16 Howard L.J. 346 (1971).
*United States v. Sanga*, 967 F.2d 1332 (9th Cir. 1992).
Nicolas Valticos and Geraldo von Potobsky, International Labour Law (1994).
*X v. Federal Republic of Germany* (Application No. 4653/70), 46 Eur. Comm'n H.R. Dec. & Rep. 22 (1974).

*Links to Consult:*

http://www.antislavery.org
http://www1.umn.edu/humanrts/instree/auof.htm
http://www1.umn.edu/humanrts/links/anti-slavery.html

## 5. Torture and Ill-Treatment (Universal Declaration, Art. 5)

The Universal Declaration of Human Rights (1948) and the Covenant on Civil and Political Rights (1966) were ahead of their time when they announced: "No one shall be subjected to torture or to cruel, inhuman or degrading treatment or punishment."[85] The Geneva Conventions of 1949 also forbid torture during armed conflicts. At that time, however, torture was commonly practiced and was rarely the subject of public comment or criticism. Torture, indeed, was a dirty secret of the police, military, and secret services throughout the world. For example, the French military regularly employed torture during Algeria's revolutionary war (1954–62).

On Human Rights Day, 1972 (December 10, the day set aside for the commemoration of the adoption of the Universal Declaration of Human Rights), Amnesty International (AI) launched its first campaign for the abolition of torture.[86] AI planned to hold a conference in Paris a year later, December 10, 1973, and issue a report detailing torture and ill-treatment in over seventy nations and territories in the early 1970s. The conference was so controversial at the time that its venue had to be changed to a less visible location. Nonetheless, the dirty secret of torture had been exposed and by 1975 Amnesty International was able to persuade the UN General Assembly to adopt by consensus the Declaration on the Protection of All Persons from Being Subjected to Torture and Other Cruel, Inhuman or Degrading Treatment or Punishment.[87] The Declaration set forth detailed measures that governments should take to prevent, investigate, punish, and remedy instances of torture. After the Civil and Political Covenant came into force in 1976, AI continued its efforts to build an international legal bulwark against torture. For example, it lobbied successfully for a Code of Conduct for Law Enforcement Officials (1979)[88] and principles of medical ethics for physicians in protecting prisoners from torture (1982).[89] In 1981 the UN General Assembly also established the UN Voluntary Fund for Victims of Torture, which provides support to rehabilitation efforts and legal advocacy for torture survivors around the world.[90]

Amnesty International began its second campaign against torture in 1984, and by the end of that year the General Assembly adopted the Convention Against Torture and Other Cruel, Inhuman or Degrading Treatment or Punishment,[91] which not only contained precepts on how governments should prohibit, prevent, investigate, punish, and remedy instances of torture, but also called for universal jurisdiction over and extradition of suspected torturers and established mechanisms for implementation through the Committee Against Torture.[92] The Convention Against Torture entered into force in 1987 and the Committee

Against Torture has since that time been reviewing the periodic reports of the 144 nations that have ratified the treaty and has been making country conclusions and recommendations. The Committee also has the authority to receive complaints about the use of torture, but that procedure is not very widely known and the Committee has only handled about 250 cases with regard to 56 nations that have accepted that procedure, as compared with the analogous procedure of the Human Rights Committee, which has handled more than 1,250 cases from the 109 nations that have agreed to be the subject of complaints.

In 2003 the General Assembly adopted an optional protocol to the Convention Against Torture, which came into force in June 2006 and established a Sub-Committee on Prevention that may visit any place of detention and interview detainees in those countries that have accepted the protocol and also requires those governments to establish national preventative mechanisms that can visit any place of detention and take other steps to stop the use of torture.[93] The optional protocol follows the similar and very successful prison visiting procedure established by the European Convention for the Prevention of Torture and Inhuman or Degrading Treatment or Punishment.

While these standard-setting efforts and international procedures have helped to prevent and remedy torture in many countries, torture remains a pervasive and troubling feature of the world scene. In initiating a third campaign against torture in 2003, Amnesty International indicated that it had received reports of torture from 150 nations. While political prisoners had been involved in seventy nations, ordinary criminals had been the victims of torture and ill-treatment in 130 nations and people had died of torture in eighty countries.

AI has found that Urgent Actions are one very effective technique for stopping torture; it has found that most torture occurs during the first hours and days after capture. Accordingly, prompt action is required. Whenever AI receives information that an individual is at risk of torture, it immediately disseminates that information to volunteers around the world, who in turn write telegrams, faxes, text messages, emails, and letters to prison wardens and other officials. Other human rights NGOs, such as the World Organization Against Torture, have developed a similar urgent action procedure.[94]

There are quite a number of other ways by which governments and NGOs have sought to prevent and remedy torture. Since torture often occurs when an individual is placed in incommunicado, solitary, or secret detention, the Committee Against Torture, human rights NGOs, and other human rights organizations, and many governments have sought to forbid such conditions of confinement, insist that detainees

## Torture and Ill-Treatment 55

are brought to court soon after arrest, guarantee the right to petition for habeas corpus, and have access to legal and medical assistance.

Another measure to prevent torture is to avoid extraditing or returning to their own country any individual who has substantial grounds for believing that he or she would be in danger of being subjected to torture if he or she is returned. The Convention Against Torture expressly provides for such a measure of prevention and the Civil and Political Covenant and the European Convention on Human Rights have been interpreted to protect against forcible return or "refoulement" of persons at substantial risk of torture.

While the Universal Declaration, Civil and Political Covenant, and Convention Against Torture forbid both torture and cruel, inhuman, and degrading treatment, some provisions (such as the duty to prosecute under the Convention and the obligation to avoid refoulement) apply only to torture. Also, accusing a government or individual of torture is far more serious in ordinary public parlance. Hence, some courts have distinguished between torture and other forms of cruel, inhuman, and degrading treatment (or more succinctly ill-treatment). Torture is defined by the Convention Against Torture to constitute (1) *severe pain or suffering*, whether physical or mental, which is (2) *intentionally inflicted* on a person (3) for such purposes as obtaining from him or a third person information or a confession, punishing him for an act he or a third person has committed or is suspected of having committed, or intimidating or coercing him or a third person, or *for any reason based on discrimination of any kind*, (4) when such pain or suffering is *inflicted by* or at the instigation of or with the consent *or acquiescence of* a public official or other person acting in an *official* capacity. (5) It does *not include* pain or suffering arising only from, inherent in or incidental to lawful sanctions. Cruel, inhuman, or degrading treatment is not defined by the Convention Against Torture, but one can infer its meaning from decisions of the Committee Against Torture, the Human Rights Committee, and other human rights bodies. For example, the Human Rights Committee has found a violation of Article 7 (torture and other cruel, inhuman or degrading treatment or punishment) of the Covenant to have occurred when a detainee was held incommunicado, blindfolded with his hands bound, and given only two cups of soup per day, and relatives were not permitted to bring food or medicine despite chronic diarrhea and frequent colds. Rape of women in detention has been found to constitute torture by the Committee Against Torture, the Inter-American Commission on Human Rights, and the European Court of Human Rights.

Torture is more likely to occur when there is a climate of impunity among perpetrators. Accordingly, torture can be prevented if there are authoritative instructions from the head of state or other high government officials that torture and ill-treatment are unacceptable. Further, the Convention Against Torture, Geneva Conventions, and national law in many countries call for the investigation, extradition, trial, and punishment of perpetrators. The Rome Statute of the International Criminal Court, which was adopted in 1998, came into force in 2002, and has more than 100 States parties, declared torture both a crime against humanity and a war crime subject to universal criminal jurisdiction.[95]

The torture and ill-treatment of detainees during 2003–4 in Abu Ghraib prison in Baghdad and other places of detention controlled by U.S. forces in Iraq and Afghanistan represents one of the most visible and troubling instances of torture in recent years. While all the facts are not yet known, several elements of the situation are instructive. Since at least the beginning of the "War on Terror" in September 2001, a number of otherwise respected individuals have begun to speculate that torture may be hypothetically necessary in particularly grave conditions, for example, when a detainee knows the location of a ticking bomb. Many have responded that torture is absolutely forbidden by national and international law—even in times of war or other national emergency; torture is morally wrong; and there is no evidence that torture actually obtains truthful information. Nonetheless, a climate of impunity began to grow in some circles in the United States. The Departments of Defense and Justice sought to interpose every legal impediment they could muster to impede judicial oversight with regard to detainees in Guantánamo and elsewhere. Further, there were memos exchanged among lawyers in the Department of Justice, Department of Defense, and White House that argued that under a skewed reading of the U.S. Constitution the U.S. President could not be held responsible for ordering torture in the cause of national defense, and that reservations to the U.S. ratification to the Convention Against Torture could be used to justify distinctions between torture and other ill-treatment and thus make permissible methods of interrogation forbidden by the Committee Against Torture, Human Rights Committee, European Court of Human Rights, Special Rapporteur on torture, and other sources of international law. It should be noted that military lawyers for the Joint Chiefs of Staff expressed concern about that approach because they feared that if detainees in Iraq were ill-treated, any U.S. soldier who might be captured would also suffer.

While the International Committee of the Red Cross (ICRC) followed its ordinary procedure in periods of armed conflict and occupation of visiting detainees in Abu Ghraib prison, it is now known that the leadership of the ICRC was expressing grave concern about the conditions in that prison and the U.S. military (with permission from the Secretary of Defense) were hiding at least some detainees from ICRC visits.

In the detention facilities themselves, U.S. soldiers and civilian translators were given ambiguous orders, for example, to keep detainees awake for long periods between interrogation sessions, but they were not given any instructions as to how such orders were to be accomplished. In those places of detention, military discipline was very lax; neither soldiers nor civilian translators were trained as to the impermissibility of torture or ill-treatment.

When the torture and other ill-treatment were first revealed by undeniable photographs at first exchanged among soldiers, then brought to the attention of higher officials, and finally leaked to the press, U.S. officials at first tried to avoid release of the information and evidently delayed informing the highest government officials, including the President. The administration sought to blame the instances on a few misguided and poorly trained troops and translators and to deny and hide any responsibility beyond Abu Ghraib Prison in Baghdad, even though there was evidence of torture in other facilities, over a far longer period of time, and with much more pervasive command responsibility. President Bush did announce, "Their treatment does not reflect the nature of the American people. That's not the way we do things in America." Initial military prosecutions were directed at a few soldiers—particularly those who had taken or posed in the photographs or had posed. Congressional and judicial investigations were long delayed as to command or political responsibility for the torture.

These events provide a cautionary lesson as to how torture and ill-treatment can occur and how important it is that the critical measures set forth in the Convention Against Torture, the Geneva Conventions, and other international provisions of international human rights law are taken to prevent torture and also to prevent recurrence.

*See also*: Genocide, War Crimes, Crimes Against Humanity, and Crimes Against Peace; Humanitarian Law; International Criminal Court

*Further Reading*:

Amnesty International, Report on Torture (1973).
Amnesty International, Torture in the Eighties (1984).
Amnesty International, Combating Torture—A Manual for Action (2003).
J. Herman Burgers and Hans Danelius, The United Nations Convention Against Torture, A Handbook on the Convention Against Torture and Other Cruel, Inhuman or Degrading Treatment or Punishment (1988).
Convention Against Torture and Other Cruel, Inhuman or Degrading Treatment or Punishment, G.A. res. 39/46, annex, 39 U.N. GAOR Supp. (No. 51) at 197, U.N. Doc. A/39/51 (1984), *entered into force* June 26, 1987.
Declaration on the Protection of All Persons from Being Subjected to Torture and Other Cruel, Inhuman or Degrading Treatment or Punishment, G.A. res.

3452 (XXX), annex, 30 U.N. GAOR Supp. (No. 34) at 91, U.N. Doc. A/10034 (1975).

Oren Gross, *Are Torture Warrants Warranted? Pragmatic Absolutism and Official Disobedience*, 88 Minnesota L. Rev. 1481 (2004).

Optional Protocol to the Convention Against Torture and Other Cruel, Inhuman or Degrading Treatment or Punishment, G.A. res. A/RES/57/199, *entered into force* June 22, 2006.

Sanford Levinson, ed., Torture: A Collection (2004).

Rita Maran, Torture: The Role of Ideology in the French-Algerian War (1989).

Nigel Rodley, The Treatment of Prisoners in International Law (2000).

Rome Statute of the International Criminal Court, 2187 U.N.T.S. 3, *entered into force* July 1, 2002.

*Links to Consult:*

http://www.amnesty.org
http://www.apt.ch
http://www.cvt.org/
http://www.omct.org
http://texscience.org/reform/torture/
http://www.unhchr.ch/html/menu2/6/cat/index.html
http://www1.umn.edu/humanrts/instree/auoy.htm
http://www1.umn.edu/humanrts/instree/h1dpast.htm
http://www1.umn.edu/humanrts/instree/h2catoc.htm
http://www1.umn.edu/humanrts/instree/optprotort.html

## 6. Procedural Fairness in the Criminal Process and the Administration of Justice (Universal Declaration, Articles 8, 9, 10, 11)

The right to a fair trial is one of the most important rights enshrined in the Universal Declaration of Human Rights and codified in the Covenant on Civil and Political Rights. Article 10 of the Universal Declaration states: "Everyone is entitled in full equality to a fair and public hearing by an independent tribunal, in the determination of his rights and obligations and of any criminal charge against him."[96] Article 11 provides for the presumption of innocence, public trial, "all guarantees necessary for [one's] defense," and the right to be free from retroactive punishment or penalties. Other provisions of the Universal Declaration—for example, as to arbitrary arrest, the right to an effective remedy or legal redress, the right to be free from torture, and the right to security of person, and privacy—relate to the fairness of the trial process in particular cases.

The Civil and Political Covenant further elaborates—particularly in Articles 14 and 15, but also in Articles 9, 2, 6, 7, and 10—upon the fair trial rights identified in the Universal Declaration. Article 14 of the Civil and Political Covenant recognizes the right to "a fair trial and public hearing by a competent, independent and impartial tribunal established by law."[97] Every person is "equal before the courts and tribunals" under Article 14(1). Article 14 also distinguishes between the sort of fair hearing required for civil cases, on the one hand, and criminal cases, on the other.

Article 14(3) deals with the "minimum guarantees" required in the determination of any criminal charge, the observance of which are not always sufficient to ensure the fairness of a hearing. Among the minimum guarantees in criminal proceedings prescribed by Article 14(3) are the right of everyone to be informed in a language that the accused understands of the charge against him/her; to have adequate time and facilities for the preparation of a defense and to communicate with counsel of one's own choosing; to be tried without undue delay; to examine or have examined the witnesses against the accused and to obtain the attendance and examination of witnesses on one's behalf under the same conditions as witnesses against the accused; to the assistance of an interpreter free of any charge, if the accused cannot understand or speak the language used in court; and not to be compelled to testify against oneself or to confess guilt. Article 14 also gives the accused the right to have one's conviction and sentence reviewed by a higher tribunal according to law; to compensation if there was a miscarriage of justice; and not to be subjected to trial or punishment for a second time (*non bis in idem*). Under Article 14(4) juvenile persons have the same right to a fair trial as adults, but are also entitled to certain additional safeguards. Article 15 codifies the principle of *nullum crimen sine lege* (no crime without law) and also gives the accused the benefit of any decrease in penalty which is promulgated after the person has committed an offense.

The Human Rights Committee has evolved a considerable jurisprudence on issues relating to the administration of justice—particularly as to the right to a fair trial.[98] For example, many prisoners have complained to the Human Rights Committee that they have not received a prompt trial and the Committee has sought to interpret that requirement. In 1984 the Human Rights Committee issued a General Comment that authoritatively interpreted Article 14 of the Covenant and stated that the right to trial without undue delay relates not only to the time by which a trial should commence, but also to the time by which it should end and judgment be rendered; all stages must take place "without undue delay."[99] It must be ensured, by means of an established procedure, that the trial will proceed "without undue delay," both in the first instance and on appeal.

The Civil and Political Covenant identifies in Article 4 certain rights as non-derogable, that is, those rights which cannot be the subject of suspension during periods of emergency that threatens the life of the nation. While Article 4 does not specify Article 14 (right to a fair trial) as expressly non-derogable, it does mention Articles 7 (prohibition of torture), 15 (*nullum crimen sine lege*; no crime without law), and 16 (recognition of every person before the law) as non-derogable. Furthermore, the Human Rights Committee has interpreted other non-derogable rights (e.g., the right not to be subjected to arbitrary deprivation of life) as implying that the basic fair trial provisions of Article 14 cannot be suspended during periods of national emergency. The Human Rights Committee has, accordingly, strengthened the non-derogable nature of the right to a fair trial by issuing a further General Comment in 2001 that stated, "any trial leading to the imposition of the death penalty during a state of emergency must conform to the provisions of the Covenant, including all the requirements of articles 14 and 15."[100] That General Comment further stated that

> Safeguards related to derogation, as embodied in article 4 of the Covenant, are based on the principles of legality and the rule of law inherent in the Covenant as a whole. As certain elements of the right to a fair trial are explicitly guaranteed under international humanitarian law during armed conflict, the Committee finds no justification for derogation from these guarantees during other emergency situations. The Committee is of the opinion that the principles of

legality and the rule of law require that fundamental requirements of fair trial must be respected during a state of emergency.[101]

The Convention on the Right of the Child elaborates on the rights of juvenile offenders in the Civil and Political Covenant and other treaties. Article 12 safeguards each child's right to be heard in legal proceedings. Article 37(b) provides that "No child shall be deprived of his or her liberty unlawfully or arbitrarily."[102] Furthermore, Article 37 (d) provides that "Every child deprived of his or her liberty shall have the right to prompt access to legal and other appropriate assistance, as well as the right to challenge the legality of the deprivation of his or her liberty before a court or other competent, independent and impartial authority, and to a prompt decision on any such action." Article 40 of the Child Convention addresses the same fair trial issues as Article 14 of the Civil and Political Covenant.

Common Article 3 of the four Geneva Conventions for the protection of victims of armed conflict and Article 6 of Additional Protocol II contain fair trial guarantees for times of non-international armed conflict.[103] Articles 96 and 99–108 of the Third Geneva Convention prescribe the rights of prisoners of war in judicial proceedings, essentially creating a fair trial standard. Articles 54, 64–74, and 117–26 of the Fourth Geneva Convention contain provisions relating to the right to fair trial in occupied territories. Article 75 of Additional Protocol I extends fair trial guarantees in an international armed conflict to all persons, including those arrested for actions relating to the conflict.

The UN has also issued a number of global nontreaty standards that relate to the right to a fair trial, including Basic Principles on the Independence of the Judiciary;[104] Basic Principles on the Role of Lawyers;[105] Code of Conduct for Law Enforcement Officials;[106] Guidelines on the Role of Prosecutors;[107] Principles on the Effective Prevention and Investigation of Extra-Legal, Arbitrary and Summary Executions;[108] and Safeguards Guaranteeing Protection of the Rights of Those Facing the Death Penalty.[109] In addition, regional human rights treaties in Africa, Europe, and the Inter-American system protect the right to a fair trial. Furthermore, the statutes of the International Criminal Court, the ad hoc criminal tribunal for the former Yugoslavia, and the ad hoc criminal tribunal for Rwanda contain provisions seeking to guarantee the right to a fair trial for the accused.

The United Nations, regional organizations, and other international structures have codified a substantial framework of fair trial standards, which have been accepted, albeit not always followed, by most nations and have begun to be used in the context of international criminal tribunals. In addition to the codified standards, several human rights institutions, including particularly the Human Rights Committee and the European Court of Human Rights, have interpreted and applied fair trial norms to particular cases and have thus generated an impressive corpus of jurisprudence which lawyers and judges worldwide should consult.

*See also*: Detention and Imprisonment, Humanitarian Law

*Further Reading*:

Amnesty International, Fair Trials Manual (1998).
S. Chernichenko & W. Treat, The right to a fair trial: Current recognition and measures necessary for its strengthening, final report, U.N. Doc. E/CN.4/Sub.2/1994/24 (1994).
Richard Clayton & Hugh Tomlinson, Fair Trial Rights (2001).
Human Rights Committee, General Comment 13, Article 14 (Twenty-first session, 1984), Compilation of General Comments and General Recommendations Adopted by Human Rights Treaty Bodies, U.N. Doc. HRI/GEN/1/Rev.1 at 14 (1994).
Human Rights Committee, General Comment 29, States of Emergency (article 4), U.N. Doc. CCPR/C/21/Rev.1/Add.11 (2001).
Office of the U.N. High Commissioner for Human Rights, Manual on Human Rights for Judges, Prosecutors and Lawyers (Professional Training Series, No. 9, 2004).
David Weissbrodt, The Right to a Fair Trial under the Universal Declaration of Human Rights and the International Covenant on Civil and Political Rights (2001).
David Weissbrodt & Rüdiger Wolfrum, eds., The Right to a Fair Trial (1997).

*Links to Consult*:

http://www1.umn.edu/humanrts/instree/auoi.htm
http://www.humanrightsfirst.org/pubs/descriptions/fair_trial.pdf
http://www.amnesty.org/ailib/intcam/fairtrial/fairtria.htm
http://www.unhchr.ch/html/menu2/issadj.htm

## 7. Detention and Imprisonment (Universal Declaration, Art. 9)

The basic protections of the rights of detained persons are found in the Universal Declaration of Human Rights and the Civil and Political Covenant.[110] In order to ensure the dignity of all human beings, including persons accused of crime, those two instruments guarantee persons accused of crime with the following basic protections: the right to a fair trial, the presumption of innocence, and the right to appeal, as discussed in the previous section of this chapter. They are also protected by the prohibition of torture and other cruel, inhuman or degrading treatment or punishment (discussed in Section 5 of this Part), the right to equal protection of the law (discussed in Section 2), and the right to freedom from arbitrary arrest or detention.

The broad protections for detained persons in the Universal Declaration and the Civil and Political Covenant have been implemented by a network of some thirty human rights instruments including treaties such as the Convention Against Torture[111] and the Convention on the Rights of the Child,[112] as well as nontreaty standards such as the Standard Minimum Rules for the Treatment of Prisoners (1955),[113] the Body of Principles for the Protection of All Persons Under Any Form of Detention or Imprisonment (1988),[114] and the Basic Principles for the Treatment of Prisoners (1990).[115]

Article 9 of the Civil and Political Covenant and the other relevant standards assure that a person who is arrested should be entitled to be informed at the time of arrest of the reasons for the arrest, and shall be promptly informed of any charges. The arrested individual should be brought promptly before a judge or similar officer authorized to exercise judicial power. Civil and Political Covenant Article 9(3) and other standards strongly discourage detention for arrested persons awaiting trial, but instead recommend guarantees to appear for trial and other noncustodial measures. The presumption of innocence requires that accused persons be given treatment appropriate to their unconvicted status. Accordingly, if accused persons are detained instead of being released pending trial, they should be separated from convicted persons. Because of their vulnerability, accused juveniles must be separated from adults.

Article 9(4) guarantees the right of anyone who is deprived of liberty to take proceedings before a court to determine the lawfulness of the detention. The Human Rights Committee has expressed the view that detention for forty-eight hours without judicial review is unreasonably long. The Committee has also indicated that the right to apply for the remedy of habeas corpus to test the legality of confinement should be extended, so that a detainee's family or friends could apply on his behalf.[116]

Detainees are entitled to communicate not only with their counsel who will represent them at trial, but also with their families and friends. Non-citizens are also entitled by the Vienna Convention on Consular Relations to be notified of their right to communicate with consular officers of their country.[117] Based on the Vienna Convention, Mexico challenged the impending execution of fifty-two Mexican nationals because they were not informed of their right to consular assistance by various states of the United States. In 2004 the International Court of Justice (ICJ) decided in favor of the Mexican claim and stated that the United States is obligated "to provide, by means of its own choosing, review and reconsideration of the convictions and sentences of the Mexican nationals . . . by taking account of . . . the violation of the rights set forth in Article 36 of the Convention."[118] The ICJ suggested that states add a Vienna Convention notice to parallel the warning required by the U.S. Supreme Court in *Miranda v. Arizona* to be given to suspects about their freedom from self-incrimination.

Pretrial detainees and sentenced prisoners are entitled to be treated with dignity and humanity. The Standard Minimum Rules for Treatment of Prisoners prescribe conditions of both pretrial and post-conviction confinement, relating to sleeping accommodation with due regard to the minimum space of the cell, lighting, heating, ventilation, a separate bed (and, in general, a separate room for untried detainees), at least one hour of open air exercise per day (weather permitting), food adequate for health and strength, drinking water, medical care, use of a library, books of religious observance, attendance at religious services (so far as practical), an opportunity to work, and an opportunity to make complaints to an officer of the institution.[119] The Standard Minimum Rules prohibit corporal punishment, punishment by placing in a dark cell, and punishment by applying instruments of restraint (such as handcuffs, chains, irons, and straitjackets). Law enforcement officials shall not use force except when strictly necessary for the maintenance of security.

Despite these standards, pretrial detainees in many countries are subjected to the worst conditions of confinement in their national prison systems. Detention facilities are often overcrowded, antiquated, unsanitary, and unsuited for human habitation. Pretrial detainees are held for months or even years while their cases are investigated and processed by the judicial system. In many countries detainees are even held for longer than the sentences would have been for the crimes with which they are charged. There is often no official or judicial authority responsible for assuring that detainees' rights are protected and their cases are promptly heard. Sentenced prisoners are far more likely than pretrial detainees to be provided educational, occupational, and physical exercise opportunities. Discipline in pretrial detention facilities is often inadequate and weaker detainees may be brutalized or sexually exploited by other detainees.

Administrative detention applies in some countries to situations outside the process of police arresting suspects and bringing them into the criminal justice system. For example, a person may be admitted involuntarily to a mental health facility if there is a serious likelihood of immediate or imminent harm to that person or others. The UN Principles for the Protection of Persons with Mental Illness and the Improveent of Mental Health Care afford some guarantees to persons who are detained and require that they be informed without delay of the grounds of admission; their detention should be decided by at least two mental health practitioners; and a review body should be informed of and review the detention.[120]

The Fourth Geneva Convention relative to the Protection of Civilian Persons in Time of War anticipates that during periods of international armed conflict or occupation individuals may be detained, but Article 43 of the Convention requires that the detention be reconsidered as soon as possible by an appropriate court or administrative board.[121] If the individual is kept in detention, the matter should be reviewed periodically—at least twice yearly.

In common law countries a petition for habeas corpus should be available to test the legality of any detention. In Latin American countries *amparo* fulfills a similar function. In 2004 the U.S. Supreme Court held that two Australians and twelve Kuwaitis captured during hostilities in Afghanistan and held in U.S. military custody at the Guantánamo Bay, Cuba, Naval Base, were entitled to file petitions for habeas corpus challenging the legality of their detention on the ground that they had never been combatants against the United States or engaged in terrorist acts, and that they had never been charged with wrongdoing, permitted to consult counsel, or provided access to courts or other tribunals.[122]

If national procedures are unavailable or unavailing, detained individuals may also seek a determination from the UN Working Group on Arbitrary Detention that their detention is arbitrary.[123] The Working Group was established in 1991 as one of the thematic procedures of the UN Commission on Human Rights, discussed in Part III. The Working Group has developed a substantial body of interpretation of what constitutes "arbitrary" detention.[124] For example, detention may be arbitrary if it has no legal basis (Category I), if it violates a human rights norm (such as the exercise of the right to freedom of expression or freedom of association) (Category II), or if the individual was deprived of fair trial procedures (Category III). In 2003 the Working Group on Arbitrary Detention considered the case of three French nationals and a Spanish

66　Particular Rights and Responsibilities

national held in Guantánamo Bay Naval Base, and found an arbitrary detention in Category I.[125]

*See also:* Equality and Nondiscrimination, Procedural Fairness in the Criminal Process and the Administration of Justice, Torture and Ill-Treatment, UN Charter-Based Procedures

*Further Reading:*

*Avena and Other Mexican Nationals (Mexico v. United States of America)*, 2004 I.C.J. (Judgment); 43 ILM 581 (2004).
Basic Principles for the Treatment of Prisoners, G.A. res. 45/111, annex, 45 U.N. GAOR Supp. (No. 49A) at 200, U.N. Doc. A/45/49 (1990).
Body of Principles for the Protection of All Persons Under Any Form of Detention or Imprisonment, G.A. res. 43/173, annex, 43 U.N. GAOR Supp. (No. 49) at 298, U.N. Doc. A/43/49 (1988).
*Miranda v. Arizona*, 384 U.S. 436 (1966).
Principles for the Protection of Persons with Mental Illnesses and the Improvement of Mental Health Care, G.A. res. 46/119, 46 U.N. GAOR Supp. (No. 49) at 189, U.N. Doc. A/46/49 (1991).
*Rasul v. Bush*, 124 S.Ct. 2686 (2004).
Nigel Rodley, The Treatment of Prisoners in International Law (2000).
United Nations Centre for Human Rights and Crime Prevention and Criminal Justice Branch, Human Rights and Pre-trial Detention, A Handbook of International Standards relating to Pre-Trial Detention, U.N. Doc. HR/P/PT/3 (1992).
United Nations, Opinions Adopted by the Working Group on Arbitrary Detention, U.N. Doc. E/CN.4/2004/3/Add.1 (2003).

*Links to Consult:*

http://ods-dds-ny.un.org/doc/UNDOC/GEN/G03/169/00/PDF/G0316900.pdf?OpenElement
http://www.ohchr.org/english/issues/detention/index.htm
http://www.unhchr.ch/html/menu2/i2adjard.htm
http://www1.umn.edu/humanrts/instree/auogs.htm
http://www1.umn.edu/humanrts/instree/g3bpppdi.htm
http://www1.umn.edu/humanrts/instree/t2pppmii.htm
http://www1.umn.edu/humanrts/instree/y4gcpcp.htm
http://212.153.43.18/icjwww/idocket/imus/imusframe.htm

## 8. Privacy (Universal Declaration, Art. 12)

Article 12 of the Universal Declaration provides:

No one shall be subjected to arbitrary interference with his privacy, family, home or correspondence, nor to attacks upon his honour and reputation. Everyone has the right to the protection of the law against such interference or attacks.[126]

Article 17 of the Civil and Political Covenant reaffirms the right to privacy in nearly the same words.[127] While one of the earliest and best known definitions of "privacy" is the "right to be left alone," the right to privacy under the Covenant has been interpreted by the Human Rights Committee (1) to permit an individual to change their surname; (2) to find a violation in construction of a hotel complex which would destroy two individuals' ancestral burial grounds, which represent an important place in their history, culture, and life, and would arbitrarily interfere with their privacy; (3) to express concern about intrusions into private telephone communications; (4) to guarantee *de jure* and *de facto* the integrity and confidentiality of correspondence; (5) to assure that correspondence should be delivered to the addressee without interception and without being opened or otherwise read; (6) to prohibit surveillance, whether electronic or otherwise, interceptions of telephonic, telegraphic, and other forms of communication, wire-tapping, and recording of conversations; (7) to make sure that searches of a person's home should be restricted to a search for necessary evidence and should not be allowed to amount to harassment; (8) to ensure that effective measures are taken such that personal and body searches are carried out in a manner consistent with the dignity of the person who is being searched; (9) to provide that persons being subjected to body search by state officials, or medical personnel acting at the request of the state, should only be examined by persons of the same sex; (10) to find a violation of the right to privacy by Mauritius where an Immigration Act did not afford resident status to non-citizen men married to Mauritian women, while Mauritian men could live in the country with their non-citizen wives; and (11) to take privacy concerns into consideration when protecting a woman from rape.[128]

The Human Rights Committee further interpreted the right to privacy in a General Comment adopted in 2000:

Another area where States may fail to respect women's privacy relates to their reproductive functions, for example, where there is a requirement for the husband's authorization to make a decision in regard to sterilization, where general requirements are imposed for the sterilization of women, such as having a certain number of children or being of a certain age, or where States impose a legal duty upon doctors and other health personnel to report cases of women who

68    Particular Rights and Responsibilities

have undergone abortion. . . . Women's privacy may also be interfered with by private actors, such as employers who request a pregnancy test before hiring a woman. . . .[129]

A General Comment adopted by the Human Rights Committee in 1988 identified several additional aspects of the right to privacy:

> The gathering and holding of personal information on computers, databanks and other devices, whether by public authorities or private individuals or bodies, must be regulated by law. Effective measures have to be taken by States to ensure that information concerning a person's private life does not reach the hands of persons who are not authorized by law to receive, process and use it, and is never used for purposes incompatible with the Covenant. In order to have the most effective protection of his private life, every individual should have the right to ascertain in an intelligible form, whether, and if so, what personal data is stored in automatic data files, and for what purposes. Every individual should also be able to ascertain which public [authorities] or private individuals or bodies control or may control their files. If such files contain incorrect personal data or have been collected or processed contrary to the provisions of the law, every individual should have the right to request rectification or elimination . . . Article 17 affords protection to personal honour and reputation and States are under an obligation to provide adequate legislation to that end.[130]

In 1994 the Human Rights Committee considered the right to privacy in considering the complaint of Nicholas Toonen against Australia with regard to two provisions of the Tasmanian Criminal Code, which prohibited private homosexual behavior. The Committee decided that

> it is undisputed that adult consensual sexual activity in private is covered by the concept of "privacy," and that Mr. Toonen is actually and currently affected by the continued existence of the Tasmanian laws. The Committee considers that Sections 122(a), (c) and 123 of the Tasmanian Criminal Code "interfere" with the author's privacy, even if these provisions have not been enforced for a decade. In this context, it notes that the policy of the Department of Public Prosecutions not to initiate criminal proceedings in respect of private homosexual conduct does not amount to a guarantee that no actions will be brought against homosexuals in the future, particularly in the light of undisputed statements of the Director of Public Prosecutions of Tasmania in 1988 and those of members of the Tasmanian Parliament. The continued existence of the challenged provisions therefore continuously and directly "interferes" with the author's privacy.[131]

The European Court of Human Rights in 1981[132] and the U.S. Supreme Court in 2003[133] used similar reasoning to reach the same conclusion as did the Human Rights Committee in 1994.[134]

*Further Reading:*

*Shirin Aumeeruddy-Cziffra and 19 other Mauritian women v. Mauritius,* Communication No. 35/1978, U.N. Doc. CCPR/C/OP/1 at 67 (1984).

Eric M. Barendt, Privacy (2001).
*Coeriel et al. v. The Netherlands,* Communication No. 453/1991, U.N. Doc. CCPR/C/52/D/453/1991 (1994).
*Dudgeon v. United Kingdom,* 45 Eur. Ct. H.R. (Ser.A) (1982), 4 Eur. H.R. Rep. 149 (1981).
Eric Heinze, Sexual Orientation, A Human Right: An Essay on International Human Rights Law (1995).
Human Rights Committee, General Comment 16 (Twenty-third session, 1988), Compilation of General Comments and General Recommendations Adopted by Human Rights Treaty Bodies, U.N. Doc. HRI\GEN\1\Rev.1 at 21 (1994).
Human Rights Committee, General Comment 28, Equality of Rights Between Men and Women (article 3), U.N. Doc. CCPR/C/21/Rev.1/Add.10 (2000).
Sarah Joseph, The International Covenant on Civil and Political Rights (2d ed. 2004).
*Lawrence v. Texas,* 123 S.Ct. 2472 (2003).
James Michael, Privacy and Human Rights: An International and Comparative Study, with Special Reference to Developments in Information Technology (1994).
Laurence Thomas & Michael E. Levin, Sexual Orientation and Human Rights (1999).
*Toonen v. Australia,* Communication No. 488/1992, U.N. Doc CCPR/C/50/D/488/1992 (1994).
Samuel Warren & Louis D. Brandeis, *The Right to Privacy,* 4 Harv. L. Rev. 193 (1890).

*Links to Consult:*

http://www.privacyinternational.org
http://www1.umn.edu/humanrts/gencomm/hrcom16.htm
http://www1.umn.edu/humanrts/gencomm/hrcom28.htm
http://www1.umn.edu/humanrts/undocs/html/vws488.htm
http://www1.umn.edu/humanrts/undocs/html/453-1991.html

70  Particular Rights and Responsibilities

## 9. Freedom of Movement—Travel (Universal Declaration, Art. 13)

Article 13 of the Universal Declaration provides:

> Everyone has the right to freedom of movement and residence within the borders of each State.... Everyone has the right to leave any country, including his own, and to return to his country.[135]

Article 12 of the Covenant on Civil and Political Rights reaffirms those provisions in slightly more precise language.[136] The Fourth Protocol, Article 2(2), of the European Convention on Human Rights also contains nearly identical wording.[137] Further, the rights to leave and return are also recognized in Article 22(2) of the American Convention on Human Rights[138] and in Article 12(2) of the African Charter on Human and Peoples' Rights.[139] These documents mention only the right to leave a nation, but one may infer that this right also includes the right to renounce one's citizenship.

### A. The Right to Movement and Residence Within National Borders

The Human Rights Committee has provided an authoritative interpretation of Article 12 of the Civil and Political Covenant with regard to the right to freedom of movement in General Comment 27:

> Everyone lawfully within the territory of a State enjoys, within that territory, the right to move freely and to choose his or her place of residence.... The right to move freely relates to the whole territory of a State, including all parts of federal States.... [P]ersons are entitled to move from one place to another and to establish themselves in a place of their choice. The enjoyment of this right must not be made dependent on any particular purpose or reason for the person wanting to move or to stay in a place.... The State party must ensure that the rights guaranteed in article 12 are protected not only from public but also from private interference. In the case of women, this obligation to protect is particularly pertinent. For example, it is incompatible with article 12, paragraph 1, that the right of a woman to move freely and to choose her residence be made subject, by law or practice, to the decision of another person, including a relative. Subject to the provisions of article 12, paragraph 3, the right to reside in a place of one's choice within the territory includes protection against all forms of forced internal displacement. It also precludes preventing the entry or stay of persons in a defined part of the territory....[140]

Using the principles enunciated by this General Comment, the Human Rights Committee found that the government of Togo to have placed an impermissible restriction on an individual's freedom of movement and residence in violation of Article 12 by forbidding him to enter his home district and native village.[141]

Forced population displacement may also be a violation of international humanitarian law if it occurs during periods of armed conflict. In international armed conflicts, including during military occupations, Article 49 of the Fourth Geneva Convention forbids individual or mass forcible transfers, as well as deportations of civilians from occupied territory to the territory of an occupying power.[142] Article 17(1) of the Protocol II to the Geneva Conventions provides that in non-international armed conflicts "the displacement of the civilian population shall not be ordered for reasons related to the conflict unless the security of the civilians involved or imperative military reasons demand," in which cases "all possible measures shall be taken in order that the civilian population may be received under satisfactory conditions of shelter, hygiene, safety, and nutrition."[143]

Around the world there are estimated to be twenty-five million people in about fifty countries who have been internally displaced because of war, famine, floods, grave human rights abuses, and related causes. While they have not crossed any national border, they face many of the same problems of dislocation and suffering as refugees. Unlike refugees, however, internally displaced persons lack effective legal protection and access to international assistance. The UN High Commissioner for Refugees (UNHCR)[144] and the International Committee of the Red Cross (ICRC)[145] are among the most prominent international organizations which have sought to provide humanitarian assistance to internally displaced persons (IDPs). In 1992 the UN Commission on Human Rights established a thematic procedure identified as the Special Representative of the Secretary-General on internally displaced persons.[146] The Special Representative reports annually to the Human Rights Council (formerly the Commission) on the very widespread problems facing IDPs, has visited a large number of countries where IDPs are located, and assisted in developing and then promulgating the Guiding Principles on Internal Displacement.[147] The Guiding Principles prohibit discrimination and other grave human rights abuses against IDPs; limit the circumstances in which they can be displaced from their homes; call for humanitarian assistance; and provide for their "return voluntarily, in safety and with dignity, to their homes or places of habitual residence, or to resettle voluntarily in another part of the country."

B. THE RIGHT TO LEAVE

The right of an individual to leave a nation first was mentioned in the Magna Carta of 1215, which stated that everyone had the right to leave

England, subject to feudal obligations.[148] Blackstone stated that there was an absolute right to leave England, subject to an injunction to remain, but he also advocated the common law doctrine of perpetual allegiance, or citizenship.[149] The Peace of Westphalia of 1648 also contained the right of departure.[150] The French Constitution of 1791 specifically proclaimed the right to leave a nation. By the middle of the nineteenth century, most European nations in practice allowed individuals to leave freely, though no generally accepted right to emigrate existed. In 1868 the U.S. Congress enacted legislation declaring that expatriation is a natural and inherent right of all people.[151]

The Human Rights Committee has elaborated on the right to leave one's country in its General Comment adopted in 1999:

> Since international travel usually requires appropriate documents, in particular a passport, the right to leave a country must include the right to obtain the necessary travel documents. The issuing of passports is normally incumbent on the State of nationality of the individual. The refusal by a State to issue a passport or prolong its validity for a national residing abroad may deprive this person of the right to leave the country of residence and to travel elsewhere. . . . It is no justification for the State to claim that its national would be able to return to its territory without a passport.[152]

### c. The Right to Return to One's Country

The right of return to one's country is also explained more fully in the Human Rights Committee's General Comment on the freedom of movement:

> The right of a person to enter his or her own country recognizes the special relationship of a person to that country. . . . It implies the right to remain in one's own country. It includes not only the right to return after having left one's own country; it may also entitle a person to come to the country for the first time if he or she was born outside the country (for example, if that country is the person's State of nationality). The right to return is of the utmost importance for refugees seeking voluntary repatriation. It also implies prohibition of enforced population transfers or mass expulsions to other countries.[153]

When refugees reenter their country, the UNHCR attempts to achieve a "durable solution" in which the former refugees return to reintegrate in "safety and dignity." It is important for the successful reintegration of returnees that they are able to reclaim ownership and possession of belongings, cars, offices, and land. The restitution of houses occupied by other individuals is often a problem faced by displaced people who return home. In the former Yugoslavia, for example, the new occupants may themselves be refugees from other countries, internally displaced persons, or bona fide purchasers who were not aware that their home originally belonged to a family that was forced to flee at some earlier stage of the conflict. A study conducted by Paulo Sérgio Pinheiro of the UN Sub-Commission on the Promotion and Protection of Human Rights has further stated that the right to return is "now understood to encompass not merely returning to one's country, but to one's home as well."[154]

*See also*: Asylum and Refugee Status, Nationality

*Further Reading:*

*Kéténguéré Ackla v. Togo*, Communication No. 505/1992, U.N. Doc. CCPR/C/51/D/505/1992 (1996).
Chaloka Beyani, Human Rights Standards and the Free Movement of People within the States (2000).
Citizenship Today: Global Perspectives and Practices (T. Alexander Aleinikoff & Douglas Klusmeyer eds., 2001).
From Migrants to Citizens: Membership in a Changing World (T. Alexander Aleinikoff & Douglas Klusmeyer eds., 2000).
Guiding Principles on Internal Displacement, U.N. Doc. E/CN.4/1998/53/Add.2 (1998), noted in Comm. Hum. Rts. res. 1998/50 (1998).
Human Rights Committee, General Comment 27, Freedom of movement (Art.12), U.N. Doc CCPR/C/21/Rev.1/Add.9 (1999).
Human Rights Protection for Refugees, Asylum-Seekers, and Internally Displaced Persons: A Guide to International Mechanisms (Joan Fitzpatrick ed., 2002).
The Movement of Persons Across Borders (Louis B. Sohn & Thomas Buergenthal eds., 1992).
The Right to Leave and to Return (Karel Vasak & Sidney Liskofsky eds., 1976).
David Weissbrodt & Laura Danielson, Immigration Law and Procedure in a Nutshell (5th ed. 2004).

*Links to Consult:*

http://www.asylumlaw.org
http://www.cicr.org/
http://www.drc.dk
http://www.forcedmigration.org
http://www.iom.int
http://www.reliefweb.int
http://www.unhcr.ch
http://www.unhchr.ch/html/menu2/7/b/interndisp/
http://www.unhcr.ch/cgi-bin/texis/vtx/home
http://www1.umn.edu/humanrts/gencomm/hrcom27.htm
http://www1.umn.edu/humanrts/instree/GuidingPrinciplesonInternal Displacement.htm
http://www1.umn.edu/humanrts/undocs/html/VWS50556.htm

## 10. Asylum and Refugee Status (Universal Declaration, Art. 14)

The Universal Declaration of Human Rights provides in Article 14 that "Everyone has the right to seek and to enjoy in other countries asylum from persecution."[155] The 1951 Convention relating to the Status of Refugees[156] and its 1967 Protocol[157] are the principal treaties implementing that provision of the Universal Declaration and focusing on both asylum and refugee status. The Office of the UN High Commissioner for Refugees (UNHCR) is the principal UN institution responsible for implementing these treaties as well as for protecting and assisting asylum seekers and refugees.

Article 1 of the Convention relating to the Status of Refugees defines a refugee as a person who "owing to well-founded fear of being persecuted for reasons of race, religion, nationality, membership of a particular social group or political opinion, is outside the country of his nationality and is unable, or owing to such fear, is unwilling to avail himself of the protection of that country; or who, not having a nationality and being outside the country of his former habitual residence . . . is unable or, owing to such fear, is unwilling to return to it."[158] The Convention focused on refugees from events surrounding World War II in Europe and thus placed both geographical limitations and temporal limits (that is, before 1 January 1951) on its definition. While there are a few countries, such as Turkey, that continue to adhere only to the Convention's geographical and temporal limitations, most countries (144) have ratified the Protocol relating to the Status of Refugees that removes those limitations.

Although refugees and asylum seekers must satisfy the same basic requirements, the refugee applicant applies from abroad, whereas the asylum applicant applies while present in the country in which asylum is sought or at its border. It should be noted that a refugee or asylee is (1) outside his or her country of origin, (2) has a well founded fear (3) of persecution, and (4) on five specified grounds.

As to the first requisite, an individual must have crossed a national frontier in order to qualify as a refugee. Accordingly, internally displaced persons cannot qualify as refugees. But it is not necessary for the individual to have possessed the requisite fear of persecution at the time of the border crossing. For example, if a student from the Central African Republic was residing in France in 2003 when there was a coup in her country and she feared political persecution if she returned, she would qualify as a refugee (sometimes known as a refugee *sur place*). Similarly, if a country, such as Yugoslavia (which had included Bosnia, Croatia, Macedonia, Montenegro, and Slovenia), broke up during a Yugoslavian traveler's holiday in the Greek islands and he was fearful of religious persecution upon return to Belgrade, he would ordinarily qualify for refugee status in Greece. If an individual has dual nationality or has been firmly resettled in a third country, however, he or she would not qualify as a refugee.

An individual must possess a well founded fear; that is, the individual must subjectively fear the persecution and must have objective grounds to justify that fear. Subjectively, the applicant must show that her or his fear is genuine. The objective component requires credible and specific evidence that would support a reasonable fear of persecution. In order to demonstrate the objective basis for an individual's fear of persecution in her home country, she may present evidence of the human rights violations occurring there for individuals with similar characteristics. For example, a union leader from Colombia might qualify under the definition of refugee by presenting information about killings, torture, and disappearances of union leaders.

The U.S. Supreme Court in two of its decisions—*INS v. Stevic* (1984)[159] and *INS v. Cardoza-Fonseca* (1987)[160]—established the two standards of proof that apply in determining whether an individual qualifies for (1) asylum or (2) for the more limited relief of *nonrefoulement* (no forcible removal), which has been known in the United States as withholding of deportation or removal. In *Stevic* the Court held that the non-citizen must show a clear probability of persecution in order to obtain withholding of deportation/removal. The Court defined the clear probability of persecution standard as inquiring whether it is more likely than not that the alien would be subject to persecution.

In *INS v. Cardoza-Fonseca* the Court considered the case of a Nicaraguan citizen who overstayed her nonimmigrant visa in the United States. The immigration authorities commenced proceedings to remove her from the U.S., and Cardoza-Fonseca requested asylum or at least withholding of removal. To support her asylum claim, she attempted to show a well-founded fear of persecution upon her return to Nicaragua with evidence that her brother had been tortured and imprisoned because of his political activities in Nicaragua. Cardoza-Fonseca claimed that she, too, would be tortured if forced to return, because the Sandinista government knew she had fled Nicaragua with her brother and would want to interrogate her about her brother's whereabouts and would become aware of her own political opposition to the Sandinistas. The Court held that in order to qualify for asylum an individual need not show the exacting burden of proof of a "clear probability of persecution" as in *Stevic*, but need only show a "well founded fear" of prosecution by demonstrating past persecution or other "good reason" to fear persecution. The UK House of Lords adopted the *Stevic* "clear probability of persecution" standard in its *Ex Parte Sivakumaran* decision for asylum applications in the United Kingdom.[161]

A refugee or asylum seeker must establish "persecution" as distinguished from prosecution for a criminal charge. The UNHCR *Handbook on Procedures and Criteria for Determining Refugee Status* has observed that

> there is no universally accepted definition of "persecution," and various attempts to formulate such a definition have met with little success. From Article 33 of the 1951 Convention, it may be inferred that a threat to life or freedom on account of race, religion, nationality, political opinion or membership of a particular social group is always persecution. Other serious violations of human rights—for the same reasons—would also constitute persecution.[162]

Accordingly, persecution includes arbitrary killing, detention, disappearance, and torture, but the UK House of Lords has approved the view of Professor James Hathaway in stating that "persecution" may include "the sustained or systemic failure of state protection in relation to one of the core entitlements which has been recognised by the international community."[163] In other words, any serious human rights violation under the Universal Declaration or the Covenants, for example, may qualify as "persecution."

Persecution must be based on one of the five specified grounds: race, religion, nationality, political opinion, or membership of a particular social group. Racial discrimination is most authoritatively defined in the Convention on the Elimination of All Forms of Racial Discrimination as

> any distinction, exclusion, restriction or preference based on race, colour, descent, or national or ethnic origin which has the purpose or effect of nullifying or impairing the recognition, enjoyment or exercise, on an equal footing, of human rights and fundamental freedoms in the political, economic, social, cultural or any other field of public life.[164]

In regard to persecution on the ground of religion, the authoritative UNHCR *Handbook* has observed:

> Differences in the treatment of various groups do indeed exist to a greater or lesser extent in many societies. Persons who receive less favourable treatment as a result of such differences are not necessarily victims of persecution. It is only in certain circumstances that discrimination will amount to persecution. This would be so if measures of discrimination lead to consequences of a substantially prejudicial nature for the person concerned, *e.g.* serious restrictions on his right to earn his livelihood, his right to practise his religion, or his access to normally available educational facilities. . . .
>
> Persecution for "reasons of religion" may assume various forms, *e.g.* prohibition of membership of a religious community, of worship in private or in public, of religious instruction, or serious measures of discrimination imposed on persons because they practise their religion or belong to a particular religious community. . . .

The question as to whether objection to performing military service for reasons of conscience can give rise to a valid claim to refugee status should also be considered in the light of more recent developments in this field. . . . In the light of these developments, it would be open to Contracting States, to grant refugee status to persons who object to performing military service for genuine reasons of conscience.[165]

The Human Rights Committee has dealt with several cases in which discrimination on the basis of nationality was alleged. For example, in *Karakurt v. Austria*, a Turkish national complained that he was holding an open-ended residence permit in Austria, and had been elected by his fellow workers to a work-council, but he was removed from his elected position because of an Austrian law that restricted membership to Austrian nationals.[166] The Human Rights Committee found that there had been discrimination on the basis of nationality.

"Political opinion" is one of the most commonly cited bases for asylum or refugee applications. In the 1992 *Elias-Zacarias* case, the U.S. Supreme Court held that a guerrilla organization's coercion to join its organization does not necessarily constitute persecution on account of political opinion.[167] In that case, Elias-Zacarias testified that he would be subject to persecution if he returned to his native Guatemala. He described how guerrillas had forced their way into his home and requested that Elias-Zacarias and his parents join their organization. When they refused, the guerrillas promised to return. Elias-Zacarias testified that he believed joining the organization would subject him to retaliation by the government. The Court rejected the asylum claim because the political opinion in question was not that of the applicant, but rather, that of the guerrilla organization (the persecutor). In response, Elias-Zacarias argued that failure to join the guerrillas was itself tantamount to expressing a political opinion, but the Court was not persuaded, holding that Elias-Zacarias had failed to show evidence sufficient to establish persecution for political opinion. Other courts have been more willing to accept such claims of "imputed" political opinion. For example, the U.S. Court of Appeals for the Ninth Circuit in *Cordon-Garcia v. INS* ruled that imputed political opinion could be found where "one party to a conflict insists to the victim that the victim is aligned with the other side."[168]

Persecution for membership in a particular social group is the least well defined or most open-ended of the five grounds for refugee status. The U.S. Court of Appeals for the Ninth Circuit has interpreted a "particular social group" as one "united by a voluntary association, including a former association, or by an innate characteristic that is so fundamental to the identities or consciences of its members that members either cannot or should not be required to change it." Using that

78   Particular Rights and Responsibilities

interpretation the Court of Appeals ruled that gay men in Mexico with female sexual identities constitute a "particular social group" for purposes of establishing eligibility for asylum.[169] The U.S. Board of Immigration Appeals in *In re Kasinga* held that the practice of female genital mutilation (FGM) can form the basis for a grant of asylum.[170] Kasinga, a nineteen-year-old native of Togo, feared that she would be subjected to FGM and forced marriage upon her return to her country. The BIA stated the applicant's testimony in *Kasinga* established that she had a well-founded fear of persecution on account of her membership in a "particular social group," young women of the Tchamba-Kunsuntu Tribe who have not suffered FGM and who oppose the practice. In *Abankwah v. INS*, the U.S. Court of Appeals for the Second Circuit reaffirmed *Kasinga* by stating that "FGM involves the infliction of grave harm" and constitutes persecution.[171] The Canadian Immigration and Refugee Board has issued guidelines on Women Refugee Claimants Fearing Gender-Related Persecution which take the same approach to claims relating to FGM.[172] Other countries, such as Australia, the United Kingdom, and the United States, have also issued gender-related guidelines for handling asylum claims.

If an individual meets the basic definition of a refugee or asylee, his or her claim for refugee or asylum status may still fail because of "cessation" and "exclusion" clauses in the Convention and Protocol relating to the Status of Refugees.[173] A refugee or asylee ceases to qualify if he or she voluntarily returns to his or her country of nationality or previous residence and accepts its protection, for example, by reacquiring nationality or establishing a home there. It is also possible for a refugee or asylee to lose status if the circumstances leading to his or her departure cease to exist. Accordingly, an individual is excluded from being considered a refugee/asylee if he or she is firmly resettled in the country where he or she presently resides, if he or she has "committed a crime against peace, a war crime, or a crime against humanity"; "has committed a serious non-political crime outside the country of refuge" prior to admission to that country as a refugee; or "has been guilty of acts contrary to the purposes and principles of the United Nations."[174]

For example, a former military officer from Sudan, who has been involved in the war crime of killing civilians in his own country and then flees that country for fear of persecution for one of the five specified grounds, cannot qualify as a refugee or asylee in Denmark or any other country that has ratified the Convention and Protocol relating to the Status of Refugees. Nonetheless, it is possible that Denmark would not be entitled to send the former army officer back to Sudan, only if he fears torture. The Convention Against Torture provides that anyone who has "substantial grounds for believing that he would be in danger of being subjected to torture" shall not be expelled, returned (*refouler*), or extradited.[175] The Convention Against Torture does not contain any exclusion clauses. The Human Rights Committee and the European Court of Human Rights have interpreted the clauses in their respective treaties that forbid torture to give similar protection against forcible return (*refoulement*) to individuals who fear torture.

Regional agreements in Africa and South America also provide a further expansion of persons who might qualify for refugee status or protection against forcible return. For example, the Convention Governing the Specific Aspects of Refugee Problems in Africa recites the basic definition of refugee found in the Convention and Protocol relating to the Status of Refugees, but adds:

> The term "refugee" shall also apply to every person who, owing to external aggression, occupation, foreign domination or events seriously disturbing public order in either part or the whole of his country of origin or nationality, is compelled to leave his place of habitual residence in order to seek refuge in another place outside his country of origin or nationality.[176]

This broad definition of refugee in Africa reflects not only the frequent armed conflicts occurring in that region, but also the large number of refugees that result from those conflicts. The UNHCR has most recently estimated that there are about 8.4 million refugees in the world, of which the greatest numbers are in Africa, Asia, and Europe. There are also about one million asylum seekers and twenty-five million internally displaced persons around the world. Of course, these data change each year as refugees are resettled, asylum applications are determined, and new individuals flee because of their fear of persecution.

*See also*: Freedom of Movement


*Further Reading*:

*Abankwah v. INS*, 185 F.3d 18 (2nd Cir. 1999).
*Asylum Case (Colombia v. Peru)*, 1950 I.C.J. 266.
Anne Bayefsky & Joan Fitzpatrick, Human Rights and Rural Development (2000).
Nathalia Berkowitz & Catriona Jarvis, Immigration Appellate Authority [United Kingdom], Asylum Gender Guidelines (2000).
Cartagena Declaration on Refugees, Nov. 22, 1984, Annual Report of the Inter-American Commission on Human Rights, OAS Doc. OEA/Ser.L/V/II.66/doc.10, rev. 1, at 190–93 (1984–85).
Convention Governing the Specific Aspects of Refugee Problems in Africa, 1001 U.N.T.S. 45, *entered into force* June 20, 1974.
Convention relating to the Status of Refugees, 189 U.N.T.S. 150, *entered into force* Apr. 22, 1954.

80  Particular Rights and Responsibilities

*Cordon-Garcia v. INS*, 204 F.3d 985 (9th Cir. 2000).
Memorandum from Phyllis Coven, International and Naturalization Service (INS) Office of International Affairs, to All INS Asylum Officers and HQASM Coordinators, Considerations for Asylum Officers Adjudicating Asylum Claims from Women (May 26, 1995).
Department of Immigration and Multicultural Affairs [Australia], Refugee and Humanitarian Visa Applicants: Guidelines on Gender Issues for Decision Makers (July 1996), *reprinted in* Gender Asylum Law in Different Countries: Decisions and Guidelines 7 (1999).
*Ex Parte Sivakumaran*, [1988] AC 958, 992G (HL).
Guy S. Goodwin-Gill, The Refugee in International Law (2nd ed. 1996).
Atle Grahl-Madsen, The Emergent International Law Relating to Refugees: Past, Present, Future (1985).
*Hernandez-Montiel v. INS*, 225 F.3d 1084 (9th Cir. 2000).
Immigration and Refugee Board of Canada, Guidelines on Women Refugee Claimants Fearing Gender-Related Persecution (Mar. 1993), *reprinted in* Gender Asylum Law in Different Countries: Decisions and Guidelines 87 (1999); Immigr. and Refugee Bd. of Can., Guideline 4: Women Refugee Claimants Fearing Gender-Related Persecution: Update (Nov. 13, 1996).
*In re Kasinga*, 21 I. & N. Dec. 357 (BIA 1996).
*INS v. Cardoza-Fonseca*, 480 U.S. 421 (1987).
*INS v. Elias-Zacarias*, 502 U.S. 478 (1992).
*Mr. Mümtaz Karakurt v. Austria*, Communication No. 965/2000, U.N. Doc. CCPR/C/74/D/965/2000 (2002).
*INS v. Stevic*, 467 U.S. 407 (1984).
International Journal of Refugee Law (Geoff Gilbert ed. 1989).
The Problem of Refugees in the Light of Contemporary International Law Issues (Vera Gowlland-Debbas ed., 1996).
Protocol Relating to the Status of Refugees, 606 U.N.T.S. 267, *entered into force* Oct. 4, 1967.
Reconceiving International Refugee Law (James C. Hathaway ed., 1997).
Refugee Protection in International Law: UNHCR's Global Consultations on International Protection (Erika Feller et al. eds., 2003).
*Shah and Islam v. Secretary of State for the Home Department*, [1999] 2 AC 629.
UNHCR, Handbook on Procedures and Criteria for Determining Refugee Status under the 1951 Convention and the 1967 Protocol relating to the Status of Refugees, U.N. Doc. HCR/IP/4/Eng/REV.1 (1992).
*Ullah & Do v. Special Adjudicator*, [2004] UKHL 26, [2004] All ER (D) 153.

*Links to Consult:*

http://uscis.gov/graphics/howdoi/RefElig.htm
http://www.asylumlaw.org
http://www.forcedmigration.org
http://www.iaa.gov.uk/32.htm
http://www.irb-cisr.gc.ca/en/about/guidelines/women_e.htm
http://www.parliament.the-stationery-office.co.uk/pa/ld199899/ldjudgmt/jd99032 5/islam01.htm
http://www.refugee.org.nz/
http://www.refugeesinternational.org
http://www.reliefweb.int

http://www.unhcr.org
http://www1.umn.edu/humanrts/instree/cartagena1984.html
http://www1.umn.edu/humanrts/instree/refugeehandbook.html
http://www1.umn.edu/humanrts/instree/v1crs.htm
http://www1.umn.edu/humanrts/instree/z2arcon.htm
http://www1.umn.edu/humanrts/undocs/965-2000.html

## 11. Nationality (Universal Declaration, Art. 15)

U.S. Supreme Court Chief Justice Earl Warren once observed, "Citizenship is man's basic right, for it is nothing less than the right to have rights. Remove this priceless possession and there remains a stateless person, disgraced and degraded in the eyes of his countrymen. He has no lawful claim to protection from any nation, and no nation may assert rights on his behalf. His very existence is at the sufferance of the state within whose borders he happens to be."[177]

On the one hand, there have been very important improvements in the protections afforded stateless persons since the late 1950s when Chief Justice Warren uttered those words. On the other hand, despite those improvements, a major gap exists between the international elaboration of the rights of stateless persons and the enjoyment of those rights in practice.

The Universal Declaration of Human Rights provides in Article 15:

1. Everyone has the right to a nationality.
2. No one shall be arbitrarily deprived of his nationality nor denied the right to change his nationality.[178]

Provisions intended to prevent or reduce statelessness are codified in several human rights treaties including the Covenant on Civil and Political Rights,[179] the Convention on the Rights of the Child,[180] the Convention on the Elimination of All Forms of Discrimination Against Women,[181] the Convention on the Reduction of Statelessness,[182] and the Convention relating to the Status of Stateless Persons.[183]

The Covenant on Civil and Political Rights addresses the problem of statelessness by providing that "Every child has the right to acquire a nationality. . . ."[184] The Convention on the Rights of the Child, which has been ratified by more states (193) than any other human rights treaty, further elaborates on the child's right to a nationality by stating that children "shall be registered immediately after birth and shall have the right from birth to a name, [and] the right to acquire a nationality. . . . States Parties shall ensure the implementation of these rights . . . in particular where the child would otherwise be stateless."[185] This right must be enforced without discrimination as to the gender of the parent. Similarly, the Convention on the Elimination of All Forms of Discrimination Against Women provides that States parties should ensure that "neither marriage to an alien nor change of nationality by the husband during marriage shall . . . render [a woman] stateless. . . ."[186]

While the treaties identified above were not principally promulgated to address the problem of statelessness, the 1961 Convention on the Reduction of Statelessness focuses exclusively on decreasing statelessness.[187] Under the 1961 Convention the twenty-seven States parties must curb situations in which persons may lose their citizenship without gaining another and States parties must also afford the means for persons born on their territory to obtain citizenship. In contrast to the 1961 Convention, which focuses on reducing statelessness, most of the 1954 Convention relating to the Status of Stateless Persons is devoted to the protection of stateless persons.[188]

Despite the widely ratified Convention on the Rights of the Child and the other treaties protecting against statelessness, there are many stateless persons who either never acquired citizenship of the country of their birth or lost their citizenship, and have no claim to the citizenship of another state. Such persons include persons native to the country of their residence who failed to register for citizenship during a specified period and have been denied it since, and persons who lost their citizenship after acquiring the citizenship of their non-citizen spouses, only to lose their adopted citizenship upon divorce. A number of persons become stateless because of the interplay of the two principal national approaches to determining citizenship. The first approach is *jus soli* (law of the place) and generally provides for citizenship based on the individual's country of birth. The second approach is *jus sanguinis* (law of blood), which determines citizenship based on family relationship. Because several governments do not comply with their obligations under the Convention on the Rights of the Child, many children are stateless if they are born in states that recognize only the *jus sanguinis* principle of acquiring citizenship to non-citizen parents of states that recognize only the *jus soli* approach. Other non-citizens are children born in a state to non-citizens and who acquire their parents' statelessness through the *jus sanguinis* principle.

The experience of a young Pakistani woman helps illustrate the kinds of problems that can arise because of different approaches to nationality. The young woman was abused by her family in the Pakistani-administered part of Kashmir. She attempted to commit suicide by throwing herself in a river. Instead of dying, however, she survived and the river took her to Indian-controlled Kashmir, where she was arrested for illegal entry and taken to jail. One of the jailers raped her and she gave birth to the jailer's child. Although DNA tests proved the paternity of the jailer, he refused to acknowledge paternity of the daughter. The Indian government attempted to deport the woman, but the Pakistani authorities refused to accept the child as a Pakistani national. The woman refused to abandon her child in order to return to Pakistan and now is living in limbo in Indian-controlled Kashmir. An Indian court in 2003 asked the Indian authorities to give her shelter and a monthly allowance until she is repatriated so she and her daughter can survive. While this case includes several unusually dramatic elements, there are many thousands of people around the world who have similarly been caught between nations.

Statelessness can cause serious problems. The increased vulnerability that often accompanies statelessness is illustrated by the plight of stateless Jews during World War II. Hannah Arendt described the situation prior the Nazi implementation of the "final solution" to the "Jewish Question," when the Nazi government began by declaring stateless all Jews in its territory.[189] This action deterred any other government from inquiring into the fate of Jews who were rounded up, deprived of their property, sent to concentration camps, and killed. Arendt also explained that when the Nazis began deporting Jews from other states, such as France and the Netherlands, the stateless Jews in those countries were more vulnerable than Jewish Dutch and French citizens. Accordingly, the Nazis almost always began the deportation process with stateless Jews. Depriving the Jews of their nationality was the precursor for their extermination.

Stateless persons must not only deal with the challenges associated with being vulnerable targets for gross human rights violators, they must also deal with the practical reality that in many states, nationality is a prerequisite for accessing political and judicial processes and obtaining economic, social, and cultural rights. One reason why stateless persons are unable to access these processes and rights is that stateless persons are often not issued identity documents by their states of habitual residence. Although the 1954 Convention on the Status of Stateless Persons does provide that States parties supply to "stateless persons such documents or certifications as would normally be delivered to aliens by or through . . . national authorities," few countries have ratified the 1954 Convention.

Being without identity documents also makes it difficult, in practice, to obtain basic social services despite the protections in the Covenant on Economic, Social and Cultural Rights for the rights of "everyone."[190] In fact, lack of identity documents often deters stateless persons from acquiring jobs, receiving medical care, marrying and starting a family, enjoying legal protection, traveling, owning property, gaining an education, or registering the birth of their children. The undocumented and stateless Bidun population of Kuwait often cannot register births, marriages, divorces, and deaths, because they lack identification and must undergo extensive security checks before the Ministry of Interior will permit them to register any of these significant life cycle events.[191] Kuwait has ratified the Covenant on Civil and Political Rights and is thus subject to Article 23 (protection of the family), but its treatment of the

Bidun does not protect the right of men and women of marriageable age to marry and found a family.

The problem of statelessness can be addressed by (a) preventive measures, (b) minimization approaches, and (c) naturalization remedies. Preventive measures, when properly implemented, stop statelessness before it develops. If all 193 states that have ratified the Convention on the Rights of the Child (and the 1961 Stateless Convention) register children born in their respective countries, statelessness will effectively be prevented in almost all situations. The Convention on the Rights of the Child requires a State party to, at birth, grant citizenship to all children born within its territory, "in particular where the child would otherwise be stateless." The 1961 Stateless Convention also forbids States parties from performing actions that would render stateless persons living within their territories. In order to pursue these preventive measures, governments must ratify the relevant treaties. The UNHCR has been the leading UN institution encouraging ratification of both the 1954 and 1961 Statelessness Conventions. Thus far, however, only 61 governments have ratified the 1954 Convention and 33 governments have ratified the 1961 Convention.

While preventive measures would avoid statelessness from occurring to newly born children or women who might be rendered stateless by marriage, minimization approaches lessen the difficulties associated with statelessness and serve to protect stateless persons from discrimination. The 1954 and 1961 Conventions call for the extension of rights to voting, employment, and ownership of property to stateless persons, so that their status is normalized. For example, Article 27 of the 1954 Convention obligates States parties to "issue identity papers to any stateless person in their territory who does not possess a valid travel document."[192] Such provisions may alleviate some of the difficulties associated with statelessness, but do not fundamentally alter one's status as a stateless person.

Statelessness can also be overcome by naturalization. The 1954 Convention, in Article 32, requires States parties to "as far as possible facilitate the assimilation and naturalization of stateless persons."[193] For example, in 2003 Sri Lanka adopted legislation intended to grant citizenship to more than 168,000 Tamils of Indian origin who were stateless. The same statute recognized the Sri Lankan nationality of children where either parent is a citizen of Sri Lanka. It is not clear, however, that adequate administrative machinery has been established to inform many Tamils who live in highland tea estates of this law or to facilitate their applications for citizenship.

*See also*: Asylum and Refugee Status, Protection of the Family

*Further Reading:*

Hannah Arendt, Eichmann in Jerusalem (1963).
Clarisa Bencomo & Human Rights Watch, Kuwait, Promises Betrayed: Denial of Rights of Bidun, Women, and Freedom of Expression (2000).
Convention on the Reduction of Statelessness, 989 U.N.T.S. 175, *entered into force* Dec. 13, 1975.
Convention relating to the Status of Stateless Persons, 360 U.N.T.S. 117, *entered into force* June 6, 1960.
Ruth Donner, The Regulation of Nationality in International Law (2d ed. 1994).
Office of the United Nations High Commissioner for Refugees, Division of Internal Protection, What Would Life Be Like if You Had No Nationality (1999).
*Perez v. Brownell,* 356 U.S. 44, 62 (1958) (Warren, C.J., dissenting).

*Links to Consult:*

http://www.hrw.org/reports/2000/kuwait/kuwait-04.htm#P168_23590
http://www.unhcr.ch/cgi-bin/texis/vtx/home
http://www.unhcr.ch/cgi-bin/texis/vtx/home?page = PROTECT&id = 3b8265c7a
http://www1.umn.edu/humanrts/instree/auow.htm

## 12. Protection of the Family (Universal Declaration, Art. 16)

The 1948 Universal Declaration of Human Rights protects the right to establish a family:

> 1. Men and women of full age, without any limitation due to race, nationality or religion, have the right to marry and to found a family. They are entitled to equal rights as to marriage, during marriage and at its dissolution.
> 2. Marriage shall be entered into only with the free and full consent of the intending spouses.
> 3. The family is the natural and fundamental group unit of society and is entitled to protection by society and the State.[194]

The Covenant on Civil and Political Rights codified these principles in its Article 23.[195] The Human Rights Committee has authoritatively interpreted Article 23 in its General Comment and stated

> that the concept of the family may differ in some respects from State to State, and even from region to region within a State, and that it is therefore not possible to give the concept a standard definition. However, the Committee emphasizes that, when a group of persons is regarded as a family under the legislation and practice of a State, it must be given the protection referred to in article 23. . . . Where diverse concepts of the family, "nuclear" and "extended," exist within a State, this should be indicated with an explanation of the degree of protection afforded to each. In view of the existence of various forms of family, such as unmarried couples and their children or single parents and their children, States parties should also indicate whether and to what extent such types of family and their members are recognized and protected by domestic law and practice.[196]

The Human Rights Committee has been asked to resolve a number of cases involving the right to protect the unity of a family, on the one hand, and the right of the government to enforce its immigration and criminal laws, on the other. For example, in *Winata v. Australia* two Indonesians of Chinese ethnicity entered Australia in 1985 and 1987 on temporary visas and remained in Australia beyond the term of their visas.[197] They met in Sydney, initiated a relationship, and gave birth to a son named "Barry" in June 1988. The son became an Australian citizen upon his birth in the country and remained in Sydney with his parents. The Australian government sought to deport Barry's parents because they lacked visas to remain in the country. The parents resisted deportation on the ground that it would violate their right to family unity under Article 23 as well as their rights under Article 17 ("No one shall be subjected to arbitrary or unlawful interference with his . . . family") and Article 24 ("Every child shall have . . . the right to such measures of protection as are required by his status as a minor, on the part of his family, society and the State"). They contended that their deportation would cause great harm to Barry because he was fully integrated into Australian society, spoke neither Indonesian or Chinese languages, should not be compelled to live in Indonesia, and should not be separated from his parents. By a divided decision, the Human Rights Committee found a violation of Articles 17, 23, and 24 reasoning:

> It is certainly unobjectionable under the Covenant that a State party may require, under its laws, the departure of persons who remain in its territory beyond limited duration permits. Nor is the fact that a child is born, or that by operation of law such a child receives citizenship either at birth or at a later time, sufficient of itself to make a proposed deportation of one or both parents arbitrary. Accordingly, there is significant scope for States parties to enforce their immigration policy and to require departure of unlawfully present persons. That discretion is, however, not unlimited and may come to be exercised arbitrarily in certain circumstances. In the present case, both authors have been in Australia for over fourteen years. The authors' son has grown in Australia from his birth 13 years ago, attending Australian schools as an ordinary child would and developing the social relationships inherent in that. In view of this duration of time, it is incumbent on the State party to demonstrate additional factors justifying the removal of both parents that go beyond a simple enforcement of its immigration law in order to avoid a characterisation of arbitrariness. In the particular circumstances, therefore, the Committee considers that the removal by the State party of the authors would constitute, if implemented, arbitrary interference with the family, contrary to article 17, paragraph 1, in conjunction with article 23, of the Covenant in respect of all of the alleged victims, and, additionally, a violation of article 24, paragraph 1, in relation to Barry Winata due to a failure to provide him with the necessary measures of protection as a minor.[198]

By way of contrast the Human Rights Committee found no violation of Articles 17 and 23 in *Stewart v. Canada*.[199] Stewart was born in Scotland and immigrated to Canada at the age of seven with his parents. Stewart was convicted of forty-two mostly petty offenses and traffic offenses, although he did suffer two convictions for possession of marijuana seeds and a prohibited martial arts weapon. He also was convicted for assault with bodily harm. Most of the convictions were attributable to Stewart's substance abuse problems, in particular alcoholism. Because Stewart's parents had never applied for his Canadian citizenship, he remained a permanent resident and the Canadian authorities sought to deport him because of his criminal convictions. At the age of thirty-six he was living with his mother who was in ill health and his disabled older brother. He also had two children living with his former wife. Canada argued that there was no violation of Article 23 in deporting Stewart:

> Canadian law provides protection for the family which is compatible with the requirements of article 23. The protection required by article 23, paragraph 1, however, is not absolute. In considering his removal, the competent Canadian courts gave appropriate weight to the impact of deportation on his family in

balancing these against the legitimate State interests to protect society and to regulate immigration. In this context the State party submits that the specific facts particular to his case, including his age and lack of dependents, suggest that the nature and quality of his family relationships could be adequately maintained through correspondence, telephone calls and visits to Canada, which he would be at liberty to make pursuant to Canadian immigration laws.[200]

The Committee concluded by a divided vote:

The Committee is of the opinion that the interference with Mr. Stewart's family relations that will be the inevitable outcome of his deportation cannot be regarded as either unlawful or arbitrary when the deportation order was made under law in furtherance of a legitimate state interest and due consideration was given in the deportation proceedings to the deportee's family connections. There is therefore no violation of articles 17 and 23 of the Covenant.[201]

While the Human Rights Committee has considered several analogous cases in the context of immigration matters, the *Winata* and *Stewart* decisions provide some insight into the way the right to protection of the family is generally implemented by the Committee. The European Court of Human Rights has had even more experience with interpreting the analogous provisions of the European Convention on Human Rights and has in some instances determined that deportation may violate a non-citizen's right to be free from interference in family life even where that non-citizen has been guilty of a criminal offense.[202] In the case of *Beldjoudi v. France*, for instance, Mr. Beldjoudi, who was considered an Algerian citizen, had been convicted of a number of criminal offenses in France—assault and battery, theft, aggravated theft, driving a vehicle without a licence, and possession of weapons—and was ordered deported.[203] Mr. Beldjoudi, however, was born in France and only lost his French citizenship while a juvenile as a result of his parents' failure to affirm their French nationality. Upon reaching adulthood, he tried to reestablish his French nationality, served in the French military, married a French citizen, and his close relatives had resided in France for several decades. Upon consideration of these factors, the European Court of Human Rights held that the deportation order was not proportionate to the legitimate aim pursued by Article 8 ("Everyone has the right to respect for his private and family life") of the European Convention and thus violated the rights of both Mr. Beldjoudi and his spouse.

The Human Rights Committee has also interpreted Article 23 of the Covenant to permit the government of New Zealand to remove a mother's six children (aged between eight and one year) from her care because she was unable to look after them adequately.[204] In addition, the Committee sustained the decision of New Zealand to refuse to confer the right to marry upon homosexual couples because Article 23 specifically refers to the right of "men and women" to marry.[205]

*See also:* Nationality

*Further Reading:*

*Beldjoudi v. France,* 234 Eur. Ct. H.R. (Ser. A) (1992).
*Margaret Buckle v. New Zealand,* Communication No. 858/1999, U.N. Doc. CCPR/C/70/D/858/1999 (2000).
Convention on Consent to Marriage, Minimum Age for Marriage and Registration of Marriages, 521 U.N.T.S. 231, *entered into force* Dec. 9, 1964.
Human Rights Committee, General Comment 19, Article 23 (Thirty-ninth session, 1990), Compilation of General Comments and General Recommendations Adopted by Human Rights Treaty Bodies, U.N. Doc. HRI/GEN/1/Rev.1 at 28 (1994).
Maja Kirilova Eriksson, The Right to Marry and to Found a Family: A World-Wide Human Right (1990).
The Family in International and Regional Human Rights Instruments (Akila Belembaogo ed., 1999).
*Juliet Joslin et al. v. New Zealand,* Communication No. 902/1999, U.N. Doc. A/57/40 at 214 (2002).
*Charles E. Stewart v. Canada,* Communication No. 538/1993, U.N. Doc. CCPR/C/58/D/538/1993 (1996).
Symposium, *Families and Children in International Law,* 12 Transnational Law & Contemporary Problems 271 (2002).
*Hendrick Winata and So Lan Li v. Australia,* Communication No. 30/2000, U.N. Doc. CCPR/C/72/D/930/2000 (2001).
Robert Wintemute and Mads Andenæs, The Legal Recognition of Same-Sex Partnerships: A Study of National, European and International Law (2001).

*Links to Consult:*

http://www.hrea.org/learn/guides/family.html
http://www.unhchr.ch/html/menu2/i2ecofam.htm
http://www1.umn.edu/humanrts/gencomm/hrcom19.htm
http://www1.umn.edu/humanrts/undocs/538-1993.html
http://www1.umn.edu/humanrts/undocs/858-1999.html
http://www1.umn.edu/humanrts/undocs/902-1999.html
http://www1.umn.edu/humanrts/undocs/930-2000.html

## 13. Property (Universal Declaration, Art. 17)

The Universal Declaration of Human Rights states: "Everyone has the right to own property alone as well as in association with others," and, "no one shall be arbitrarily deprived of his property."[206]

Unlike other provisions of the Universal Declaration, however, these principles were not codified in the two Covenants of 1966. Accordingly, neither the Covenant on Economic, Social and Cultural Rights nor the Covenant on Civil and Political Rights included a right to own property. The two Covenants did provide that property cannot be a basis for discrimination. Both Covenants also declared within the principle of self-determination that "All peoples may, for their own ends, freely dispose of their natural wealth and resources . . . , based upon the principle of mutual benefit, and international law. In no case may a people be deprived of its own means of subsistence."[207]

These statements represented a compromise among the drafters who reflected the divergent views of developed and developing countries. On the one hand, many developed countries generally respected the right to property, although they recognized that property may be taken by the government for a public purpose if fair procedures are followed and the owner is compensated. Developing and socialist countries wanted to protect their right to nationalize property—particularly property owned by non-citizens. There have been a number of very visible nationalizations of foreign-held properties: Russia (1917—private property), Mexico (1938—oil properties), Iran (1951—oil industry), Egypt (1956—Suez Canal Company), Indonesia (1956—Dutch properties), Cuba (1959-60—telephone company), Chile (1971—copper mine), Saudi Arabia (1970s—oil industry), Libya (1973—oil), Venezuela (1974-75—oil industry), United Kingdom (1975-77—shipbuilding industries), and France (1982—banks). The U.S. government responded to such nationalization efforts by contending that U.S. investors should be entitled to "prompt, adequate, and effective" compensation, but that view has not been shared by many countries. For example, a very visible 1962 resolution of the UN General Assembly on "Permanent Sovereignty over Natural Resources," called only for "appropriate compensation":

Nationalization, expropriation or requisitioning shall be based on grounds or reasons of public utility, security or the national interest which are recognized as overriding purely individual or private interests, both domestic and foreign. In such cases the owner shall be paid appropriate compensation, in accordance with the rules in force in the State taking such measures in the exercise of its sovereignty and in accordance with international law.[208]

Decisions of arbitral tribunals and the Permanent Court of International Justice have variously called for "fair compensation," "just compensation," and "appropriate compensation" for nationalized property.[209]

Given these divergent views—particularly in the 1960s when the Covenants were being drafted, it is not surprising that the Covenants do not provide for a right to property. The inclusion of the word "arbitrarily" in the Universal Declaration, however, might be interpreted to limit nationalizations at least to those situations in which property is taken for public good and possibly with such other concerns such as fair procedures and compensation.

While the Covenant on Civil and Political Rights does not comprehend the right to property, the Human Rights Committee has dealt indirectly with this right in cases (such as in Namibia) involving "the right of members of a minority to enjoy their culture under article 27 [which] includes protection to a particular way of life associated with the use of land resources through economic activities, such as hunting and fishing, especially in the case of indigenous peoples."[210] The Human Rights Committee also found discrimination between a husband and a wife in Peru because only the husband had standing in the courts to sue for collection of rent on matrimonial property.[211] In its General Comment on the equality of rights between men and women, the Human Rights Committee has further emphasized that

the capacity of women to own property, to enter into a contract or to exercise other civil rights may not be restricted on the basis of marital status or any other discriminatory ground. It also implies that women may not be treated as objects to be given together with the property of the deceased husband to his family. ... Women should also have equal inheritance rights to those of men when the dissolution of marriage is caused by the death of one of the spouses.[212]

In addition, the Human Rights Committee found that a former resident of Equatorial Guinea had been deprived of some of his lands because he did not adhere to the ruling party and did not belong to the president's clan. The Committee found political discrimination against that individual in violation of the Covenant and urged the government "to guarantee the security of his person, to return confiscated property to him or to grant him appropriate compensation, and that the discrimination to which he has been subjected be remedied without delay."[213]

Although the Covenant on Economic, Social and Cultural Rights does not guarantee the right to property, it does protect the cognate right to adequate housing.[214] In defining the right to adequate housing, the Committee on Economic, Social and Cultural Rights has set forth in its General Comment several critical attributes that would also apply in some circumstances to the right to property: (a) legal security of tenure; (b) availability of services, materials, facilities, and infrastructure; (c) affordability; (d) habilitability; (e) accessibility; (f) location; and (g) cultural adequacy.[215] The Covenant on Economic, Social and Cultural

Rights also protects intellectual property interests by calling on States parties to "recognize the right of everyone . . . to [both] enjoy the benefits of scientific progress and its applications," on the one hand, and to "benefit from the protection of the moral and material interests resulting from any scientific, literary or artistic production of which he is the author," on the other.[216] Hence, international human rights law recognized the property rights of inventors and authors as well as simultaneously focusing on the public right to benefit from their inventions and works of art. In addition, the Committee on Economic, Social and Cultural Rights has expressed concern about the process, for example in the Czech Republic, whereby formerly government property has been privatized or re-privatized without adequate "social safety nets . . . and . . . have negatively affected the enjoyment of economic, social and cultural rights, in particular by the most disadvantaged and marginalized groups."[217]

While neither of the two Covenants specifically protects the right to property, there are several other human rights treaties that protect against discrimination in regard to the right to property. For example, the Convention on the Elimination of All Forms Racial Discrimination forbids racial discrimination in regard to the "right to own property alone as well as in association with others" and "the right to inherit."[218] The Convention on the Elimination of All Forms of Discrimination Against Women provides for equality of spouses as to "ownership, acquisition, management, administration, enjoyment and disposition of property."[219] The right to property for refugees and stateless persons is protected by the Convention and Protocol relating to the status of refugees[220] as well as the Convention relating to the Status of Stateless Persons.[221]

In its 2005 judgment in the case of *Armed Activities in the Territory of the Congo*, the International Court of Justice found that the armed forces of the Democratic Republic of the Congo attacked the diplomatic property of Uganda and thus violated its oblicgations under the 1961 Vienna Convention on Diplomatic Relations.

Land plays a central role in the daily life, customs, culture, and religious life of many indigenous peoples. Accordingly, the International Labor Organization Convention concerning Indigenous and Tribal Peoples in Independent Countries provides, "governments shall respect the special importance for the cultures and spiritual values of the peoples concerned of their relationship with the lands or territories, or both as applicable, which they occupy or otherwise use, and in particular the collective aspects of this relationship."[222] Similarly, the draft Declaration on the Rights of Indigenous Peoples focuses on that aspect of the right to property in stating:

94   Particular Rights and Responsibilities

Indigenous peoples shall not be forcibly removed from their lands or territories. No relocation shall take place without the free and informed consent of the indigenous peoples concerned and after agreement on just and fair compensation and, where possible, with the option of return.[223]

As a concrete application of these principles the Inter-American Commission on Human Rights in October 2004 held that the "Maya people [in the Toledo District of Belize] have a communal property right, in accordance with their customary land use practices."[224] The Commission called on the government of Belize to

delimit, demarcate and title or otherwise clarify and protect the corresponding lands of the Maya people without detriment to other indigenous communities and, until those measures have been carried out, abstain from any acts that might lead the agents of the State itself, or third parties acting with its acquiescence or its tolerance, to affect the existence, value, use or enjoyment of the property located in the geographic area occupied and used by the Maya people.[225]

The right to property was not initially protected by the European Convention on Human Rights[226] when it was promulgated in 1950, for reasons similar to the impediments encountered in drafting a right to property clause for the Civil and Political Covenant. Two years later in 1952, however, the Council of Europe added the right to property in the first Protocol to the European Convention. The first Protocol states:

Every natural or legal person is entitled to the peaceful enjoyment of his possessions. No one shall be deprived of his possessions except in the public interest and subject to the conditions provided for by law and by the general principles of international law. The preceding provisions shall not, however, in any way impair the right of a State to enforce such laws as it deems necessary to control the use of property in accordance with the general interest or to secure the payment of taxes or other contributions or penalties.[227]

The European Court of Human Rights in *Sporrong and Lönnroth* decided that Sweden had violated the right to property under the first Protocol as well as Article 6 (right to a fair hearing within a reasonable time) of the European Convention when the city of Stockholm prohibited construction on two properties for more than twenty-three years while the city government was engaged in town planning. The Court observed that it "must determine whether a fair balance was struck between the demands of the general interest of the community and the requirements of the protection of the individual's fundamental rights."[228]

*See also:* Culture, Equality and Nondiscrimination, Housing, Procedural Fairness in the Criminal Process and the Administration of Justice, Asylum and Refugee Status

*Further Reading:*

*Armed Activities in the Territory of the Congo (Dem. Rep. Congo v. Uganda)*, 2005 I.C.J. No. 116 (Dec. 19).
*Graciela Ato del Avellanal v. Peru*, Communication No. 202/1986, U.N. Doc. Supp. No. 40 (A/44/40) at 196 (1988).
*Chorzów Factory Case*, 1928 PCIJ (ser. A), No. 17.
Committee on Economic, Social and Cultural Rights, Conclusions and Recommendations, Cultural Rights, Czech Republic, U.N. Doc. E/C.12/1/Add.76 (2002).
Committee on Economic, Social and Cultural Rights, General Comment 4, The Right to Adequate Housing (Sixth session, 1991), U.N. Doc. E/1992/23, annex III at 114 (1991).
Committee on Economic, Social and Cultural Rights, General Comment 17, The Right of Everyone to Benefit from the Protection of the Moral and Material Interests Resulting from any Scientific, Literary or Artistic Production of Which He or She is the Author (article 15, paragraph 1 (c), of the Covenant), U.N. Doc. E/C.12/GC/17 (2006).
Committee on Economic, Social and Cultural Rights, *Human Rights and Intellectual Property: Statement of the Committee on Economic, Social and Cultural Rights*, U.N. Doc. E/C.12/2001/15 (2001).
Committee on the Elimination of Discrimination Against Women, General Recommendation 21, Equality in Marriage and Family Relations (Thirteenth session, 1992), U.N. Doc. A/49/38 at 1 (1994).
Juan C. Consuegra-Barquin, *Cuba's Residential Property Ownership Dilemma: A Human Rights Issue Under International Law*, 46 Rutgers L. Rev. 873 (Winter 1994).
Convention concerning Indigenous and Tribal Peoples in Independent Countries (ILO No. 169), 72 ILO Official Bull. 59, *entered into force* Sept. 5, 1991.
Convention on the Elimination of All Forms of Discrimination Against Women, G.A. res. 34/180, 34 U.N. GAOR Supp. (No. 46) at 193, U.N. Doc. A/34/46, *entered into force* Sept. 3, 1981.
Convention Relating to the Status of Refugees, 189 U.N.T.S. 150, *entered into force* Apr. 22, 1954.
Convention Relating to the Status of Stateless Persons, 360 U.N.T.S. 117, *entered into force* June 6, 1960.
*J.G.A. Diergaardt (late Captain of the Rehoboth Baster Community) et al. v. Namibia*, Communication No. 760/1997, U.N. Doc. CCPR/C/69/D/760/1997 (2000)
Draft Declaration on the Rights of Indigenous Peoples, U.N. Doc. A/HRC/1/L.10 (1994).
Helene Ruiz Fabri, *The Approach Taken by the European Court of Human Rights to the Assessment of Compensation for 'Regulatory Expropriations' of the Property of Foreign Investors*, 11 N.Y.U. Envtl. L.J. 148 (2002).
Ralph H. Folsom, Michael Wallace Gordon, & John A. Spanogle, International Trade and Investment in a Nutshell (2000).
Rosalyn Higgins, *The Taking of Property by the State: Recent Developments in Interna-*

*tional Law*, 176 Recueil des cours, Collected Courses of the Hague Academy of International Law 363 (1983).

Human Rights Committee, General Comment 28, Equality of rights between men and women (article 3), U.N. Doc. CCPR/C/21/Rev.1/Add.10 (2000).

Inter-American Commission on Human Rights, Maya Indigenous Community of the Toledo District, Belize, Report No. 40/04, Case 12.053 (Oct. 12, 2004).

*Littgow and Others v. United Kingdom* (9006/80), [1986] ECHR 8 (July 8, 1986).

*Ol' Bahamonde v. Equatorial Guinea*, Communication No. 468/1991, U.N. Doc. CCPR/C/49/D/468/1991 (1993).

Permanent Sovereignty over Natural Resources, G.A. res. 1803 (XVII), 17 U.N. GAOR Supp. (No.17) at 15, U.N. Doc. A/5217 (1962).

*Sporrong and Lönnroth* (7151/75), [1982] ECHR 5 (Sept. 23, 1982).

Luis Valencia Rodríguez, The Right of Everyone to Own Property Alone as Well as in Association with Others, U.N. Doc. E/CN.4/1993/15 (1992).

Edwin D. Williamson, *U.S.-EU Understanding on Helms-Burton: A Missed Opportunity to Fix International Law on Property Rights*, 48 Cath. U.L. Rev. 293 (1999).

*Links to Consult:*

http://www1.umn.edu/humanrts/esc/czechrepublic2002.html
http://www1.umn.edu/humanrts/gencomm/epcomm4.htm
http://www1.umn.edu/humanrts/gencomm/generl21.htm
http://www1.umn.edu/humanrts/gencomm/hrcom28.htm
http://www1.umn.edu/humanrts/instree/c2psnr.htm
http://www1.umn.edu/humanrts/instree/declra.htm
http://www1.umn.edu/humanrts/instree/d1cerd.htm
http://www1.umn.edu/humanrts/instree/e1cedaw.htm
http://www1.umn.edu/humanrts/instree/v1crs.htm
http://www1.umn.edu/humanrts/instree/w3cssp.htm
http://www1.umn.edu/humanrts/undocs/html/vws468.htm
http://www1.umn.edu/humanrts/undocs/session44/202-1986.htm
http://www1.umn.edu/humanrts/undocs/session69/view760.htm

## 14. Freedom of Religion and Belief (Universal Declaration, Art. 18)

The Universal Declaration of Human Rights provides in Article 18:

> Everyone has the right to freedom of thought, conscience and religion; this right includes freedom to change his religion or belief, and freedom, either alone or in community with others and in public or private, to manifest his religion or belief in teaching, practice, worship and observance.[229]

In adopting the Universal Declaration, the freedom to change one's religion or belief was very controversial—particularly among Muslims who believed that it was not possible to leave Islam—and caused Saudi Arabia to abstain from voting in favor of the final text. In codifying this provision in the Covenant on Civil and Political Rights, the right to change one's religion was omitted and significant limitations were introduced as to the right to manifest one's belief. Accordingly, Article 18 of the Civil and Political Covenant states,

> 1. Everyone shall have the right to freedom of thought, conscience and religion. This right shall include freedom to have or to adopt a religion or belief of his choice, and freedom, either individually or in community with others and in public or private, to manifest his religion or belief in worship, observance, practice and teaching.
> 2. No one shall be subject to coercion which would impair his freedom to have or to adopt a religion or belief of his choice.
> 3. Freedom to manifest one's religion or beliefs may be subject only to such limitations as are prescribed by law and are necessary to protect public safety, order, health, or morals or the fundamental rights and freedoms of others.
> 4. The States Parties to the present Covenant undertake to have respect for the liberty of parents and, when applicable, legal guardians to ensure the religious and moral education of their children in conformity with their own convictions.[230]

The Human Rights Committee has authoritatively interpreted this provision by noting that the right to freedom of conscience and religion is absolute, but there are significant limitations on the right to manifest one's religion or belief.[231] The Committee has also indicated that "Article 18 protects theistic, nontheistic and atheistic beliefs, as well as the right not to profess any religion or belief. The terms 'belief' and 'religion' are to be broadly construed."[232] At the same time the Committee decided in *M.A.B. et al. v. Canada* that "a belief consisting primarily or exclusively in the worship and distribution of a narcotic drug cannot conceivably be brought within the scope of article 18 of the Covenant."[233]

Even though the Covenant does not mention the right to "change" one's religion or belief, the Committee's General Comment has observed "that the freedom to 'have or to adopt' a religion or belief necessarily entails the freedom to choose a religion or belief, including the right to replace one's current religion or belief with another or to adopt atheistic views, as well as the right to retain one's religion or belief."[234]

The Committee's General Comment has also issued an interpretation of the freedom to manifest religion or belief:

The freedom to manifest religion or belief may be exercised "either individually or in community with others and in public or private." The freedom to manifest religion or belief in worship, observance, practice and teaching encompasses a broad range of acts. The concept of worship extends to ritual and ceremonial acts giving direct expression to belief, as well as various practices integral to such acts, including the building of places of worship, the use of ritual formulae and objects, the display of symbols, and the observance of holidays and days of rest. The observance and practice of religion or belief may include not only ceremonial acts but also such customs as the observance of dietary regulations, the wearing of distinctive clothing or headcoverings, participation in rituals associated with certain stages of life, and the use of a particular language customarily spoken by a group. In addition, the practice and teaching of religion or belief includes acts integral to the conduct by religious groups of their basic affairs, such as the freedom to choose their religious leaders, priests and teachers, the freedom to establish seminaries or religious schools and the freedom to prepare and distribute religious texts or publications.[235]

The Human Rights Committee found a violation of Article 18 (freedom to manifest religion or belief in worship, observance, practice) when a prisoner in Trinidad was subjected to disciplinary measures whereby he was "forbidden from wearing a beard and from worshipping at religious services, and that his prayer books were taken from him."[236] The Committee found no violation, however, in the case of a Sikh in Canada who was required for reasons of worker safety to wear a hard hat at his job site work rather than a turban.[237]

The European Court of Human Rights has decided several cases interpreting the analogous freedom of religion or belief clause in the European Convention on Human Rights. For example, in June 2004 the European Court ruled that a Turkish student could be barred from attending the Istanbul University medical school in 1998 because her headscarf violated the official dress code. The court stated, "Measures taken in universities to prevent certain fundamentalist religious movements from pressuring students who do not practice the religion in question or those belonging to another religion can be justified."[238] Similar issues about wearing headscarves in schools have arisen in Belgium, France, Germany, and the United Kingdom.

Freedom of religion has also been construed to manifest one's belief by exercising the right to conscientious objection to military service. The Human Rights Committee's General Comment stated,

> Many individuals have claimed the right to refuse to perform military service (conscientious objection) on the basis that such right derives from their freedoms under article 18. In response to such claims, a growing number of States have in their laws exempted from compulsory military service citizens who genuinely hold religious or other beliefs that forbid the performance of military service and replaced it with alternative national service. The Covenant does not explicitly refer to a right to conscientious objection, but the Committee believes that such a right can be derived from article 18, inasmuch as the obligation to use lethal force may seriously conflict with the freedom of conscience and the right to manifest one's religion or belief. When this right is recognized by law or practice, there shall be no differentiation among conscientious objectors on the basis of the nature of their particular beliefs; likewise, there shall be no discrimination against conscientious objectors because they have failed to perform military service. . . .[239]

The Human Rights Committee refused, however, to find that individuals who were conscientious objectors to nuclear weapons had a right under Article 18 to refuse to pay a percentage of their assessed taxes to the Netherlands in so far as those taxes were used for military expenditures, including procurement and maintenance of nuclear weapons.[240]

Neither Article 18 of the Civil and Political Covenant nor the analogous provision in the European Convention forbid establishment of religion so long as individuals who do not belong to the established religion cannot demonstrate that they were subjected to discrimination. There is considerable diversity among nations as to whether they have an established church or provide for separation of church and state. For example, the Jordanian Constitution expressly provides that Islam is the official religion of Jordan. The Icelandic Constitution provides that the Evangelical Lutheran Church is the state Church and that it should receive support from the state. Ethiopia's Constitution specifically declares the separation of church and state. Japan's and Angola's Constitutions declare the states to be secular. Liberia's Constitution states that there is no state religion. While not formally taking a position one way or the other on a state religion, Singapore's Constitution expressly bans any tax that requires a person to support a religion that is not their own. The Human Rights Committee's General Comment provides in this respect:

> The fact that a religion is recognized as a state religion or that it is established as official or traditional or that its followers comprise the majority of the population, shall not result in any impairment of the enjoyment of any of the rights under the Covenant, including articles 18 and 27 [minorities' right to profess and practice their own religion], nor in any discrimination against adherents to

other religions or nonbelievers. In particular, certain measures discriminating against the latter, such as measures restricting eligibility for government service to members of the predominant religion or giving economic privileges to them or imposing special restrictions on the practice of other faiths, are not in accordance with the prohibition of discrimination based on religion or belief and the guarantee of equal protection under article 26 [no discrimination based on religion].[241]

Following the approach set forth in this General Comment, the Human Rights Committee has applied its principled opposition to discrimination between religions in a case arising in Canada in which the Committee

observes that the Covenant does not oblige States parties to fund schools which are established on a religious basis. However, if a State party chooses to provide public funding to religious schools, it should make this funding available without discrimination. This means that providing funding for the schools of one religious group and not for another must be based on reasonable and objective criteria. In the instant case, the Committee concludes that the material before it does not show that the differential treatment between the Roman Catholic faith and the author's religious denomination is based on such criteria. Consequently, there has been a violation of the author's rights under article 26 of the Covenant to equal and effective protection against discrimination.[242]

The 1981 UN Declaration on the Elimination of All Forms of Intolerance and of Discrimination Based on Religion or Belief also forbids religious discrimination.[243] In 1986 the UN Commission on Human Rights established a Special Rapporteur on freedom of religion or belief, who reports annually to the Commission and its successor Human Rights Council on information he has received on religious discrimination and other violations of religious freedom.[244]

*See also:* Asylum and Refugee Status; Clothing; Equality and Nondiscrimination, Genocide, War Crimes, Crimes Against Humanity, Crimes Against Peace

*Further Reading:*

*Karnel Singh Bhinder v. Canada*, Communication Nos. 208/1986, U.N. Doc. CCPR/C/37/D/208/1986 (1989).
*Clement Boodoo v. Trinidad and Tobago*, Communication No. 721/1996, U.N. Doc. CCPR/C/74/D/721/1996 (2002).
Convention on the Prevention and Punishment of the Crime of Genocide, 78 U.N.T.S. 277, *entered into force* Jan. 12, 1951.
Declaration on the Elimination of All Forms of Intolerance and of Discrimination Based on Religion or Belief, G.A. res. 36/55, 36 U.N. GAOR Supp. (No. 51) at 171, U.N. Doc. A/36/684 (1981).
Human Rights Committee, General Comment 22, Article 18 (Forty-eighth session, 1993), Compilation of General Comments and General Recommenda-

## Freedom of Religion and Belief 101

tions Adopted by Human Rights Treaty Bodies, U.N. Doc. HRI/GEN/1/Rev.1 at 35 (1994).
*J.v.K. and C.M.G.v.K.-S. v. The Netherlands,* Communication No. 483/1991, U.N. Doc. CCPR/C/45/D/483/1991 (1992).
Natan Lerner, Religion, Beliefs, and International Human Rights (2000).
*M.A.B., W.A.T. and J.-A.Y.T. v. Canada,* Communication No. 570/1993, U.N. Doc. CCPR/C/50/D/570/1993 (1994).
Elizabeth Odio Benito, Elimination of All Forms of Intolerance and Discrimination Based on Religion or Belief, U.N. sales no. E.89.XIV.3 (1989).
*Leyla Şahin v. Turkey,* App. No. 44774/98 (June 29, 2004).
Freedom of Religion & Belief: World Report (Juliet Sheen ed., 1997).
Religious Human Rights in Global Perspective, Legal Perspectives (Johan D. van der Vyver & John Witte Jr. eds., 1996).
Bahiyyih G. Tahzib, Freedom of Religion or Belief: Ensuring Effective International Legal Protection (1996).
U.S. Department of State, The International Religious Freedom Report (2001–) [annual].
*Arieh Hollis Waldman v. Canada,* Communication No. 694/1996, U.N. Doc. CCPR/C/67/D/694/1996 (1999).

*Links to Consult:*

http://hrw.org/doc/?t=religion
http://religiousfreedom.lib.virginia.edu/nationprofiles/
http://web.hamline.edu/law/lawrelign/jlr/
http://www.echr.coe.int
http://www.paradigmpub.com/guest.htm
http://www.starlightsite.co.uk/keston/
http://www.state.gov/g/drl/irf
http://www.unesco.org/most/rr2int.htm
http://www.unhchr.ch/html/menu2/i2othrel.htm
http://www.unhchr.ch/html/menu2/7/b/religion/
http://www.unhchr.ch/html/menu2/7/b/religion/documents.htm
http://www.uscirf.gov/index.php3?SID=28f80d60e171193d006ad9b8b296edff
http://www1.umn.edu/humanrts/edumat/studyguides/religion.html
http://www1.umn.edu/humanrts/gencomm/hrcom22.htm
http://www1.umn.edu/humanrts/instree/d4deidrb.htm
http://www1.umn.edu/humanrts/instree/d5drm.htm
http://www1.umn.edu/humanrts/instree/x1cppcg.htm
http://www1.umn.edu/humanrts/undocs/html/483-1991.html
http://www1.umn.edu/humanrts/undocs/html/570-1993.html
http://www1.umn.edu/humanrts/undocs/session37/208-1986.html

## 15. Freedom of Expression (Universal Declaration, Art. 19)

Article 19 of the Universal Declaration of Human Rights establishes the freedoms of opinion and expression in quite sweeping terms:

> Everyone has the right to freedom of opinion and expression; this right includes freedom to hold opinions without interference and to seek, receive and impart information and ideas through any media and regardless of frontiers.[245]

In codifying this provision, the Covenant on Civil and Political Rights, also in Article 19, distinguishes between the unqualified right to hold opinions and the far more limited freedom of expression which "carries with it special duties and responsibilities" and is subject to "certain restrictions" in Article 19(3) which must be provided by law and are necessary:

> (a) For respect of the rights or reputations of others;
> (b) For the protection of national security or of public order (*ordre public*), or of public health or morals.[246]

Nearly all constitutions protect freedom of expression or the essentially identical freedom of speech and the press. For example, the constitutions of Angola (Article 32), Ethiopia (Article 29), Iceland (Article 73), Japan (Article 21), Liberia (Article 15), Mexico (Article 6), New Zealand (Section 14 of the Bill of Rights Act of 1990), Poland (Article 54 of the Constitution of 1997), Singapore (Article 14), and South Africa (Article 16) contain language similar to Article 19 of the Civil and Political Covenant.

The Human Rights Committee in a General Comment has noted the important relationship of Article 19 with Article 25 of the Covenant (right to participate in public affairs):

> In order to ensure the full enjoyment of rights protected by Article 25, the free communication of information and ideas about public and political issues between citizens, candidates and elected representatives is essential. This implies a free press and other media able to comment on public issues without censorship or restraint and to inform public opinion. It requires the full enjoyment and respect for the rights guaranteed in Articles 19, 21 [peaceful assembly] and 22 [freedom of association] of the Covenant, including freedom to engage in political activity individually or through political parties and other organizations, freedom to debate public affairs, to hold peaceful demonstrations and meetings, to criticize and oppose, to publish political material, to campaign for election and to advertise political ideas.[247]

Freedom of expression problems are often found in cases involving issues of national security, public morals, protection of the justice system, hate speech, and defamation because these areas often give rise to possible justifications for placing limitations on freedom of expression.

The Human Rights Committee has considered several cases in which the government contended that freedom of expression should be limited for reasons of national security. For example, *Park v. Republic of Korea* concerned a Korean student who attended college in the United States. While there, Park belonged to a youth organization that promoted the unification of the Republic of Korea (South Korea) and the Democratic People's Republic of Korea (North Korea) and that voiced criticism toward the South Korean government and its U.S. support. When Park returned to South Korea, he was arrested and convicted under the Korean National Security Law for supporting an organization which benefitted the "enemy," that is, North Korea. The Committee observed that the government had failed to explain how the National Security Law's restrictions on the freedom of expression were "necessary . . . [for] the protection of national security":

> The Committee considers that the State party has failed to specify the precise nature of the threat which it contends that the author's exercise of freedom of expression posed and finds that none of the arguments advanced by the State party suffice to render the restriction of the author's right to freedom of expression compatible with paragraph 3 of article 19. The Committee has carefully studied the judicial decisions by which the author was convicted and finds that neither those decisions nor the submissions by the State party show that the author's conviction was necessary for the protection of one of the legitimate purposes set forth by article 19 (3). The author's conviction for acts of expression must therefore be regarded as a violation of the author's right under article 19 of the Covenant.[248]

The Committee's ruling is consistent with the Johannesburg Principles on National Security, Freedom of Expression and Access to Information.[249] Those principles indicate that if a government appeals to national security as a justification for limiting freedom of expression, the government bears the burden of demonstrating (a) the threat to national security and (b) that the manner in which freedom of expression is being limited has the effect of reducing or removing the threat.

Questions of public morality and freedom of expression have also come before the Human Rights Committee. *Hertzberg et al. v. Finland* concerned the question of whether a government-controlled broadcasting company could censor segments of radio and TV programs which contained material dealing with homosexuality, for fear of violating a Finnish law which prohibited the public encouragement of "indecent behavior between members of the same sex." The Committee agreed with the State's position that government is the better judge of what restrictions are necessary to protect public morals:

public morals differ widely. There is no universally applicable common standard. Consequently, in this respect, a certain margin of discretion must be accorded to the responsible national authorities. The Committee finds that it cannot question the decision of the responsible organs of the Finnish Broadcasting Corporation that radio and TV are not the appropriate forums to discus issues related to homosexuality.[250]

As this Human Rights Committee decision reflects, the standards for protection of public morals are neither universal, nor static. A government cannot, however, close all forums to a topic that it views as offending public morals, but it can bar access to some.

In interpreting the freedom of expression provision in the European Convention on Human Rights, the European Court of Human Rights has balanced the values underlying freedom of expression and the need to protect the independence and impartiality of the judicial system. In *Sunday Times v. United Kingdom*, the government requested an injunction to prevent the *Sunday Times* from publishing an exposé of the extremely protracted legal settlement of an ongoing lawsuit by individuals who were born with severe birth defects because their mothers had taken medical prescriptions for the drug thalidomide. The government defended the injunction on the grounds that publishing the article would negatively impact the ongoing judicial process by creating a sort of separate trial in the media. The Court disagreed:

freedom of expression constitutes one of the essential foundations of a democratic society. [This] principle is of particular importance . . . to the field of the administration of justice, which . . . requires the cooperation of an enlightened public. . . . [While] the mass media must not overstep the bounds imposed in the interests of the proper administration of justice, it is incumbent on them to impart information and ideas concerning matters that come before the courts just as in other areas of public interest.[251]

As cornerstones of democracy, freedom of expression, and the judicial system must coexist with one another. In some instances the judicial system may need to be protected from certain exercises of the freedom of expression. For example, newspapers or television may issue news reports that have the consequence of undermining an accused's right to be presumed innocent.

The use of hate speech is another domain in which freedom of expression must be balanced against other societal norms. Article 20 of the Civil and Political Covenant and Article 4 of the Convention on the Elimination of All Forms of Racial Discrimination forbid hate speech. The Human Rights Committee has sought to interpret these hate speech provisions so as to be consistent with freedom of expression in its General Comment:

Article 20 of the Covenant states that any propaganda for war and any advocacy of national, racial or religious hatred that constitutes incitement to discrimination, hostility or violence shall be prohibited by law. In the opinion of the Committee, these required prohibitions are fully compatible with the right of freedom of expression as contained in article 19, the exercise of which carries with it special duties and responsibilities.[252]

The Committee on the Elimination of Racial Discrimination has similarly observed in its General Recommendation on hate speech that "the prohibition of the dissemination of all ideas based upon racial superiority or hatred is compatible with the right to freedom of opinion and expression," and further noted the duties and rights established by Article 20 of the Civil and Political Covenant.[253] Legal prohibitions against hate speech are not only commanded by Article 20 of the Covenant and by Article 4 of the Race Convention, but they fit within the limitations of Article 19(3) as "necessary . . . [f]or respect of the rights . . . of others. . . . "[254]

The U.S. Supreme Court interprets the First Amendment to the U.S. Constitution in a way which is more protective of freedom of expression than the Covenant's Article 19. The First Amendment is worded in absolute terms: "Congress shall make no law . . . abridging the freedom of speech." The U.S. Constitution also protects against racial discrimination, but in balancing racial harmony with free speech, the Supreme Court clearly favors freedom of expression. For example, in its 2003 decision in *Virginia v. Black*, the Supreme Court found that a cross-burning at the home of an African American family could not be the subject of criminal sanction unless the prosecution demonstrated an intent to harm.[255] Even under this more restrictive approach focusing on the intent of the individual, however, both the Covenant and U.S. law would have permitted the Rwandan government to prosecute the radio announcers on Radio Milles Collines who broadcast calls to kill members of the Tutsi minority in 1994.

The approach of the U.S. Supreme Court in *Virginia v. Black* can be contrasted with the Human Rights Committee's views on *Faurisson v. France*. Mr. Faurisson was convicted under the French "Gayssot Act" for expressing his doubts about the Nazi use of gas chambers in the Holocaust in a published interview. In its analysis the Human Rights Committee declined to examine Mr. Faurisson's intent, and instead focused on the impact of his statements on the "interests of other persons or . . . of the *community as a whole*. Since the statements made by the author, read in their full context, were of a nature as to raise or strengthen antisemitic feelings, [the restriction on freedom of expression preserved the ability] of the Jewish community to live free from fear of an atmosphere of anti-semitism" (emphasis original).[256]

## 106   Particular Rights and Responsibilities

The European Commission on Human Rights used similar reasoning in defamation cases, such as *D.I. v. Germany*, which involved an individual who sought to invoke the protections of freedom of expression for his denial of the existence of gas chambers during the Holocaust. The Commission's decision in *D.I. v. Germany* noted the safety interests of the Jewish community, but also declared that

> the requirements of protecting [the Jewish community's] reputation and rights, outweigh, in a democratic society, the applicant's freedom to impart publications denying the existence of the gassing of Jews under the Nazi regime....[257]

Both the Human Rights Committee decision in *Faurisson v. France* and the European Commission decision in *D.I. v. Germany* required that freedom of expression must yield to such competing interests such as respect of the rights or reputations of others. It is not clear that U.S. courts, given their greater interest in freedom of expression, would come to the same conclusion.

The Human Rights Committee has considered other freedom of expression issues, ruling for example that (1) the Finnish government may not characterize public display of a protest banner as a demonstration so as to remove that display from Article 19 protection[258] and (2) a letter in support of a labor strike does not constitute a threat to Korean national security such that it can be punishable by law.[259]

*See also:* Freedom of Association and Assembly, Freedom of Religion or Belief

*Further Reading:*

Article 19 World Report 1988 (Kevin Boyle ed., 1988).
Sandra Coliver, The Article 19 Freedom of Expression Handbook: International and Comparative Law, Standards and Procedures (1993).
Committee on the Elimination of Racial Discrimination, General Recommendation 15, Measures to eradicate incitement to or acts of discrimination (Forty-second session, 1993), U.N. Doc. A/48/18 at 114 (1994).
*D.I. v. Germany,* App. No. 26551/95, Eur. Comm'n H.R. (June 26, 1996).
*Robert Faurisson v. France,* Communication No. 550/1993, U.N. Doc. CCPR/C/58/D/550/1993(1996).
Human Rights Committee, General Comment 10, Article 19 (Nineteenth session, 1983), Compilation of General Comments and General Recommendations Adopted by Human Rights Treaty Bodies, U.N. Doc. HRI/GEN/1/Rev.1 at 11 (1994).
Human Rights Committee, General Comment 11, Article 20 (Nineteenth session, 1983), Compilation of General Comments and General Recommendations Adopted by Human Rights Treaty Bodies, U.N. Doc. HRI/GEN/1/Rev.1 at 12 (1994).
Human Rights Committee, General Comment 25 (57), General Comments under article 40, paragraph 4, of the International Covenant on Civil and

Political Rights, Adopted by the Committee at its 1510th meeting, U.N. Doc. CCPR/C/21/Rev.1/Add.7 (1996).
*J.R.T. and the W.G. Party v. Canada,* Communication No. 104/1981, U.N. Doc. CCPR/C/OP/2 at 25 (1984).
*Leo R. Hertzberg, Uit Mansson, Astrid Nikula and Marko and Tuovi Putkonen, represented by SETA (Organization for Sexual Equality) v. Finland,* Communication No. R.14/61, U.N. Doc. Supp. No. 40 (A/37/40) at 161 (1982).
The International Covenant on Civil and Political Rights: Cases, Materials, and Commentary (Sarah Joseph, Jenny Schultz, & Melissa Castan eds., 2d ed. 2004).
The Johannesburg Principles on National Security, Freedom of Expression and Access to Information, Freedom of Expression and Access to Information, U.N. Doc. E/CN.4/1996/39 (1996).
*J.R.T. and the W.G. Party v. Canada,* Communication No. 104/1981, U.N. Doc. Supp. No. 40 (A/38/40) at 231 (1983).
Thomas David Jones, Human Rights: Group Defamation, Freedom of Expression, and the Law of Nations (1998).
*Kivenmaa v. Finland,* Communication No. 412/1990, U.N. Doc. CCPR/C/50/D/412/1990 (1994).
*Tae Hoon Park (represented by Mr. Yong-Whan Cho of Duksu Law Offices in Seoul) v. Republic of Korea,* Communication No. 628/1995, U.N. Doc. CCPR/C/64/D/628/1995 (1998).
*Malcolm Ross v. Canada,* Communication No. 736/1997, U.N. Doc. CCPR/C/70/D/736/1997 (2000).
Secrecy and Liberty: National Security, Freedom of Expression and Access to Information (Sandra Coliver, Paul Hoffman, Joan Fitzpatrick, & Stephen Bowen eds., 1999).
*Jong-Kyu Sohn v. Republic of Korea,* Communication No. 518/1992, U.N. Doc. CCPR/C/54/D/518/1992 (1995).
*The Sunday Times v. The United Kingdom,* 30 Eur. Ct. H.R. (ser. A), 2 E.H.R.R. 245 (1979).
*Virginia v. Black,* 538 U.S. 343 (2003).

*Links to Consult:*

http://confinder.richmond.edu/
http://hrw.org/doc/?t=press_freedom
http://hudoc.echr.coe.int/Default.htm
http://hudoc.echr.coe.int/Hudoc2doc%5Chedec%5Csift%5C3049.txt http://www.article19.org
http://www.hrw.org/advocacy/internet/index.htm
http://www.ifex.org
http://www.ifj.org
http://www.rsf.fr
http://www.supremecourtus.gov/opinions/02pdf/01-1107.pdf
http://www.unhchr.ch/html/menu2/7/b/mfro.htm
http://www.worldlii.org/eu/cases/ECHR/1979/1.htmlhttp://www1.umn.edu/humanrts/gencomm/genrxv.htm
http://www1.umn.edu/humanrts/gencomm/hrcom10.htm
http://www1.umn.edu/humanrts/gencomm/hrcom11.htm
http://www1.umn.edu/humanrts/gencomm/hrcom25.htm

108    Particular Rights and Responsibilities

http://www1.umn.edu/humanrts/instree/johannesburg.html
http://www1.umn.edu/humanrts/links/expression.html
http://www1.umn.edu/humanrts/undocs/736-1997.html
http://www1.umn.edu/humanrts/undocs/html/vws412.htm
http://www1.umn.edu/humanrts/undocs/html/vws518.htm
http://www1.umn.edu/humanrts/undocs/html/VWS55058.htm
http://www1.umn.edu/humanrts/undocs/html/104-1981.htm
http://www1.umn.edu/humanrts/undocs/session37/14-61.htm
http://www1.umn.edu/humanrts/undocs/session38/104-1981.htm
http://www1.umn.edu/humanrts/undocs/session64/view628.htm

## 16. Freedom of Association and Assembly (Universal Declaration, Art. 20)

The Universal Declaration of Human Rights states, "Everyone has the right to freedom of peaceful assembly and association."[260] Article 21 of the Civil and Political Covenant codifies the freedom of peaceful assembly with a number of significant "restrictions . . . imposed in conformity with the law and which are necessary in a democratic society in the interests of national security or public safety, public order (*ordre public*), the protection of public health or morals or the protection of the rights and freedoms of others."[261] Both Article 22 of the Civil and Political Covenant and Article 8 of the Covenant on Economic, Social and Cultural Rights[262] codify the right to freedom of association and particularly establish the rights to form and join trade unions, which are also protected by the International Labor Organization (ILO).[263]

The Human Rights Committee has dealt with relatively few cases that help define freedom of peaceful assembly in light of the limitations imposed by Article 21 of the Civil and Political Covenant. One such case arose when a foreign head of state was meeting with the president of Finland; twenty-five members of an organization, amid a larger crowd, gathered across from the Presidential Palace where the leaders were meeting, distributed leaflets, and raised a banner critical of the human rights record of the visiting head of State. The police immediately took the banner down and asked who was responsible. The author identified herself and was subsequently charged with violating the Finnish Act on Public Meetings by holding a "public meeting" without prior notification. The Committee found a violation of the Covenant's Article 21 (right of peaceful assembly) with the following explanation:

The Committee finds that a requirement to notify the police of an intended demonstration in a public place six hours before its commencement may be compatible with the permitted limitations laid down in article 21 of the Covenant. In the circumstances of this specific case, it is evident from the information provided by the parties that the gathering of several individuals at the site of the welcoming ceremonies for a foreign head of State on an official visit, publicly announced in advance by the State party authorities, cannot be regarded as a demonstration. Insofar as the State party contends that displaying a banner turns their presence into a demonstration, the Committee notes that any restrictions upon the right to assemble must fall within the limitation provisions of article 21. A requirement to pre-notify a demonstration would normally be for reasons of national security or public safety, public order, the protection of public health or morals or the protection of the rights and freedoms of others. Consequently, the application of Finnish legislation on demonstrations to such a gathering cannot be considered as an application of a restriction permitted by article 21 of the Covenant.[264]

110   Particular Rights and Responsibilities

The Committee found inadmissible, however, a complaint from a Dutch antiwar protestor who was charged with the offense of obstructing the free flow of traffic on a public road while participating in a sit-down demonstration on a road leading to a military base that was preparing for the deployment of cruise missiles.[265]

Based on the principles in the Universal Declaration, Article 22 of the Covenant on Civil and Political Rights guarantees the "right to freedom of association with others, including the right to form and join trade unions," but the Covenant does not mention the right to strike.[266] The Covenant on Economic, Social and Cultural Rights also assures "the right of everyone to form trade unions and join the trade union of his choice," but also sets forth the "right to strike, provided that it is exercised in conformity with the laws of the particular country."[267] The Human Rights Committee was asked by a trade union in Canada to find the right to strike implied within the freedom of association provision of the Civil and Political Covenant, but the Committee noted the difference between the language in the two Covenants and thus did not accept the union's claim.[268]

The ILO has been much more forceful in protecting the right to strike as an aspect of freedom of association. The two principal ILO treaties guaranteeing freedom of association are the Freedom of Association and Protection of the Right to Organize Convention (ILO No. 87)[269] and the Right to Organize and Collective Bargaining Convention (ILO No. 98).[270] ILO Convention No. 87 protects the right, without previous authorization, to organize workers and employers, except that armed forces and the police may be exempted by national laws from organizing. Workers and employers are assured their right to choose a union or employer association that shall be free from interference by the public authorities when drawing up their constitutions and rules, electing their representatives, organizing their administration, and deciding upon activities and programs. Unions and employer associations cannot be dissolved or suspended by governments, but may establish and join national and international federations, confederations, or associations.

ILO Convention No. 98 protects workers from acts of anti-union discrimination when they are employed or during their employment. Employers may not require workers to abstain from joining a union or quit a union in order to seek employment; employers may not dismiss or discriminate against a worker for union membership or because of union activities outside of working hours. Nor may employers interfere in the control of unions. ILO Convention No. 98 also establishes the basic principles in respect of collective bargaining encouraging development and utilization of voluntary negotiation between employers or

## Freedom of Association and Assembly  111

employers' organizations and trade unions in both pubic and private sectors.

One of the principal institutions for assuring the implementation of these two treaties is the ILO Committee on Freedom of Association (CFA), which is comprised of nine individuals nominated in equal parts by governments, employers, and unions. The CFA was established in 1951 following the entry into force of the ILO Freedom of Association and Protection of the Right to Organize Convention. The Committee receives allegations principally from trade unions directly involved and occasionally from organizations of employers. The Committee has, for example, concluded, "The right to strike and to organize union meetings are essential aspects of trade union rights, and measures taken by the authorities to ensure the observance of the law should not, therefore, prevent unions from organizing meetings during labour disputes."[271]

The ILO Committee on Freedom of Association applied this principle in handling the complaint of the New Zealand Council of Trade Unions that the New Zealand Employment Contracts Act violated Conventions 87 and 98 in the collective bargaining process and by its restrictions on the right to strike. Even though New Zealand had not ratified either ILO Convention 87 or 98, the Committee on Freedom of Association was authorized under the ILO system to consider the complaint. The Committee found that "trade union organizations ought to have the possibility of recourse to protest strikes in particular where aimed at criticizing a government's economic and social policy. However, strikes that are purely political in character do not fall within the scope of the principles of freedom of association."[272]

The ILO Committee on Freedom of Association also found the United States to be in violation of the freedom of association in permitting employers to hire permanent replacements during a strike:

The right to strike is one of the essential means through which workers and their organisations may promote and defend their economic and social interests. The Committee considers that this basic right is not really guaranteed when a worker who exercises it legally runs the risk of seeing his or her job taken up permanently by another worker, just as legally. The Committee considers that, if a strike is otherwise legal, the use of labour drawn from outside the undertaking to replace strikers for an indeterminate period entails a risk of derogation from the right to strike which may affect the free exercise of trade union rights.[273]

The ILO Committee came to a similar conclusion in regard to the United Kingdom stating

That the relevant legislation in the United Kingdom should be amended to give effective protection to workers who have been dismissed for having participated

112   Particular Rights and Responsibilities

in a strike and in particular to enable workers who are dismissed in the course of, or at the conclusion of, a strike or other industrial action to challenge their dismissal before a judicial authority.[274]

*See also*: Work-Related Rights and Rest, Specialized and Other Agencies

*Further Reading:*

*E.C.W. v. The Netherlands*, Communication No. 524/1992, U.N. Doc. CCPR/C/49/D/524/1992 (1993).
Freedom of Association and Protection of the Right to Organize Convention (ILO No. 87), 68 U.N.T.S. 17, *entered into force* July 4, 1950.
ILO Committee on Freedom of Association, Complaint Against the Government of New Zealand Presented by the New Zealand Council of Trade Unions (NZCTU), Report No. 292, Case No. 1698 (1994).
ILO Committee on Freedom of Association, Complaint Against the Government of the United Kingdom presented by the National Union of Seamen (NUS) Report No. 277, Case No. 1540 (1991).
ILO Committee on Freedom of Association, Complaint Against the Government of the United States presented by the American Federation of Labor and Congress of Industrial Organizations (AFL-CIO) Report No. 278, Case No. 1543 (1991).
ILO, Freedom of Association, Digest of Decisions and Principles of the Freedom of Association Committee of the Governing Body of the ILO (4th ed. 1996).
ILO, Freedom of Association, Digest of Decisions and Principles of the Freedom of Association Committee of the Governing Body of the ILO (3d ed. 1985).
*J.B. et al. v. Canada*, Communication No. 118/1982, U.N. Doc. Supp. No. 40 (A/41/40) at 151 (1986).
*Kivenmaa v. Finland*, Communication No. 412/1990, U.N. Doc. CCPR/C/50/D/412/1990 (1994).
Right to Organize and Collective Bargaining Convention (ILO No. 98), 96 U.N.T.S. 257, *entered into force* July 18, 1951.

*Links to Consult:*

http://www.ilo.org/public/english/standards/norm/enforced/foa/index.htm
http://www.ilo.org/public/english/standards/norm/sources/cfa_proc.htm#compo
http://www.unhchr.ch/html/menu2/i2civfra.htm
http://www1.umn.edu/humanrts/instree/m1fapro.htm
http://www1.umn.edu/humanrts/instree/m2rocb.htm
http://www1.umn.edu/humanrts/undocs/html/dec524.htm
http://www1.umn.edu/humanrts/undocs/html/412-1990.html
http://www1.umn.edu/humanrts/undocs/session41/118-1982.htm

## 17. Political Participation and Voting (Universal Declaration, Art. 21)

The Universal Declaration of Human Rights in Article 21 states:

1. Everyone has the right to take part in the government of his/her country, directly or through freely chosen representatives.
2. Everyone has the right of equal access to public service in his country.
3. The will of the people shall be the basis of the authority of government; this will shall be expressed in periodic and genuine elections which shall be by universal and equal suffrage and shall be held by secret ballot or by equivalent free voting procedures.[275]

While the Universal Declaration does not contain a provision guaranteeing democracy, it does provide for public participation in government and voting rights and assumes in Article 29 that any limitations on human rights must be for the "general welfare in a democratic society." Article 25 of the Covenant on Civil and Political Rights[276] codifies the principles of public participation and voting first pronounced in the Universal Declaration.

The Human Rights Committee, which monitors compliance with the Civil and Political Covenant, has in a General Comment affirmed that "Article 25 lies at the core of democratic government based on the consent of the people."[277] Article 25 is also consistent with the right of peoples to self-determination, which comprehends "the right to freely determine their political status and to enjoy the right to choose the form of their constitution or government."[278]

The Civil and Political Covenant does not promote a single system of government over others, and its principles can be upheld under different political systems as long as they allow for public participation and free and fair elections. While the Covenant's Article 25 stipulates that every citizen has the right to "take part in the conduct of public affairs, directly or through freely chosen representatives," the Human Rights Committee decision in *Marshall v. Canada* confirmed that Article 25 does not guarantee the right to direct participation.[279] Further, the Human Rights Committee recognized that, regardless of the particular system of government, a democratic system must provide for the participation of minority groups. In its General Comment on minority rights, the Human Rights Committee insisted that whatever the political system selected, a government must adopt "measures to ensure the effective participation of members of minority communities in decisions which affect them."[280]

The Universal Declaration and the Civil and Political Covenant protect a number of basic rights, the enjoyment of which is crucial to a meaningful electoral process.[281] The right to participate in free and fair elections implicates the rights to freedom of expression, the right to freedom of opinion, the right to peaceful assembly, and the right to freedom of association. Other rights relevant to the electoral process include the rights to freedom of movement, to organize trade unions, to participate in one's government, to be free from discrimination on political grounds, and—in particularly difficult circumstances—the right to be free from arbitrary killing.

Article 25 of the Covenant establishes that "every citizen" shall have the right to participate in public affairs, to vote and hold office, and to have access to public service. Accordingly, while the Covenant generally prohibits discrimination against non-citizens, Article 25 constitutes an exception to that rule. In some countries, even citizens are denied the right to vote. In the United States, all mentally competent adults have the right to vote with the exception of convicted criminal offenders. Nearly four million U.S. citizens are denied the right to vote, including over one million who have fully completed their sentences. In its General Comment adopted in 1996, the Human Rights Committee has indicated that restrictions on the right to vote should only be based on grounds that are "objective and reasonable."[282] As to criminal disenfranchisement laws, the Committee stated that if "conviction for an offence is the basis for suspending the right to vote, the period of such suspension should be proportionate to the offence and the sentence."[283] Seven states of the United States—Alabama, Florida, Iowa, Kentucky, Mississippi, Nebraska, and Virginia—deny the right to vote to all criminal offenders after completion of their sentences. Over thirty states prohibit felony offenders from voting while they are on parole or probation. Many states have established complex and difficult procedures for former prisoners to obtain restoration of their voting rights. Accordingly, very few former offenders in the U.S. have regained their voting rights.

There is a racially disproportionate impact of disenfranchisement laws in the United States: 13 percent of African American men (1.4 million) are denied the right to vote because they had previously been convicted of a criminal offense. Article 25 of the Civil and Political Covenant guarantees that the right to vote "without distinction of any kind, such as race, colour, sex, language, religion, political or other opinion, national or social origin, property, birth or other status."[284] The practical impact of the disenfranchisement laws in the United States certainly falls most heavily on racial minorities. In addition, status as a former criminal offender could be classified as an "other status" as to which no discrimination is permissible with regard to the right to vote.

Similarly, Article 5 of the Convention on the Elimination of Racial Discrimination requires States parties to guarantee, without distinction as to race, color or national or ethnic origin: "Political rights, in particular the right to participate in elections—to vote and to stand for election—on the basis of universal and equal suffrage. . . ."[285] After the United States appeared before the Committee on the Elimination of Racial Discrimination to present its periodic report in 2001, the Committee expressed concern about

> the political disenfranchisement of a large segment of the ethnic minority population who are denied the right to vote by disenfranchising laws and practices based on the commission of more than a certain number of criminal offences, and also sometimes by preventing them from voting even after the completion of their sentences. The Committee recalls that the right of everyone to vote on a nondiscriminatory basis is a right contained in article 5 of the Convention.[286]

In addition to disenfranchisement for former criminal offenders, the Human Rights Committee has in its General Comment outlined further standards for ensuring the right to vote:

> Positive measures should be taken to overcome specific difficulties, such as illiteracy, language barriers, poverty or impediments to freedom of movement which prevent persons entitled to vote from exercising their rights effectively. Information and materials about voting should be available in minority languages. Specific methods, such as photographs and symbols, should be adopted to ensure that illiterate voters have adequate information on which to base their choice.[287]

The latest developments in electronic voting technology reveal new potential for the elimination of discrimination during the voting process. For example, some persons with physical disabilities or limited language proficiency have historically been unable to cast a secret ballot, but electronic voting may give them easier access to the ballot. While rectifying previous problems, the implementation of electronic voting machines, however, poses new challenges to the principles of fair and legitimate elections. There is concern that computer voting systems may be subject to tampering—particularly where there is no paper record of citizens' votes to verify computer files.

The right to stand for election is arguably just as crucial to a democracy as the right to vote. In its General Comment on political participation, the Human Rights Committee stated:

> The effective implementation of the rights and the opportunity to stand for elective office ensures that persons entitles to vote have a free choice of candidates. Any restrictions on the right to stand for election, such as minimum age, must be justifiable on objective and reasonable criteria. Persons who are otherwise eligible to stand for election should not be excluded by unreasonable or discriminatory requirements such as education, residence or descent, or by reason of political affiliation.[288]

116   Particular Rights and Responsibilities

The Committee has on several occasions dealt with issues regarding the right to stand for election. For example, in *M.A. v. Italy*, a prohibition on the reestablishment of the Italian Fascist Party was held compatible with the principles of Article 25 because of the party's history of pursuing policies that undermined civil and political rights.[289] In addition, in its Concluding Observations on India, the Committee approved of India's "quota" system that reserved at least one-third of elected local positions for women, suggesting that measures of positive discrimination within the context of the right to stand for election are compatible with Article 25.[290] India's quota system is also an example of how a state might begin to redress systematic inequality in political participation. In its Concluding Observations on the United States, however, the Committee expressed concern at the "considerable financial costs that adversely affect the right of persons to be candidates at elections."[291]

For decades after the Universal Declaration and the Civil and Political Covenant pronounced the right to vote in periodic and genuine elections, most of the world did not practice free and fair elections. In Central and Eastern Europe there were no democracies. Most of the countries in Africa and the Middle East were ruled by single-party governments or hereditary rulers. Military dictatorships controlled most of Latin America. In 1982, U.S. President Ronald Reagan addressed the British parliament, cited the Universal Declaration, and proposed "to foster the infrastructure of democracy—the system of a free press, unions, political parties, universities—which allows a people to choose their own way to develop their own culture." Out of President Reagan's speech came a historic initiative for free nations to work together to support democracy around the world. Today, more countries than ever are working to build democratic governance.

Some of the greatest progress has been made in Latin America where there are now democratically elected governments in almost all countries. The Charter of the Organization of the American States (OAS) states "that representative democracy is an indispensable condition for the stability, peace and development of the region" and that one of its purposes is "to promote and consolidate representative democracy, with due respect for the principle of nonintervention."[292] Article 20 of the American Declaration of the Rights and Duties of Man[293] and Article 23(b) of the American Convention on Human Rights[294] guarantee the right of citizens to vote and be elected in genuine periodic elections. The OAS General Assembly has adopted several general and country-specific resolutions on promoting and strengthening representative democracy. When there were attempted coups against democratic governments in Latin America, for example, in Guatemala (1997), Paraguay (1999), and Venezuela (2002) concerted OAS pressure compelled

## Political Participation and Voting 117

coup leaders to permit democratically led governments to return to office. The OAS confirmed and strengthened these developments in 2001 by adopting the Inter-American Democratic Charter, which appears to be the first instrument to declare democracy a human right: "The peoples of the Americas have a right to democracy and their governments have an obligation to promote and defend it."[295] This landmark document is used by the OAS when responding to challenges regarding democratic transition and sustainability in the region.

Efforts to promote democracy have been bolstered by social science research that demonstrates a significant correlation between democratic countries that experience a high degree of public participation and competitiveness in the political process with strong respect for civil and political rights. An additional advantage of democratic governments is that they do not often engage in wars with each other and are thus unlikely to suffer from the serious human rights abuses incident to armed conflict.

Around the world, governments struggle to meet the challenge of the Universal Declaration related to free and fair elections. Election monitoring groups include local or party monitors and international monitors, for example, organized by the UN, the Organization of American States Unit for the Promotion of Democracy, U.S.-related institutions (the National Democratic Institute, the International Republican Institute, the Carter Center—founded by former President Jimmy Carter), the Commonwealth (former British colonies), and the International Institute for Democracy and Electoral Assistance (IDEA). These monitors and organizations assist in assuring free and fair elections by their presence during the election process—from the beginning (voter education, candidate campaigns, planning for the ballot) to the final vote count as well as by promoting improvements in election structures, election administration, and in international election work. By declaring an election "free and fair" monitors can appropriately legitimize the outcome of that election. Conversely, by identifying unfairness, legitimacy of the vote may necessarily be withheld.

*See also*: Equality and Nondiscrimination, Organization for Security and Cooperation in Europe

*Further Reading*:

African Charter on Human and Peoples' Rights, adopted June 27, 1981, OAU Doc. CAB/LEG/67/3 rev. 5, 21 I.L.M. 58 (1982), *entered into force* Oct. 21, 1986.
Stephen Ansolabehere, *Voting Machines, Race and Equal Protection*, 1 Election Law Journal 61 (2002).

## 118    Particular Rights and Responsibilities

*Baker vs. Pataki*, 85 F.3d 919 (2nd Cir. 1996).
Concluding Observations of the Human Rights Committee, India, U.N. Doc. CCPR/C/79/Add.81 (1997).
Conclusions and recommendations of the Committee on the Elimination of Racial Discrimination, United States of America, U.N. Doc. A/56/18, paras. 380–407 (2001).
*Diergaardt v. Namibia*, Communication No. 760/1997, U.N. Doc. CCPR/C/69/D/760/1997 (2000).
Alec C. Ewald, Civil Death: The Ideological Paradox of Criminal Disenfranchisement Laws in the United States (2000).
Jamie Fellner and Marc Mauer, Losing the Vote: The Impact of Felony Disenfranchisement Laws in the United States (1998).
*Fischer v. Governor*, 749 A.2d 321 (N.H. 2000).
Thomas M. Franck, *The Emerging Right to Democratic Governance*, 86 A.J.I.L. 46 (1992).
Michael J. Gottlieb, *One Person, No Vote: The Laws of Felon Disenfranchisement*, 115 Harvard L. Rev. 1939 (2002).
Guy Goodwin-Gill, Free and Fair Elections: International Law and Practice (1994).
Human Rights Committee, General Comment 23, Article 27 (Fiftieth session, 1994), U.N. Doc. CCPR/C/21/Rev.1/Add.5 (1994).
Human Rights Committee, General Comment 25, Article 25 (Fifty-seventh session, 1996), U.N. Doc. CCPR/C/21/Rev.1/Add.7 (1996).
International Institute for Democracy and Electoral Assistance, The International IDEA Handbook on Democracy Assessment (2001).
Louis Massicotte, Establishing the Rules of the Game: Election Laws in Democracies (2004).
*M.A. v. Italy*, Communication No. 117/1981, U.N. Doc. CCPR/C/OP/2 at 31 (1990).
*Marshall v. Canada*, Communication No. 205/1986, U.N. Doc. CCPR/C/43/D/205/1986 (1991).
Pippa Norris, Electoral Engineering: Voting Rules and Political Behavior (2004).
O.A.S. Charter, Charter of the Organization of American States, 119 U.N.T.S. 3, *entered into force* Dec. 13, 1951; *amended by* Protocol of Buenos Aires, 721 U.N.T.S. 324, O.A.S. Treaty Series, No.1-A, *entered into force* Feb. 27, 1970; *amended by* Protocol of Cartagena, O.A.S. Treaty Series, No. 66, 25 I.L.M. 527, *entered into force* Nov. 16, 1988; *amended by* Protocol of Washington, 1-E Rev. OEA Documentos Oficiales OEA/Ser.A/2 Add. 3 (SEPF), 33 I.L.M. 1005, *entered into force* Sept. 25, 1997; *amended by* Protocol of Managua, 1-F Rev. OEA Documentos Oficiales OEA/Ser.A/2 Add.4 (SEPF), 33 I.L.M. 1009, *entered into force* Jan. 29, 1996.
Office of the United Nations High Commissioner for Human Rights, Training Manual on Human Rights Monitoring (Professional Training Series No. 7), U.N. Doc. HR/P/PT/7 (2001).
Protocol to the European Convention for the Protection of Human Rights and Fundamental Freedoms, 213 U.N.T.S. 262, *entered into force* May 18, 1954.
Andrew Reeve, Electoral Systems: A Comparative and Theoretical Introduction (1992).
Andrew L. Shapiro, *Challenging Criminal Disenfranchisement Under the Voting Rights Act: A New Strategy*, 103 Yale Law Journal 537 (1993).
United Nations, Human Rights and Elections: A Handbook on the Legal, Technical and Human Rights Aspects of Elections (1994).

*Links to Consult:*

http://www.cartercenter.org
http://www.civilrights.org/issues/voting/index.html
http://www.idea.int/
http://www.iri.org/
http://www.ndi.org/
http://www.sentencingproject.org/pubs_05.cfm
http://www.thenation.com/docprint.mhtml?i = 20040816&s = dugger
http://www.truthout.org/voting.rights.htm
http://www.un.org/Depts/dpa/ead/eadhome.htm
http://www.upd.oas.org
http://www.vote.caltech.edu/
http://www1.umn.edu/humanrts/country/usa2001.html
http://www1.umn.edu/humanrts/euro/z20prot1.html
http://www1.umn.edu/humanrts/gencomm/hrcom25.htm
http://www1.umn.edu/humanrts/instree/b3ccpr.htm
http://www1.umn.edu/humanrts/instree/d1cerd.htm
http://www1.umn.edu/humanrts/undocs/923-2000.html

## 18. Economic, Social, and Cultural Rights (Universal Declaration, Articles 4, 22–27)

In his 1941 State of the Union Address, President Franklin D. Roosevelt set out "Four Freedoms" that became the World War II aims of the United States, the United Kingdom, and their allies. President Roosevelt's third freedom established the basis for later efforts to understand and apply economic, social, and cultural rights:

> The third [freedom] is the freedom from want, which, translated into world terms, means economic understandings which will secure to every nation a healthy peace-time life for its inhabitants everywhere in the world.[296]

Later during World War II, Roosevelt's State of the Union message on January 11, 1944, more specifically addressed the freedoms he had previously enumerated. They included the right to a job; the right to enough money for adequate food, clothing, and recreation; the right to a decent home; the right to decent medical care; the right to protection in the event of old age, sickness, accident, and disability; and the right to a good education. President Roosevelt, of course, presided over the New Deal, a series of programs by which the federal government combated the effects of the Depression of the 1930s. At the end of World War II the international community began through the United Nations to focus on the rights discussed by President Roosevelt.

Article 55 of the UN Charter reflects the importance given to economic, social, and cultural rights: the "United Nations shall promote higher standards of living, full employment, and conditions of economic and social progress and development; solutions of international economic, social, health, and related problems; and international cultural and educational co-operation. . . ."[297] In Article 56, all members pledge "to take joint and separate action . . . for the achievement of the purposes set forth in Article 55."[298]

The first task of the newly created UN Commission on Human Rights, under the leadership of Mrs. Eleanor Roosevelt was to draft the Universal Declaration of Human Rights and thus to define the general human rights obligations established by the UN Charter.[299] The Universal Declaration was adopted by the UN General Assembly in 1948, including Articles 22 and 25 that set forth the seminal protection of economic, social, and cultural rights:

### Article 22
Everyone, as a member of society, has the right to social security and is entitled to realization, through national effort and international cooperation and in accordance with the organization and resources of each State, of the economic,

social and cultural rights indispensable for his dignity and the free development of his personality.

Article 25(1)

Everyone has the right to a standard of living adequate for the health and well-being of himself and of his family, including food, clothing, housing and medical care and necessary social services, and the right to security in the event of unemployment, sickness, disability, widowhood, old age or other lack of livelihood in circumstances beyond his control.[300]

The Universal Declaration also provides for the right to work and join trade unions (Article 23); rest and leisure (Article 24); education (Article 26); and participate freely in cultural life (Article 27).

In 1966, the General Assembly completed the Covenant on Economic, Social and Cultural Rights, which codified in treaty form and elaborated upon the principles in the Universal Declaration.[301] This Covenant, which entered into force January 3, 1976, is the main source of international standards covering those rights. Originally, it was contemplated that both economic, social, and cultural as well as civil and political rights would be included in one treaty, but two Covenants were eventually promulgated due to Cold War political tensions, the difficulty of establishing one system to implement both sets of rights, and the desire to encourage ratification even among those states that might be willing to accept only one of the two treaties. Nonetheless, numerous international bodies have reaffirmed that both sets of rights are indivisible and interdependent and must be implemented.

In Article 2 of the Covenant, each State party "undertakes to take steps . . . to the maximum of its available resources, with a view to achieving progressively the full realization of the rights recognized in [the Covenant] by all appropriate means. . . ."[302] While that language could be interpreted to mean that it provides for no concrete obligations, the Committee on Economic, Social and Cultural Rights, the body charged with implementing the Covenant, has explained in its General Comment 3 that the steps toward the realization of the rights should be taken within a reasonably short time and should be "deliberate, concrete and targeted as clearly as possible towards meeting the obligations" in the Covenant.[303] Further, while the phrase "by all appropriate means" imparts a flexible approach by giving states discretion in determining what action to take, the Committee ultimately determines what is appropriate.[304] And, while the rights need not be achieved all at once, States parties must begin immediately to work toward implementing the rights even if they cannot all be implemented at once. Reductions in spending for social services constitute a violation of the Covenant if there is no compelling reason for them. In addition, the obligation to avoid discrimination as to economic, social, and cultural rights is applicable without regard to progressive realization or available resources. Hence, there would also be a violation of the Covenant if a State party does not guarantee against discrimination on the basis of race, color, sex, language, religion, political or other opinion, national or social origin, property, birth or other status with regard to economic, social, and cultural rights.

In General Comment 9, the Committee provides that if implementation of these obligations is going to differ from the approach taken to civil and political rights, there needs to be a pressing reason. In that General Comment, the Committee rejected the idea that civil and political rights are justiciable while economic, social, and cultural rights are not. The General Comment distinguished the concept of justiciability from the role of the court in implementing a self-executing treaty obligation. On the one hand, the Committee noted that the justiciability refers to matters which are appropriately resolved by the courts and noted that, despite differences in legal systems, "there is no Covenant right which could not . . . be considered to possess at least some significant justiciable dimensions."[305] Otherwise, the courts would be unable to protect rights of the most vulnerable and disadvantaged groups in society. On the other hand, the Committee noted that treaty-based norms which are self-executing are those which are capable of being applied by courts without further elaboration. The Committee observed in General Comment 9 that each national legal system may determine whether particular treaty clauses are self-executing, but "adoption of a rigid classification of economic, social and cultural rights which puts them, by definition, beyond the reach of the courts would thus be arbitrary and incompatible with the principle that the two sets of human rights are indivisible and interdependent."[306]

The Committee on Economic, Social and Cultural Rights has identified the need to develop benchmarks or indicators for monitoring economic and social rights violations. The Committee has requested that governments identify the indicators and benchmarks they consider essential minimum requirements for the realization of the rights identified in the Covenant as well as information on vulnerable or disadvantaged groups that have not achieved the relevant standards. During its periodic review of state reports the Committee engages in a process of joint consideration by the States parties and the Committee of the indicators and national benchmarks which will then be used to provide the targets to be achieved during the next reporting period.

It is within these basic principles that the specific economic, social, and cultural rights should be considered below as to the right to housing, food, water, health, education, work, social security, and culture. The standards will include not only pronouncements by the UN treaty body, discussed above, but those made by other UN bodies such as the

Commission on Human Rights and its successor Human Rights Council and in regional treaties as well. (The various bodies are described in greater detail in Part III.) Where appropriate, reference will be made to national pronouncements regarding the international standards.

*See also:* Clothing, Culture, Education, Food, Freedom of Association and Assembly, Health, Housing, Social Security, Water, Work-Related Rights and Rest

*Further Reading:*

Philip Alston, *U.S. Ratification of the Covenant on Economic, Social and Cultural Rights: The Need for an Entirely New Strategy,* 84 A.J.I.L. 365 (1990).
Committee on Economic, Social and Cultural Rights, General Comment 3, The Nature of States Parties' Obligations (Fifth session, 1990), U.N. Doc. E/1991/23, annex III at 86 (1991).
Committee on Economic, Social and Cultural Rights, General Comment 9, The Domestic Application of the Covenant (Nineteenth session, 1998), U.N. Doc. E/C.12/1998/24 (1998), *reprinted in* Compilation of General Comments and General Recommendations Adopted by Human Rights Treaty Bodies, U.N. Doc. HRI/GEN/1/Rev.6 at 54 (2003).
Matthew C. R. Craven, The International Covenant on Economic, Social, and Cultural Rights: A Perspective on Its Development (1995).
Dignity and Human Rights: The Implementation of Economic, Social and Cultural Rights (Berma Klein Goldewijk et al. eds., 2002).
Economic, Social, and Cultural Rights: A Textbook (Asbjørn Eide et al. eds., 1995).
Giving Meaning to Economic, Social, and Cultural Rights (Isfahan Merali & Valerie Oosterveld eds., 2001).
International Covenant on Economic, Social and Cultural Rights, G.A. res. 2200A (XXI), 21 U.N. GAOR Supp. (No. 16) at 49, U.N. Doc. A/6316 (1966), 993 U.N.T.S. 3, *entered into force* Jan. 3, 1976.
A. Glenn Mower, Jr., International Cooperation for Social Justice: Global and Regional Protection of Economic/social Rights (1985).
Franklin D. Roosevelt, *"Four Freedoms" Speech,* 87 Cong. Rec. 44 (1941).
Franklin D. Roosevelt, *State of the Union Message,* 90 Cong. Rec. 55 (1944).
M. Magdalena Sepúlveda, The Nature of the Obligations under the International Covenant on Economic, Social and Cultural Rights (2003).
Willem van Genugten & Camilo Perez-Bustillo, The Poverty of Rights: Human Rights and the Eradication of Poverty (2001).

*Links to Consult:*

http://www.escr-net.org
http://www.hrw.org/esc
http://www.unhchr.ch/html/menu2/6/cescr.htm
http://www1.umn.edu/humanrts/gencomm/epcomm3.htm
http://www1.umn.edu/humanrts/gencomm/escgencom9.htm
http://www1.umn.edu/humanrts/instree/b2esc.htm

A. WORK-RELATED RIGHTS (UNIVERSAL DECLARATION ART. 23) AND REST (ART. 24)

Article 23 of the Universal Declaration of Human Rights sets out the various components of the right to work: free choice of employment; just and favorable conditions, protection against unemployment, the right to equal pay for equal work without discrimination; the right to just compensation that ensures an existence worthy of human dignity for the workers and their families, supplemented by social protection if necessary, and the right to form and join trade unions.[307] Article 24 provides for the right to rest and leisure, including reasonable limitation of working hours and paid holidays.

The Covenant on Economic, Social and Cultural Rights expands on those rights in Articles 6, 7, and 8.[308] Article 6 describes the steps States parties can take to achieve the full realization of the right to work. They include technical and vocational guidance and training programs; policies and techniques to achieve steady economic, social, and cultural development; and full and productive employment under conditions safeguarding fundamental political and economic freedoms to the individual. Article 7 expands on the right to the enjoyment of just and favorable conditions. Working conditions should be safe and healthy. Remuneration includes fair wages and equal remuneration, that provide for a decent living for workers and their families. In this context Article 11 recognizes the right of everyone to an adequate standard of living for themselves and their family. Equality is emphasized in particular for women, who should enjoy equal pay for equal work. Everyone should have an equal opportunity to job promotion based on seniority and competence. The right to rest, leisure, reasonable working hours, and paid holidays and vacations are reiterated.

Article 8 expands on the right of everyone to form trade unions, which includes the right to establish national and international trade union organizations. Limits on trade unions must be prescribed by law and should be only those necessary for the protection of national security or public order. The right to strike is acknowledged as long as it is exercised in conformity with national laws. Allowance is made for lawful restrictions on the exercise of union rights by members of the armed forces, the police, or the administration of the state. The right to form and join trade unions is also recognized as part of the right to freedom of association in Article 22 of the Covenant on Civil and Political Rights.[309]

The International Labor Organization (ILO) has drafted, promulgated, and now monitors a number of treaties and recommendations assuring a safe and healthy working environment for workers, which are far more detailed than the provisions of the Covenant on Economic, Social and Cultural Rights; the Covenant on Civil and Political Rights; and other general human rights treaties. Those ILO conventions include Nos. 110 (Plantations, 1958), 115 (Radiation Protection Convention, 1960), 119 (Guarding of Machinery Convention, 1963), 120 (Hygiene (Commerce and Offices) Convention, 1964), 127 (Maximum Weight Convention, 1967), 136 (Benzene Convention, 1971), 139 (Occupational Cancer Convention, 1974), 147 (Merchant Shipping, 1976), 148 (Working Environment (Air Pollution, Noise, and Vibration) Convention, 1977), 155 (Occupational Safety and Health Convention, 1981), 161 (Occupational Health Services Convention, 1985), 162 (Asbestos Convention, 1986), 167 (Safety and Health in Construction Convention, 1988), 170 (Chemicals Convention, 1990), 174 (Prevention of Major Industrial Accidents Convention, 1993), 176 (Safety and Health in Mines Convention, 1995), 183 (Maternity Protection, 2000), and other relevant recommendations; as well as ensuring their application under ILO Conventions Nos. 81 (Labour Inspection Convention, 1947), 129 (Labour Inspection (Agriculture) Convention, 1969), 135 (Workers' Representatives Convention, 1971), and their successor conventions.[310]

A safe and healthy work environment for workers under these ILO conventions and related recommendations aids in the prevention of accidents and injuries arising out of, linked with, or occurring within the course of work. Employers also have the obligation under these treaties and recommendations to make available information about health and safety standards relevant to their local activities. Such information includes arrangements for training in safe working practices and details on the effects of all substances used in manufacturing processes. It is particularly important for employers to make known any special hazards that tasks or conditions of work involve and the related measures available to protect the workers. Similarly, employers are required to provide, where necessary, measures to deal with emergencies and accidents, including first-aid arrangements. They also are obligated to provide personal protective clothing and equipment when necessary. Further, they should incur expenses for occupational health and safety measures. In addition, employers should consult and cooperate fully with health, safety and labor authorities, workers' representatives and their organizations, and established safety and health organizations on matters of occupational health and safety. They should cooperate in the work of international organizations concerned with the preparation and adoption of international safety and health standards. Where appropriate, matters relating to safety and health should be incorporated in agreements with the representatives of the workers and their organizations.

Employers should examine the causes of safety and health hazards in their industry and work to implement improvements and solutions to those conditions, including the provision of safe equipment at least consistent with industry standards. Furthermore, they should monitor the working environment and the health of workers liable to exposure to specified hazards and risks. ILO treaties and recommendations also call for employers to investigate work-related accidents, keep records of incidents stating their cause and remedial measures taken to prevent similar accidents, and ensure the provision of remedies for the injured. Employers ought also to respect the right of workers to (1) remove themselves from work situations in which there is a reasonable basis for concern about present, imminent, and serious danger to life or health; (2) not subject them to consequences as a result; and further (3) not require them to return to work situations as long as the condition continues.

A great deal of the monitoring of the right to work is left to the ILO, which protects workers' rights and the right to organize in various conventions. The ILO Convention (No. 122) concerning Employment Policy requires States parties to protect the right to work by pursuing full employment.[311] ILO Convention No. 117 concerning Basic Aims and Standards of Social Policy of 1962 states that "wages shall normally be paid in legal tender only."[312] The convention stipulates that wages must be paid regularly "at such intervals as will lessen the likelihood of indebtedness among the wage earners."[313] It also places responsibility on a "competent authority" to ensure that, when food, housing, clothing, or other essential supplies and services are being used to pay the worker their cash value is fairly assessed. The convention places responsibility on the States parties to establish mechanisms to monitor and control payments of wages made through non-cash transactions, and is intended to ensure that employers do not abuse their dominant position by charging inflated prices for goods provided in lieu of wages.

The ILO Declaration on Fundamental Principles and Rights at Work also establishes that all member states of the ILO have an obligation arising from their membership to respect, promote, and realize the principles concerning the fundamental rights to work even if they have not separately ratified the separate conventions.[314] In 2003 the ILO Committee on Freedom of Association ruled that a 2002 decision issued by the U.S. Supreme Court that said that undocumented workers could not receive back pay as compensation for a violation of their right to unionize violated the right of freedom of association to be provided to all workers regardless of their legal status, even though the United States had not ratified key ILO conventions regarding the right to freedom of association.[315] Hence, equality for all workers is one of the primary underlying principles in the enjoyment of that right.

The regional human rights treaties likewise protect various aspects of workers' rights. The African Charter on Human and Peoples' Rights provides for the right to work under equitable and satisfactory conditions, with equal pay for equal work (Article 15); the right to free association (Article 10); and the right to assemble freely with others subject only to restrictions provided by law in the interest of national security, the safety, health, ethics, as well as the rights and freedoms of others (Article 11).[316]

Article 34(g) of the Charter of the Organization of American States provides for "Fair wages, employment opportunities, and acceptable working conditions for all."[317] Article 45(b) provides for the right to work, with fair wages that "ensure life, health, and a decent standard of living for the worker and his family" both while working, in old age, or when unable to work. Article 45(c) provides for the right of employers and workers to associate and to promote the right to collective bargaining in accordance with the law. The American Convention on Human Rights Article 16 protects the right to associate freely for various purposes including labor subject only to restrictions necessary for protecting national security, public safety, public health or morals or the rights and freedoms of others.[318] Rights of the armed forces and police to associate can be limited. The American Declaration of the Rights and Duties of Man also mentions the right to work with sufficient remuneration to assure an adequate standard of living and the right to leisure time; wholesome recreation; and the opportunity to use free time for spiritual, cultural, and physical benefit.[319] The Protocol of San Salvador provides more detailed articles on the right to work (Article 6); the right to just, equitable, and satisfactory conditions of work, including rest, leisure, and paid vacations (Article 7); and trade union rights, including the right to strike (Article 8).[320] Many of the provisions are similar to others discussed above. The Protocol, however, adds the prohibition of certain work for persons under eighteen and limits on the hours for those under sixteen so they can attend school, as well as reasonable limits for both daily and weekly work. States parties are also obliged to implement and strengthen programs that help to ensure suitable family care so that "women may enjoy a real opportunity to exercise the right to work."[321]

In response to a request for an advisory opinion by the government of Mexico on whether States parties to the OAS could deem a specific migratory status to be a prerequisite for the enjoyment of labor rights, the Inter-American Court of Human Rights ruled that members of the Organization of American States could not put undocumented migrant workers at a legal disadvantage in terms of labor rights as compared with legal residents or citizens.[322] It also found that American states could not subordinate fundamental human rights, such as the right to equality

## 128 Particular Rights and Responsibilities

before the law and to equal and effective protection of the law without discrimination, to achieving its migration policies.

The European Convention for the Protection of Human Rights and Fundamental Freedoms provides for the right to freedom of association including the right to form and join trade unions.[323] They can be limited only for certain specified reasons and the exercise of the rights by members of the armed forces, the police, or the administration of the state can be restricted by law. The European Social Charter includes extensive protections for work-related rights, including the right to work (Article 1), the right to just conditions of work (Article 2), the right to safe and healthy work conditions, the right to a fair remuneration (Article 4), the right to organize (Article 5), and the right to bargain collectively (Article 6).[324] Protections are specified for specific groups, such as disabled persons' right to vocational training, rehabilitation and resettlement, the rights of nationals of any of the European States parties to work in the territory of any of the others on "a footing of equality," and the rights of migrant workers to protection and assistance from States parties.

*See also*: Education, Freedom of Association, Slavery, Social Security, Specialized and Other Agencies

*Further Reading*:

Hector Bartolomei de la Cruz, Geraldo von Potobsky, and Lee Swepston, The International Labor Organization: The International Standards System and Basic Human Rights (1996).
Ryszard I. Cholewinski, Migrant Workers in International Human Rights Law: Their Protection in Countries of Employment (1997).
Convention concerning Employment Policy (ILO No. 122), 569 U.N.T.S. 65, *entered into force* 15 July 1966.
Convention concerning Forced or Compulsory Labour (ILO No. 29), 39 U.N.T.S. 55, *entered into force* May 1, 1932 .
Corte Interamericana de Derechos Humanos, *Condicion Juridica y Derechos de los Migrantes Indocumentados*, Opinion Consultiva OC-08/03 de 17 de septiembre de 2003, solicitada por los Estados Unidos Mexicanos.
Discrimination (Employment and Occupation) Convention (ILO No. 111), 362 U.N.T.S. 31, *entered into force* June 15, 1960.
Ernst B. Haas, Human Rights and International Action; The Case of Freedom of Association (1970).
*Hoffman Plastic Compounds, Inc. v. NLRB*, 535 U.S. 137 (2002).
ILO Committee on Freedom of Association, Complaints Against the Government of the United States presented by the American Federation of Labor and the Congress of Industrial Organizations (AFL-CIO) and the Confederation of Mexican Workers (CTM), Report No. 2227, Case No. 332 (2003).
International Labor Office, Fundamental Rights at Work and International Labour Standards (2003).

International Labor Standards: Globalization, Trade, and Public Policy (Robert J. Flanagan & William B. Gould IV eds., 2003).
International Labour Organization, Constitution of the International Labour Organization and Standing Orders of the International Labour Conference (2001).
International Labour Organization, Promoting Better Working Conditions: A Guide to the International Labour Standards System (2003).
International Labour Standards: History, Theory, and Policy Options (Kaushik Basu et al. eds., 2003).
Ozay Mehmet, Errol Mendes, and Robert Sinding, Towards a Fair Global Labour Market: Avoiding a New Slave Trade (1999).
Richard Lewis Siegel, Employment and Human Rights: The International Dimension (1994).
The Terms of Labor: Slavery, Serfdom, and Free Labor (Stanley L. Engerman ed., 1999).

*Links to Consult:*

http://www.ilo.org
http://www.ilo.org/ilolex/english/index.htm
http://www.ilo.org/public/english/about/iloconst.htm
http://www1.umn.edu/humanrts/edumat/IHRIP/circle/modules/module10.htm
http://www1.umn.edu/humanrts/instree/auon.htm
http://www1.umn.edu/humanrts/links/commentary-Aug2003.html

B. SOCIAL SECURITY (UNIVERSAL DECLARATION, ARTICLES 22, 25)

Increasing globalization and trade liberalization have created insecurity for many income earners. A growing number of workers—especially women and migrant workers—are exposed to unstable working conditions that, in turn, cause precarious living conditions in general. In many countries a large proportion, sometimes a majority, of workers and their families lack or are excluded from access to employment, social security, or social insurance that would provide citizens access to basic necessities, such as food, housing, education, and medical care. The United Nations and the International Labor Organization (ILO) have formulated standards that require national social security programs to support or supplement income in the event of old age, disability, bearing and raising children, and unemployment. These standards emphasize that priority should be given by civil society and the state to provide social protection to vulnerable groups that, without the right to social security, would also be denied other basic economic rights. In addition to women and migrant families, vulnerable groups include, for example, the elderly, persons with disabilities, and impoverished children.

In developing countries, billions of people face extreme poverty without any form of social security programs to provide relief. Many rural workers, in particular, earn less than $2.00 per day during their employable years and then have no social security programs when they are no longer able to work. The growing trend of migration into urban areas has caused many of the traditional support systems, such as family and kinship, to collapse. People in developing countries are especially vulnerable during crises caused by natural disasters, armed conflict, and economic fluctuations. Although social security programs are needed most in the poorest countries, implementation of such programs in these countries suffer from poor administrative infrastructure and corruption.

Social security systems in industrialized countries consist of social insurance programs (that is, "earned" benefits for workers and their families financed by employment contributions) or social assistance programs (that is, noncontributory mechanisms designed to provide a safety net for persons unable to access social insurance). There remain, even in developed countries, many who lack social security or insurance—particularly because programs tend to target special groups or to focus on emergency relief during calamities.

Social security is included as a human right in the International Bill of Human Rights, as well as in the more specific human rights treaties that protect the rights of particularly vulnerable groups, such as minority populations, women, and children. Articles 22 and 25 of the Universal Declaration of Human Rights provide:

> Everyone, as a member of society, has the right to social security and is entitled to realization, through national effort and international co-operation and in accordance with the organization and resources of each State, of the economic, social and cultural rights indispensable for his dignity and the free development of his personality.
>
> Everyone has the right to a standard of living adequate for the health and well-being of himself and of his family, including food, clothing, housing and medical care and necessary social services, and the right to security in the event of unemployment, sickness, disability, widowhood, old age or other lack of livelihood in circumstances beyond his control.[325]

Social security is also protected by the Covenant on Economic, Social and Cultural Rights Article 9, which requires that, "The States Parties to the present Covenant recognize the right of everyone to social security, including social insurance."[326] The right to social security is interrelated and interdependent with other economic, social, and cultural rights, such as the right of everyone to an adequate standard of living (including food, clothing, and housing); the right to the enjoyment of the highest attainable standard of health; the right to the enjoyment of just and favorable conditions of work; and protection of the family.

The Committee on Economic, Social and Cultural Rights has elaborated on how the right to social security should be implemented in several of its General Comments. In 1995, for example, the Committee noted that social security and income-maintenance schemes are of particular importance for persons with disabilities:

Such support should reflect the special needs for assistance and other expenses often associated with disability. In addition, as far as possible, the support provided should also cover individuals (who are overwhelmingly female) who undertake the care of a person with disabilities. Such persons, including members of the families of persons with disabilities, are often in urgent need of financial support because of their assistance role. . . . Institutionalization of persons with disabilities, unless rendered necessary for other reasons, cannot be regarded as an adequate substitute for the social security and income-support rights of such persons.[327]

In 1996 the Committee commented on the particular relevance of the right to social security to elderly persons, calling on States parties to "establish [a] retirement age so that it is flexible, depending on the occupations performed and the working ability of elderly persons, with due regard to demographic, economic and social factors."[328] As an economic right, of course, social security should be made available "to the maximum of its available resources, with a view to achieving progressively the full realization of the right," as the Committee recommended:

States parties should, within the limits of available resources, provide non-contributory old-age benefits and other assistance for all older persons, who, when reaching the age prescribed in national legislation, have not completed a qualifying period of contribution and are not entitled to an old-age pension or other social security benefit or assistance and have no other source of income.[329]

Although the Covenant on Civil and Political Rights[330] does not specifically mention social security as a human right, the Human Rights Committee has determined in several of its views on individual cases and one General Comment that the prohibition on discrimination (Article 26) applies to social and economic rights, including the right to social security. Article 26 states that

All persons are equal before the law and are entitled without any discrimination to the equal protection of the law. In this respect, the law shall prohibit any discrimination and guarantee to all persons equal and effective protection against discrimination on any ground such as race, colour, sex, language, religion, political or other opinion, national or social origin, property, birth or other status.[331]

132   Particular Rights and Responsibilities

In *S.W.M. Broeks v. The Netherlands*, the Human Rights Committee determined that Dutch employment insurance legislation applied discriminatory conditions to a married woman by requiring her to submit evidence that she was a breadwinner in order to qualify for unemployment benefits, while not imposing the same requirement on men.[332] The Committee held that this legislation violated Article 26 of the Covenant by discriminating on the basis of sex. Similarly, the Human Rights Committee, in its 2000 General Comment on equality of rights between men and women, mentioned social security as an area where women are often the subject of discrimination.[333] In *Gueye et al v. France*, the Committee found that France, in paying Senegalese soldiers lower pensions than retired French soldiers, had discriminated against retired Senegalese soldiers of the French army on the ground of nationality (which the Committee inferred from the phrase "other status" in Article 26).[334]

The Convention on the Elimination of Racial Discrimination states in Article 5 that States parties must prohibit and eliminate racial discrimination in all of its forms, and to guarantee the right of everyone "without distinction as to race, colour, or national or ethnic origin, to equality before the law, notably in the enjoyment of . . . [t]he right to public health, medical care, social security and social services. . . ."[335] In 2000 the Committee on the Elimination of Racial Discrimination issued a General Recommendation on discrimination against the Roma, calling on States parties to consider the Roma a particularly vulnerable group, and to "ensure Roma equal access to health care and social security services and to eliminate any discriminatory practices against them in this field."[336]

The Convention on the Elimination of All Forms of Discrimination Against Women requires in Article 11 that women have the "the right to social security, particularly in cases of retirement, unemployment, sickness, invalidity and old age and other incapacity to work, as well as the right to paid leave."[337] Article 11 also seeks to ensure women's right to the same employment opportunities as men, equal remuneration, and the right of free choice of employment, which includes the "the right to promotion, job security, and the right to receive vocational training."[338] Other social security rights of women include the right to the "protection of health and to safety in working conditions, including the safeguarding of the function of reproduction."[339] In addition, the Convention prohibits discrimination against women on the grounds of marriage or maternity status. In its 1991 General Recommendation on the protection of unpaid women workers in rural and urban family enterprises, the Committee on the Elimination of Discrimination Against Women urged states to "take the necessary steps to guarantee payment, social security and social benefits for women who work without such benefits in enterprises owned by a family member."³⁴⁰

The Convention on the Rights of the Child describes the duty of States parties to protect children's right to social security in Article 26:

> States Parties shall recognize for every child the right to benefit from social security, including social insurance, and shall take the necessary measures to achieve the full realization of this right in accordance with their national law . . . The benefits should, where appropriate, be granted, taking into account the resources and the circumstances of the child and persons having responsibility for the maintenance of the child, as well as any other consideration relevant to an application for benefits made by or on behalf of the child.³⁴¹

In addition to the general guarantees of Article 26 regarding the right to social security, the Children's Convention also elaborates in Article 18 on the particular obligation of States parties to ensure access to services necessary to the fulfillment of social security rights of children of working parents:

> For the purpose of guaranteeing and promoting the rights set forth in the present Convention, States Parties shall render appropriate assistance to parents and legal guardians in the performance of their child-rearing responsibilities and shall ensure the development of institutions, facilities and services for the care of children. . . . States Parties shall take all appropriate measures to ensure that children of working parents have the right to benefit from child-care services and facilities for which they are eligible.³⁴²

Similarly, the Children's Convention in Article 20 indicates that States parties are required to provide care for children without parents. The state's obligation to care for orphans could also be considered part of a child's right to social security:

> A child temporarily or permanently deprived of his or her family environment, or in whose own best interests cannot be allowed to remain in that environment, shall be entitled to special protection and assistance provided by the State. . . . Such care could include, inter alia, foster placement, *kafalah* of Islamic law, adoption or if necessary placement in suitable institutions for the care of children. When considering solutions, due regard shall be paid to the desirability of continuity in a child's upbringing and to the child's ethnic, religious, cultural and linguistic background.³⁴³

The Committee on the Rights of the Child, in response to the report submitted by Nigeria in 1996, stated that "the general lack of financial resources cannot be used as a justification for neglecting to establish social security programmes and social safety nets to protect the most vulnerable groups of children."³⁴⁴ The Committee also noted in its concluding comments on Greece in 2002 that "many children and families

134   Particular Rights and Responsibilities

from some distinct ethnic, religious, linguistic or cultural groups, such as the Roma, are not fully aware of their rights to social security and welfare and are consequently unable to claim such assistance."[345]

Since its establishment in 1919 a major objective of the ILO has been to enable countries to extend social protection to all groups in society by improving and protecting working conditions. The ILO has developed international labor standards that assist member states in the design, reform, and implementation of social security policies. In 1952 it adopted the Social Security (Minimum Standards) Convention (No.102), which provided minimum standards for nine distinct types of social security: medical care, sickness, unemployment, old-age, employment injury, family, maternity, disability, and survivors' benefits.[346] In order to fulfill its responsibilities under Convention No. 102, a State party was obliged to provide at least three of those categories of social security. As of 2006, forty-two countries at varying levels of development have ratified Convention No. 102.

Since the adoption of Convention No. 102, the ILO has created new instruments to supplement or revise the earlier convention. Some of those instruments include the Maternity Protection Convention of 1962 (No. 103); Equality of Treatment (Social Security) Convention of 1962 (No. 118); the Employment Injury Benefits Convention of 1964 (No. 121); the Invalidity, Old-age and Survivors' Benefits Convention of 1967 (No. 128); the Medical Care and Sickness Benefits Convention of 1969 (No. 130); the Maintenance of Social Security Rights Convention of 1982 (No. 157); and the Employment Promotion and Protection Against Unemployment Convention of 1988 (No. 168).[347]

In addition to the social security standards developed by the UN and the ILO, there have been several regional conventions that include social security as a human right. Adopted by the Council of Europe in 1961, the European Social Charter requires in Article 12 the establishment of a system of social security that complies with the minimum standards established by the ILO.[348] More recently, the European Code of Social Security of 1964 defined the specific needs of vulnerable groups and requires States parties to implement social security systems that progressively respond to those needs. The European Code of Social Security also requires governments to take steps through bilateral and multilateral agreements to ensure equal treatment when protected persons move among European nations.

Although the European Convention on Human Rights does not mention social security as a human right, the European Court has determined in several cases, such as in *Schuler-Zgraggen v. Switzerland*, that certain civil and political rights can be relevant to the protection of the right to social security, particularly regarding the right to a fair hearing procedure in the determination of their social security.[349] The European Court also ruled in *Gaygusuz v. Austria* that a violation of Article 14 (right to nondiscrimination) of the European Convention and Article 1 of the First Protocol (right to the peaceful enjoyment of one's possessions) had occurred when an Austrian resident received different treatment under the rules of his employment insurance on the ground that he was not an Austrian citizen.[350]

The Preamble of the Charter of the Organization of American States recognized that "social justice and social security are bases of lasting peace," and Article 45 requires that "Member States agree to dedicate every effort to development of a social security policy."[351] The Protocol of San Salvador further provided in Article 9 that elderly and disabled persons be particularly protected by social security, and

in the event of the death of a beneficiary, social security benefits shall be applied to his dependents . . . In the case of persons who are employed, the right to social security shall cover at least medical care and an allowance or retirement benefit in the case of work accidents or occupational disease and, in the case of women, paid maternity leave before and after childbirth.[352]

Social security rights have also been recognized in state constitutions and by national legal systems. South Africa's constitution, for example, contains a comprehensive set of socioeconomic rights—including the right to social security—that are justiciable, that is, capable of application by the courts. Further examples of countries that have constitutional provisions relating to social security include: Chile, Colombia, Ghana, Hungary, India, Iran, Ireland, Italy, Japan, the Netherlands, Portugal, and Spain.

*See also*: Health, Work-Related Rights and Rest

*Further Reading*:

Robin Burgess & Nicholas Stern, *Social Security in Developing Countries: What, Why, Who and How?* in Social Security in Developing Countries (Ehtisham Ahmed ed., 1991).
Committee on Economic, Social and Cultural Rights, General Comment No. 5, Persons with Disabilities (Eleventh session, 1994), U.N. Doc E/1995/22 at 19 (1995).
Committee on Economic, Social and Cultural Rights, General comment No. 6, The Economic, Social and Cultural Rights of Older Persons (Thirteenth session, 1995), U.N. Doc. E/1996/22 at 20 (1996).
Committee on the Elimination of Discrimination Against Women, General Recommendation 16, Unpaid Women Workers in Rural and Urban Family Enterprises (Tenth session, 1991), U.N. Doc. A/46/38 at 1 (1993).
Committee on the Elimination of Racial Discrimination, General Recommenda-

tion 27, Discrimination Against Roma, (Fifty-seventh session, 2000), U.N. Doc. A/55/18, annex V at 154 (2000).
Concluding Observations of the Committee on the Rights of the Child, Greece, U.N. Doc. CRC/C/15/Add.170 (2002).
Concluding Observations of the Committee on the Rights of the Child, Nigeria, U.N. Doc. CRC/C/15/Add.61 (1996).
Convention Concerning the Establishment of an International System for the Maintenance of Rights in Social Security (No. 157), June 23, 1982, 1932 U.N.T.S. 29.
Equality of Treatment (Social Security) Convention (No. 118), June 30, 1962, 494 U.N.T.S. 271.
*Gaygusuz v. Austria*, Application No. 17371/90, European Court of Human Rights, September 16, 1996.
*Ibrahima Gueye et al. v. France*, Communication No. 196/1985, U.N. Doc. CCPR/C/35/D/196/1985 (1989).
Human Rights and Social Security (Roger Blanpain ed., 1998).
Human Rights Committee, General Comment 28, Equality of rights between men and women (article 3), U.N. Doc. CCPR/C/21/Rev.1/Add.10 (2000).
International Labour Organization, Introduction to Social Security (1984).
*Schuler-Zgraggen v. Switzerland*, Application No. 14518/89, European Court of Human Rights, June 24, 1983.
Social Security (Minimum Standards) Convention (No. 102), June 28, 1952, 210 U.N.T.S. 131.
*S.W.M. Broeks v. The Netherlands*, Communication No. 172/1984, U.N. Doc. CCPR/C/OP/2 at 196 (1990).
Welfare: Need, Rights and Risks (Mary Langan ed., 1998).

*Links to Consult*:

http://www1.umn.edu/humanrts/edumat/IHRIP/circle/modules/module11.htm
http://www.frontlinedefenders.org/manuals/104
http://www.ilo.org/public/english/standards/norm/whatare/stndards/secsoc.htm
http://www.issa.int/engl/homef.htm

C. HEALTH (UNIVERSAL DECLARATION, ART. 25)

Article 25 of the Universal Declaration states:

Everyone has the right to a standard of living adequate for the health and well-being of himself and of his family, including food . . . and medical care and necessary social services, and the right to security in the event of . . . sickness, disability, . . . or other lack of livelihood in circumstances beyond his control.[353]

Elaborating on that provision of the Universal Declaration, the Covenant on Economic, Social and Cultural Rights includes an article on the right to health separate from the right to an adequate standard of living. Article 12 recognizes the "right of everyone to the enjoyment of the highest attainable standard of physical and mental health."³⁵⁴ It further stipulates that the steps that should be taken to achieve the right include

(a) The provision for the reduction of the stillbirth-rate and of infant mortality and for the healthy development of the child;
(b) The improvement of all aspects of environmental and industrial hygiene;
(c) The prevention, treatment and control of epidemic, endemic, occupational and other diseases;
(d) The creation of conditions which would assure to all medical service and medical attention in the event of sickness.³⁵⁵

In 2000 the Committee on Economic, Social and Cultural Rights issued a General Comment that addressed the right to the highest attainable standard of health, providing an authoritative interpretation of the Covenant's Article 12. As it has done with other rights, the Committee notes the interdependency of this right with other rights, in particular the right to food, nutrition, housing, access to safe and potable water and adequate sanitation, safe and healthy working conditions, and a healthy environment. The Committee notes that poverty impedes the goal of attaining the right and recognizes the "formidable structural and other obstacles resulting from international and other factors beyond the control of States that impede the full realization" of the right in many countries.³⁵⁶

The General Comment identifies several attributes of the right to health, including the right to control one's health and body, sexual and reproductive freedom, and freedom from torture and nonconsensual medical treatment and experimentation. The right to health also includes entitlement to a system of health protection that provides equality of opportunity for people to enjoy the highest attainable level of health. In addition, the General Comment mentions access to health-related education and information, including on sexual and reproductive health.

The Committee takes note of the change in conditions that have taken place since 1966 when the Covenant was adopted that must be considered when determining the meaning of the right. They include determinants of health such as resource distribution and gender differences, socially related concerns such as violence and armed conflict, the increase in diseases such as cancer, and the appearance of Human Immunodeficiency Virus (HIV) and Acquired Immunodeficiency Syndrome (AIDS).

As with other rights, the interrelated and essential elements are identified: availability, including safe and potable drinking water; adequate sanitation facilities, hospitals, clinics and other health-related buildings; trained medical and professional personnel receiving domestically competitive salaries; essential drugs; physical, economic, and information accessibility, as well as nondiscrimination; acceptability, including culturally appropriate care and respect for confidentiality; and scientifically and medically appropriate goods and services of good quality.

The specific steps identified in the Covenant are further defined to include measures to improve child and maternal health as well as sexual and reproductive services including family planning; preventive measures in respect to occupational accidents, diseases, and harmful substances; and promotion of social determinants of good health, including discouraging substance abuse and preventive care.

Nondiscrimination is one of the important aspects of the right that is stressed throughout the General Comment. States have an obligation to provide for individuals who do not have sufficient means for necessary health care. In this regard, investments should not disproportionately favor expensive curative health services, which are often accessible only to a small, privileged fraction of the population. Primary and preventive care should be stressed. Special measures are encouraged for women, children, adolescents, older persons, persons with disabilities, and indigenous peoples. With respect to the latter, not only do they have the right to specific measures to improve their access to health care services, but their natural resources, such as medicinal plants, animals, and minerals, must also be protected.

As with the other economic, social, and cultural rights, the Covenant implies obligations to respect, protect, and fulfill. Included in the right to respect is the right to equal access and to refrain from (1) prohibiting or impeding traditional preventive care, healing practices, and medicines; and (2) marketing unsafe drugs, and applying coercive medical treatments, unless necessary in certain restricted situations. States should also refrain from limiting access to contraceptives and from denying access to sexual and reproductive health. Pollution of air, water, and soil by state-owned facilities is also prohibited.

The obligation to protect includes the duty to adopt legislation and take other measures to ensure equal access to health care provided by third parties and ensure that privatization does not affect the availability, accessibility, acceptability, and quality of health care. Governments also have an obligation to ensure that harmful social or traditional practices do not interfere with access to health care, including family planning, or to prevent third parties from coercing women to undergo traditional practices such as female genital mutilation.

The obligation to fulfill requires States parties to recognize the right in their political and legal systems, and to adopt a national health policy with a detailed plan for realizing the right to health. Specifically required are information campaigns, immunization programs, proper training of personnel, provision of an affordable insurance system—whether private, public, or mixed. Measures against environmental and occupational hazards are also required, as are policies aimed at reducing pollution.

Also in conformity with General Comment 3, the Committee emphasizes the obligation of international cooperation to achieve the right to health, including prevention of third parties from violating it in other countries and greater attention to the right when participating in international financial institutions.[357] Embargos restricting the supply of medicines and medical equipment are prohibited.

As with other rights, General Comment 14 distinguishes between inability and unwillingness to comply with obligations.[358] Retrogressive measures are prohibited. Failure to regulate individuals, groups, or corporations to prevent them from violating the health of others constitutes a violation of the right. Individuals and groups have the right to participate in the decision-making process and states should ensure it.

In applying Covenant Article 12 and its related General Comment 14, the Committee on Economic, Social and Cultural Rights has identified a number of nations where health rights problems have occurred. For example, in reviewing the report of Finland, the Committee stated that it "regrets the weakening of the public health care system as a result of cuts in the Government's health spending. . . . The Committee is particularly concerned that certain municipalities allocate insufficient funds to health care services. This has resulted in inequality with regard to levels of health care service provision depending on the place of residence, to the detriment in particular of children, persons with physical and mental disabilities and older persons."[359]

The right to health is addressed in several other human rights treaties. The rights to public health and medical care are among the economic, social, and cultural rights to be enjoyed without distinction as to race, color, or national or ethnic origin in the International Convention for the Elimination of Racial Discrimination.[360] The Convention on the Elimination of All Forms of Discrimination Against Women refers to the right in two contexts: (1) the right to protection of health and to safety in working conditions, including the safeguarding of the function of reproduction (Article 11); and (2) the right of women to equality in the field of health care services, including those related to family planning, as well as to appropriate services in connection with pregnancy, confinement, and the postnatal period, granting free services where necessary (Article 12).[361]

The Convention on the Rights of the Child in Article 24 provides an extensive list of measures for implementation of the right "to the enjoyment of the highest attainable standard of health and facilities for the treatment of illness and rehabilitation of health."³⁶² The measures should: (1) diminish infant and child mortality; (2) ensure the provision of necessary medical assistance and health care with an emphasis on development of primary health care; (3) combat disease and malnutrition through the provision of adequate nutritious foods and clean drinking water, taking into consideration the dangers of pollution; (4) ensure pre- and postnatal health care for mothers; (5) ensure information and education on child health and nutrition, breastfeeding, hygiene, environmental sanitation, and the prevention of accidents; and (6) develop preventive health care, guidance for parents, and family planning education. States must also take steps to abolish traditional practices that are prejudicial to the health of children (such as female genital mutilation) and undertake to promote and encourage international cooperation to achieve the right progressively, taking the needs of developing countries into particular account.

The Covenant on Civil and Political Rights contains a provision relating to the right to health in prohibiting in Article 7 medical or scientific experimentation on human beings without full understanding of the extent of the experiment and prior consent.³⁶³ The UN General Assembly has also adopted the Principles of Medical Ethics relevant to the Role of Health Personnel, particularly Physicians, in the Protection of Prisoners and Detainees Against Torture and Other Cruel, Inhuman or Degrading Treatment or Punishment.³⁶⁴

All the major regional human rights systems cover the right to health. The African Charter on Human and Peoples' Rights refers to the right to enjoy the best attainable state of physical and mental health.³⁶⁵ States parties must take necessary measures to protect the health of their people and ensure that they receive medical attention when they are sick. The American Declaration of the Rights and Duties of Man recognizes the right to the preservation of health through sanitary and social measures relating to food, clothing, housing, and medical care, to the extent permitted by public and community resources.³⁶⁶ The Additional Protocol to the American Convention on Human Rights in the Area of Economic, Social and Cultural Rights (Protocol of San Salvador) provides that the right to health means the enjoyment of the highest level of physical, mental, and social well-being.³⁶⁷ Measures to implement the right include: primary health care available to all individuals and families; health services to all people in the states' jurisdiction; universal immunization against the principal infectious diseases; prevention and treatment of endemic, occupational, and other diseases; education on the prevention and treatment of health problems; and provision of the health needs of the highest risk groups and those whose poverty makes them most vulnerable. The European Social Charter provides for the right to protection of health.[368] Measures to be taken include removing the causes of ill-health; providing advisory and educational facilities for the promotion of health and encouragement of individual responsibility in matters of health; and prevention of epidemics, endemic and other diseases, and accidents.

In addition to the work of the Committee on Economic, Social and Cultural Rights in reviewing and questioning periodic reports from the 156 governments that have ratified the Covenant as well as issuing broad interpretive Comments, there are several other international institutions that protect the right to the highest attainable standard of health. The most prominent of those institutions is the World Health Organization (WHO), centered in Geneva, whose Constitution was the first treaty to provide, in 1946, a right to health: "The enjoyment of the highest attainable standard of health is one of the fundamental rights of every human being without distinction of race, religion, political belief, economic or social condition."[369] The WHO has programs and standards for preventing and treating HIV/AIDS, preventing the use of tobacco, encouraging breastfeeding of infants rather than infant formula where there is insufficient clean water and where there is not a significant risk of transmitting HIV to the infant, and so on.

Right to health issues have also arisen in the context of the World Trade Organization (WTO). The Agreement on the Application of Sanitary and Phytosanitary Measures (SPS Agreement) is an integral part of the WTO agreements aiming to prevent governments from using sanitary measures as a pretext for banning or inhibiting foreign imports. Accordingly, the SPS Agreement subjects national health standards to scrutiny whenever they may affect trade, requiring that a risk assessment be made so as to assure that health standards are based on scientific evidence and are thus not discriminatory against imports. Under the SPS Agreement, the WTO prefers national health measures that are consistent with international standards. In the "hormone-beef" dispute, Canada and the United States complained to the WTO Dispute Settlement Mechanism (DSM) against a European Union (EU) ban imposed in the 1980s on the sale of meat produced with several growth hormones, on the grounds that the hormones might be carcinogenic.[370] The ban was not discriminatory against imports because it applied to the same hormones anywhere in the EU. Nonetheless, the WTO dispute settlement panel and Appellate Body determined that the EU import ban was not consistent with the SPS Agreement as the EU sanitary measures were not based on an adequate risk assessment. The Appellate Body did acknowledge that hormones could constitute a health risk, but the WTO placed the burden of proof on consumers and consuming nations to support protective measures that might inhibit imports. If the WTO had followed the precautionary principle as a matter of customary international law, the burden of proof or the lack of scientific certainty would, instead, sustain health measures.

In 2002 the Commission on Human Rights recognized the right to health and appointed a Special Rapporteur on that right.[371] Like other thematic rapporteurs of the Commission (now the Human Rights Council), the Special Rapporteur on the right of everyone to the enjoyment of the highest attainable standard of physical and mental health receives complaints from all over the world about violations of the right to health, visits nations where there are particularly grave problems, advocates for improvements in health conditions, and prepares an annual report that summarizes developments. The Special Rapporteur has focused particularly on the right to sexual and reproductive health, poverty and the right to health, neglected diseases, and the right to health and violence prevention. The Special Rapporteur has visited Mozambique, Peru, and Romania to assess the situation in those countries.

The right to health is most importantly implemented, however, nearer to home. While most international protections for the right to health rely upon persuasion, threats of embarrassment, embarrassment, and expectations of professionalism, there have been developments in turning the international right to health into enforceable practice in particular countries. A number of national constitutions protect the right to health. One of the earliest was the 1925 Chilean Constitution; others include the constitutions of Cuba, Haiti, Hungary, and South Africa. In 2002 the Constitutional Court of South Africa used international right to health principles and the South African Constitution to sustain a trial court order to the national and provincial governments to "make Nevirapine available to pregnant women with HIV who give birth in the public sector, and to their babies, in public health facilities to which the [government's] programme for the prevention of mother-to-child transmission of HIV has not yet been extended."[372] The government of South Africa had refused to provide this very inexpensive and indispensable treatment to women with HIV. The South African courts decided that the right to health required the government to change its policies and protect the babies from HIV/AIDS.

*See also*: Equality and Nondiscrimination, Food, Healthy Environment, Housing, Life, Social Security, Torture and Inhuman Treatment, Work-Related Rights and Rest

*Further Reading*:

Committee on Economic, Social and Cultural Rights, General Comment 14, The Right to the Highest Attainable Standard of Health (Twenty-second session, 2000), U.N. Doc. E/C.12/2000/4 (2000), *reprinted in* Compilation of General Comments and General Recommendations Adopted by Human Rights Treaty Bodies, U.N. Doc. HRI/GEN/1/Rev.6 at 85 (2003).

Committee on the Elimination of Discrimination Against Women, General Recommendation 24, Women and Health (Twentieth session, 1999), U.N. Doc. A/54/38 at 5 (1999).

Committee on the Rights of the Child, General Comment 3, HIV/AIDS and the Right of the Child, U.N. Doc. CRC/GC/2003/3 (2003).

Committee on the Rights of the Child, General Comment 4, Adolescent Health and Development in the Context of the Convention on the Rights of the Child, U.N. Doc. CRC/GC/2003/4 (2003).

Conclusions and Recommendations of the Committee on Economic, Social and Cultural Rights, Finland, U.N. Doc. E/C.12/1/Add.52 (2000).

Constitution of the World Health Organization, 14 U.N.T.S. 185, *entered into force* Apr. 7, 1948; WHO Basic Documents, Official Document No. 240 (1991).

Rebecca J. Cook, Bernard M. Dickens, and Mahmoud F. Fathall, Reproductive Health and Human Rights: Integrating Medicine, Ethics, and Law (2003).

Caroline Dommen, *Balancing Global Trade with Social Need a Role for Human Rights Norms and Mechanisms?* in Balancing Global Trade with Social Need (Ellen Rosskam & Gregory Loos eds., 2001)

European Communities—Measures Affecting Meat and Meat Products (Hormones), Report of the Appellate Body, WT/DS26/AB/R & WT/DS48/AB/R (1998).

European Scientific Co-Operation Network "Medicine and Human Rights" of the European Federation of Scientific Networks, The Human Rights, Ethical and Moral Dimensions of Health Care (1998).

David P. Fidler, International Law and Public Health: Material on and Analysis of Global Health Jurisprudence (2000).

Lawrence O. Gostin, The AIDS Pandemic: Complacency, Injustice, and Unfulfilled Expectations (2004).

Lawrence O. Gostin & Zita Lazzarini, Human Rights and Public Health in the AIDS Pandemic (1997).

Health and Human Rights: A Reader (Jonathan M. Mann et al. eds., 1999).

*Minister of Health and Others v. Treatment Action Campaign and Others*, CCT9/02 (2002), 2002 (5) SA 721 (CC); 2002 (10) BCLR 1033 (CC).

Helena Nygren-Krug/World Health Organization, 25 Questions & Answers on Health & Human Rights (2002).

Principles of Medical Ethics relevant to the Role of Health Personnel, particularly Physicians, in the Protection of Prisoners and Detainees Against Torture and Other Cruel, Inhuman or Degrading Treatment or Punishment, G.A. res. 37/194, annex, 37 U.N. GAOR Supp. (No. 51) at 211, U.N. Doc. A/37/51 (1982).

A Thematic Guide to Documents on Health and Human Rights: Global and Regional Standards Adopted by Intergovernmental Organizations, International Non-Governmental Organizations and Professional Associations (Gudmundur Alfredsson & Katarina Tomaevski eds., 1998).

*Links to Consult*:

http://policy.who.int/cgi-bin/om_isapi.dll?infobase = Basicdoc&softpage = Browse_Frame_Pg42

144   Particular Rights and Responsibilities

http://www.concourt.gov.za/date2002.html
http://www.doctorsoftheworld.org
http://www.doctorswithoutborders.org/
http://www.msf.org/
http://www.ohchr.org/english/issues/health/right/index.htm
http://www.phrusa.org/
http://www.phrusa.org/healthrights
http://www.who.int/hhr/en
http://www.wto.org/english/tratop_e/dispu_e/dispu_e.htm
http://www1.umn.edu/humanrts/crc/comment3.htm
http://www1.umn.edu/humanrts/crc/crc-generalcomment4.html
http://www1.umn.edu/humanrts/edumat/IHRIP/circle/modules/module14.htm
http://www1.umn.edu/humanrts/esc/finland2000.html
http://www1.umn.edu/humanrts/gencomm/escgencom14.htm
http://www1.umn.edu/humanrts/gencomm/generl24.htm
http://www1.umn.edu/humanrts/instree/h3pmerhp.htm

D. FOOD (UNIVERSAL DECLARATION, ART. 25)

The right to food is identified in Article 25 of the Universal Declaration of Human Rights as another component of the right to an adequate standard of living.[373] Article 11 of the Covenant on Economic, Social and Cultural Rights emphasizes the right further in "recognizing the fundamental right of everyone to be free from hunger."[374] Also pursuant to Article 11, States parties agree to take individual measures and to cooperate at the international level:

(a) To improve methods of production, conservation and distribution of food by making full use of technical and scientific knowledge, by disseminating knowledge of the principle of nutrition and by developing or reforming agrarian systems in such a way as to achieve the most efficient development and utilization of natural resources; (b) Taking into account the problems of both food-importing and food exporting countries, to ensure an equitable distribution of world food supplies in relation to need.[375]

In order to further delineate the right to food, the UN General Assembly, in 1974, convened a World Food Conference, which issued the Universal Declaration on the Eradication of Hunger and Malnutrition, that provides:

Every man, woman and child has the inalienable right to be free from hunger and malnutrition. . . . It is a fundamental responsibility of Governments to work together for higher food production and a more equitable and efficient distribution of food between countries and within countries. Governments should initiate immediately a greater concerted attack on chronic malnutrition and deficiency diseases among the vulnerable and lower income groups.[376]

In 1996 the UN General Assembly and the Food and Agriculture Organization convened a second world conference, the World Food Summit, in response to the continued existence of widespread under nutrition and growing concern about the capacity of agriculture to meet future food needs. The World Food Conference, World Food Summit, and similar international efforts have concentrated on implementation techniques that promote this right by such measures as development programs, education, agrarian policies, the promotion of co-operatives, technical and financial assistance, the provision of fertilizers and high-quality seeds, and arrangements for stabilizing world food markets to avoid famine. These measures are not so much a subject for lawyers and courts which are important to the implementation of political rights. Instead, the right to food is largely implemented by programs run by agronomists, biologists, doctors, engineers, farmers, managers, trade experts, and other technicians. In September 2004, the Committee on World Food Security of the Food and Agriculture Organization also adopted extensive Voluntary Guidelines for the progressive implementation of the right to adequate food.[377]

In 1999, the Committee on Economic, Social and Cultural Rights adopted General Comment 12 on the right to adequate food.[378] It did so in response to a request by the 1996 World Food Summit. The Committee also referred to the Rome Declaration of the World Food Summit, as well as reports and documentation of the Commission on Human Rights, the Sub-Commission on Prevention of Discrimination and Protection of Minorities, and other UN bodies, and a draft code of conduct on the human right to adequate food prepared by international nongovernmental organizations.

General Comment 12 affirms that the right to food is indivisibly linked to the inherent dignity of the human person and indispensable for the fulfillment of other human rights. It observes that the problem of hunger and malnutrition are not lack of food but lack of access to available food because of poverty. Hence, the right is realized when everyone has physical and economic access at all times to adequate food or means for its procurement. While the right is to be achieved progressively, states have an obligation to mitigate and alleviate hunger, even in times of natural or other disasters.

General Comment 12 identifies the core content of the right to adequate food as "The availability of food in a quantity and quality sufficient to satisfy the dietary needs of individuals, free from adverse substances, and acceptable within a given culture; the accessibility of such food in ways that are sustainable and that do not interfere with the enjoyment of other human rights."[379] It reiterates the legal obligation to achieve the right progressively and identifies three levels of obligations that states have: to respect, to protect, and to fulfill. The obligation to respect requires that States parties not take measures that prevent existing access to food. The obligation to protect requires that the state ensure that enterprises or individuals do not deprive individuals access to adequate food. The obligation to fulfill requires activities to strengthen people's access to resources so they can ensure their livelihood, including food security. The prohibition against discrimination is an important component of the right. While only states are parties to the Covenant and thus ultimately accountable for compliance with the right, all members of society have responsibilities in relation to the right. It is the states' responsibility to facilitate implementation of those responsibilities, including the adoption of a code of conduct to provide a framework for the private business sector at both the national and international level.

One concrete step required by the General Comment is the adoption of a national strategy to ensure food and nutrition security for all. The strategy should address all aspects of the food system, including the production, processing, distribution, marketing, and consumption of safe food, as well as measures in the fields of health, education, employment, social security, and sustainable management of natural resources. It should include the formulation of policies and corresponding benchmarks to facilitate national and international monitoring, as well as identification of resources available to meet the goals and the most efficient way to use them.

General Comment 12 also calls for recourse procedures whereby persons or groups have access to effective judicial or other appropriate remedies at both national and international levels. Victims are entitled to adequate reparation, which can include restitution, compensation, satisfaction, or guarantees of nonrepetition. Courts should be empowered to adjudicate the violations. National ombudsmen and human rights commissions are urged to address violations of the right to food.

States are also urged to recognize the role of international cooperation to comply with their obligations. General Comment 12 reiterates the mandate of the Rome Declaration that food should not be used as an instrument of political or economic pressure, thus food embargoes are proscribed. Cooperation should include disaster relief and humanitarian assistance in times of emergencies. Food aid should avoid negative effects on local producers and markets, as well as be safe and culturally acceptable. Requests are made to the international financial institutions to pay greater attention to the protection of the right to food in lending policies, credit agreements, and measures to deal with the debt crisis.

In 2000 the Committee on Economic, Social and Cultural Rights issued a further General Comment on the right to the highest attainable standard of health in which the Committee viewed "the right to health . . . as an inclusive right extending . . . to the underlying determinants of health, such as access to safe and potable water and adequate sanitation, an adequate supply of safe food."[380]

The Human Rights Committee has also referred to the right to life provision in the Covenant on Civil and Political Rights to make conclusions and recommendations relating to the lack of adequate food. For example, in reviewing the report of the Democratic People's Republic of Korea, the Committee observed in 2001:

Given the State party's obligation, under article 6 of the Covenant, to protect the life of its citizens and to take measures to reduce infant mortality and increase life expectancy, the Committee remains seriously concerned about the lack of measures by the State party to deal with the food and nutrition situation in the Democratic People's Republic of Korea and the lack of measures to address, in cooperation with the international community, the causes and consequences of the drought and other natural disasters which seriously affected the country's population in the 1990s.[381]

The Convention on the Rights of the Child also mentions "adequate nutritious food" in order to implement the right to health.[382] In Article 27, nutrition is included as a component of the right of every child to a standard of living adequate for the child's physical, mental, spiritual, moral, and social development. States parties agree to assist parents and others responsible for the child to implement the right.

In addition, the World Health Organization has noted how lack of food affects the right to health. As a result of malnutrition over 200 million people are stunted, more than 900 million suffer from goiter, 16 million are severely retarded, and an additional 50 million suffer from brain damage due to iodine deficiency.

In 2000, the UN Commission on Human Rights first appointed a Special Rapporteur to address the right to food.[383] The mandate of the Special Rapporteur was based on many of the policies and standards of both the Rome Declaration and the General Comment. The Commission did urge the special rapporteur to mainstream a gender perspective in the fulfillment of his mandate. In authorizing the Special Rapporteur, the Commission stated that it is intolerable that there are approximately 840 million undernourished people in the world and that every seven seconds a child under ten dies of hunger somewhere in the world. The Commission invited international financial and developmental institutions as well as UN agencies to give priority and funding to halve by the year 2015 the proportion of people who suffer from hunger.

The Special Rapporteur on the right to food has addressed a number of serious food problems around the world. For example, in 2004 he called attention to the humanitarian catastrophe particularly affecting children and older people in the Democratic People's Republic of Korea where millions are suffering from hunger, severe malnutrition and violations of their right to food. The Special Rapporteur's observations are consistent with the insight of Nobel Prize winning economist Amartya Sen, who noted that starvation does not occur in the context of democracy and freedom of expression where people can complain about hunger and misdistribution of food. The Special Rapporteur also called for urgent efforts to stop destruction of food and water by Janjaweed militias in the Western Darfur region of Sudan, where 1.2 million are at risk and there are hundreds of thousands of internally displaced persons. In 2004 the Special Rapporteur also visited and reviewed the food situation in Ethiopia and Mongolia.

In addition to efforts at the global level, the right to food has been the subject of attention in the Organization of American Statess. Article 34 of the Charter of the Organization of American States provides that one of the goals that States parties agree to accomplish is "proper nutrition, especially through the acceleration of national efforts to increase the production and availability of food."[384] The American Declaration of the Rights and Duties of Man of 1948 identifies food as one of the components of the right to the preservation of health.[385] The American Convention does not provide for a specific right to food, but the Protocol of San Salvador recognizes the "right to adequate nutrition which guarantees the possibility of enjoying the highest level of physical, emotional and intellectual development."[386] To promote the right and eradicate malnutrition, States parties "undertake to improve methods of production, supply and distribution of food, and to this end agree to promote greater international cooperation in support of the relevant national policies."[387]

The African Commission on Human and Peoples' Rights has also dealt with the right to food in a case relating to Nigeria and the

> irresponsible oil development that has poisoned much of the soil and water upon which Ogoni farming and fishing depended.... The destruction of farmlands, rivers, crops, and animals has created malnutrition and starvation among certain Ogoni Communities.... The government's treatment of the Ogonis has violated three minimum duties of the right to food. The government has destroyed food sources through its security forces and State Oil Company; has allowed private oil companies to destroy food sources; and through terror, has created significant obstacles to Ogoni communities trying to feed themselves.[388]

The right to food has also been the subject of national litigation. For example, the People's Union for Civil Liberties petitioned the Supreme

Court of India for enforcement of the Famine Code arguing that the government had failed to allocate its large grain supply to respond to the needs of many starving individuals in Rajasthan.[389] The Court reasoned that the right to food can be derived from the constitutional protection for the right to life and ordered that the Famine Code ought to be implemented for a period of three months.

*See also*: Economic, Social, and Cultural Rights, Health, Social Security, Water

*Further Reading*:

Additional Protocol to the American Convention on Human Rights in the Area of Economic, Social and Cultural Rights, "Protocol of San Salvador," O.A.S. Treaty Series No. 69 (1988), *entered into force* November 16, 1999, *reprinted in* Basic Documents Pertaining to Human Rights in the Inter-American System, OEA/Ser.L.V/II.82 doc.6 rev.1 at 67 (1992).
American Declaration of the Rights and Duties of Man, O.A.S. Res. XXX, adopted by the Ninth International Conference of American States (1948), *reprinted in* Basic Documents Pertaining to Human Rights in the Inter-American System, OEA/Ser.L.V/II.82 doc.6 rev.1 at 17 (1992).
Committee on Economic, Social and Cultural Rights, General Comment 12, Right to Adequate Food (Twentieth session, 1999), U.N. Doc. E/C.12/1999/5 (1999).
Committee on Economic, Social and Cultural Rights, General Comment 14, The Right to the Highest Attainable Standard of Health (Twenty-second session, 2000), U.N. Doc. E/C.12/2000/4 (2000).
Concluding Observations of the Human Rights Committee, Democratic People's Republic of Korea, U.N. Doc. CCPR/CO/72/PRK (2001).
Convention on the Rights of the Child, G.A. res. 44/25, annex, 44 U.N. GAOR Supp. (No. 49) at 167, U.N. Doc. A/44/49 (1989), *entered into force* Sept. 2, 1990.
Lorenzo Cotula & Margaret Vidar/FAO, The Right to Adequate Food in Emergencies (2003).
Declaration of Principles and the Programme of Action, Report of the World Conference on Agrarian Reform and Rural Development, Rome, July 12–20, 1979, U.N. Doc. WCCARD/REP (1979).
Asbjørn Eide, Report on the Right to Adequate Food as a Human Right, U.N. Doc. E/CN.4/Sub.2/1987/23 (1987).
Asbjørn Eide, The Right to Adequate Food and to be Free from Hunger, U.N. Doc. E/CN.4/Sub.2/1999/12 (1999).
Food and Agriculture Organization, The Right to Food: In Theory and Practice (1998).
FoodFirst Information and Action Network (FIAN International) et al., International Code of Conduct on the Human Right to Adequate Food (1997).
Susan George and Nigel Paige, Food for Beginners (1982).
Malcolm Langford and Aoife Nolan, 50 Leading Cases on Economic, Social and Cultural Rights: Summaries (2003).
*People's Union for Civil Liberties v. Union of India & Others* (Supreme Court of India) 2001, Unreported, 2 May 2003.

The Right to Food (Philip Alston & Katarina Tomaevski eds., 1984).
Rome Declaration on World Food Security and the World Food Summit Plan of Action, adopted Nov. 17, 1996, FAO, WFS 96/REP (Part I) (1997).
Amartya Sen, Poverty and Famines: An Essay on Entitlement and Deprivation (1987).
*Social and Economic Rights Action Center and the Center for Economic and Social Rights v. Nigeria,* Communication No. 155/96, African Commission on Human and Peoples' Rights (2001).
United Nations, Right to Adequate Food as a Human Right, U.N. Sales No. E.89.XIV.2 (1989).
Universal Declaration on the Eradication of Hunger and Malnutrition, adopted by the World Food Conference, Rome, U.N. Doc. E/CONF. 65/20, at 1 (1974).
Voluntary Guidelines to Support the Progressive Realization of the Right to Adequate Food in the Context of National Food Security, Report of the 30th Session of the Committee on World Food Security (CFS), Supplement, FAO Doc. CL 127/10-Sup.1, Annex 1 (2004).

*Links to Consult:*

http://www.fao.org/docrep/003/w3613e/w3613e00.htm
http://www.fao.org/docrep/u8719e/u8719e00.htm
http://www.fao.org/Legal/rtf/rtf-e.htm
www.righttofood.com
http://www.righttofoodindia.org/orders/may203.html
http://www.cohre.org/downloads/50leadingcases.pdf
http://www.fao.org/
http://www.fao.org/wfs/homepage.htm
http://www.fian.org/fian/index.php
http://www.unhchr.ch/html/menu2/7/b/mfood.htm
http://www1.umn.edu/humanrts/africa/comcases/155-96.html
http://www1.umn.edu/humanrts/edumat/IHRIP/circle/modules/module12.htm
http://www1.umn.edu/humanrts/gencomm/escgencom12.htm
http://www1.umn.edu/humanrts/gencomm/escgencom14.htm
http://www1.umn.edu/humanrts/hrcommittee/korea2001.html
http://www1.umn.edu/humanrts/instree/k2crc.htm
http://www1.umn.edu/humanrts/instree/q1udehm.htm
http://www1.umn.edu/humanrts/oasinstr/zoas2dec.htm
http://www1.umn.edu/humanrts/oasinstr/zoas10pe.htm

E. CLOTHING (UNIVERSAL DECLARATION, ART. 25)

*i. The Right to Adequate Clothing*

Article 25 of the Universal Declaration mentions the right to clothing as an aspect of the right to an adequate standard of living.[390] The Covenant on Economic, Social and Cultural Rights specifies a number of rights emanating from, and indispensable for, the realization of the right to an adequate standard of living, "including adequate food, clothing and housing, and to the continuous improvement of living conditions."[391] The right to clothing is, however, more than a physical necessity; it is a manifestation of culture and custom. The right to cultural development and culture are mentioned in Articles 1 and 17 of the Economic, Social and Cultural Covenant.

The Committee on Economic, Social and Cultural Rights interprets the Covenant and has addressed the right to clothing in several of its General Comments. In its interpretation of Article 12 of the Covenant (the right to the highest attainable standard of health), the Committee recommended that States parties minimize the risk of occupational accidents through the provision of "adequate protective clothing."[392] The Committee also articulated the issue of access to adequate and appropriate clothing in its General Comment on the rights of elderly persons.[393] Furthermore, in its 1991 General Comment the Committee determined that "The right to adequate clothing also assumes a special significance in the context of persons with disabilities who have particular clothing needs, so as to enable them to function fully and effectively in society."[394] In several of its Concluding Comments on the reports submitted by States parties, the Committee has expressed concern that governments have not afforded the right to adequate clothing. For example, in its 1998 concluding comments on Canada, the Committee expressed concern that people living in poverty (usually women with children) are not guaranteed an adequate means of subsistence, including clothing.[395] In addition, the Committee noted in its 1998 comments on Sri Lanka that thousands of internally displaced persons were denied access to sufficient clothing.[396]

The Convention on the Rights of the Child also includes clothing as part of an adequate standard of living. Article 27 of the Convention states that every child has a right to a

> standard of living adequate for the child's physical, mental, spiritual, moral and social development.... States Parties, in accordance with national conditions and within their means, shall take appropriate measures to assist parents and others responsible for the child to implement this right and shall in case of need provide material assistance and support programmes, particularly with regard to nutrition, clothing and housing.[397]

In Concluding Comments on State reports submitted by Georgia, Haiti, Jordan, and Mozambique, the Committee on the Rights of the Child has specified the particular obligation of States parties to provide adequate clothing to street children and orphans living in government institutions.[398]

While the Covenant on Economic, Social and Cultural Rights and the

152   Particular Rights and Responsibilities

Convention on the Rights of the Child deal with the right to clothing as a minimum requirement for an adequate standard of living, the issue of clothing has raised issues that implicate other human rights, such as freedom of thought, religion, and belief. Clothing is often a visible expression of cultural, religious, and sometimes even political identity. The visibility and public nature of such expressions has raised questions about states' obligations under international human rights law to protect freedoms of expression and religion.

*ii. Clothing and Freedom of Religion*

On February 10, 2004, the French National Assembly voted to ban public school pupils from wearing obvious religious symbols on school premises, including large Christian crosses, Jewish skull caps, Sikh turbans, and Islamic head scarves. The ban has aroused controversy regarding the absolute prohibition on the wearing of clothing suffused with religious symbolism, such as headscarves and turbans. The provisions of this legislation will require many observant members of the Sikh, Islamic, and Orthodox Jewish faiths to choose between practicing fundamental aspects of their chosen religions and beliefs or adhering to government regulations about clothing. The law, which forbids signs and dress that conspicuously show the religious affiliation of students, exemplifies the tension between respect for manifestations of religious beliefs through the clothing students and teachers wear, on the one hand, and the authority of the state to protect civil order and the avoidance of religious pressure on other students to conform to the dress requirements of particular religions.

French Muslims constitute the largest Islamic presence in any European country, although Muslims in several other European countries are facing similar restrictions on dress. In 2004, Germany's highest administrative court ruled that German states were allowed to ban religiously motivated clothing in state schools, including Muslim headscarves and Catholic habits. Belgium is also considering a similar legislative ban on headscarves. Since 1997 Turkey has imposed and enforced a ban on the wearing of headscarves in Turkish universities.

Most women's rights groups assert that women should not be forced to wear traditional or religious clothing, as they are in Iran and Saudi Arabia. In those countries women are compelled to wear the burka or chador (usually covering the whole body and head), and/or the hijab (covering the hair or neck). They contend that women should not be subjected to discrimination requiring that they wear certain clothing that limit their choice of employment and their manifestations of identity. At the same time, however, these groups are concerned that women

Economic, Social, and Cultural Rights    153

who wish to wear manifestations of religious belief should be permitted to do so.

France, Germany, and Turkey have imposed bans on religious clothing because they are concerned that young women are being compelled to wear the chador or other religious symbols and that they should not be subjected to such religious compulsion. They point out that more and more women have been wearing the chador as a way of manifesting their religious commitment to Islam. The French government, however, believes that such religious symbols of Islam undermine the French principles of democratic civil order and secularism. Similarly, the Turkish government is concerned that such manifestations of Islam will make it more difficult to achieve the separation of religion and state which is the basis for the Turkish government.

Persons who wish to express their religious identity through clothing have received protection under the principal international human rights treaties and other instruments as part of freedom of religion. Article 18 of the Covenant on Civil and Political Rights affirms, "Everyone shall have the right to freedom of thought, conscience and religion. This right shall include freedom to have or to adopt a religion or belief of his choice, and freedom, either individually or in community with others and in public or private, to manifest his religion or belief in worship, observance, practice and teaching."[399] Article 27 of the same Convention requires, "In those States in which ethnic, religious or linguistic minorities exist, persons belonging to such minorities shall not be denied the right, in community with the other members of their group, to enjoy their own culture, to profess and practice their own religion."[400] Religious attire can also be protected by Article 19 of the Covenant, which states: "Everyone shall have the right to freedom of expression; this right shall include freedom to seek, receive and impart information and ideas of all kinds, regardless of frontiers."[401]

In 1993 the Human Rights Committee issued a General Comment that elaborated on the issues of clothing, freedom of thought, conscience, and religion. According to the Committee's interpretation,

The observance and practice of religion or belief may include not only ceremonial acts but also such customs as the observance of dietary regulations, the wearing of distinctive clothing or head coverings, participation in rituals associated with certain stages of life, and the use of a particular language customarily spoken by a group.[402]

With regard to paragraph 3 of Article 18, the General Comment reads, "Restrictions may not be imposed for discriminatory purposes or applied in a discriminatory manner."[403]

154   Particular Rights and Responsibilities

Children are also allowed freedom to manifest their religion or beliefs. Article 14 of the Convention on the Rights of the Child requires:

> States Parties shall respect the right of the child to freedom of thought, conscience and religion. . . . Freedom to manifest one's religion or beliefs may be subject only to such limitations as are prescribed by law and are necessary to protect public safety, order, health or morals, or the fundamental rights and freedoms of others.[404]

Article 30 of the same Convention guarantees:

> In those States in which ethnic, religious or linguistic minorities or persons of indigenous origin exist, a child belonging to such a minority or who is indigenous shall not be denied the right, in community with other members of his or her group, to enjoy his or her own culture, to profess and practice his or her own religion, or to use his or her own language.[405]

Freedom of religion is mentioned in the European Convention of Human Rights, and religious clothing has also been the topic of several cases before the European Court on Human Rights. Article 9 of the European Convention provides:

> Everyone has the to freedom of thought, conscience, and religion, this right includes the freedom to change his religion or belief and freedom, either alone, or in community with others and in public or private, to manifest his religion or belief, in worship, teaching practice and observance. . . . Freedom to manifest one's religion or beliefs shall be subject to such limitations as are prescribes by law and are necessary in a democratic society in the interest of public safety, for the protection of public order, health or morals, or for the protection of rights and freedom of others.[406]

In addition, Article 2 of the first Protocol to the European Convention states, "No person shall be denied the right to education. In the exercise of any functions which it assumes in relation to education and to teaching, the State shall respect the right of parents to ensure such education and teaching in conformity with their own religious and philosophical convictions."[407] This provision is particularly pertinent to the instances where students are forced to choose between pursing their education, on the one hand, and, on the other hand, manifesting their religious beliefs through clothing that has been banned in educational institutions.

In the 1993 case *Karaduman v. Turkey* the European Commission of Human Rights ruled as inadmissible a case in which a university student had refused to remove her headscarf in order to obtain a degree certificate.[408] The Commission took the view that a student joining a secular institution would be obligated to comply with the rules of that institution. The Commission also pointed to the rights and freedoms of the other students not to be pressured into wearing the headscarf. In addition, in the 2001 case *Dahlab v. Switzerland* the European Court of Human Rights upheld a ban on the Islamic headscarf being worn by a teacher in a state infant school.[409] The Court argued that the measures taken by Switzerland were justified on the grounds that "the ordinance did not target the plaintiff's religious beliefs, but rather it aimed to protect others' freedom and security of public order" given the role of the teacher of very young children.

In the European Court case *Leyla Şahin v. Turkey*, the applicant alleged that the ban on wearing the Islamic headscarf in higher education institutions had infringed on her right under Article 2 of the first Protocol to the European Convention.[410] As discussed in the chapter on freedom of religion and belief, the Court assessed that in democratic societies in which several religions coexist within the same population, "it may be necessary to place restrictions on freedom to manifest one's religion or belief in order to reconcile the interests of the various groups and ensure that everyone's beliefs are respected."[411] Further, the Court reasoned that

A margin of appreciation is particularly appropriate when it comes to the regulation by the Contracting States of the wearing of religious symbols in teaching institutions, since rules on the subject vary from one country to another depending on national traditions and there is no uniform European conception of the requirements of "the protection of the rights of others" and of "public order."[412]

The Court additionally stated that secularism in Turkey was the guarantor of democratic values, and that secularism protects the individual from external pressures. It added that "restrictions could be placed on freedom to manifest one's religion in order to defend those democratic values and principles."[413]

The *Leyla Şahin* case further initiated controversy because the applicant was, in essence, being forced to choose between religion and education. Following the judgment, some human rights advocates argued that protection of religious freedoms is consistent with secularism in state institutions, and that protecting these freedoms demonstrates respect for the diversity of religious conscience on which the secularism of public institutions is founded. Further, advocates have claimed that the impact of absolute bans on visible religious symbols fall disproportionately on Muslim women who wear headscarves as a sign of their religious devotion, thus violating the antidiscrimination and equal educational opportunity provisions of international human rights law.

The UN Special Rapporteur on the elimination of all forms of religious intolerance visited Turkey in 1999, and in 2000 published a report that strongly questioned the Turkish Republic's representation of itself as a secular state. In particular, the Special Rapporteur noted that the Directorate of Religious Affairs wields "excessive powers of religious management such that religious practice appears to be regimented by the government and Islam is treated as if it were a 'State affair'."[414] The report additionally recommended that "concerns over the political exploitation of religion" should be reconciled and delineated by laws that allow for the free expression of dress within legitimate limitations.[415] The report did not, however, elaborate on the legitimate limits to free expression of dress.

*See also*: Culture, Economic, Social, and Cultural Rights, Freedom of Religion and Belief

*Further Reading:*

Committee on Economic, Social and Cultural Rights, General Comment 14, The Right to the Highest Attainable Standard of Health (Twenty-second session, 2000), U.N. Doc. E/C.12/2000/4 (2000).
Conclusions and Recommendations of the Committee on Economic, Social and Cultural Rights, Canada, U.N. Doc. E/C.12/1/Add.31 (1998).
Conclusions and Recommendations of the Committee on Economic, Social and Cultural Rights, Sri Lanka, U.N. Doc. E/C.12/1/Add.24 (1998).
*Dahlab v. Switzerland*, Application No. 42393/98, 2001-V Eur. Ct. H.R. 447.
Human Rights Committee, General Comment 22, Article 18, Compilation of General Comments and General Recommendations Adopted by Human Rights Treaty Bodies, U.N. Doc. HRI/GEN/1/Rev.1 at 35 (1994).
Interim report of the Special Rapporteur of the Commission on Human Rights on the elimination of all forms of intolerance and of discrimination based on religion or belief, U.N. Doc. A/55/280/Add.1 (2000).
*Karaduman v. Turkey*, Application No. 16278/90, 74 Eur. Comm'n H.R. Dec. & Rep. 93 (1993).
*Leyla Şahin v. Turkey*, Application No. 44774/98, European Court of Human Rights (2004).

*Links to Consult:*

http://news.bbc.co.uk/1/hi/world/europe/3459963.stm
http://www.hrw.org/backgrounder/eca/turkey/2004/index.htm
https://webmcdev.oddl.fsu.edu/human-rights/ch12/ch12.html

F. HOUSING (UNIVERSAL DECLARATION, ART. 25)

The Universal Declaration states, "Everyone has the right to a standard of living adequate for the health and well-being of himself and of his family, including . . . housing. . . ."[416] Article 11 of the Covenant on Economic, Social and Cultural Rights does not expand on this right.[417] The Committee on Economic, Social and Cultural Rights, however, in 1991, further defined the right in its General Comment 4.[418] The General Comment relied in part on the codification of the right to housing included in UN instruments such as the Convention on the Elimination of All Forms of Racial Discrimination,[419] the Convention on the Elimination of All Forms of Discrimination Against Women,[420] and the Convention on the Rights of the Child.[421] The right to housing is also found in regional instruments such as the American Declaration on the Rights and Duties of Man[422] and the Charter of the Organization of American States.[423]

In General Comment 4, the Committee noted that the right to adequate housing is of "central importance for the enjoyment of all economic, social and cultural rights."[424] Further, each person should have the right to live somewhere in security, peace, and dignity in adequate housing.

Two components of the right are identified in the various international instruments: (1) it is part of an adequate standard of living, and (2) there can be no discrimination in how it is provided. General Comment 4 identified seven ways in which housing may be considered to be adequate: legal security of tenure; availability of services, materials, facilities, and infrastructure; affordability; habitability; accessibility; location; and cultural adequacy.

In regard to housing discrimination, General Comment 4 relies upon the Convention for the Elimination of All Forms of Discrimination Against Women, in which States parties agree to take measures to eliminate discrimination against rural women regarding the enjoyment of adequate living conditions, in particular in relation to housing, sanitation, electricity, and water supply. The Convention on the Elimination of All Forms of Racial Discrimination, Article 5, likewise provides that States parties undertake not only to prohibit and eliminate discrimination but to guarantee specifically the right to housing without distinction as to race, color, or national or ethnic origin, equally before the law. The Convention on the Rights of the Child in Article 27 recognizes housing as a component of the right to a standard of living adequate for the child's physical, mental, spiritual, moral, and social development. As to regular migrants and their families, the International Convention on the Protection of the Rights of All Migrant Workers and Their Families similarly calls for equality with regard to access to "housing, including social housing schemes, and protection against exploitation in respect of rents."

The Committee on Economic, Social and Cultural Rights has been particularly active in combating forced evictions. In 1997 it adopted

158   Particular Rights and Responsibilities

General Comment 7, confirming that forced evictions violate the Covenant.[425] States parties have an obligation not to carry out forced evictions as well as to prevent such evictions by nonstate actors such as landlords, developers, and paramilitary forces. The Committee expressed heightened concern about forced evictions motivated by discrimination or permitted without procedural protections. It also referred to the interrelationship with civil and political rights and lists the procedural protections which should be applied in relation to forced evictions.

For example, the Committee on Economic, Social and Cultural Rights in 1991 was able to convince the government of the Dominican Republic to desist from a plan of forced evictions of 70,000 slum dwellers in a Santo Domingo community.[426] The government had begun to remove thousands of slum dwellers in order to build a monument to celebrate the 500th anniversary of the landing of Christopher Columbus on the island in 1492. No alternative housing was provided the forcibly removed slum dwellers. Based on information provided by two Dominican NGOs and the Geneva-based NGO Centre on Housing Rights and Evictions, the Committee declared that the forced evictions violated Article 11 of the Covenant and persuaded the government to stop the forced evictions. As a result of the efforts of the NGOs and the Committee, the community in Santo Domingo has received more secure tenure and better social services.

The UN Commission on Human Rights and its successor, the Human Rights Council, has begun to emphasize economic rights, including the right to adequate housing. The Commission reaffirmed in 1993 that "the practice of forced evictions constitutes a gross violation of human rights, in particular the right to adequate housing."[427] Effectively lobbying as a NGO in the Commission on Human Rights and the Committee on Economic, Social and Cultural Rights, the Centre on Housing Rights and Evictions has identified eight ways in which forced evictions are distinguished from the coerced removal or flight of persons from their homes in eight different ways:

—forced evictions raise issues of human rights;
—forced evictions are planned, foreseen or publicly announced and thus part of a state policy or legal regime;
—forced evictions often involve the use of physical force;
—forced evictions raise issues of State responsibility;
—forced evictions affect both individuals and groups;
—forced evictions are regulated or legitimized by national or local law;
—forced evictions almost always involve an attempt to rationalize the process by those supporting or sponsoring them;
—not all evictions constitute forced evictions, as evictions may be justified for reasons of public order, the safety and security of the dwellers and threats to public health and thereby be consistent with human rights.[428]

Beginning in 2000, the UN Commission on Human Rights appointed a special rapporteur for three years to focus on adequate housing as a component of the right to an adequate standard of living.[429] The Special Rapporteur has prepared annual reports to the Commission on various aspects of housing rights. He has also undertaken investigative visits to various nations. For example, in February 2004 he went to Kenya where he observed the housing situation of vulnerable groups such as minorities, migrants, internally displaced persons, slum dwellers, women who may not be entitled to inherit property, and indigenous people (including the Ogieks who are aboriginal forest dwellers in western Kenya). The Special Rapporteur discussed the housing situation in Kenya and his recommendations with government officials and reported to the Office of the High Commissioner for Human Rights, so that his views could be made available to the Commission on Human Rights. The Special Rapporteur has undertaken and reported upon similar visits to such places as Afghanistan, Brazil, Iran, and Palestine.

The Special Rapporteur on adequate housing has also sought to coordinate his work with the Plan of Implementation of the World Summit on Sustainable Development, the Special Session of the UN General Assembly on Children, the Global Campaign for Secure Tenure launched by the UN Human Settlements Program (Habitat), and other efforts following the last major world conference on housing (Habitat II) which was held in Istanbul during June 2001. In reviewing the Special Rapporteur's reports the Commission on Human Rights has focused attention on housing rights of women and children living in extreme poverty as well as indigenous peoples and persons with disabilities. In addition, the Commission has also looked at the relationship between the right to adequate housing and violence against women, the difficulty that women have leaving violent family situations because of poverty and lack of housing options, and the disproportionate impact forced evictions have on women. The Commission has expressed concern about discrimination against women in access to, acquiring, and securing land, property, and housing. Similarly, the Commission on the Status of Women has urged governments to revise laws as to the right of women to inherit, receive credit, get access to markets and information, obtain capital, and benefit from appropriate technologies.

From its inception, the Inter-American regional system focused on the importance of economic, social, and cultural rights, including the right to housing. In Article 34 of the Charter of the Organization of American States, governments in the Western Hemisphere "agree that equality of opportunity, the elimination of extreme poverty, equitable distribution of wealth and income and the full participation of their peoples in decisions relating to their own development are, among others, basic objectives of integral development."⁴³⁰ In that context, they agree to "devote their utmost efforts" to accomplishing certain goals, which include "Adequate housing for all sectors of the population."⁴³¹ In May 1948—a few months before the UN completed work on the Universal Declaration of Human Rights, the Western Hemisphere governments adopted the American Declaration of the Rights and Duties of Man which includes housing as an aspect of the right to the preservation of health (Article XI) and also recognizes the right to the inviolability of the home (Article IX).⁴³² Interestingly, neither the American Convention on Human Rights,⁴³³ which includes a general commitment to achieving the economic, social, educational, scientific, and cultural rights, nor the Additional Protocol to the American Convention in the Area of Economic, Social and Cultural Rights (Protocol of San Salvador)⁴³⁴ includes a specific reference to housing rights. More recently, however, in the context of drafting a new treaty addressing violence against women, OAS governments have agreed to provide—through private and public sector agencies—shelter for women who have been subjected to violence.

The European countries have codified the right to housing in Article 31 of the European Social Charter.⁴³⁵ Parties to the 1996 revision to the European Social Charter undertake to (1) promote access to housing of an adequate standard, (2) to prevent and reduce homelessness with a view to its gradual elimination, and (3) to make the price of housing accessible to those without adequate resources. Housing is also mentioned in the context of the right to protection against poverty and social exclusion and a right of the family. In addition, the Charter of Fundamental Rights of the European Union mentions that there is a "right to social and housing assistance so as to ensure a decent existence for all those who lack sufficient resources."⁴³⁶

National courts can also play an important role in the further elaboration of the right to housing. For example, the Constitutional Court of South Africa in 2000 considered the rights of people who left the appalling conditions in which they were living and occupied someone else's land.⁴³⁷ The owners of that land obtained an eviction order, and before mediation took place the occupants were forcibly removed by having their homes bulldozed and burned and their possessions destroyed at the beginning of winter. They had nowhere to go at the time the order was served on them. At issue was whether the eviction by the government violated Section 26 of the South African Constitution that provides that everyone has the right of access to adequate housing. The Court decided that socioeconomic rights were justiciable under the Constitution and that at minimum they can be protected from improper action by the government. The Court also affirmed that all the rights in the South African Bill of Rights are interrelated and mutually supporting, and need to be interpreted in the context of historical events, which in that case involved laws and policies under *apartheid* that had resulted in numerous inequities and large numbers of homeless people.

The Court considered international law in interpreting its constitutional provision because it was required to do so under Section 39 of the Constitution. It thus referred to the Covenant on Economic, Social and Cultural Rights, which South Africa had signed but not yet ratified at the time the case was being considered. While the Court noted that the Covenant provided for the right to adequate housing, the South African Constitution guaranteed only the right of access to adequate housing. The Court nonetheless found the Committee's General Comment 3 helpful in determining the nature of the legal obligation under national law, including what constitutes reasonable measures toward fulfilling the obligation. In this case, it concluded that the government was obligated to ensure a minimum essential level of socioeconomic rights, including the right to adequate housing. While the Court was not able to determine what was minimally required, it did determine that there were other aspects of the right that it could identify. First, it found that the government and other entities were required to desist from preventing or impairing the right of access to adequate housing, which includes a prohibition against arbitrary evictions. Second, there is a positive obligation to address the content of the right of access requiring land, services, and a dwelling. The Court noted that other agents and individuals must be enabled by legislative and other measures to provide housing for people at all economic levels. What is reasonable must be analyzed in the context of the various levels of government that are involved, but what is essential is a program that coordinates responsibility for the various tasks to the different spheres of government. The courts' task then would be to determine whether the measures adopted are reasonable.

The Court also cited General Comment 3 of the Committee on Economic, Social and Cultural Rights, in determining that "progressive realization" connotes "an obligation to move as expeditiously and effectively as possible" to ensure the full realization of the right and that the validity of cutbacks would have to be "justified by reference to the totality of the rights provided in the Covenant and in the context of the full use of the maximum available resources."[438] With respect to the mandate that the right be provided "within available resources," the Court acknowledged that availability of resources would be an important factor in assessing what was reasonable. Nonetheless, in this case it found a constitutional violation of the right and noted the failure to provide relief to the categories of people in desperate need. The Court found a violation in the failure to carry out the eviction humanely, as evidenced by the destruction of the property.

162   Particular Rights and Responsibilities

This case demonstrates how a national court used international human rights standards to interpret its own constitutional norms. The Constitutional Court of South Africa interpreted and imbued with meaning the right to adequate housing. It also demonstrated how economic, social, and cultural rights can be justiciable and thus applicable by courts in concrete situations.

*See also*: Clothing, Economic, Social, and Cultural Rights, Food, Social Security, Water

*Further Reading*:

American Declaration of the Rights and Duties of Man, O.A.S. Res. XXX, adopted by the Ninth International Conference of American States (1948), *reprinted in* Basic Documents Pertaining to Human Rights in the Inter-American System, OEA/Ser.L.V/II.82 doc.6 rev.1 at 17 (1992).

Centre on Housing Rights and Evictions, Forced Evictions: Violations of Human Rights (2003).

Charter of Fundamental Rights of the European Union, 2000 O.J. (C 364) 1, *entered into force* Dec. 7, 2000.

Charter of the Organization of American States, 119 U.N.T.S. 3, *entered into force* Dec. 13, 1951; *amended by* Protocol of Buenos Aires, 721 U.N.T.S. 324, O.A.S. Treaty Series, No. 1-A, *entered into force* Feb. 27, 1970; *amended by* Protocol of Cartagena, O.A.S. Treaty Series, No. 66, 25 I.L.M. 527, *entered into force* Nov. 16, 1988; *amended by* Protocol of Washington, 1-E Rev. OEA Documentos Oficiales OEA/Ser.A/2 Add. 3 (SEPF), 33 I.L.M. 1005, *entered into force* September 25, 1997; *amended by* Protocol of Managua, 1-F Rev. OEA Documentos Oficiales OEA/Ser.A/2 Add.4 (SEPF), 33 I.L.M. 1009, *entered into force* Jan. 29, 1996.

Committee on Economic, Social and Cultural Rights, General Comment 4, The Right to Adequate Housing (Sixth session, 1991), U.N. Doc. E/1992/23, annex III at 114 (1991), *reprinted in* Compilation of General Comments and General Recommendations Adopted by Human Rights Treaty Bodies, U.N. Doc. HRI/GEN/1/Rev.6 at 18 (2003).

Convention on the Elimination of All Forms of Discrimination Against Women, G.A. res. 34/180, 34 U.N. GAOR Supp. (No. 46) at 193, U.N. Doc. A/34/46, *entered into force* Sept. 3, 1981.

Convention on the Rights of the Child, G.A. res. 44/25, annex, 44 U.N. GAOR Supp. (No. 49) at 167, U.N. Doc. A/44/49 (1989), *entered into force* Sept. 2, 1990.

European Social Charter (revised) (ETS No. 163), *entered into force* Jan. 7, 1999.

*Government of the Republic of South Africa et al. v. Grootboom*, Constitutional Court of South Africa, Case CCT 11/00, (11) BCLR 1169, Judgment of October 4, 2000).

Inter-American Convention on the Prevention, Punishment, and Eradication of Violence Against Women, 33 I.L.M. 1534 (1994), *entered into force* Mar. 5, 1995.

International Convention on the Protection of the Rights of All Migrant Workers and Members of Their Families, G.A. res. 45/158, annex, 45 U.N. GAOR

Supp. (No. 49A) at 262, U.N. Doc. A/45/49 (1990), *entered into force* July 1, 2003.

Scott Leckie, *The UN Committee on Economic, Social and Cultural Rights and the Right to Adequate Housing: Towards an Appropriate Approach*, 11 Hum. Rts. Q. 522 (1989).

U.N. Centre for Human Rights, *The Human Right to Adequate Housing: Fact Sheet No. 21* (1996).

*Links to Consult:*

http://www.concourt.gov.za/files/grootboom1/grootboom1.pdf
http://www.un.org/ga/Istanbul+5/
http://www.unhchr.ch/html/menu2/7/b/mhous.htm
http://www.unhchr.ch/html/menu2/7/b/mhousintro.htm
http://www1.umn.edu/humanrts/euro/ets163.html
http://www1.umn.edu/humanrts/edumat/IHRIP/circle/modules/module13.htm
http://www1.umn.edu/humanrts/gencomm/epcomm4.htm
http://www1.umn.edu/humanrts/iachr/oascharter.html
http://www1.umn.edu/humanrts/instree/brazil1994.html
http://www1.umn.edu/humanrts/instree/d1cerd.htm
http://www1.umn.edu/humanrts/instree/europeanunion2.html
http://www1.umn.edu/humanrts/instree/e1cedaw.htm
http://www1.umn.edu/humanrts/instree/forcedevictions
http://www1.umn.edu/humanrts/instree/k2crc.htm
http://www1.umn.edu/humanrts/instree/n8icprmw.htm
http://www1.umn.edu/humanrts/oasinstr/zoas2dec.htm

G. WATER

The right to water is not mentioned specifically in the Universal Declaration of Human Rights[439] or the Covenant on Economic, Social and Cultural Rights.[440] Nonetheless, the Committee on Economic, Social and Cultural Rights issued General Comment 15 in 2002 to address the right to water. To support its position that the right to water is covered by the Covenant, it referred to Article 11 which provides for the right to an adequate standard of living "including adequate food, clothing, and housing."[441] The Committee determined that the word "including" meant that the cataloging of rights was not exhaustive and that water is one of the "guarantees essential for securing an adequate standard of living, particularly since it is one of the most fundamental conditions for survival."

The Committee also noted that the right to water had previously recognized the right in General Comment 6 (1995) on the economic, social and cultural rights of older persons. In addition, the Committee supported its General Comment 15 by referring to such treaties as the Convention on the Elimination of All Forms of Discrimination Against

Women[442] and the Convention on the Rights of the Child (discussed below);[443] the Geneva Conventions for the protection of victims of armed conflict;[444] and such other standards as resolutions adopted at the UN Conference on Environment and Development and the UN International Conference on Population and Development, as well as resolutions and reports of the UN Sub-Commission on the Promotion and Protection of Human Rights. The Committee had also consistently addressed the right to water in its review of States parties reports.

The General Comment establishes that water is needed to realize a number of other rights in the Covenant, such as the right to food (necessary for its production), the right to health (necessary to ensure environmental hygiene), the right to gain a living by work, and the right to enjoy certain cultural practices. It notes that the right to water includes the right to maintain access to existing water supplies and the right to be free from interference, for example, to be free from arbitrary disconnections and contamination of water supplies. The right to water also requires a system of supply and management that provides equality of opportunity in the enjoyment of the right. It emphasizes that water should be treated as a social and cultural good, and not primarily an economic good, and its realization must be sustainable so that future generations as well as the present can enjoy it.

General Comment 15 identifies three factors that apply in all circumstances regarding the adequacy of water: availability, quality, and accessibility. Regarding accessibility, nondiscrimination in the provision of water is emphasized, as well as physical and economic accessibility and information accessibility. States parties are asked to give special attention to individuals and groups that have traditionally faced difficulties in exercising this right, including women, children, minority groups, indigenous peoples, refugees, asylum seekers, internally displaced persons, migrant workers, prisoners, and detainees.

The General Comment reaffirms the general legal obligations established in General Comment 3 (1990) with respect to the right to water, including the obligation to take immediate steps even though the right is to be realized progressively and retrogressive measures are presumptively prohibited. It also lists the three types of obligations the Committee has recognized in relation to other human rights: to respect, to protect, and to fulfill. While the obligations are similar to those related to food, the Committee noted the additional responsibility that States parties have under international humanitarian law codified by the Geneva Convention to protect the right to water during armed conflicts, emergency situations, and natural disasters. The Committee specifically referred to international humanitarian law for "protection of objects indispensable for survival of the civilian population . . . protection of the natural environment against widespread, long-term and severe damage and ensuring that civilians, internees and prisoners have access to adequate water."[445] To fulfill their obligations, states are required, among other things, to recognize the right in their political and legal systems; adopt a national water strategy and plan of action; ensure that water is affordable for everyone; and facilitate improved and sustainable access to water, particularly in rural and deprived areas. Adequate sanitation is also an important mechanism for protecting the quality of drinking water and resources. Specific violations of these obligations include: arbitrary disconnection or exclusion from water services or facilities, discriminatory or unaffordable increases in the price of water, pollution and diminution of water resources affecting health, and failure to control or regulate third parties in regard to provision or pollution of water.

The national strategy or plan must set targets, goals, and a timeframe for achieving them. States parties must formulate corresponding benchmarks and indicators. Full and equal access to information concerning water for individuals and groups should also be an integral part of the plan. An independent and transparent judiciary is essential for the effective implementation of this and all other human rights. Victims should be entitled to adequate reparation, including restitution, compensation, satisfaction, or guarantees or nonrepetition through the courts, but national ombudsmen and human rights commissions should also be permitted to address the violations of this right.

International cooperation and assistance is also stressed by the Committee, including the obligation to refrain from actions that interfere with the enjoyment of the right to water in other countries. In line with General Comment 8 (on economic sanctions), use of water as an instrument of political or economic pressure is also prohibited. States parties are also urged to take steps to prevent their own citizens and companies from violating the right to water of individuals and communities in other countries. States parties are further urged to take due account of the right in their roles as members of international financial institutions.

The other major human rights treaties that refer to the right to water are the Convention on the Elimination of All Forms of Discrimination Against Women and the Convention on the Rights of the Child. In Article 14 of the Women's Convention, States parties agree to eliminate discrimination against women in rural areas in order to ensure, on a basis of equality with men, water supply as part of the right to enjoy adequate living conditions.[446] Article 24 of the Children's Convention refers to clean drinking water as a component of the right to the enjoyment of the highest attainable standard of health.[447]

Several UN conferences have made reference to the right to water: Mar Del Plata Action Plan of the UN Water Conference of 1977, the

1992 UN Conference on Environment and Development, and the 1994 UN International Conference on Population and Development. The Sub-Commission on the Promotion and Protection of Human Rights recognized the right in 2002 and appointed a Special Rapporteur on the right to drinking water supply and sanitation.

At the regional level, the African Charter on the Rights and Welfare of the Child provides that States parties shall undertake "to ensure the provision of adequate nutrition and safe drinking water. . . ."[448] Similarly, the Committee of Ministers of the Council of Europe in 2001 adopted the European Charter on Water Resources that declared "Everyone has the right to a sufficient quantity of water for his or her basic needs."[449] A European Union directive of 2000 has recognized that "Water is not a commercial product like any other, but, rather, a heritage which must be protected, defended and treated as such. . . ."[450]

A number of national constitutions explicitly guarantee the right to water (or potable/clean water) or obligate the government to safeguard water resources, including Cambodia, Colombia, Ecuador, Eritrea, Ethiopia, Gambia, Laos, Nigeria, Panama, South Africa, Uganda, Venezuela, and Zambia.

It is estimated that a billion individuals around the globe do not have access to enough water for drinking and household requirements. The World Health Organization has indicated that contaminated water often causes such preventable diseases as infectious diarrhoea accounting for about 1.7 million deaths per year—particularly among children.

The Committee on Economic, Social and Cultural Rights has identified a number situations in which the right to water is a matter of concern. For example, the Committee noted "the living conditions of prisoners and detainees in [Yemen], especially women, with regard to access to health-care facilities, adequate food and safe drinking water."[451] The Committee also observed that "some 1,200 families of the traveler community [in Ireland] are living in roadside encampments without access to water and adequate sanitary facilities, and are liable to be forcibly evicted."[452]

In addition, the African Commission on Human and Peoples' Rights has dealt with the right to water as an aspect of the right to food in a case relating to Nigeria and the "irresponsible oil development that has poisoned much of the soil and water upon which Ogoni farming and fishing depended. . . . The destruction of farmlands, rivers, crops, and animals has created malnutrition and starvation among certain Ogoni Communities. . . ."[453]

National courts have also dealt with the right to water. For example, the Indian Supreme Court considered a petition on behalf of water consumers in New Delhi as against upstream farmers who were using water for irrigation of their crops. The court held:

> Water is a gift of nature. Human hand cannot be permitted to convert this bounty into a curse, an oppression. The primary use to which the water is put being drinking, it would be mocking the nature to force the people who live on the bank of a river to remain thirsty, whereas others incidentally placed in an advantageous position are allowed to use the water for non-drinking purposes. A river has to flow through some territory; and it would be travesty of justice if the upper-riparian States were to use its water for purposes like irrigation, denying the lower riparian States the benefit of using the water even for quenching the thirst of its residents.[454]

In 2003 the Office of the High Commissioner for Human Rights issued a report on trade and investment mentioning several national situations that illustrate how the right to water can be implemented or violated:

> Private sector participation in the water and sanitation sector—as with public sector provision—has produced successes and failures. In Uganda, successes in private sector participation have resulted in the implementation of village-level water supply projects by private contractors on a massive scale across the country and the connection of about 1 million people to wells between 1998 and 2001. In contrast, the provision of services free of charge by the public sector in the United Republic of Tanzania not only crippled the water system, it has pushed the country deeper into debt, leaving at least 120,000 households in one of the poorest areas of the capital completely unconnected. . . .
> However, in some cases, private sector participation has led to real problems from a human rights perspective. In Cochabamba, Bolivia, the water and sanitation sector had suffered in public hands. While international aid had assisted some communities to dig wells and establish water cooperatives, water purity was often poor, there was chronic water shortage and the poorest neighbourhoods were not connected to the water mains. In 1999, the Bolivian Government conducted an auction of the Cochabamba water system which drew only one bidder—a consortium called Aguas del Tunari, the controlling partner of which was wholly owned by a foreign investor, Bechtel Corporation. The concession agreement gave the corporation exclusive rights to the water, a guarantee of a minimum fifteen percent return on its investment, and allowed the corporation to install water meters and charge for water. Shortly afterwards, water tariffs increased with a view to expanding and upgrading the water network. However, the company shortly introduced increases of up to thirty-five percent and cut people off from water connections if they did not pay their bills. This in turn led to violent demonstrations and, ultimately, the departure of the water company and a reversal of the Government's decision to liberalize the water supply. The Government assumed responsibility for the provision of water services, but services still require enhancement. The foreign investor since commenced proceedings against the Bolivian Government before the International Centre for the Settlement of Investment Disputes under the bilateral investment agreement between the Netherlands and Bolivia. The arbitration is ongoing.[455]

*See also:* Clothing, Economic, Social, and Cultural Rights, Food, Health, Housing, Social Security

*Further Reading:*

African Charter on the Rights and Welfare of the Child, OAU Doc. CAB/LEG/ 24.9/49 (1990), *entered into force* Nov. 29, 1999.
Committee on Economic, Social and Cultural Rights, General Comment 12, Right to adequate food (Twentieth session, 1999), U.N. Doc. E/C.12/1999/5 (1999).
Committee on Economic, Social and Cultural Rights, General Comment 15, The right to water (Twenty-ninth session, 2003), U.N. Doc. E/C.12/2002/11 (2002).
Conclusions and Recommendations of the Committee on Economic, Social and Cultural Rights, Ireland, U.N. Doc. E/C.12/1/Add.77 (2002).
Conclusions and Recommendations of the Committee on Economic, Social and Cultural Rights, Yemen, U.N. Doc. E/C.12/1/Add.92 (2003).
Council of Europe, European Charter on Water Resources, CO-DBP/documents/codbp2001/08e (2001).
*Delhi Water Supply v. State of Haryana*, 1996 SOL Case No. 556 (1996).
Dublin Statement on Water and Sustainable Development, International Conference on Water and the Environment: Development Issues for the 21st Century, Dublin, Ireland (1992).
El Hadji Guissé, Relationship Between the Enjoyment of Economic, Social and Cultural Rights and the Promotion of the Realization of the Right to Drinking Water Supply and Sanitation, U.N. Doc. E/CN.4/2002/10 (2002).
European Union Directive 2000/60/EC (2000).
Mar Del Plata Action Plan of the United Nations Water Conference; Report of the United Nations Water Conference, Mar del Plata, Mar. 14–25 1977, U.N. Doc. E/CONF.70/29, U.N. Sales No. E.77.II.A.12 (1977).
Office of the High Commissioner for Human Rights, Human Rights, Trade and Investment, U.N. Doc. E/CN.4/Sub.2/2003 (2003).
Report of the 1992 United Nations Conference on Environment and Development, June 3–14, U.N. Doc. A/CONF.151/26/Rev. 1 (Vol. I and Vol. I/Corr.1, Vol. II, Vol. III and Vol. III/Corr.1), Sales No. E.93.I.8 and corrigenda (1992).
*Social and Economic Rights Action Center and the Center for Economic and Social Rights v. Nigeria*, Communication No. 155/96, African Commission on Human and Peoples' Rights (2001).
World Declaration on Education for All, World Conference on Education for All, Jomtien, Thailand, Mar. 5–9, 1990.
World Health Organization et al., The Right to Water (2003).

*Links to Consult:*

http://www.coe.int/T/E/Cultural_Co-operation/Environment/Nature_and_biological_diversity/Biodiversity/Water_Charter.asp
http://www.cohre.org/downloads/water_res_8.pdf
http://www.cohre.org/water
http://www.ecouncil.ac.cr/about/ftp/riodoc.htm

http://www.johannesburgsummit.org/html/documents/
  nowater_nofuture_eng. pdf
http://www.supremecourtonline.com/cases/8493.html
http://www.unesco.org/education/efa/ed_for_all/background/
  jomtien_declaration.shtml
http://www.unhchr.ch/html/menu2/6/water/index.htm
http://www.unhchr.ch/Huridocda/Huridoca.nsf/0/
  5ba923c98b7f221ec1256c05002c3ebc ?Opendocument
http://www.unhchr.ch/Huridocda/Huridoca.nsf/
  e06a5300f90fa0238025668700518ca4/9
  b2b4fed82c88ee2c1256d7b002e47da/$FILE/G0314847.pdf
http://www.who.dk/watsan/Issues/20030903_1
http://www.wmo.ch/web/homs/documents/english/icwedece.html
http://www.world.water-forum3.com/jp/mc/md_final.pdf
http://www1.umn.edu/humanrts/africa/comcases/155-96.html
http://www1.umn.edu/humanrts/esc/yemen2003.html
http://www1.umn.edu/humanrts/gencomm/escgencom12.htm
http://www1.umn.edu/humanrts/gencomm/escgencom15.htm

## H. EDUCATION (UNIVERSAL DECLARATION, ART. 26)

The Universal Declaration of Human Rights addresses the right to education in Article 26. First, it provides that elementary education shall be free and compulsory. Further, "Technical and professional education shall be made generally available and higher education shall be equally accessible to all on the basis of merit."[456] The second paragraph of Article 26 delineates that the content of education shall be directed toward the full development of the human personality and strengthen respect for human rights as well as promote understanding, tolerance, and friendship among nations and further the activities of the United Nations for the maintenance for peace. The third paragraph provides that parents have the right to choose the kind of education for their children.

In Article 13, the Covenant of Economic, Social and Cultural Rights emphasizes the content of education in the Universal Declaration adding that it should enable "all persons to participate effectively in a free society" among other goals.[457] It also reiterates the language of the Universal Declaration regarding primary and higher education, but adds that secondary education, including technical and vocational, "shall be made generally available and accessible to all by every appropriate means, and in particular by the progressive introduction of free education."[458] It also expands on the rights to attend nonpublic schools and to set up private schools as long as they conform to the principles of the Covenant and minimum standards set by the state. In Article 14, States parties agree to work out and adopt a plan for the progressive imple-

170  Particular Rights and Responsibilities

mentation of the principle of compulsory education free of charge for all.

The Committee on Economic, Social and Cultural Rights has adopted two General Comments on the right to education: General Comment 11 on plans of action for primary education and General Comment 13 on the right to education. In General Comment 11, the Committee notes that education can be classified as an economic right, a social right, and a cultural right, but in many ways it is also a civil and political right, "since it is central to the full and effective realization of those rights as well."[459] It epitomizes the indivisibility and interdependence of all human rights.

The Committee notes that many factors have made it difficult for States parties to fulfill their obligation to provide a plan of action pursuant to Article 14 of the Covenant, including the structural adjustment programs that began in the 1970s, the debt crises that followed in the 1980s, and the financial crises of the late 1990s. Those difficulties do not relieve States parties from their obligation to adopt and submit a plan of action to the Committee. The plans of action are especially important because the lack of educational opportunities for children often reinforces the violation of other rights.

The Committee in General Comment 11 asks that States parties include information in their periodic reports on the following elements: compulsory and free of charge education as well as adoption of the plan of action within two years of ratification of the Covenant. In General Comment 13, the Committee explains and expands upon the requirements of Article 13 of the Covenant. It begins by noting that education is a right in itself but also an indispensable means of realizing other rights. It is not only a tool for empowerment of marginalized adults and children, but is one of the "joys and rewards of human existence."[460] Hence, Article 13 is the longest provision in the Covenant and must also be considered in conjunction with Article 14, as well as the fundamental purposes and principles of the United Nations as enshrined in Articles 1 and 2 of the UN Charter,[461] the Universal Declaration,[462] the Convention on the Rights of the Child,[463] the World Declaration on Education for All,[464] the Vienna Declaration and Programme of Action,[465] and the Plan of Action for the United Nations Decade for Human Rights Education, which add references to gender equality and respect for the environment.

As with the other rights, the Committee identifies essential features of the right with respect to accessibility, including nondiscrimination, physical accessibility, and economic accessibility; acceptability; and adaptability. The Committee also refers to basic learning needs as defined in the World Declaration on Education for All as: "essential learning tools (such as literacy, oral expression, numeracy, and problem solving) and the basic learning content (such as knowledge, skills, values, and attitudes) required by human beings to be able to survive, to develop their full capacities, to live and work in dignity, to participate fully in development, to improve the quality of their lives, to make informed decisions, and to continue learning." General Comment 13 also emphasizes the requirement that primary education is "compulsory" and "available free to all."

With respect to secondary education, General Comment 13 notes that the term "in its different forms" recognizes the need for flexible curricula and varied delivery systems to respond to different social and cultural settings.[466] The phrase "generally available" means that it is not dependent on the student's capacity or ability and that it should be available on the same basis to all. While the States parties must prioritize elementary education, they still have an obligation to take steps to achieving free secondary and higher education.

Technical and vocational education (TVE) is a part of both the right to education and the right to work. The Committee notes the interrelationship with the provisions of Article 13, which presents TVE as part of secondary education, and Article 6 as part of the means for achieving "steady economic, social and cultural development and full and productive employment."[467] In addition, TVE is mentioned in the Universal Declaration, the UNESCO Convention on Technical and Vocational Education, and ILO Conventions and thus the Committee concludes that it is an integral element of all levels of education. Hence, the Committee identifies the various aspects of TVE as including enablement of personal development; taking into account differences in the educational, social, and cultural background of the population; training for adults to learn about changes in technology, employment, and the like; programs to give students, especially in developing countries, the opportunity to receive appropriate transfer and adaptation of technology; and nondiscrimination and equality for disadvantaged groups.

Regarding higher education, the Committee notes that both secondary education and higher education should be available in "different forms," including TVE. Higher education shall be "equally accessible to all, on the basis of capacity."[468] The Committee determines that "capacity" should be assessed as to relevant expertise and experience.

In developing systems of schools at all levels, the Committee notes the right of teachers to organize and bargain collectively and draws attention to UNESCO and ILO recommendations in this regard. The Committee also expands on the rights of parents to ensure the religious and moral education of their children and thus subjects such as general history of religion and ethics must be taught in an unbiased and objective way, respectful of the freedoms of opinion, conscience, and expression. Public schools that include instruction in religion is inconsistent with the Covenant unless provision is made for nondiscriminatory exemptions or alternatives that would accommodate the wishes of parents and guardians. With regard to the right of parents and guardians to choose non-public schools for their children, the Committee emphasizes that such schools must comply with minimum educational standards set down by the State and should not lead to extreme disparities of educational opportunity for some groups in society.

The Committee addresses nondiscrimination and equal treatment, academic freedom and institutional autonomy, discipline in schools, and other topics. With respect to the first, the Committee notes that special measures (known in the United States and some other countries as affirmative action or positive discrimination measures) designed to bring about actual equality between various groups in society, such as men and women, is not a violation of the right to nondiscrimination as long as they do not lead to the maintenance of unequal or separate standards for the different groups and they are not continued after the objectives are achieved. Also, sharp disparities in spending that result in different qualities of education for persons residing in different geographical locations may constitute discrimination.

With respect to the second topic, the right to education can be enjoyed only if the staff and students have academic freedom, which includes freedom of expression and freedom from fear of retaliation for expressing one's views. It also requires the autonomy of institutions of higher education as well as accountability. The Committee determines that corporal punishment in the schools is inconsistent with various provisions of the Covenants and the Universal Declaration. Public humiliation and the denial of the right to food are also incompatible and the Committee urges States parties to encourage the schools to use positive, nonviolent approaches to discipline.

The right to education is enshrined in other international treaties. The International Convention on the Elimination of All Forms of Racial Discrimination requires in Article 5 that States parties agree to prohibit and eliminate discrimination and to equality before the law in the enjoyment of the right to education and training.[469] The Women's Convention in Article 10 provides that States parties shall take measures to eliminate discrimination and ensure education on the basis of equality for men and women in career and vocational guidance; access to the same curricula, examinations, and teachers; the elimination of stereotyped roles; scholarships and grants; adult and continuing education which should be aimed at reducing any gaps between men and women; the reduction of dropout rates; the opportunities to participate in sports and physical education; and access to information to ensure the health and well-being of families, including advice on family planning.[470]

The Convention on the Rights of the Child has two articles that address the right to education. Article 28 lists various factors for achieving the right to education progressively on the basis of equal opportunity: that it be compulsory and free; that secondary education include different forms, including general and vocational, and that measures be undertaken to make it free; that higher education be accessible on the basis of capacity; that educational and vocational information and guidance be available to all children; and that measures be taken to encourage regular attendance and reduce dropout rates. In Article 29, States parties agree that education shall be directed to the development of the child's personality, talents, and mental and physical abilities to their fullest potential; the development of respect for human rights and fundamental freedoms; the development of respect for the child's parents, cultural identity, language, and values, for the national values of the countries where he or she is living or is from, and for different civilizations; the preparation of the child for responsible life in a free society; and development of respect for the environment.[471]

The International Convention on the Protection of the Rights of All Migrant Workers and Their Families provides that States parties shall respect the right of parents who are migrant workers to ensure the religious and moral education of their children in conformity with their own convictions. The Convention also assures that "each child of a migrant worker shall have the basic right of access to education on the basis of equality of treatment with nationals" and access "to public preschool educational institutions or schools shall not be refused or limited by reason of the irregular situation" of the child or parent.[472]

All major regional systems recognize the right to education. For example, the Charter of the Organization of American States provides in Article 34 that one of its basic goals is to eradicate illiteracy rapidly and expand educational opportunities for all.[473] Further, Articles 47–52 refer to various aspects of the right to education including development plans that encourage inclusion of education, efforts to guarantee free and compulsory primary education, progressive extension of middle education to as much of the population as possible, and higher education available to all who meet academic standards. The American Convention on Human Rights in Article 26 refers to progressive realization of the education standards set forth in the Charter.[474] The American Declaration of the Rights and Duties of Man provides in Article XII that "Every person has the right to an education, which should be based on the principles of liberty, morality, and human solidarity."[475] The Protocol of San Salvador defines the right to education in great detail in Article 13, including for special education and training for handicapped persons or those with physical or mental disabilities.[476] It also provides for the rights of parents to select the type of education for their children and the right of individuals and entities to establish educational institutions in accordance with the law.

The African Charter on Human and Peoples' Rights provides for the right to education in Article 17.[477] Two major instruments provide for the right to education in the European system. Protocol No. 1 to the [European] Convention for the Protection of Human Rights provides that "No person shall be denied the right to education" and ensures respect for the right of parents to ensure education in conformity with their own religious and philosophical convictions.[478] Education is also mentioned in various articles of the European Social Charter with regard to the employment of children, vocational guidance and training, and training for disabled persons.[479]

The primary international institution concerned about education, the UN Educational, Scientific, and Cultural Organization (UNESCO), has estimated that there are 680 million children enrolled in primary schools, but more than 130 million children, including about sixty-five million girls, have no access to primary schooling. In some countries, such as Nepal and Oman, the government has ratified the Convention on the Rights of the Child guaranteeing free and compulsory primary education, but primary education is not, in fact, compulsory. In other countries, such as Bhutan and Vanuatu, primary education is not compulsory and there is a considerable gender gap between boys and girls in attendance. In other countries, such as Cameroon and Indonesia, primary education is not free. In Zambia primary education is neither free nor compulsory.

Even in countries in which there are legal protections for free and compulsory primary education, children are practically deterred from attending school. Many children in Morocco, for example, lack shoes, uniform, school books, school supplies, transportation, or other requirements to attend. Children—particularly girls—are often required to work rather than attend school. In some countries, such as Côte d'Ivoire, there is a high incidence of domestic abuse, including sexual abuse, and neglect of children; insufficient efforts have been made to protect children; there is accordingly a high rate of primary and secondary school dropout. In Guatemala only 30 percent of children living in rural communities and 20 percent of indigenous children complete primary education; indigenous children do not enjoy education in their mother tongue.

Without education these children will be condemned to lives of poverty and deprivation. The level of literacy and education in a country are also primary determinants of the economic development and prosperity of the nation. It has been estimated that assuring universal primary education in the world would cost only about eight million dollars above present expenditures, that is, about the same amount spent in four days by the military around the world or less than Europeans spend on computer games.

UNESCO is a specialized agency of the United Nations which, among other things, promotes education as a fundamental right, seeks to improve the quality of education, and promotes educational innovation.[480] The United Nations International Children's Emergency Fund (UNICEF) focuses particularly on encouraging the education of girls.[481] The International Labor Organization (ILO) works to end child labor, because there are estimated to be more than 246 million child laborers between the ages of five and seventeen in the world—many of whom do not go to school.[482] The ILO monitors compliance with the ILO Convention (No. 138) on Minimum Age for Admission to Employment (1973) and the ILO Convention (No. 182) concerning the Prohibition and Immediate Action for the Elimination of the Worst Forms of Child Labor (1999).[483] The ILO also manages the International Programme on the Elimination of Child Labor (IPEC), which focuses on bonded child laborers, children in hazardous working conditions and occupations, and children who are particularly vulnerable, such as very young working children (under age twelve), and working girls. IPEC has projects to end child labor and return children to school in Bangladesh, Brazil, Cambodia, Costa Rica, El Salvador, India, Kenya, Nepal, Nicaragua, Pakistan, Tanzania, Thailand, Turkey, and other countries.

The UN Commission on Human Rights in 1998 established a Special Rapporteur on the right to education to make recommendations on appropriate measures to promote and protect the realization of the right to education based on information from relevant sources, and to intensify efforts aimed at identifying ways and means to overcome obstacles and difficulties in the realization of the right to education.[484] The Special Rapporteur is also mandated to apply a gender perspective in his work and to present proposals and recommendations to the Commission (now the Human Rights Council) each year. The Special Rapporteur has visited and reported on China, Colombia, Indonesia, Turkey, Uganda, the United Kingdom, and the United States.

*See also*: Economic, Social, and Cultural Rights, ILO, UNESCO

*Further Reading*:

Committee on Economic, Social and Cultural Rights, General Comment 11, Plans of Action for Primary Education (Twentieth session, 1999), U.N. Doc. E/C.12/1999/4 (1999).

176   Particular Rights and Responsibilities

Committee on Economic, Social and Cultural Rights, General Comment 13, the Right to Education (Twenty-first session, 1999), U.N. Doc. E/C.12/1999/10 (1999).
Committee on the Rights of the Child, General Comment No. 1, The Aims of Education, U.N. Doc. CRC/GC/2001/1 (2001).
Convention Against Discrimination in Education, 429 U.N.T.S. 93 *entered into force* May 22, 1962.
Convention Concerning the Prohibition and Immediate Action for the Elimination of the Worst Forms of Child Labor (ILO No. 182), 38 I.L.M. 1207 (1999), *entered into force* Nov. 19, 2000.
Douglas Hodgson, The Human Right to Education (1998).
Convention on Technical and Vocational Education, *entered into force* Aug. 29, 1991, *reprinted in* 37 Select Documents on International Affairs 11 (1989).
Connie de la Vega, *The Right to Equal Education: Merely a Guiding Principle or Customary International Legal Rights?* 11 BlackLetter Law Journal 37 (1994).
Education for All: Meeting Our Collective Commitments, Adopted by the World Education Forum, Dakar, Senegal, Apr. 26–28, 2000.
Human Rights and Education (Norma Bernstein Tarrow ed., 1987).
Joel Spring, The Universal Right to Education: Justification, Definition and Guidelines (2000).
Katarina Tomaevski, Education Denied: Costs and Remedies (2003).
Understanding Human Rights, Manual on Human Rights Education (Wolfgang Benedek and Minna Nikolova eds., 2003).
University of Minnesota Human Rights Center, This Is My Home: A Minnesota Human Rights Education Experience (2005).
World Declaration on Education for All, World Conference on Education for All, Jomtien, Thailand, Mar. 5–9, 1990.

*Links to Consult*:

http://portal.unesco.org/
http://www.hrusa.org/thisismyhome
http://www.ilo.org
http://www.ilo.org/public/english/standards/ipec/index.htm
http://www.right-to-education.org
http://www.ohchr.org/english/issues/education/rapporteur/
http://www.unesco.org/education/efa/ed_for_all/background/jomtien_declaration.shtml
http://www.unesco.org/education/efa/ed_for_all/dakfram_eng.shtml
http://www.unevoc.unesco.org/convention/
http://www.unhchr.ch/education/main.htm
http://www.unhchr.ch/html/menu2/i2ecored.htm
http://www.unicef.org/
http://www1.umn.edu/humanrts/crc/bhutan2001.html
http://www1.umn.edu/humanrts/crc/comment1.htm
http://www1.umn.edu/humanrts/crc/indonesia2004.html
http://www1.umn.edu/humanrts/crc/morocco2003.html
http://www1.umn.edu/humanrts/crc/crc-Nepal96.htm
http://www1.umn.edu/humanrts/crc/oman2001.html
http://www1.umn.edu/humanrts/crc/vanuatu1999.html
http://www1.umn.edu/humanrts/crc/zambia2003.html

http://www1.umn.edu/humanrts/edumat/IHRIP/circle/modules/
 module16.htm
http://www1.umn.edu/humanrts/edumat/introduction.shtm
http://www1.umn.edu/humanrts/esc/cameroon1999.html

i. CULTURE (UNIVERSAL DECLARATION, ART. 27)

Cultural rights are among the least understood and developed of the rights that have been guaranteed by international human rights law. In part, the complexity arises from the many definitions of "culture." Nonetheless, the Universal Declaration, the two Human Rights Covenants, and other human rights treaties recognize the right to culture, including everyone's right to take part in cultural life, to enjoy the benefits of scientific progress, and to develop international contacts and cooperation in the area of science and culture.

*i. International Principles That Protect the Right to Culture*

There are several references to culture in the International Bill of Human Rights. Article 27 of the Universal Declaration guarantees that

Everyone has the right freely to participate in the cultural life of the community, to enjoy the arts and to share in scientific advancement and its benefits. . . . Everyone has the right to the protection of the moral and material interests resulting from any scientific, literary or artistic production of which he is the author.[485]

Article 15 of the Covenant on Economic, Social and Cultural Rights elaborates on the right to culture in treaty language by stating that

The States Parties to the present Covenant recognize the right of everyone . . . [t]o take part in cultural life . . . [t]o benefit from the protection of the moral and material interests resulting from any scientific, literary or artistic production of which he is the author . . . The steps to be taken by the States Parties to the present Covenant to achieve the full realization of this right shall include those necessary for the conservation, the development and the diffusion of science and culture.[486]

Articles 1 of both the Covenant on Economic, Social and Cultural Rights and the Covenant on Civil and Political Rights guarantee the right to self-determination and the right of peoples to their respective cultures:

All peoples have the right of self-determination. By virtue of that right they freely determine their political status and freely pursue their economic, social and cultural development . . . All peoples may, for their own ends, freely dispose of their natural wealth and resources without prejudice to any obligations arising out of international economic co-operation, based upon the principle of mutual benefit, and international law. In no case may a people be deprived of its own means of subsistence.[487]

In addition, Article 27 of the Civil and Political Covenant provides cultural rights for minorities:

> In those States in which ethnic, religious or linguistic minorities exist, persons belonging to such minorities shall not be denied the right, in community with the other members of their group, to enjoy their own culture, to profess and practise their own religion, or to use their own language.[488]

The Human Rights Committee, in its 1994 General Comment that elaborated on minority rights guaranteed by Article 27 of the Covenant, stated that

> With regard to the exercise of the cultural rights protected under article 27, the Committee observes that culture manifests itself in many forms, including a particular way of life associated with the use of land resources, especially in the case of indigenous peoples. That right may include such traditional activities as fishing or hunting and the right to live in reserves protected by law. The enjoyment of those rights may require positive legal measures of protection and measures to ensure the effective participation of members of minority communities in decisions which affect them. . . . The protection of these rights is directed towards ensuring the survival and continued development of the cultural, religious and social identity of the minorities concerned, thus enriching the fabric of society as a whole.[489]

Although the Convention on the Elimination of All Forms of Racial Discrimination does not specifically protect the right to culture, the Convention requires that "States Parties undertake to prohibit and to eliminate racial discrimination in all its forms and to guarantee the right of everyone, without distinction as to race, colour, or national or ethnic origin, to equality before the law."[490] The Committee on the Elimination of Racial Discrimination has taken a particular interest in the situation of indigenous peoples in its 1997 General Recommendation calling upon States parties to "provide indigenous peoples with conditions allowing for a sustainable economic and social development compatible with their cultural characteristics," including the right to full participation in public life; the right to practice cultural traditions, customs, and languages; and the rights of indigenous peoples to "own, develop, control and use their communal lands, territories and resources and, where they have been deprived of their lands and territories traditionally owned or otherwise inhabited or used without their free and informed consent, to take steps to return those lands and territories."[491]

Article 30 of the Convention on the Rights of the Child protects the right to culture not only for indigenous children but also others:

Economic, Social, and Cultural Rights    179

In those States in which ethnic, religious or linguistic minorities or persons of indigenous origin exist, a child belonging to such a minority or who is indigenous shall not be denied the right, in community with other members of his or her group, to enjoy his or her own culture, to profess and practise his or her own religion, or to use his or her own language.[492]

Article 2 of the Convention on the Prevention and Punishment of the Crime of Genocide has been interpreted to forbid the deliberate destruction of a people and thus their culture. In addition, the UN Educational, Scientific and Cultural Organization (UNESCO) in 2001 adopted the Universal Declaration on Cultural Diversity. Article 5 of the Declaration affirms:

All persons have therefore the right to express themselves and to create and disseminate their work in the language of their choice, and particularly in their mother tongue; all persons are entitled to quality education and training that fully respect their cultural identity; and all persons have the right to participate in the cultural life of their choice and conduct their own cultural practices, subject to respect for human rights and fundamental freedoms.[493]

The Declaration additionally elaborates on the interrelated nature of cultural diversity and other human rights, especially those rights pertaining to equal access of information and expression:

Freedom of expression, media pluralism, multilingualism, equal access to art and to scientific and technological knowledge, including in digital form, and the possibility for all cultures to have access to the means of expression and dissemination are the guarantees of cultural diversity.[494]

The Declaration was derived from a number of earlier attempts to define and protect cultural rights, including the UNESCO Principles on International Cultural Cooperation of 1966; the Declaration of Principles on International Cultural Cooperation of 1966; the Convention on the Means of Prohibiting and Preventing the Illicit Import, Export and Transfer of Ownership of Cultural Property of 1970; the Convention for the Protection of World Cultural and Natural Heritage of 1972; and the Recommendation on Safeguarding Traditional and Popular Culture of 1989. Each of these instruments promoted the principles (1) that each culture has a dignity and value which must be protected and preserved; (2) that every people has the right and duty to develop its culture; (3) and that all cultures form part of the common heritage belonging to all mankind.

The right to culture was also articulated in the declarations produced at several world conferences. The Mexico City Declaration on Cultural Policies of 1982 states that "The assertion of cultural identity . . . contributes to the liberation of peoples. Conversely, any form of domination constitutes a denial or an impairment of that identity."[495] The Vienna Declaration and Programme of Action of 1993 states that

All human rights are universal, indivisible and interdependent and interrelated. The international community must treat human rights globally in a fair and equal manner, on the same footing, and with the same emphasis. While the significance of national and regional particularities and various historical, cultural and religious backgrounds must be borne in mind, it is the duty of States, regardless of their political, economic and cultural systems, to promote and protect all human rights and fundamental freedoms.[496]

In addition, the Vienna Declaration emphasizes the equal status of women in the context of traditional cultures:

the World Conference stresses the importance of working towards . . . the eradication of any conflicts which may arise between the rights of women and the harmful effects of certain traditional or customary practices, cultural prejudices and religious extremism. . . .[497]

There have been several regional human rights treaties that contain provisions on the right to culture. Article 17 of the African Charter on Human and Peoples' Rights states that "Every individual may freely, take part in the cultural life of his community" and that "the promotion and protection of morals and traditional values recognized by the community shall be the duty of the State."[498] In addition, Article 20 of the African Charter recognizes the right of peoples to self-determination and the related right to be free from domination: "All peoples shall have the right to the assistance of the States parties to the present Charter in their liberation struggle against foreign domination, be it political, economic or cultural."[499] Further, Article 22 of the African Charter promises all persons the right to their "economic, social and cultural development with due regard to their freedom and identity and in the equal enjoyment of the common heritage of mankind."[500]

Article 14 of the Additional Protocol to the American Convention on Human Rights in the Area of Economic, Social and Cultural Rights (Protocol of San Salvador) contains one of the narrowest descriptions of the right to benefit from culture, including the right to take part in the cultural and artistic life of the community, the right to enjoy the benefits of scientific and technological progress, and the right to benefit from the protection of moral and material interests deriving from any scientific, literary or artistic production of which she or he is the author. The Protocol also requires States parties to respect "the freedom indispensable for scientific research and creative activity" and to "recognize the benefits to be derived from the encouragement and development of international cooperation and relations in the fields of science, arts and culture, and accordingly agree to foster greater international cooperation in these fields."[501]

*ii. Problems That Arise Regarding the Right to Culture*

Cultural rights demonstrate the interdependence and indivisibility of all human rights. For example, the freedom to think within a cultural framework is protected by the freedom of conscience and opinion. The freedom of religion protects the rights to believe and practice the religion of one's choice. Further, the freedom to express one's culture publicly is protected by the right to political participation as well as the freedoms of expression, assembly, and association. At the same time, cultural rights often exist in juxtaposition with other human rights. Women's rights, intellectual property rights, and the rights of indigenous peoples are several areas in which the right to culture sometimes conflicts with other interests and rights.

Culture may be understood as the customary beliefs and social norms of an ethnic, religious, or social group. Certain cultural practices contradict international human rights standards. For example, cultural practices in many countries violate the dignity and integrity of women. Female genital mutilation (FGM) or female genital cutting (FGC)—the removal of part or all of the external female genitalia—has been identified as a cultural practice that is physically and psychologically harmful to women. FGM is practiced in twenty-eight countries in Africa, some Arab countries, in parts of Asia, and has been practiced among migrant populations in Australia, Europe, and North America. The procedure is practiced by some Muslims, some Christians, some Ethiopian Jews, and within other African religions on the pretext of cultural tradition or hygiene. Some Muslims believe that Islam requires FGM, although FGM is not practiced in many Muslim countries. Supporters of FGM have explained this cultural practice as necessary for preservation of virginity, marital fidelity, family honor, protection from rape, cleanliness, beauty, and increased fertility. Many women choose to undergo FGM because they believe they will not be marriageable without the procedure. FGM has been condemned by the World Health Organization (WHO) as well as the UN Declaration on the Elimination of Violence Against Women.[502]

Other cultural practices that violate women's human rights include forced or child marriages; honor killings; denial of access to education; deprivation of food in preference of males; female infanticide; inaccessibility of health services; and discriminatory laws that prohibit women from participating in government, inheriting, and owning property. Groups or individuals who defend certain cultural practices may argue that the right of peoples to enjoy their own culture trumps the conflicting universal human rights enshrined in the treaties. These arguments of "cultural specificity" or "cultural relativism" contend that extracultural standards of moral judgments are not possible, and that moral judgments can only be determined through the standards of a culture's perspectives. Universal women's rights are thus labeled extracultural standards (and often as Western standards), as opposed to the cultural norms and practices—however harmful their effects on women—that have been traditionally accepted by a culture as "values."

Human rights advocates have responded to arguments based on cultural relativism by pointing out that cultural practices may not reflect everyone within a cultural group, but only a dominant sector. Further, cultural practices do change and cannot be considered to be permanent. In addition, there is a danger of using culture in such a way as to glorify some aspects (and conveniently ignore others), thereby justifying the denial of fundamental human rights.

In such contexts the right to cultural preservation may conflict with other rights, such as the right to freedom of expression or to manifest one's religious belief. As with all potential conflicts among international legal principles, one must first try to avoid any conflict by interpreting those principles so that they do not impinge upon one another. For example, a societal interest in worker safety may conflict with a Jewish or Sikh worker's wish to wear a large hat or turban in a factory. Article 18 of the Civil and Political Covenant states that "freedom to manifest one's religion or beliefs may be subject only to such limitations as are prescribed by law and are necessary to protect public safety, order, health, or morals or the fundamental rights and freedoms of others."[503] These two concerns—worker health/safety and manifestation of religious belief—can both be respected if the factory allows smaller head coverings. If it is not possible to avoid a direct conflict, one must inquire as to whether one principle should prevail over another. While there is, in general, no hierarchy among various rights, it is generally thought that non-derogable rights (rights that cannot be the subject of exception even in times of emergency) should be given preference over other rights in the case of direct conflict. Non-derogable rights are specified in Article 4 of the Covenant on Civil and Political Rights, and include the right to be free from discrimination, along with the right to be free from torture and arbitrary killing. Accordingly, if there is a conflict between religious rights and the right to be free from racial or gender discrimination, the right to avoid discrimination should prevail. For example, if a government imposes a duty on women to cover themselves with the burka and some women object on the ground of gender discrimination, this cultural/religious conflict should be resolved in favor of the nondiscrimination principle.

The realization of cultural rights is also problematic within the context of intellectual property protection schemes. Article 15 of the Covenant on Economic, Social and Cultural Rights recognizes "the right of everyone . . . to [both] enjoy the benefits of scientific progress and its applications," on the one hand, and to "benefit from the protection of the moral and material interests resulting from any scientific, literary or artistic production of which he is the author," on the other.[504] Hence, international human rights law recognizes the rights of inventors and authors while simultaneously focusing on the public right to benefit from their inventions and works of art. Article 15 does not, however, indicate how a balance may be struck among the creators, the economic interests that acquire their intellectual property, and the beneficiaries of creativity.

In 2000 the UN Sub-Commission on the Promotion and Protection of Human Rights adopted a resolution that expressed a fundamental concern that the Agreement on Trade-Related Aspects of Intellectual Property (TRIPS) did not adequately recognize human rights norms, particularly economic, social, and cultural rights:

actual or potential conflicts exist between the implementation of the TRIPS Agreement and the realization of economic, social and cultural rights in relation to, *inter alia*, impediments to the transfer of technology to developing countries, the consequences for the enjoyment of the right to food, or plant variety rights and the patenting of genetically modified organisms, "bio-piracy" and the reduction of communities' (especially indigenous communities') control over their own genetic and natural resources and cultural values, and restrictions on access to patented pharmaceuticals and the implications for the enjoyment of the right to health. . . .[505]

TRIPS was a product of the Uruguay Round of the General Agreement on Tariffs and Trade (GATT) held in 1994.[506] Broadly speaking, TRIPS extended intellectual property rights by creating a new World Trade Organization (WTO) enforcement mechanism with the availability of reciprocal trade sanctions. TRIPS requires that WTO states protect intellectual property by enacting national legislation and regulatory procedures.

There are several provisions of TRIPS that reveal a fundamental tension between the interests of intellectual property holders, on the one hand, and state and public interests in promoting public health and economic development, on the other. For example, Article 7 of TRIPS notes that "protection and enforcement of intellectual property rights should contribute to the promotion of technological innovation," yet should do so "in a manner conducive to social and economic welfare."[507] Article 8, however, explicitly mentions that WTO states may take into account the "protect[ion] of public health and nutrition, and promot[ion of] the public interest in sectors of vital importance to their socioeconomic and technological development" when tailoring their intellectual property regimes to the norms mandated by TRIPS.[508] Both of these general intellectual property provisions give a government wide authority to resolve any potential conflicts between intellectual property interests and other human rights concerns.

The TRIPS copyright provisions focus on rights involving computer programs, cinematographic works, sound recordings, and broadcasting. These protections are more valuable to copyright holders in developed nations than to literary and artistic creators seeking to protect traditional knowledge and indigenous cultural rights. The TRIPS refusal to recognize moral rights of authors partially explains why some indigenous artists have difficulty in protecting their creations from undesirable modifications or uses. In addition, differing conceptions of the desirability of claiming exclusive rights often underlie the inadequacy of protection. In their report submitted to the UN Sub-Commission on the Promotion and Protection of Human Rights, the Special Rapporteurs on globalization and its impact on the full enjoyment of human rights characterized the TRIPS guarantee of the patentability of plant varieties and life forms as a "legal act of economic hijack." Furthermore, the Special Rapporteurs recommended that if the WTO really wanted to commit to a balanced trade liberalization scheme, it "must not only include intellectual property protections of interest to the developed countries, but also address issues of current or potential concern for developing countries, such as property rights for knowledge embedded in traditional medicines, or the pricing of pharmaceuticals in developing country markets."

There have been several instances of indigenous cultures clashing with intellectual property regimes. One case that has received a fair amount of publicity is related to the validity of a patent on an extract from the oil of an Asian tree. The neem tree is indigenous to the Indian subcontinent, and neem bark has been used for centuries as a traditional medicine, insecticide and fungicide. The pharmaceutical manufacturer W.R. Grace Co. initially obtained a patent from the European Patent Office (EPO) on the fungicidal properties of a neem oil extract, and then tried to sell the patented product on the Indian market. Upon appeal by the Green Party of the European Parliament and an Indian nongovernmental organization, the EPO revoked the patent on the grounds that it did not qualify as a novel invention, in light of the traditional use of neem bark in Indian society. The EPO's revocation of a patent on neem tree oil extract was a rare victory for traditional scientific knowledge over modern patent schemes.[509]

While the neem tree case demonstrates the occasional conflict between the cultural rights of indigenous peoples and intellectual property regimes, human rights advocates have argued for decades that the process of globalization in general endangers the cultural rights and interests of indigenous peoples.

An estimated 300 million indigenous persons live in the world today. Indigenous populations include the Indians of South and Central America and the United States; the First Nations of Canada; the Aborigines of Australia; the Maori of New Zealand; the Sami of Scandinavia; and the Inuit of the far north of Canada, Greenland, and Russia. Historically, the cultural rights of indigenous peoples have often come into conflict with neighboring communities, especially regarding their rights to possess and use traditional lands, control their lives, enforce treaties that have been made in the past, pursue their religious practices, and resist encroachments.

The Committee on Economic, Social and Cultural Rights has frequently expressed concern over the conflicts between indigenous persons' right to culture and states' protection of the majority culture. In comments on reports submitted by Argentina, Australia, Colombia, Guatemala, Honduras, Israel, New Zealand, and Russia, the Committee noted that many indigenous persons are denied their economic, social, and cultural rights, including the means of subsistence and respect for indigenous languages and cultures.[510] The Committee's General Comment 17 calls for protecting the "knowledge, innovations and practices of indigenous and local communities."[511]

The International Bill of Human Rights and the Convention on the Elimination of All Forms of Racial Discrimination forbid discrimination on the grounds of "race, colour, sex, language, religion, political or other opinion, national or social origin, property, birth or others status," which could be construed to include indigenous persons. In addition, the Convention on the Rights of the Child mentions the rights of indigenous children in Articles 17, 29, and 30. There have been several cases adjudicated by the Human Rights Committee under Article 27 (minority rights) of the Civil and Political Covenant, specifically regarding the rights of the Sami people—in accordance with their cultural traditions—to raise reindeer in Sweden and Finland (*Kitok v. Sweden*[512] and *Lansman v. Finland*[513]). In both cases, the Human Rights Committee balanced the rights of the indigenous Sami people with the rights of the dominant government, arguably demonstrating the inadequacy of a minority rights framework for protecting indigenous lands and other cultural rights.

186   Particular Rights and Responsibilities

The UN, while giving considerable visibility to indigenous issues, was rather slow in adopting international standards for the protection of indigenous cultures. The Declaration on the Rights of Indigenous Peoples is an attempt to protect the integrity of indigenous peoples and cultures through protections against land dispossession, population transfers, propaganda, and cultural assimilation.[514] The Declaration was in the process of preparation by the UN Working Group on Indigenous Populations from 1985 and was submitted to the Commission on Human Rights in 1994. It was finally adopted by the newly created Human Rights Council in June 2006. The delay in adoption was principally the result of disagreements between states and indigenous representatives over the clauses relating to self-determination and the definition of indigenous.

In addition to the UN's attention to the cultural rights of indigenous peoples, the Inter-American Court of Human Rights and the Inter-American Commission on Human Rights within the Organization of American States (OAS) have interpreted the American Convention on Human Rights so as to recognize indigenous rights to their lands and culture. Indigenous communities generally hold their lands in common and embrace their lands as a fundamental aspect of their religious and cultural identity. The OAS is engaged in drafting the American Declaration on the Rights of Indigenous Peoples, which includes protections for indigenous lands and cultural integrity. Furthermore, in 2001 the Inter-American Court found in *The Mayagna (Sumo) Awas Tingni Community v. Nicaragua* that Nicaragua had violated the right of the Awas Tingni people under the American Convention to judicial protection (Article 25) and to property (Article 21), specifically holding that indigenous peoples possess collective rights to the lands and natural resources they have traditionally occupied and used.[515] In 2002 the Inter-American Commission on Human Rights found in *Mary and Carrie Dann v. United States* that the Indian Claims Commission, a quasi-judicial organ established by the U.S. Congress to resolve Native American land claims, had improperly determined the Danns' claim since the tribe, despite efforts to intervene, was not allowed to participate in the resolution of the claim. Accordingly, the Commission found a violation of Articles 2 (right to equality before the law), 18 (right to a fair trial), and 23 (right to property) of the American Declaration of the Rights and Duties of Man.[516] The United States has refused to comply with the findings of the Commission.

*See also*: Clothing, Self-Determination

*Further Reading*:

Additional Protocol to the American Convention on Human Rights in the Area of Economic, Social and Cultural Rights, "Protocol of San Salvador," O.A.S.

Treaty Series No. 69 (1988), *entered into force* November 16, 1999, *reprinted in* Basic Documents Pertaining to Human Rights in the Inter-American System, OEA/Ser.L.V/II.82 doc.6 rev.1 at 67 (1992).

African Charter on Human and Peoples' Rights, adopted June 27, 1981, OAU Doc. CAB/LEG/67/3 rev. 5, 21 I.L.M. 58 (1982), *entered into force* Oct. 21, 1986.

Agreement on Trade-Related Aspects of Intellectual Property Rights, Apr, 15, 1994, Marrakesh Agreement Establishing the World Trade Organization, Annex 1C, Legal Instruments-Results of the Uruguay Round vol. 31, 33 I.L.M. 81 (1994).

Committee on Economic, Social and Cultural Rights, General Comment 17, The Right of Everyone to Benefit from the Protection of the Moral and Material Interests Resulting from Any Scientific, Literary or Artistic Production of Which He or She is the Author (article 15, paragraph 1 (c), of the Covenant), U.N. Doc. E/C.12/GC/17 (2006).

Committee on the Elimination of Racial Discrimination, General Recommendation 23, Rights of Indigenous Peoples (Fifty-first session, 1997), U.N. Doc. A/52/18, annex V at 122 (1997).

Convention for the Protection of World Cultural and Natural Heritage, Nov. 13, 1972, 27 U.S.T. 37, 1037 U.N.T.S. 151.

Convention on the Means of Prohibiting and Preventing the Illicit Import, Export and Transfer of Ownership of Cultural Property [UNESCO], Nov. 14, 1970, 823 U.N.T.S. 231, 10 I.L.M. 289.

*Mary and Carrie Dann v. United States*, Case 11.140, Report No. 75/02, Inter-Am. C.H.R., Doc. 5 rev 1 at 860 (2002).

Convention on the Prevention and Punishment of the Crime of Genocide, 78 U.N.T.S. 277, *entered into force* Jan. 12, 1951.

Declaration of the Principles of International Cultural Cooperation, U.N. Educational, Scientific and Cultural Organization, UNESCO Doc. 14C/8.I., 14th Sess. (1966), *reprinted in* U.N. Doc. ST/HR/1/rev.4, Sales No. E.93. XIV.1 (1993), vol. 1, pt. 2, at 591.

Declaration on Race and Racial Prejudice, UNESCO Gen. Conf. Res. 20 C/Res.3/1.1/2, 20th Sess. (1978), U.N. Doc. E/CN.4/Sub.2/1982/2/Add.1, annex V (1982).

*Human Rights and Intellectual Property: Statement of the Committee on Economic, Social and Cultural Rights*, Comm. on Econ., Social and Cultural Rights, 27th Sess., Agenda item 3, U.N. Doc. E/C.12/2001/15 (2001).

Human Rights Committee, General Comment 23, Article 27 (Fiftieth session, 1994), Compilation of General Comments and General Recommendations Adopted by Human Rights Treaty Bodies, U.N. Doc. HRI/GEN/Rev.1 at 38 (1994).

*Ivan Kitok v. Sweden*, Communication No. 197/1985, U.N. Doc. CCPR/C/33/D/197/1985 (1988).

Gabrielle Marceau, *WTO Dispute Settlement and Human Rights*, Eur. J. Int'l L. 17 (2003).

*The Mayagna (Sumo) Awas Tingni Community v. Nicaragua*, Judgment of August 31, 2001, Inter-Am. Ct. H.R. (Ser. C) No. 79 (2001).

Mexico City Declaration on Cultural Policies, in the final report of World Conference on Cultural Policies, Mexico City, Jul. 26-Aug. 6, 1982, UNESCO Doc. CLT/MD/1 (1982).

J. Oloka-Onyango & Deepika Udagama, *The Realization of Economic, Social and*

188   Particular Rights and Responsibilities

*Cultural Rights: Globalization and its Impact on the Full Enjoyment of Human Rights*, ESCOR, Sub-Comm'n on the Promotion and Protection of Human Rights, 52nd Session, item 4, U.N. Doc. E/CN.4/Sub.2/200/13 (2000).

Prevention of Discrimination and Protection of Indigenous Peoples, Report of the Working Group on Indigenous Populations, U.N. Doc. E/CN.4/Sub.2/2004/28 (2004).

Patrick Thornberry, Indigenous Peoples and Human Rights (2002).

Patrick Thornberry, International Law and the Protection of Minorities (1991).

United Nations Declaration on the Rights of Indigenous Peoples, U.Sn. Doc. A/HRC/1/L,10 at 58 (2006).

Universal Copyright Convention, Sept. 6, 1952, 6 U.S.T. 2731, 216 U.N.T.S. 132, revised by 25 U.S.T. 1341, 943 U.N.T.S. 193 (1971).

Universal Declaration on Cultural Diversity, UNESCO Doc. 31C/Res 25, 31st Sess., Annex 1 (2001).

United Nations Declaration on the Rights of Indigenous Peoples, U.N. ESCOR, Comm. on Human Rights, 11th Sess., Annex 1, U.N. Doc. E/CN.4/Sub.2 (1993).

Vienna Declaration and Programme of Action, World Conference on Human Rights, Vienna, June 14–25, 1993, U.N. Doc. A/CONF.157/24 (Part I) at 20 (1993).

*Links to Consult:*

http://www.indianlaw.org
http://cesr.org/culture
http://portal.unesco.org/
http://www.unesco.org/culture/laws/artist/html_eng/page2.shtml
http://www.unesco.org/culture/laws/paris/html_eng/page1.shtml
http://www.un.org/era/vocdev/unpfii/index.html

## 19. Healthy Environment

The Universal Declaration of Human Rights protects the right to life and the right to a standard of living adequate for health and well-being.[517] From these basic rights can be inferred the right to a healthy environment.

Many national constitutions already contain language recognizing the importance of a healthy environment. For example, the constitutions of Bulgaria (Chapter 2, Article 31), Burkina Faso (Article 30), Chile (Article 19), the Democratic People's Republic of Korea (Chapter 2, Article 35), Ecuador (Article 19), Germany (Article 9), Greece (Article 24), Honduras (Chapter 7, Article 145), India (Article 48 A), the Islamic Republic of Iran (Chapter 4, Article 50), Mozambique (Chapter 4, Article 37), the Netherlands (Article 20), Nicaragua (Article 60), the Russian Federation (Article 49), Spain (Chapter 3, Article 45), Sri Lanka (Chapter 6, Article 27), Thailand (Chapter 5, Article 65), and Turkey (Chapter 8, Article 56) have provisions assuring the protection/preservation of the environment. Some constitutions provide for the right to a healthy environment and others place a duty on the state to conserve the environment.

International interest in the environment arose in the 1960s, particularly as a result of the 1962 publication of Rachel Carson's *Silent Spring*, an exposé on the effects of chemical pollution on the environment and human health. The international community addressed environmental rights for the first time in 1972 at the UN Conference on the Human Environment, which produced the Stockholm Declaration. The issue did not return to the international forum in a meaningful way, however, until the decision was made in 1989 to hold the UN Conference on Environment and Development (UNCED) in Rio de Janeiro during 1992.

In preparation for the Rio conference the UN Sub-Commission on the Prevention of Discrimination and Protection of Minorities selected a Special Rapporteur on human rights and the environment. The General Assembly also adopted a resolution recognizing the "Need to Ensure a Healthy Environment for the Well-being of Individuals" in 1990. The Rio Conference of 1992 then produced the path-breaking Rio Declaration on Environment and Development. The Sub-Commission received the final report of its Special Rapporteur in 1994, which included the Draft Declaration of Principles on Human Rights and the Environment and a recommendation for a Commission on Human Rights thematic rapporteur on human rights and the environment. Neither of those recommendations has been accepted by the Commission, but the Commission in 1995 authorized a Special Rapporteur on the adverse effects of the illicit movement and dumping of toxic and dangerous products and wastes on the enjoyment of human rights.

190   Particular Rights and Responsibilities

The right to a healthy environment has also been considered in regional human rights instruments, such as the African Charter of Human and Peoples' Rights, the Additional Protocol to the American Convention on Human Rights in the Area of Economic, Social and Cultural Rights, Declaration by the European Council on the Environmental Imperative, and the UN Economic Commission for Europe Convention on Access to Information, Public Participation in Decision-Making and Access to Justice in Environmental Matters (the Aarhus Convention) have also sought to address environmental rights.

The Covenant on Civil and Political Rights and the Covenant on Economic, Social and Cultural rights do not contain the right to a healthy environment. Instead, the Civil and Political Covenant guarantees the right to life (Article 6) and the Economic and Social Covenant provides for the right to an "adequate standard of living . . . including . . . the continuous improvement of living conditions" (Article 11) and the right to "the highest attainable standard of physical and mental health" (Article 12).[518] One cannot enjoy these rights in the absence of a healthy environment. The Committee on Economic, Social and Cultural Rights further delineated the right to a healthy environment in its General Comments 14 and 15. In General Comment 14 the Committee elaborated on the right to health (Article 12):

the reference in article 12.1 of the Covenant to "the highest attainable standard of physical and mental health" is not confined to the right to health care. On the contrary, the drafting history and the express wording of article 12.2 acknowledge that the right to health embraces a wide range of socio-economic factors that promote conditions in which people can lead a healthy life, and extends to the underlying determinants of health, such as food and nutrition, housing, access to safe and potable water and adequate sanitation, safe and healthy working conditions, and a healthy environment.[519]

The Committee reasoned further that the right to health should be interpreted

as an inclusive right extending not only to timely and appropriate health care but also to the underlying determinants of health, such as access to safe and potable water and adequate sanitation, an adequate supply of safe food, nutrition and housing, healthy occupational and environmental conditions. . . .[520]

Using a similar approach, the Committee addressed the "underlying determinants" of the right to water in General Comment 15:

Environmental hygiene, as an aspect of the right to health under article 12, paragraph 2(b), of the Covenant, encompasses taking steps on a non-discriminatory basis to prevent threats to health from unsafe and toxic water conditions. . . . [S]tates parties should monitor and combat situations where aquatic eco-systems serve as a habitat for vectors of diseases wherever they pose a risk to human living environments.[521]

While General Comments 14 and 15 address the Economic and Social Covenant, the same reasoning can be used to understand the right to life and other provisions in the Civil and Political Covenant. In 1972 the United Nations Conference on the Human Environment produced the Stockholm Declaration recognizing that "man's environment [is] essential to his well-being and to the enjoyment of basic human rights [such as] the right to life itself."[522] The Declaration clarified that notion with a set of principles, the first of which identified the individual's

> fundamental right to freedom, equality and adequate conditions of life, in an environment of a quality that permits a life of dignity and well-being, and . . . solemn responsibility to protect and improve the environment for present and future generations.[523]

World leaders met again in 1992 at the United Nations Conference on Environment and Development, held in Rio de Janeiro. In preparing for the conference, the General Assembly reaffirmed the principles of the Stockholm Declaration and recognized "that all individuals are entitled to live in an environment adequate for their health and well-being."[524] The Conference produced the Rio Declaration, which sought to build on the Stockholm Declaration and "equitably meet developmental and environmental needs of present and future generations." Like the Stockholm Declaration, the Rio Declaration began by proclaiming that "Human beings are . . . entitled to a healthy and productive life in harmony with nature."[525]

Preparation for the UN Conference on Environment and Development also included the authorization and appointment in 1989 of a Special Rapporteur on Environment and Development by the UN Sub-Commission on the Prevention of Discrimination and Protection of Minorities. The final report of the Special Rapporteur, Ms. Fatma Zohra Ksentini, submitted in 1994, examined the "relationship between human rights and the environment" and included an "analysis of the effects of the environment on the enjoyment of fundamental rights" such as the right to life, the right to health, and the right to food.[526] The report also recommended the Draft Declaration of Principles on Human Rights and the Environment. Drawing upon the Stockholm and Rio Declarations, the Draft Declaration recognized the relationship between the right to a healthy environment and other fundamental human rights:

> 1. Human rights, an ecologically sound environment, sustainable development and peace are interdependent and indivisible.

2. All persons have the right to a secure, healthy and ecologically sound environment. This right and other human rights, including civil, cultural, economic, political and social rights are universal, interdependent and indivisible.⁵²⁷

The proposed Draft Declaration also included such rights as the right of individuals to freedom from pollution (Principle 5), to safe and healthy food and water (Principle 8), to information concerning the environment (Principle 15), and to effective remedies and redress for environmental harm (Principle 20). To date, however, the Commission on Human Rights (now the Human Rights Council) has declined to act on the Special Rapporteur's recommendation.

The Special Rapporteur on Environment and Development, as part of her final report, also recommended that the Commission on Human Rights appoint a thematic rapporteur to examine human rights and the environment. While the Commission has also ignored that recommendation, it did authorize in 1995 a Special Rapporteur on the adverse effects of the illicit movement and dumping of toxic and dangerous products and wastes on the enjoyment of human rights.⁵²⁸ The Chairperson of the Commission appointed Ms. Fatma Zohra Ouhachi-Vesely (formerly Ksentini) as the Special Rapporteur who, in the course of her duties, has visited Brazil, Canada, Costa Rica, Ethiopia, Germany, Kenya, Mexico, the Netherlands, Paraguay, South Africa, the United Kingdom, and the United States. Her 2004 report dealt with "Trends in the Illicit Traffic and Dumping of Toxic and Dangerous Products and Wastes," "Transnational Corporations," and the "Human Rights Impact" of such activities on the right to life and the right to health. The report observed:

On the one hand, illicit practices violate human rights such as the right to life and the right to health; on the other, the denial of rights such as freedom of expression, assembly and association or the right to information encourages illicit transfers, which in turn give rise to other human rights violations.⁵²⁹

Accordingly, the Commission on Human Rights in 2004 indicated its awareness that toxic wastes have adverse consequences not only for the rights to health and life but also the rights to water, food, adequate housing, and work.⁵³⁰ Hence, the international community is gradually recognizing aspects of the right to a healthy environment.

More progress has been achieved at the regional level. The African Charter of Human and Peoples' Rights declares in Article 24, "All peoples shall have the right to a general satisfactory environment favorable to their development."⁵³¹ The African Commission on Human and Peoples' Rights had an opportunity to consider this right in *The Social and*

*Economic Rights Action Center and the Center for Economic and Social Rights v. Nigeria.* The case challenged the Nigerian government's involvement in severe environmental damage caused by oil exploitation, particularly as it affected the Ogoni people. The African Commission ruled that the government's involvement constituted a breach of Article 24 of the African Charter, noting in the process the connection to Article 12 of the Economic and Social Covenant:

The right to a general satisfactory environment or the right to a healthy environment, as it is widely known, . . . obliges the State to take reasonable and other measures to prevent pollution and ecological degradation, to promote conservation, and to secure an ecologically sustainable development and use of natural resources. Article 12 of the International Covenant on Economic, Social and Cultural Rights (ICESCR), to which Nigeria is a party, requires governments to take necessary steps for the improvement of all aspects of environmental and industrial hygiene. Reduced to their most basic level, however, the rights to health . . . and a healthy environment . . . serve to prohibit governments from directly threatening the health and environment of their citizens.[532]

The African Commission then appealed to the Nigerian government to compensate and resettle the affected Ogoni people and to clean up the lands and waters polluted by the oil exploitation activities.

The European Council, meeting in Dublin during 1990, considered the right to a healthy environment and issued the Environmental Imperative setting guidelines for future action and explaining that

The development of higher levels of knowledge and understanding of environmental issues will facilitate more effective action by the Community and its Member States to protect the environment. The objective of such action must be to guarantee citizens the right to a clean and healthy environment. . . . Acceptance at all levels of this concept must be promoted.[533]

The European Court of Human Rights indirectly considered the right to a healthy environment in *Lopez Ostra v. Spain.* The European Convention on Human Rights states in Article 8, "Everyone has the right to respect for his private and family life, his home and his correspondence."[534] The complainant contended that the Spanish government had violated Article 8 by subsidizing the construction of a waste treatment plant 12 meters from her home. The Court agreed that the noxious fumes produced, while not life threatening, were nonetheless a violation of the right:

Naturally, severe environmental pollution may affect individuals' well-being and prevent them from enjoying their homes in such a way as to affect their private and family life adversely, without, however, seriously endangering their health.[535]

In 1998, the UN Economic Commission for Europe adopted the Convention on Access to Information, Public Participation in Decision-making and Access to Justice in Environmental Matters, or the Aarhus Convention. The objective of the Convention is to "contribute to the protection of the right of every person of present and future generations to live in an environment adequate to his or her health and well-being."[536]

Furthermore, in the Organization of American States, the Additional Protocol to the American Convention on Human Rights in the Area of Economic, Social and Cultural Rights (the Protocol of San Salvador), was signed in 1988 and also provides for a right to a healthy environment. Article 11 of the Protocol states:

1. Everyone shall have the right to live in a healthy environment and to have access to basic public services.
2. The States Parties shall promote the protection, preservation, and improvement of the environment.[537]

The Protocol came into force in 1999, though to date only fourteen states have ratified the treaty.

Nationally, India presents a valuable example of how environmental rights may be understood in the absence of explicit provisions. Like many international instruments, the Indian constitution does not specifically grant the right to a healthy environment, but does grant the right to life in Article 21. The Indian Supreme Court has interpreted the right to life so as to include the right to a healthy environment. Such reasoning was demonstrated in *M.C. Mehta v. Union of India*, which found that a chemical plant in Delhi that had violated its duty to the community by accidentally releasing oleum gas into the atmosphere:

[any] enterprise which is engaged in a hazardous or inherently dangerous industry which poses a potential threat to the health and safety of persons working in the factory and residing in the surrounding areas, owes an *absolute* and non-derogable duty to the community to ensure that no harm results to anyone on account of [its activities].[538]

*See also*: Health, Life, Water

*Further Reading*:

Additional Protocol to the American Convention on Human Rights in the Area of Economic, Social and Cultural Rights, "Protocol of San Salvador," O.A.S. Treaty Series No. 69 (1988), *entered into force* November 16, 1999, *reprinted in* Basic Documents Pertaining to Human Rights in the Inter-American System, OEA/Ser.L.V/II.82 doc.6 rev.1 at 67 (1992).

Adverse effects of the illicit movement and dumping of toxic and dangerous products and wastes on the enjoyment of human rights, Comm. on Human Rts. res. 2004/17, U.N. Doc. E/CN.4/2004/23 at 70 (2004).

African Charter on Human and Peoples' Rights, adopted June 27, 1981, OAU Doc. CAB/LEG/67/3 rev. 5, 21 I.L.M. 58 (1982), *entered into force* Oct. 21, 1986.

Committee on Economic, Social and Cultural Rights, General Comment 14, The Right to the Highest Attainable Standard of Health (Twenty-second session, 2000), U.N. Doc. E/C.12/2000/4 (2000), *reprinted in* Compilation of General Comments and General Recommendations Adopted by Human Rights Treaty Bodies, U.N. Doc. HRI/GEN/1/Rev.6 at 85 (2003).

Committee on Economic, Social and Cultural Rights, General Comment 15, The Right to Water (Twenty-ninth session, 2003), U.N. Doc. E/C.12/2002/11 (2002), *reprinted in* Compilation of General Comments and General Recommendations Adopted by Human Rights Treaty Bodies, U.N. Doc. HRI/GEN/1/Rev.6 at 105 (2003).

Declaration by the European Council on the Environmental Imperative, Bull. Eur. Comm., No. 6, at 17 (1990).

Draft Principles on Human Rights and the Environment, in Human Rights and the Environment: Final Report Prepared by Mrs. Fatma Zohra Ksentini, Special Rapporteur, U.N. ESCOR Commission on Human Rights, Sub-Commission on Prevention of Discrimination and Protection of Minorities, U.N. Doc. E/CN.4/Sub.2/1994/9 (1994), annex I.

Environmental Victims: New Risks, New Injustice (Christopher Williams ed., 1998).

Human Rights and the Environment: Compendium of Instruments and Other International Texts on Individual and Collective Rights Relating to the Environment in the International and European Framework (Maguelonne Déjeant-Pons & Marc Pallemaerts eds., 2002).

Human Rights and the Environment: Conflicts and Norms in a Globalizing World (Lyuba Zarsky ed., 2002).

Human Rights Approaches to Environmental Protection (Alan E. Boyle & Michael R. Anderson ed., 1996).

Barbara Rose Johnston, Life and Death Matters: Human Rights and the Environment at the End of the Millennium (1997).

Linking Human Rights and the Environment (Romina Picolotti & Jorge Daniel Taillant eds., 2003).

*Lopez Ostra v. Spain*, European Court of Human Rights, 20 EHRR 277 (1994).

*M.C. Mehta v. Union of India*, AIR 1987 SC 1086 (1987).

*The Social and Economic Rights Action Center and the Center for Economic and Social Rights v. Nigeria*, Communication No. 155/96, African Commission on Human and Peoples' Rights.

*Links to Consult*:

http://cmiskp.echr.coe.int/tkp197/view.asp?item=1&portal=hbkm&action=htm l&highlight=lopez%20%7C%20ostra&sessionid=605491&skin=hudoc-en

http://documents-dds-ny.un.org/doc/UNDOC/PRO/G04/147/34/pdf/G0414734.pd f?OpenE lement

http://shr.aaas.org/hrenv

## 196   Particular Rights and Responsibilities

http://www.cedha.org.ar/en
http://www.ciel.org/Hre/programhre.html
http://www.earthrights.org
http://www.europarl.eu.int/summits/dublin/du2_en.pdf
http://www.oas.org/juridico/english/Sigs/a-52.html
http://www.ohchr.org/english/issues/food/
http://www.ohchr.org/english/issues/health/right/
http://www.un.org/esa/sustdev/documents/agenda21/english/agenda21chapter1.htm
http://www.unece.org/env/pp/documents/cep43e.pdf
http://www.unhchr.ch/html/menu2/i2ecotow.htm
http://www.unhchr.ch/html/menu2/7/b/mtow.htm
http://www1.umn.edu/humanrts/africa/comcases/155-96b.html
http://www1.umn.edu/humanrts/gencomm/escgencom14.htm
http://www1.umn.edu/humanrts/gencomm/escgencom15.htm
http://www1.umn.edu/humanrts/instree/z1afchar.htm
http://www1.umn.edu/humanrts/instree/1994-dec.htm
http://www1.umn.edu/humanrts/oasinstr/zoas10pe.htm

## 20. Sustainable Development

Sustainable development fulfills the needs of the present without compromising the ability of future generations to meet their needs. None of the global human rights instruments contain an express right to development or sustainable development, however, Article 55 of the UN Charter does commit the United Nations to the promotion of "conditions of economic and social progress and development."[539] The right to development or sustainable development can be viewed as the sum of all civil, cultural, economic, political, and social rights with a particular focus on the right to a healthy environment.

The international community considered sustainable development at environmental conferences such as those held in Stockholm, Rio de Janeiro, and Johannesburg. In 1972 the UN Conference on the Human Environment was held in Stockholm and produced the Stockholm Declaration, which captured the essence of sustainable development in its observation that

> To defend and improve the human environment for present and future generations has become an imperative goal for mankind—a goal to be pursued together with, and in harmony with, the established and fundamental goals of peace and of worldwide economic and social development.[540]

In 1986 the General Assembly adopted the Declaration on the Right to Development with a vote of 146 in favor, one against (the United States), and eight countries (principally in Northern Europe plus Israel) abstaining. The Declaration sets out the right of all human beings "to participate in, contribute to, and enjoy economic, social, cultural and political development, in which all human rights and fundamental freedoms can be fully realized," and the duty of States "to formulate appropriate national development policies that aim at the constant improvement of the well-being of the entire population and of all individuals. . . ."[541] The United States opposed and some European countries abstained due to their concern that the Declaration would establish a right of governments to receive economic assistance. Article 4 of the Declaration reads, "As a complement to the efforts of developing countries, effective international co-operation is essential in providing these countries with appropriate means and facilities to foster their comprehensive development."[542]

The UN Conference on Environment and Development in 1992 sought to build on the Stockholm Declaration, and culminated in the adoption of the Rio Declaration and Agenda 21. The Rio Declaration made the international community's commitment to sustainable development more explicit in its Principles 1, 3, and 4:

198   Particular Rights and Responsibilities

> 1. Human beings are at the centre of concerns for sustainable development. They are entitled to a healthy and productive life in harmony with nature. . . .
> 3. The right to development must be fulfilled so as to equitably meet developmental and environmental needs of present and future generations.
> 4. In order to achieve sustainable development, environmental protection shall constitute an integral part of the development process and cannot be considered in isolation from it.[543]

Agenda 21 provided a framework for meeting the substantive challenges of sustainable development, such as protecting the atmosphere, caring for land-resource use, combating deforestation, halting the spread of deserts, protecting mountain ecosystems, meeting agricultural needs without destroying the land, sustaining biological diversity, establishing environmentally sound management of biotechnology, safeguarding the ocean's resources, protecting and managing freshwater resources, instituting safe use of toxic chemicals, managing hazardous wastes, seeking solutions to solid waste problems, and managing radioactive wastes.

In 1992 the General Assembly established the Commission on Sustainable Development with a mandate to

> ensure effective follow-up to the [Rio] Conference, as well as to enhance international cooperation and rationalize the intergovernmental decision-making capacity for the integration of environment and development issues and to examine the progress of the implementation of Agenda 21 at the national, regional and international levels, fully guided by the principles of the Rio Declaration on Environment and Development and all other aspects of the Conference, in order to achieve sustainable development in all countries. . . .[544]

The General Assembly convened a special session in 1997 to review the progress made since the Rio Conference. The General Assembly adopted the Programme for Further Implementation of Agenda 21 and reaffirmed its commitment to Agenda 21 as the "fundamental programme of action for achieving sustainable development," and to "all the principles contained in the Rio Declaration on Environment and Development."[545] The General Assembly in 2000 again reaffirmed its commitment to Agenda 21 as part of its Millennium Declaration, a comprehensive document intended to guide the activities of the United Nations going forward in the third millennium. In identifying the protection of the environment as a key goal, the Assembly observed that

> Prudence must be shown in the management of all living species and natural resources, in accordance with the precepts of sustainable development. Only in this way can the immeasurable riches provided to us by nature be preserved and passed on to our descendants. The current unsustainable patterns of production

and consumption must be changed in the interest of our future welfare and that of our descendants.[546]

The international community met to address sustainable development most recently at the World Summit on Sustainable Development held in Johannesburg during 2002, and issued the Johannesburg Declaration[547] and the Johannesburg Plan of Implementation[548] reaffirming the previous pronouncements and building on Agenda 21. In particular, the Johannesburg Plan of Implementation sought to address poverty eradication, unsustainable consumption and production practices, managing natural resource bases, globalization, and the necessary institutional framework.

In the wake of the 2002 Summit, the Commission on Sustainable Development has used the Johannesburg Plan of Implementation to guide its activities in the form of a multi-year program of work on issues such as water, sanitation, drought, mining, Africa, and transport. In addition to the Commission on Sustainable Development the Economic and Social Council in 1998 authorized the Commission on Human Rights to establish an open-ended working group on the right to development and to appoint an independent expert on the right to development. Together, the working group and the independent expert have attempted to establish a more precise understanding of these very general concepts and problems.

The human rights treaty bodies have also demonstrated their respect for the concept of sustainable development. For example, in interpreting the right to education in Article 29 of the Convention on the Rights of the Child the Committee on the Rights of the Child noted that for "the development of respect for the natural environment, education must link issues of environment and sustainable development with socio-economic, sociocultural and demographic issues."[549] The Committee on the Elimination of Discrimination Against Women addressed discrimination against women in marital and family relations and observed,

There is general agreement that where there are freely available appropriate measures for the voluntary regulation of fertility, the health, development and well-being of all members of the family improves. Moreover, such services improve the general quality of life and health of the population, and the voluntary regulation of population growth helps preserve the environment and achieve sustainable economic and social development.[550]

Sustainable development has also played a role in the conclusions and recommendations of the Committee on Economic, Social and Cultural Rights in response to country reports, as seen in the Committee's response to the 1999 report of Tunisia:

200  Particular Rights and Responsibilities

The Committee welcomes the success achieved in the promotion of sustainable human development, as evidenced by the reduction in the number of persons living below the national poverty line, the increase in life expectancy, the decrease in illiteracy and the decrease in infant mortality, as indicated by the overall human development index.[551]

The Committee on the Rights of the Child was more critical in its response to the 2000 report of South Africa:

Concern is expressed at the increase in environmental degradation, especially as regards air pollution. The Committee recommends that the State party increase its efforts to facilitate the implementation of sustainable development programmes to prevent environmental degradation, especially as regards air pollution.[552]

In order to achieve the right to development, the United Nations Development Program (UNDP) assists in reaching the Millennium Development Goals, fulfilling national poverty strategies, providing technical advice, building global partnerships, and advocating for trade reform, debt relief, economic reform, and investment opportunities. The annual report of the UNDP documents its accomplishments and the UNDP also publishes the Human Development Index seeking to rank the efforts and relative success of nations in achieving various aspects of development. The most recent UNDP annual report, issued in 2004, focuses on efforts to eradicate extreme poverty and hunger, achieve universal primary education, promote gender equality and empower women, reduce child mortality, improve maternal health, combat HIV/AIDS, malaria and other diseases, ensure environmental sustainability, and develop a global partnership for development.

The World Bank provides loans and monetary assistance to developing nations and has begun to consider the human rights implications of its efforts. Additional assistance comes from regional development banks such as the African Development Bank Group, the Asian Development Bank, the Central American Bank for Economic Integration, and the Inter-American Development Bank.

Regional human rights institutions have also strived to establish a right to development or sustainable development. For example, the right to development is proclaimed in Article 22 of the African Charter on Human and Peoples' Rights and Article 24 states, "All peoples shall have the right to a general satisfactory environment favorable to their development." In *The Social and Economic Rights Action Center and the Center for Economic and Social Rights v. Nigeria*, the African Commission on Human and Peoples' Rights found a violation of the Ogoni People's rights under the Charter where their lands had been heavily polluted as the result of government condoned oil exploitation. As discussed in the previous chapter on healthy environments, the African Commission in its decision explained that

The right to a general satisfactory environment or the right to a healthy environment, as it is widely known, therefore imposes clear obligations upon a government. It obliges the State to take reasonable and other measures to prevent pollution and ecological degradation, to promote conservation, and to secure an ecologically sustainable development and use of natural resources.[553]

The Protocol to the African Charter on Human and Peoples' Rights on the Rights of Women in Africa, signed in 2003, goes further and makes the right to sustainable development explicit in its Article 19, which states, "Women shall have the right to fully enjoy their right to sustainable development."[554] Considering that the African Charter, like all international human rights treaties, prohibits discrimination of any sort, it can be inferred that the Protocol views the right to sustainable development as a right held by all. The Protocol came into force in 2005. Further, the Constitutive Act of the African Union, which entered into force in 2001, states sustainable development as one of its goals.

In Europe, the European Commission regards sustainable development as a key issue, and addressed the matter at the European Council in Göteborg in 2001. There, the Council adopted the European Union Sustainable Development Strategy, which seeks to encourage sustainable development through clarifying policy initiatives, improving market pricing, investing in science and technology, improving communication regarding sustainable development, and so forth. The Commission plans to revisit the issue in 2005.

*See also*: Food, Healthy Environment, Water


*Further Reading*:

Agenda 21, Report of the United Nations Conference on Environment and Development, Rio de Janeiro, June 3–14, 1992, chap. I, resolution 1, annex II, A/CONF.151/26 (1992).
Declaration on the Right to Development, G.A. res. 41/128, annex, 41 U.N. GAOR Supp. (No. 53) at 186, U.N. Doc. A/41/53 (1986).
Committee on the Elimination of Discrimination Against Women, General Recommendation 21, Equality in Marriage and Family Relations (Thirteenth session, 1992), U.N. Doc. A/49/38 at 1 (1994).
Committee on the Rights of the Child, General Comment No. 1, The Aims of Education, U.N. Doc. CRC/GC/2001/1 (2001).
Concluding Observations of the Committee on the Rights of the Child, South Africa, U.N. Doc. CRC/C/15/Add.122 (2000).
Conclusions and Recommendations of the Committee on Economic, Social and Cultural Rights, Tunisia, U.N. Doc. E/C.12/1/Add.36 (1999).

Human Rights and the Environment as Part of Sustainable Development, C.H.R. res. 2003/71, U.N. Doc. E/CN.4/2003/L.11/Add.6 (2003).

Implementing the Right to Development in the Current Global Context, C.H.R, Consideration of the Sixth Report of the Independent Expert on the Right to Development, U.N. Doc. E/CN.4/2004/WG.18/2 (2004).

Johannesburg Declaration on Sustainable Development, Report of the World Summit on Sustainable Development, Johannesburg, Aug. 26–Sept. 4, 2002, chap. I, res. 1, annex I, A/CONF.199/20 (2002).

Plan of Implementation of the World Summit on Sustainable Development, Report of the World Summit on Sustainable Development, Johannesburg, 26 Aug. 26–Sept. 4, 2002, chap. I, res. 2, annex I, A/CONF.199/20 (2002).

Programme for the Further Implementation of Agenda 21, G.A. res. S-19/2, U.N. Doc. A/RES/S-19/2 (1997).

The Right to Development, C.H.R. res. 2004/7, U.N. Doc. E/CN.4/2004/127 (2004).

Right to Development, C.H.R. Report of the Working Group on the Right to Development on its fifth session, U.N. Doc. E/CN.4/2004/23 (2004).

Rio Declaration on Environment and Development, Report of the United Nations Conference on Environment and Development, Rio de Janeiro, June 3–14, 1992, chap. I, resolution 1, annex I, A/CONF.151/26 (1992).

United Nations Millennium Declaration, G.A. Res. 55/2, U.N. GAOR, 55th Sess., Supp. No. 49, at 4, U.N. Doc. A/55/49 (2000).

World Commission on Environment and Development (Brundtland Commission), Our Common Future (1987).

*Links to Consult:*

http://ap.ohchr.org/documents/E/CHR/resolutions/E-CN_4-RES_2004_7.doc
http://www.johannesburgsummit.org/html/documents/summit_docs/131302_wssd_report_reissued.pdf
http://www.un.org/documents/ga/confl51/aconf15126_1annex1.htm
http://www.un.org/documents/ga/res/47/ares47_191.htm
http://www.un.org/documents/ga/res/spec/aress19_2.htm
http://www.un.org/esa/sustdev/documents/agenda21/english/agenda21toc.htm
http://www.unep.org/DPDL/cso/New_files_under_guidelines/Resolution_2003_71_Human_rights_and_the_environment.doc
http://www.unhchr.ch/Huridocda/Huridoca.nsf/(Symbol)/E.CN.4.2004.23+and+Corr.1.En?Opendocument
http://www.unhchr.ch/Huridocda/Huridoca.nsf/(Symbol)/E.CN.4.2004.WG.18.2.En?Op endocument
http://www1.umn.edu/humanrts/crc/comment1.htm
http://www1.umn.edu/humanrts/crc/southafrica2000.html
http://www1.umn.edu/humanrts/esc/tunisia1999.html
http://www1.umn.edu/humanrts/gencomm/generl21.htm
http://www1.umn.edu/humanrts/instree/aunchart.htm
http://www1.umn.edu/humanrts/instree/millennium.html
http://www1.umn.edu/humanrts/instree/s3drd.htm
http://www.un.org.ora/sustdev/csd/policy.htm

## 21. Peace

The founders of the United Nations had two principal objectives—the preservation of peace and the protection of human rights. The UN Charter in Article 1 identifies peace as one main purpose of the United Nations:

> To maintain international peace and security, and to that end: to take effective collective measures for the prevention and removal of threats to the peace, and for the suppression of acts of aggression or other breaches of the peace, and to bring about by peaceful means, and in conformity with the principles of justice and international law, adjustment or settlement of international disputes or situations which might lead to a breach of the peace.[555]

Article 1 also indicates that self-determination and other human rights are among the main purposes of the UN:

> (2) To develop friendly relations among nations based on respect for the principle of equal rights and self-determination of peoples, and to take other appropriate measures to strengthen universal peace;
> (3) To achieve international cooperation in solving international problems of an economic, social, cultural, or humanitarian character, and in promoting and encouraging respect for human rights and for fundamental freedoms for all without distinction as to race, sex, language, or religion; . . .[556]

The UN Charter expresses a strong international preference that peace can be achieved if military force should only be used upon authorization of the Charter. Article 2 of the Charter states:

> (3) All Members shall settle their international disputes by peaceful means in such a manner that international peace and security, and justice, are not endangered.
> (4) All Members shall refrain in their international relations from the threat or use of force against the territorial integrity or political independence of any state, or in any other manner inconsistent with the Purposes of the United Nations.[557]

When peacemaking efforts fail, Chapter VII of the UN Charter provides that "the Security Council shall determine the existence of any threat to the peace, breach of the peace, or act of aggression and shall . . . decide what measures shall be taken" including the use of military force.[558] The Security Council's actions to preserve the peace under Chapter VII can take two forms: nonmilitary enforcement pursuant to Article 41, and military enforcement according to Article 42.

Article 41 identifies nonmilitary measures the Security Council may take to deal with threats to the peace, for example "complete or partial interruption of economic relations and of rail, sea, air, postal, telegraphic, radio, and other means of communication, and the severance of diplomatic relations."[559] The Security Council has used such measures, commonly referred to as sanctions, in a number of situations in order to maintain or restore international peace and security.

Following Iraq's invasion of Kuwait in 1990, the Security Council imposed sanctions against Iraq, banning all financial transactions with Iraq, international flights to Iraq, and trade in all goods except medicine and humanitarian food aid. In 1991, after the sanctions did not result in Iraq's withdrawal from Kuwait, the Security Council authorized military action. After the Gulf War in which Iraqi forces were removed from Kuwait in 1991, the Security Council determined that the sanctions would continue until Iraq met several conditions relating particularly to disarmament. Those sanctions were controversial because they were not calibrated to respond to Iraqi actions and they had serious consequences for the health and well-being of the Iraqi people. In 2003, the United States, the United Kingdom, and several other countries invaded Iraq, removing the Iraqi government from power without new Security Council authority; the Security Council later ended all sanctions against Iraq, except those regarding the sale or supply of arms and related material.

In 1992 and 1993, travel, economic, and other sanctions were also imposed against Libya because of its involvement in the crash of Pan Am Flight 103 over Lockerbie, Scotland, in 1988. The United States and Britain accused two Libyan nationals of placing a bomb on the Pan Am flight. Eventually, in 1999, Libya extradited the two Libyan perpetrators for trial in the Hague, and in 2003 the Security Council lifted the sanctions against Libya. The Security Council also imposed sanctions against Afghanistan in 1999, by freezing financial resources and boycotting Taliban aircraft, after the Taliban refused to extradite Osama bin Laden for trial in connection with the bombing of U.S. embassies in Kenya and Tanzania.

If nonmilitary actions do not succeed in maintaining or restoring international peace and security, Article 42 of the UN Charter authorizes the Security Council to "take such action by air, sea or land forces as may be necessary to maintain or restore international peace and security...."[560] For example, the Security Council invoked Chapter VII of the Charter in mounting a peacekeeping operation in the Democratic Republic of Congo (DRC). The humanitarian crisis and ethnic conflict in the DRC has resulted in the loss of more than four million lives. Beginning in 1999 the Security Council sent UN peacekeepers to the DRC in order to protect endangered ethnic groups and encourage an end to the conflict which has involved several neighboring countries.

In 2003 the Security Council determined that the situation in Liberia constituted a threat to international peace and security in the region and to the peace process for Liberia. The Security Council found that the prolonged conflict resulted in atrocities against civilians, widespread sexual violence against women and children, and the use of child soldiers by armed rebel militias, government forces, and other militias. Accordingly, the Security Council acted under Chapter VII to authorize a military force to contribute toward international efforts to protect human rights in Liberia.

The Security Council occasionally has authorized an alliance of governments or a regional organization to use military action under Chapter VII of the UN Charter for a humanitarian intervention. For example, in 1992 the Security Council was motivated by the threat of famine to the lives of a million residents of Somalia to authorize a U.S.-led multinational intervention that was authorized to "use all necessary means to establish a secure environment for humanitarian relief operations in Somalia."[561]

The use of military force for self-defense is also authorized under the UN Charter pursuant to Article 51:

Nothing in the present Charter shall impair the inherent right of individual or collective self-defense if an armed attack occurs against a Member of the United Nations, until the Security Council has taken measures necessary to maintain international peace and security.[562]

Another possible basis for the use of military action might focus on the role of regional organizations, such as the North Atlantic Treaty Organization (NATO). In this context Article 52 of the UN Charter states:

Nothing in the present Charter precludes the existence of regional arrangements or agencies for dealing with such matters relating to the maintenance of international peace and security as are appropriate for regional action, provided that such arrangements or agencies and their activities are consistent with the Purposes and Principles of the United Nations.[563]

In the UN Secretary-General's Agenda for Peace "Preventive diplomacy, peacemaking and peace-keeping" of 1992, he stated that

under the Charter, the Security Council has and will continue to have primary responsibility for maintaining international peace and security, but regional action as a matter of decentralization, delegation and cooperation with the United Nations efforts could not only lighten the burden of the Council but also contribute to a deeper sense of participation, consensus and democratization in international affairs.[564]

For example, after the attacks of September 11, 2001, NATO declared that it would act in defense of the United States, if the U.S. had been subject to external military attack and requested assistance. That provision, however, is still subject to the purposes and principles of the United Nations, including the limitations in the Charter on the use of military force and the preeminent role of the Security Council.

To the extent that military force is authorized, however, the means of war are limited. The International Court of Justice (ICJ) in its Advisory Opinion on the Legality of the Threat or Use of Nuclear Weapons stated that under the customary laws of war military force must be necessary and proportional to the threat.[565] The four Geneva Conventions for the protection of the victims of armed conflict provide that soldiers may direct deadly force against an enemy, but not against civilians, civilian targets, or other persons taking no active part in the hostilities, including members of armed forces who have laid down their arms and others placed out of combat by sickness, wounds, detention, or any other cause.[566]

After the brutal 9/11 attacks, the United States, the United Kingdom, and several other countries initiated a "war on terror." There are treaties against various aspects of terrorism, such as the hijacking of airplanes, but there is no internationally accepted definition of terrorism. Amnesty International, in its 2004 report, criticized the "war on terrorism" by stating: "Governments and armed groups have launched a war on global values, destroying human rights of ordinary people."[567] The U.S. government on 20 September 2002, issued a National Security Strategy in which the U.S. declared that it had a right to preemptive self-defense, that is, to attack before it had been subjected to an armed attack, as required by Article 51 of the UN Charter.

In addition to the UN Charter, human rights treaties and other instruments also emphasize the significant relationship between peace and human rights. The Universal Declaration on Human Rights states that "recognition of the inherent dignity and of the equal and inalienable rights of all members of the human family is the foundation of freedom, justice and peace in the world."[568] Similarly, both the Covenant on Civil and Political Rights and the Covenant on Economic, Social and Cultural Rights as well as the Convention Against Torture and Other Cruel, Inhuman or Degrading Treatment or Punishment state that "in accordance with the principles proclaimed in the Charter of the United Nations, recognition of the inherent dignity and of the equal and inalienable rights of all members of the human family is the foundation of freedom, justice and peace in the world."[569] The significant relationship between peace and human rights can also be found in some other widely ratified human rights treaties. The Convention on the Elimination of All Forms of Racial Discrimination reaffirms that "that discrimination between human beings . . . is an obstacle to friendly and peaceful relations among nations and is capable of disturbing peace and security among peoples and the harmony of persons living side by side even within one and the same State."[570]

The Covenant on Civil and Political Rights establishes a further relationship between human rights and peace in providing for derogation of certain rights in times of public emergency threatening the life of a nation. International and non-international armed conflict may constitute such a public emergency. Article 4 indicates that certain rights may be subject to derogation, but others may not be the subject of derogation even in times of armed conflict:

> In time of public emergency which threatens the life of the nation and the existence of which is officially proclaimed, the States Parties to the present Covenant may take measures derogating from their obligations under the present Covenant to the extent strictly required by the exigencies of the situation, provided that such measures are not inconsistent with their other obligations under international law and do not involve discrimination solely on the ground of race, colour, sex, language, religion or social origin.[571]

The authors of Article 4 were probably thinking of armed conflict as the principal "public emergency" that might threaten "the life of the nation."

Article 4 further prescribes that no derogation, that is no exception, may be made from particularly important rights including the right to life; prohibition of torture or cruel, inhuman, or degrading punishment, or of medical or scientific experimentation without consent; prohibition of slavery, slave trade, and servitude; prohibition of imprisonment because of inability to fulfill a contractual obligation; the principle that no one shall be convicted of an offense that was not legally proscribed at the time of the conduct for which the individual is charged; the recognition of everyone as a person before the law; and freedom of thought, conscience, and religion. The same approach applies to States parties of the Second Optional Protocol to the Covenant, aiming at the abolition of the death penalty, as determined in Article 6 of that Protocol.

The Human Rights Committee in its General Comment 29, States of Emergency, has interpreted Article 4 and the Covenant as a whole to identify several further non-derogable rights, such as

> 11. States parties may in no circumstances invoke article 4 of the Covenant as justification for acting in violation of humanitarian law or peremptory norms of international law, for instance by taking hostages, by imposing collective punishments, through arbitrary deprivations of liberty or by

208   Particular Rights and Responsibilities

> deviating from fundamental principles of fair trial, including the presumption of innocence . . .
>
> 13. . . . (a) All persons deprived of their liberty shall be treated with humanity and with respect for the inherent dignity of the human person . . .
> (b) The prohibitions against taking of hostages, abductions or unacknowledged detention are not subject to derogation . . .
> (c) . . . the international protection of the rights of persons belonging to minorities includes elements that must be respected in all circumstances . . .
> (d) . . . deportation or forcible transfer of population without grounds permitted under international law, in the form of forced displacement by expulsion or other coercive means from the area in which the persons concerned are lawfully present, constitutes a crime against humanity. The legitimate right to derogate from article 12 of the Covenant during a state of emergency can never be accepted as justifying such measures.
> (e) No declaration of a state of emergency made pursuant to article 4, paragraph 1, may be invoked as justification for a State party to engage itself . . . propaganda for war, or in advocacy of national, racial or religious hatred that would constitute incitement to discrimination, hostility or violence, . . .[572]

Regional human rights treaties in Europe and the Western Hemisphere similarly contain provisions for derogation in cases of war or other public emergency threatening the life of a nation, and also identify rights that are non-derogable.

In the 1984 Declaration on the Right of Peoples to Peace, the General Assembly proclaimed that there is a right to peace. In that Declaration the General Assembly has emphasized that

> ensuring the exercise of the right of peoples to peace demands . . . the elimination of the threat of war . . . the renunciation of the use of force in international relations and the settlement of international disputes by peaceful means on the basis of the Charter of the United Nations.[573]

Some scholars have identified the right to peace as a "solidarity right" along with the right to development, the right to respect for the common heritage of humankind, the right to a healthy environment, and the right of peoples to self-determination.

The relationship between peace and human rights is also supported by social science studies indicating that there is a significant correlation between international and non-international armed conflicts and human rights abuses by both governments and armed opponents. Some scholars have claimed that governments, when faced with threats, consider responding to the threats with repressive practices that violate human rights. It is expected that repression will increase as governments are faced with a domestic threat in the form of a civil war, or when a country is involved in international armed conflict.

A number of nongovernmental organizations (NGOs) have cooperated with the United Nations in working for the achievement of peace and security through disarmament. NGOs such as Oxfam, Amnesty International, and the International Action Network on Small Arms have particularly campaigned against the manufacture and trade of small arms and anti-personnel landmines. The proliferation of weapons make wars more likely and more deadly, encourage violence, and obstruct peacemaking. In recent conflicts around the world, most casualties were caused by small arms and light weapons, and many of those casualties were children. In countries and regions emerging from violent conflict, the clearing of landmines is often a prerequisite for the return of refugees, internally displaced people (IDPs), humanitarian aid, reconstruction, and development. NGOs and coalitions, including Human Rights Watch and the International Campaign to Ban Landmines, advocate for cease-fire agreements and peace accords that properly address landmine concerns.

*See also*: Genocide, War Crimes, Crimes Against Humanity, and Crimes Against Peace; Humanitarian Law; Security/Terrorism and Human Rights

*Further Reading*:

Advisory Opinion on the Legality of the Threat or Use of Nuclear Weapons, 1996 I.C.J. 226, (1996).
An Agenda for Peace: Preventive diplomacy, peacemaking and peace-keeping, Report of the Secretary-General pursuant tot the statement adopted by the Summit Meeting of the Security Council Jan. 31, 1992, June 17, 1992, U.N. Doc. A/47/277-S/24111 (1992).
David P. Barash and Charles P. Webel, Peace and Conflict Studies (2002).
Antonio Cassese, *Ex Iniuria Ius Oriter: Are we Moving Towards International Legitimation of Forcible Humanitarian Countermeasures in the World Community?*, 10 European Journal of International Law 23 (1999).
Christine M. Chinkin, *Kosovo a "Good" or "Bad" War*, 93 A.J.I.L. 841 (1999).
Convention for the Protection of Human Rights and Fundamental Freedoms as amended by Protocol No. 11 with Protocols Nos. 1, 4, 6, 7, 12 and 13, Registry of the European Court of Human Rights, February 2003.
Convention Relating to the Status of Refugees, adopted on 28 July 1951 by the United Nations Conference of Plenipotentiaries on the Status of Refugees and Stateless Persons Convened Under General Assembly Resolution 429 (V) of 14 December 1950, *entered into force* Apr. 22, 1954.
Convention Against Torture and Other Cruel, Inhuman or Degrading Treatment or Punishment, G.A. res. 39/46, Annex, 39 U.N. GAOR Supp. (No. 51) at 197, U/N/ Doc. A/39/51 (1984), *entered into force* June 26, 1987.
Yael Danieli, Nigel S. Rodley & Lars Weisaeth, International Responses to Traumatic Stress (1996).
Declaration on the Right of Peoples to Peace, G.A. res. 39/11, annex, 39 U.N. GAOR Supp. (No. 51) at 22, U.N. Doc. A/39/51 (1984).

## 210   Particular Rights and Responsibilities

David P. Forsythe, Human Rights and Peace: International and National Dimensions (1993).
Richard J. Goldstone, *Whither Kosovo? Whither Democracy?*, 8 Global Governance 143 (2002).
Raija Hanski & Markku Suksi, An Introduction to the International Protection of Human Rights (1999).
Joan Hartman, *Derogations from Human Rights in Public Emergencies*, 22 Harv. Int'l L.J. 1 (1981).
Roman Herzog, Preventing the Clash of Civilizations: A Peace Strategy for the Twenty-First Century (1999).
Human Rights Committee, General Comment 29, States of Emergency (article 4), U.N. Doc. CCPR/C/21/Rev.1/Add.11 (2001).
Mari Katayanagi, Human Rights Functions of United Nations Peacekeeping Operations (2002).
Tom Lansford, All for One: Terrorism, NATO and the United States (2002).
Peter Malanczuk, Akehurst's Modern Introduction to International Law (1997).
*Military and Paramilitary Activities in and Against Nicaragua (Nicaragua v. U.S.)*, 1986 I.C.J. 14, June 27 (1986).
Edward Newman & Joanne van Selm, Refugees and Forced Displacement International Security, Human Vulnerability, and the State (2003).
Prevention of Armed Conflict, Report of the Secretary-General on the Work of the Organization, General Assembly fifty-fifth session agenda item 10, June 7, 2001, U.N. Doc. A/55/985-S/2001/574 (2001).
Resolution 827 on the Tribunal (former Yugoslavia), adopted by the Security Council at its 3217th meeting on May 25, 1993, U.N. Doc. S/RES/827 (1993).
Resolution 794 on the situation in Somalia, adopted by the Security Council at its 3145th meeting on Dec. 3, 1992, U.N. Doc. S/RES/794 (1992).
Resolution 955 on the Establishment of an International Tribunal and Adoption of the Statute of the Tribunal, adopted by the Security Council at its 3453rd meeting on Nov. 8, 1994, U.N. Doc. S/RES/955 (1994).
Resolution 1244 on the Situation Relating to Kosovo, adopted by the Security Council at its 4011th meeting on June 10, 1999, U.N. Doc. S/RES/1244 (1999).
Resolution 1267 on the situation in Afghanistan, adopted by the Security Council at its 4051st meeting on Oct. 15, 1999, U.N. Doc. S/RES/1267 (1999).
Resolution 1291 on the Situation Concerning the Democratic Republic of Congo, adopted by the Security Council at its 4104th meeting on 24 Feb. 24, 2000, U.N. Doc. S/RES/1291 (2000).
Resolution 1386 on the Situation in Afghanistan, adopted by the Security Council at its 4443rd meeting on Dec. 20, 2001, U.N. Doc. S/RES/1386 (2001).
Resolution 1509 on the Situation in Liberia, adopted by the Security Council at its 4830th meeting on Sept. 19, 2003, U.N. Doc. S/RES/1509 (2003).
Luc Reychler & Thania Paffenholz, Peace-Building: A Field Guide (2001).
Bruno Simma with Hermann Mosler et al., The Charter of the United Nations: A Commentary (2002).
Supplement to an Agenda for Peace: Position Paper of the Secretary-General on the Occasion of the Fiftieth Anniversary of the United Nations Report of the Secretary-General on the work of the Organization, Jan. 3, 1995, U.N. Doc. A/50/60-S/1995/1 (1995).
Vienna Convention on the Law of Treaties, 1155 U.N.T.S. 331, *entered into force* Jan. 27, 1980.

Jennifer M. Welsh, *From Right to Responsibility: Humanitarian Intervention and International Society*, 8 Global Governance 503 (2002).

*Links to Consult:*

http://disarm.igc.org
http://globalpolicy.igc.org/security/sanction/
http://peace.sandiego.edu.
http://web.amnesty.org/report2004/index-eng
http://www.globalissues.org/Geopolitics/WarOnTerror.asp
http://www.hri.org/docs/ECHR50.html
http://www.hrni.org
http://www.icj-cij.org
http://www.icj-cij.org/icjwww/icases/iunan/iunanframe.htm
http://www.ictr.org
http://www.icty.org
http://www.ifhv.de
http://www.ifsh.de
http://www.javier-leon-diaz.com/docs/humanIntervIssues_Status.htm
http://www.peacebrigades.org
http://www.ruhr-uni-bochum.de/ifhv/news/Tashkent_Speech%20Heintze.pdf
http://www.unhcr.ch
http://www.un.org
http://www.un.org/News/ossg/sanction.htm
http://www.un.org/Depts/dpko/dpko/faq/index.htm
http://www.whitehouse.gov/nsc/nss.pdf
http://www1.umn.edu/humanrts/gencomm/hrc29.html
http://www1.umn.edu/humanrts/instree/auoq.htm
http://www1.umn.edu/humanrts/links/peace.html
http://www1.umn.edu/humanrts/monitoring/index.html

## 22. Humanitarian Law

International humanitarian law is mainly designed to ensure respect for general principles of humanity during periods of international and non-international armed conflict. International humanitarian law principally protects soldiers and sailors wounded in armed conflict, prisoners of war, and civilians in times of war or military occupation. As Article 4 of the Covenant on Civil and Political Rights makes clear, both human rights and humanitarian law principles apply in the context of armed conflict, but international humanitarian law provides a stronger and far more detailed basis for the protection of human rights in armed conflict than the more general provisions in the International Bill of Human Rights and other UN human rights instruments.

The principal multilateral treaties that constitute the core of international humanitarian law—the four Geneva Conventions of 1949—have been ratified by more governments (194) than other human rights treaties—even more than the UN Charter (191) and the Convention on the Rights of the Child (193). The two Additional Protocols of 1977 (ratified by 167 and 163 nations respectively) extend and make more specific the protections of the 1949 Geneva Conventions to international and non-international armed conflicts.[574] Many provisions of the four Geneva Conventions, the two Protocols, and the Hague Conventions of 1899 and 1907 are broadly accepted as restating customary international humanitarian law applicable to all countries.

A. FOUR CATEGORIES OF ARMED CONFLICTS

The four Geneva Conventions and two Protocols identify four categories of armed conflict: (a) international armed conflict or occupation, (b) wars of national liberation or self-determination, (c) non-international armed conflict under Common Article 3, and (d) non-international armed conflict under Additional Protocol II. In regard to the first category, most of the four Geneva Conventions "apply to all cases of declared war or any other armed conflict which may arise between two more of the High Contracting Parties, even if the state of war is not recognized by one of them."[575] The Geneva Conventions and particularly the Fourth Convention apply to partial or total occupation of the territory of a High Contracting Party, that is, a state that has ratified the Geneva Conventions. Even if one or more of the parties to an armed conflict have not ratified the treaties, the ratifying parties are nonetheless bound to obey the Geneva Conventions.

Additional Protocol I to the Geneva Conventions identifies a second category of international armed conflicts—wars of national liberation or self-determination—that is, "armed conflicts in which peoples are fighting against colonial domination an alien occupation and against racist regimes in the exercise of their right of self-determination. . . ."[576]

In all four of the Geneva Conventions there is an identical or "common" Article 3 that applies a limited number of very basic protections to "armed conflicts not of an international character." Common Article 3 does not define non-international armed conflict so as to distinguish it from unorganized and short-lived insurrection or a mere act of banditry. Nonetheless, the authoritative commentary prepared by the International Committee of the Red Cross mentions a number of factors that bear upon the application of Common Article 3, including for example: (a) whether the armed opposition group possesses an organized military force, (b) the government is obliged to use regular military force in responding to the insurgents, (c) the government has recognized the insurgents as belligerents, (d) the conflict has been admitted to the agenda of the Security Council, (e) the armed opposition have an organization purporting to have the characteristics of a state, (f) the armed opposition exercises de facto authority over persons within a determinate territory, and (g) the armed opposition group is prepared to observe the ordinary laws of war.

Additional Protocol II to the Geneva Conventions more narrowly defines "armed conflicts not of an international character" but then expands upon the humanitarian protections available in such conflicts.[577] Accordingly, Additional Protocol II specifies as more rigid criteria several of the factors that have been used to interpret Common Article 3 for determining the existence of non-international armed conflicts "which take place in the territory of a High Contracting Party between its armed forces and dissident armed forces or other organized armed groups which, under responsible command, exercise such control over a part of its territory as to enable them to carry out sustained and concerted military operations and to implement this Protocol."[578]

Since the brutal attacks perpetrated by Al Qaeda on September 11, 2001, there have been questions as to whether the "war on terror" qualifies as an international armed conflict or a non-international armed conflict under international humanitarian law, on the one hand, or an entirely new form of armed conflict as to which new rules must be developed, on the other. On October 6, 2001, the United States, the United Kingdom, and several other countries began a military action against Afghanistan to destroy Al Qaeda and the Taliban government closely associated with Al Qaeda and to assist the Northern Alliance forces that had been opposing the Taliban. The U.S. forces removed the Taliban from power in Afghanistan and assisted in installing a government comprised of Northern Alliance forces and others who had opposed the Taliban's rule. The U.S. forces remained in Afghanistan looking for Al

Qaeda fighters, Osama bin Laden, and Taliban leaders. Since Afghanistan, the United States, and the United Kingdom are High Contracting Parties to the Geneva Conventions, the combat of those three military forces qualified as international armed conflict. An internal U.S. Justice Department memo argued, however, that Afghanistan was a failed state and thus the Taliban could not qualify as a High Contracting Party. Such a hypertechnical and narrow reading of the Geneva Conventions would undermine the comprehensive coverage of international humanitarian law and was rejected by the ICRC and interested governments. Similarly, the U.S./UK invasion of Iraq in 2003 was an international armed conflict under the Geneva Conventions.

Once the U.S./UK forces removed the Taliban and Saddam Hussein governments from Afghanistan and Iraq, the new Iyad Allawi and Hamid Karzai governments cooperated with the U.S./UK forces in combating remaining elements of the Taliban/Qaeda forces in Afghanistan and the insurgents in Iraq. One might assess the situation in 2004 in both countries as an occupation by foreign forces in which the full panoply of humanitarian law applies, particularly the Fourth Geneva Convention Relative to the Protection of Civilian Persons in Time of War. Alternatively, as the new governments in Afghanistan and Iraq gain authority and permanency, one should assess the on-going armed conflict as a non-international armed as to which the very limited protections of Common Article 3 apply. The United States has not ratified the Second Additional Protocol and its conditions are probably too narrow to fit the conditions in either Afghanistan and Iraq, at least as of 2006.

As one can see from the above analysis, it is possible to fit the principal conditions arising under the "war on terror" into the traditional humanitarian law categories of armed conflict and related protections of noncombatants. Furthermore, there is a lack of international consensus as to what might be the limits of or standards applicable to the purported new category of conflict relating the "war on terror." Accordingly, the four Geneva Conventions and two Additional Protocols continue to constitute the most reliable standard of international humanitarian law in regard to armed conflicts, including the "war on terror." The U.S. contention that there exists a new category of persons ("enemy combatant") without protection under the Geneva Convention Relative to the Treatment of Prisoners of War (Third Geneva Convention) is discussed below.

B. SUMMARY OF HUMANITARIAN LAW PROTECTIONS UNDER DIFFERENT KINDS OF ARMED CONFLICT

In regard to international armed conflicts the four Geneva Conventions and first Additional Protocol provide extremely detailed protections for the wounded and sick in armed forces in the field (First Geneva Convention), the wounded and sick in armed forces in at sea (Second Geneva Convention), prisoners of war (Third Geneva Convention), and civilian persons (Fourth Geneva Convention). For example, the First Geneva Convention for the Amelioration of the Condition of the Wounded and Sick in Armed Forces in the Field assures that members of the armed forces and militia who are wounded or sick, shall be respected, protected, and treated humanely by the party to the conflict in whose power they may be without any adverse discrimination based on sex, race, nationality, religion, political opinions, or any other similar criteria. Accordingly, "Any attempts upon their lives, or violence to their persons, shall be strictly prohibited; in particular, they shall not be murdered or exterminated, subjected to torture or to biological experiments; they shall not wilfully be left without medical assistance and care, nor shall conditions exposing them to contagion or infection be created."[579]

In the context of international armed conflicts, the Third Geneva Convention relative to the Treatment of Prisoners of War applies to members of the armed forces of a party to the conflict as well as members of militias or volunteer corps forming part of such armed forces. After the U.S. army invaded Afghanistan in 2001, the U.S. captured a large number of combatants and refused to accord them prisoner of war status even though many of them were part of the regular Taliban forces defending the Taliban government. Other detainees had evidently been Al Qaeda fighters who may not have been wearing a distinctive uniform or otherwise fulfilling the requirements of the Third Geneva Convention relating to militia or spontaneous volunteers. The Geneva Conventions are intended to be comprehensive in protecting prisoners of war or civilians who are detained in armed conflicts. Indeed, in the case of any doubt as to the status of any individuals who has fallen into the hands of an enemy, Article 5 requires that "such persons shall enjoy the protection of the present Convention until such time as their status has been determined by a competent tribunal."[580]

Under the Third Geneva Convention, prisoners of war captured in an international armed conflict are entitled to be humanely treated and are not to be subjected to any unlawful act or omission causing death or seriously endangering their health; physical mutilation or medical or scientific experiments of any kind; or acts of violence, intimidation, insults, and public curiosity. Prisoners of war may be interned in a safe location; "quartered under conditions as favorable as those for the forces of the detaining power who are billeted in the same area"; provided with sufficient bedding, clothing, health care, facilities for religious observance, necessary facilities for correspondence (two letters and four cards monthly); and must be repatriated upon the cessation of active hostilities.[581] A prisoner of war may be tried only by a military court or by a civil court if a member of the armed forces of the detaining power would have jurisdiction by such a civil court. In no circumstances may a prisoner of war be tried by a court of any kind that does not offer the essential guarantees of independence, impartiality, no double jeopardy, and respect for rights of the defense. Prisoners of war may be tried only for offenses for which a member of the armed forces of the detaining power may be tried. Hence a prisoner of war may be tried for war crimes, but not for engaging in military activities as an active duty combatant.

Under the Fourth Geneva Convention, High Contracting Parties undertake to assure that hospitals and medical supplies shall not be the object of attack in an international armed conflict. Protected persons, such as civilians who are nationals of the occupied country, are further entitled to "respect for their persons, their honour, their family rights, their religious convictions and practices, and their manners and customs. They shall at all times be humanely treated, and shall be protected especially against all acts of violence or threats thereof and against insults and public curiosity. . . . Women shall be especially protected against any attack on their honour, in particular against rape, enforced prostitution, or any form of indecent assault."[582] The Fourth Convention also forbids "physical or moral coercion" against civilians "to obtain information from them or from third parties" as well as "any measure of such a character as to cause the physical suffering or extermination of protected persons in their hands [including] murder, torture, corporal punishment, mutilation and medical or scientific experiments. . . ."[583] Children are also entitled to particular protection.

The Fourth Geneva Convention does not allow a party to an international armed conflict to use civilians as human shields to make certain places immune from military operations. Article 46 of the same Convention prohibits individual or mass "forcible transfers, as well as deportations of protected persons from occupied territory to the territory of the Occupying Power or to that of any other country, occupied or not, are prohibited, regardless of their motive."[584] If absolutely necessary for the security of a party to the conflict, civilians may be interned or assigned to particular residences, but the need for their internment or assigned residence must be reconsidered by a court or administrative board at least every six months, and they should be released as soon as possible after end of hostilities. Internees may receive, by post or any other means, individual parcels or collective shipments containing, in particular, food, clothing, medical supplies, and books and objects of a devotional, educational, or recreational character. Internees are entitled to communicate with the outside world by at least two letters and four cards monthly. If an individual is definitely suspected of activities hostile to the security of the state, such individual person may not exercise rights prejudicial to the security of the state. Accordingly, if an individual is detained as a spy, saboteur, or person suspected of activity hostile to the security of the occupying power, such person may, in cases where absolute military security so requires, be regarded as having forfeited rights of communication. "In each case, such persons shall nevertheless be treated with humanity, and in case of trial, shall not be deprived of the rights of fair and regular trial prescribed by the present Convention. They shall also be granted the full rights and privileges of a protected person under the present Convention at the earliest date consistent with the security of the State or Occupying Power, as the case may be."[585]

The most important contribution of Additional Protocol I to the humanitarian protections in international armed conflict is its affirmation that "the right of the Parties to the conflict to choose methods or means of warfare is not unlimited . . . . It is prohibited to employ weapons, projectiles and material and methods of warfare of a nature to cause superfluous injury or unnecessary suffering. . . . It is prohibited to employ methods or means of warfare which are intended, or may be expected, to cause widespread, long-term and severe damage to the natural environment."[586] Additional Protocol I also affirms the fundamental principle that "Parties to the conflict shall at all times distinguish between the civilian population and combatants and between civilian objects and military objectives and accordingly shall direct their operations only against military objectives."[587] Furthermore, Protocol I forbids attacks against civilians, civilian objects, "historic monuments, works of art or places of worship which constitute the cultural or spiritual heritage of peoples," as well as indiscriminate attacks.[588] Among others, the following types of attacks are to be considered as indiscriminate:

(a) An attack by bombardment by any methods or means which treats as a single military objective a number of clearly separated and distinct military objectives located in a city, town, village or other area containing a similar concentration of civilians or civilian objects; and
(b) An attack which may be expected to cause incidental loss of civilian life, injury to civilians, damage to civilian objects, or a combination thereof, which would be excessive in relation to the concrete and direct military advantage anticipated.

Additional Protocol I also prohibits attacks against a person who is *hors de combat*, that is, a person who may have previously been engaged in combat as a soldier but who has been injured, detained, or otherwise unable to take an active part in the hostilities. Protocol I further prohibits attacks on any person who is parachuting from an aircraft in distress or is a member of a civil defense organization, as well as attacks against "installations containing dangerous forces, namely dams, dykes and nuclear electrical generating stations, . . . even where these objects are military objectives, if such attack may cause the release of dangerous forces and consequent severe losses among the civilian population."[589] Protocol I further elaborates on the rights of prisoners of war, persons who have taken part in hostilities, mercenaries, and spies. In addition, Protocol I prohibits such perfidious acts of war as feigning of incapacitation by wounds or sickness; feigning of civilian, noncombatant status; misuse of the emblem of the red cross; and wearing uniforms or emblems of neutral parties. The Protocol also prohibits giving an order that there shall be no survivors or threatening to give such an order as well as starvation of civilians as a method of war.

Additional Protocol I assures more precise protection in international armed conflicts for civilian medical units, ships, aircraft, other transports, and personnel unless they are used to commit, outside their humanitarian function, acts harmful to the enemy. Protocol I also calls for measures to locate and return persons missing or deceased as a result of an international armed conflict. Article 75 of Additional Protocol I guarantees that "persons who are in the power of a Party to the conflict and who do not benefit from more favourable treatment under the Conventions or under this Protocol shall be treated humanely in all circumstances and shall enjoy, as a minimum," protection from violence "to the life, health, or physical or mental well-being of persons. . . ."[590] Article 75 elaborates on those protections and guarantees, for example, that

Any person arrested, detained or interned for actions related to the armed conflict shall be informed promptly, in a language he understands, of the reasons why these measures have been taken. . . .

No sentence may be passed and no penalty may be executed on a person found guilty of a penal offence related to the armed conflict except pursuant to a conviction pronounced by an impartial and regularly constituted court respecting the generally recognized principles of regular judicial procedure, which include the following:

(a) The procedure shall provide for an accused to be informed without delay of the particulars of the offence alleged against him and shall afford the accused before and during his trial all necessary rights and means of defence; . . .

(d) Anyone charged with an offence is presumed innocent until proved guilt according to law;

(e) Anyone charged with an offence shall have the right to be tried in his presence;

(f) No one shall be compelled to testify against himself or to confess guilt;

(g) Anyone charged with an offence shall have the right to examine, or have examined, the witnesses against him and to obtain the attendance and examination of witnesses on his behalf under the same conditions as witnesses against him. . . .[591]

Common Article 3 to the Four Geneva Conventions provides a few very fundamental protections during armed conflicts not of an international character occurring in the territory of one of the High Contracting Parties for persons taking no active part in the hostilities, including members of armed forces who have laid down their arms and those placed *hors de combat* by sickness, wounds, detention, or any other cause. Protected persons "shall in all circumstances be treated humanely, without any adverse" discrimination; nor shall they be subjected to

(a) Violence to life and person, in particular murder of all kinds, mutilation, cruel treatment and torture;
(b) Taking of hostages;
(c) Outrages upon personal dignity, in particular humiliating and degrading treatment;
(d) The passing of sentences and the carrying out of executions without previous judgment pronounced by a regularly constituted court, affording all the judicial guarantees which are recognized as indispensable by civilized peoples. . . .[592]

The International Committee of the Red Cross (ICRC) monitors compliance with the four Geneva Conventions and two Additional Protocols by visiting places of detention, making approaches to authorities, using its right of humanitarian initiative, and receiving complaints about breaches of international humanitarian law. The ICRC visits prisoners of war and civilian internees, interviews them without witnesses; repeats such visits to assure that the detainees are not killed or ill-treated; and are supplied with basic supplies of blankets medicines, medical care, clothing, food, and so on. The ICRC brings to the attention of the authorities any problems. The ICRC occasionally uses its right of humanitarian initiative to organize exchanges of prisoners, reunion of families, and truces to bring care for the wounded or refugees.

In October 2003 the ICRC publicly criticized the U.S. government for the prolonged detention (without apparent end) of over 600 detainees in Guantánamo Bay, Cuba. ICRC delegates were the only outsiders with access to the detainees the U.S. military captured in Afghanistan, Bosnia, and elsewhere. The ICRC normally visits places of detention resulting from armed conflict under the assurance that it will reveal its findings only to the detaining government. Accordingly, the ICRC public announcement of concern about the Guantánamo detainees was remarkable and represented an external manifestation about problems of prolonged detention. It was later learned that the ICRC had confidentially expressed even greater concerns about the way the detainees were put through extraordinarily lengthy and repeated interrogations, in which they were required to stand for prolonged periods of time, as well as being subjected to sleep deprivation and other disorienting tactics. Additional information became public about deaths, torture, and other ill-treatment of detainees at U.S. detention facilities in Iraq and Afghanistan (Bagram and Kandihar), as well as places where the ICRC was not allowed to visit (such as naval ships in the Indian Ocean).

*See also*: Genocide, War Crimes, Crimes Against Humanity, and Crimes Against Peace; International Criminal Procedures; Peace; Security/Terrorism and Human Rights; Torture and Inhuman Treatment

*Further Reading*:

Assisting the Victims of Armed Conflict and other Disasters (Frits Kalshoven ed., 1989).
Commentary on the Geneva Conventions of 12 August 1949 (Jean Pictet ed., 1952).
Joan Fitzpatrick, Agora: Military Commissions, *Jurisdiction of Military Commissions and the Ambiguous War on Terrorism*, 96 A.J.I.L. 345 (2002).
Geneva Convention for the Amelioration of the Condition of the Wounded and Sick in Armed Forces in the Field, 75 U.N.T.S. 31, *entered into force* Oct. 21, 1950.
Geneva Convention for the Amelioration of the Condition of Wounded, Sick and Shipwrecked Members of Armed Forces at Sea, 75 U.N.T.S. 85, *entered into force* Oct. 21, 1950.
Geneva Convention relative to the Treatment of Prisoners of War, 75 U.N.T.S. 135, *entered into force* Oct. 21, 1950.
Geneva Convention relative to the Protection of Civilian Persons in Time of War, 75 U.N.T.S. 287, *entered into force* Oct. 21, 1950.
Oren Gross, *Chaos and Rules: Should Responses to Violent Crises Always Be Constitutional?* 112 Yale L.J. 1011 (2003).
Oren Gross & Fionnuala Ní Aoláin, Law in Times of Crisis (2006).
Detainees in Guantanamo Bay, Cuba, Request for Precautionary Measures, Inter-Am. C.H.R. (Mar. 13, 2002).
Harold Hongju Koh, Agora: Military Commissions, *The Case Against Military Commissions*, 96 A.J.I.L. 337 (2002).
Theodor Meron, *Human Rights and Humanitarian Norms as Customary Law* (1989).
Sean D. Murphy, *Decision Not to Regard Persons Detained in Afghanistan as POWs*, 96 A.J.I.L. 475 (2002).
*Prosecutor v. Tadic*, Decision on the Defense Motion for Interlocutory Appeal on Jurisdiction, Case No. IT-94-1-AR72 (1995), 35 I.L.M. 32 (1995).
Diane F. Orentlicher & Robert Kogod Goldman, *When Justice Goes to War: Prosecuting Terrorists Before Military Commissions* 25 Harv. J.L. & Pub. Pol'y 653 (2002).
Protocol Additional to the Geneva Conventions of 12 August 1949, and Relating to the Protection of Victims of International Armed Conflicts (Protocol I), 1125 U.N.T.S. 3, *entered into force* Dec. 7, 1978.
Protocol Additional to the Geneva Conventions of 12 August 1949, and Relating to the Protection of Victims of Non-International Armed Conflicts (Protocol II), 1125 U.N.T.S. 609, *entered into force* Dec. 7, 1978.

Michael Ratner, *Moving Away from the Rule of Law: Military Tribunals, Executive Detentions and Torture*, 24 Cardozo L. Rev. 1513 (2003).
Marco Sassòli, *Use and Abuse of the Laws of War In the "War on Terrorism,"* 22 Journal of Law & Inequality 195 (2004).
Anne-Marie Slaughter, *Beware the Trumpets of War: A Response to Kenneth Anderson*, 25 Harv. J.L. & Pub. Pol'y 965 (2002).
David Weissbrodt, *The Role of International Organizations in the Implementation of Human Rights and Humanitarian Law in Situations of Armed Conflict*, 21 Vanderbilt J. Trans. L. 313 (1988).

*Links to Consult:*

http://web.amnesty.org/ai.nsf/recent/AMR510532002
http://www.asil.org/insights/insigh81.htm
http://www.crimesofwar.org
http://www.icrc.org/web/eng/siteeng0.nsf/iwpList2/Humanitarian_law?OpenDo cum ent
http://www.un.org/icty/tadic/appeal/decision-e/51002.htm
http://www1.umn.edu/humanrts/cases/guantanamo-2003.html
http://www1.umn.edu/humanrts/instree/auoy.htm
http://www1.umn.edu/humanrts/links/afghanistan.html
http://www1.umn.edu/humanrts/links/Iraq.html
http://www1.umn.edu/humanrts/links/response.html

## 23. Genocide, War Crimes, Crimes Against Humanity, and Crimes Against Peace

At the conclusion of World War II, France, the Soviet Union, the United States, and the United Kingdom embarked upon an unprecedented international response to genocide, war crimes, crimes against humanity, and crimes against peace by initiating the development of international criminal responsibility. On August 8, 1945, those four governments signed the Agreement for the Prosecution and Punishment of the Major War Criminals of the European Axis and Charter of the International Military Tribunal (Nuremberg Charter).[593] The Nuremberg Charter prescribed for prosecution "crimes against peace," "war crimes," and "crimes against humanity." Crimes against humanity were interpreted to include the Holocaust during World War II, that is, the deliberate and systematic killing of six million Jews, three million Russian prisoners of war, one-half million Roma (Gypsies), as well as thousands of persons with mental illness, Jehovah's Witnesses, homosexuals, and Communists.

### A. Genocide

Although genocide has been practiced throughout history, the word "genocide," which means the "killing" (derives from the Latin, *cide*) of a "people" (Greek, *genos*), was added to the English language in 1944 as an attempt to describe crimes against humanity involving the deliberate and systematic killing of racial and national groups during World War II. The concept of "genocide" was then used by the prosecutors at Nuremberg. Shortly after the Nuremberg trials the UN General Assembly adopted a resolution that defined genocide as "a denial of the right of existence of entire human groups," and affirmed that genocide was a "crime under international law."[594]

On December 9, 1948,—one day before the adoption of the Universal Declaration of Human Rights—the General Assembly unanimously adopted the Convention on the Prevention and Punishment of the Crime of Genocide, defining genocide in Article 2 more precisely to mean

> any of the following acts committed with intent to destroy, in whole or in part, a national, ethnical, racial or religious group, as such:
> (a) Killing members of the group;
> (b) Causing serious bodily or mental harm to members of the group;
> (c) Deliberately inflicting on the group conditions of life calculated to bring about its physical destruction in whole or in part;
> (d) Imposing measures intended to prevent births within the group;
> (e) Forcibly transferring children of the group to another group.[595]

Although genocide in common parlance focuses particularly on the killing of groups of individuals, the Genocide Convention covers a number of other criminal acts, including for example, imposing measures to prevent births within a group. The Convention also requires a criminal mental component, that is, the acts must have been committed with "the intent to destroy, in whole or in part, a national, ethnic, racial, or religious group, as such."[596] In addition to the crime of genocide itself, Article 3 of the Convention states that the following acts are also punishable: conspiracy to commit genocide, direct and public incitement to commit genocide, attempt to commit genocide, or complicity in genocide. The definition of genocide in the 1948 Convention was later incorporated verbatim in the statutes of the Yugoslavia (1993)[597] and Rwanda (1994)[598] tribunals, as well as that of the International Criminal Court (ICC)[599] (adopted 1998, came into force 2002).

Although earlier drafts of the Genocide Convention included the killing of political groups, this category was omitted during the final drafting stages because of concern that frequent claims of political genocide might undermine the gravity of the other offenses covered by the Convention. Further, as described during the International Criminal Tribunal of the Former Yugoslavia (ICTY) in *Prosecutor v. Jelisic*, the Convention sought to protect "'stable' groups objectively defined and to which individuals belong regardless of their own desires."[600] In addition to the omission of political groups, the concept of cultural genocide—the destruction of a group through forcible assimilation into a dominant culture—was also omitted in order to focus solely on acts involving the physical destruction of a group. The Convention's reference to forcibly transferring children of a targeted group to another group may, however, be considered a feature of cultural genocide.

The narrow terms of the Genocide Convention have caused dispute about its application. For example, even a massacre of large numbers of people may not constitute genocide unless one can find an intent by the perpetrators to destroy the group in whole or in part. Such a massacre would still be forbidden as arbitrary killings, however. Governments have shown considerable reluctance to identify situations as involving genocide because Articles 1 and 8 of the Convention appear to require preventative, possibly even military, action. Article 1 requires States parties to "prevent and punish" genocide.[601] Article 8 states, "Any Contracting Party may call upon the competent organs of the United Nations to take such action under the Charter of the United Nations as they consider appropriate for the prevention and suppression of acts of genocide or any other acts enumerated in article 3."[602]

In addition to the Holocaust, there have been a number of genocides during the twentieth and the beginning of the twenty-first century—

some of them more clearly qualify as genocide than others. The extermination of Armenians by the Turks beginning in 1915 is commonly recognized as the first genocide of the twentieth century, although the Turkish government still denies that a genocide occurred. More recent situations include: the Turkish killing of the Dersim Kurds (1937–38); the killing of Hutus by Tutsis in Burundi (1972); the Khmer Rouge killing of Cambodians (mid-1970s); the Anfal campaign against Iraqi Kurds (1988); the killing of Tutsis by Hutus in Rwanda (1994); the killing of Bosnians and Albanians by the Serbian military during the dissolution of Yugoslavia (1991–95); and the killing of the Fur, Zaghawas, and Massalit ethnic communities in the Darfur region of Sudan (2003–7).

The death of one and a half million Cambodians (out of a population of seven million) during the rule of the Khmer Rouge illustrates difficulties in applying the 1948 Convention definition of genocide. Part of the problem with identifying what happened in Cambodia as genocide is that both the perpetrators and victims were Khmer. Some scholars have argued that the Convention definition applies even when the victims and perpetrators are of the same ethnic/national group, which might be identified as "auto-genocide." Others, however, have more narrowly reasoned that the majority of victims were killed for largely political motivations, but certain religious or minority groups, such as the Muslim Cham and the Khmer Buddhists, were definitely targets of genocide.

Similar ambiguities over the application of the term "genocide" have surfaced in regard to other situations. For example, in Rwanda during 1994 Hutus associated with the government and the Interahamwe killed not only members of the Tutsi and Twa ethnic communities, but also moderate Hutus who were sympathetic to the Tutsi cause. At first there was even some reluctance to identify the killing of Tutsis as genocide, partly because of the unwillingness of the international community to intervene militarily to stop the killings.

At times the term "ethnic cleansing" has been used as a euphemism for genocide. In the Balkans, for example, about 250,000 people were killed during the break-up of Yugoslavia. The war was initiated when Bosnia and Herzegovina—composed of a mixed ethnic population, declared independence from Yugoslavia in 1991. Croatian president Franjo Tudjman and Serbian president Slobodan Milošević, however, had planned to partition Bosnia between Croatia and Serbia. Attempting to carve out their own enclaves, the Serbian minority in Bosnia, with the help of the Serbian Yugoslav army, took the offensive and laid siege, particularly on Sarajevo. It then began its campaigns of ethnic cleansing, which involved rape, expulsion, and massacre of Muslim civilians. Croats also began carving out communities by employing many of the same techniques. By 1992, rebel Bosnian Serbs had conquered over 60 percent of Bosnia. Even after NATO intervention in 1995, Serb militia groups entered the UN safe areas of Tuzla, Zepa, and Srebrenica, where they murdered thousands of Croat and Muslim civilians. A number of individuals have been indicted and convicted by the International Criminal Tribunal for the former Yugoslavia for their role in the genocide, and the International Court of Justice found in 2007 that Serbia violated its obligations under the Genocide Convention to prevent genocide in Srebenica and to cooperate with the ICTY.[603]

Since the beginning of the twenty-first century, violence committed in the Democratic Republic of Congo and in Sudan have persisted and the international community remains ineffective in halting genocide. For example, more than four million people have died in the Democratic Republic of Congo since the beginning of a complex civil war involving numerous rebel groups and seven foreign armies, making this war more deadly to civilians than any other since World War II. Government and dissident forces have committed war crimes, including killing or displacing civilians in their struggle to gain control of regions such as the Northern Katanga province, south Kivu, and Ituri. The massacre of targeted ethnic groups in the Ituri district caused Amnesty International, Human Rights Watch, and other human rights organizations in 2003 to warn about genocide. Women and girls have been particular targets of violence in the Congo, and the UN estimates that more than 40,000 women and girls—some as young as three years of age—have been raped since the year 2000. Luis Moreno Ocampo, the International Criminal Court prosecutor, announced in June 2004 that the first-ever investigation by the ICC prosecutor's office would be conducted in the Democratic Republic of Congo.

Since February 2003, Sudanese government forces and government-backed ethnic militias known as "Janjaweed" have committed war crimes, crimes against humanity, and "ethnic cleansing" in the Darfur region of Sudan. Under the pretext of controlling a counterinsurgency campaign against two rebel groups, the Janjaweed have systematically targeted civilian communities that share the same ethnicity as the rebel groups and have committed massacres, as well as looting, raping, forcibly displacing civilians, and destroying hundreds of villages.

B. War Crimes

The Hague Conventions of 1899 and 1907 identified "violations of the laws or customs of war" that became the basis of individual criminal responsibility for war crimes.[604] The Nuremberg Charter of 1945 was the first instrument that identified specific violations as war crimes, including

> murder, ill-treatment or deportation to slave labor or for any other purpose of civilian population of or in occupied territory, murder or ill-treatment of prisoners of war or persons on the seas, killing of hostages, plunder of public or private property, wanton destruction of cities, towns or villages, or devastation not justified by military necessity.[605]

The four Geneva Conventions specify that certain violations shall be considered grave breaches that are subject to criminal sanctions.[606] Grave breaches include the following acts if committed against protected persons (principally civilians and soldiers who are *hors de combat*) or property protected by the relevant Geneva Convention: willful killing, torture, or inhuman treatment, including biological experiments; willfully causing great suffering or serious injury to body or health; unlawful deportation or transfer; unlawful confinement or compulsion to serve in the forces of a hostile Power; willfully depriving a protected person of the rights of fair and regular trial; taking of hostages; and extensive destruction and appropriation of property, not justified by military necessity and carried out unlawfully and wantonly. In the four Geneva Conventions, the High Contracting Parties have undertaken to adopt necessary legislation to provide for effective penal sanctions; to search for persons alleged to have committed, or to have ordered to be committed, grave breaches; and to bring such persons, regardless of their nationality, before their own courts. They may also extradite offenders for trial by another High Contracting Party. Persons accused of grave breaches are entitled to at least the safeguards of proper trial and defense, which are extensively defined by the Geneva Conventions.

Additional Protocol I adds further grave breaches in the context of international armed conflicts, including, among others, (a) making the civilian population or individual civilians the object of attack; (b) launching an indiscriminate attack affecting the civilian population or civilian objects in the knowledge that such attack will cause excessive loss of life, injury to civilians, or damage to civilian objects; (c) launching an attack against works or installations containing dangerous forces (e.g., a hydroelectric dam) in the knowledge that such attack will cause excessive loss of life, injury to civilians, or damage to civilian objects; (d) making a person the object of attack in the knowledge that he is *hors de combat*; (e) transfer by the occupying power of parts of its own civilian population into the territory it occupies, or the deportation or transfer of all or parts of the population of the occupied territory within or outside this territory; (f) unjustifiable delay in the repatriation of prisoners of war or civilians; (g) practices of *apartheid* and other inhuman and degrading practices involving outrages upon personal dignity, based on racial discrimination; (h) making the clearly recognized historic monuments, works of art, or places of worship that constitute the cultural or spiritual heritage of people the object of attack, causing as a result extensive destruction thereof, when such places are not located in the immediate proximity of military objectives; and (i) depriving protected persons of the rights of fair and regular trial.[607]

Additional Protocol I further specifies that grave breaches of the Geneva Conventions and Protocols shall be regarded as war crimes. War crimes have been subject to criminal prosecution by the Nuremberg and Tokyo Tribunals after World War II as well as the International Criminal Tribunals for Rwanda and the former Yugoslavia initiated in the 1990s, and have been subject to prosecution by the International Criminal Court since 2002. Furthering the jurisprudence of and provisions establishing those tribunals and court, Additional Protocol 1 indicates that superior officers will not be absolved of responsibility for a grave breach/war crime committed by a subordinate if the superior officers knew, or had information which should have enabled them to conclude in the circumstances at the time, that the subordinate was committing or was going to commit such a breach, and if they did not take all feasible measures within their power to prevent or repress the breach.

Additional Protocol II omits any reference to grave breaches for humanitarian law violations committed in non-international armed conflicts.[608] The Appeals Chamber of the ICTY, however, has indicated in *Prosecutor v. Tadic* that "customary international law imposes criminal liability for serious violations of common Article 3, as supplemented by other general principles and rules on the protection of victims of internal armed conflict."[609]

The Statute of the ICC comprehends and makes more specific the previous definitions of war crimes and clearly indicates that "violations of the laws and customs of war" can be perpetrated during noninternational armed conflicts.[610] Among the most significant additional war crimes specified by the ICC Statute are crimes of sexual violence, including forced pregnancy and forced sterilization.

C. CRIMES AGAINST HUMANITY

Crimes against humanity are often committed during armed conflict, although experts have argued that the link is not necessary. For example, many crimes against humanity were committed during peacetime, including Stalin's purges, much of the Khmer Rouge's terror, and the forced collectivization of Chinese peasants under Mao.

228   Particular Rights and Responsibilities

The Nuremberg Charter was the first international agreement to identify what actions would be considered crimes against humanity:

> murder, extermination, enslavement, deportation, and other inhumane acts committed against any civilian population, before or during the war, or persecutions on political, racial or religious grounds in execution of or in connection with any crime within the jurisdiction of the Tribunal, whether or not in violation of the domestic law of the country where perpetrated.[611]

While the August 1945 Nuremberg definition of crimes against humanity and the similar definition for the Tokyo War Crimes Tribunal of 1946 limited prosecutions of the major war criminals to events "before or during the war," the four Allies of World War II concluded a second agreement (Control Council Law No. 10) in December 1945 that broadened the definition to include

> Atrocities and offences, including but not limited to murder, extermination, enslavement, deportation, imprisonment, torture, rape, or other inhumane acts committed against any civilian population, or persecutions on political, racial or religious grounds whether or not in violation of the domestic laws of the country where perpetrated.[612]

Not only does the Control Council Law No. 10 omit any reference or specific connection to World War II, but it also includes rape within the jurisdiction of the courts in Germany that tried thousands of lower rank offenders.

Although there is no specific treaty on crimes against humanity, since the Nuremberg Charter and Control Council Law No. 10 of 1945, the statutes of the ICTY, the ICTR, and the International Criminal Court ICC have included within their jurisdiction crimes against humanity. For example, the ICC Statute defines a crime against humanity so as to include torture, rape, "sexual slavery, enforced prostitution, forced pregnancy, enforced sterilization, or any other form of sexual violence of comparable gravity," *apartheid*, forcible transfer of population, severe deprivation of physical liberty, and the enforced disappearance of persons as well as to define more precisely the application of such terms as extermination, enslavement, deportation (or forcible population transfer), torture, and forced pregnancy.[613]

In addition to the description of crimes against humanity included in the statutes of the international criminal tribunals, the Convention on the Non-Applicability of Statutory Limitations to War Crimes and Crimes Against Humanity of 1968 established that there was no statutory or period of limitation to war crimes or crimes against humanity due to the international priority of prosecuting such crimes.[614] Accordingly, an offender can be brought to justice even many years after committing a crime against humanity.

D. CRIMES AGAINST PEACE

The Nuremberg Charter defined a crime against peace as the "planning, preparation, initiation or waging of a war of aggression, or a war in violation of international treaties, agreements or assurances, or participation in a common plan or conspiracy for the accomplishment of any of the foregoing."[615] Seven of the twenty-three major war criminals at Nuremberg were tried for crimes against peace. The Statute of the International Criminal Court also prescribes the crime of aggression, but prosecutions are awaiting authoritative definition of that phrase.

E. CRIMINAL TRIBUNALS

Recognizing that serious violations of humanitarian law were committed in Rwanda, the UN Security Council created the ICTR by Resolution 955 in November 1994, although the first trial began only in January 1997. The tribunal is responsible for the prosecution of persons who committed genocide and other serious violations of international humanitarian law in the territory of Rwanda, as well as in the territory of neighboring states, from January 1, 1994 to December 31, 1994. Located in Arusha, United Republic of Tanzania, the tribunal is governed by its statute and consists of three organs: the Chambers and the Appeals Chamber; the Office of the Prosecutor; and the Registry. As of 2006, the ICTR has completed cases involving twenty-one individuals, seven more accused are on appeal, while another twenty-six accused are on trial, and twelve more are awaiting trial. The International Criminal Tribunal for Rwanda delivered the first-ever judgment on the crime of genocide by an international tribunal.

The International Criminal Tribunal for the former Yugoslavia was established in May 1993 by Security Council Resolution 827 in response to war crimes, crimes against humanity, and genocide committed in the territory of the former Yugoslavia since 1991, and as a response to the threat to international peace and security posed by those serious violations.[616] The ICTY is located in the Hague, Netherlands. As of 2006, the ICTY had indicted 161 individuals for serious violations of humanitarian law, and ninety-nine judgments have been handed down. There are sixty-two accused as to which proceedings are continuing, and six arrest warrants for suspects at large.

The idea of a permanent court that could hold individuals accountable for the worst international crimes was first proposed in the late nineteenth century, after World War I, and in response to the genocide committed by the Turkish government against the Armenians, and again following World War II in response to the Holocaust. After the establishment of the international criminal tribunals for Rwanda and the former Yugoslavia in the 1990s, the idea evolved into the International Criminal Court, which has jurisdiction over genocide, war crimes, and crimes against humanity. The Rome Statute of the International Criminal Court entered into force on July 1, 2002, with sixty States parties, but now has more than 100 States parties.[617] Although the ICC cannot prosecute people for crimes committed before it came into existence, the Court is intended to deter and punish crimes committed in states that fall within the Court's jurisdiction, that is, states that have ratified the Rome Statute. Nonetheless, the ICC does have jurisdiction not only over crimes committed by people from states that are party to the Rome Statute, but also over crimes committed on the territory of a State party. The Court has jurisdiction only over individuals, not governments, armed groups, or companies, although members of governments or armed groups as well as corporate officers may be prosecuted as individuals.

One important feature of the ICC is that any prosecution may be blocked by the UN Security Council for a renewable period of one year if the Security Council determines that the prosecution would be a threat to international peace and security. While allowing the Security Council to retain the ultimate authority over peace and security, this provision prohibits a single Security Council member from blocking a prosecution by the Court.

Another important aspect of the ICC is that, unlike the ICTY and the ICTR, it does not have precedence over national courts. According to the Rome Statute's Article 17, the Court can pursue cases only as a measure of last resort when the country involved shows itself to be "unwilling or unable genuinely to carry out the investigation or prosecution."[618] This principle, known as "complementarity," allows a state with a legitimately functioning legal system to investigate allegations itself, as long as the state's interest in the case is not for "the purpose of shielding the person concerned from criminal responsibility."[619]

Perhaps the single reason why the ICC has gained so much international support is the efforts of nongovernmental organizations (NGOs) to assist in drafting the ICC Statute as well as in mobilizing public opinion. Still, the ICC has a number of opponents that have sought to undermine the Court. The United States, for example, has expressed concern that the ICC may launch politically motivated prosecutions of U.S. citizens. Evoking Article 98 of the Rome Statute, the U.S. has secured signatures and ratifications to bilateral immunity agreements with 100 countries as of 2006. Although the U.S. signed the Rome Statute in 2000, the Bush administration sought in 2002 to withdraw the U.S. signature. Because there exists no procedure for withdrawing a signature, the U.S. could only indicate its unwillingness to proceed with ratification.

F. SAMPLE OF JURISPRUDENCE

The Nuremberg Tribunal, the ICTY, and the ICTR have established some important principles regarding the process of establishing individual criminal responsibility for war crimes, crimes against humanity, and genocide. For example, during the prosecution of several Nazi officers, the Nuremberg Court rejected the defense claim that they were "only acting under orders," in favor of a the idea that certain crimes can never be justified, even when a government authorizes their practice.

In the ICTR case *Prosecutor v. Nahimana, Barayagwiza and Ngeze (Media Case)*, the founders and ideologists of the Radio Television Libre des Milles Collines (RTLM)—after 1994 known as "Radio Machete"—and the newspaper *Kangura* were convicted of genocide, in particular, of direct and public incitement to commit genocide.[620] The tribunal distinguished incitement from legitimate uses of the media by noting how radio and print media were used in these cases to promote ethnic hatred and the killing of Tutsis and Hutus who sympathized with the Tutsis.

The ICTR in the case of *Prosecutor v. Akayesu* (2001)[621] and the ICTY in the case of *Prosecutor v. Kunarac, Kovac and Vokovic* (2002) were the first prosecutions for rape as a war crime in the history of international tribunals. The ICTY recognized that wartime rape is often encouraged as official military strategy, although it noted that "the armed conflict need not have been causal to the commission of the crime, but the existence of an armed conflict must, at a minimum, have played a substantial part in the perpetrator's ability to commit it."[622] The defendants' criminal conduct was part of a systematic attack on the non-Serb population which included the specific targeting of 20,000 Muslim women who were detained, raped, and tortured by military units. The *Akayesu* and the *Kunarac, Kovac and Vokovic* cases contain important standards for the prosecution of sexual violence, especially with the creation of a permanent International Criminal Court.

*See also*: Humanitarian Law, International Criminal Procedures, Security/Terrorism and Human Rights

*Further Reading*:

Accountability for Atrocities: National and International Responses (Jane E. Stromseth ed., 2003).

Agreement for the Prosecution and Punishment of the Major War Criminals of the European Axis, and Charter of the International Military Tribunal, 82 U.N.T.S. 280, *entered into force* Aug. 8, 1945.

Application of the Convention on the Prevention and Punishment of the Crime of Genocide *(Bosn. & Herz. v. Yugo. (Serb. & Mont.))*, Judgment, Feb. 16, 2007.

M. Cherif Bassiouni, The Statute of the International Criminal Court: A Documentary History (1998).

Yves Beigbeder, Judging War Criminals: The Politics of International Justice (1999).

Machteld Boot, Genocide, Crimes Against Humanity, War Crimes: Nullum Crimen Sine Lege and the Subject Matter Jurisdiction of the International Criminal Court (2002).

Charter of the International Military Tribunal, 82 U.N.T.S. 279; 59 Stat. 1544; 3 Bevans 1238 (1945).

Roger S. Clark & Madeleine Sann, The Prosecution of International Crimes (1996).

Control Council Law No. 10, Punishment of Persons Guilty of War Crimes, Crimes Against Peace and Against Humanity, 3 Official Gazette Control Council for Germany 50–55 (1946).

Convention on the Non-Applicability of Statutory Limitations to War Crimes and Crimes Against Humanity, G.A. res. 2391 (XXIII), annex, 23 U.N. GAOR Supp. (No. 18) at 40, U.N. Doc. A/7218 (1968); 754 U.N.T.S. 73; 18 I.L.M. 68.

Convention on the Prevention and Punishment of the Crime of Genocide, 78 U.N.T.S. 277 *entered into force* Jan. 12, 1951.

Crimes of War: A Legal, Political-Documentary, and Psychological Inquiry into the Responsibility of Leaders, Citizens, and Soldiers for Criminal Acts in Wars (Richard A. Falk et al. eds., 1971).

Draft Code of Crimes Against the Peace and Security of Mankind, 1996, 51 UN GAOR Supp. (No. 10) at 14, U.N. Doc. A/CN.4/L.532, corr.1, corr.3 (1996).

G.A. res. 96(I), U.N. GAOR, 1st Sess., pt. 2, at 188, U.N. Doc. A/64/Add.1 (1946).

Genocide and Human Rights: A Global Anthology (Jack Nusan Porter ed., 1982).

Genocide: Conceptual and Historical Dimensions (George J. Andreopoulos ed., 1994).

John Hagan, Justice in the Balkans: Prosecuting War Crimes in the Hague Tribunal (2003).

Irving Louis Horowitz, Taking Lives: Genocide and State Power (4th ed. 1997).

Kurt Jonassohn and Karin Solveig Björnson, Genocide and Gross Human Rights Violations in Comparative Perspective (1998).

Justice for Crimes Against Humanity (Mark Lattimer & Philippe Sands eds., 2003).

Peter Karsten, Law, Soldiers, and Combat (1978).

Leo Kuper, The Prevention of Genocide (1985).

The Law of War Crimes: National and International Approaches (Timothy L.H. McCormack and Gerry J. Simpson eds., 1997).

Howard S. Levie, Terrorism in War, the Law of War Crimes (1993).

Theodor Meron, War Crimes Law Comes of Age: Essays (1998).

Principles of International Co-operation in the Detection, Arrest, Extradition and Punishment of Persons Guilty of War Crimes and Crimes Against Human-

ity, G.A. res. 3074 (XXVIII), 28 U.N. GAOR Supp. (30A) at 78, U.N. Doc. A/9030/Add.1 (1973).
Principles of International Law Recognized in the Charter of the Nuremberg Tribunal and in the Judgment of the Tribunal, 5 U.N. GAOR Supp. (No. 12) at 11, U.N. Doc. A/1316 (1950).
*Prosecutor v. Akayesu*, Case No. ICTR-96-4-T (Appeals Chamber), June 1, 2001.
*Prosecutor v. Jelisic*, Case No. IT-95-10 (Trial Chamber), Dec.14, 1999.
*Prosecutor v. Kunarac, Kovac and Vokovic*, Case No. IT-96-23 and IT-96-23/1 (Appeals Chamber), June 12, 2002.
*Prosecutor v. Nahimana, Barayagwiza and Ngeze*, Case No. ICTR-99-52-T (Trial Chamber), Dec. 3, 2003.
Steven R. Ratner & Jason S. Abrams, Accountability for Human Rights Atrocities in International Law: Beyond the Nuremberg Legacy (2d. ed. 2001).
Rome Statute of the International Criminal Court, U.N. Doc. A/CONF. 183/9; 37 I.L.M. 1002 (1998), *entered into force* July 1, 2002.
William A. Schabas, An Introduction to the International Criminal Court (2001).
William A. Schabas, Genocide in International Law: The Crimes of Crimes (2000).
Statute of the International Criminal Tribunal for Rwanda, S.C. res. 955, UN SCOR 49th sess., 3453rd mtg, U.N. Doc. S/Res/955 (1994); 33 I.L.M 1598.
Statute of the International Tribunal for the Prosecution of Persons Responsible for Serious Violations of International Humanitarian Law Committed in the Territory of the Former Yugoslavia Since 1991, SC res. 827, U.N. SCOR 48th sess., 3217th mtg. at 1–2 (1993); 32 I.L.M. 1159.
Lyal S. Sunga, Individual Responsibility in International Law for Serious Human Rights Violations (1992).
War Crimes in International Law (Yoram Dinstein & Mala Tabory eds., 1996).
Eric D. Weitz, A Century of Genocide: Utopias of Race and Nation (2003).
Donald A. Wells, War Crimes and Laws of War (2d ed. 1991).

*Links to Consult:*

http://www.crimesofwar.org
http://www.hrw.org/reports/2004/ij/
http://www.icc-cpi.int
http://www.icrc.org
http://www.ihlresearch.org/ihl
http://www.irinnews.org
http://www.preventgenocide.org
http://socrates.berkeley.edu/%7Ewarcrime/index2.htm
http://www.yale.edu/lawweb/avalon/lawofwar/lawwar.htm
http://www1.umn.edu/humanrts/instree/auox.htm

## 24. Security/Terrorism and Human Rights

Since the attacks of September 11, 2001, the international community has devoted increased attention to the issues of terrorism and security. That incident and the U.S. response to the attacks have raised questions about the adequacy of international law and tools for responding to the increased virulence of transnational terrorism, particularly considering that modern terrorist networks are increasingly enabled by technological modes of communication and organization. In addition, the U.S. response to the attacks has raised awareness of the need to balance the right to security with other fundamental human rights.

The main purpose of government and human rights law is to protect the security of everyone who lives in that society. All human beings are born equal in dignity and in rights, including the right to life, to be free from torture, and the right to be free from arbitrary killing. Those rights are non-derogable, that is, they cannot be subject to limitation or violation even in times of public emergency threatening the life of the nation. Although most of the development of human rights law has focused on protecting individuals from violations by governments, there are other forces in society that may also abuse human rights, including armed opposition groups, human trafficking networks, corporations, and even individuals (as in the case of domestic violence). Hence, international human rights law must respond to abuses by states and non-state actors, including terrorist groups.

The international human rights norms governing abuses committed by non-state actors, however, have not kept pace with those pertaining to state or even individual responsibility, thus inhibiting the ability of the UN to develop a comprehensive counterterrorism strategy. Another impediment to developing an international response to terrorism has been the lack of a universal definition of that word or concept. The UN has thus far failed to produce a common definition of terrorism or a general convention on terrorism—in part because one person's freedom fighter is another person's terrorist. The International Convention for the Suppression of the Financing of Terrorism, however, which entered into force April 10, 2002, offers a somewhat indirect definition of terrorism by describing the acts that constitute the financing of terrorism in the context of an armed conflict. Article 2 states:

Any person commits an offence within the meaning of this Convention if that person by any means, directly or indirectly, unlawfully and wilfully, provides or collects funds with the intention that they should be used or in the knowledge that they are to be used, in full or in part, in order to carry out . . . [any] act intended to cause death or serious bodily injury to a civilian, or to any other person not taking an active part in the hostilities in a situation of armed conflict, when the purpose of such act, by its nature or context, is to intimidate a population, or to compel a Government or an international organization to do or to abstain from doing any act.[623]

In addition to that convention, the UN has produced eleven conventions that criminalize specific acts of terrorism, including the Convention for the Suppression of Unlawful Seizure of Aircraft (1970), the Convention for the Suppression of Unlawful Acts Against the Safety of Civil Aviation (1971), the Convention on the Prevention and Punishment of Crimes Against Internationally Protected Persons, including Diplomatic Agents (1973), the Convention Against the Taking of Hostages (1979), the Convention on the Physical Protection of Nuclear Material (1980), the Protocol on the Suppression of Unlawful Acts of Violence at Airports Serving International Civil Aviation, supplementary to the Convention for the Suppression of Unlawful Acts Against the Safety of Civil Aviation (1988), the Convention for the Suppression of Unlawful Acts Against the Safety of Maritime Navigation (1988), the Protocol for the Suppression of Unlawful Acts Against the Safety of Fixed Platforms Located on the Continental Shelf (1988), and the Convention for the Suppression of Terrorist Bombings (1997).[624] Despite the seemingly piecemeal manner by which the conventions address terrorism, most legal scholars agree that virtually all forms of terrorism are prohibited by one of these conventions, in addition to the Geneva Conventions and the Rome Statute. Others have argued that a comprehensive convention on terrorism that offers a universal definition of terrorism is necessary in order for the UN to achieve the same degree of normative strength concerning the use of force by non-state actors as it has concerning the use of force by states.

Several regional organizations have attempted to formulate a response to terrorism by defining the acts that constitute terrorism. The Council of Europe adopted the European Convention on the Suppression of Terrorism in 1977, which identifies (in Article 1) the following terrorist acts as punishable:

1. an offence within the scope of the Convention for the Suppression of Unlawful Seizure of Aircraft, signed at The Hague on 16 December 1970;
2. an offence within the scope of the Convention for the Suppression of Unlawful Acts Against the Safety of Civil Aviation, signed at Montreal on 23 September 1971;
3. a serious offence involving an attack against the life, physical integrity or liberty of internationally protected persons, including diplomatic agents;
4. an offence involving kidnapping, the taking of a hostage or serious unlawful detention;
5. an offence involving the use of a bomb, grenade, rocket, automatic firearm or letter or parcel bomb if this use endangers persons;
6. an attempt to commit any of the foregoing offences or participation as an

accomplice of a person who commits or attempts to commit such an offence.[625]

In addition, the Organization of American States adopted in 2002 the Inter-American Convention Against Terrorism, which considers an offense of terrorism to include any crime already established in the international instruments (mentioned above). Further, in 1998 the Council of Arab Ministers of the Interior and the Council of Arab Ministers of Justice adopted the Arab Convention on the Suppression of Terrorism, which defined terrorism as

Any act or threat of violence, whatever its motives or purposes, that occurs in the advancement of an individual or collective criminal agenda and seeking to sow panic among people, causing fear by harming them, or placing their lives, liberty or security in danger, or seeking to cause damage to the environment or to public or private installations or property or to occupying or seizing them, or seeking to jeopardize a national resources.[626]

Some human rights advocates, however, have expressed concern that this definition, as well as the Arab Convention in general, could be subject to imprecise interpretation and abuse, and do not satisfy the requirements of legality in international human rights and humanitarian law.

In 2003, UN Secretary-General Kofi Annan initiated the High-Level Panel on Threats, Challenges and Change in order to generate new ideas about the kinds of security policies and institutions required for the UN to be effective in the twenty-first century. Recognizing that the failure to agree on a definition of terrorism had caused an obstruction to the formulation of counter-terrorism standards, the High-Level Panel offered a clear definition of terrorism that included the following elements:

(a) Recognition, in the preamble, that State use of force against civilians is regulated by the Geneva Conventions and other instruments, and, if of sufficient scale, constitutes a war crime by the persons concerned or a crime against humanity;
(b) Restatement that acts under the 12 preceding anti-terrorism conventions are terrorism, and a declaration that they are a crime under international law; and restatement that terrorism in time of armed conflict is prohibited by the Geneva Conventions and Protocols;
(c) Reference to the definitions contained in the 1999 International Convention for the Suppression of the Financing of Terrorism and Security Council resolution 1566 (2004);
(d) Description of terrorism as "any action, in addition to actions already specified by the existing conventions on aspects of terrorism, the Geneva Conventions and Security Council resolution 1566 (2004), that is intended to cause death or serious bodily harm to civilians or non-combatants, when the purpose

of such an act, by its nature or context, is to intimidate a population, or to compel a Government or an international organization to do or to abstain from doing any act."[627]

It is very significant that the High-Level Panel's definition of terrorism mentions a state's use of force against civilians, despite the reluctance of governments to accept responsibility for doing so. Hence, through these efforts and a strong international desire to achieve progress in this field, a definition of terrorism is beginning to emerge.

Meanwhile, the UN Security Council and the General Assembly have adopted resolutions that focus on improving the international response to terrorism. On September 28, 2001, the Security Council, acting under Chapter VII of the UN Charter, declared in Resolution 1373 that "acts, methods and practices of terrorism are contrary to the purposes and principles of the United Nations" and called upon states to "become parties as soon as possible to the relevant international conventions and protocols" as well as "to increase cooperation and fully implement the relevant international conventions and protocols."[628] Resolution 1373 also established the Counter-Terrorism Committee (CTC) to coordinate international efforts against terrorism, including bringing states to an increased level of compliance with the terrorism-related conventions and protocols.[629] While Resolution 1373 did not mention human rights, the Security Council in January 2003 adopted Resolution 1456 calling on the CTC to consider human rights in its work.[630] Unfortunately, the CTC continues to ignore human rights implications of its activities, even though such nations as China, Russia, Tunisia, and Uzbekistan have been using their effort to combat terrorism as an excuse for repressing political or ethnic opposition.

Resolution 1373 and the CTC have encouraged states to report on whatever measures they are taking to combat terrorism. There are at least two models for analyzing how a state can respond to the threat of terrorism and/or an international terrorist attack. First, terrorism can be perceived as a form of criminal conduct that must be prevented, prosecuted, and punished. Second, terrorist incidents may be seen as analogous to military attacks, which require an armed response. With both of these models, there are rules and limitations contained in international human rights and humanitarian law that constrain state responses to terrorism.

Under the criminal justice model, governments are required to establish criminal jurisdiction over and severely punish any individuals or groups who commit violent acts against civilians for political aims. According to the Convention for the Suppression of Unlawful Acts Against the Safety of Civil Aviation, for example, a person may be tried and punished if he or she "performs an act of violence against a person on board an aircraft in flight if that act is likely to endanger the safety of that aircraft" or "destroys an aircraft in service."[631] In addition, many acts of terrorism—for example, the deliberate use of an aircraft to kill thousands of civilians—constitute crimes against humanity. According to the Rome Statute of the International Criminal Court, a "crime against humanity" includes murder and other inhumane acts "when committed as part of a widespread or systematic attack directed against any civilian population. . . ."[632] Such crimes are the subject of prosecution, extradition, and universal jurisdiction in many countries. Many countries have statutes covering such crimes as hijacking of airplanes, hostage-taking, and attacks on diplomats. It is possible that transnational terrorists may one day be tried by the International Criminal Court for crimes against humanity or war crimes, although the Court lacks the resources to handle a significant number of cases at one time and is already fully occupied by the three investigations it has undertaken with regard to the Democratic Republic of Congo, Sudan, and Uganda. It is more likely that terrorists will be tried either in national courts or by ad hoc tribunals, similar to the tribunals for Rwanda and the former Yugoslavia.

The criminal justice model focuses on individual responsibility for proven past criminal acts, and must respect the fair trial and other rights protected by international human rights law. In addition to fair trial rights, the Covenant on Civil and Political Rights requires that states not subject persons to torture, other ill-treatment, arbitrary detention, and discrimination.[633]

Terrorist attacks may also be perceived as acts of war which require armed action in self-defense by any nation and also may require military measures authorized by the UN Security Council to deal with threats to the peace, breaches of the peace, and acts of aggression. To the extent that military force is authorized, however, means of war are not unlimited. Under the laws of war, military force must be proportional to the threat. The International Court of Justice (ICJ), in its Advisory Opinion on the Legality of the Threat or Use of Nuclear Weapons, stated that under the customary laws of war military force must be necessary and proportional to the threat.[634] In addition, international humanitarian law provides a minimal safety net for the protection of prisoners of war. The four Geneva Conventions for the protection of the victims of armed conflict—to which most nations are parties—provide that soldiers may direct deadly force against an enemy, but not against civilians, civilian targets, or other persons taking no active part in the hostilities, including members of armed forces who have laid down their arms and others placed out of combat by sickness, wounds, detention, or any other cause.[635]

An armed response to terrorism does not perfectly fit existing legal paradigms and presents some special problems regarding the applicability of the laws and customs of war. The four Geneva Conventions and two Protocols identify four categories of armed conflict: (a) international armed conflict or occupation, (b) wars of national liberation or self-determination, (c) noninternational armed conflict under Common Article 3, and (d) noninternational armed conflict under Additional Protocol II. Since the terrorist attacks on September 11, 2001, there have been questions as to whether the "war on terror"—or any armed response to terrorism—qualifies as an international armed conflict or a noninternational armed conflict under international humanitarian law, on the one hand, or an entirely new form of armed conflict as to which new rules must be developed, on the other.

International humanitarian law, while applying only to armed conflicts, cannot provide protection to those persons held in connection to "war on terror" that do not meet the threshold of either international or non-international armed conflicts. Although the U.S. hostilities against Afghanistan and Iraq do qualify as international armed conflicts, the "war on terror"—an international armed conflict against a non-state actor—has caused much concern about the implications of the use of armed force in response to terrorism, because it has purported to deny all of those detained as accused terrorists—or "unlawful combatants"— their full protection of the humanitarian law. This problem has arisen with the detention of Taliban fighters captured in Afghanistan and detained at a U.S. military base in Guantánamo Bay, Cuba, as well as with captured Al Qaeda members and other persons labeled as "terrorists." Such persons have thus been denied their status as either a combatant (or, if captured, a prisoner of war) or a civilian. Importantly, the International Committee of the Red Cross (ICRC) has stated in its authoritative commentary on the Fourth Geneva Convention:

Every person in enemy hands must have some status under international law: he is either a prisoner of war and, as such, covered by the Third Convention, a civilian covered by the Fourth Convention, or again, a member of the medical personnel of the armed forces who is covered by the First Convention. There is no intermediate status; nobody in enemy hands can be outside the law.[636]

Another dangerous implication of characterizing "the war on terror" as an international armed conflict against a non-state actor is that any member of a terrorist group may purportedly be attacked, regardless of their physical location. For example, in November 2002 the U.S. Central Intelligence Agency (CIA) used a missile to kill a suspected Al Qaeda member in a car driving with several other individuals in Yemen, causing Amnesty International to classify the assassinations as extrajudicial executions, which are forbidden under international human rights law.

The armed conflict model also raises questions about the use of force in general. Article 51 of the UN Charter establishes the right of a state to engage in individual or collective self-defense. It is unclear, however, if the attacks on the U.S. by Al Qaeda constitute an attack by another state, and if the U.S. response could be considered self-defense. It is similarly unclear if the U.S. war against the Taliban government could be considered a necessary and proportionate response directed against an imminent attack. Further, the U.S. government on September 20, 2002, issued a National Security Strategy, in which the U.S. declared that it had a right to pre-emptive self-defense, that is, to attack even before it had been subjected to an armed attack as required by Article 51 of the UN Charter. Many critics have reacted to this new strategy by claiming that preemptive self-defense undermines the approach of the Charter in regard to the use of force, particularly because preemptive self-defense could be used indiscriminately.

It has been suggested that a new convention be formulated that specifically describes the rules by which a state may respond to an incident of transnational terrorism. A new convention on terrorism would require time to develop the requisite degree of consensus and might actually undermine the existing principles of human rights and humanitarian law. Many human rights advocates insist that, while transnational terrorism does not perfectly fit the categories of armed conflict, the existing humanitarian law standards governing armed conflict are sufficient when supplemented by the broader norms of international human rights law.

*See also*: Detention and Imprisonment, Equality and Nondiscrimination, International Humanitarian Law, Peace, Procedural Fairness in the Criminal Process and the Administration of Justice, Torture and Ill-Treatment

*Further Reading*:

Advisory Opinion on the Legality of the Threat or Use of Nuclear Weapons, 1996 I.C.J. 226 (1996).
Arab Convention on the Suppression of Terrorism, Apr. 22, 1998, *entered into force* May 7, 1999.
Jonathan L. Black-Branch, *Powers of Detention of Suspected International Terrorists Under the United Kingdom Anti-Terrorism, Crime and Security Act 2001: Dismantling the Cornerstones of a Civil Society*, 27 Eur. L. Rev. 19 (2002).
David Bonner, *Managing Terrorism While Respecting Human Rights? European*

*Aspects of the Anti-Terrorism Crime and Security Act 2001*, 8 Eur. Pub. L. 497 (2002).
Alan Clarke, *Terrorism, Extradition, and the Death Penalty*, 29 Wm. Mitchell L. Rev. 783 (2003).
Combating Terrorism and Respect for Human Rights, Eur. Parl. Ass. Res. 1271 (2002).
Convention Against the Taking of Hostages, 1316 U.N.T.S. 205, *entered into force* June 3, 1983.
Convention for the Suppression of Terrorist Bombings, U.N. Doc. A/RES/52/164 (1997), 37 I.L.M. 249, *entered into force* May 23, 2001.
Convention for the Suppression of the Financing of Terrorism, U.N. Doc. A/RES/54/109 (1999), 39 I.L.M. 270, *entered into force* Apr. 1, 2002.
Convention for the Suppression of Unlawful Acts Against the Safety of Civil Aviation, Sept. 23, 1971, 974 U.N.T.S. 177, 24 U.S.T. 564, 10 I.L.M. 1151, *entered into force* Jan. 26, 1973.
Convention for the Suppression of Unlawful Acts Against the Safety of Maritime Navigation, Mar. 10, 1988, 1678 U.N.T.S. 221, 27 I.L.M. 668, *entered into force* Mar. 1, 1992.
Convention for the Suppression of Unlawful Seizure of Aircraft, 860 U.N.T.S. 105, *entered into force* Oct. 14, 1971.
Convention of the Organization of the Islamic Conference on Combating International Terrorism, July 1, 1999, *not in force*.
Convention on Offences and Certain Other Acts Committed on Board Aircraft, Sept. 14, 1963, 704 U.N.T.S. 219, 20 U.S.T. 2941, 2 I.L.M. 1042, *entered into force* Dec. 4, 1969.
Convention on the Marking of Plastic Explosives for the Purpose of Detection, Mar. 1, 1991, 30 I.L.M. 721, *entered into force* June 21, 1998.
Convention on the Physical Protection of Nuclear Material, Mar. 3, 1980, 1456 U.N.T.S. 101, T.I.A.S. 11080, 18 I.L.M. 1419, *entered into force* Feb. 8, 1987
Convention on the Prevention and Punishment of Crimes Against Internationally Protected Persons, Including Diplomatic Agents, 1035 U.N.T.S. 167, 13 I.L.M. 41, *entered into force* Feb. 20, 1977.
Council of Europe, Guidelines on Human Rights and the Fight Against Terrorism: adopted by the Committee of Ministers July 11, 2002 at the 804th meeting of the Ministers' Deputies (2002).
Declaration on Measures to Eliminate International Terrorism, G.A. Res. 49/60, U.N. GAOR, 49th Sess., Supp. No. 49, at 303, U.N. Doc. A/RES/49/60 (1994).
Declaration on the Global Effort to Combat Terrorism, S.C. Res. 1377, U.N. SCOR, 4413th mtg., Supp. 1, at 295, U.N. Doc. S/RES/1377 (2001).
Declaration on the Issue of Combating Terrorism, S.C. Res. 1456, U.N. SCOR, 57th Sess., 4688th mtg., U.N. Doc. S/Res/1456 (2003).
Declaration to Supplement the 1994 Declaration on Measures to Eliminate International Terrorism, G.A. res. 51/210, U.N. GAOR, 51st Sess., Supp. No. 49, at 346, U.N. Doc. A/RES/51/210 (1996).
European Convention on the Suppression of Terrorism, Jan. 27, 1977, 1137 U.N.T.S. 93, Europ. T.S. No. 90, 15 I.L.M. 1272, *entered into force* Aug. 4, 1978.
James Finsten, Note, *Extradition or Execution? Policy Constraints in the United States' War on Terror*, 77 S. Cal. L. Rev. 835 (2004).
Joan Fitzpatrick, *Speaking Law to Power: The War Against Terrorism and Human Rights*, 14 Eur. J. Int'l L. 241 (2003).
Rosemary Foot, Human Rights and Counter-Terrorism in America's Asia Policy (2004).

Conor Gearty, *Terrorism and Human Rights: A Case Study in Impending Legal Realities*, 19 Legal Stud. 367 (1999).

Virginia Helen Henning, Note and Comment, *Anti-Terrorism, Crime and Security Act 2001: Has the United Kingdom Made a Valid Derogation from the European Convention on Human Rights?*, 17 Am. U. Int'l L. Rev. 1263 (2002).

International Committee of the Red Cross, Commentary IV, Geneva Convention Relative to the Protection of Civilian Persons in Time of War (Jean S. Pictet ed., Ronald Griffin trans., 1958).

Elena Katselli & Sangeeta Shah, *September 11 and the U.K. Response*, 52 Int'l & Comp. L.Q. 245 (2003).

Dana Keith, *In the Name of National Security or Insecurity? The Potential Indefinite Detention of Noncitizen Certified Terrorists in the United States and the United Kingdom in the Aftermath of September 11, 2001*, 16 Fla. J. Int'l L. 405 (2004).

Kevin Dooley Kent, *Basic Rights and Anti-Terrorism Legislation: Can Britain's Criminal Justice (Terrorism and Conspiracy) Act 1998 Be Reconciled with Its Human Rights Act?*, 33 Vand. J. Transnat'l L. 221 (2000).

Human Rights and Comparative Foreign Policy (David P. Forsythe ed., 2000).

Heinz Klug, *The Rule of Law, War, or Terror*, 2003 Wis. L. Rev. 365, 383–84 (2003).

Kalliopi K. Koufa, Terrorism and human rights, Final report of the Special Rapporteur, U.N. Doc. E/CN.4/Sub.2/2004/40 (2004).

Seth F. Kreimer, *Too Close to the Rack and the Screw: Constitutional Constraints on Torture in the War on Terror*, 6 U. Pa. J. Const. L. 278, 280 (2003).

Legal Instruments in the Fight Against International Terrorism: A Transatlantic Dialogue (Cyrille Fijnaut, Jan Wouters, and Frederik Naert eds., 2004).

Juan E. Méndez & Javier Mariezcurrena, *Prospects for Human Rights Advocacy in the Wake of September 11, 2001*, 22 Law & Ineq. 223 (2004).

OAS Convention to Prevent and Punish Acts of Terrorism Taking the Form of Crimes Against Persons and Related Extortion That Are of International Significance, Feb. 2, 1971, 27 U.S.T. 3949, 1986 U.N.T.S. 195, OAS Treaty Series, No. 37, *entered into force* Oct. 16, 1973.

OAU Convention on the Prevention and Combating of Terrorism, July 14, 1999, *not in force*

Steve Peers, *EU Responses to Terrorism*, 52 Int'l & Comp. L.Q. 227 (2003).

Catherine Powell, *The Role of Transnational Norm Entrepreneurs in the U.S. "War on Terrorism,"* 5 Theoretical Inquiries L. 47, 57 n.37 (2004).

Protocol for the Suppression of Unlawful Acts Against the Safety of Fixed Platforms Located on the Continental Shelf, Mar. 10, 1988, 1678 U.N.T.S. 304, 27 I.L.M. 685, *entered into force* Mar. 1, 1992.

Protocol on the Suppression of Unlawful Acts of Violence at Airports Serving International Civil Aviation, supplementary to the Convention for the Suppression of Unlawful Acts Against the Safety of Civil Aviation, Feb. 24, 1988, 27 I.L.M. 627, *entered into force* Aug. 6, 1989.

SAARC Regional Convention on Suppression of Terrorism, Nov. 4, 1987, *reprinted in* 8 GAOR, 44th Sess., Doc. A/51/136, *entered into force* Aug. 22, 1988.

Kim Lane Scheppele, *Law in a Time of Emergency: States of Exception and the Temptations of 9/11*, 6 U. Pa. J. Const. L. 1001 (2004).

Daniel J. Sharfstein, *Human Rights Beyond the War on Terrorism: Extradition Defenses Based on Prison Conditions in the United States*, 42 Santa Clara L. Rev. 1137 (2002).

Roberta Smith, Note, *America Tries to Come to Terms with Terrorism: The United States Anti-Terrorism and Effective Death Penalty Act of 1996 v. British Anti-Terrorism Law and International Response*, 5 Cardozo J. Int'l & Comp. L. 249 (1997).

Sabine von Schorlemer, *Human Rights: Substantive and Institutional Implications of the War Against Terrorism*, 14 Eur. J. Int'l L. 265 (2003).

Treaty on Cooperation Among States Members of the Commonwealth of Independent States in Combating Terrorism, June 4, 1999, *entered into force* June 4, 1999.

Colin Warbrick, *The European Convention on Human Rights and the Prevention of Terrorism*, 32 Int'l & Comp. L.Q. 82 (1983).

Jeremie J. Wattellier, Note, *Comparative Legal Responses to Terrorism: Lessons from Europe*, 27 Hastings Int'l & Comp. L. Rev. 397 (2004).

Sir David Williams, *The United Kingdom's Response to International Terrorism*, 13 Ind. Int'l & Comp. L. Rev. 683 (2003).

Jan Wouters & Frederik Naert, *The European Union and "September 11,"* 13 Ind. Int'l & Comp. L. Rev. 719 (2003).

*Links to Consult*:

http://www.state.gov/r/pa/ho/pubs/fs/5902.htm
http://www.un.org/Docs/sc/committees/1373/
http://www.un.org/secureworld/report.pdf
http://www.un.org/terrorism/
http://www1.umn.edu/humanrts/links/afghanistan.html
http://www1.umn.edu/humanrts/links/Iraq.html
http://www1.umn.edu/humanrts/links/response.html
http://www1.umn.edu/humanrts/links/terrorism.html

## B. Groups at Risk

Human rights concerns may not only be categorized and reviewed by focusing on core human rights principles, but also by looking at the groups or categories of individuals who may be at risk. Some kinds of individuals have been identified as requiring protection by treaty, for example, racial minorities, women, migrants, and children. Others individuals have been accorded protection by declarations or other non-treaty instruments; for example, the Declaration on the Elimination of All Forms of Intolerance and of Discrimination Based on Religion or Belief. Some particular groups and kinds of individuals have concerns and problems that touch upon many aspects of human rights. In order to understand the risks that these individuals or groups face, it is better to focus not upon categories of rights (as done above), but upon the overall human rights difficulties of each group at risk. While it is not possible to cover the rights of each of the groups, it is important to recognize that certain groups need special protection. Those groups include: refugees and asylum seekers; children and youth; persons infected with, affected by, or vulnerable to HIV/AIDS; indigenous peoples; lesbian, gay, bisexual, or transgendered persons; linguistic, ethnic, racial, and religious minorities; migrants; older persons; persons with disabilities; trafficked persons; and women.

Most human rights treaties and other instruments pronounce rights of individuals or of individuals in the context of groups. For example, freedom of religion and belief may be exercised in churches, mosques, synagogues, temples and other group settings, but that freedom is expressed as an individual right in the Universal Declaration of Human Rights:

Everyone has the right to freedom of thought, conscience and religion; this right includes freedom to change his religion or belief, and freedom, either alone or in community with others and in public or private, to manifest his religion or belief in teaching, practice, worship and observance.[637]

Similarly, freedom of association and the right to join trade unions may be perceived as group rights, but they are expressed in Articles 20 and 23 of the Universal Declaration and the Covenants as individual rights:

Everyone has the right to freedom of peaceful assembly and association.
Everyone has the right to form and to join trade unions for the protection of his interests.[638]

The two Covenants further identify responsibilities of states, as well as groups and persons:

Nothing in the present Covenant may be interpreted as implying for any State, group or person any right to engage in any activity or to perform any act aimed at the destruction of any of the rights or freedoms recognized herein, or at their limitation to a greater extent than is provided for in the present Covenant.[639]

There are, however, a few human rights that are expressed as belonging to groups. For example, Article 16 of the Universal Declaration protects the rights of the family:

The family is the natural and fundamental group unit of society and is entitled to protection by society and the State.[640]

Similarly, the two Human Rights Covenants protect the right of peoples to self-determination:

All peoples have the right of self-determination. By virtue of that right they freely determine their political status and freely pursue their economic, social and cultural development. . . . All peoples may, for their own ends, freely dispose of their natural wealth and resources without prejudice to any obligations arising out of international economic co-operation, based upon the principle of mutual benefit, and international law. In no case may a people be deprived of its own means of subsistence.[641]

Following a similar approach, ILO Convention 169 concerning Indigenous and Tribal Peoples in Independent Countries recognized collective rights, for example: "Indigenous and tribal peoples shall enjoy the full measure of human rights and fundamental freedoms without hindrance or discrimination."[642]

In assuring rights of human rights defenders, the General Assembly noted that everyone has the right, individually and in association with others, to promote and to strive for the protection and realization of human rights, but also "an important role and a responsibility in contributing, as appropriate, to the promotion of the right of everyone to a social and international order in which the rights and freedoms set forth in the Universal Declaration of Human Rights and other human rights instruments can be fully realized."[643]

The recognition of collective rights, particularly for such areas as religious freedom, union rights, and indigenous issues, is helpful in creating conditions for the realization of individual rights, and also in supporting rights for groups where appropriate.

Some groups have been successful in securing group protection through treaties, for example, children and youth, individuals with disabilities, migrants, and women. It took years of effort for indigenous peoples to lobby for a UN declaration to protect their rights, though they have been more successful in the International Labor Organization. Some groups are the subject of special procedures under various international human rights bodies. For example, the UN Commission on Human Rights established—and the successor Human Rights Council continued—thematic procedures relating to people of African descent, sale of children, indigenous people, internally displaced persons, migrants, minority issues, trafficking in persons, and violence against women. Still other groups struggle for basic recognition for their rights as a group at the international level, as is the case for lesbian, gay, bisexual, or transgendered persons.

*See also*: Protection of the Family, Self-Determination, International Procedures, Regional Institutions and Procedures

*Further Reading*:

Convention Concerning Indigenous and Tribal Peoples in Independent Countries (ILO No. 169), 72 ILO Official Bull. 59, *entered into force* Sept. 5, 1991.

Declaration on the Right and Responsibility of Individuals, Groups and Organs of Society to Promote and Protect Universally Recognized Human Rights and Fundamental Freedoms, G.A. res.53/144, annex, 53 U.N. GAOR Supp., U.N. Doc. U.N. Doc. A/RES/53/144 (1999).

Minority and Group Rights in the New Millennium (Deirdre Fottrell & Bill Bowring eds., 1999).

Natan Lerner, Group Rights and Discrimination in International Law (1991).

International Human Rights in the 21st Century: Protecting the Rights of Groups (Gene M. Lyons and James Mayall eds., 2003).

# Part III
# Procedures for Implementation of Human Rights

The most effective means of achieving human rights in practice depend on the government and people of each country. When human rights are incorporated within the laws, institutions, and customs of a nation, the residents of that nation can be best assured that their rights will be respected. In many countries, however, the laws, institutions, and customs do not reflect the international human rights obligations to which those nations have committed themselves by accepting the UN Charter and other treaties guaranteeing human rights. In such situations, the residents of those countries can utilize international mechanisms to persuade, embarrass, or put more forceful pressure on their governments to protect human rights.

A wide range of procedures exist for implementing human rights both at the national and international levels. Without question, national laws and procedures are the most important mechanisms for achieving human rights compliance in daily life. Nonetheless, this section begins by looking at international human rights institutions and procedures because they demonstrate global standards and provide a vital system of last resort when national structures fail. Accordingly, the content of this part progresses from the global to the local. The first section examines the international procedures that have developed under the United Nations Charter and other human rights treaties within the United Nations system. It also looks at the role of specialized international agencies and world conferences in promoting and protecting human rights. It concludes by tracing the development of international criminal procedures. The second section covers the regional institutions and their human rights mechanisms. It looks first at the European human rights system, then at the systems in the Americas and Africa. The third section discusses the national institutions and procedures established to safeguard human rights, including constitutional protections, courts and legislatures, and national human rights institutions. The fourth section focuses on the role of truth and reconciliation commissions in restoring respect for human rights in post-conflict societies. The fifth and final section examines the important role of nongovernmental organizations (NGOs) in human rights advocacy. The text concludes by contemplating the progress human rights have made over the past sixty years and calling attention to some of the challenges ahead.

# A. International Procedures

It is important to keep in mind when studying or using the United Nations and regional procedures that very few mechanisms exist to enforce the country-specific decisions or resolutions of the various international institutions. Even so, governments often feel compelled to perform what is requested of them by international bodies. This sense of obligation arises from their formal commitment to protect human rights coupled with the mobilization of shame that can result from the use of such procedures. In addition, the procedures serve an important function in elaborating human rights standards and providing means to raise awareness of human rights violations.

Still, international human rights procedures can appear complex and daunting to understand. It is tempting to become so absorbed in the intricacies of the various procedures that one loses sight of the principal objective—that is, to improve human rights conditions in concrete situations. Given this predicament, one is advised to continually ask the question: How will using a UN or regional human rights procedure help me in achieving my client's or my own human rights objectives? Indeed, one of the best reasons for using UN procedures is that there is no adequate national remedy available. For example, there may be no way to communicate with national authorities about human rights violations without a significant risk of retaliation. A UN complaint may make the national authorities aware that the UN, and presumably others outside the country, care about what is happening. The UN may also be able to shield the identity of the complainant or function as an ombudsman seeking to encourage ways to resolve the problem. In general, the UN and other international institutions can play an important role in: (1) persuading a government to stop violations, (2) threatening embarrassment (which may be more effective than embarrassment itself because the government is not sure what will happen if the violation is made public), or (3) causing public embarrassment and focusing an international spotlight of shame on human rights violators.

Even if the country *does* have procedures for resolving the problem, there may still be reasons to use a UN or other international procedure. For example, one may want to publicize the case and demonstrate to a national legislature, court, or administrator that there is international interest in the matter. One may also file a UN complaint in order to find out what the government's argument might be, so that the information can be used in domestic litigation or lobbying. For example, lawyers representing the Guantánamo detainees used the Inter-American Commission on Human Rights procedures to obtain discovery of the U.S. Government's arguments for later successful use in U.S. federal court litigation. In any case, one should ask: How can I use UN or other international procedures to improve my chances of success at the national level?

## 1. UN Charter-Based Procedures

There is a fundamental division between (1) the Charter-based institutions of the United Nations that were responsible for drafting and adopting as well as implementing human rights standards and (2) the other treaty-based committees that implement seven of the principal human rights treaties. This chapter introduces the principal UN Charter-based organs of the United Nations, including the General Assembly, the Security Council, the former UN Commission on Human Rights, its Sub-Commission, and the newly created Human Rights Council. The chapter then focuses on the Commission, its subsidiary mechanisms, and the procedures that were transferred to the Human Rights Council. These procedures include public discussions of country situations, machinery on specific countries, the confidential "1503 procedure," and thematic procedures. Turning to an overview of the newly created Human Rights Council, the chapter addresses the Council's relationship to the Commission's legacy. The chapter further discusses the work of other relevant UN bodies, including the Commission on the Status of Women and the Commission on Crime Prevention and Criminal Justice. In conclusion, the chapter examines the human rights activities of the UN Secretary-General, the Office of the High Commissioner for Human Rights, and the International Court of Justice.

The next chapter discusses one of the principal human rights treaty bodies—the Human Rights Committee—as representative of the function of all seven treaty bodies that were developed under the aegis of the United Nations. These treaty bodies are staffed by the UN, but are independently founded upon their respective multilateral treaties.

### A. GENERAL ASSEMBLY

The General Assembly,[1] established by Chapters III and IV of the UN Charter, is the world's most authoritative source of international declarations and conventions.² Human rights issues are generally discussed in the Assembly's Third Committee. The General Assembly is also the most representative decision-making organ of the UN, where all 191 members of the UN are entitled to vote. Furthermore, the General Assembly elects the 10 nonpermanent members of the Security Council, the 54 members of the Economic and Social Council (ECOSOC), and the 47 members of the Human Rights Council, regularly reviews ECOSOC recommendations, and receives reports from several of the human rights treaty bodies.³ The General Assembly usually meets from September through December and considers resolutions on several hundred matters.

The General Assembly (GA) is often the "last stop" for UN human rights treaties, declarations, and other instruments, which must ultimately work their way up to the GA for approval from its subsidiary bodies. The General Assembly ordinarily approved the human rights initiatives begun in the Commission on Human Rights. Occasionally, human rights initiatives (e.g., work on the rights of the disabled and rights of children in armed conflict) are centered in the GA. In 1993, the GA created the post of the High Commissioner for Human Rights.⁴ Over the years, the General Assembly has focused on a number of human rights issues, such as human rights education, protection of internally displaced persons, religious intolerance, the right of Palestinian people to self-determination, the right to food, the rights of the child, the rights of minorities, violence against women, and globalization and its impact on human rights.

Despite a longstanding tension in the Charter between Article 2(7)'s prohibition against invading states' "domestic jurisdiction" and the universal human rights protections set forth in Charter Articles 1, 55, and 56, the GA has increasingly called attention to the situation of human rights in specific countries. That tension was significantly challenged in the mid-1970s when the General Assembly and the Commission on Human Rights reached a consensus that a working group must be established to investigate human rights violations in Chile. Following that important step, almost all governments have accepted that human rights constitute a matter of international concern, and that UN investigations and hortatory resolutions do not, in any case, invade a country's domestic jurisdiction. Domestic jurisdiction arguments under Article 2(7) are occasionally raised by specific governments accused of violations, but are not met with widespread approval. In fact, offending governments often undermine their arguments by supporting condemnatory resolutions with regard to other offending countries. Since the mid-1970s the General Assembly and other UN organs have more regularly expressed concern and taken other actions with regard to situations in countries, including Afghanistan, Bosnia and Herzegovina, Cambodia, Cuba, Democratic Republic of Congo, El Salvador, Estonia, Haiti, Iraq, the Islamic Republic of Iran, Kosovo, Latvia, Myanmar (Burma), Nigeria, Rwanda, Somalia, the Sudan, Turkmenistan, and the former Yugoslavia. Nonetheless, such country-specific resolutions are often controversial.

### B. SECURITY COUNCIL

The Security Council is the principal organ of the UN, on which the Charter confers primary responsibility for the maintenance of international peace and security.[5] The Council is composed of fifteen members, including five permanent members (China, France, Russia, the United Kingdom, and the United States) and ten nonpermanent members elected for two-year terms by the General Assembly. Under Chapter VII of the Charter, the Security Council makes recommendations or decides what measures should be taken to maintain or restore international peace and security. Council measures may include humanitarian aid, economic sanctions, and military intervention. With the end of the Cold War, the Security Council's role has become more visible as the permanent members have more frequently agreed on action.

The Security Council's increasing activism becomes apparent when contrasting the number of actions taken during and after the Cold War. During the Cold War, the Security Council considered on merely five occasions whether human rights violations qualified as threats to the peace so as to justify measures under Chapter VII. In fact, during the thirty-nine-year period from 1948 to 1987, the Security Council established only thirteen peacekeeping operations. In contrast, during the 18 years from 1988 to 2006 the Security Council had authorized an additional forty-eight peacekeeping operations. In addition, onsite U.N. activities with a significant human rights dimension—based principally on Security Council decisions—have taken place in at least twenty-four countries since 1988, including Angola, Bosnia-Herzegovina, Burundi, Cambodia, Côte d'Ivoire, Democratic Republic of Congo, East Timor (Timor-Leste), El Salvador, Georgia, Guatemala, Haiti, Iraq, Kosovo, Liberia, Mozambique, Namibia, Nicaragua, Rwanda, Sierra Leone, Somalia, South Africa, Sudan, Western Sahara, and the former Yugoslavia.

In 1993 the Security Council further contributed to the development of human rights law when it authorized an international tribunal to prosecute persons responsible for serious violations of international humanitarian law committed in the former Yugoslavia. In addition, following widespread killings in Rwanda during April 1994, the Security

Council established a second tribunal using the same basic approach as in the former Yugoslavia and focusing on bringing perpetrators of the Rwandan genocide to justice. Those two *ad hoc* tribunals are discussed below in Chapter 5 of this part. In 1991 the Security Council notably created a Compensation Commission to assist victims of the Iraqi invasion of Kuwait, which has distributed more than $15 billion. Additionally, shortly after the attacks of September 11, 2001, the Security Council established the Counter-Terrorism Committee.[6] The Counter-Terrorism Committee tries to increase the capacity of states to fight terrorism, but has been criticized for not focusing on the human rights consequences of terrorism and efforts to combat terrorism.

c. COMMISSION ON HUMAN RIGHTS AND ITS SUB-COMMISSION

The founders of the United Nations anticipated in Charter Article 68 that the principal work on human rights would be accomplished by the UN Commission on Human Rights.[7] After drafting the Universal Declaration of Human Rights, the two Human Rights Covenants, and many other human rights treaties, the Commission continued to elaborate on those norms in further treaties, declarations, and other instruments. It also began to develop mechanisms for the implementation of those norms.

The Commission on Human Rights met annually in Geneva, Switzerland, for six weeks beginning in mid-March. It consisted of fifty-three member governments which were elected by the Economic and Social Council for staggered three-year terms. The elected government delegations made statements and voted on proposed resolutions and decisions. The Commission reported to ECOSOC, which in turn reports to the GA. The Commission held its last meeting on March 27, 2006. It was replaced by the Human Rights Council, discussed below. As the Council took over the functions of the Commission, it is still helpful to understand the Commission's work and mandates.

When the Commission met, its sessions were attended by nonvoting representatives from nearly all the other members of the UN as well as representatives from other intergovernmental organizations, such as the UN High Commissioner for Refugees and the International Labor Organization, and many nongovernmental organizations, such as Amnesty International and the International Commission of Jurists. All in all, 3,000 people routinely attended Commission sessions. The Commission was often criticized for the political nature of its deliberations and decisions. Indeed, because Commission members were government officials, they reflected the policies and attitudes of their respective nations. Nonetheless, the Commission contributed very substantially to the protection of human rights by drafting international standards, developing monitoring mechanisms, and applying its concerns to some of the countries where violations took place.

Very early in the history of the UN, the Sub-Commission on the Promotion and Protection of Human Rights was established (known from 1946 to 1999 as the Sub-Commission on the Prevention of Discrimination and Protection of Minorities).[8] The Sub-Commission met annually in Geneva for three to four weeks beginning in late July or early August. At its first session in June 2006, the Human Rights Council authorized the continuation of the Sub-Commission for at least one more year. The Sub-Commission has been composed of twenty-six individual experts, nominated by their governments and elected by the Commission. In practice, some Sub-Commission members and their alternates have been well attuned to the policies of their governments and take positions that are consistent with those policies. It was not unusual for such members to have official positions or to serve in their government's delegation at the Commission. On the whole, the Sub-Commission could be expected to act somewhat more on the merits than on the politics of human rights issues.

The Sub-Commission has proven itself innovative in the advancement of human rights. Over the years, for example, the Sub-Commission has been responsible for the drafting of the International Convention on the Protection of all Persons from Enforced Disappearance, the United Nations Declaration on the Rights of Indigenous Peoples, the Declaration of the Rights of Persons Belonging to National or Ethnic, Religious and Linguistic Minorities, and the Norms on the Responsibilities of Transnational Corporations and Other Business Enterprises with Regard to Human Rights. It has also issued groundbreaking studies on such diverse subjects as the right to adequate housing, the right to food, the rights of non-citizens, the right to a fair trial, and states of emergency. In 2000, however, the Commission limited the Sub-Commission's capacity to adopt country-specific resolutions and emphasized that its role was that of an independent advisory body to the Commission. In 2006 the Human Rights Council replaced the Sub-Commission with an 18-member Advisory Committee.

*i. Public Discussion of Country Situations*

As the primary UN human rights organ, the Commission on Human Rights—and now its successor, the Human Rights Council—derive their authority from Articles 55 and 56 of the UN Charter, in which States parties "pledge themselves to take joint and separate action" . . . "to promote . . . higher standards of living . . . development . . . solutions of international economic . . . and related problems; and . . . universal respect for, and observance of, human rights and fundamental freedoms."⁹ It is worth noting that the proposal to include protection along with promotion of human rights was defeated in drafting the Charter, and when the Commission first met in 1947 it decided that it did not have power to take any enforcement actions in regard to complaints of human rights violations. ECOSOC, its parent body, confirmed that decision. Nonetheless, over the past half century, the "no-action" position slowly eroded as UN member states realized that protection of human rights is fundamental to the UN's central mandate of safeguarding international peace and security.

The first step in expanding the authority of the Commission occurred in ECOSOC Resolution 728F, which was adopted in 1959. It requested the Secretary-General to compile a confidential list of communications received by the UN regarding human rights violations for the Commission and to give copies to any governments identified in such communications. The Commission was authorized to look at the communications and any replies the governments submitted.

While this initial measure now seems a very minor step, it did establish a process for gathering information and seeking responses from governments, which later developed into more concrete procedures as will be described below. Meanwhile, however, the Commission on Human Rights focused its efforts on establishing the principal norms of international human rights, which included the Universal Declaration of Human Rights (1948), the Convention on the Prevention and Punishment of the Crime of Genocide (1948), the International Covenant on Civil and Political Rights (1966), and the International Covenant on Economic, Social and Cultural Rights (1966).

Upon the adoption of the two Human Rights Covenants in 1966, the Commission anticipated that it would take several years for those treaties to come into force (it actually took ten years). ECOSOC adopted resolution 1235 in 1967 authorizing the Commission and Sub-Commission "to examine information relevant to gross violations of human rights and fundamental freedoms."¹⁰ The Commission on Human Rights and ECOSOC were particularly motivated to adopt resolution 1235 in 1967 principally in response to *apartheid* and other racial discrimination occurring in South Africa. In July 1966 the International Court of Justice had rendered a very disappointing decision in the South West Africa cases,¹¹ which so distressed the African delegations in the UN that they pressed for the adoption of resolution 1235 to encourage the Commission and Sub-Commission to place gross violations of human rights on their agendas.

In fact, resolution 1235 was another step toward weakening the "no action" doctrine. It was interpreted as giving broad authority to the Commission and Sub-Commission to debate particular country situations and adopt resolutions on them. The Commission could also authorize appointment of a special rapporteur or other mechanism for studying a given country situation or thematic issue, subject to the approval of ECOSOC if there were financial implications. Similar powers are retained by the Human Rights Council, as discussed below.

When the Commission adopted a resolution on a particular issue, it did not necessarily mention a country, but it still could have an impact on the reputation of a specific government. Take, for example, when it adopted its resolution in opposition to juvenile executions. Although the Commission did not name the United States, the U.S. was implicitly targeted as nearly the only country at the time still executing juvenile offenders. In 2005, the juvenile death penalty was declared unconstitutional by the U.S. Supreme Court, citing the Commission's resolutions along with other international documents. Similarly, a Sub-Commission resolution that did not identify a country by name, but did express concern about a particular issue that might relate to a country's human rights situation—especially where the Commission had not yet dealt with the situation—could serve three important functions: (1) it gave political impetus to further action by the Commission or other human rights bodies; (2) even if the Commission was unwilling to act, a Sub-Commission resolution represented the opinion of a formally constituted UN body of human rights experts; and (3) it could build up an official documentary record by requesting a report by the Secretary-General or a member of the Sub-Commission on the issue. In 2000, for example, the Sub-Commission adopted a resolution on "Discrimination based on work and descent" and requested one of its members to prepare a working paper on that subject. The working paper, which contained extensive information supplied by NGOs, discussed, among other things, discrimination based on caste in India, Japan, and Nepal. Adoption of the resolution and the Sub-Commission working paper contributed to the efforts of the Committee on the Elimination of Racial Discrimination to adopt a General Recommendation based on descent in 2002, which continues to have considerable political impact.[12]

*ii. Commission Machinery on Specific Countries*

Beyond plenary discussions or adoption of resolutions not mentioning a specific country, the Commission also investigates human rights violations in specific states and territories. At its last regular meetings in 2005, the Commission was able to take its most visible possible action by authorizing Special Rapporteurs on the human rights situations in

Belarus, the Occupied Palestinian Territories, Myanmar (Burma), the Democratic People's Republic of Korea, and Sudan. The Special Rapporteurs were authorized to receive information from individuals, groups, organizations, and governments; make appeals to the government with regard to particular cases; seek to visit the country they are assigned to investigate; and produce an authoritative report for the following session of the Commission (now the Council) on the human rights situation in that nation. The overall objective of these country rapporteurs has been to mobilize shame and pressure recalcitrant governments to improve human rights conditions in their countries.

Slightly less visible have been country resolutions without the appointment of a rapporteur or representative. The Commission in 2005 adopted a resolution or decision without appointing a rapporteur or representative on Cyprus and the Syrian Golan. With regard to Cuba the High Commissioner for Human Rights selected a personal representative and the Commission referred to that mandate in its rather terse resolution. During the same last regular session, the Commission's Chairperson announced still less potent statements on Afghanistan, Colombia, Haiti, and Western Sahara. Furthermore, the Commission authorized advisory services with regard to several countries in which there are serious human rights problems but where the governments have been considered—sometimes unrealistically—to be cooperating with international measures to improve the situations. This view was taken for Burundi, Cambodia, Chad, the Democratic Republic of Congo, Nepal, Sierra Leone, and Somalia. Although advisory service experts do not report on the human rights situations as such in the countries with which they are concerned, they often use information about human rights conditions as a context for their advisory work and in their reports.

*iii. Confidential "1503 Procedure"*

When ECOSOC resolution 1235 was adopted in 1967, it was intended primarily to allow the Commission to consider the situations in South Africa, Namibia, Rhodesia, and the African colonies of Portugal. At that time, NGOs were not allowed to make oral interventions or circulate written statements complaining about human rights violations in UN member states. It came as something of a shock to the Commission when, later in 1967, the Sub-Commission, on the basis of information supplied by NGOs, recommended that the Commission establish a Special Committee of Experts to consider the human rights situations in southern Africa. The Special Committee of Experts was also asked to consider the situations in Greece (after the 1967 colonels' coup) and

Haiti (under the rule of François Duvalier). This initiative goaded the Commission into developing a procedure under which information from nongovernmental sources could be considered in a less directly challenging manner.

The result was the adoption by ECOSOC in 1970 of Resolution 1503. The "1503 procedure," as it is known, provides that nongovernmental allegations concerning "situations which appear to reveal a consistent pattern of gross and reliably attested violations of human rights" are discussed in closed sessions of the Commission (now the Council).[13] A "communication" (UN euphemism for complaint) can be sent to the Office of the High Commissioner for Human Rights (OHCHR) in Geneva.[14] The OHCHR acknowledges receipt but usually does not otherwise correspond with the author of the communication. Unless the communication is screened out as "manifestly ill-founded," the OHCHR sends it to the government concerned and summarizes it in a confidential monthly list. A Working Group on Communications composed of five members, one from each of the five UN geographic regions—Africa, Asia, Eastern Europe, Latin America, and Western Europe and Other (including the United States, Canada, Australia, and New Zealand), meets in private for two weeks in August to review the confidential communications (the group also has access to the full texts of communications) and any corresponding government replies.

In 1971 the Sub-Commission adopted standards for the admissibility of 1503 communications that are still being used by the Working Group on Communications. The first requirement is that "there are reasonable grounds to believe that they may reveal a consistent pattern of gross and reliably attested violations of human rights and fundamental freedoms, including policies of racial discrimination and segregation and of *apartheid* in any country, including colonial and other dependent countries and peoples."[15] The 1971 Sub-Commission resolution also provides that anonymous communications are not admissible (though the author can request that his or her name not be revealed to the government); the description of the facts must indicate what rights have been violated; secondhand information may be included as long as it is accompanied by clear evidence; abusive language, insulting references to the State involved, or complaints that have "manifestly political motivations" are not permitted; and communications cannot be "based exclusively on reports disseminated by mass media."[16] Domestic remedies, if they exist and are not "ineffective or unreasonably prolonged" must be exhausted although if there really exists a consistent pattern of gross violations, it is doubtful that domestic remedies would be effective. Further, the communication must be submitted within "a reasonable time after the exhaustion of domestic remedies."[17]

If at least three members of the Working Group on Communications agree that a communication appears to reveal a consistent pattern of gross violations of human rights, the group forward it to the Commission, now replaced by the Human Rights Council. The Working Group may also keep the matter pending for a year. The situations in eighty-four different countries have been referred to the Commission/Council since the procedure's creation, although no public announcement is made at this stage about which countries are involved.

A similar Working Group on Situations, appointed from among the states that are members of the Commission, regularly met for one week before the Commission's annual session. It examined the country dossiers; determined whether to refer a particular situation to the Commission, keep the matter pending, or discontinue consideration; and made recommendations to the Commission about how to deal with the situations referred by the Working Group on Situations. The Commission was free to accept or reject the Working Group's recommendations. The Commission considered the "situations" (note that it was no longer dealing only with the forwarded "communications") in closed session. Resolution 1503 empowered it to make a "thorough study" or institute an "investigation by an *ad hoc* committee."[18] No such *ad hoc* committee is known to have been created, however, and it would appear (although it has not been publicly confirmed) that only one thorough study has been initiated.

In practice, however, the Commission developed a wide range of techniques short of a "thorough study" to investigate particular situations. The primary methods included (1) referring the situation to the Commission for consideration in public session (as occurred with regard to both Chad and Liberia in 2003); (2) appointing an independent expert or rapporteur (as occurred in 2004 with respect to Uzbekistan); (3) asking the Secretary-General to establish direct contacts with the government concerned; (4) asking the government for further information; and (5) keeping the situation "under review." In each of these cases, the situation was reported on and considered the following year.

At the end of the Commission's closed discussions, the Chairperson announced publicly the names of the countries in which situations had been considered and those which had been discontinued. The public was thereby informed of the countries that the Commission was reviewing under the 1503 procedure, but not of the action taken or the nature of the alleged violations. For example, in 2004 the Commission decided to discontinue consideration of the situation in Bolivia, Djibouti, and Honduras. Also, as mentioned above, the Commission decided to keep the situation in Uzbekistan under review and to mandate an independent expert to report during its closed 1503 sessions in 2005 about human rights conditions in that country. The mandate of the independent expert on Uzbekistan was continued by the Human Rights Council in 2006. Eventually, the Commission (and the Council) could recommend that ECOSOC put any such situation on the public record. For example, the human rights situation was placed on the public record either at the request of a new government in the country concerned (e.g., Argentina after democracy was restored under Alfonsín) or when the Commission was faced by flat noncooperation by the government (e.g., Equatorial Guinea's refusal to supply any defense to the accusations against it). In 1988, ECOSOC failed to act on a Commission recommendation to make the file of Albania public, although it did pave the way for the Commission to publicly consider the situation.

*iv. Thematic Procedures of the Commission*

One of the most positive developments in the UN work in the late twentieth century was the development of thematic machinery to deal with violations of specific human rights. Unlike the public and confidential procedures that dealt with general situations, the thematic mechanisms deal with individual cases of human rights violations or threatened violations, particularly when violations appear to be widespread. The thematic rapporteurs and working groups have the ability to respond quickly to information about individual cases and have been successful in preventing or stopping violations.

The Commission created twenty-six thematic procedures.[19] The earliest mandates were focused on civil and political rights. Due to demands by developing countries, there was a move toward the establishment of procedures that focused on economic rights. The names of the procedures and the year they were established are Working Group on Enforced or Involuntary Disappearances (1980); Special Rapporteur on summary or arbitrary executions (1982); Special Rapporteur on torture (1985); Special Rapporteur on religious intolerance (1986); Special Rapporteur on mercenaries (1987); Special Rapporteur on the sale of children (established in 1990 and recognized as a thematic procedure in 1992); Working Group on Arbitrary Detention (1991); Special Representative on internally displaced persons (established in 1992 and recognized as a thematic procedure in 1993); Special Rapporteur on racism and xenophobia (1993); Special Rapporteur on freedom of opinion and expression (1993); Special Rapporteur on violence against women (1994); Special Rapporteur on the independence of judges and lawyers (1994); Special Rapporteur on toxic waste (1995); Special Rapporteur on the right to education (1998); Independent expert on human rights and extreme poverty (1998); Independent expert on the right to development (1998); Special Rapporteur on the human rights of migrants 1999 (the creation of this procedure was preceded by a Working Group on Migrants which met from 1996–99); Independent expert on structural adjustment policies and foreign debt (in 2000 the Commission decided to merge the 1998–2000 mandates of the independent experts on foreign debt and structural adjustment); Special Rapporteur on human rights defenders (2000); Special Rapporteur on the right to food (2000); Special Rapporteur on the situation of human rights and fundamental freedoms of indigenous people (2001); Special Rapporteur on the right of everyone to the enjoyment of the highest attainable standard of physical and mental health (2002); Working Group on people of African descent (2002); Special Rapporteur on trafficking in persons (2004); Special Rapporteur on human rights in countering terrorism (2004); Special Representative of the Secretary-General on human rights and transnational corporations and other business enterprises (2005); Independent Expert on human rights and international solidarity (2005); and Independent Expert on minority issues (2005). The Special Rapporteurs and working groups are generally appointed for three year terms with a limit of two terms, although the Commission, and now the Council, reviews their work yearly.

These mechanisms have been genuinely impartial to date. Their annual reports to the Commission indicate that cases and problems are taken up, regardless of the identity of the state whose behavior is called into question. This approach is a radical departure from the practice of some other UN bodies, including the former Commission, where actions are partly (if not primarily) determined by political considerations. These thematic procedures generally analyse the human rights problem, its causes, measures for prevention, remedies, and the like. They receive information from individuals and nongovernmental organizations who seek their intervention in concrete situations. Each year Special Rapporteurs endeavour to visit at least a couple of nations where there are human rights concerns falling within their mandate. They reported to the Commission on Human Rights, and now report to the Human Rights Council. A few have reported to the General Assembly and occasionally to the Security Council.

D. HUMAN RIGHTS COUNCIL

Reform of human rights mechanisms is presently an issue of major concern at the United Nations. The creation of the Human Rights Council in 2006 was the most substantial change made to UN Charter-based human rights machinery since the organization was founded in 1945. Although high-level discussions concerning human rights reform had been ongoing at the United Nations for several years, a report issued in March 2005 by UN Secretary-General Kofi Annan reinvigorated the reform effort.[20] The report, entitled "In Larger Freedom," set forth the Secretary-General's agenda for the UN World Summit in September 2005. The report argued that the Commission on Human Rights suffered from declining credibility and professionalism and should be replaced by a new Human Rights Council. Negotiations were conducted over the course of the ensuing year, and on March 15, 2006, the General Assembly approved the creation of the Council with a vote of 170 to 4. (The United States, Israel, the Marshall Islands, and Palau voted against the proposal, while Belarus, Iran, and Venezuela abstained.) The resolution adopted by the General Assembly officially replaced the Commission with the Council and detailed the mandate and scope of the new human rights body.[21]

In many ways, the Council continues the Commission's key strengths and intended role intact. Speaking to the criticism that the Commission had become too politicized, GA Resolution 60/251—the resolution that created the Council—stresses the importance of nonselectivity in the consideration of human rights issues and the need to eliminate double standards. During its inaugural session in June 2006, the Council continued the mandates of the Sub-Commission, all the special procedures of the Commission on Human Rights, and the 1503 complaints procedure for one year (creating a working group to review these procedures at the same time). The Council also retained mechanisms for NGO participation, a core strength of the Commission.

Nonetheless, there are several important differences between the Human Rights Council and the Commission on Human Rights. Four of these differences are especially significant. First, the Council enjoys a higher status than the Commission. Whereas the Commission on Human Rights was a subsidiary body of ECOSOC, the Human Rights Council is a subsidiary body of the General Assembly.

Second, the election procedure and member composition for the Human Rights Council has been considerably altered. The forty-seven-member Council replaced the fifty-three-member Commission with members elected by an absolute majority of the GA (requiring ninety-seven votes). The GA also has the power, by a two-thirds majority vote, to suspend membership of a Council member that commits gross and systematic violations of human rights. Moreover, Council membership is governed by a new regional distribution formula. The Council's forty-seven member governments are to be comprised of thirteen states from both Africa and Asia (including the Middle East), eight from Latin American and the Caribbean, seven from Western Europe and other states, and six from Eastern Europe. This distribution increases the relative strength of the African and Asian delegations and decreases that of Latin America and Western European and other groups of states. Members are elected to staggered three-year terms and are not eligible for immediate reelection after two consecutive terms. This change prohibits *de facto* permanent membership for a few countries. Elections for the first Human Rights Council were held in May 2006. Human rights NGOs raised concerns over the human rights records of certain elected members, such as China, Cuba, Russia, and Saudi Arabia, although there are human rights problems in every country.

A third significant change under the Human Rights Council is the institution of a new universal periodic review procedure to monitor all states' fulfilment of human rights obligations and commitments. Elected Council members will be subject to review during their term. It is expected that this mechanism will eliminate some of the political positioning that blocked certain Commission members' human rights records from scrutiny in the past. At the same time, however, universal periodic review is likely to diminish attention to countries with serious human rights problems. For example, there is a possibility that the advent of universal periodic review will be used as an argument for abolishing the country resolutions and country rapporteurs established under ECOSOC resolution 1235. There is also concern that universal periodic review may duplicate work undertaken by the human rights treaty bodies. During its first session the Council formed a working group on procedures for the universal periodic review.

The fourth major difference between the Council and the Commission is the frequency of its sessions. In contrast to the Commission's single annual session of six weeks, in his "In Larger Freedom" report, the Secretary-General proposed that the Human Rights Council be a permanent standing body. After much negotiation in the General Assembly, it was ultimately agreed that the Council would be convened for a minimum of ten weeks per year in no fewer than three sessions. Because of the intermittent nature of the Council's sessions, NGOs with offices in Geneva will find it easier to attend than NGOs with offices in other parts of the world.

The Council also has the power to call special sessions for urgent human rights problems at the request of a member of the Council and with the support of one-third of Council membership. The Commission could only convene a special session if two-thirds of the members agreed. Accordingly, special sessions will become an important mechanism for focusing on grave country situations. Indeed, after its first meeting in June 2006, the Council convened two brief special sessions relating to the human rights situations in Palestine and Lebanon. The special sessions resulted in the dispatch of an urgent fact-finding mission to the Occupied Territories and the establishment of a high-level inquiry commission for Lebanon. Both resolutions to call special sessions divided generally along regional lines, with developing countries voting for—and developed countries voting against—the resolutions. Later in 2006 the Council convened similar special sessions about Israeli attacks on Palestinian sites and also about the human rights situation in Darfur—resulting in authorization of factfinding/assessment missions.

The Human Rights Council functions as an intergovernmental body with many of the same objectives, procedures, and limitations of its predecessor, the Commission on Human Rights. The great anticipation which accompanied the establishment of the Council may not, in practice, be realized, but only time will tell.

E. COMMISSION ON THE STATUS OF WOMEN

The Commission on the Status of Women (CSW) was created by ECOSOC in 1946.[22] It was first established as a sub-commission, but after one year its importance was acknowledged when it became a full commission. It is composed of representatives from forty-five governments, elected for four-year terms by ECOSOC. It prepares recommendations and reports to ECOSOC on women's rights in civil, economic, educational, political, and social fields. It may also make recommendations to ECOSOC on problems that require immediate attention and has two procedures analogous to the confidential 1503 procedure for reviewing communications alleging violations of women's rights. It has not, however, been very effective at prodding governments to address the violations. The CSW provides a forum for government delegates and NGOs to discuss issues affecting women's rights, but since it only meets for two weeks in March, it is not able to consider many issues at each session. Indeed, due to lack of time, it rotates consideration of various topics over the course of several years so it is not a useful mechanism for reviewing progress in a particular area from year to year. The CSW served as a preparatory body for the UN world conferences on women and also drafted the Optional Protocol to the Convention on the Elimination of Discrimination against Women establishing a procedure for individual communications. Those communications may be submitted to the Committee on the Elimination of Discrimination Against Women (CEDAW). The role of CEDAW as a human rights treaty body is discussed below in Part III.A.2 below.

F. COMMISSION ON CRIME PREVENTION AND CRIMINAL JUSTICE

The Commission on Crime Prevention and Criminal Justice was established in 1992 by ECOSOC to replace the Committee on Crime Prevention and Control, a subsidiary organ of ECOSOC comprised of twenty-seven experts.[23] As an expert body the Committee was an energetic source of international standards in regard to the administration of justice and human rights, including the Standard Minimum Rules for the Treatment of Prisoners, the Basic Principles on the Independence of the Judiciary, the UN Rules for the Protection of Juveniles Deprived of Their Liberty, and other useful human rights standards in the field of criminal justice. The Commission on Crime Prevention, with its forty governmental members, however, has not been effective in standard-setting, but it does consider such issues as the fight against corruption, international crime, assistance to victims of crime, abuse of power, and implementation of UN standards.

G. SECRETARY-GENERAL

The Secretary-General is authorized by Chapters III and XV of the UN Charter to serve as the chief administrative officer of the United Nations.[24] The office of the Secretary-General staffs the Security Council, General Assembly, and other UN organs. The Secretariat includes a number of departments and programs whose activities are relevant to human rights, but human rights are not explicitly central to the mandates of the Department of Political Affairs,[25] the Department of Peace-Keeping Operations,[26] and the UN Development Program.[27] The Secretary-General has, however, been encouraged by the General Assembly—and considers himself to have the inherent power—to contact governments regarding issues that fall within the purview of the United Nations. Hence, it is now typical for the Secretary-General to raise serious human rights issues with governments, usually on urgent humanitarian grounds. Most such exercises of the Secretary-General are done diplomatically and without publicity.

H. HIGH COMMISSIONER FOR HUMAN RIGHTS

In 1993, the General Assembly approved the creation of the post of UN High Commissioner for Human Rights.[28] The Office of the United Nations High Commissioner for Human Rights (OHCHR) has the principal responsibility for overseeing UN human rights activities, including staffing of the meetings of most human rights bodies, promoting universal ratification and implementation of international standards, exercising good offices, and maintaining a number of UN human rights field operations.

Although the Office of the High Commissioner for Human Rights plays an extremely important role in the implementation of UN human rights mandates, the OHCHR has lacked adequate personnel, independence, funding, and the capacity to function effectively in the field. Generally speaking, the OHCHR and the UN human rights procedures have been severely understaffed. For example, the Special Rapporteur Against Torture has been authorized to monitor and attempt to prevent torture throughout the world, but the Special Rapporteur is only a single individual assisted, at best, by two or possibly three OHCHR staff members. Although the OHCHR staff size has significantly increased, a much larger staff would be required to begin to respond to that mandate. In fact, often such thematic procedures must share staff, so that some special rapporteurs do not even benefit from a single full-time staff person.

Whereas the title of the High Commissioner for Human Rights and the OHCHR share a nomenclature with the High Commissioner for Refugees and the related UNHCR—a separate and specialized UN agency—the High Commissioner for Human Rights and the OHCHR are really only parts of the UN Secretariat. Accordingly, the OHCHR must rely significantly on the regular budget of the United Nations and the number of posts at the OHCHR must be approved by the UN Secretariat. Furthermore, when former High Commissioner Mary Robinson used her position as a strong advocate for human rights in concrete situations, her position was undermined by several powerful governments and by the UN Secretary-General.

The OHCHR budget is a few percent of the total cost of the UN, even though the UN often identifies human rights as one of the two or three primary purposes of the organization. The OHCHR lacks a level of regular funding necessary to train and maintain a competent and effective core of substantive staff, as well as to undertake a role in mainstreaming human rights throughout the UN system, implementing human rights in the field, and offering technical assistance to national governments. With the doubling of its budget in 2006, as part of the revamping of the human rights bodies, it is hoped that the OHCHR will be able to make greater headway in these areas.

I. INTERNATIONAL COURT OF JUSTICE

The International Court of Justice (ICJ) was created by Chapter XIV of the UN Charter and is the judicial branch of that body.[29] It is the successor to the Permanent Court of International Justice that was established under the League of Nations after World War I and began to function in 1922. The ICJ sits at the Peace Palace in The Hague, Netherlands. It consists of fifteen judges elected to nine-year terms (one-third are elected every three years) by the General Assembly and the Security

Council. The Charter provides for both contentious or adversary and advisory jurisdiction. Adversary jurisdiction applies only in cases where the States parties have referred to it and in situations where treaties provide for adjudication by the ICJ. Article 38(1) of the ICJ Statute specifies that the sources of law that the Court is to use in making its decisions are: international conventions, international custom, and general principles of international law. Decisions of the ICJ are only binding between the immediate parties and only in respect to that particular case. Hence, they are not precedential for other matters. Nonetheless, in practice the decisions are often relied upon as statements of international law. The ICJ has issued a number of important opinions—some detailed below—in both advisory and contentious cases regarding human rights.

In 1951 the ICJ rendered its first advisory opinion related to a human rights issue. It held that a reservation to the Convention on the Prevention and Punishment of the Crime of Genocide was not valid unless it was consistent with the object and purpose of the treaty.[30] In 1970, in another advisory opinion, the ICJ found that South Africa's continued presence in Namibia was a violation of international law because the government of South Africa had "pledged itself to observe and respect, in a territory having an international status, human rights and fundamental freedoms for all without distinction as to race. To establish instead, and to enforce, distinctions . . . based on grounds of race . . . which constitute a denial of fundamental human rights is a flagrant violation of the purposes and principles of the Charter. . . ."[31] In 1980 regarding the holding of U.S. diplomatic staff in Iran, it held that to deprive persons of their freedom and to hold them in conditions of hardship was a violation of the Charter and the Universal Declaration of Human Rights.[32] In 1986 it found the United States responsible for violating customary international law by failing to give notice of its mining of Nicaraguan ports.[33] In the same case, the ICJ found that U.S. publication and dissemination of a manual on "Psychological Operations in Guerrilla Warfare," which advised the Contras to "neutralize" certain judges, police officers, and state security officials, to be "contrary to the . . . prohibition in Article 3 of the Geneva Conventions, with respect to . . . executions without . . . judicial guarantees. . . ."[34]

Notably, the ICJ has issued a number of decisions in cases involving U.S. compliance with the Vienna Convention on Consular Relations.[35] In 1998 the ICJ unanimously issued provisional measures asking that Paraguayan prisoner Angel Francisco Breard would not be subjected to capital punishment pending a determination of whether his right to contact his consular representatives after arrest had been violated. The U.S. government and Supreme Court ignored the request and executed Mr. Breard, and Paraguay discontinued the case later that year. In June

2001, however, the ICJ decided on the merits that the United States had violated the Vienna Convention on Consular Relations by failing to comply with its requirements and by failing to take measures in regard to provisional measures to prevent the execution of two German nationals in Arizona.[36] Furthermore, in March 2004 the ICJ decided in favor of a Mexican government claim against the U.S. challenging the impending execution of fifty-two Mexican nationals because they had failed to receive their rights to be informed of consular assistance under the Vienna Convention on Consular Relations. The ICJ refused to invalidate the convictions, but it found that the United States is obligated "to provide, by means of its own choosing, review and reconsideration of the convictions and sentences of the Mexican nationals . . . by taking account of the violation of the rights set forth in Article 36 of the Convention. . . ."[37] In 2007, the ICJ also found that Serbia violated its obligations under the Genocide Convention to prevent genocide in Srebrenica during 1995 and to cooperate with the International Criminal Tribunal for the former Yugoslavia.

The ICJ has also supported the privileges and immunities of UN human rights officials, one who was prevented by his government from attending UN meetings and another who was threatened with a defamation action for words spoken regarding his country.[38] It did not, however, give much consideration to human rights concerns in its advisory opinion on the threat or use of nuclear weapons.[39]

*Further Reading:*

Advisory Opinion on the Legality of the Threat or Use of Nuclear Weapons, 1996 I.C.J. 226 (July 8).
Advisory Opinion on Reservations to the Convention on the Prevention and Punishment of the Crime of Genocide, 1951 I.C.J. 15 (May 28).
Philip Alston, The United Nations and Human Rights: A Critical Appraisal (2d ed. 2002).
Applicability of Article VI, Section 22, of the Convention on Privileges and Immunities of the United Nations, 1989 I.C.J. 177 (Dec. 15).
Application of the Convention on the Prevention and Punishment of the Crime of Genocide *(Bosn. & Herz. v. Yugo. (Serb. & Mont.))*, Judgment, Feb. 26, 2007.
*Avena and Other Mexican Nationals (Mex. v. U.S.),* 2003 I.C.J. 2 (Provisional Measures, Order of February 5), 2004 I.C.J. 1 (Judgment), 43 I.L.M. 581.
*Case Concerning Military and Paramilitary Activities in and Against Nicaragua (Nicaragua v. United States of America),* 1986 I.C.J. 14 (June 27).
*Difference Relating to Immunity from Legal Process of a Special Rapporteur of the Commission of Human Rights,* 1999 I.C.J. 61 (Apr. 29).
Economic and Social Council res. 728F (XXVIII), 28 U.N. ESCOR Supp. (No. 1) at 19, U.N. Doc. E/3290 (1959).
Economic and Social Council res. 1235 (XLII), 42 U.N. ESCOR Supp. (No. 1) at 17, U.N. Doc. E/4393 (1967).

Economic and Social Council res. 1503 (XLVIII), 48 U.N. ESCOR (No. 1A) at 8, U.N. Doc. E/4832/Add.1 (1970).
Legal Consequences for States of the Continued Presence of South Africa in Namibia (South West Africa) Notwithstanding Security Council Resolution 276 (1970), 1971 I.C.J. 15 (June 21).
*LeGrand Case (Germany v. United States of America)*, 1999 I.C.J. 9 (Provisional Measures, Order of Mar. 3) and 1999 I.C.J. 28 (Mar. 5).
Optional Protocol to the Convention on the Elimination of Discrimination Against Women, G.A. res. 54/4, annex, 54 U.N. GAOR Supp. (No. 49) at 5, U.N. Doc. A/54/49 (Vol. I) (2000), *entered into force* Dec. 22, 2000.
Nigel Rodley & David Weissbrodt, *United Nations Nontreaty Procedures for Dealing with Human Rights Violations*, in Guide to International Human Rights Practice (Hurst Hannum ed., 4th ed. 2004).
Security Council res. 827 of May 25, 1993.
*South West Africa Cases (Second Phase) (Eth. v. S. Afr.; Liber. v. S. Afr.)*, 1966 I.C.J. 4 (July 18).
UN Charter, June 26, 1945, 59 Stat. 1031, T.S. 993, 3 Bevans 1153, *entered into force* Oct. 24, 1945.
UN Centre for Human Rights, United Nations Action in the Field of Human Rights (1994).
*United States Diplomatic and Consular Staff in Tehran (U.S. v. Iran)*, 1980 I.C.J. 3 (May 24).
*Vienna Convention on Consular Relations (Paraguay v. United States of America)*, 1998 I.C.J. 248 (Provisional Measures, Order of 9 Apr.) and 1998 I.C.J. 266 (Apr. 9); 1998 I.C.J. 426 (Nov. 10); 1998 I.C.J. 272 (June 8).

*Links to Consult*:

http://www.ohchr.org/english/
http://www.ohchr.org/english/bodies/chr/index.htm
http://www.uncjin.org/
http://www.unhchr.ch/html/menu2/7/b/tm.htm
http://www.unhchr.ch/html/menu2/8/stat1.htm
http://www.un.org/
http://www.un.org/Depts/dhl/resguide/gares1.htm
http://www.un.org/Depts/dpko/dpko/bnote.htm
http://www.un.org/womenwatch/daw/csw/
http://www1.umn.edu/humanrts/instree/aunchart.htm
http://www1.umn.edu/humanrts/procedures/reports.html

## 2. Human Rights Treaty-Based Procedures

Including the Convention on the Rights of Migrant Workers and Members of Their Families, which came into force in 2003, there are now seven treaty-based committees that play a monitoring role in the protection of human rights. They are (1) the Committee on Migrant Workers; (2) the Human Rights Committee, which monitors the International Covenant on Civil an Political Rights; (3) the Committee on the Elimination of All Forms of Racial Discrimination; (4) the Committee on the

Elimination of Discrimination Against Women; (5) the Committee Against Torture; (6) the Committee on the Rights of the Child; and (7) the Committee on Economic, Social and Cultural Rights.[40] Two more treaties are on the way. The International Convention on the Rights of Persons with Disabilities and its Optional Protocol will establish a Committee on the Rights of Persons with Disabilities. The International Convention for the Protection of All Persons from Enforced Disappearance will establish the Committee on Enforced Disappearances.

With the exception of the Committee on Economic, Social and Cultural Rights—which was established under ECOSOC—the committees were created under the treaties they monitor to review reports by States parties. The Committee on Economic, Social and Cultural Rights was created in 1986 and modeled on the Human Rights Committee after several efforts to monitor the International Covenant on Economic, Social and Cultural Rights through ECOSOC working groups were deemed unsatisfactory.

Committee members for all seven treaty bodies are expected to be experts in the field covered by the treaty creating the committee. Members are typically elected to four-year terms by States parties to the treaty and can be reelected if nominated. Because committee members act in their personal capacity to review reports by States parties, the treaty bodies tend to avoid accusations of playing politics. In addition to monitoring reports, the committees issue statements regarding further interpretations of rights. These statements are called "General Comments" or "General Recommendations." NGOs and specialized agencies are allowed to submit information regarding states' reports and attend most committee meetings.

A major problem for all committees is the tardiness (sometimes extreme tardiness involving delays of many years) of governments in submitting reports required by the treaties and the backlog that the committees have in reviewing the numerous reports. There are on-going efforts to address these shortfalls, which are part of a larger push for UN human rights reform. For example, one treaty body reform proposal involves the harmonization of reporting requirements. Proponents of this idea argue that "harmonizing" reporting—essentially collapsing States parties' separate reports into a single, comprehensive document—would increase efficiency and reduce duplication. Critics, in turn, caution that combining reports risks producing less complete and overly generalized documents. Another reform proposal entails the consolidation of all treaty body committees into a unified standing treaty body or a unified committee for adjudicating complaints. Because ratification of treaties is not universal, however, there are significant legal obstacles to such a change. There is also concern that combining reports and their evaluation will deprive the process of the subject matter expertise now available through the human rights treaty bodies. Still others argue that it makes more sense to focus on strengthening and coordinating treaty body machinery as it currently exists by providing more staff and funding.

This chapter discusses in detail one of the principal human rights treaty bodies—the Human Rights Committee—as representative of the function of all seven treaty bodies. Readers interested in the specific areas covered by the other six treaties, however, should consult the work of the relevant committees and the chapters of this book relating to those subjects. For example, the Committee on Economic, Social and Cultural Rights has developed extensive General Comments elaborating the provisions of the Covenant on Economic, Social and Cultural Rights, as discussed above in the chapters on food, health, housing, and other rights. It should also be noted that the Human Rights Committee—given its burden of adjudicating many communications and its reputation for high quality work—is often regarded as the standard-bearer of the human rights treaty body system. In this way, the Human Rights Committee may not be perfectly representative of the committee system as a whole.

The Human Rights Committee consists of eighteen members from eighteen different nations elected by the States parties to the International Covenant for Civil and Political Rights.[41] Half are elected every two years by the 160 States parties to the Covenant. None of the members are government officials. Rather, most of the Committee members are academics, judges, or retired ambassadors. They are presently from such countries as Australia, Benin, Colombia, Ecuador, Egypt, France, India, Ireland, Japan, Mauritius, Paraguay, Romania, South Africa, Sweden, Switzerland, Tunisia, the United Kingdom, and the United States. Most are experts in relevant aspects in the field of human rights and act in their individual capacity even though they are nominated by their governments. The Committee meets three times a year for three weeks each time, alternating their meetings between New York (generally in March) and Geneva (generally in July and October).

The Committee has two main functions: (1) to review the compliance reports by states and (2) to adjudicate individual complaints filed by individuals in countries that have ratified the First Optional Protocol to the International Covenant on Civil and Political Rights. It also issues General Comments on issues concerning the implementation of the Covenant and elaborating the content of the specific rights delineated in the treaty.

The Committee has developed detailed reporting procedures for States parties. The initial report—due within one year after a state becomes a party—usually focuses on the constitution, laws, and structures of the nation as they relate to the fulfillment of the Covenant provisions. The Committee also expects information about actual practices, including in the first report, but more emphatically in subsequent reports. The Committee has determined that further periodic reports are ordinarily due every five years.

After a government submits its report, the Committee usually decides at which meeting it will review the report. The Committee selects a member or several members to serve as Special Rapporteurs on the country and lead the questioning of the national representatives when they appear before the Committee. The Human Rights Committee and its special rapporteurs have developed a practice of identifying key issues that the national representatives should address when they appear before the Committee to present their report. In preparing issue papers and questions, the Committee has developed a practice of consulting with nongovernmental organizations—particularly national NGOs—that can alert the Special Rapporteur and the Committee members to any problems with (1) the compliance of the government with its treaty obligations; (2) the failures of the government to involve civil society in preparing the report; and (3) inaccuracies in the report, which might be the subject of questions when the government representative appears before the Committee. In many cases, NGOs prepare their own parallel reports, sometimes referred to as "shadow reports," to answer the official government reports. These shadow reports are often taken into consideration by Committee members.

On the day the Committee begins to hear the government report in question, government representatives present usually include high-level officials from the capital as well as diplomats from Geneva or New York. Also in the meeting room are the eighteen members of the Committee, a small Committee staff of perhaps five or six employees of the Office of the High Commissioner for Human Rights, interpreters, official note-takers, and NGO representatives. With the exception of a few countries for which there is a great deal of NGO interest, the treaty bodies function without much NGO attendance or media attention. Generally speaking, the Human Rights Council and some of the other Charter-based organs receive far more media and NGO participation than the Human Rights Committee and other treaty bodies.

The principal government representative begins the consideration of his or her country report by giving an introductory statement addressing questions raised by the Committee's issue paper or addressing the Committee about recent developments since the government's report was produced. The Committee's Special Rapporteur raises questions about human rights concerns he or she has identified in the state report or from the information available from NGOs and other sources. The government representatives do not endeavor to answer right away. Instead, the other members of the Committee are each given the opportunity to ask further questions and raise individual concerns. The government representatives are usually given a window of time—for example, an afternoon or an evening—before attempting responses to the questions. There may be follow-up exchanges during which Committee members express their views and concerns regarding the government's official responses.

Although the Committee does not issue a legally binding judgment on violations by the government, the Committee has, since 1992, developed a practice of issuing "concluding observations" on each state report. These country conclusions identify positive developments, note concerns, and offer recommendations. In effect, country conclusions set an agenda for government action until the next reporting deadline, which may be as long as five years later. In their next periodic report, states are asked to address the concluding observations, in particular the concerns and recommendations, and report on progress regarding the protection and enjoyment of rights. For states that are party to the Optional Protocol, the Committee also requests information on remedies provided for any individual cases that have been decided.

The Committee occasionally asks for supplementary or more prompt reports when it determines that the initial and periodic reports are incomplete. It has also asked for emergency reports or follow-up reports within one year when it ascertained that events in a particular country indicated that the enjoyment of rights under the Covenant had been seriously affected or there is a need for follow-up on Committee recommendations. The Committee has established specific guidelines for such reports in order to get away from the tendency that governments have had of being self-congratulatory and not self-critical.

The greatest strength of the periodic reporting process is that it involves a painstaking, professional evaluation of each State party's progress in fulfilling the treaty provisions. The principal limitation is that the treaty bodies and their conclusions rarely receive the publicity they warrant, therefore significantly weakening their impact. Another major limitation is that many governments are late in fulfilling their reporting responsibilities. Several of the treaty bodies have experimented with ways to encourage governments to reply more promptly. For example, a committee might inform the government that if they do not produce their report, the Committee will invite the government to appear without having prepared a report and the treaty body will produce country conclusions without the attendance of the government. Such pressures have generally resulted in greater government reporting and cooperation.

In addition to their country conclusions, the Human Rights Committee has developed a practice of preparing General Comments to provide governments with authoritative guidance as to the meaning of the provisions of the Covenant or on other major issues facing the Committee. For example, in 1982—before the adoption of the Convention Against Torture and Other Cruel, Inhuman or Degrading Treatment—the Human Rights Committee issued a General Comment interpreting Covenant Article 7 on the prohibition of torture. The General Comment offered an expansive reading of the prohibition of torture to include the prohibition of cruel, inhuman, or degrading treatment or punishment. The Committee further noted that it is not sufficient to merely prohibit such treatment or punishment. Instead, governments should make effective

provisions against detention incommunicado, granting, without prejudice to the investigation, persons such as doctors, lawyers and family members access to the detainees; provisions requiring that detainees should be held in places that are publicly recognized and that their names and places of detention should be entered in a central register available to persons concerned, such as relatives; provisions making confessions or other evidence obtained through torture or other treatment contrary to article 7 inadmissible in court; and measures of training and instruction of law enforcement officials not to apply such treatment.[42]

This General Comment was an important step in defining the prohibition of torture set forth by Article 7. It laid the foundation for further development of the interpretation of that right by the drafting of the Convention Against Torture, decisions of regional human rights bodies, national legislation, and judicial decisions.

In addition to the state reporting procedure with its country conclusions and the General Comments, the Human Rights Committee is authorized under the Optional Protocol to receive and adjudicate complaints by individuals alleging that their rights have been violated. This complaint mechanism is available to individuals in the 109 nations that have ratified the Optional Protocol.[43] The Human Rights Committee also has the power—pursuant of Article 41—to consider complaints by one state against another relating to violations of the Covenant. To date, however, no State party has invoked this provision.

Before determining that an individual communication is admissible under the Optional Protocol, the Human Rights Committee decides whether certain requirements have been fulfilled. For example, the Committee decides whether domestic remedies have been exhausted. This requirement involves verifying whether the individual has previously sought relief from national courts or any other available procedure at the national level. Since 1989, the Human Rights Committee has requested one of its members to serve as the Special Rapporteur on New Communications in determining whether additional information is needed or whether to refer the communication to the State party for its observations on admissibility and the merits. The Special Rapporteur can also make recommendations regarding admissibility, but the Committee as a whole has the ultimate authority to make determinations regarding both admissibility and the merits. Meetings concerning individual complaints are not open to the public. When the Committee has determined whether there has been a violation of the Covenant, its judgments—which are referred to as "views"—are transmitted to the State party concerned and are eventually published. In all, the Human Rights Committee has handled hundreds of cases and developed a very impressive body of human rights jurisprudence.[44]

While the individual decisions and views of the Human Rights Committee are not enforceable as a matter of law, most governments comply with Committee views in individual cases, though sometimes only after the urging of a member of the Committee designated as the Special Rapporteur for the Follow-up of Views. In their periodic reports, States parties are required to detail compliance with Committee views about individual cases. For example, individuals have been released from detention, governments have paid compensation for violations, laws have been improved, non-citizens have been allowed to remain in the country where they were residing rather than being deported.

The great advantage of these procedures is that they can result in a well considered judgment on the merits of human rights claims. The disadvantage is that all of these procedures are entirely handled through the exchange of written communications. Without the capacity to hear evidence, receive oral arguments, or visit the country concerned, the Human Rights Committee is unable to handle significant factual disputes.

The Human Rights Committee is one of the four human rights treaty bodies that may adjudicate complaints about human rights violations. The other three committees that are authorized to consider individual communications—if the State party has agreed—are the Committee Against Torture, the Committee on the Elimination of Racial Discrimination, and the Committee on the Elimination of Discrimination Against Women. These three committees receive far fewer communications because they are less well known and have thus not developed such a rich jurisprudence as the Human Rights Committee. The new International Convention on the Rights of Persons with Disabilities and its Optional Protocol will authorize individual communications to the

Committee on the Rights of Persons with Disabilities, when those treaties come into force. Similarly, the new International Convention for the Protection of All Persons from Enforced Disappearance will authorize individual communications to the Committee on Enforced Disappearances, when the convention comes into force. There is also presently a working group under the Human Right Council tasked with elaborating an Optional Protocol on individual complaints for the International Covenant on Economic, Social and Cultural Rights.

There are several additional differences among the various treaty bodies. For example, the Committee Against Torture is authorized to initiate an inquiry in a country where there are well-founded indications that torture is being systematically practiced.[45] Furthermore, the 2002 Protocol to the Convention Against Torture, which has been ratified by thirty-two nations and came into force on June 22, 2006, establishes a system of regular visits undertaken by independent international and national bodies.[46] Nonetheless, the human rights treaty bodies—with their state reporting mechanisms and General Comments—are largely similar. Taken together, the treaty bodies represent perhaps the most authoritative, respected, and effective aspect of the UN human rights system.

*See also*: Economic, Social, and Cultural Rights; International Procedures

*Further Reading*:

Anne Bayefsky, The UN Human Rights Treaty System: Universality at the Crossroads (2001).
Convention Against Torture and Other Cruel, Inhuman or Degrading Treatment or Punishment, G.A. res. 39/46, annex, 39 U.N. GAOR Supp. (No. 51) at 197, U.N. Doc. A/39/51 (1984), *entered into force* June 26, 1987.
The Future of UN Human Rights Treaty Monitoring (Philip Alston & James Crawford eds., 2000).
Human Rights Committee, General Comment 7, Article 7 (Sixteenth session, 1982), Compilation of General Comments and General Recommendations Adopted by Human Rights Treaty Bodies, U.N. Doc. HRI/GEN/1/Rev.1 at 7 (1994).
The International Covenant on Civil and Political Rights: Cases, Materials, and Commentary (Sarah Joseph, Jenny Schultz, and Melissa Castan eds., 2d ed. 2004).
Optional Protocol to the Convention Against Torture and Other Cruel, Inhuman or Degrading Treatment or Punishment, G.A. res. A/RES/57/199, *adopted* Dec. 18, 2002, *reprinted in* 42 I.L.M. 26 (2003).
Optional Protocol to the International Covenant on Civil and Political Rights, G.A. res. 2200A (XXI), 21 U.N. GAOR Supp. (No. 16) at 59, U.N. Doc. A/6316 (1966), 999 U.N.T.S. 302, *entered into force* Mar. 23, 1976.

*Links to Consult:*

http://www.ohchr.org/english/bodies/treaty/index.htm
http://www1.umn.edu/humanrts/gencomm/hrcomms.htm
http://www1.umn.edu/humanrts/hrcommittee/hrc-page.html

## 3. Specialized and Other Agencies

In addition to the international human rights procedures based on the UN Charter and the seven human rights treaty bodies, there are several international organizations whose work relates to human rights. Some of those organizations, such as the International Labor Organization (ILO) and the UN Educational, Scientific and Cultural Organization (UNESCO), are considered UN specialized agencies. They have been established on the basis of their own treaties (or constitutions) to which states have become members. In contrast, the Statute of the Office of the UN High Commissioner for Refugees (UNHCR) was promulgated as a resolution of the UN General Assembly. The High Commissioner is elected by the General Assembly and the UNHCR possesses considerable functional independence from the UN Secretary-General and the UN Secretariat. Additionally, international financial institutions such as the International Monetary Fund, the World Bank, and the World Trade Organization are specialized agencies whose functions have significant bearing on human rights conditions. Each of the agencies noted above is reviewed briefly in this chapter.

### A. INTERNATIONAL LABOR ORGANIZATION (ILO)

The International Labor Organization was authorized in 1919 by the Treaty of Versailles. It was an agency of the League of Nations and became the first specialized agency of the UN in 1946.[47] The ILO was established as a partnership between employers and employees and has a unique tripartite system which enables the representatives of workers and employers to participate on an equal footing with governments in discussions and decision-making. The ILO is comprised of the International Labor Conference (its general assembly), the Governing Body (its executive council), and the International Labor Office (its secretariat). The International Labor Organization employs a staff of about 2,000 from 110 nations at its Geneva headquarters and in 40 field offices around the world. At the International Labor Conference each of the 180 member governments is represented by two individuals selected by the government, one employer delegate, and one labor delegate. The International Labor Conference meets every year for three weeks in

June and adopts the budget, establishes international labor standards, passes resolutions for setting general policy, provides a forum for discussion of social and labor issues, and—every three years—elects the Governing Body for a three-year term.

The Governing Body of the ILO is composed of fifty-six persons—twenty-eight government representatives, fourteen employer representatives, and fourteen worker representatives. It meets three times a year, draws up the agenda for the Conference and other ILO meetings, and supervises the daily functioning of the International Labor Office. The major international trade union organizations have full consultative status with the ILO, the International Trade Union Confederation, which is comprised of the previous International Confederation of Free Trade Unions and the previous World Confederation of Labor; the World Federation of Trade Unions; and the Organization of African Trade Union Unity. Employers are represented by the International Organization of Employers.

The ILO has adopted labor standards in 187 conventions and 198 recommendations. Among the most important are those standards that relate to (a) freedom of association and the effective recognition of the right to collective bargaining; (b) the elimination of all forms of forced or compulsory labor; (c) the effective abolition of child labor; and (d) the elimination of discrimination in respect of employment and occupation. In 1998, the ILO determined in the Declaration on Fundamental Principles and Rights at Work and its Follow-Up that all ILO member States, "even if they have not ratified the Conventions in question, have an obligation arising from the very fact of membership in the Organization, to respect, to promote and to realize, in good faith and in accordance with the Constitution, the principles concerning the fundamental rights which are the subject of those Conventions," particularly relating to those four basic principles.[48]

The 1998 Declaration calls for an annual review of countries that have not ratified one or more of the conventions relating to the four categories of fundamental rights. The Declaration also provides for a global report to be produced annually on one of the four categories of fundamental rights. Accordingly, the first global report on the situation of freedom of association and recognition of the right to collective bargaining (entitled,"Your Voice at Work") was issued in 2000, both to countries that had ratified the relevant conventions and those which had not. Further reports cycle through the four categories, for example, "Stopping Forced Labour" (2001), "A Future Without Child Labour" (2002), "Time for Equality at Work" (2003), "Organizing for Social Justice" (2004), "A Global Alliance Against Forced Labour" (2005), and "The End of Child Labour: Within Reach" (2006).

Article 22 of the ILO Constitution establishes another very important mechanism of implementation of the ILO's labor conventions, in which each member State is required to make periodic reports to the International Labor Office detailing measures it has taken to give effect to provisions of conventions to which it is party. Since the ILO has obtained more than thousands of ratifications of its 187 conventions, it receives about 1,500 periodic reports each year. The ILO now requests reports every other year for the most important labor conventions—for example, those relating to human rights (e.g., forced labor, freedom of association). For most other conventions, the ILO expects state reports every five years. Some conventions have become outmoded or have been subsumed within more recent standards, such that the ILO no longer requests specific reporting on them unless the ILO becomes aware of particular problems. The periodic state reports include information on (1) how a nation's laws comply with the convention; (2) what enforcement procedures have been implemented if required; (3) measures that have been taken to reach goals of the convention and obstacles that have to be overcome; (4) decisions made by courts of law relating to the application of the convention; (5) a general description of how the convention is applied in practice; and (6) the organizations of workers and employers that have been sent copies of the reports and any replies received from them.

The government reports for each convention are reviewed by the staff of the Standards and Fundamental Principles and Rights at Work Branch of the International Labor Office, together with the country's legislation, decisions of other ILO bodies, and comments from employer and worker groups. The staff prepares recommendations for the Committee of Experts on the Application of Conventions and Recommendations comprised of twenty individuals with expert qualifications in legal and social fields and knowledge of labor conditions and administration. The members of the Committee of Experts are nominated by the ILO Director-General for approval by the Governing Body. They serve for renewable terms of three years and they meet each year for three weeks in November/December. If the Committee of Experts finds that a government is not complying with the ratified convention or its obligations under the ILO Constitution regarding conventions and recommendations, it can issue comments in the form of observations or direct requests. The former are published in its report and are used for serious cases of failure to comply. Direct requests are sent directly to the concerned government, workers' organizations, and employer's organizations, but are not published. The report of the Committee of Experts is published during the following March and that report is then reviewed by the tripartite Conference Committee on the Application of Standards in June at the time of the International Labor Conference.

The Conference Committee starts with a general discussion and then examines particular countries. Governments mentioned in the report of the Committee of Experts may make a statement. Government delegates can also be asked questions by workers' and employers' representatives. The factual exchanges between delegates are seen as valuable tools for attaining compliance with the labor standards.

Another ILO procedure is founded upon Article 19 of the ILO Constitution. Under this procedure the Governing Body may request reports from each member state on its laws and practices in regard to the subject matter of particular conventions which that member state has not ratified. Article 19 is intended to encourage ratification of conventions and states are asked to indicate "the difficulties which prevent or delay the ratification" of conventions.[49] Based on information generated by Articles 19 and 22 reporting, the ILO prepares a General Survey on particular aspects of labor standards and national practices. For example in 2003, the ILO requested information about implementation and ratification of two conventions and two recommendations relating to employment policies. As a result of the information gathered, the ILO in published a General Survey in 2004 entitled "Promoting Employment: Policies, Skills, Enterprises."

In addition, the ILO manages several complaint mechanisms. For example, Article 24 of the ILO Constitution authorizes any national or international workers' or employers' organization to make a "representation" claiming that a particular government has failed to comply with an ILO convention it has ratified. The Governing Body must determine whether the representation is receivable, for example, whether it provides sufficient information to indicate in what respect the government has failed to secure the effective observance of the relevant ILO convention. If the representation is receivable, the Governing Body will ordinarily refer the matter to a tripartite committee that gathers information from the complaining party and the government. The Committee makes conclusions and recommendations to the Governing Body, which hears presentations from the government and publishes its decision. One possible decision would be to invoke Article 26 of the ILO Constitution for establishing a Commission of Inquiry. Article 26 may also be invoked by one ILO member State against another indicating that the latter government had failed to secure "the effective observance of any Convention which both have ratified. . . ."

The Article 26 procedure, however, is considered so important that it has rarely been invoked. For example, during the period 1934 to 1998 the Commission of Inquiry procedure was only pursued in 26 situations. For example, in 1997 the ILO established a Commission of Inquiry of three distinguished individuals (from Australia, Barbados, and India) in regard to complaints of forced labor in Myanmar (Burma). The Commission of Inquiry visited the country and found forced labor was widespread and systematic. The Commission recommended several measures to Myanmar aimed at reducing forced labor pursuant to ILO Convention No. 29 and stopping the use of child labor. Nonetheless, according to a report of an ILO technical team in October 2000, the government of Myanmar failed to fulfill the Commission's recommendations. As a result, for the first time in its more than eighty years the ILO decided to invoke sanctions in calling on "governments, employers and workers to review their relationships with Myanmar 'and take appropriate measures to ensure that [Myanmar] cannot take advantage of such relations to perpetuate or extend the system of forced or compulsory labor'; and to 'contribute as far as possible to the implementation' of the recommendations of the Committee of Inquiry."[50]

If a complaint filed pursuant to Article 24 relates to trade union rights, it is referred to the ILO Committee on Freedom of Association (CFA), which is comprised of nine individuals—three each from government, unions, and employers. The CFA can consider complaints even in regard to governments that have not ratified the relevant ILO treaties. The Committee ordinarily receives complaints from trade unions and makes recommendations to the Governing Body. It has handled about 2,000 cases and amassed a considerable jurisprudence interpreting the two principal ILO treaties guaranteeing freedom of association—the Freedom of Association and Protection of the Right to Organise Convention (ILO No. 87) and the Right to Organise and Collective Bargaining Convention (ILO No. 98).

The ILO also has a high-level procedure for investigating infringements of trade union rights—the Fact-Finding and Conciliation Commission—which follows procedures similar to those followed by a Commission of Inquiry. The Fact-Finding and Conciliation Commission is composed of nine independent experts selected by the Governing Body. The Commission ordinarily works in panels of three members and has, since 1964, dealt with six cases arising in Chile, Greece, Japan, Lesotho, South Africa, and the United States/Puerto Rico.

In 1977 the ILO adopted the Tripartite Declaration of Principles concerning Multinational Enterprises (known as the Multinational Declaration), which calls upon businesses to follow the relevant ILO conventions and recommendations principally related to worker rights. The Multinational Declaration was updated in 2000. Since 1980 the Governing Body has established a procedure, revised in 1986, for interpretation of the Multinational Declaration in regard to cases where there may be a dispute as to its meaning or application. Only five interpretations have been issued pursuant to that procedure. Since 1985 the Governing Body has also asked governments to report every three years on the implementation of the Multinational Declaration. The information received from governments, employers' organizations, and workers' organizations is compiled in triennial surveys for consideration by the Governing Body.

The ILO has utilized *ad hoc* procedures or special studies, for reporting on issues such as labor concerns in *apartheid* South Africa and in the Occupied Arab Territories, or studying discrimination in particular countries. The Director-General has further selected independent experts to undertake direct contacts with governments as to issues raised by the Committee of Experts and other supervisory mechanisms. Among its many other functions, the ILO maintains the International Programme on the Elimination of Child Labour (IPEC), which supports projects in more than ninety countries to protect bonded child laborers, children in hazardous working conditions, and other vulnerable children from being compelled to work instead of going to school. For example, IPEC has been successful in removing hundreds of child carpet weavers in India from work and in providing them with nonformal education.

B. UN EDUCATIONAL, SCIENTIFIC AND CULTURAL ORGANIZATION (UNESCO)

The Constitution of the UN Educational, Scientific and Cultural Organization was issued in 1945 and came into force in 1946.[51] Its secretariat is located in Paris, and it also has about fifty national offices. UNESCO has 192 member States, which are members of the General Conference. As a specialized agency of the United Nations, UNESCO's purpose is

> to contribute to peace and security by promoting collaboration among the nations through education, science and culture in order to further universal respect for justice, for the rule of law and for the human rights and fundamental freedoms which are affirmed for the peoples of the world, without distinction of race, sex, language or religion, by the Charter of the United Nations.

It has promulgated treaties related to human rights such as the Convention Against Discrimination in Education in 1960 and the Convention for the Protection of Cultural Property in the Event of Armed Conflict in 1954. In 1997 it adopted the Universal Declaration on the Human Genome and Human Rights, which is the first international instrument on this topic, and which rejects the cloning of human beings. UNESCO encourages international educational exchanges and programs relating to human rights. For example, it assists university and secondary human rights programs in many countries to improve and coordinate their activities.

UNESCO established a Committee on Conventions and Recommendations in 1978, which examines violations against teachers, artists, poets, authors, scientists, and teachers. Victims or persons with reliable knowledge may file a petition. Before the complaints are found to be admissible, the Director-General may initiate consultations with the government or take humanitarian action if needed. The complaints are transmitted to the concerned governments, which may submit replies. The parties may appear before the Committee, which can then propose measures to the state. The procedure emphasizes friendly settlement and is confidential. UNESCO reports that in the first twenty years the Committee handled 460 communications and settled 274 of them. Because the UNESCO procedure functions almost entirely in secrecy and does not report on its results, it is very difficult to evaluate its success. One study, however, obtained access to 64 case files relating to 36 countries. It found that the situation of 93 individuals had improved as a result of the Committee's actions. Nonetheless, it concluded that the procedure is very slow, is subject to political manipulation, prefers to delay decisions rather than reaching conclusions, accepts government responses at face value, and dismisses cases when some positive results are reached—for example, when an individual is released from prison, rather than insisting on restitution (e.g., compensation for torture or allowing a teacher to return to the classroom).

c. UN High Commissioner for Refugees (UNHCR)

The UN High Commissioner for Refugees protects refugees, asylum seekers, and stateless persons.[52] It pursues long-term solutions for them, including repatriation, third country resettlement, and host country integration. The UNHCR has become a major provider of humanitarian assistance to refugees, broadly defined—in certain circumstances—to include victims of persecution and armed conflict, as well as internally displaced persons (people fleeing for "refugee-like" reasons who have not crossed an internationally recognized border). The Office of the UNHCR was established in 1950 by a resolution of the UN General Assembly which adopted its Statute. Although it has many organizational characteristics of a UN specialized agency, the UNHCR was not founded upon its own treaty as were specialized agencies such as the ILO and UNESCO. The UNHCR does, however, encourage ratification of the 1951 United Nations Convention Relating to the Status of Refugees and its 1967 Protocol. The High Commissioner for Refugees is elected by the General Assembly upon nomination of the UN Secretary-General. The

Office of the UNHCR employs a staff of more than 6,500 at its Geneva headquarters and in 277 offices in 120 countries, working to assist nearly twenty-one million people in about 115 nations with the support of hundreds of humanitarian agencies. Policy for the UNHCR is established by its Executive Committee (known as EXCOM), comprised of seventy nations.

D. INTERNATIONAL FINANCIAL INSTITUTIONS—INTERNATIONAL MONETARY FUND, WORLD BANK, AND WORLD TRADE ORGANIZATION

Major intergovernmental financial institutions such as the International Monetary Fund (IMF),[53] the International Bank for Reconstruction and Development (World Bank),[54] and the World Trade Organization (WTO)[55] have increasing impact on the promotion and protection of human rights. As international trade grows in scale and significance, the activities of these organizations have profound effects on people and economies all over the world—particularly in poor or developing nations.

The IMF and World Bank were created contemporaneously in the latter years of World War II, via the Bretton Woods Agreements. As stated in the Articles of Agreement of the International Monetary Fund, the purposes of the Fund are

(I) To promote international monetary cooperation.
(ii) To facilitate the expansion and balanced growth of international trade, and to contribute thereby to the promotion and maintenance of high levels of employment and real income and to the development of the productive resources of all members as primary objectives of economic policy. . . .
(iv) To assist in the establishment of a multilateral system of payments in respect of current transactions between members and in the elimination of foreign exchange restrictions which hamper the growth of world trade. . . .[56]

According to the Articles of Agreement of the International Bank for Reconstruction and Development, the purposes of the World Bank are

(I) To assist in the . . . development of territories of members. . . .
(ii) To promote private foreign investment. . . .
(iii) To promote the long-range balanced growth of international trade and the maintenance of equilibrium in balances of payments. . . .
(v) To conduct its operations with due regard to the effect of international investment on business conditions in the territories of its members . . . .[57]

The World Trade Organization was created in 1994 to oversee the operation and implementation of several multilateral and plurilateral trade agreements, foremost among them was the General Agreement on

Tariffs and Trade (GATT). The Agreement Establishing the World Trade Organization opens with the recognition that States parties'

relations in the field of trade and economic endeavor should be conducted with a view to raising standards of living, ensuring full employment and a large and steadily growing volume of real income and effective demand, and expanding the production of and trade in goods and services, while allowing for the optimal use of the world's resources in accordance with the objective of sustainable development. . . .[58]

Article 3(5) of the Agreement further instructs that

With a view to achieving greater coherence in global economic policy-making, the WTO shall cooperate, as appropriate, with the International Monetary Fund and with the International Bank for Reconstruction and Development and its affiliated agencies.[59]

These provisions illustrate the common goals of the IMF, World Bank, and WTO—furthering international trade and economic development. The efforts of these organizations, collectively and individually, affect fundamental rights such as the rights to food, a healthy environment, health, freedom of association to form trade unions, work, and the like. The founding documents of the IMF, World Bank, and WTO do not explicitly mention the role human rights should play in organizational activities, but all call for "development" or "balanced growth," which could be read to include human rights. Furthermore, these founding instruments should be read together with the UN Charter and the human rights treaties that member States have ratified.

The UN Charter has been ratified by all the nations that are States parties to the founding documents of the IMF, World Bank, and WTO. Article 55 of the Charter states:

With a view to the creation of conditions of stability and well-being which are necessary for peaceful and friendly relations among nations . . . the United Nations shall promote:
a. higher standards of living, full employment, and conditions of economic and social progress and development
b. solutions of international economic, social, health, and related problems; and international cultural and educational cooperation; and
c. universal respect for, and observance of, human rights and fundamental freedoms for all without distinction as to race, sex, language, or religion.[60]

Article 56 then declares: "All Members pledge themselves to take joint and separate action in co-operation with the Organization for the achievement of the purposes set forth in Article 55."[61] Read together, Articles 55 and 56 demonstrate that all the states that are members of the IMF, World Bank, and WTO are obliged to honor human rights.

288  International Procedures

Other international human rights treaties contain similar provisions that implicate the international responsibilities of cooperation among states participating in the IMF, World Bank, and WTO. For example, the Covenant on Economic, Social and Cultural Rights provides in Article 2 that

> Each State Party to the present Covenant undertakes to take steps, individually and through international assistance and co-operation, especially economic and technical, to the maximum of its available resources, with a view to achieving progressively the full realization of the rights recognized in the present Covenant by all appropriate means. . . .[62]

Similarly, the Convention on the Rights of the Child provides in Article 4 that

> States Parties shall undertake all appropriate legislative, administrative, and other measures for the implementation of the rights recognized in the present Convention. With regard to economic, social and cultural rights, States Parties shall undertake such measures to the maximum extent of their available resources and, where needed, within the framework of international co-operation.[63]

Like the UN Charter, these provisions support the notion that there is a duty on states to observe their human rights obligations when participating in organizations such as the IMF, World Bank, and WTO. Gabrielle Marceau, Counsellor for the Legal Affairs Division of the WTO Secretariat, has expressed her view that

> the WTO Agreement [does not exist] in an hermetically sealed system, closed off from general international law and human rights law. On the contrary, States must implement all their obligations in good faith, including human rights and WTO treaty obligations.[64]

An analogous observation would be appropriate for seeing the work of the IMF and World Bank in a human rights context. An alternative means of reaching a similar conclusion can be found through the treaty interpretation provisions of the Vienna Convention on the Law of Treaties. The Vienna Convention provides in Article 31(3)(c) that when interpreting a treaty, one must consider "any relevant rules of international law applicable in the relations between the parties."[65] Hence, the agreements creating the IMF, World Bank, WTO, and United Nations, as well as human rights treaties, should be read together so that none conflicts or impinges on another. For example, each of these treaties encourages development that should be read as consistent with the objective to achieve human rights. Indeed, the right to development is an aspect of human rights.

If it is not possible to avoid a direct conflict between two treaties, there is a basic principle of international law that states that a government cannot exempt itself from its obligations under a first treaty by ratifying another treaty. There is an exception, of course, if all the parties to the first treaty ratify the second treaty and thus essentially amend the first treaty. This exception does not apply in regard to the IMF, World Bank, WTO, UN, and human rights treaties because there is not a complete congruence among the States parties.

Moreover, if there is a conflict between the UN Charter and other treaties, the UN Charter provisions must be followed. Article 103 of the Charter states that "In the event of a conflict between the obligations of the Members of the United Nations under the present Charter and their obligations under any other international agreement, their obligations under the present Charter shall prevail."[66]

Following this unified approach to interpreting the UN Charter and the founding instruments of the international economic institutions, the OHCHR has proposed a unified "human rights approach" to trade treaties. The High Commissioner's "human rights approach"

Sets the promotion and protection of human rights as objectives of trade liberalization, not exceptions;
Examines the effects of trade liberalization on individuals and seeks to devise trade law and policy to take into account the rights of all individuals, in particular vulnerable individuals and groups;
1. Emphasizes the role of the State in the process of liberalization—not only as negotiators of trade law and setters of trade policy, but also as the primary duty bearer of human rights;
2. Seeks consistency between the progressive liberalization of trade and the progressive realization of human rights;
3. Requires a constant examination of the impact of trade liberalization on the enjoyment of human rights; and
4. Promotes internal cooperation for the realization of human rights and freedoms in the context of trade liberalization.

Despite the human rights obligations of the IMF, World Bank, and WTO, as read together with the UN Charter and human rights treaties, the activities of the institutions in practice have been the focus of much pointed criticism. Professor Joe Oloka-Onyango has pointed out that in the context of globalization—substantially powered by the efforts of the IMF, World Bank, and WTO—much attention has been paid to, "policies pursued in the quest for economic reform [that] have rendered the state incapable of fulfilling many of its human rights obligations."[67] For example, the World Bank and IMF have principally sought to increase the overall wealth in developing countries without considering the unequal distribution of the benefits of economic growth. They promote privatization schemes that impair the rights to health, education, work, and an adequate standard of living and they emphasize exports that undermine the right to adequate food.

Professors Oloka-Onyango and Deepika Udagama produced a detailed report on the IMF, World Bank, and WTO for the UN Sub-Commission on the Promotion and Protection of Human Rights as Special Rapporteurs on Globalization and its impact on the full enjoyment of human rights. Commenting on the activities of the WTO, Professors Oloka-Onyango and Udagama noted positively that "human rights considerations do find their way into the negotiations as well as into dispute settlement." They observed, however, that such considerations are, "not necessarily done in a systematic or deliberate manner ... [and] ... there is no guarantee that the imperative of trade concerns does not get superior treatment."[68]

In discussing the IMF and World Bank, Professors Oloka-Onyango and Udagama expressed criticisms about the institutions' inadequate attention to "transparency, participation and the enhanced inclusion of both marginalized groups and countries."[69] The UN Special Rapporteurs observed that "the Bank appears much more responsive to the pressures [of promoting and protecting human rights] than does the Fund."[70] Specifically, the UN report states that

> In terms of issues such as the situation of women, child labour, the HIV/AIDS pandemic, "governance," increased transparency and the consequences of forced (environmental or developmental) displacement, the Bank has in many respects moved beyond what it used to argue was its essential mandate.... [T]he Bank has sought to ". . . increase staff awareness of human rights issues and legal framework, their implications for Bank operations and the extent to which human rights issues are being, or should be, addressed in World Bank operations."[71]

Professors Oloka-Onyango and Udagama concluded that the ultimate outcome of these efforts will likely be determined by an ongoing debate within the World Bank between "traditionalists" who "assert that the Bank is principally bound by its Articles of Agreement and that this instrument specifies specialized functions, which do not include any human rights," and those World Bank officials who counter that, "there is a compelling need for the development of a more comprehensive approach to human rights that recognizes economic policies do not 'have a neutral impact on individual or collective rights.'"[72]

As noted by the two Special Rapporteurs, the IMF has been much less receptive to human rights concerns. The IMF has imposed structural adjustment programs as conditions for providing loan assistance to countries with problems meeting their debts. While there may be some variation in the structural adjustment conditions applied to particular countries, an ILO study of the consequences of structural adjustment on trade union rights has noted that conditions often include significant decreases in the number of civil service employees and in their salaries; increases in the cost of utilities, food, and housing; declines in incomes and social services in the society as a whole; and increases in the suffering of the poor. Policies motivated by structural adjustment conditions, such as the withdrawal of food subsidies, have caused strong (and sometimes violent) public opposition in such countries as Argentina, Bangladesh, Egypt, Tunisia, and Zambia.

The American Federation of Labor-Congress of Industrial Organizations (AFL-CIO) has criticized IMF and World Bank loan conditions as "anti-worker," pointing out that such conditions weaken collective bargaining agreement laws and reduce real wages. In addition, a report on economic development in Africa by the United Nations Conference on Trade and Development has noted that growing wage inequality has accompanied the rapid trade liberalization in developing countries. Such critiques have typically been countered by the IMF and World Bank with the notion that if there was growth it did not matter who benefitted or what inequality effects resulted. Recently, however, the Word Bank's own Operations Evaluation Department detailed how income inequality grew in the vast majority of former Soviet-bloc countries during the period they received World Bank assistance.

An ILO study recommended that structural adjustment programs should be designed in such a way that the government does not violate its commitments under international human rights and labor conventions.[73] The structural adjustment program should also be developed in consultation with principal sectors of civil society including trade unions and employers. The UN Development Program has advocated that such adjustment programs should also focus on human development, poverty reduction, and long term sustainability.

E. OTHER SPECIALIZED AGENCIES

The Food and Agriculture Organization (FAO),[74] the United Nations Children's Fund (UNICEF),[75] and the World Health Organization (WHO)[76] also have programs and policies relating to human rights within their respective fields.

*See also*: Asylum and Refugee Status, Food, Health, Slavery and Forced Labor, Work-Related Rights and Rest

*Further Reading:*

Articles of Agreement of the International Monetary Fund, Dec. 27, 1945, 60 Stat. 1401, 2 U.N.T.S. 39, *entered into force* Dec. 27, 1945.
Steve Charnovitz, Trade Law and Global Governance (2002).
Convention Against Discrimination in Education, 429 U.N.T.S. 93, *entered into force* May 22, 1962.
Convention Concerning Forced or Compulsory Labour (ILO No. 29), 39 U.N.T.S. 55, *entered into force* May 1, 1932.
Convention for the Protection of Cultural Property in the Event of Armed Conflict, 249 U.N.T.S. 240, *entered into force* Aug. 7, 1956.
Convention Relating to the Status of Refugees, 189 U.N.T.S. 150, *entered into force* Apr. 22, 1954.
Mac Darrow, Between Light and Shadow: The World Bank, the International Monetary Fund and International Human Rights Law (2003).
Freedom of Association and Protection of the Right to Organise Convention (ILO No. 87), 68 U.N.T.S. 17, *entered into force* July 4, 1950.
General Agreement on Tariffs and Trade, Oct. 30, 1947, 61 Stat. A-11, T.I.A.S. 1700, 55 U.N.T.S. 194, *entered into force* Jan. 1, 1948.
Global Trade and Global Social Issues (Annie Taylor & Caroline Thomas eds., 1999).
Robert Howse and Makau Mutua, Protecting Human Rights in a Global Economy: Challenges for the World Trade Organization (2000).
International Bank for Reconstruction and Development, Articles of Agreement of the International Bank for Reconstruction and Development, Dec. 27, 1945, 60 Stat. 1440, T.I.A.S. No. 1502, 2 U.N.T.S. 134, *entered into force* Dec. 27, 1945, *amended* Dec. 16, 1965, 16 U.S.T. 1942, T.I.A.S. No. 5929.
International Development Association, Articles of Agreement of the International Development Association, Jan. 26, 1960, art. I, 11 U.S.T. 2284, T.I.A.S. No. 4607, 439 U.N.T.S. 249, *entered into force* Sept. 24, 1960.
International Finance Corporation, Articles of Agreement of the International Finance Corporation, May 25, 1955, 7 U.S.T. 2197, T.I.A.S. No. 3620, 264 U.N.T.S. 117, *entered into force* July 20, 1956.
ILO Declaration on Fundamental Principles and Rights at Work and its Follow-Up, *adopted* June 18, 1998, 37 I.L.M. 1233.
ILO, Report of the Commission of Inquiry Appointed under Article 26 of the Constitution of the International Labour Organisation to Examine the Observance by Myanmar of the Forced Labour Convention, 1930 (No. 29), 81 Off. Bull., Series B, para. 536 (1998).
International Labor Organization, International Labor Standards Department, Handbook of procedures relating to international labour Conventions and Recommendations (Rev. 2, 1998).
International Labor Organization, Tripartite Declaration of Principles concerning Multinational Enterprises and Social Policy, 17 ILM 422 (1978).
Kent Albert Jones, Who's Afraid of the WTO? (2004).
Joe Oloka-Onyango and Deepika Udagama, Final Report, Globalization and Its Impact on the Full Enjoyment of Human Rights, U.N. Doc. E/CN.4/Sub.2/2003/14 (2003).
Protocol Relating to the Status of Refugees, 606 U.N.T.S. 267, *entered into force* Oct. 4, 1967.
Right to Organize and Collective Bargaining Convention (ILO No. 98), 96 U.N.T.S. 257, *entered into force* July 18, 1951.

Statute of the Office of the United Nations High Commissioner for Refugees, G.A. res. 428 (V), annex, 5 U.N. GAOR Supp. (No. 20) at 46, U.N. Doc. A/1775 (1950).
UNESCO Doc. 154 EX/16, Annex II, Summary of the Results of the Application of the Procedures Laid Down by 104 EX/Decision 3.3 (1998).
Universal Declaration on the Human Genome and Human Rights, UNESCO Gen. Conf. Res. 29 C/Res.16, *reprinted in* Records of the General Conference, UNESCO, 29th Sess., 29 C/Resolution 19, at 41 (1997) (adopted by the UN General Assembly, G.A. res. 152, U.N. GAOR, 53rd Sess., U.N. Doc. A/RES/53/152 (1999)).
C. S. Venkata Ratnam, Trade Unions and Structural Adjustment (ILO 1996).
Gary P. Sampson, ed., The Role of the World Trade Organization in Global Governance (2001).
Sigrun I. Skogly, The Human Rights Obligations of the World Bank and the International Monetary Fund (2001).
World Bank, IMF and Human Rights: Including the Tilburg Guiding Principles on World Bank, IMF and Human Rights (Willem van Genugten, Paul Hunt, & Susan Mathews eds., 2003).
David Weissbrodt & Rose Farley, *The UNESCO Human Rights Procedure: An Evaluation*, 16 Human Rights Quarterly 391 (1994).


*Links to Consult*:

http://portal.unesco.org
http://www.aflcio.org/issuespolitics/globaleconomy/wbimf.cfm
http://www.ejil.org/journal/Vol13/No4/art1.pdf
http://www.eldis.org/cf/search/disp/DocDisplay.cfm?Doc = DOC16264& Resource = f 1wbimf
http://www.fao.org
http://www.ilo.org/
http://www.ilo.org/public/english/dialogue/actrav/publ/strucadj.pdf
http://www.unctad.org/en/docs/pogdsafricad2.en.pdf
http://www.unhcr.org
http://www.unicef.org
http://www.who.int
http://www.worldbank.org/oed/transitioneconomies/docs/transition_economies.p df
http://www1.umn.edu/humanrts/instree/auov.htm


## 4. World Conferences

United Nations world conferences on human rights have become an important way of strengthening and further developing international human rights law. While the concluding documents from these conferences are not usually binding on countries, they have played an important role in molding the relevant law and programs of the UN in this field.

The first World Conference on Human Rights was held in Teheran during 1968 to celebrate the twentieth anniversary of the Universal Declaration of Human Rights. The conference proclaimed that the Universal Declaration "states a common understanding of the peoples of the world concerning the inalienable and inviolable rights of all members of the human family and constitutes an obligation for the members of the international community. . . ."[77] In 1993 the Second World Conference was held in Vienna. Seven thousand persons representing 171 countries and more than 800 nongovernmental organizations participated. The Vienna Declaration and Programme of Action of the World Conference on Human Rights expressed "commitment to women's equality and the human rights of women."[78] The 1993 World Conference also recommended establishing the UN High Commissioner for Human Rights and the General Assembly created the High Commissioner's office that same year. After considerable discussion as to whether certain rights are more significant than other rights and as to whether rights should be limited by their cultural context, the World Conference declared, "All human rights are universal, indivisible and interdependent."[79]

Other conferences relevant to human rights have included (1) the UN Conference on Environment and Development (UNCED, Earth Summit) (Rio de Janeiro, 1992); (2) the International Conference on Population Development (Cairo, 1994); (3) the World Conference on Women (Beijing, 1995); (4) the World Summit on Social Development (Copenhagen, 1995); (5) the World Food Summit (Rome, 1996); (6) Habitat II (Istanbul, 1996); (7) and the World Conference Against Racism, Racial Discrimination, Xenophobia and Related Intolerance (Durban, 2001); (8) the World Summit on Sustainable Development (Johannesburg, 2002); and (9) the Small Arms Review Conference (New York, 2006).

The Racism Conference in Durban was attended by nearly 19,000 people and representatives of 146 states took the floor during the plenary sessions of the conference. 125 representatives from nongovernmental organizations also spoke. The Racism Conference was controversial in that media attention focused initially on the walk-out by the United States and certain NGO procedures and proposals that were marred by anti-Semitism. At the same time, however, the Declaration and Program of Action of the World Conference Against Racism recognized with "deep concern the increase in anti-Semitism and Islamophobia in various parts of the world, as well as the emergence of racial and violent movements based on racism and discriminatory ideas against Jewish, Muslim and Arab communities. . . ."[80]

The Durban Declaration and Program of Action called upon states "to combat the scourges of racism, racial discrimination, xenophobia and related intolerance. United Nations bodies and specialized agencies, international and regional organizations, national human rights institutions, nongovernmental organizations, youth and civil society at large are called upon to take an active part in the implementation process."[81] The Durban Conference discussed at length reparations for slavery and the transatlantic slave trade, acknowledged the "untold suffering" inflicted on millions, noted that some states have apologized and paid reparations, and invited the international community to honor the memory of the victims and to find further ways to restore the dignity of the victims. The Declaration and Program of Action of the World Conference Against Racism included recommendations for national plans and programs to fight racism, for better treatment of victims, for tougher antidiscrimination legislation and administrative measures, and for implementation of the International Convention for the Elimination of All Forms of Racial Discrimination, and for strengthening education. In addition to laying the foundation for UN activities, the Durban Program has provided impetus for action at the national level.

Follow up conferences to assess progress on the various subjects discussed at the principal conferences have been held every five or ten years. Outcome documents from those conferences further help to define standards and encourage progress on the specific issues.

*See also*: Equality and Nondiscrimination; Food; Healthy Environment; Housing

*Further Reading:*

Marc Bossuyt & Stef Vandeginste, *The Issue of Reparation for Slavery and Colonialism and the Durban World Conference Against Racism*, 22 Human Rights Law Journal 341 (2002).
J. A. Lindgren Alves, *The Durban Conference Against Racism and Everyone's Responsibilities*, 37 U.S.F. Law Review 971 (2003):.
Proclamation of Teheran, Final Act of the International Conference on Human Rights, Teheran, Apr. 22–May 13, 1968, U.N. Doc. A/CONF. 32/41 at 3 (1968).
Vienna Declaration, World Conference on Human Rights, Vienna, June 14–25, 1993, U.N. Doc. A/CONF.157/24 (Part I) at 20 (1993).
World Conference Against Racism, Racial Discrimination, Xenophobia and Related Intolerance, Programme of Action, Agenda item 9, *adopted* Sept. 8, 2001, in Durban South Africa, U.N. Doc. A/CONF.189/5 (2001).

*Links to Consult:*

http://www1.umn.edu/humanrts/instree/auol.htm
http://www1.umn.edu/humanrts/un-orgs.htm

## 5. International Criminal Procedures

Shortly after World War II, the Nuremberg and Tokyo Tribunals determined the criminal responsibility and punishment of major war criminals. Thousands of less visible war criminals were tried in Germany during the years following the war. Still, despite more than forty years of advocacy from lawyers and scholars pushing for the establishment of further international criminal tribunals to punish grave human rights abuses and war crimes, no progress was made in this realm until 1993–94, when the UN Security Council established two *ad hoc* tribunals for the former Yugoslavia and Rwanda. In addition, national courts began to apply "universal jurisdiction" to war criminals and perpetrators of genocide and crimes against humanity who committed offenses in other countries. Two very important milestones in this process have been the 1998 adoption of the Statute of the International Criminal Court and the 2002 celebration of the coming into force of the International Criminal Court in the Hague. There have also been "mixed tribunals" (sometimes called "hybrids") which combine international personnel and standards together with national legal systems. This chapter covers each of these developments in turn.

### A. Nuremberg, Tokyo, and Other Post-World War II Developments

After World War II, the Allied governments of the Soviet Union, United Kingdom, United States, and the provisional government of the French Republic created the International Military Tribunal to sit in Nuremberg in response to the numerous reports they received of Nazi atrocities involving civilians. The Agreement for the Prosecution and Punishment of the Major War Criminals of the European Axis (the "London Agreement") set forth the Tribunal's jurisdiction for individual responsibility for crimes against peace, war crimes, and crimes against humanity.[82] The London Agreement provided that under the principle of individual responsibility the official position of defendants as heads of state or responsible government officials would not shield them from trial or punishment.

The trials of twenty-two Nazi military and political leaders under the London Agreement began on November 20, 1945. The prosecution presented thirty-three witnesses and placed over 4,000 documents into evidence. The defense presented sixty-one witnesses in addition to the testimony of nineteen defendants, and 143 witnesses provided testimony by way of interrogatories. More than 100 witnesses testified regarding the indictments of criminal organizations such as the S.S., S.A., and

Gestapo. The judgments were announced on September 30 and October 1, 1946. Nineteen of the accused were convicted; three were acquitted. Twelve of the convicted were sentenced to death; the remaining received sentences in prison ranging from ten years to life.

The International Military Tribunal for the Far East was established by Special Proclamation of the Allied Supreme Commander of the Pacific on January 19, 1946. On May 3 of that year representatives from eleven states considered war crime indictments against twenty-five defendants. On November 12, 1948, all defendants were convicted. Seven were sentenced to death and the others received prison sentences ranging from seven and a half years to life.

In addition to those two courts, the Allies established several national courts under Control Council Law No. 10 to try less visible defendants in Germany for crimes against peace, war crimes, and crimes against humanity.[83]

B. FORMER YUGOSLAVIA AND RWANDA

For nearly fifty years after the signing of the London Agreement, Cold War divisions on the Security Council prevented the international community from applying the Nuremberg principles when faced with widespread human rights abuses. Only after the Cold War ended was the Security Council able to approve military intervention to address threats to international peace and security, impose economic sanctions, send peacekeepers to unstable regions of the world, establish a compensation commission for damages caused by the Iraq invasion of Kuwait in 1991, and create international tribunals for the former Yugoslavia and Rwanda. Those tribunals are the subject of this section.

*i. The International Criminal Tribunal for the Former Yugoslavia (ICTY)*

The territory formerly known as Yugoslavia has for centuries been divided along cultural and religious lines, which resulted from divisions by successive empires including the Romans, Turks, and Austro-Hungarians, as well as from the conversion of Christians to Islam during Turkish rule. The Kingdom of Serbs, Croats, and Slovenes was founded in 1918 and adopted the name Yugoslavia in 1930. The dictatorship of Josip Broz Tito suppressed most ethnic divisions. But, after his death in 1980, ultra-nationalist politicians exploited ethnic differences. Years of escalating intolerance and hostility erupted into armed conflict when Croatia declared its independence from Yugoslavia in 1991. These events led to conflicts between Croats and Serbs as well as the formation of independent republics in Slovenia and Macedonia.

The most devastating armed conflict occurred in Bosnia-Herzegovina, where none of the three major ethnic groups of Croats, Muslims, or Serbs constituted a majority. The armed conflict resulted in widespread violations of human rights and international humanitarian law (also known as the laws of war). In 1993 a Special Rapporteur of the UN Commission on Human Rights reported on ethnic cleansing measures, including harassment, discrimination, beatings, torture, summary executions, expulsion, and forced work affecting all three ethnic groups. On October 6, 1992, in response to media and public outcry over the violence in Bosnia, the UN Security Council adopted Resolution 780, establishing a Commission of Experts to investigate and document grave breaches of the Geneva Conventions and other violations of international humanitarian law committed in the former Yugoslavia. The Experts' report concluded that there had been grave breaches and that an *ad hoc* tribunal would be consistent with the direction of its work. On February 22, 1993, the Security Council established the international criminal tribunal for the prosecution of persons responsible for serious violations of international humanitarian law in the former Yugoslavia since 1991. The mandate was finalized in Resolution 827 of May 25, 1993, following the Secretary-General's report with a proposed statute for the tribunal. The statute provided that the international tribunal would apply rules of international humanitarian law that had risen to the level of customary law, including the Geneva Conventions, the Convention on the Prevention and Punishment of the Crime of Genocide, and the Charter of the International Military Tribunal of August 8, 1945.[84]

The International Criminal Tribunal for the former Yugoslavia had jurisdiction over grave breaches of the Geneva Conventions, violations of the laws or customs of war, genocide, and crimes against humanity.[85] Persons accused of planning, ordering, or committing those crimes were to be held individually responsible. Persons would not be relieved of criminal responsibility for acting pursuant to superior orders, though that could be a mitigating factor in determining the punishment. Unlike Nuremberg, no defendant could be tried *in abstentia*, penalties were limited to imprisonment (excluding the death penalty), and there were provisions for appeal.

While there was a debate about whether the tribunal could be established by Security Council resolution instead of a treaty, the Secretary-General's report made clear that drafting a treaty would take too long and it was not clear that the necessary ratifications would be obtained. By basing the tribunal upon a Security Council resolution, member States of the UN were compelled to comply with orders of the ICTY relating to the arrest or detention of accused persons.

As of 2006, more than 161 accused have been indicted by the ICTY and forty-five individuals had received their final sentence. Five had been found not guilty or acquitted by the trial or appeal chamber of the tribunal. Sentences were as long as forty years. Three died while in custody during proceedings including Slobodan Milošević, who had been President of Serbia and Yugoslavia and who had been accused of war crimes and crimes against humanity.

Critics of the ICTY note that its establishment did not prevent later atrocities in the former Yugoslavia, for example, during 1995 in Srebrenica or during 1998 in Kosovo. Its supporters, however, argue that it has developed a very significant jurisprudence of international humanitarian law, including decisions relating to command responsibility, the permissibility of defenses to the crimes based on reprisal and duress, and the rights of suspects to counsel, cross-examination of witnesses, and the treatment of victims and witnesses. Most important, the ICTY is the first functioning international criminal tribunal since Nuremberg and Tokyo that provides a forum for victims, creates a historical record of the events in the former Yugoslavia, and has forced some perpetrators out of power.

*ii. The International Criminal Tribunal for Rwanda (ICTR)*

The International Criminal Tribunal for Rwanda was also created in response to armed conflict between rival ethnic groups.[86] At the beginning of 1994, approximately seven million people lived in Rwanda, about 80 percent of them Hutu, 20 percent Tutsi, and 1 percent Twa. The two main groups share a language and most cultural and religious traditions. There were sharp divisions across economic and ethnic lines established by German colonial authorities and maintained by Belgian administrators.

In 1959, three years prior to Rwandan independence, the Hutu majority ousted Tutsi leaders in a bloody rebellion. Tens of thousands of Tutsi fled to neighboring nations, with the largest number fleeing to Uganda. The exiled Tutsi refugees formed the Rwandan Patriotic Front (RPF), based in Uganda, and invaded Rwanda in 1990. Both sides then engaged in peace talks and signed an accord in August 1993 providing for power sharing and the return of Tutsi refugees.

On April 6, 1994, massive violence followed the mysterious crash of an airplane carrying the presidents of Burundi and Rwanda. An organized effort led by the Hutu-dominated government and its allies to slaughter the Tutsi population immediately followed. Moderate Hutus opposed to the government and Twa were also targeted. Human rights investigators believe that government extremists had been promoting

300  International Procedures

anti-Tutsi paranoia and planning the mass murders for nearly two years. Estimates of the number of persons killed during the roughly 100 days of conflict range from 500,000 to one million. At the same time, more than two million were displaced to neighboring countries.

The Tutsi-dominated government of Rwanda, which came into power after the killings, actively supported the establishment of an international tribunal for persons responsible for the genocide and other crimes in Rwanda. Rwanda was a member of the UN Security Council and was among the first countries to propose the creation of the tribunal. On July 1, 1994, the Security Council adopted Resolution 935 which requested that the Secretary-General establish a Commission of Experts to investigate "the grave violations of international humanitarian law committed in the territory of Rwanda, including the evidence of possible acts of genocide."[87]

Three months later the Commission of Experts submitted a report concluding that both sides of the conflict had committed serious breaches of international humanitarian law as well as crimes against humanity. The report also found that acts of genocide against Tutsi had been perpetrated in a concerted, planned, systematic, and methodical way. In order that the people who had committed the violations be brought to justice, the Commission recommended that the Statute for the International Criminal Tribunal for Yugoslavia be amended to extend its jurisdiction to cover crimes committed in Rwanda beginning on April 6, 1994. Instead, on November 8, 1994, the Security Council adopted Resolution 955, establishing a second *ad hoc* tribunal centered in Arusha, Tanzania.[88] The purpose of the tribunal was to prosecute persons responsible for genocide and other serious violations of international humanitarian law committed in Rwanda between January 1 and December 31, 1994.

The ICTR Statute is similar to the ICTY Statute in that it establishes that both the prosecutor and the Appeals Chamber of the ICTY shall also serve the ICTR, to provide consistency in the legal approach and to share resources.[89] While the ICTR has jurisdiction over acts of genocide and crimes against humanity, however, its jurisdiction is limited to violations of international standards governing internal armed conflict. The ICTR Statute is also different than the ICTY Statute in its definition of crimes against humanity in that it does not require proof of the existence of an armed conflict.

Various problems arose with the ICTR. The first problem related to difficulty of traveling from Rwanda to the court in Arusha, Tanzania. Second, the death penalty was not allowed under the ICTR, but was a punishment under Rwandan law. Third, the ICTR jurisdiction was limited to crimes committed in 1994 only, impeding the prosecution of persons who planned the genocide before 1994 as well as prosecution for similar crimes committed after that year. Fourth, the ICTR lacked sufficient resources to try the 130,000 suspects. Fifth, there was resistance from some African countries to handing over important suspects within their jurisdiction. Four years after the ICTR issued its first indictment against eight accused persons on November 28, 1995, only twenty-eight persons had been indicted and only seven accused had been convicted.

Following a report of the various problems faced by the ICTR, UN Secretary-General Kofi Annan made changes in the administration of the court and a third trial chamber was established by the Security Council in 1998. At this point, the ICTR's work began to improve. As of 2004, the ICTR had completed eleven cases, nine cases were on appeal, five had been released, and one had died in custody. By 2006, the ICTR had completed thirty cases, twenty-five accused had been sentenced, and five had been acquitted. The longest sentences were for thirty years and for the remainder of the accused's life. Despite the problems faced by the ICTR, it made contributions in the evolution of international criminal law. In the case of *Prosecutor v. Akayesu*, the ICTR was the first international tribunal to impose a conviction for rape as a crime against humanity. The ICTR held that the rapes encouraged by Akayesu, a local burgomaster (or mayor), constituted the crime of genocide.[90] On June 16, 2006, the Appeals Chamber in *Prosecutor v. Karemera* ruled that it was common knowledge that a genocide took place in Rwanda against the Tutsi ethnic group and that the lower courts had to take judicial notice of this fact, thus obviating the need by the prosecutor to prove that point in each case.[91] In addition, many of the 130,000 suspects were detained in Rwanda and were being tried by traditional Gacaca courts in Rwanda.

C. THE INTERNATIONAL CRIMINAL COURT (ICC)

The International Criminal Court was anticipated by the Nuremberg and Tokyo Tribunals after World War II as well as the Genocide Convention of 1948.[92] The International Law Commission (ILC), the legal drafting body of the United Nations, submitted a draft statute for an international criminal court to the General Assembly in 1954, but disagreement over the definition of aggression prevented further consideration of the statute. The ICC project remained dormant until 1990, when the General Assembly asked the ILC to reopen its consideration of a permanent criminal court partially in response to a request by the government of Trinidad and Tobago to explore means of combating the international narcotics trade. The conflict in the former Yugoslavia and the experiences of the ICTY and ICTR helped galvanize support for a permanent forum for prosecuting violations of international humanitarian law. In 1994, the ILC presented a Draft Statute for an International Criminal Court to the General Assembly.[93]

In response, the General Assembly established an *ad hoc* committee to review the issues in the draft statute and consider arrangements for a diplomatic conference. Over the next three and a half years, government experts held nineteen weeks of meetings where 500 amendments to the proposed statute were discussed. In the summer of 1998, diplomats representing over 150 countries convened in Rome to finalize the treaty to establish a permanent international criminal court. The Rome Treaty was approved by a vote of 120 to 7, with twenty-one abstentions. It created a tribunal for the most serious crimes of international concern—genocide, crimes against humanity, and war crimes. The treaty came into force on July 1, 2002, when it obtained the sixty required ratifications. As of early 2007, 104 nations had become States parties.

The ICC has its headquarters in The Hague. It deals only with crimes committed after the Rome Treaty came into force. Because it is created by a multilateral treaty, it is not an organ of the United Nations. Still, the two organizations have formal relations and the UN Security Council plays a significant role in the Court's operation because of its authority to initiate or defer investigations.

One fundamental principle of the Rome Treaty is that the jurisdiction of the ICC is complementary to national criminal jurisdiction. Hence, the Court must defer to national systems unless they are unwilling or unable to investigate or prosecute a crime that would otherwise be under its jurisdiction. The principle of complementarity highlights the fact that the Court is an alternative to impunity where independent and effective judicial systems are not available.

The ICC has jurisdiction over genocide (as defined by the 1948 Genocide Convention), crimes against humanity, and war crimes. The ICC will also have jurisdiction over the crime of aggression, once the Rome Treaty is amended to define that crime (amendments cannot be considered until seven years after the treaty entered into force and will require a two-thirds vote of the Assembly of States parties and ratification by seven-eighths of States parties to be enacted). Crimes against humanity can be charged against state and non-state actors, whether committed in peacetime or armed conflict. The jurisdiction of the Court applies to widespread or systematic attacks directed against civilian populations pursuant to or in furtherance of a state or organizational policy. To be charged, individuals must have acted with knowledge of the attack.

The ICC Statute reflects an important confirmation in international law that rape, sexual slavery, enforced prostitution, forced pregnancy, enforced sterilization, or any other form of sexual violence of comparable gravity constitute crimes against humanity and war crimes. The

Rome Statute also gives the Court jurisdiction over both international and internal armed conflicts. Under the Rome Statute, defendants can avoid criminal responsibility if they establish that they had a legal obligation to obey the order, they did not know the order was unlawful, and the order was not manifestly unlawful. This approach to superior orders is a departure from principles developed at the Nuremberg, Yugoslav, and Rwandan tribunals.

Jurisdiction of the Court can be triggered by referral from the Security Council or initiation of an investigation by the prosecutor. The Security Council can refer a situation involving the territory or nationals of any state that is party to the UN Charter. The initiation of an investigation by the prosecutor is subject to rigorous safeguards. In order to proceed, the prosecutor must convince a panel of judges that "there is a reasonable basis to proceed with an investigation and that the case appears to fall withing the jurisdiction of the Court." In addition, the prosecution must defer to national procedures unless a panel of judges decides that national authorities are either unwilling or unable genuinely to investigate or prosecute. Proceedings must also be deferred for a renewable twelve-month period upon request of the Security Council. The prosecutor is limited to initiating an investigation in cases involving either conduct on the territory of states that have accepted the Court's jurisdiction or acts committed by nationals of those states. By the end of 2006, only two investigations had been initiated by the prosecutor—the Democratic Republic of the Congo and Northern Uganda. On March 31, 2005, in Resolution 1593, the Security Council voted to refer perpetrators of human rights abuses in Darfur to the ICC. The Sudanese government, however, has refused to cooperate or turn over Sudanese citizens to the jurisdiction of the ICC.

D. MIXED (INTERNATIONAL AND NATIONAL) TRIBUNALS

In addition to the purely international tribunals discussed above, some nations have begun to use mixed tribunals in which international personnel and standards are joined or otherwise associated with the national legal system to try war crimes, crimes against humanity, genocide, and systematic criminal offenses, such as murder, rape, and torture. Three examples of these hybrid tribunals can be found in Sierra Leone, Cambodia, East Timor (Timor-Leste), Kosovo, and Bosnia.

*i. The Special Court for Sierra Leone*

During 1991, the Revolutionary United Front (RUF) began a nationwide insurgency in Sierra Leone. Beginning November 30, 1996, several peace and ceasefire agreements were signed between the RUF, the government of Sierra Leone, and other armed groups, but the agreements were often not respected. In 1997, former members of the Sierra Leone military created the Armed Forces Ruling Council (AFRC) and overthrew the elected government. During this period, the Civil Defense Forces (CDF) fought on the side of and were supported by the government of Sierra Leone. The RUF fought against the CDF, the government, and the AFRC. None of these parties respected basic principles of human rights and humanitarian law. By January 2002, when fighting abated, nearly 75,000 people had reportedly died and an estimated two million had been displaced from their homes.

The Special Court for Sierra Leone was established on January 16, 2002, by an agreement between the United Nations and the government of Sierra Leone.[94] The court was given the power to prosecute persons who bear the greatest responsibility for the serious violations of international humanitarian law and Sierra Leonean law since November 30, 1996. The Court's founding statute defines these "serious violations" to include crimes against humanity, violations of Common Article 3 of the Geneva Convention and Additional Protocol II, other violations of international humanitarian law—including attacks on civilians or peacekeepers, and offenses against Sierra Leone statutes relating to arson and abuse of girl children. The prosecutor has chosen, however, not to prosecute under Sierra Leone statutes.

Acting under its mandate the Court has indicted eleven individuals. Ten of these persons were members of the AFRC, CDF, and RUF. The court has also indicted Charles Taylor, the former president of Liberia, who is accused of supporting the RUF. Taylor, who presently faces prosecution under the auspices of the Special Court in the chambers of the ICC in The Hague, is only the second head of state in history to be indicted for war crimes. Having indicted only a few individuals, the Special Court has been careful to stress that its mission is limited to trying persons who bear the greatest responsibility, and that many others who are culpable do not fall within the jurisdiction of the Special Court.

The Special Court is comprised of eight judges. Three judges sit on the Trial Court and five sit on the Appeals Court. Two of the Trial Court judges and three of the Appeals Court judges are appointed the by the UN Secretary-General. The Secretary-General appointed appeals court judges from Austria, Nigeria, and Sri Lanka as well as trial court judges from Sri Lanka and the United Kingdom. The government of Sierra Leone appointed one appeals court judge from Sierra Leone and another from the United Kingdom. The Secretary-General also appointed an initial Chief Prosecutor from the United States, who was replaced by an attorney from Australia, and then a third prosecutor from the United States. The government of Sierra Leone selected two judges from that country plus an appeals court judge from Sri Lanka.

The Special Court follows the ICTR rules as they existed at the time the Special Court was created. These rules can be amended or additional rules adopted by unanimous consent of the judges. The rules have been amended five times since their adoption.

*ii. The Cambodian Extraordinary Chambers*

In April 1975 the military government of Cambodia fell to the forces of the Communist Party of Kampuchea, or Khmer Rouge, led by Pol Pot. Once in power, the Khmer Rouge set out to transform Cambodia into a collective agrarian society. All preexisting social, economic, and cultural institutions were abolished, and the Khmer Rouge forcibly relocated between two and three million inhabitants of the country's cities and towns to newly established agricultural collectives. Hundreds of thousands died of exhaustion, disease, and starvation, or were killed by their overseers. In addition, the Khmer Rouge targeted several groups as potential enemies of the revolution and undertook to eliminate their members. During the first few months of Khmer Rouge rule, thousands of former government officials, army officers, and bureaucrats were summarily executed. A similar fate befell thousands of intellectuals, Buddhist monks, and ethnic minorities including Vietnamese, Chinese, and Cham (a Muslim people present in Cambodia for more than 500 years). In all, during four years (1975-79) of Khmer Rouge rule at least 1.5 million Cambodians were killed or died as a result of the actions of or conditions created by the Khmer Rouge. This number equaled approximately 20 percent of the total population of Cambodia. The Khmer Rouge was ultimately ousted when Vietnamese forces took control of the country in 1979.

The Cambodian government sought the help of the UN in 1997 to bring Khmer Rouge officials responsible for crimes against humanity to justice. The UN assembled a "Group of Experts" (from Australia, Mauritius, and the United States) who first proposed a purely international tribunal. The UN was concerned that the Cambodian judiciary was ill-equipped to meet international standards. Cambodia rejected the proposal.

The Cambodians proposed a mixed tribunal within the Cambodian judiciary. This court would be known as the Extraordinary Chambers. The Extraordinary Chambers would be comprised of the Trial Court (with five judges), the Appeals Court (seven judges), and the Supreme Court (nine judges). At each level, the Cambodian government would provide the majority of the judges and the UN Secretary-General the remaining judges. The prosecutor's office would have one Cambodian national and one international member. The Extraordinary Chambers would be given the power to prosecute murder, torture, religious persecution, violations of the Geneva Convention, and crimes against humanity. The UN agreed to the proposal in 2000, and the Cambodian legislature adopted a law authorizing the Extraordinary Chambers in 2001.

The Group of Experts and Amnesty International criticized the 2001 law. In January 2004, amendments to the law were accepted by the UN and adopted by the Cambodian legislature. Nonetheless, the Group of Experts continued to criticize the Extraordinary Chambers law, because it limits prosecutions under the Geneva Conventions and relies upon Cambodian laws that may not provide adequate basis for prosecution. Amnesty International (AI) has also expressed concern that Cambodia appears unwilling to incorporate international standards for criminal prosecution. In addition, AI has observed that Cambodia's judicial system appears too weak to participate in the process. AI's further concern is that a proposed ban on the death penalty was omitted from the final agreement.

Despite these concerns, the UN funded part of the staffing for the Extraordinary Chambers. On July 3, 2006, seventeen Cambodian (sixteen men and one woman) and thirteen international judges and prosecutors took office. Problems started to arise immediately. These included the fact that thirty years have passed since the crimes were committed and many of those responsible have died. The lengthy delay also makes it difficult to produce reliable evidence. Additional issues raised by the Open Society Institute include problems concerning inadequate funding, lack of transparency in hiring, a reported corrupt arrangement in which Cambodian employees of the tribunal remitted some of their salaries to the government, the need for qualified interpreters, the need to adopt clear rules of procedure, and the fact that—unlike other hybrid tribunals—the international judges constitute a minority.

*iii. The Serious Crimes Panel for East Timor*

East Timor, a territory under the control of Portugal, was undergoing on process of decolonization and self-determination in 1975. On December 7 of that year, Indonesian forces invaded the country. Indonesia later declared East Timor its twenty-seventh province. The occupation of East Timor lasted twenty-four years during which the Indonesian army and pro-Indonesian militia fought with East Timorese insurgents and sought to control the territory. Almost 200,000 East Timorese were killed during the Indonesian occupation. After Haji Mohammad Suharto stepped down as Indonesia's President in 1998, the Indonesian government offered the residents of East Timor an opportunity to vote for independence. When the residents of East Timor voted by more than a three-to-one margin for independence, pro-Indonesian militias launched a brutal campaign of property destruction and human rights abuses. Sixteen days after the abuses began the Indonesian government—with strong UN backing—allowed an Australian-led UN force to land in East Timor and restore order. Upon arriving in East Timor the UN found no functioning government and no judiciary. The UN established the United Nations Transitional Administration in East Timor (UNTAET) with the stated purpose of reestablishing the rule of law and institutions for its maintenance.[95]

At a special session in September 1999, the UN Commission on Human Rights created a Commission of Inquiry to investigate breaches of humanitarian law committed in East Timor after January 1999. The Commission (comprised of five distinguished individuals from Costa Rica, Germany, India, Nigeria, and Papua New Guinea) identified incidents in which Indonesian military, police, and militia were involved in intimidation and terror, killings and massacres, gender violence, other forms of torture and ill-treatment, targeting of international staff and journalists, destruction of property, displacement of people, destruction of evidence, and other human rights and humanitarian law violations. The Commission recommended in a report issued in 2000 that the UN set up a tribunal comprised of judges appointed by the UN with participation from East Timor and Indonesia to try and sentence persons who had committed human rights and humanitarian law violations since January 1999. That tribunal was never created, however, because investigations and some prosecutions were pursued instead through UNTAET and by the Indonesian authorities.

In 2000, UNTAET created a commission to recommend candidates for judicial and prosecutorial offices. That commission consisted of three East Timor nationals and two international experts. The same year, UNTAET reestablished the court system in East Timor. The courts were to consist of regional district courts and one appeals court in Dili. The Dili district court was given the power to hear "serious crimes," which included war crimes, crimes against humanity, murder, sexual offenses, and torture. Jurisdiction over the latter three was limited to the period from January 1 to October 25, 1999. Later in 2000, UNTAET established the first Serious Crimes Panel and attached it to the Dili district. This panel was comprised of two international judges (from Brazil and Burundi) and one East Timorese judge. The prosecutorial team is mainly composed of non-nationals.

The Serious Crimes Panel applied East Timorese law as it was expressed by UNTEAT in regulation 1999/1. The definition of war crimes and crimes against humanity were nearly identical to those of the Rome Statute of the International Criminal Court. The Panel, however, faced the same problems as the Cambodian Extraordinary Chambers—to prosecute war crimes under the Geneva Convention, the crimes must have been committed during an armed conflict. The generally accepted view is that war was ongoing from the 1975 Indonesian invasion. Indonesia counters that it was asked to restore order, while few UN members have accepted this view, with the exception of Australia. If the prosecutors cannot establish the existence of an armed conflict, prosecution of war crimes cannot occur.

In addition, after East Timor—now Timor-Leste—was recognized as a state by the United Nations in 2002, the fledgling judicial system struggled to operate even without the burden of international criminal prosecutions. Trying international crimes takes skills and resources that may be lacking in the newly rebuilt judicial system. The courts have worked through these difficulties and began issuing opinions at the end of 2002.

The final difficulty facing the Serious Crimes Panel has been the location of many of the accused inside of West Timor and other parts of Indonesia. The government of Indonesia has refused to extradite individuals to stand trial in Timor-Leste and instead chose to conduct trials within Indonesia. The Indonesian government appointed a National Commission of Inquiry on Human Rights Violations in East Timor (*Komisi Penyelidik Pelanggaran HAM di Timor Timur,* KPP HAM) to investigate human rights abuses perpetrated by Indonesians in East Timor.

The KPP HAM recommended prosecutions within the Indonesian legal system and cited 670 cases of human rights abuses. Indonesian authorities decided, however, to pursue investigations of only six of the incidents, all of which involved killings. Eventually, only five incidents resulted in indictments. The Indonesian authorities ignored incidents of rape, torture, and property destruction. The KPP HAM publicly identified thirty-two individuals, but Indonesian authorities only sought indictments against eighteen. Of the eighteen indicted only six were convicted. Amnesty International has criticized those trials for failing to reflect the extent of abuses, to present key evidence, to employ experienced prosecutors and judges, and to provide adequate protection for victims and witnesses.

*iv. Mixed Tribunals in the Balkans*

In June 1999 the UN Security Council established the United Nations Mission Interim Administration in Kosovo (UNMIK).[96] A month later the Secretary-General asked UNMIK to re-establish a multi-ethnic judiciary. At first UNMIK did not use international judges, but after a period of unrest in 2000, UNMIK began to appoint international judges and prosecutors to serve in the Kosovo judicial system. By 2004 there were twelve international judges and a same number of prosecutors working within the local court system.

Unlike the international judges in Cambodia, Sierra Leone, and Timor-Leste who can only hear cases involving violations of human rights and humanitarian law, the international judges in Kosovo may adjudicate any case brought before the Kosovo courts. The international judges are perceived to be impartial and less subject to pressure in dealing with cases involving the different ethnic communities.

Bosnia has also utilized a mixed tribunal, known as the Human Rights Chamber, to address human rights abuses. The Human Rights Chamber had civil, rather than criminal, jurisdiction over human rights abuses occurring after the signing of the Dayton Peace Accord on December 14, 1995, through the expiration of the Chamber's mandate on December 31, 2003. The Chamber had the authority to issue cease and desist orders, as well as issue awards for compensatory damages. The Human Rights Chamber's fourteen members consisted of four individuals from the Federation of Bosnia and Herzegovina, two from the Republic Srpska, and eight international members appointed by the Council of Europe (from Austria, France, Germany, Hungary, Iceland, Italy, Turkey, and the United Kingdom). Any cases still pending before the Human Rights Chamber on December 21, 2003, were then addressed by the Human Rights Commission that operated during 2004. The Human Rights Commission is also a mixed tribunal with two members appointed by the Federation of Bosnia and Herzegovina, one member appointed by the Republic Srpska, and two appointed by the Council of Europe (from Iceland and the United Kingdom).

*See also*: Genocide, War Crimes, Crimes Against Humanity, and Crimes Against Peace; Torture and Ill-Treatment

*Further Reading:*

John E. Ackerman & Eugene O'Sullivan, Practice and Procedure of the International Criminal Tribunal for the former Yugoslavia: With Selected Materials from the International Criminal Tribunal for Rwanda (2000).
Payam Akhavan, *The International Criminal Tribunal for Rwanda: The Politics and Pragmatics of Punishment*, 90 A.J.I.L. 501 (1996).
Yves Beigbeder, Judging War Criminals: The Politics of International Justice (1999).
Antonio Cassese, International Criminal Law (2003).
Claire De Than & Edwin Shorts, International Criminal Law and Human Rights (2003).

Jerry Fowler, *The Rome Treaty for an International Criminal Court: A Framework of International Justice for Future Generations*, 6 Hum. Rts. Brief 1 (Fall 1998).

Richard J. Goldstone, *Prosecuting Rape as a War Crime*, 34 Case W. Res. J. Int'l L. 277 (2002).

John Hagan, Justice in the Balkans: Prosecuting War Crimes in the Hague Tribunal (2003).

International Criminal Law (M. Cherif Bassiouni ed., 2d ed. 1999).

International Criminal Law Conventions and Their Penal Provisions (M. Cherif Bassiouni ed., 1997).

Suzannah Linton, *Cambodia, East Timor and Sierra Leone: Experiments in International Justice*, 12 Crim. L. F. 185 (2001).

John R.W.D. Jones & Steven Powles, International Criminal Practice: The International Criminal Tribunal for the Former Yugoslavia, the International Criminal Tribunal for Rwanda, the International Criminal Court, the Special Court for Sierra Leone, the East Timor Special Panel for Serious Crimes, War Crimes Prosecutions in Kosovo (3d ed. 2003).

Sean D. Murphy, *Progress and Jurisprudence of the International Criminal Tribunal for the Former Yugoslavia*, 93 A.J.I.L. 57 (1999).

The Permanent International Criminal Court: Legal and Policy Issues (Dominic McGoldrick, Peter Rowe, & Eric Donnelly eds., 2004).

*Prosecutor v. Akayesu*, ICTR-96-4-T (1998).

Report Int'l L. Comm'n, 49 U.N. GAOR Supp. (No. 10) at 29–140, U.N. Doc. A/RES/49/10 (1994), *reprinted in* 33 I.L.M. 253 (1994).

Rome Statute of the International Criminal Court, U.N. Doc. A/CONF.183/9 (1999).

The Rome Statute of the International Criminal Court: A Commentary (Antonio Cassese, Paola Gaeta, & John R.W.D. Jones eds., 2002).

Leila Nadya Sadat, The International Criminal Court and the Transformation of International Law: Justice for the New Millennium (2002).

William A. Schabas, An Introduction to the International Criminal Court (2001).

Security Council Resolution 935, S.C. res. 935, 49 U.N. SCOR at 2, U.N. Doc. S/RES/935 (1994).

Security Council Resolution 955, S.C. res. 955, 49 U.N. SCOR at 1, U.N. Doc. S/RES/955 (1994).

Universal Jurisdiction: National Courts and the Prosecution of Serious Crimes under International Law (Stephen Macedo ed., 2004).

Beth Van Schaack & Ronald C. Slye, International Criminal Law and Its Enforcement (2007).

Robert K. Woetzel, The Nuremberg Trials in International Law (1962).

*Links to Consult:*

http://web.amnesty.org/library/index/engasa230052003
http://www.cambodia.gov.kh/krt/english/
http://www.hrc.ba/
http://www.icc-cpi.int
http://www.sc-sl.org/
http://www.unmikonline.org
http://www.un.org/ictr/
http://www.un.org/icty/

# B. Regional Institutions and Procedures

Chapter VIII of the UN Charter encourages regional arrangements or agencies so long as their activities are consistent with the purposes and principles of the United Nations.[97] Indeed, members of the United Nations are encouraged to settle local disputes through such institutions. Countries in most regions of the world have established regional bodies with procedures for addressing human rights violations. Moreover, whereas UN human rights machinery can seem remote and detached, regional systems are often more accessible and are frequently better informed about local issues. Regional human rights treaties are also more culturally specific than universal human rights treaties.

The regional systems have different strengths and weaknesses. For example, the European human rights system has a very successful procedure for dealing with individual complaints, but has not been particularly effective in addressing massive violations of human rights. In contrast, some of the human rights mechanisms developed in the Americas have been very effective in helping focus attention on widespread human rights violations. It has been difficult, however, to get countries in the Americas to comply with decisions in individual cases. Long hampered by funding and logistical problems, the African human rights system is gradually improving in effectiveness within the new context of the African Union. Asian and Middle Eastern countries, it must be noted, have yet to establish overall regional organizations, much less mechanisms for protecting human rights. This section transitions from examining international procedures for protecting human rights and provides an overview of regional human rights protection mechanisms. It looks at the European, American, and African human rights system in turn.

## 1. European Mechanisms

Three principal institutions in Europe have procedures for protecting human rights: (1) the Council of Europe,[98] (2) the European Union,[99] and (3) the Organization for Security and Cooperation in Europe

(OSCE).[100] The various human rights treaties and procedures associated with each body are considered separately in this chapter.

For example, the member states of the Council of Europe developed the European Court of Human Rights[101] and the Committee of Ministers, which together implement the European Convention on Human Rights.[102] The Council of Europe also has a Parliamentary Assembly that elects—in tandem with the Committee of Ministers—members of the European Court of Human Rights and adopts hortatory resolutions on human rights issues and situations of human rights concern. Furthermore, the Council of Europe promulgated the European Social Charter, which entered into force in 1965 (its revised version came into force in 1999).[103] Whereas the European Convention on Human Rights sets forth principally civil and political rights, the European Social Charter and its implementation procedures guarantee social and economic rights.

The Council of Europe has also established a Commissioner for Human Rights as an independent institution aiming to promote awareness of and respect for human rights. Other bodies created by the region's human rights treaties include the European Commission Against Racism and Intolerance (ECRI)[104]—which reviews member states' laws, policies, and measures to combat racism and intolerance—and the Committee for the Prevention of Torture (CPT)[105]—which undertakes visits to places of detention in order to assure compliance with the European Convention for the Prevention of Torture and Inhuman or Degrading Treatment or Punishment.

A. COUNCIL OF EUROPE (COE)

The Council of Europe was established in 1949. Following World War I, the Western European governments wanted a regional mechanism for protecting human rights. Hopes for a united Europe and fear of communism provided additional motivation for enforcing a limited set of human rights norms. Accordingly, COE states approved the European Convention on Human Rights in 1950 and it entered into force in 1953.[106] There have been fourteen subsequent protocols to the European Convention adding rights and improving implementation procedures.[107] For example, protocols have added the rights to education, free elections, and property, as well as abolishing the death penalty.

While COE members were not initially required to ratify the European Convention, all Council members eventually did. When the Cold War ended and the Eastern European countries requested membership, ratification of the Convention became mandatory. As of 2007, the following forty-six countries had become parties to the European Convention: Albania, Andorra, Armenia, Austria, Azerbaijan, Belgium, Bosnia and Herzegovina, Bulgaria, Croatia, Cyprus, Czech Republic, Denmark, Estonia, Finland, France, Georgia, Germany, Greece, Hungary, Iceland, Ireland, Italy, Latvia, Liechtenstein, Lithuania, Luxembourg, Malta, Moldova, Monaco, Netherlands, Norway, Poland, Portugal, Romania, Russia, San Marino, Serbia and Montenegro, Slovakia, Slovenia, Spain, Sweden, Switzerland, the former Yugoslav Republic of Macedonia, Turkey, Ukraine, and the United Kingdom.

The European Convention originally included three organs for implementing rights—the European Commission on Human Rights, the European Court of Human Rights, and the Committee of Ministers. The Commission determined admissibility, established facts, encouraged friendly settlement, and issued opinions as to whether petitions alleged violations of the Convention. After a Commission decision, cases were referred to the European Court or the Committee of Ministers. On November 1, 1998, Protocol No. 11 to the European Convention entered into force, creating a single permanent European Court of Human Rights. In 2004, Protocol No. 14 was opened for signature to modify the procedures of the European Court, in particular to restrict admissibility for the increasing number of individual applications and by 2006 only one nation—Russia—had failed to ratify the protocol. Due to the 1998 changes, the European Convention on Human Rights now functions only through the strengthened European Court and the Committee of Ministers.

*i. European Court of Human Rights*

The European human rights system has the oldest human rights court and is highly respected around the globe for its well developed case law. Under the European Convention, the European Court of Human Rights is comprised "of a number of judges equal to that of the High Contracting Parties."[108] Under Protocol No. 14 of 2004, judges will be elected for non-renewable terms of nine years by the Parliamentary Assembly of the Council of Europe. They must retire at age seventy. Each member state is allowed to nominate three persons for consideration by the Assembly. Under Article 21(1) of the Convention, the judges serve in their individual capacity and must be persons of high moral character, "who possess the qualifications required for appointment to high judicial office or be jurisconsults of recognized competence."[109] The judges are ordinarily—although not necessarily—nationals of the member states of the Council. They serve full-time during their term. Both the Council and the Court sit in Strasbourg, France.

The Court addresses three types of cases. First, it accepts complaints by individuals, groups of individuals, and nongovernmental organizations (NGOs) who allege that they are victims of violations of the Convention and its protocols by one of the States parties. Second, under Article 33 of the Convention, the Court considers allegations of violations between States parties. Third, the Court has limited advisory jurisdiction, conferred in 1970. These three types of cases are described below.

(a) Individual Cases

Under the system established by Protocol No. 11 (which will be implemented under Protocol No. 14 of 2004), a single judge may declare inadmissible any application where such a decision may be made without further examination. A decision of a single judge to declare an application inadmissible is final. Single judges may not, however, consider cases with regard to countries of which they are a national. Criteria for admissibility include such issues as whether the applicant is a victim, the violation was by a State party to the Convention, the applicant has exhausted available domestic remedies, the issue is not the same as one previously rejected by the Court, the complaint is well-founded, the violation is within the scope of the Convention, and the application was filed within six months of the final effective national decision.

There was considerable concern before the adoption of Protocol No. 11 about the backlog of cases being considered by the European Court, which, at the time, was reaching five- and six-year delays before final decision by the Court. After Protocol No. 11 came into force in 1998, the streamlined procedures succeeded in bringing the delay down to three or four years. Nonetheless, because of further concern about delays which were expected as a result of the large number of new cases filed by residents of Turkey and Russia, the COE decided in adopting Protocol No. 14 to restrict admissibility further by adding two additional criteria: (1) if the application is incompatible with the provisions of the Convention or the Protocols thereto, is manifestly ill-founded, or is an abuse of the right of individual application; or (2) when the applicant has not suffered a significant disadvantage, unless respect for human rights as defined in the Convention and the Protocols thereto requires an examination of the application on the merits and provided that no case may be rejected on this ground which has not been duly considered by a domestic tribunal.[110]

If an application is not declared inadmissible by a single judge, it is ordinarily considered next by a three-judge committee which may unanimously decide that it is inadmissible. If at least one committee member finds the case admissible, the committee of three judges may declare the case admissible and at the same time render judgment on the merits if the issues in the case are already the subject of well-established case law of the Court. Alternatively, the case is assigned to a Court Chamber, which consists of seven judges. The Chamber considers written submissions by the parties and may hold oral hearings. Friendly settlement discussions are then held, and if they are unsuccessful, the Chamber issues a judgment. Applicants may apply for leave to appeal to a Grand Chamber consisting of seventeen judges. Five judges determine the request and whether to refer it to the full Grand Chamber, which is rare in individual cases.

Article 41 of the Convention provides that the Court shall "afford just satisfaction to the injured party."[111] Despite this clear authority to grant pecuniary relief, the Court did not do so until 1974 in *Neumeister v. Austria*.[112] There the Court found that pre-trial detention of two years and four months violated Article 5 (the right to liberty and security), but awarded legal fees only because time spent in pre-trial detention counted toward the final sentence that had been imposed. After that case, the Court slowly began to award damages for the injuries suffered by the applicants, though it still focuses primarily on reimbursing them for their costs and expenses. In addition to the latter, which can include legal fees, travel, and accommodations, the Court awards pecuniary damages when it can quantify economic harm, and nonpecuniary or moral damages to compensate for emotional suffering or interference with protected rights. Awards have ranged from 100 guilders (U.S.$37) in 1976 for violations by Dutch military proceedings in *Engel and Others v. the Netherlands*[113] (the first time indemnity for damages was awarded) to $16,000,000 in 1994 in *Stran Greek Refineries and Straits Andreadis v. Greece*,[114] where the applicant oil refinery owners successfully challenged the Greek government's enactment of legislation that prevented them from filing further appeals in a contract dispute.

While the Court lacks power to grant equitable relief or order revisions of national law, most governments usually comply with its orders. The general willingness of European nations to comply with the Court's judgments may stem from the authority that the Committee of Ministers has to enforce compliance with the Court's decisions, as explained below. Compliance, however, may also reflect the development of European legal culture and a desire of governments to make the system work. Governments often change their national laws following a Court decision. Also, most States parties to the European Convention have incorporated the norms outlined in the Convention or the actual Convention language itself into national laws. Accordingly, those governments follow Convention law without recourse to the Strasbourg procedures. With its many decisions, the European Court has produced a significant jurisprudence that provides states and individuals considerable guidance as to their conduct. Part II relating to particular human rights refers frequently to European jurisprudence and includes the European Court precept that governments are entitled to a margin of appreciation where rules vary from one country to another depending on national traditions and there is no uniform European conception of the requirements of such ideas as "the protection of the rights of others" and of "public order."[115]

(b) Inter-State Cases

While several human rights treaties provide for inter-state complaints, the European system is one of the few where such complaints have actually been filed. Still, they are rare. Only twenty-one inter-state applications have been filed in thirteen cases regarding seven situations. These situations include: (1) Cyprus (two applications by Greece against Great Britain during 1956–57; (2) Italy (a complaint by Austria regarding the right to a fair trial of six youths in the early 1960s); (3) Greece (four applications by Denmark, Netherlands, Norway, and Sweden regarding torture by the Greek colonels in the late 1960s); (4) Turkey (two applications by 1970s); (5) subsequent applications by Cyprus regarding violations by Turkey in Northern Cyprus in the early 1980s and late 1990s and applications concerning torture in Cyprus filed by Denmark, France, Netherlands, Norway, and Sweden in the early 1980s; (6) Northern Ireland (complaint filed by Ireland against Great Britain for interrogation techniques used against suspected I.R.A. members in the mid-1970s); and (7) Turkey (complaint by Denmark regarding the treatment of a Danish citizen by Turkish authorities settled in 2000).

As can be seen from these situations, the applicant state does not have to have any direct relationship to the victim addressed in the complaint or to the subject matter. They also do not have to meet the admissibility requirements that apply to individual applications, except for exhaustion of remedies. Most of the cases involved countries that had not recognized the right of individual petition, so the only way to hold them accountable for a violation of the Convention was by an inter-state case. A few of the cases may have had political motivations, despite the general reluctance by states to file inter-state complaints for fear that they will have a negative affect on their diplomatic relationships. The majority of cases, however, have been filed for humanitarian reasons. Inter-state cases are assigned directly to a Grand Chamber.

(c) Advisory Jurisdiction

Limited advisory jurisdiction was added in 1970 by Protocol No. 2 and extended by the Convention on Human Rights and Biomedicine.[116] Advisory jurisdiction was incorporated into Article 47 of the European

Convention, which requires that the Council of Ministers make a request that is limited to "legal questions concerning the interpretation of the Convention and the protocols thereto." It also excludes advisory opinions regarding the Court's contentious jurisdiction.

*ii. Committee of Ministers*

Under Article 46(2) of the European Convention, the Committee of Ministers helps to oversee compliance with the Court's judgments. States found to be in violation have generally complied with orders and taken corrective action. If a state refuses to do so, the Committee may suspend or expel the state from the Council of Europe. The Council has never had to take such action, but Greece did withdraw from the European Convention from 1969 to 1974 to avoid being suspended following the Commission's decision on an inter-state case filed by Denmark, the Netherlands, Norway, and Sweden. The Committee also oversees compliance with the European Social Charter as discussed below.

When judgments involve payment of money damages, it is easy for the Committee to monitor compliance. It has had a harder time, however, monitoring compliance when judgments declare that certain states' laws are in conflict with the Convention. Changes in national legislation usually take longer to implement and are harder to monitor. It has also been difficult for the Committee to determine whether changes in legislation comply with the Court's judgments since the Committee is not a judicial body. These and other problems have led to the creation of an Assembly Monitoring Committee to verify compliance with human rights obligations of all members of the Council of Europe. Actions that the Assembly Monitoring Committee can take include adoption of resolutions regarding states that consistently do not comply, non-approval of a national parliamentary delegation, and recommending action to the Committee of Ministers. In 1994, the Committee of Ministers adopted a declaration on compliance and follow-up procedure for thematic monitoring. As a result, the following themes have been studied: freedom of expression and information, the functioning of the judicial system, the functioning and protection of democratic institutions, local democracy, and police and security forces. For each study, reports were submitted to the Committee of Ministers which adopted conclusions and recommendations for follow-up action.

*iii. European Committee of Social Rights (ECSR)*

The European Social Charter was opened for signature on October 18, 1961, and entered into force on February 26, 1965.[117] Twenty-seven

318    Regional Institutions and Procedures

of the forty-six states of the COE are parties to the original Charter. Most of the countries that have not ratified are new member states of the COE. The member states undertake to report on both domestic implementation of the rights they have accepted under the Charter and on the status of rights they did not accept. By ratifying the Charter, governments accept as an aim of their policy the attainment of conditions in which nineteen rights and principles may be effectively realized. The Charter, however, permits States parties to limit their responsibilities to at least five of seven core principles as well as at least ten of the forty-five paragraphs in the Charter.

There have been several protocols and one revision gradually broadening the economic and social rights guaranteed by the Charter and strengthening the implementation procedures. In 1988, the COE adopted the Additional Protocol to the European Social Charter, which entered into force in 1992. The Additional Protocol now has thirteen States parties. It added several new rights, including the right to gender equality in the workplace, the right of workers to be consulted as to decisions that might have an important impact on the employment situation, the right of workers and their representatives to participate in decisions as to improvements in working conditions, and the right of elderly persons to social protection.

In 1991 the COE adopted the Protocol Amending the European Social Charter to improve the supervisory system of the Charter.[118] The 1991 Protocol will only come into force when it has been ratified by all States parties to the European Social Charter and has been ratified by twenty-two states, but the Committee of Ministers has decided to implement the Protocol's procedures immediately to the extent possible.

In 1995 the COE adopted the Additional Protocol to the European Social Charter Providing for a System of Collective Complaints, which has been ratified by twelve states and entered into force in 1998. This protocol expands the categories of rights and provides for a system of collective complaints by international organizations of employers and trade unions that participate in the work of the Governmental Committee, international NGOs that have consultative status with COE and are on a list prepared by the Governmental Committee, and national organizations of employers and trade unions from contracting parties. Each state may also accept the right of its national nongovernmental organizations to file complaints against it.

In 1996 the Council of Europe produced a revised European Social Charter, which came into force in 1999 and has been ratified by twenty-three European states.[119] Under the Revised Charter, states report on how they implement the Charter in law and practice with regard to the provisions they have accepted. State reports are reviewed by ESCR. The

Committee consists of fifteen members elected for a six-year term by the Committee of Ministers. They should be experts of the highest integrity and of recognized competence in national and international social questions and are nominated by States parties. The members may serve for a period of six years and may be reelected for one additional term of six years. The Committee determines whether States parties are in compliance with their undertakings and its conclusions are made public. If a State party fails to take action on a Committee conclusion, the matter is transmitted to the Governmental Committee—a body including representatives of the States parties to the Charter as well as observers from organizations of employers and unions. The Governmental Committee then prepares a recommendation for the Committee of Ministers to transmit to the State party concerned asking it to improve the situation.

With regard to the twelve States parties to the 1995 Additional Protocol to the European Social Charter Providing for a System of Collective Complaints, the ECSR receives complaints from organizations of employers and unions as well as recognized NGOs. The ECSR examines the complaints to determine whether they are admissible. For example, the complaint must identify the submitting organization, provide proof of the authority of the person submitting the complaint to represent the organization, give the name of the state concerned, indicate the provisions of the Charter allegedly violated, and explain the substance of the complaint. If the complaint is found admissible, the ECSR requests the parties to engage in an exchange of written information and views. The ECSR may also hold a public hearing before it makes a decision on the case. The ECSR then prepares a report on its review and conclusions and refers them to the Committee of Ministers, the complaining organization, and the States parties. The Committee of Ministers may adopt a resolution with recommendations. The state must submit information on its efforts to comply. At the time of the resolution or four months after the Committee of Ministers receives the report, the Parliamentary Assembly also receives the report, which is made public.

Since its establishment in 1998, the collective complaint procedure has been invoked in thirty-six cases.[120] Allegations raised in the complaints included discriminatory fees charged to independent medical doctors in France; racial discrimination in housing against the Roma in Greece and Italy; impediments on the freedom to organize among workers in the higher education institutions of France; impediments on the right to collective bargaining in the public sector of Belgium; corporal punishment of school children in Greece, Ireland, Italy, and Portugal; deprivation of the right not to join a trade union in Sweden; and loss of the right to special leave for hospital workers exposed to radiation in Finland. A further example of the ECSR's handling of collective complaints can be found in a case in which the ECSR found admissible in 2002 a collective complaint filed against France alleging insufficient educational facilities for autistic persons. In 2003, ECSR concluded that there was a violation of the Charter in that case. In 2004, the French government undertook a series of measures to increase the number of educational places for autistic children, teenagers, and adults and otherwise to bring the situation into conformity with the Revised Charter. Later in 2004, the Committee of Ministers adopted a resolution looking forward to reports by France that the situation had improved.

While the Revised Charter has helped foster improvements in respect for economic, social, and cultural rights, the Charter is given less attention than the European Convention on Human Rights or the European Union. Governments, for example, are often delayed in submitting their reports under the Charter. Furthermore, the European Union's directives and recommendations often overlap with and are given much more respect than the Charter's provisions. Still, the Charter has accorded new attention and prominence to economic, social, and cultural rights in the European context.

### iv. *Council of Europe Commissioner for Human Rights*

The Committee of Ministers established the terms of reference for the Commissioner for Human Rights in 1999 after it was initially discussed by the Parliamentary Assembly.[121] The Commissioner is elected for a nonrenewable term of six years by the Parliamentary Assembly from a list of three candidates proposed by the Committee of Ministers. The Commissioner seeks to visit member states of the Council of Europe to examine the human rights situation, to identify shortcomings, to promote effective implementation of standards, to encourage establishment of ombudsmen and other human rights institutions, to promote human rights education, and to report to the Committee of Ministers and Parliamentary Assembly. The Commissioner focuses his visits particularly on crisis situations, such as the Chechen Republic in the Russian Federation. As to the Chechen Republic, the Commissioner has recommended the establishment of a Special Representative of the President of the Russian Federation for Human Rights in the Chechen Republic, the creation of joint military and civil prosecution service inspection teams for places of detention, the formation of a consultative Council of NGOs and Civil Society representatives, and the development of other mechanisms for monitoring the human rights situation. The Commissioner also cooperates with the Council of Europe's monitoring mechanism in establishing contacts with the authorities of states under review. In addition, the Commissioner may not only issue reports, but also may make recommendations, give opinions (either on the request of national bodies or on his own initiative), and organize meetings.

B. EUROPEAN UNION

Until 2004, the European Union consisted of fifteen member states: Austria, Belgium, Denmark, Finland, France, Germany, Greece, Ireland, Italy, Luxembourg, Netherlands, Portugal, Spain, Sweden, and the United Kingdom. They were joined by ten central and eastern European states on May 1, 2004. The new members are: Cyprus (the Greek part), the Czech Republic, Estonia, Hungary, Latvia, Lithuania, Malta, Poland, Slovakia, and Slovenia. With Bulgaria and Romania joining in 2007, five other nations are expected to join in the future.

The basis for European integration lies in three foundational treaties: (1) the European Coal and Steel Community Treaty of 1952,[122] (2) the Treaty Establishing the European Economic Community of 1958,[123] and (3) the Treaty Establishing the European Atomic Energy Community of 1958.[124] These treaties have been amended as the organization has grown, and extensive reforms have been instituted through four additional treaties: (1) the Single European Act, (2) the Treaty on European Union, (3) the Treaty of Amsterdam, and (4) the Treaty of Nice. Each successive treaty has elevated the position of human rights among the organization's basic principles.

The Single European Act (SEA) of 1986 established a free internal market and mentioned human rights.[125] In the preamble, member states pledged to promote democracy on the basis of their national constitutions and laws, the European Convention for the Protection of Human Rights and Fundamental Freedoms, and the European Social Charter. Human rights were further emphasized in the Treaty on European Union, which was concluded at Maastricht in 1992.

The EU has issued directives and developed policies relevant to human rights, including education, employment discrimination, equality, fair application of the law, freedom of association, and migrant workers. Moreover, the Treaty on European Union expanded the rights of free movement, residence, and transportation within the Union for citizens of member states. The member states have also created institutions to implement the political and policy functions of the E.U. The four most important institutions playing a role in shaping human rights policies have been the European Court of Justice (ECJ), the Council of the European Union, the European Commission, and the European Parliament.

The ECJ sits in Luxembourg and interprets and applies EU law. It applies general principles of national and international law. It has established human rights doctrines as a matter of Community law, including protection against gender and other discrimination, the right to be heard, and the right to a fair hearing. In 1974 in *Nold v. Commission*,[126] the Court began to cite the European Convention as a guideline to be followed within the framework of European Community law. Since then, in *Cinéthèque S.A. v. Fédération National des Cinémas Français*, the ECJ has cited the European Convention in most of its relevant cases.[127] It has also recognized limits on its power to review national legislation.

There has been some question as to the relationship of the EU to the European Convention on Human Rights. Various member states and EU officials have proposed that the EU, as an institution, should accede to the European Convention. Accession would allow individuals to challenge EU laws and directives before the European Court of Human Rights. The ECJ determined in a 1996 opinion that EU treaties do not confer a power to ratify international human rights instruments. In the Treaty Establishing a Constitution for Europe, adopted by consensus in 2003 and awaiting uncertain ratification by member states, the EU would apparently be given authority to ratify the European Convention. Further, Protocol No. 14 of the European Convention on Human Rights contains a provision that the European Union may accede to that Convention.

The Constitution for Europe contains a Charter of Fundamental Rights of the Union with forty-six articles setting forth rights to human dignity, life, integrity of the person, marriage, family, liberty, security, private and family life, property, asylum, equality before the law, equality between men and women, nondiscrimination, cultural and religious diversity, linguistic diversity, education, social security and assistance, health care, access to services, environmental protection, consumer protection, political participation, good administration, access to documents, access to the European Ombudsman, petition, effective remedy, fair trial, presumption of innocence, defense, and legality and proportionality of criminal offenses and penalties. The Charter also contains prohibitions of torture and inhuman or degrading treatment or punishment, slavery, forced labor, and double jeopardy and freedoms of thought, conscience, religion, expression, information, assembly, association, arts and sciences, movement, residence, occupation, work, business, and property. Further, it includes protection in the event of removal, expulsion, or extradition, and rights of the child, the elderly, persons with disabilities, workers, and the family. This extensive listing of rights for the E.U. raises the question of whether the E.U. will focus on complying with the human rights provisions of the Charter of Fundamental Rights or with the European Convention on Human Rights. The

Constitution of Europe's Charter of Rights begins to answer that question in Article II-112(3):

> Insofar as this Charter contains rights which correspond to rights guaranteed by the Convention for the Protection of Human Rights and Fundamental Freedoms, the meaning and scope of those rights shall be the same as those laid down by the said Convention. This provision shall not prevent Union law providing more extensive protection.[128]

In 2007 the EU established the EU Agency for Fundamental Rights, located in Vienna. The Agency is expected to produce an annual report based on information provided by EU states, respond to requests for advice from the European Parliament on the impact of new legislation on human rights, and advise on the human rights performance of governaments that are seeking EU membership. The EU Commission also reviews fundamental rights in the candidate countries. The Fundamental Rights Agency will not receive complaints from individuals.

C. ORGANIZATION FOR SECURITY AND COOPERATION IN EUROPE (OSCE)

The Organization for Security and Cooperation in Europe is a regional organization comprising fifty-five European, Central Asian, and North American states. It addresses a wide range of issues including arms control, election monitoring, human rights, and preventive diplomacy. The OSCE grew out of the Conference on Security and Cooperation in Europe (CSCE), established in 1973. The thirty-four governments that created the CSCE sought a means for addressing various Cold War concerns by entering into a nonbinding agreement called the Helsinki Final Act (or Helsinki Accords) in 1975.[129] Eastern European governments sought confirmation of the territorial status quo and development of economic relations, while Western governments hoped to achieve security and advance humanitarian issues. Instead of a treaty or institution, they developed a statement of principles of behavior for governments and a negotiating process that established a unique linkage between security and human rights concerns.

The Final Act included four categories known as "baskets." Basket I outlined ten principles involving relations among governments, security, and confidence building. Basket II addressed cooperation in economics, technology, and the environment. Basket III applied to cooperation in humanitarian and other fields. Basket IV established the follow-up process which resulted in several meetings between 1977 and 1989. Those meetings resulted in various documents addressing security concerns and protecting human rights such as trade union freedoms, religious freedoms, free flow of information, protection against terrorism, and family unification. Exchanges of information and bilateral meetings to discuss human rights were also encouraged. The CSCE played a key role in establishing the normative framework and political environment for ending the Cold War.

At the end of the Cold War, the CSCE struggled to find a place in the new Europe. In 1990, government leaders convened a summit meeting that resulted in the Charter of Paris for a New Europe.[130] That document created permanent administrative organs and decision-making bodies. It also provided for *ad hoc* meetings and reflected an intent to create a parliamentary body. The governments agreed to hold follow-up meetings called "review conferences" every two years. In 1992, the first review conference was held in Helsinki. The participants adopted the "Helsinki Summit Declaration," which included the "Helsinki Decisions."[131] The latter emphasized substantive issues of conflict prevention and management and described potential peacekeeping activities. The review conference also established new institutions including a Chairman in Office, a CSCE Secretary-General, the CSCE Forum for Security Cooperation, and the High Commissioner on National Minorities.

At the 1994 review conference in Budapest the CSCE changed its name to the OSCE. The new name reflected the development of permanent administrative structures and personnel. At that time, the Office for Free Elections was also restructured into the Office for Democratic Institutions and Human Rights (ODIHR). That office, headquartered in Warsaw, has the primary responsibility for overseeing the OSCE's human dimension activities, including human rights and fair elections. At the Helsinki Summit in 1992 it was decided that ODIHR help participating states "to ensure full respect for human rights and fundamental freedoms, to abide by the rule of law, to promote principles of democracy and . . . tolerance throughout society."[132] Its work is divided into four areas: (1) election observation, (2) democratization assistance, (3) monitoring/early warning, and (4) Roma and Sinti issues. The OSCE created the Contact Point for Roma and Sinti Issues (CPRSI) within ODIHR in response to increasing acts of violence committed against Europe's largest ethnic minority group. The CPRSI advises governments on policy-making toward Roma and Sinti, promotes networking and capacity building among Roma and Sinti civil society organizations, and encourages the participation of Roma and Sinti representatives in policy-making bodies at the local, national, and international levels. Through the efforts of the CPRSI and the High Commissioner on National Minorities, the OSCE assumed a leading role among European intergovernmental institutions in preventing ethnic conflict and combating discrimination.

For other human rights issues, the OSCE's Human Dimension Mechanism follows a multistage process of negotiations, mediation, and fact-finding involving bilateral and multilateral negotiations, OSCE experts, and rapporteurs assisted by the ODIHR. The process begins with one or more states filing claims that another state is not living up to its Human Dimension commitments. Resolution of the problem is attempted through diplomatic means within certain time periods. If the matter is not resolved, it can be brought to the attention of all states by placing it on the agenda of OSCE follow-up or human dimension conferences. Fact-finding by experts or rapporteurs can follow. There can also be mediations. Usually the fact-finding and mediation missions require consent of the states concerned, but in serious situations, a mission may be assembled if a group of states or the OSCE Senior Council (a periodic high-level meeting of political directors) deems it necessary.

Two OSCE procedures deserve particular attention for their specific human rights impact. First, the High Commissioner on National Minorities (HCNM) addresses minority problems before they degenerate into conflicts. The HCNM conducts on-site missions, engages in preventive diplomacy, mediates between concerned parties, and makes recommendations to governments. The High Commissioner has issued recommendations to Albania, Croatia, Estonia, the former Yugoslav Republic of Macedonia, Hungary, Kazakhstan, Kyrgyzstan, Latvia, Lithuania, Moldova, Romania, Russian Federation, Slovak Republic, and Ukraine. For example, in 2001 the HCNM wrote a letter to the Foreign Minister of the Russian Federation encouraging the government to establish Ukrainian language schools for Ukrainian children and recommending that the Russian Federation should become a party to the European Charter for regional or minority languages. Second, the Representative on Freedom of the Media was created in 1997 to address problems caused by "obstruction of media activities and unfavorable working conditions for journalists."[133] The Media Representative is an advocate, observing developments and promoting compliance with commitments regarding freedom of expression and free media, including hate speech. The Representative has the power to contact states and seeks to resolve violations. The Representative reports to the Permanent Council and can recommend further action where appropriate.

## 2. Mechanisms for the Americas

The human rights system in the Western Hemisphere has developed in the context of countering the spread of communism, military dictatorships, and chronic states of emergency. The Charter of the Organization of American States (OAS) was opened for signature in 1948, and entered into force in 1951.[134] It has been amended several times by the

Protocol of Buenos Aires in 1970,[135] the Protocol of Cartagena de Indias in 1988,[136] the Protocol of Managua in 1996,[137] and the Protocol of Washington in 1997.[138] In addition to establishing the regional system, the Charter contains many provisions that pertain to human rights issues, in particular with relation to economic, social, and cultural rights. For example, Article 34 provides:

The Member States agree that equality of opportunity, the elimination of extreme poverty, equitable distribution of wealth and income and the full participation of their peoples in decisions relating to their own development are, among others, basic objectives of integral development.[139]

Article 45 of the OAS Charter sets forth a number of other rights, which include collective bargaining, dignity, economic security, equality of opportunity, liberty, and work as well as mechanisms such as the provision of legal aid in order to secure rights.

Another major OAS instrument is the American Declaration of the Rights and Duties of Man, which was adopted in 1948 by the Ninth International Conference of American States. The preamble provides that "the international protection of the rights of man should be the principal guide of an evolving American law."[140] It provides for twenty-seven human rights, one limitation clause, and ten duties. The rights include civil and political rights as well as economic, social, and cultural rights. While the Declaration was drafted as a non-binding resolution, it has gradually developed into a binding interpretation of the OAS Charter obligations. The Inter-American Court of Human Rights ruled in 1989 that the Declaration "is the text that defines the human rights referred to in the Charter of the Organization."[141]

A third major document in the Inter-American system is the American Convention on Human Rights, which was opened for signature on November 20, 1969, and entered into force on July 18, 1978.[142] It has been ratified by twenty-five countries of the Americas: Argentina, Barbados, Bolivia, Brazil, Chile, Colombia, Costa Rica, Dominica, Dominican Republic, Ecuador, El Salvador, Grenada, Guatemala, Haiti, Honduras, Jamaica, Mexico, Nicaragua, Panama, Paraguay, Peru, Suriname, Trinidad, Uruguay, and Venezuela. Left to ratify remain only Canada, the United States, and some of the smaller English-speaking Caribbean countries. In 1998, Trinidad and Tobago denounced—in other words, withdrew from—the Convention, effective 1999, due to Court decisions taken that limited the application of the death penalty.

Like the European Convention, the American Convention guarantees civil and political rights. Unlike its European counterpart, however, Article 26 of the American Convention's contains undertakings for States parties to take progressive measures to realize "economic, social, educational, scientific, and cultural standards set forth in the Charter of the Organization of American States as amended by the Protocol of Buenos Aires." That pledge is further elaborated by the Protocol of San Salvador,[143] which sets out more specific rights in the economic, social, and cultural areas.

The American Convention establishes procedures for its implementation by the Inter-American Commission on Human Rights and the Inter-American Court of Human Rights. Both are discussed below. Other treaties in the Americas—such as the Inter-American Convention to Prevent and Punish Torture and the Inter-American Convention on Forced Disappearance of Persons—also use the Inter-American Commission and/or Court for implementation. The Inter-American Convention on the Prevention, Punishment and Eradication of Violence Against Women authorizes the Inter-American Commission of Women to receive reports as to compliance but also gives the Inter-American Court of Human Rights jurisdiction to issue advisory opinions on the interpretation of that treaty.

A. INTER-AMERICAN COMMISSION ON HUMAN RIGHTS (IACHR)

The Inter-American Commission on Human Rights was initially established in 1959 by the OAS General Assembly. In 1970, the entry into force of the Protocol of Buenos Aires amended the OAS Charter to establish the Commission as a Charter-based institution implementing the American Declaration on the Rights and Duties of Man. When the American Convention on Human Rights came into force in 1978, the Commission also attained a role in implementing the Convention for States parties.

The IACHR is headquartered in Washington, D.C. It is one of the two principal organs of the OAS that promotes and protects human rights in the Western Hemisphere. It is composed of seven members elected in their personal capacity by the General Assembly of the OAS from a list of candidates proposed by member states. The Commission members are elected for a term of four years and may be reelected once. No two nationals of the same state may be members of the Commission at any one time. The functions of the IACHR include promoting awareness of human rights in the Americas, providing member states with advisory services in the field of human rights, monitoring the situation of human rights in each member state and undertaking on-site observations, acting on individual petitions alleging human rights violations, preparing studies and reports, and making recommendations to OAS member states for the adoption of progressive measures for human rights.

### i. Individual Petition System

The IACHR has one of the broadest standing requirements of all the international procedures. Any person or group can file a petition alleging the violation of the American Convention (against countries that are party) or of the American Declaration. Indeed, the Commission may initiate a case on its own motion as a result of information of which it becomes aware in the media or elsewhere. While it is usually necessary for a petition to identify the victim so the state involved can investigate and respond to the allegations, the identity of the petitioner may be kept in confidence. The petition must be in writing, be signed, and set forth facts that tend to show the violation of a protected right. Other admissibility requirements include exhaustion of domestic remedies unless the state's laws do not provide due process, the party was denied access to those remedies, or there has been unwarranted delay; and submission in a timely manner, either within six months of notification of a final judgment by a domestic court or within a reasonable time of the occurrence. The petition cannot duplicate a case pending or previously settled by the Commission or another international governmental organization of a similar nature. A ruling on admissibility by the Commission is final and not subject to appeal.

Under Article 48(1)(f) of the American Convention, the Commission is authorized to facilitate a "friendly settlement" of the situation if the parties are willing. Once the initial written proceedings are completed, the Commission notifies parties that the Commission is at their disposal for a limited time period. It can assist with arrangement of meetings, transmittal of communications, and mediation. Any agreement reached by the parties will be reviewed by the Commission to ensure that it is in accord with respect for the human rights recognized in the American Convention before the matter can be finalized.

Pursuant to Article 29 of its Regulations,[144] the Commission may—in urgent cases—on its own initiative or at the request of a petitioner, ask that the state concerned adopt precautionary measures to prevent irreparable harm to persons. The Commission may request that the Court order the adoption of provisional measures under grave circumstances in a matter that has not yet been submitted to the Court. Emergency action is taken without prejudice to any future decision on the merits of the situation, and is generally taken to protect the life and/or physical and mental integrity of individuals.

When a case is not resolved through friendly settlement, the Commission draws up an initial report of its findings, which are sent to the state in question. In carrying out this function, the Commission has been very flexible and informal in the evidence it considers. It has permitted the admission of affidavits, videotaped testimony, personal documents, technical expert testimony, and newspaper accounts. When the Commission undertakes a fact-finding visit, it may also gather information about individual petitions. It has occasionally held oral arguments. If a violation is established, the Commission makes recommendations to the state aimed at obtaining a full investigation of the facts, the prosecution and punishment of those found responsible, and action to remedy the situation for the victim. The state is first given a chance to act on the recommendations without publicity and is given a set time to report on measures taken. The Commission then evaluates any response and can either adopt a final report, which is sent to both parties, or submit the case to the Inter-American Court of Human Rights for adjudication if the state has accepted its compulsory jurisdiction.

The Commission has experienced difficulty in assuring compliance with its decisions—particularly with regard to countries (such as the United States) that have not ratified the American Convention and are thus not subject to the jurisdiction of the Court. Although the Commission does transmit its annual reports including its decisions on cases to the OAS General Assembly, that body has not done much to urge compliance with Commission decisions on individual petitions. In order to address these problems, the Commission has adopted follow-up measures, which include holding hearings to verify compliance and the preparing of reports that draw as much attention as possible to cases.

The Commission also has jurisdiction to hear petitions under the American Convention, including inter-state communications. About one-half the States parties to the Convention have recognized inter-state jurisdiction, although no inter-state communication has yet been lodged.

*ii. Country Studies and On-Site Investigations*

The Inter-American Commission can initiate a study on the human rights conditions in a particular country as a result of information received in petitions or other evidence submitted usually by nongovernmental organizations indicating large-scale violations of human rights. It also conducts studies upon invitation from a particular state or political bodies of the OAS. The studies often involve on-site visits, but they require the consent of the state concerned. The first country reports were pursued in the early 1960s on Cuba, the Dominican Republic, and Haiti. The Dominican Republic was the only one of the three that allowed the Commission to enter and was thus the first country to have an on-site visit. In that case, the Commission held hearings, met with government and opposition leaders, and interviewed representatives of churches, businesses, union groups, and individuals all over the country. It also set up places for persons to provide oral and written complaints. That visit set the framework for future on-site Commission visits. In the case of Cuba, the Commission heard from witnesses and received evidence in Miami where many refugees from Cuba had fled.

On-site investigations are one of the major strengths of the Commission. Such investigations and country reports were very effective in preventing, stopping, or at least drawing world attention to the massive violations of human rights during the 1970s and 1980s when there were numerous military governments in Latin America. On-site investigations to prisons resulted in finding missing persons. Most importantly, on-site visits and the resulting country reports have been successful in exposing violations of human rights. The reports alert the domestic and international community to particular practices and often have been the foundation for debates in the UN General Assembly and Commission on Human Rights.

*iii. Other Commission Activities*

The Inter-American Commission on Human Rights[145] has drafted or cooperated in drafting various treaties and other human rights instruments, including the Inter-American Convention to Prevent and Punish Torture; the Additional Protocol to the American Convention on Human Rights Relevant to Economic, Social and Cultural Rights; the Inter-American Convention on Forced Disappearances of Persons; the American Convention on Human Rights to Abolish the Death Penalty, and the Proposed American Declaration on the Rights of Indigenous Peoples.[146] It has also submitted proposals on issues such as the independence of the judiciary and refugee rights. In addition, in 1997 the Commission created the Office of the Special Rapporteur for Freedom of Expression.[147] The Special Rapporteur began to function a year later. The Special Rapporteur visits countries, organizes seminars on freedom of expression, assists the Commission in handling individual cases, and issues reports on the situation of freedom of expression in the Western Hemisphere. Similarly, in 1998 the Commission established the Special Rapporteur for Migrant Workers and Their Families, with analogous functions to the Freedom of Expression Rapporteur. The Special Rapporteur for Migrants began work in May 1998 by sending a questionnaire on migrant workers to states in the region, visiting various facilities in the United States—including factories, border posts, and detention facilities—and undertaking research on the rights of migrant workers.

B. INTER-AMERICAN COURT OF HUMAN RIGHTS

The Inter-American Court of Human Rights was established by the American Convention on Human Rights, and was first elected in 1979.[148] It consists of seven part-time judges who are nominated and elected by the parties to the Convention. The judges must be nationals of a member of the OAS, but not necessarily of a party to the Convention. Because they are part-time, they are free to have other employment that would be compatible with their judicial functions. The term of judges is six years, and they may be reelected for one additional term. The General Assembly voted to make the permanent seat in San José, Costa Rica, but it may convene in any other location with the prior consent of the state concerned when the majority of the Court considers it desirable. The Court has contentious and advisory jurisdiction.

*i. Contentious or Adjudicatory Jurisdiction*

In order for the Court to decide a case, the States parties to the American Convention have to accept its jurisdiction. Peru accepted the jurisdiction of the Court and then tried to withdraw from contentious jurisdiction after a case was decided against it, but the Court ruled that it could not withdraw because the American Convention did not permit a withdrawal once jurisdiction was accepted. Pursuant to Article 61, the IACHR may submit a case to the Court, but individuals have no standing. To date, general declarations accepting the Court's jurisdiction are in effect with regard to Argentina, Barbados, Bolivia, Brazil, Chile, Colombia, Costa Rica, Dominican Republic, Ecuador, El Salvador, Guatemala, Haiti, Honduras, Mexico, Nicaragua, Panama, Paraguay, Peru, Suriname, Uruguay, and Venezuela.

The Court's procedures include consideration of preliminary objections (including failure to exhaust domestic remedies), the merits phase (in which the parties present their cases in written submissions), a public hearing of testimony, deliberation in private, and issuance of an unappealable decision. The Court may enter a final judgment in cases which can include declaratory relief and damages. Under Article 63(c) of the American Convention, it can also grant provisional measures, even before referral of a case by the IACHR, in "cases of extreme gravity and urgency, and when necessary to avoid irreparable damage to persons. . . ."[149] There is no formal enforcement procedure except that the Court reports to the OAS General Assembly and specifies "cases in which a state has not complied with its judgments, making any pertinent recommendations."[150] Hence, enforcement is left to the General Assembly, which can discuss cases publicly and use political measures.

By 2006, the court had decided, or at least taken cognizance of, 155 cases under its contentious jurisdiction and delivered 20 advisory opinions. The cases covered a wide range of issues, from the banning of movies in Chile to kidnapping and disappearances in Argentina, Guatemala, and Honduras. In the Guatemala case, the Court ruled that the government had violated the American Convention and ordered reparations of $222,000. In *Garrido and Baigorria Judgment*,[151] a case against Argentina, the Court ordered the equivalent of $175,000 in reparations and $45,000 in cost and expenses, as well as set forth steps the government had to take to investigate and prosecute the responsible officials. In *Velásquez Rodriguez Judgment*,[152] *Godínez Cruz Judgment*,[153] and *Fairen and Solis Judgment*[154]—three cases against Honduras—the Court awarded damages for loss of income and moral harm (similar to the pecuniary and nonpecuniary relief under the European system), but ruled that punitive damages were not authorized under the American Convention. It also did not award costs and expenses because it found that the applicants had not proved them.[155] In the *Velásquez Rodriguez* case, the best-known opinion of the Inter-American Court, he Court held that the Government of Honduras had a duty of "due diligence" to prevent disappearances:

> An illegal act which violates human rights and which is initially not directly imputable to a State (for example, because it is the act of a private person or because the person responsible has not been identified) can lead to international responsibility of the State, not because of the act itself, but because of the lack of due diligence to prevent the violation or to respond to it as required by the Convention.[156]

In contrast with the European cases, the States parties to the American Convention often fail to comply with the awards issued by the Court or are very slow in responding. It usually takes continued monitoring by the Court for years to ensure that payments are made. Because ultimate enforcement lies with the OAS General Assembly, States parties are often able to forestall the political measures that the Assembly could take to enforce the Court's rulings, as was done by Honduras in the cases mentioned above. Unlike the European system, however, under Article 68(2), victims and their representatives can enforce the Court's judgments directly under the domestic procedures governing the execution of judgments.

*ii. Advisory Jurisdiction*

Article 64 of the American Convention provides that members of the OAS and its organs may consult the Court regarding the interpretation of the Convention itself or other treaties concerning the protection of human rights in the Western Hemisphere. Member states may also ask for opinions regarding the compatibility of their domestic laws with those instruments.

The question of what treaties are subject to interpretation by the Court was addressed in its first advisory opinion in response to a request by Peru. The Court ruled that it had "the power to interpret any treaty as long as it is directly related to the protection of human rights in a Member State of the inter-American system."[157] That principle has been interpreted to cover a broad set of treaties that include any kind of treaty, bilateral or multilateral, within or outside of the Inter-American system, and not necessarily a human rights treaty, as long as the provisions relate to the protection of human rights.

C. OTHER OAS PROCEDURES

The Charter of the OAS states "that representative democracy is an indispensable condition for the stability, peace and development of the region" and that one of its purposes is "to promote and consolidate representative democracy, with due respect for the principle of nonintervention."[158] In 2001, the OAS General Assembly adopted the Inter-American Democratic Charter, which appears to be the first instrument to declare democracy a human right.[159] The OAS assists its member states in improving democratic institutions by providing training in drafting legislation and running elections, by observing elections, and by organizing conferences to strengthen political parties. For example, the OAS has since 1990 observed eighty-five elections in half the nations of the Western Hemisphere.

At the Sixth International Conference of American States, held in Havana during 1928, more than a thousand women demanded the right that a woman be permitted to speak before the conference. After more than a month of protests and campaigning, a woman was allowed to address the conference for the first time. At that conference, the Inter-American Commission of Women was established. The Commission of Women has drafted several path-breaking treaties, including the Convention on the Nationality of Women, the Inter-American Convention on the Granting of Civil Rights to Women, and the Inter-American Convention on the Granting of Political Rights to Women. The Commission also helped to draft—and now implements—the Inter-American Convention on the Prevention, Punishment and Eradication of Violence Against Women.

## 3. African Mechanisms

The African human rights system has developed in the context of countering one-party systems, preventing mass violations of human rights, and addressing a unique need for a "home-grown" system. The African Union is a regional intergovernmental organization established in 2002 as a successor to the Organization of African Unity (OAU) that had been formed in 1963.[160] Two of the objectives of the African Union are (1) to encourage international cooperation, taking due account of the Charter of the United Nations and the Universal Declaration of Human Rights, and (2) to promote and protect human and peoples' rights in accordance with the African Charter on Human and Peoples' Rights and other relevant human rights instruments.[161]

The African Charter on Human and Peoples' Rights (also referred to as the Banjul Charter) was adopted in Banjul, Gambia, during 1981 and entered into force on October 21, 1986.[162] As of 2006, fifty-three African countries had ratified the Charter. The African Charter contains many clauses comparable to other human rights instruments. It covers civil and political rights and stresses economic, social, and cultural rights. It is notably innovative for including the right to development and various duties of the individual—to family, state, society, and recognized communities—and duties of the state to strengthen national independence and contribute to its own defense. The Charter has no derogation clause during times of emergency. It does contain numerous "claw-back" clauses, however, which have occasionally been invoked by governments perpetrating violations of human rights.

The African Charter established the African Commission on Human and Peoples' Rights, discussed below. On June 9, 1998, the OAU also adopted a Protocol to the African Charter for the establishment of the African Court on Human and Peoples' Rights.[163] The Protocol entered into force in January 2004. Twenty-three countries have ratified the Protocol: Algeria, Burkina Faso, Burundi, Côte d'Ivoire, Comoros, Gabon, Gambia, Ghana, Kenya, Lesotho, Libya, Mali, Mauritania, Mauritius, Mozambique, Niger, Nigeria, Rwanda, Senegal, South Africa, Tanzania, Togo, and Uganda.

### a. African Commission on Human and Peoples' Rights

The African Commission on Human and Peoples' Rights consists of eleven members who serve in their individual capacity.[164] They are nominated by States parties to the African Charter and are elected by the Assembly of Heads of State and Government. The members must be nationals of the States parties, but the Commission cannot include more than one national of the same state. Members are elected for six years and may be reelected. The Commission has its office in Banjul, The Gambia.

Under Article 45 of the African Charter, the mandate of the Commission includes taking measures to promote human rights such as researching specific situations, on-site missions, organizing seminars and conferences, giving recommendations to states, setting out human rights principles, and cooperating with other international organizations. It monitors states' compliance through review of reports that are required every two years. It can also receive communications from states as well as other communications which have been submitted primarily by individuals and NGOs.

In reviewing reports by States parties, the Commission conducts an oral examination of the state's representatives, and gives opinions and recommendations to the governments. Unfortunately, the process has not been effective in part because as of 2006, only thirty-five of fifty-three states had submitted reports to the Commission since ratifying the Charter. Moreover, those states that had reported were often significantly overdue in submitting their reports. Still, despite such obstacles, the Commission is making considerable headway in strengthening the human rights protection system in Africa. While no inter-state communications have yet been received, the Commission has begun to develop a body of jurisprudence on the basis of complaints filed by NGOs on behalf of African residents. For example, the Commission found that Nigeria had violated the rights to life, integrity of person, fair trial, freedom of expression and association, in detaining and executing environmental activist Ken Saro-Wiwa.[165]

Communications (that is, complaints) are compiled by the Secretary of the Commission and a simple majority of the members have to agree for a communication to be considered. Admissibility requirements include that they cannot be anonymous (although the authors can request anonymity), are not written in disparaging or insulting language, cannot be based exclusively on news disseminated by the mass media, local remedies are exhausted as long as the procedures are not unduly prolonged, are submitted within a reasonable time after exhaustion, and do not deal with cases that have been settled by the states under the UN Charter, the Charter of the OAU (now the Constitutive Act of the AU), or provisions of the African Charter.

The Commission makes decisions regarding admissibility and the merits. Its decisions are communicated to the applicant and the state. Remedies for violations are limited. When the communications reveal a series of serious violations, the Assembly could request an in-depth study and report from the Commission. Other potential remedies include publicity, fact-finding missions, and the use of special rapporteurs. In a path-breaking decision in 2001, African Commission appealed to the Government of Nigeria

> to ensure protection of the environment, health and livelihood of the people of Ogoniland by . . . [s]topping all attacks on Ogoni communities and leaders . . . [and by] ensuring adequate compensation to victims of the human rights violations, including relief and resettlement assistance to victims of government sponsored raids, and undertaking a comprehensive cleanup of lands and rivers damaged by oil operations.[166]

It remains to be seen whether the African Commission will make such compensation a regular feature of its decision making, and whether the Assembly of Heads of State and Government will assist the Commission in assuring that its decisions are implemented. The Commission has noted that it has generally failed to provide methods of compensation to the victims who thereby find themselves without any remedy. Such concerns led to the adoption of the Protocol designed to create the African Court on Human and Peoples' Rights.

B. AFRICAN COURT ON HUMAN AND PEOPLES' RIGHTS

The Protocol to the African Charter for the establishment of the African Court on Human and Peoples' Rights came into force on January 25, 2004. The Protocol indicates that the Court of eleven judges who are nationals of member

> States of the OAU [now AU), elected in an individual capacity from among jurists of high moral character and of recognized practical, judicial or academic competence and experience in the field of human and peoples' rights. No two judges shall be nationals of the same State.[167]

The African Court on Human and Peoples' Rights has both advisory and contentious jurisdiction. It is expected to hear cases brought by AU member states and African intergovernmental organizations, as well as receive requests from NGOs. Individuals can bring a case only with the agreement of the country that is party to the case or through the African Commission for Human and Peoples' Rights. In July 2004, the AU Assembly of Heads of State and Government at its third Ordinary Session decided to integrate the African Court on Human and Peoples' Rights and the African Union Court of Justice into one Court. The AU Assembly appeared to be motivated by concerns about the costs of establishing two courts.

The African Union Court of Justice is expected to have seventeen judges that will be nationals of member states. There cannot be two judges from the same country. Since the judges are supposed to reflect the principal legal systems in Africa, each of the five regions (Northern, Eastern, Central, Southern, and Western Africa) shall be represented by at least two judges. The judges are to be impartial, independent, and possess the qualifications required in their countries for judicial office or jurists of international law. The judges cannot exercise any political or administrative function or engage in other professional occupations. They will be elected for seven years and will be eligible for reelection once. The Protocol provides for "adequate gender representation" in the nomination process. The African Union Court is expected to have jurisdiction over all disputes and applications referred to it in accordance with, *inter alia,* the Constitutive Act of the African Union; the interpretation of the Constitutive Act; the interpretation, application, or validity of Union treaties, and all subsidiary legal instruments adopted within the framework of the Union; any question of international law; all acts, decisions, regulations and directives of the organs of the Union. This very broad jurisdictional mandate has the potential for giving the African Court the authority to hear matters involving international human rights matters.

Since the two courts have some overlapping jurisdiction for human rights matters, the AU Assembly apparently decided to join the two bodies. Amnesty International, however, has expressed concern about difficulties in such a restructuring. There is no legal authority in the two protocols for such a combination. While the Protocol establishing the African Court on Human and Peoples' Rights came into force, the July 2004 decision did not take into account that the Protocol of the Court of the African Union had only received five of the fifteen ratifications necessary to bring it into force. The two courts are expected to have different numbers of judges (eleven and seventeen respectively). More important, the members of the African Court on Human and Peoples' Rights are supposed to be experts in that field, while the AU Court of Justice should have members with different legal qualifications. There is a risk that the human rights functions of the African Court on Human and Peoples' Rights will be subsumed or possibly even lost in combining the two courts. Recognizing at least some of these difficulties, the AU Assembly at its third Ordinary Session in July 2004 requested the Chairperson of the AU Commission to work out the modalities for implementing its decision and to report back at its fourth Ordinary Session expected to be held in 2005, though by 2006 there had been no resolution on the merger.

Still, on July 2, 2006, the eleven judges of the African Court on Human and Peoples' Rights were inaugurated. There were criticisms of the procedure used to select the judges because they were apparently selected in secret after the 39th Session of the AU meeting in May 2006. The Court will be based in Arusha, Tanzania. Questions remain as to how the African Court on Human and Peoples' Rights will be merged with the African Union Court of Justice, which was designed to address inter-state conflicts.

## 4. Other Regional Mechanisms

Asian and Middle Eastern governments have not yet created human rights norm-setting instruments or implementation procedures. In other regions, human rights treaties arose from regional institutions, such as the Council of Europe, the Organization of American States, and the African Union. There are no such regional institutions covering the entire continent of Asia. There are also a great variety of governmental systems, religions, philosophies, and cultural traditions in the vast region. There are a number of subregional organizations that address political, economic, and security concerns. Some of these subregional institutions could eventually develop human rights structures and standards. For example, the Pacific sub-region, has taken steps toward developing a human rights system, with a Pacific Charter on Human Rights and a commission to enforce it. In 1998, the NGO Asian Human Rights Commission finalized an Asian Human Rights Charter that has been adopted by other Asian NGOs, but so far no governments have accepted that document.

The Arab and Islamic states have also worked on regional human rights standards and bodies. In 1990 the Nineteenth Islamic Conference of Foreign Ministers adopted the Cairo Declaration on Human Rights in Islam. The League of Arab States established a Human Rights Commission in 1968, adopted an Arab Charter on Human Rights in 1994, and revised it in 2004. Only Iraq ratified the 1994 version and again the 2004 Arab Charter. These documents reflect rights such as those involving education, equality, fair trial, health, life, property, and travel, but offer a more limited range of rights than the Universal Declaration of Human Rights and two Human Rights Covenants. The Human Rights Commission of the League of Arab States has not yet reviewed any country situations.

*See also*: Economic, Social, and Cultural Rights; Freedom of Expression; Political Participation and Voting

*Further Reading:*

African [Banjul] Charter on Human and Peoples' Rights, OAU Doc. CAB/LEG/67/3 rev.5, 21 I.L.M. 58 (1982).

African Commission, Non-Compliance of States Parties to Adopted Recommendations of the African Commission: A Legal Approach, ¶ 6, adopted at the 24th Ord. Sess. of the Commission Banjul, The Gambia, Oct. 1998, OAU DOC/os/50b (XXIV).
American Convention on Human Rights, O.A.S. Treaty Series No. 36, 1144 U.N.T.S. 123 *entered into force* July 18, 1978, *reprinted in* Basic Documents Pertaining to Human Rights in the Inter-American System, OEA/Ser.L.V/II.82 doc.6 rev.1 at 25 (1992).
American Declaration of the Rights and Duties of Man, O.A.S. Res. XXX, adopted by the Ninth International Conference of American States (1948), *reprinted in* Basic Documents Pertaining to Human Rights in the Inter-American System, OEA/Ser.L.V/II.82 doc.6 rev.1 at 17 (1992).
Amnesty International, Open Letter to the Chairman of the African Union (AU) seeking clarifications and assurances that the Establishment of an effective African Court on Human and Peoples' Rights will not be delayed or undermined, AI Index: IOR 63/008/2004 (2004).
Arab Charter on Human Rights, adopted by the League of Arab States, *reprinted in* 18 Human Rights Law Journal 151 (1997).
*Autisme-Europe v. France*, Council of Europe, Committee of Ministers, Resolution ResChS(2004), Collective complaint No. 13/2002.
*The Baby Boy Opinion*, Case 2141, Inter-Am. C.H.R. 25, OEA.Ser.L/V/II.54, doc. 9 rev. 1 (1981).
Thomas Buergenthal, *The Inter-American Court of Human Rights*, 76 A.J.I.L. 211 (1982).
Thomas Buergenthal, *The Advisory Practice of the Inter-American Human Rights Court*, 79 A.J.I.L. 1 (1985).
Cairo Declaration on Human Rights in Islam, Aug. 5, 1990, U.N. GAOR, World Conf. on Hum. Rts., 4th Sess., Agenda Item 5, U.N. Doc. A/CONF.157/PC/62/Add.18 (1993) [English translation].
Antonio Augusto Cancado Trindade, *Current State and Perspectives of the Inter-American System of Human Rights Protection at the Dawn of the New Century*, 8 Tul. J. Int'l. & Comp.L 5 (2000).
*Cinéthèque S.A. v. Fédération National des Cinémas Français*, Cases 60 and 61/84, 1985 E.C.R. 2604).
Convention for the Protection of Human Rights and Dignity of the Human Being with Regard to the Application of Biology and Medicine: Convention on Human Rights and Biomedicine, ETS No. 164, *entered into force* Dec. 1, 1999.
CSCE, Declaration and Decisions from Helsinki Summit, July 10, 1992, 31 I.L.M. 1385 (1992).
*Engel and Others v. the Netherlands*, 22 Eur. Ct. H.R. (ser. A) (1976).
*Fairen and Solis Judgment*, Inter-Am. Ct. H.R. (ser. C) No. 6 (1989).
*Garrido and Baigorria Judgment*, Inter-Am. Ct. H.R. (ser. C) No. 39 (1998).
*Godínez Cruz Judgment*, Inter-Am. Ct. H.R. (ser. C) No. 5 (1989).
Inter-American Commission on Human Rights, Annual Report of 1998, OEA/Ser.L/V/II.102 Doc. 6 rev. (1999).
Inter-American Commission on Human Rights, The Organization of American States and Human Rights 1960–1967, at 202–557 (1972).
Interpretation of the American Declaration of the Rights and Duties of Man Within the Framework of Article 64 of the American Convention on Human Rights, Advisory Opinion OC-10/89, July 14, 1989, Inter-Am. Ct. H.R. (Ser. A) No. 10 (1989).

Mandate of the OSCE Representative on Freedom of the Media (November 5, 1997), PC Journal No. 137, Decision No. 193, para. 2.

Rachel Murray, The African Commission on Human and People's Rights and International Law (2000).

*Neumeister v. Austria*, 17 Eur. Ct. H.R. (ser. A) (1974).

*Nold v. Commission*, Case 4/73, E.C.R. 491 (1974).

Opinion 2/94, [1996] 2 C.M.L.R. 265, 290 (1996).

The Organization of American States and Human Rights 1960–1967, Part III (1972).

"Other Treaties" Subject to the Advisory Jurisdiction of the Court (art. 64 American Convention on Human Rights), Advisory Opinion OC-1/82, Sept. 24, 1982, Inter-Am. Ct. H.R. (Ser. A) No. 1 (1982).

Jo M. Pasqualucci, The Practice and Procedure of the Inter-American Court of Human Rights (2003).

Soren C. Prebensen, *Inter-State Complaints Under Treaty Provisions—The Experience Under the European Convention on Human Rights*, 20 Human Rights Law Journal 445 (1999).

Protocol of Buenos Aires, OAS Charter, *as amended*, arts. 51(e) and 112, now arts. 53(e) and 106.

Rules adopted by the Committee of Ministers for the application of Article 46, paragraph 2, of the European Convention on Human Rights, *reprinted in* Appendix I, Report: Implementation of decisions of the European Court of Human Rights, Council of Europe, Committee on Legal Affairs and Human Rights, Doc. 9307 (2001).

Dinah Shelton, *The Inter-American System for the Protection of Human Rights: Emergent Law*, in International Human Rights Law: Theory and Practice, 369 (Irwin Cotler & F. P. Eliadis eds., 1992).

Kathryn Sikkink, Mixed Signals: U.S. Human Rights Policy and Latin America (2004).

Single European Act, O.J. (L 169/1) (1987).

*The Social and Economic Rights Action Center and the Center for Economic and Social Rights v. Nigeria*, Communication No. 155/96, African Commission on Human and Peoples' Rights (2001).

*Stran Greek Refineries and Straits Andreadis v. Greece*, 301 Eur. Ct. H.R. (ser. A) 61 (1994).

Treaty Establishing a Constitution for Europe, Oct. 29, 2004, O.J. (C310) 1 (2004).

Treaty on European Union, Feb. 7, 1992, O.J. (C191) 1 (1992).

Nsongurua J. Udombana, *An African Human Rights Court and an African Union Court: A Needful Duality or a Needless Duplication?* 28 Brooklyn J. of International Law 811 (2003).

P. Van Dijk and G. J. H. Van Hoof, Theory and Practice of the European Convention on Human Rights (1990).

*Velásquez Rodriguez Judgment*, Inter-Am. Ct. H.R. (ser. C) No. 4 (1988).

Claude Emerson Welch, *Protecting Human Rights in Africa: Roles and Strategies of Non-Governmental Organizations* (1995).

Richard J. Wilson, *The Index of Individual Case Reports of the Inter-American Commission on Human Rights: 1994–1999*, 16 American University International Law Review 353 (2001).

*Links to Consult:*

http://www.achpr.org/
http://www.africa-union.org/
http://www.coe.int/
http://www.corteidh.or.cr/
http://www.cpt.coe.int/en/
http://www.echr.coe.int/
http://www.oas.org/
http://www.osce.org/
http://www1.umn.edu/humanrts/euro/eurocon-all.html
http://www1.umn.edu/humanrts/regional.htm

# C. National Institutions and Procedures

Eleanor Roosevelt, who presided over the drafting of the Universal Declaration of Human Rights, understood that if universal human rights were to have meaning they must be upheld and respected in daily life. She expressed this principle eloquently when she said:

> Where do universal human rights begin? In small places, close to home. So close and so small that they cannot be seen on any maps of the world. Yet they are the world of the individual person; the neighbourhood he lives in; the school or college he attends; the factory, farm, or office where he works. Such are the places where every man, woman, and child seeks equal justice, equal opportunity, equal dignity without discrimination. Unless these rights have meaning there, they have little meaning anywhere. Without concerted citizen action to uphold them close to home, we shall look in vain for progress in the larger world.[168]

National and local human rights norms and procedures are usually better understood and more accessible than treaties and international procedures. In most countries, human rights issues are initially resolved by reference to the national constitution, laws, governmental structures, and practices. Only if those systems fail is there a need for recourse to international norms and procedures. National constitutions ordinarily recite fundamental rights as basic precepts for the government. Indeed, one of the principal reasons for the existence of a national government is to protect the rights of the country's residents.

## 1. Constitutional Protections for Human Rights

A sample of constitutional provisions in such diverse countries as Angola, Canada, Ethiopia, Iceland, Japan, Jordan, Liberia, Mexico, Netherlands, New Zealand, Poland, Singapore, South Africa, and the United States indicate that some of the most frequently protected rights are freedom of expression, freedom of religion and belief, rights of the accused, and rights of persons who are in detention. Several constitutions also state that a goal of the national government is to promote economic, social, and cultural rights. Some constitutions take an extra step and expressly guarantee certain economic, social, and cultural rights.

Poland, for example, guarantees the right to support for involuntary unemployment, sickness, or infirmity. Poland also guarantees the right and freedom of minorities to preserve their languages and cultures. New Zealand guarantees the rights of their minorities to enjoy their cultures, practice their religions, and speak their languages. Iceland makes economic guarantees in the event of sickness, infirmity, unemployment, and similar circumstances. Angola and Ethiopia provide for a right to enjoy a clean and healthy environment.

Similarities among the various declarations of rights in national constitutions partially occur because countries learn from one another and also because many governments have ratified the principal human rights treaties and are compelled to conform their constitutions to international human rights provisions. There are, however, two important caveats. First, in some countries, rights may be identified in the constitution, but may not be enforced by the courts—particularly in countries lacking a tradition for judicial review of executive and legislative actions. Second, just because a right is not guaranteed in a constitution of one of the respective countries does not mean that the country does not protect that right through legislation or other means.

## 2. Role of Courts and Legislatures in Applying International Human Rights Law

As discussed in the section entitled "Introduction to Human Rights as Part of International Law" above, courts play an important role in enforcing international human rights law in some countries or at least in interpreting national law in light of international human rights obligations. Human rights treaties such as the International Covenant on Civil and Political Rights, require States parties to "take the necessary steps, in accordance with its constitutional processes and with the provisions of the . . . Covenant, to adopt such legislative or other measures as may be necessary to give effect to the rights recognized in the . . . Covenant."[169]

There are two principal models for fulfilling such treaty obligations and for understanding the place of treaties in national legal systems. These are the "monist" and "dualist" approaches. While no country perfectly conforms to either model, the two approaches do help in conceptualizing the way treaties are incorporated within the national legal order. Monist nations view all laws—national or international—as part of an overall legal system. In monist nations, courts may directly apply international law in the same way that they apply national law. Dualist nations distinguish between the national and international legal systems, such that courts may not ordinarily apply a treaty unless it has been incorporated in national legislation. A dualist nation is still bound by any treaties it ratifies, but violations may be the subject of concern only at the international level and may not be asserted in national courts.

The Netherlands and the Czech Republic, for example, have not only adopted the monist view, but also have given priority to some treaties (such as human rights conventions) over their own constitutions and statutes. Other countries that generally follow the monist model are Argentina, Austria, and Sweden. Austria, Sweden, and other monist countries in Europe have incorporated the European Convention on Human Rights into their national law. Australia and the United Kingdom, in contrast, generally follow the dualist approach and require legislation in order to bring treaties into domestic effect. Canada follows the dualist approach within its federal structure in that the national parliament may adopt a treaty provision in a statute only to the extent that the treaty's subject matter falls within the legislative competence of the national government. If the treaty's subject matter falls within the legislative competence of the provincial government, however, the provincial governments must each enact the treaty to make it applicable in that province. Canada's constitution, however, incorporates many human rights provisions that are applicable nationally.

The South African Constitution, in comparison, requires that the courts interpret rights in light of international law. The South African Constitutional Court has interpreted the South African constitution in accord with international agreements whether or not they are binding on South Africa. Similarly, Spain's Constitution contains an express provision that, "The norms relative to basic rights and liberties which are recognized by the Constitution, shall be interpreted in conformity with the Universal Declaration of Human Rights and the international treaties and agreements on those matters ratified by Spain."[170]

Following the dualist approach, the British Parliament adopted the UK Human Rights Act in 1998.[171] It incorporates almost all of the European Convention on Human Rights into British law so that it can be asserted by British residents in the courts. Furthermore, the Human Rights Act requires the Minister in charge of any proposed legislation to issue a statement as to the compatibility of the bill with the European Convention on Human Rights. The Joint Parliamentary Committee on Human Rights then reviews the legislation together with the Minister's statement, compatibility with the European Convention on Human Rights and other treaties to which the UK government is party, and the comments of nongovernmental organizations and scholars. The Human Rights Act also authorizes British courts to interpret laws in such a way that they, wherever possible, are construed to be consistent with the European Convention. In reading the legislation, courts may take into account the comments of the Joint Parliament Committee on Human Rights. Where a consistent reading is not possible, the courts may make declarations of incompatibility. Laws incompatible with the European Convention are not annulled by such judicial declarations, but Parliament is put under considerable pressure to reconsider the legislation.

New Zealand also follows the dualist tradition. New Zealand's Bill of Rights Act of 1990 incorporates provisions of the International Covenant on Civil and Political Rights and the courts interpret legislation in light of international human rights jurisprudence. Ombudsmen and the national Human Rights Commission in New Zealand also take into account international human rights law in exercising their functions.

The United States partakes of both the monist and dualist approaches to international law. Article III of the U.S. Constitution provides that treaties—together with federal statutes—are the "the supreme law of the land and the judges in every state shall be bound thereby. . . ."[172] Accordingly at least in principle, an earlier federal statute, a state constitutional provision, or a state law must yield to an inconsistent treaty. The U.S. Supreme Court has sought to integrate treaties into the domestic legal order. Since 1804, for example, the Supreme Court has consistently held that "an Act of Congress ought never to be construed to violate the law of nations, if any other possible construction remains. . . ."[173] Some treaty provisions can be applied directly in U.S. courts if they are considered to be self-executing, that is, they do not require legislation to put them into effect. Further, in *The Paquete Habana* decision of 1900, the Supreme Court addressed the power of courts to enforce customary international law. In invalidating the wartime seizure of fishing vessels as contrary to the law of nations, the Court observed that "International law is part of our law, and must be ascertained and administered by the courts."[174] Where no treaty or other legal authority is controlling, resort must be had to the customs of nations. Nonetheless, U.S. and state judges have—with few exceptions—generally exhibited great reticence in applying Article III's Supremacy Clause to treaties and in making more general use of international standards in their decisions. In fact, some U.S. judges have even appeared ignorant as to the application of international law. One example of how international law and practice can be relevant to at least some justices can be found in the Supreme Court's 2002 decision in *Atkins v. Virginia*. In holding that executions of mentally retarded criminals are "cruel and unusual punishments" prohibited by the Eighth Amendment, Justice Stevens supported the decision of six justices by noting that "within the world community, the imposition of the death penalty for crimes committed by mentally retarded offenders is overwhelmingly disapproved."[175]

### 3. National Human Rights Institutions

In addition to the role of constitutions, courts, and legislatures, human rights may be protected (or endangered) by an array of human rights institutions. These include national, regional, provincial, and local structures of government; human rights commissions and ombudsmen offices; military forces and internal security forces; and criminal justice, prison, and law enforcement systems. Officials of such institutions have a responsibility to learn about and comply with human rights obligations under both national and international law.

In many countries there are national and local institutions specifically mandated with protecting human rights. National human rights institutions (NHRIs) are generally autonomous, quasi-governmental institutions tasked with advising governments regarding human rights protection, reviewing human rights legislation, preparing human rights reports, and investigating complaints of human rights abuses. NHRIs have played a significant role at the national level in promoting and protecting human rights and in encouraging public awareness of those rights. The majority of NHRIs take the form of human rights commissions and ombudsmen. There are also some specialized NHRIs that function to protect the rights of particular vulnerable groups, such as ethnic and linguistic minorities, indigenous populations, children, refugees, or women.

At a 1991 UN-sponsored meeting of NHRI representatives, a detailed set of principles on the status of national institutions was developed. These principles, commonly known as the Paris Principles, were subsequently endorsed by the Commission on Human Rights and the General Assembly, and have become the foundation for the establishment and operation of NHRIs. The Paris Principles state that national institutions should be given as broad a mandate as possible that is legitimized by a constitution or by legislation. Some of the specific tasks described by the Paris Principles include submission of recommendations or reports, harmonization of national legislation with the international human rights instruments, encouragement of ratification of human rights instruments, contribution to state reports submitted to UN bodies and committees, and assistance with the formulation of human rights education programs. In addition, the Paris Principles emphasize the necessity for NHRIs to be as autonomous from the government as possible, to represent the pluralist interests of civil society, and to be given adequate powers of investigation, as well as sufficient resources.[176]

There have been several world and regional conferences at which a growing interest in the creation and strengthening of NHRIs has been expressed. Most prominently, the Vienna Declaration and Programme of Action, which was adopted at 1993 World Conference on Human Rights, stated that

Governments, the United Nations system as well as other multilateral organizations are urged to increase considerably the resources allocated to programmes aiming at the establishment and strengthening of national legislation, national institutions and related infrastructures which uphold the rule of law and democracy, electoral assistance, human rights awareness through training, teaching and education, popular participation and civil society.[177]

Some NHRIs have been more effective than others. In general, NHRIs have been most successful if they are independent from the executive branch, are well funded, concentrate on key problem areas (as opposed to focusing only on whatever complaints may be submitted), and achieve broad public legitimacy. The role of the typical human rights institution is to investigate actions by the executive branch of government that may have violated human rights. Since NHRIs are established by the government, it is important to put in place safeguards to ensure that these institutions can act independently. Some NHRIs have been criticized for not devoting sufficient effort to matters concerning economic, social, and cultural rights—such as alleviating extreme poverty and ensuring equal access to education, housing, and health care.

Over eighty nations have established an office of ombudsman or an institution possessing characteristics of the nineteenth-century Swedish model in which an independent official receives complaints or acts on his or her own motion to investigate the basis of any claim against the government as to which other remedies have been exhausted. Typically, the institution with ombudsman functions promptly makes non-enforceable—but very influential—recommendations to the government for resolution of the problem. Such an institution may be known not only as an ombudsman, but may be a parliamentary committee or commissioner, an individual legislator with similar functions, a public defender, a public or citizen's advocate, and so on. In a number of countries the institution with ombudsman functions has been expressly given a human rights mandate.

In some countries national and local human rights institutions focus on discrimination in regard to education, employment, housing, obtaining credit, public accommodations, and public services. They process claims by individuals pertaining to discrimination on the basis of color, creed, disability, family status, gender, marital status, national origin, receipt of public assistance, race, sexual orientation, victims of domestic abuse, and discrimination due to the fact that the individual petitioned for assistance from a human rights commission. These national and local human rights commissions may have the authority to adjudicate claims, assess responsibility, impose sanctions, or offer other relief. Some commissions may also provide mediation services for discrimination claims or have the authority to bring claims in court.

*See also*: International Institutions and Procedures, Introduction to Human Rights as Part of International Law, Nongovernmental Organizations, Regional Institutions and Procedures

*Further Reading:*

Mirna E. Adjami, *African Courts, International Law, and Comparative Case Law: Chimera or Emerging Human Rights Jurisprudence*, 24 Mich. J. Int'l L. 103 (2002).

Ibrahim Al-Wahab, The Swedish Institution of Ombudsman: An Instrument of Human Rights (1979).

African Commission on Human and Peoples' Rights, Resolution on Granting Observer Status to National Human Rights Institutions in Africa (1998).

Amnesty International, National Human Rights Institutions: Amnesty International's Recommendations for Effective Protection and Promotion of Human Rights (2001).

*Atkins v. Virginia*, 536 US 304 (2002).

Anne Bayefsky, International Human Rights Law: Use in Canadian Charter of Human Rights and Freedoms Litigation (1992).

Thomas Buergenthal, *Modern Constitutions and Human Rights Treaties*, 36 Colum. J. Transnat'l L. 211 (1997).

Brian Burdekin & Anne Gallagher, *The United Nations and National Human Rights Institutions*, in International Human Rights Monitoring Mechanisms: Essays in Honour of Jacob Th. Möller (Gudmundur Alfredsson et al. eds., 2001).

Sonia Cardenas, *Emerging Global Actors: The United Nations and National Human Rights Institutions*, 9 Global Governance 23 (2003).

Committee on Economic, Social and Cultural Rights, General Comment 10, the Role of National Human Rights Institutions in the Protection of Economic, Social and Cultural Rights (Nineteenth session, 1998), U.N. Doc. E/1999/22 at 18 (1998).

Close to Home: Case Studies of Human Rights Work (Larry Cox & Dorothy Q. Thomas eds., 2004).

Committee on the Rights of the Child, General Comment No. 2, the Role of Independent National Human Rights Institutions in the Promotion and Protection of the Rights of the Child (Thirty-second session, 2003), U.N. Doc. CRC/GC/2002/2 (2002).

Compilation of Documents and Materials on National Human Rights Institutions for the Promotion and Protection of Human Rights, U.N. Doc. ST/]HR/NONE/2001/86 HR/NONE/2001/86 (2001).

Council on International Human Rights Policy, Performance and Legitimacy: National Human Rights Institutions (2000).

The Danish Ombudsman (Hans Gammeltoft-Hansen & Flemming Axmark eds.,1995).

Brice Dickson, *Ireland's Human Rights Commission*, 36 Irish Jurist 265 (2001).
David Feldman, *Human Rights and International Law and Institutions*, in Common Law, Common Values, Common Rights 85 (2000).
Mehmet Semih Gemalmaz, *Constitution, Ombudsperson and Human Rights Chamber in "Bosnia Herzegovina,"* 17 Netherlands Q. Hum. Rts. 277 (1999).
Mario Gomez, *Social Economic Rights and Human Rights Commissions*, 17 Hum. Rts. Q. 155 (1995).
Mario Gomez, *Sri Lanka's New Human Rights Commission*, 20 Hum. Rts. Q. 281 (1998).
Brigid Hadfield, *The Human Rights Commission and the Civic Forum in the Devolved Northern Ireland*, 7 Eur. Pub. L. 143 (2001).
John Hatchard, National Human Rights Institutions: Best Practice (2001).
Human Rights Commissions and Ombudsman Offices: National Experiences Throughout the World (Kamal Hossain et al. eds., 2000).
International Human Rights Law in the Commonwealth Caribbean (A. D. Byre & B. Y. Byfeild eds., 1991).
The International Ombudsman Anthology (Linda C. Reif ed., 1999).
Jeno Kaltenbach, The Role of Ombudspersons and National Human Rights Institutions in the Protection and the Promotion of the Rights of Persons Belonging to National, Ethnic, Religious and Linguistic Minorities: Background Paper, U.N. Doc. [ST]/HR/PRAGUE/SEM.4/2003/BP.3; HR/PRAGUE/SEM.4/2003/BP.3 (2003).
Morten Kjaerum, *National Human Rights Institutions Implementing Human Rights*, in Human Rights and Criminal Justice for the Downtrodden: Essays in Honour of Asbjørn Eide 631–53 (Morten Bergsmo ed., 2003).
C. Raj Kumar, *National Human Rights Institutions: Good Governance Perspectives on Institutionalization of Human Rights*, 19 Am. U. Int'l L. Rev. 259 (2004).
Anthony Lester, *Parliamentary Scrutiny of Human Rights under the Human Rights Act 1998*, 2002 Eur. Hum. Rts. L. Rev. 432.
Stephen Livingstone, *The Northern Ireland Human Rights Commission*, 22 Fordham Int'l L.J. 1465 (1999).
Paul Mageean & Martin O'Brien, *From the Margins to the Mainstream: Human Rights and the Good Friday Agreement*, 22 Fordham Int'l L.J. 1499 (1999).
Stephen P. Marks, *The New Cambodian Constitution: From Civil War to a Fragile Democracy*, 26 Colum. Hum. Rts. L. Rev. 45 (1994).
Vincent Meerabux, *The Ombudsman and Human Rights Institutions in the Caribbean: an Overview*, 25 Comm. L. Bull. 79 (1999).
[*Murray v. Schooner*] *Charming Betsy*, 6 U.S. (2 Cranch) 34 (1804).
Willy Mutunga & Alamin Mazrui, *Rights Integration in an Institutional Context: The Experience of the Kenya Human Rights Commission*, 8 Buff. Hum. Rts. L. Rev. 123 (2002).
National Human Rights Institutions: A Handbook on the Establishment and Strengthening of National Institutions for the Promotion and Protection of Human Rights, U.N. Doc. HR/P/PT/4, U.N. Sales No. E.95.XIV.2 (1995).
National Institutions for the Promotion and Protection of Human Rights: Note by the Secretariat, U.N. Doc. E/CN.4/2002/196 (2002).
National Institutions for the Promotion and Protection of Human Rights: Report of the Secretary-General, U.N. Doc. E/CN.4/2003/110 (2002).
National Institutions for the Promotion and Protection of Human Rights, Report of the Secretary-General, U.N. Doc. A/58/261 (2003).
National Institutions for the Promotion and Protection of Human Rights: Report of the Secretary-General, U.N. Doc. E/CN.4/2004/60 (2004).

Gerald L. Neuman, *Human Rights and Constitutional Rights: Harmony and Dissonance*, 55 Stan. L. Rev. 1863 (2003).

The New Zealand Bill of Rights (Paul Rishworth, Grant Huscroft, Scott Optican & Richard Mahoney eds., 2003).

Charles Norchi, *The National Human Rights Commission of India as a Value-Creating Institution*, in Human Rights: Positive Policies in Asia and the Pacific Rim 113 (John D. Montgomery ed., 1998).

Office of the High Commissioner for Human Rights, National Institutions for the Promotion and Protection of Human Rights, Fact Sheet No. 19 (1993).

J. Oloka-Onyango, *Beyond the Rhetoric: Reinvigorating the Struggle for Economic and Social Rights in Africa*, 26 Cal. W. Int'l L.J. 1 (1995).

*The Paquete Habana*, 175 U.S. 677 (1900).

Principles Relating to the Status and Functioning of National Institutions [Paris Principles], G.A. Res. 48/134, U.N. ESCOR, Annex (1993).

Rights and Freedoms, The New Zealand Bill of Rights Act 1990 and the Human Rights Act 1993 (Grant Huscroft & Paul Rishworth eds., 1995).

Mary Robinson, *From Rhetoric to Reality: Making Human Rights Work*, 2003 E.H.R.L.R. 1.

The Role of the Judiciary in the Protection of Human Rights (Eugene Cotran & Adel Omar Sherif eds., 1997).

Anna Rotman, Note, *Benin's Constitutional Court: An Institutional Model for Guaranteeing Human Rights*, 17 Harv. Hum. Rts. J. 281 (2004).

George Slyz, *International Law in National Courts*, 28 N.Y.U. J. Int'l L. & Pol. 65 (1996).

Vijayashri Sripati, *India's National Human Rights Commission: A Shackled Commission?* 18 B.U. Int'l L.J. 1 (2000).

Strengthening Ombudsman and Human Rights Institutions in Commonwealth Small and Island States: The Caribbean Experience (Victor Ayeni, Linda Reif, & Hayden Thomas eds., 2000).

Mary Ellen Tsekos, *Human Rights Institutions in Africa*, Hum. Rts. Brief, Winter 2002, at 21.

Vienna Declaration and Programme of Action, U.N. GAOR World Conference on Human Rights, 23d Sess., 157th mtg., U.N. Doc. A/CONF.157/23 (1993).

V. Vijayakumar, *The Working of the National Human Rights Commission: A Perspective*, in Human Rights in India: Historical, Social and Political Perspectives 211 (Chiranjivi J. Nirmal ed., 1999).

Amanda Whiting, *Situating Suhakam: Human Rights Debates and Malaysia's National Human Rights Commission*, 39 Stan. J. Int'l L. 59 (2003).

The Work and Practice of Ombudsman and National Human Rights Institutions: Articles and Studies (Lisbeth Garly Andersen ed., 2002).

A. H. Young, *Keeping the Courts at Bay: The Canadian Human Rights Commission and Its Counterparts in Britain and Northern Ireland: Some Comparative Lessons*, 43 Univ. Toronto L.J. 65 (1993).

*Links to Consult:*

http://www.oefre.unibe.ch/law/icl/index.html
http://www.asiapacificforum.net
http://www.hrdc.net/nhris
http://www.hrw.org/reports/2001/africa
http://www.ichrp.org/index.html?project=102

http://www.nhri.net/default.asp
http://www.nhri.net/pdf/nhribook.pdf
http://www.ohchr.org/english/about/publications/docs/fs19.htm
http://www.spainemb.org/information/constitucionin.htm
http://www1.umn.edu/humanrts/crc/comment2.htm
http://www1.umn.edu/humanrts/instree/nhri-denmark2003.html

# D. Truth and Reconciliation Commissions

During a transition from a period of widespread violence and repression to a society in which democracy and the rule of law prevail, a number of countries have confronted the difficult legacy of human rights abuse through efforts to promote reconciliation and justice. In countries as diverse as Bosnia and Herzegovina, Peru, Sierra Leone, and East Timor (Timor-Leste), government officials, nongovernmental organization (NGO) advocates, and the United Nations have responded to past human rights violations by establishing truth-seeking initiatives. These have at times helped to prosecute individual perpetrators as well as provide reparations to victims.

As of 2006, Truth and Reconciliation Commissions—also known as truth commissions—have been established in order to facilitate the process of reconciliation in societies that have been divided during periods of violence and grave human rights abuses. The principal objectives of such commissions are to give individuals who have suffered serious human rights violations an opportunity to communicate their experiences to persons in authority and to receive collective acknowledgment of responsibility for their suffering. These temporary commissions focus on a defined period of time during which the abuses occurred and typically conclude with the publication of a report on their findings.

Since 1973, truth commissions have been established by presidential decree, legislative decision, NGOs, or the United Nations. Typically, a strong mandate is necessary in order to access sensitive files, subpoena powerful political figures, and protect truth commission members during the investigative process. The mandate must also properly define the truth commission's scope, allowing inquiries into the relevant time period, areas of the country, and types of acts to be investigated. Examples of nations where truth commissions have been established by presidential decree are Argentina, Bolivia, Chad, Chile, Ecuador, Germany, Ghana, Haiti, Malawi, Nepal, Nigeria, Panama, Peru, the Philippines, Serbia and Montenegro, South Africa, South Korea, Sri Lanka, Uganda, Uruguay, and Zimbabwe. The truth commissions of El Salvador, Guatemala, and Sierra Leone were created by parliamentary order, but were authorized by peace agreements negotiated between those governments and opposition forces. Other truth commissions have been established by the UN, as in El Salvador, Guatemala, and Timor-Leste; by the legislature, as in Liberia; and by NGOs, as was the case in Brazil.

The first truth commission took place in Uganda in 1974. Its mandate was to investigate and report on the 308 disappearances that occurred during the government of Idi Amin. Since then, and including four commissions proposed in 2004, there have been fourteen truth commissions proposed or established in Latin America, fourteen in Africa, six in Asia, two in Europe and Central Asia, and one in the Middle East and Northern Africa. By decade, the number of truth commissions increased from one in the 1970s to six in the 1980s, thirteen in the 1990s, and seventeen from 2000 to 2006. Each commission has built upon previous models, which attempted to improve and elaborate the truth-seeking and reconciliation process.

The ways in which truth commissions are created and composed and the scope of their activities vary greatly. Some commissions are comprised of prominent individuals in the country, as in the case of Argentina. Other commissions are entirely or partially composed of distinguished persons from other countries, for example, in El Salvador and Timor-Leste. International commissions have both strengths and weaknesses. On the one hand, they can provide impartiality and objectivity. On the other hand, their recommendations may not always be accepted and their activities may be regarded as an imposition of the international community's will on the country concerned. National commissions, in comparison, may have better contextual understanding of the situation in the country, but their members are sometimes accused of bias. Mixed commissions may draw on the advantages of both the national and international commissions. The composition of a commission is determined by its establishing entity.

In some instances, NGOs have created their own truth commissions—particularly when governments have failed to act. For example, the archbishop of São Paulo, with the support of the NGO the World Council of Churches, investigated human rights abuses under Brazil's military government after the government refused the public's demand for a formal inquiry. Moreover, the International Center for Transitional Justice (ICTJ) was established as an NGO in March 2001 to propagate truth commissions and has since helped disseminate the expertise developed in previous commissions to new efforts. The ICTJ is currently working in many countries, including Ghana, Guatemala, Liberia, Northern Ireland, Peru, Sierra Leone, South Africa, Sri Lanka, Timor-Leste, the United States, and the former Yugoslavia. Minnesota Advocates for Human Rights is assisting the Liberian Truth and Reconciliation Commission by collecting information from thousands of Liberian refugees throughout the United States.

In pursuit of reconciliation, truth commissions usually strive to investigate past human rights abuses, provide an official forum where victims and perpetrators alike can tell their stories and offer evidence, and prepare an authoritative report that documents the events, makes conclusions, and suggests ways in which similar atrocities can be avoided in the future. The final reports of a truth commission are almost always made public and contain the commission's observations, conclusions, and recommendations. The final report does not seek to establish the "truth"—an arguably impossible task. Rather, it formally documents the truth in such a way that it must be acknowledged by the state. The publication of the final report establishes the documented events as part of the state's historical record, which, along with the report's recommendations, attempts to prevent reoccurrences. The final report may also name those responsible for or involved in the human rights violations, although at times may refrain from doing so for fear of backlash or even a return to the violence of the past.

Public hearings held by truth commissions serve the three purposes of furthering information collection, permitting individual victims to tell their stories, and enabling national catharsis. Some truth commissions entice public testimony from human rights violators by offering the possibility of amnesty in exchange—collecting valuable information in the process. The hearings, sometimes publicly broadcast throughout the country, allow individuals affected by human rights violations to tell their stories of grief and suffering—often for the first time. Although truth commissions do not normally have the power to prosecute, they can make recommendations for prosecution as was possible in Peru and South Africa. Truth commissions, however, usually do not identify individuals responsible for human rights abuses, and some perpetrators have been granted amnesty. For example, the South African Truth and Reconciliation Commission was authorized to grant amnesty to those perpetrators who provided a full account of their wrongdoing. The issue of amnesty is extremely controversial because amnesty may give past and future perpetrators impunity for their misconduct. The decision whether to grant amnesty calls into question the purpose of truth commissions and whether there is a duty to prosecute offenders. Amnesty considerations aside, public hearings force a country to confront and accept its past, and provide truth commissions with invaluable data from which it can construct its final report.

A truth commission may also make recommendations for reparations to be given to victims, which usually take the form of cash payments, pensions, free access to health care and psychiatric treatment, or public memorials and national remembrance days. Due to governmental resource constraints, however, reparations may not involve substantial payments of compensation. There have, however, been some efforts to seek compensation from the perpetrators rather than relying entirely on the government, as was the case in Argentina.

Of the thirty-six truth commissions, the truth commissions in Argentina, Chile, and South African have been the most visible models. The National Commission of the Disappeared of Argentina was created by Argentinean President Raúl Alfonsín in 1983 to address the disappearances of more than 9,000 individuals during the period of military rule from 1976 to 1983, known as the "dirty war." The commission was comprised of thirteen members. Ten were selected by the President and six were to be nominated by the two houses of the legislature, but only the chamber of deputies responded by nominating three members. One of the ten members selected by President Alfonsín was a U.S. citizen who had previously worked in Argentina helping people during the dirty war. The commission heard testimony from thousands of individuals, conducted its own investigations, and in 1984 produced a final report, "Nunca Más: Informe de la Comisión Nacional sobre la Desaparición de Personas," that implicated more than 1,300 military officers.

In 1985 the former leaders of the Argentine military junta, General Jorge Videla and Admiral Emilio Massera, were tried and sentenced to life in prison by the Buenos Aires Federal Appeals Court for their role in the atrocities. The convictions stood as a testament to the role truth commissions could play in holding human rights violators accountable. Unfortunately, justice was short-lived as both Videla and Massera were pardoned by President Alfonsín's successor, Carlos Menem, in 1990. Also in 1990, however, the Argentine Congress passed a law establishing a pension for the relatives of the disappeared (*los desaparecidos*), which was equal to 75 percent of the minimum lifetime salary. Some families were reluctant to claim these funds because they did not want to acknowledge that their relatives had died. In 1991 the government enacted another law enabling individuals who were detained without trial during the period 1976–79 to receive significant compensation. Many victims have been unable to claim this money, however, because of their inability to provide the required evidence that proves they were detained. In 1995 the Federal Court of Appeals of Buenos Aires opened its first "truth trial," to ascertain the fate of the victims of the dirty war. In 1998 General Jorge Videla was again detained and investigations were initiated because the judges ruled that kidnapping of babies from people detained or "disappeared" during the dirty war was outside the scope of the various laws and decrees (Ley de Punto Final [Full Stop Law], Due Obedience Law, and various pardons) that sought to absolve perpetrators of responsibility. Judges also ordered the restitution of the sons and daughters of the "disappeared" to their biological families.

The military dictatorship that ruled Chile from 1973 until 1990 resulted in massive human rights abuses causing thousands of deaths, disappearances, torture, and arbitrary arrests. In 1990, Chilean President Patricio Aylwin established the National Commission for Truth and Reconciliation, comprised of eight distinguished Chileans. The Commission sought to provide an officially sanctioned forum in which the victims and relatives could give testimony. Although seeking to gain government acknowledgment of its responsibility for the violations, the Commission faced significant obstacles to the complete exposure of "truth," primarily due to the continued presence of Augusto Pinochet as Commander-in-Chief of the Chilean Army. The Commission published its report in 1991 and proposed reparations procedures, which were later implemented by the Congress, but the Commission stopped short of recommending individuals for prosecution. Recent developments in Chile, however, suggest that barriers to the exposure of individual responsibility for human rights violations may be diminishing over time. For example, after many decades, the Chilean Supreme Court ruled that Pinochet could be tried for his involvement in several disappearances and deaths and he was placed under house arrest.

The Commission of Truth and Reconciliation of South Africa is considered to be another very visible model for truth commissions. The South African Parliament established the Commission in 1995 to examine the human rights violations associated with the *apartheid* era, which gripped South Africa from 1960 to 1994. The Commission was authorized to have seventeen members and was allowed no more than two persons who were not South African citizens to be appointed as commissioners. Ultimately, all members of the Commission were South African nationals, although one or two were born outside of the country. The Commission was well-funded and had a mandate to hold public hearings, consider applications for amnesty, and determine necessary reparations for victims. The public hearings, held across South Africa, were successful in collecting information and allowing the nation to acknowledge more than thirty years of *apartheid*. The Commission's power to grant amnesty in exchange for full disclosure by applicants was highly controversial, but was considered politically necessary in order for the Commission to come into existence. In any case, the Commission found that most perpetrators failed to provide a full account of their wrongdoing and thus the Commission refused more than 85 percent of immunity applications.

*See also*: Genocide, War Crimes, Crimes Against Humanity, Crimes Against Peace, International Criminal Procedures, Nongovernmental Organizations

*Further Reading:*

Amnesty International, Argentina: The Right to the Full Truth, AI Index: AMR 13/03/95 (1995).
Amnesty International, Ethiopia: Accountability Past and Present: Human Rights in Transition, AI Index: AFR 25/06/95 (1995).
Amnesty International, Guatemala: All the Truth, Justice for All, AI Index: AMR 34/02/98 (1998)
Christine Bell, Colm Campbell, Fionnuala Ní Aoláin, and Terry Bell, *Justice Discourses in Transition*, 13 Social Leg. Stud. 305 (2004).
David A. Crocker, *Reckoning with Past Wrongs: A Normative Framework*, 13 Ethics and Int'l Aff. 47 (1999).
Joan Fitzpatrick, *Nothing But the Truth? Transitional Regimes Confront the Past*, 16 Mich. J. Int'l L. 713 (1995).
María José Guembe, The Argentinean Experience with Economic Reparations for Serious Human Rights Violations (2005).
Priscilla B. Hayner, *Fifteen Truth Commissions—1974 to 1994: A Comparative Study*, 16 Hum. Rts. Q. 600 (1994).
Luc Huyse, *Justice After Transition: On the Choices Successor Elites Make in Dealing with the Past*, 20 L. & Social Inquiry 51 (1995).
Impunity and Human Rights in International Law and Practice (Naomi Roht-Arriaza ed., 1995).
Neil J. Kritz, *A Review of Accountability Mechanisms for Mass Violations of Human Rights*, 59 Law & Contemp. Prob. 127 (Fall 1996).
Jamie Malamud-Goti, *Transitional Governments in the Breach: Why Punish State Criminals*, 12 Hum. Rts. Q. 1 (1990).
Martha Minow, Between Vengeance and Forgiveness: Facing History After Genocide and Mass Violence (1998).
Aryeh Neier, War Crimes: Brutality, Genocide, Terror, and the Struggle for Justice (1998).
Fionnuala Ní Aoláin, The Politics of Force: Conflict Management and State Violence in Northern Ireland (2000).
Carlos S. Nino, *The Duty to Punish Past Abuses of Human Rights Put into Context: The Case of Argentina*, 100 Yale L.J. 2619 (1991).
Diane F. Orentlicher, *Settling Accounts: The Duty to Prosecute Human Rights Violations of a Prior Regime*, 100 Yale L.J. 2537 (1991).
Mike Oquaye, *Human Rights and the Transition to Democracy Under the PNDC in Ghana*, 17 Hum. Rts. Q. 556 (1995).
Jo M. Pasqualucci, *The Whole Truth and Nothing But the Truth: Truth Commissions, Impunity and the Inter-American Human Rights System*, 12 B.U. Int'l L.J. 321 (1994).
Past Imperfect: Dealing With the Past in Northern Ireland and Societies in Transition (Brandon Hamber ed., 1998).
Margaret Popkin & Naomi Roht-Arriaza, *Truth as Justice: Investigatory Commissions in Latin America*, 20 L. & Social Inquiry 79 (1995).
Margaret Popkin & Nehal Bhuta, *Latin American Amnesties in Comparative Perspective: Can the Past be Buried?* 13 Ethics & Int'l Aff. 100 (1999).
Steven R. Ratner & Jason S. Abrams, Accountability For Human Rights Atrocities in International Law: Beyond the Nuremberg Legacy (1997).
Jeremy Sarkin, Carrots and Sticks: The TRC and the South African Amnesty Process (2004).

Kathryn Sikkink and Carrie Booth Walling, Truth Commissions (Draft July 14, 2004).

Symposium, *Transitions to Democracy and the Rule of Law,* 5 Am. U. J. Int'l L. & Pol'y 965 (1990).

Ruti Teitel, Transitional Justice (2000).

Transitional Justice: How Emerging Democracies Reckon with Former Regimes (vols. I–III) (Neil J. Kritz ed., 1995).

Transitional Justice and the Rule of Law in New Democracies (James McAdams ed., 1997).

David Weissbrodt and Paul W. Fraser, *Book Review: Report of the Chilean National Commission on Truth and Reconciliation,* 14 Human Rights Q. 601 (1992).

José Zalaquett, *Balancing Ethical Imperatives and Political Constraints: The Dilemma of New Democracies Confronting Past Human Rights Violations,* 43 Hastings L.J. 1425 (1992).

*Links to Consult:*

www.doj.gov.za/trc/
www.ictj.org
www.truthcommission.org
www.usip.org/library/truth.html#background

# E. Nongovernmental Organizations (NGOs)

There are thousands of nongovernmental organizations engaged in the promotion and protection of human rights at the international, regional, national, and local levels. They engage in development of standards, monitoring, advocacy, campaigning, education, conciliation, and assistance to victims.

From the beginning of the United Nations, NGOs were active in lobbying for human rights standards. The drafters of the UN Charter benefitted from the lobbying of a dozen or more human rights organizations—most based in the United States—that successfully advocated for human rights provisions in Articles 1 and 55 of the Charter. NGOs participated in the drafting of the Universal Declaration of Human Rights, the two Human Rights Covenants, and all subsequent human rights treaties and other instruments. Their expertise as to particular subjects and their perseverance in the drafting process have made them very influential in preparing treaties, such as the Convention on the Rights of the Child.

In order to be effective in advocating for human rights standards, NGOs must be informed of human rights conditions and applicable legal principles. NGOs receive information from human rights victims, families, and friends; interview witnesses; visit places of detention, refugee camps, camps for internally displaced persons, hospitals, morgues, and psychiatric institutions; examine injuries and physical evidence; videotape incidents or distribute video cameras to those willing to videotape abuses; disinter and help perform autopsies on the bodies of persons who have been killed; observe events such as elections, trials, and demonstrations; perform tests as to housing or job discrimination; undertake meetings with government officials; monitor the conduct of corporations or other non-state actors; assess governmental budgets to determine how they will provide for children, women, or other human rights concerns; pursue legal research; and formulate recommendations for corrective action.

Human rights NGOs work toward the improvement of human rights situations in a number of ways. They meet with or lobby governments and international governmental organizations, testify in favor of legislation, issue media statements and reports, publish newsletters, post material on websites, prepare videotapes, initiate law suits, file *amicus curiae* and other briefs in court, promote international tribunals and truth commissions, petition or provide information to UN human rights bodies, and encourage investors, banks, universities, and city councils to avoid investing in companies that abuse human rights.

NGOs also mobilize their members and others to support and promote human rights campaigns. This is done, for example, by organizing individuals and groups to write letters, telegrams, faxes, emails, text messages, and blogs; getting petitions signed and submitted; running listservs; posting information on websites; holding meetings, teach-ins, seminars, and other discussions; distributing leaflets; putting up posters; holding rallies and demonstrations; organizing silent vigils, debates, and mock trials; running film screenings and theater performances; erecting historical monuments to commemorate abuses or resistance; creating museums; and engaging in nonviolent civil disobedience. Some NGOs develop and distribute curricula and educational materials. They might even teach classes and seminars and provide training for teachers, police, prison guards, military officers, and other government officials.

Because of their knowledge of human rights conditions and reputation for impartiality, NGOs may become involved in reconciliation and mediation. They may help to resolve conflicts or other disputes, facilitate negotiations between ethnic communities, develop confidence-building measures, and encourage exchanges of prisoners in the context of armed conflict.

NGOs further assist human rights victims by responding to requests for emergency aid, food aid, food production techniques and tools, housing or emergency shelter, medicine, health care, water, sanitation, protection, and logistics. They provide rehabilitation to torture victims and give psychological care to other human rights survivors. NGOs also help feed and house refugees and displaced persons, provide blankets and other necessities to prisoners, seek compensation for human rights victims, give legal advice and assistance, and accompany persons at risk in traveling to dangerous locations.

Some NGOs are very small—essentially just the lengthened shadow of one individual focusing on a single issue. Others have millions of members in many countries with democratic decision-making procedures and many activities. There is tremendous diversity among human rights NGOs in their structures, activities, and supporters. Most NGOs, however, have a central office or secretariat. International NGOs usually have national sections or chapters in several countries. National NGOs may be located in the country's capital city or other large city. Most NGOs are led by a Secretary-General, Executive Director, or other head officer, who directs the staff and is guided as to policy matters by a board, executive committee, or similar group. Many NGOs make use of volunteers.

There is a complex relationship between the work of local, national, and international NGOs. International NGOs—centered mainly in Geneva, London, New York, Paris, and Washington—often rely upon information and inspiration from grassroots organizations that are aware of local conditions. Local and national organizations are often at greater risk and rely upon international organizations for credibility, support, and access to the media and intergovernmental organizations such as the United Nations.

The United Nations Economic and Social Council (ECOSOC), the International Labor Organization, UNESCO, and several regional organizations have developed consultative arrangements with NGOs. Article 71 of the UN Charter authorizes ECOSOC to make "suitable arrangements for consultation with nongovernmental organizations."[178] In order to participate in the UN Commission on Human Rights—and now the Human Rights Council—NGOs must seek consultative status through the ECOSOC Committee on NGOs, which is comprised of nineteen government representatives. Almost all the human rights procedures of the United Nations rely heavily or exclusively upon information and arguments supplied by NGOs.

Over the last thirty years, there has been a tremendous increase in the number of NGOs that focus on human rights. One way of measuring the growth in the number of NGOs is to note that in 1974 there were about 600 international NGOs in consultative status with ECOSOC; by 2006, there were more than 2,500 international and national NGOs in consultative status.

*See also*: UN Charter-Based Procedures, Human Rights Treaty-based Procedures, Regional Institutions and Procedures, Specialized and Other Agencies, World Conferences

*Further Reading*:

Taj I. Hamad & Frederick A. Swarts, Culture of Responsibility and the Role of NGOs (2003).
William Korey, NGOs and the Universal Declaration of Human Rights: A Curious Grapevine (1998).
NGOs and Human Rights: Promise and Performance (Claude E. Welch, Jr. ed., 2001).
Office of the High Commissioner for Human Rights, Training Manual on Human Rights Monitoring, Professional Training Series No. 7 (2001).
Office of the High Commissioner for Human Rights, Working with the Office

of the United Nations High Commissioner for Human Rights, A Handbook for NGOs (2006).

The Power of Human Rights: International Norms and Domestic Change (Kathryn Sikkink, Thomas Risse, and Stephen C. Ropp eds., 1999).

Kathryn Sikkink and Margaret E. Keck, Activists Beyond Borders: Advocacy Networks in International Politics (1998).

*Links to Consult:*

http://www.newtactics.org
http://www.un.org/esa/coordination/ngo/
http://www1.umn.edu/humanrts/links/ngolinks.html
http://www1.umn.edu/humanrts/links/tortcenters.html

# Part IV
# Conclusion

During 1945, in the wake of a horrific world war in which nearly sixty million persons perished, the community of nations came together to adopt the United Nations Charter. Two of the main objectives of the Charter are the maintenance of peace and the promotion of human rights. Over the past sixty years, the UN authoritatively defined human rights in the Universal Declaration of Human Rights of 1948 and dozens of subsequent treaties and instruments. Essentially, human rights standards allow people to live with dignity as human beings.

At first, the international community focused on the protection of civil and political rights—the right to be free from arbitrary detention, political and religious discrimination, torture, unfair trials, and so on. Since the mid-1980s, however, many nations and human rights advocates have devoted increased attention to strategies for achieving economic, social, and cultural rights. Perhaps now more than ever, human rights have attained an unprecedented level of international legitimacy. At the same time, new challenges have emerged that seek to undercut that legitimacy and the institutions charged with protecting human rights. As the international community—in particular, the government of the United States—becomes more and more enmeshed in the politics and rhetoric of combating terrorism, governments around the world are seeking ways in which to redefine, reinvent, and effectively dilute critical human rights principles, including protections against torture, other ill-treatment, "disappearance," and arbitrary detention. In pursuing their "war on terror," some governments have also taken actions that undercut and delegitimize the institution of the United Nations and the paramountcy of international law.

Given these developments, two key questions arise as to the relevance and potency of human rights today. First, why should activists for justice at home and abroad consider their work from a "human rights" point of view? Simply put, the idea of human rights provides a common language for action. It helps us identify and formulate responses to problems at home and abroad. It also provides a framework to orient the work of government and set minimum standards of achievement. Moreover, a proactive, rights-based approach to issues of social justice enables advocates for adequate housing, women's rights, freedom of expression, and other critical rights to identify a common agenda and gain greater power by working together, rather than competing for attention and resources. Further, as an internationally accepted world-view, a human rights perspective allows advocates to link their work in local communities with action at national and international levels. Ideas and efforts are informed and reinforced by such dynamic synergy.

Second, has progress been achieved in the protection of human rights over the last sixty years? Across the globe, there has been a tremendous evolution of standards. There has been increased recognition of the human rights responsibilities not only of governments but also of non-state actors such as armed opposition groups, individuals, and businesses. For all these actors there has been gradual acceptance of the principle that with power comes responsibility. Some governments and international organizations have significantly improved their procedures for implementing human rights standards. There has been a remarkable increase in the number of human rights advocates and their ability to coordinate work through NGOs. There has also been increased awareness of human rights principles thanks to the efforts of NGOs and educators.

Still, the following examples—responding to matters raised in the preface—reveal that, although some human rights situations have improved, progress is achieved slowly and there remains much to be accomplished.

- Myanmar's (Burma's) democracy leader, Aung San Suu Kyi, continues to be one of several political prisoners held in Myanmar under an administrative detention law. On November 12, 2004, more than twenty Nobel Laureates demanded the unconditional release of Aung San Suu Kyi from house arrest, strongly urging the government to restore civil and political rights by releasing Aung San Suu Kyi and her supporters.

- There have been several trials of low-ranking soldiers involved in torture at Iraq's Abu Ghraib prison, and some of the convicted have been subject to military punishment. These measures, however, represent only the first steps toward accountability for abuses against detainees by U.S. forces, and it remains to be seen if those at higher levels who approved or condoned torture and ill-treatment against detainees will also be brought to justice.

- Almost a quarter century after the assassination of El Salvador's Archbishop Oscar Romero, a California federal court in September 2004 found former Salvadoran Air Force Captain Alvaro Rafael Saravia liable under the U.S. Alien Tort Claims Act (ATCA) for the 1980 murder. The $10 million judgment in *Doe v. Saravia*[1] marks the first occasion in which anyone has been held responsible for one of the most notorious assassinations in Latin American history. Additionally, on June 29, 2004, the U.S. Supreme Court in *Sosa v. Alvarez-Machain*,[2] while rejecting the petitioner's specific claim, upheld the use of the ATCA as an important measure to promote accountability for serious human rights violations.

• Major progress toward establishing democratic institutions has taken place in Central and South America even as governments and NGOs address past injustices resulting from massive human rights violations and deal with current concerns.

• The Statute of the International Criminal Tribunal for the Former Yugoslavia (ICTY) of 1993 considered rape a crime against humanity, marking the first time that rape had been explicitly codified as a crime within the jurisdiction of an international court. Building upon this precedent, the Rome Statute of the International Criminal Court, which came into force in 2002, confirmed that rape, sexual slavery, enforced prostitution, forced pregnancy, enforced sterilization, or any other form of sexual violence constitute crimes against humanity and war crimes.

• In 1992, the International Labor Organization (ILO) established the International Programme on the Elimination of Child Labor (IPEC). IPEC has developed partnerships in nearly ninety countries. More than 140,000 children have directly benefitted from IPEC's work to combat the worst forms of child labor. Across the globe, however, there remain more than 150 million children who are employed in hazardous conditions.

• Since its founding in 1950, the UN High Commissioner for Refugees (UNHCR) has helped an estimated fifty million refugees from more than 116 countries restart their lives in countries where they can live free from persecution.

• National courts and governments have become engaged in the struggle against HIV/AIDS by turning the international right to health into an enforceable norm. For example, on April 4, 2002, the Constitutional Court of South Africa used international right to health principles and the South African Constitution to sustain a trial court order to the national and provincial governments to make a medicine available to pregnant women with HIV for the prevention of mother-to-child transmission of HIV. The government of South Africa had refused to provide

368  Conclusion

this very inexpensive treatment to women with HIV. The South African courts decided that the right to health required the government to change its policies and protect the babies from HIV/AIDS.

- The Declaration on the Rights of Indigenous Peoples, one of the most important set of standards in regard to indigenous peoples and their rights, is currently working its way through the UN system. At its first session in June 2006, the Human Rights Council adopted the document and forwarded it to the General Assembly for adoption. Among many rights, the Declaration recognizes that indigenous peoples have the right to manifest, practice, develop, and teach their spiritual and religious traditions, as well as to maintain, protect, and have access in privacy to their religious and cultural sites.

- The Committee on Economic, Social and Cultural Rights has achieved some progress on the issues of adequate housing and forced evictions in a number of countries. For instance, in 1991 when the government of the Dominican Republic attempted to evict and relocate more than 680 families in a shantytown called Los Alcarrizos, the Committee intervened before the plan could be fully implemented. Since then, the Dominican Republic has reportedly given housing preference to low-income groups, in addition to establishing housing projects in low-income communities.

- In March 2005, the U.S. Supreme Court held that the death penalty for juvenile offenders violated the U.S. Constitution and cited international treaties and standards as well as the laws of other nations to support its decision.

The idea of human rights is clearly gaining currency around the globe. As the language of human rights is increasingly used, however, it is helpful to recall the core features of human rights. Human rights are

> *Inherent*: They do not have to be bought, earned, or inherited. They belong to individuals simply because they are human.
> *Universal*: They are the same for all people, regardless of race, sex, religion, political or other opinions, national or social origins, and other characteristics or status.
> *Inalienable*: They cannot be taken away. They exist even when not upheld.
> *Indivisible*: All humans are entitled to freedom, security, and decent standards of living concurrently.

Conclusion 369

These immutable aspects underscore the promise and power of human rights.

*See also:* Housing, International Criminal Procedures, Torture and Ill-Treatment

*Links to Consult:*

http://hrw.org/english/docs/2005/01/05/usint9945.htm
http://www.humanrightsfirst.org/international_justice/w_context/w_cont_e14.htm
http://www.humanrightsfirst.org/Issues/ATCA/oscar_romero_090904.htm
http://www.ilo.org/public/english/standards/ipec/publ/download/implementation_2004_en.pdf
http://www.ohchr.org/english/issues/indigenous/index.htm
http://www.unhcr.org/
http://www1.umn.edu/humanrts/esc/DOMINICA.htm
http://www1.umn.edu/humanrts/icty/statute.html
http://www1.umn.edu/humanrts/instree/declra.htm
http://www1.umn.edu/humanrts/instree/Rome_Statute_ICC/Rome_ICC_toc.htm l

# Notes

*Part I. Basic Introduction to International Human Rights*

1. Universal Declaration of Human Rights, G.A. res. 217A (III), U.N. Doc A/ 810 at 71 (1948), available at http://www1.umn.edu/humanrts/instree/b1udhr.htm.
2. Charter of the United Nations, June 26, 1945, 59 Stat. 1031, T.S. 993, 3 Bevans 1153, *entered into force* Oct. 24, 1945, available at http://www1.umn.edu/humanrts/instree/aunchart.htm.
3. International Covenant on Economic, Social and Cultural Rights, G.A. res. 2200A (XXI), 21 U.N.GAOR Supp. (No. 16) at 49, U.N. Doc. A/6316 (1966), 993 U.N.T.S. 3, *entered into force* Jan. 3, 1976, available at http://www1.umn.edu/humanrts/instree/b2esc.htm.
4. International Covenant on Civil and Political Rights, G.A. res. 2200A (XXI), 21 U.N. GAOR Supp. (No. 16) at 52, U.N. Doc. A/6316 (1966), 999 U.N.T.S. 171, *entered into force* Mar. 23, 1976, available at http://www1.umn.edu/humanrts/instree/b3ccpr.htm.
5. Articles 92–95, Constitution of the Netherlands, adopted February 17, 1983, available at http://www.oefre.unibe.ch/law/icl/nl00000.html.
6. Human Rights Act 1998, 1998 Ch. 42, available at http://www.hmso.gov.uk/acts/acts1998/19980042.htm.
7. European Convention for the Protection of Human Rights and Fundamental Freedoms, 213 U.N.T.S. 222, *entered into force* Sept. 3, 1953, as amended by Protocols Nos. 3, 5, 8, 11, *entered into force* Sept. 21, 1970, Dec. 20, 1971, Jan. 1, 1990, Nov. 1, 1998 respectively, available at http://www1.umn.edu/humanrts/instree/z17euroco.html.
8. Article 6, U.S. Constitution, available at http://www1.umn.edu/humanrts/education/usconstitution.html.
9. Advisory Opinion on Reservations to the Convention on the Prevention and Punishment of the Crime of Genocide, 1951 I.C.J. 15 (May 28).
10. [European] Convention for the Protection of Human Rights and Fundamental Freedoms, 213 U.N.T.S. 222, *entered into force* Sept. 3, 1953, *as amended by* Protocols Nos. 3, 5, 8, 11, *entered into force* Sept. 21, 1970, Dec. 20, 1971, Jan. 1, 1990, Nov. 1, 1998 respectively, available at http://www1.umn.edu/humanrts/instree/z17euroco.html. European Convention for the Prevention of Torture and Inhuman or Degrading Treatment or Punishment, E.T.S. 126, *entered into force* Feb. 1, 1989, available at http://www1.umn.edu/humanrts/euro/z34eurotort.html.
11. Official website of the International Committee of the Red Cross (ICRC), http://www.icrc.org.
12. Geneva Conventions available at http://www1.umn.edu/humanrts/instree/auoy.htm

13. Optional Protocol to the International Covenant on Civil and Political Rights, G.A. res. 2200A (XXI), 21 U.N. GAOR Supp. (No. 16) at 59, U.N. Doc. A/6316 (1966), 999 U.N.T.S. 302, *entered into force* Mar. 23, 1976, available at http://www1.umn.edu/humanrts/instree/b4ccprp1.htm.

14. Convention Against Torture and Other Cruel, Inhuman or Degrading Treatment or Punishment, G.A. res. 39/46, [annex, 39 U.N. GAOR Supp. (No. 51) at 197, U.N. Doc. A/39/51 (1984)], *entered into force* June 26, 1987.

15. Canada Criminal Code (R.S. 1985, c. C-46 ), available at http://laws.justice.gc.ca/en/C-46/

16. Criminal Justice Act 1988, 1988 c. 33, available at http://www.legislation.hmso.gov.uk/acts/acts1988/Ukpga_19880033_en_1.htm.

17. Official website of the International Criminal Tribunal for the Former Yugoslavia, http://www.un.org/icty.

18. Official website of the International Criminal Tribunal for Rwanda, http://www.ictr.org.

19. Rome Statute of the International Criminal Court, 2187 U.N.T.S. 3, *entered into force* July 1, 2002.

20. *Prosecution v. Refik Saric*, Danish High Court, Third Chamber, Eastern Division, Nov. 25, 1994.

21. *Prosecution v. Darko Knezevic*, Sup. Ct. Neth., 11 Nov. 1997.

22. *See* Human Rights Watch, "The Pinochet Precedent: How Victims Can Pursue Human Rights Criminals Abroad," available at http://www.hrw.org/campaigns/chile98/precedent.htm.

23. Official website for the Special Court for Sierra Leone, http://www.sc-sl.org.

24. Available at http://www.wsu.edu/~dee/MESO/CODE.HTM (law as a means of preventing the strong from oppressing the weak).

25. An excellent summary and analysis of the philosophical roots of modern human rights is Jerome J. Shestack, *The Jurisprudence of Human Rights*, in Human Rights in International Law: Legal and Policy Issues (Theodor Meron, ed., 1984), 1: 69.

26. Magna Carta (Eng., 1215), available at http://www1.umn.edu/humanrts/education/magnacarta.html.

27. English Bill of Rights, 1689, An Act Declaring the Rights and Liberties of the Subject, and Settling the Succession of the Crown (Bill of Rights), 1689, 1 W. & M., c. 2 (Eng.), available at http://www1.umn.edu/humanrts/education/engbillofrights.html.

28. Declaration of Independence (U.S. 1776), available at http://www1.umn.edu/humanrts/education/usdeclaration.html.

29. French Declaration of the Rights of Man and of the Citizen (Aug. 26, 1789), available at http://www1.umn.edu/humanrts/education/frdeclaration.html.

30. Available at http://www1.umn.edu/humanrts/education/usbillofrights.html.

31. Official website of the Anti-Slavery Society, http://www.antislavery.org.

32. Official website of the International Committee of the Red Cross (ICRC), http://www.icrc.org.

33. Available at http://www.icrc.org/IHL.nsf/0/.87a3bb58c1c44f0dc125641a005a06e0?OpenDocument.

34. Available at http://www.yale.edu/lawweb/avalon/lawofwar/lawwar.htm.

35. Available at http://www.yale.edu/lawweb/avalon/wilson14.htm.

36. Available at http://www.yale.edu/lawweb/avalon/imt/menu.htm.
37. Official website of the International Labor Organization (ILO), http://www.ilo.org.
38. "The Four Freedoms"—President Franklin Delano Roosevelt, State of the Union Address [the "Four Freedoms Speech"] (Jan. 6, 1941), 87 Cong. Rec. 44 (1941), available at http://www1.umn.edu/humanrts/education/FDR4freedoms.html.
39. The Atlantic Charter, Joint Declaration by the President and The Prime Minister, Declaration of Principles, Aug. 14, 1941, U.S.-U.K., 55 Stat. app. 1603, available at http://www1.umn.edu/humanrts/education/FDRjointdec.html.
40. Available at http://www.yale.edu/lawweb/avalon/decade/decade03.htm.
41. Available at http://www.yale.edu/lawweb/avalon/imt/proc/imtchart.htm.
42. Available at http://www.yale.edu/lawweb/avalon/imtfem.htm.
43. Control Council Law No. 10, Punishment of Persons Guilty of War Crimes, Crimes Against Peace and Against Humanity, Dec. 20, 1945, *Official Gazette Control Council for Germany* 3 (1946): 50–55, available at http://www1.umn.edu/humanrts/instree/ccno10.htm.
44. Jacob Robinson, Human Rights and Fundamental Freedoms in the Charter of the United Nations: A Commentary, From War to Peace Series 4 at 17 (1946).
45. A.J.C. News Release, June 13, 1945.
46. Preamble, Charter of the United Nations, June 26, 1945, 59 Stat. 1031, T.S. 993, 3 Bevans 1153, *entered into force* Oct. 24, 1945, available at http://www1.umn.edu/humanrts/instree/aunchart.htm.
47. Official website of the U.N. Commission on Human Rights, http://www.ohchr.org/english/bodies/chr/index.htm.
48. Article 2, International Covenant on Economic, Social and Cultural Rights, G.A. res. 2200A (XXI), 21 U.N.GAOR Supp. (No. 16) at 49, U.N. Doc. A/6316 (1966), 993 U.N.T.S. 3, *entered into force* Jan. 3, 1976.

*Part II. Human Rights Categorized by Particular Rights, Responsibilities, and Groups*

1. Universal Declaration of Human Rights, G.A. res. 217A (III), U.N. Doc A/810 at 71 (1948), available at http://www1.umn.edu/humanrts/instree/b1udhr.htm.
2. Charter of the United Nations, June 26, 1945, 59 Stat. 1031, T.S. 993, 3 Bevans 1153, *entered into force* Oct. 24, 1945, available at http://www1.umn.edu/humanrts/instree/aunchart.htm.
3. International Covenant on Economic, Social and Cultural Rights, G.A. res. 2200A (XXI), 21 U.N.GAOR Supp. (No. 16) at 49, U.N. Doc. A/6316 (1966), 993 U.N.T.S. 3, *entered into force* Jan. 3, 1976, available at http://www1.umn.edu/humanrts/instree/b2esc.htm. International Covenant on Civil and Political Rights, G.A. res. 2200A (XXI), 21 U.N. GAOR Supp. (No. 16) at 52, U.N. Doc. A/6316 (1966), 999 U.N.T.S. 171, *entered into force* Mar. 23, 1976, available at http://www1.umn.edu/humanrts/instree/b3ccpr.htm.
4. Official website of the Human Rights Committee: http://www.ohchr.org/english/bodies/hrc/index.htm.

5. Official website of the Committee on Economic, Social and Cultural Rights: http://www.ohchr.org/english/bodies/cescr/index.htm.

6. See Hurst Hannum, *Autonomy, Sovereignty, and Self-Determination* (1992).

7. Charter of the United Nations, June 26, 1945, 59 Stat. 1031, T.S. 993, 3 Bevans 1153, *entered into force* Oct. 24, 1945, available at http://www1.umn.edu/humanrts/instree/aunchart.htm.

8. Legal Consequences of the Construction of a Wall in the Occupied Palestinian Territory (2003–2004), Advisory Opinion, I.C.J. Reports (2004), available at http://www.icj-cij.org/icjwww/idecisions.htm.

9. Committee on the Elimination of Racial Discrimination, General Recommendation 21, The right to self-determination (Forty-eighth session, 1996), U.N. Doc. A/51/18, annex VIII at 125 (1996), *reprinted in* Compilation of General Comments and General Recommendations Adopted by Human Rights Treaty Bodies, U.N. Doc. HRI/GEN/1/Rev.6 at 209 (2003), available at http://www1.umn.edu/humanrts/gencomm/genrexxi.htm.

10. Draft Declaration on the Rights of Indigenous Peoples, U.N. Doc. E/CN.4/Sub.2/1994/2/Add.1 (1994), available at http://www1.umn.edu/humanrts/instree/declra.htm.

11. *Id.*

12. Charter of the United Nations, June 26, 1945, 59 Stat. 1031, T.S. 993, 3 Bevans 1153, *entered into force* Oct. 24, 1945, available at http://www1.umn.edu/humanrts/instree/aunchart.htm.

13. Article 2, Universal Declaration of Human Rights, G.A. res. 217A (III), U.N. Doc A/810 at 71 (1948), available at http://www1.umn.edu/humanrts/instree/b1udhr.htm.

14. Available at http://www1.umn.edu/humanrts/instree/b2esc.htm and http://www1.umn.edu/humanrts/instree/b3ccpr.htm.

15. African [Banjul] Charter on Human and Peoples' Rights, *adopted* June 27, 1981, OAU Doc. CAB/LEG/67/3 rev. 5, 21 I.L.M. 58 (1982), *entered into force* Oct. 21, 1986, available at http://www1.umn.edu/humanrts/instree/z1afchar.htm.

16. American Convention on Human Rights, O.A.S.Treaty Series No. 36, 1144 U.N.T.S. 123 *entered into force* July 18, 1978, *reprinted in* Basic Documents Pertaining to Human Rights in the Inter-American System, OEA/Ser.L.V/II.82 doc.6 rev.1 at 25 (1992), available at http://www1.umn.edu/humanrts/oasinstr/zoas3con.htm.

17. American Declaration of the Rights and Duties of Man, O.A.S. Res. XXX, adopted by the Ninth International Conference of American States (1948), *reprinted in* Basic Documents Pertaining to Human Rights in the Inter-American System, OEA/Ser.L.V/II.82 doc.6 rev.1 at 17 (1992), available at http://www1.umn.edu/humanrts/oasinstr/zoas2dec.htm.

18. Convention for the Protection of Human Rights and Fundamental Freedoms, 213 U.N.T.S. 222, *entered into force* Sept. 3, 1953, *as amended by* Protocols Nos. 3, 5, 8, 11, *entered into force* Sept. 21, 1970, Dec. 20, 1971, Jan. 1, 1990, Nov. 1, 1998 respectively, available at http://www1.umn.edu/humanrts/instree/z17euroco.html.

19. Protocol No. 12 to the Convention for the Protection of Human Rights and Fundamental Freedom, E.T.S. 177, *opened for signature* Apr. 11, 2000, available at http://www1.umn.edu/humanrts/euro/z31prot12.html.

20. *H. A. E. d. J. [name deleted] v. The Netherlands*, Communication No. 297/1988, U.N. Doc. CCPR/C/37/D/297/1988 (1989), available at http://www1.umn.edu/humanrts/undocs/session37/297-1988.html.

21. International Convention on the Elimination of All Forms of Racial Discrimination, G.A. res. 2106 (XX), Annex, 20 U.N. GAOR Supp. (No. 14) at 47, U.N. Doc. A/6014 (1966), 660 U.N.T.S. 195, *entered into force* Jan. 4, 1969, available at http://www1.umn.edu/humanrts/instree/d1cerd.htm.
22. *Id.*, Article 5.
23. *Id.*
24. *Id.*, Article 2. See also Article 4 of the Convention on the Elimination of All Forms of Discrimination Against Women, G.A. res. 34/180, 34 U.N. GAOR Supp. (No. 46) at 193, U.N. Doc. A/34/46, *entered into force* Sept. 3, 1981, available at http://www1.umn.edu/humanrts/instree/e1cedaw.htm.
25. Article 2, International Convention on the Elimination of All Forms of Racial Discrimination, G.A. res. 2106 (XX), Annex, 20 U.N. GAOR Supp. (No. 14) at 47, U.N. Doc. A/6014 (1966), 660 U.N.T.S. 195, *entered into force* Jan. 4, 1969, available at http://www1.umn.edu/humanrts/instree/d1cerd.htm.
26. *Gratz v. Bollinger*, 123 S.Ct. 2411 (2003), available at http://caselaw.lp.findlaw.com/scripts/getcase.pl?court=US&vol=000&invol=02-516.
27. *Grutter v. Bollinger*, 123 S.Ct. 2325 (2003), available at http://caselaw.lp.findlaw.com/scripts/getcase.pl?court=US&vol=000&invol=02-241.
28. Article 3, Universal Declaration of Human Rights, G.A. res. 217A (III), U.N. Doc A/810 at 71 (1948), available at http://www1.umn.edu/humanrts/instree/b1udhr.htm.
29. International Covenant on Civil and Political Rights, G.A. res. 2200A (XXI), 21 U.N. GAOR Supp. (No. 16) at 52, U.N. Doc. A/6316 (1966), 999 U.N.T.S. 171, *entered into force* Mar. 23, 1976, available at http://www1.umn.edu/humanrts/instree/b3ccpr.htm.
30. Convention on the Prevention and Punishment of the Crime of Genocide, 78 U.N.T.S. 277, *entered into force* Jan. 12, 1951, available at http://www1.umn.edu/humanrts/instree/x1cppcg.htm.
31. Article 6, International Covenant on Civil and Political Rights, G.A. res. 2200A (XXI), 21 U.N. GAOR Supp. (No. 16) at 52, U.N. Doc. A/6316 (1966), 999 U.N.T.S. 171, *entered into force* Mar. 23, 1976, available at http://www1.umn.edu/humanrts/instree/b3ccpr.htm.
32. Official website of the Human Rights Committee: http://www.ohchr.org/english/bodies/hrc/index.htm
33. Human Rights Committee, General Comment 6, Article 6 (Sixteenth session, 1982), Compilation of General Comments and General Recommendations Adopted by Human Rights Treaty Bodies, U.N. Doc. HRI/GEN/1/Rev.1 at 6 (1994), available at http://www1.umn.edu/humanrts/gencomm/hrcom6.htm.
34. Second Optional Protocol to the International Covenant on Civil and Political Rights, aiming at the abolition of the death penalty, G.A. res. 44/128, annex, 44 U.N. GAOR Supp. (No. 49) at 207, U.N. Doc. A/44/49 (1989), *entered into force* July 11, 1991, available at http://www1.umn.edu/humanrts/instree/b5ccprp2.htm.
35. Article 37, Convention on the Rights of the Child, G.A. res. 44/25, annex, 44 U.N. GAOR Supp. (No. 49) at 167, U.N. Doc. A/44/49 (1989), *entered into force* Sept. 2, 1990, available at http://www1.umn.edu/humanrts/instree/k2crc.htm.
36. Article 9, International Convention on the Protection of the Rights of All Migrant Workers and Members of Their Families, G.A. res. 45/158, annex, 45 U.N. GAOR Supp. (No. 49A) at 262, U.N. Doc. A/45/49 (1990), *entered into force* July 1, 2003, available at http://www1.umn.edu/humanrts/instree/n8icprmw.htm.

37. Official website of the Commission on Human Rights: http://www.ohchr-.org/english/bodies/chr/index.htm; official website of the Sub-Commission on Promotion and Protection of Human Rights: http://www.ohchr.org/english/bodies/subcom/56th/56sub.htm.

38. *Roper v. Simmons*, 125 S.Ct. 1183 (2005).

39. Official website of the Special Rapporteur on extrajudicial, summary or arbitrary executions: http://www.ohchr.org/english/issues/executions/index.htm.

40. Report of the Special Rapporteur on Extrajudicial, Summary or Arbitrary Executions, U.N. Doc. E/CN.4/2004/7 (2003).

41. Article 4, African [Banjul] Charter on Human and Peoples' Rights, adopted June 27, 1981, OAU Doc. CAB/LEG/67/3 rev. 5, 21 I.L.M. 58 (1982), *entered into force* Oct. 21, 1986, available at http://www1.umn.edu/humanrts/instree/z1afchar.htm.

42. Article 1, American Declaration of the Rights and Duties of Man, O.A.S. Res. XXX, adopted by the Ninth International Conference of American States (1948), *reprinted in* Basic Documents Pertaining to Human Rights in the Inter-American System, OEA/Ser.L.V/II.82 doc.6 rev.1 at 17 (1992), available at http://www1.umn.edu/humanrts/oasinstr/zoas2dec.htm.

43. Article 4, American Convention on Human Rights, O.A.S.Treaty Series No. 36, 1144 U.N.T.S. 123, *entered into force* July 18, 1978, *reprinted in* Basic Documents Pertaining to Human Rights in the Inter-American System, OEA/Ser.L.V/II.82 doc.6 rev.1 at 25 (1992), available at http://www1.umn.edu/humanrts/oasinstr/zoas3con.htm.

44. Article 2, Convention for the Protection of Human Rights and Fundamental Freedoms, 213 U.N.T.S. 222, *entered into force* Sept. 3, 1953, as amended by Protocols Nos. 3, 5, 8, 11, *entered into force* 21 Sept. 21, 1970, Dec. 20, 1971, Jan. 1, 1990, Nov. 1 1998 respectively, available at http://www1.umn.edu/humanrts/instree/z17euroco.html.

45. Protocol No. 6 to the 1950 European Convention for the Protection of Human Rights and Fundamental Freedoms, E.T.S. 114, *entered into force* Mar. 1, 1985, available at http:// www1.umn.edu/humanrts/euro/z25prot6.html.

46. The Anti-Slavery Society is today known as Anti-Slavery International; official website: http://www.antislavery.org.

47. Declaration Relative to the Universal Abolition of the Slave Trade, 8 February 1815, Consolidated Treaty Series, vol. 63, No. 473.

48. *Barcelona Traction, Light and Power Co, Ltd. (Belgium v. Spain)*, Judgment of 5 February 1971, I.C.J. Reports, 1970, at 32.

49. The World Conference Against Racism, Racial Discrimination, Xenophobia and Related Intolerance in September 2001 noted in its final declaration: "We further acknowledge that slavery and the slave trade are a crime against humanity and should always have been so, especially the trans-Atlantic slave trade."

50. Slavery, Servitude, Forced Labour and Similar Institutions and Practices Convention of 1926 (hereinafter Slavery Convention of 1926), League of Nations Treaty Series, vol. 60, p. 253; *entered into force* Mar. 9, 1927, available at http://www1.umn.edu/humanrts/instree/f1sc.htm.

51. International Agreement for the Suppression of the White Slave Trade of 1904, League of Nations Treaty Series, vol. 1, p. 83; *entered into force* on July 18, 1905, available at http://www1.umn.edu/humanrts/instree/whiteslavetraffic1904.html.

52. The International Convention for the Suppression of the White Slave Traffic of 4 May 1910, United Nations Treaty Series, vol. 98, p. 101, available at http://www1.umn.edu/humanrts/instree/whiteslavetraffic1910.html.

53. International Convention for the Suppression of the Traffic of Women of Full Age, 150 League of Nations Treaty Series 431, *entered into force* Aug. 24, 1934.

54. Convention for the Suppression of the Traffic in Persons and of the Exploitation of the Prostitution of Others, 96 U.N.T.S. 271, *entered into force* July 25, 1951, available at http://www1.umn.edu/humanrts/instree/trafficinperson.htm.

55. Convention on the Rights of the Child, G.A. res. 44/25, annex, 44 U.N. GAOR Supp. (No. 49) at 167, U.N. Doc. A/44/49 (1989), *entered into force* Sept. 2, 1990, available at http://www1.umn.edu/humanrts/instree/k2crc.htm.

56. Supplementary Convention on the Abolition of Slavery, the Slave Trade, and Institutions and Practices Similar to Slavery, 226 U.N.T.S. 3, *entered into force* Apr. 30, 1957, available at http://www1.umn.edu/humanrts/instree/f3scas.htm.

57. Article 7, Rome Statute of the International Criminal Court, U.N. Doc. 2187 U.N.T.S. 90, *entered into force* July 1, 2002, available at http://www1.umn.edu/humanrts/instree/Rome_Statute_ICC/Rome_ICC_toc.html.

58. Article 4, Universal Declaration of Human Rights, G.A. res. 217A (III), U.N. Doc A/810 at 71 (1948), available at http://www1.umn.edu/humanrts/instree/b1udhr.htm.

59. International Covenant on Civil and Political Rights, G.A. res. 2200A (XXI), 21 U.N. GAOR Supp. (No. 16) at 52, U.N. Doc. A/6316 (1966), 999 U.N.T.S. 171, *entered into force* Mar. 23, 1976, available at http://www1.umn.edu/humanrts/instree/b3ccpr.htm.

60. Article 6, International Covenant on Economic, Social and Cultural Rights, G.A. res. 2200A (XXI), 21 U.N.GAOR Supp. (No. 16) at 49, U.N. Doc. A/6316 (1966), 993 U.N.T.S. 3, *entered into force* Jan. 3, 1976, available at http://www1.umn.edu/humanrts/instree/b2esc.htm.

61. United Nations Convention Against Transnational Organized Crime, G.A. Res. 25, annex I, U.N. GAOR, 55th Sess., Supp. No. 49, at 44, U.N. Doc. A/45/49 (Vol. I) (2001), *not in force*, available at http://www1.umn.edu/humanrts/instree/organizedcrime.html.

62. Article 3, Protocol to Prevent, Suppress and Punish Trafficking in Persons, Especially Women and Children, Supplementing the United Nations Convention Against Transnational Organized Crime, G.A. Res. 25, annex II, U.N. GAOR, 55th Sess., Supp. No. 49, at 60, U.N. Doc. A/45/49 (Vol. I) (2001), *entered into force* Sept. 9, 2003, available at http://www1.umn.edu/humanrts/instree/trafficking.html.

63. Article 5, Supplementary Convention on the Abolition of Slavery, the Slave Trade, and Institutions and Practices Similar to Slavery, 226 U.N.T.S. 3, *entered into force* Apr. 30, 1957, available at http://www1.umn.edu/humanrts/instree/f3scas.htm.

64. Official website of the ILO: http://www.ilo.org.

65. Convention concerning Forced or Compulsory Labour (ILO No. 29), 39 U.N.T.S. 55, *entered into force* May 1, 1932, available at http://www1.umn.edu/humanrts/instree/n0ilo29.htm.

66. *Id.*, Article 1.

67. Report of the Commission of Inquiry appointed under article 26 of the Constitution of the International Labour Organization to examine the obser-

vance by Myanmar of the Forced Labour Convention, 1930 (No. 29), 2 July 1998, available at http://www.ilo.org/public/english/standards/relm/gb/docs/gb273/myanmar.htm.

68. Abolition of Forced Labour Convention (ILO No. 105), 320 U.N.T.S. 291, *entered into force* Jan. 17, 1959, available at http://www1.umn.edu/humanrts/instree/n2ilo105.htm.

69. Convention concerning Forced or Compulsory Labour (ILO No. 29), 39 U.N.T.S. 55, *entered into force* May 1, 1932, available at http://www1.umn.edu/humanrts/instree/n0ilo29.htm.

70. International Covenant on Civil and Political Rights, G.A. res. 2200A (XXI), 21 U.N. GAOR Supp. (No. 16) at 52, U.N. Doc. A/6316 (1966), 999 U.N.T.S. 171, *entered into force* Mar. 23, 1976, available at http://www1.umn.edu/humanrts/instree/b3ccpr.htm.

71. Convention for the Protection of Human Rights and Fundamental Freedoms, 213 U.N.T.S. 222, *entered into force* Sept. 3, 1953, *as amended by* Protocols Nos 3, 5, 8, 11, *entered into force* Sept. 21, 1970, Dec. 20, 1971, Jan. 1, 1990, Nov.1, 1998 *respectively*, available at http://www1.umn.edu/humanrts/instree/z17euroco.html.

72. *X v. Federal Republic of Germany* (Application No. 4653/70), 46 Eur. Comm'n H.R. Dec. & Rep. 22 (1974).

73. Convention Concerning Forced or Compulsory Labour (ILO No. 29), 39 U.N.T.S. 55, *entered into force* May 1, 1932, available at http://www1.umn.edu/humanrts/instree/n0ilo29.htm.

74. ILO Convention No. 131 Concerning Minimum Wage Fixing with Special Reference to Developing Countries, available at http://www.ilo.org/ilolex/cgi-lex/convde.pl?C131. R135 Minimum Wage Fixing Recommendation, 1970, available at http://www.ilo.org/ilolex/cgi-lex/convde.pl?R135

75. ILO Convention No. 117 Concerning Basic Aims and Standards of Social Policy of 1962, available at http://www.ilo.org/ilolex/cgi-lex/convde.pl?C117.

76. Convention Concerning the Prohibition and Immediate Action for the Elimination of the Worst Forms of Child Labour (ILO No. 182), 38 I.L.M. 1207 (1999), *entered into force* Nov. 19, 2000, available at http://www1.umn.edu/humanrts/instree/ilo182.html.

77. Convention Concerning the Protection of Wages (ILO No. 95), *entered into force* Sept. 24, 1952, available at http://www1.umn.edu/humanrts/instree/ilo95.html; Convention Concerning Basic Aims and Standards of Social Policy (ILO No. 117), *entered into force* Apr. 23, 1964, available at http://www1.umn.edu/humanrts/instree/ilo117.html.

78. *United States v. Sanga*, 967 F.2d 1332 (9th Cir. 1992).

79. Slavery, Servitude, Forced Labour and Similar Institutions and Practices Convention of 1926 (Slavery Convention of 1926), 60 U.N.T.S. 253, *entered into force* Mar. 9, 1927, available at http://www1.umn.edu/humanrts/instree/f1sc.htm. Supplementary Convention on the Abolition of Slavery, the Slave Trade, and Institutions and Practices Similar to Slavery, 226 U.N.T.S. 3, *entered into force* Apr. 30, 1957, available at http://www1.umn.edu/humanrts/instree/f3scas.htm.

80. Working paper prepared by Mr. David Weissbrodt and Anti-Slavery International, Updated review of the implementation of and follow-up to the conventions on slavery, U.N. Doc. E/CN.4/Sub.2/2000/3 (2000); official website of the UN Working Group on Contemporary Forms of Slavery: http://www.ohchr.org/english/issues/slavery/group.htm.

81. Convention concerning Forced or Compulsory Labour (ILO No. 29), 39 U.N.T.S. 55, *entered into force* May 1, 1932, available at http://www1.umn.edu/humanrts/instree/n0ilo29.htm.
82. Abolition of Forced Labour Convention (ILO No. 105), 320 U.N.T.S. 291, *entered into force* Jan. 17, 1959, available at http://www1.umn.edu/humanrts/instree/n2ilo105.htm.
83. The ILO Constitution is available at http://www.ilo.org/public/english/about/iloconst.htm.
84. Report of the Commission of Inquiry Appointed Under Article 26 of the Constitution of the International Labour Organization to Examine the Observance by Myanmar of the Forced Labour Convention, 1930 (No. 29), 2 July 1998, available at http://www.ilo.org/public/english/standards/relm/gb/docs/gb273/myanmar.htm.
85. Article 5, Universal Declaration of Human Rights, G.A. res. 217A (III), U.N. Doc A/810 at 71 (1948), available at http://www1.umn.edu/humanrts/instree/b1udhr.htm. Article 7, International Covenant on Civil and Political Rights, G.A. res. 2200A (XXI), 21 U.N. GAOR Supp. (No. 16) at 52, U.N. Doc. A/6316 (1966), 999 U.N.T.S. 171, *entered into force* Mar. 23, 1976, available at http://www1.umn.edu/humanrts/instree/b3ccpr.htm.
86. Official website of Amnesty International: http://www.amnesty.org.
87. Declaration on the Protection of All Persons from Being Subjected to Torture and Other Cruel, Inhuman or Degrading Treatment or Punishment, G.A. res. 3452 (XXX), annex, 30 U.N. GAOR Supp. (No. 34) at 91, U.N. Doc. A/10034 (1975), available at http://www1.umn.edu/humanrts/instree/h1dpast.htm.
88. Code of Conduct for Law Enforcement Officials, G.A. res. 34/169, annex, 34 U.N. GAOR Supp. (No. 46) at 186, U.N. Doc. A/34/46 (1979), available at http://www1.umn.edu/humanrts/instree/i1ccleo.htm.
89. Principles of Medical Ethics relevant to the Role of Health Personnel, particularly Physicians, in the Protection of Prisoners and Detainees Against Torture and Other Cruel, Inhuman or Degrading Treatment or Punishment, G.A. res. 37/194, annex, 37 UN GAOR Supp. (No. 51) at 211, U.N. Doc. A/37/51 (1982), available at http://www1.umn.edu/humanrts/instree/h3pmerhp.htm.
90. Official website of the U.N. Voluntary Fund for Victims of Torture: http://www.ohchr.org/english/about/funds/torture.
91. Convention Against Torture and Other Cruel, Inhuman or Degrading Treatment or Punishment, G.A. res. 39/46, [annex, 39 U.N. GAOR Supp. (No. 51) at 197, U.N. Doc. A/39/51 (1984)], *entered into force* June 26, 1987, available at http://www1.umn.edu/humanrts/instree/h2catoc.htm.
92. Official website of the Committee Against Torture: http://www.ohchr.org/english/bodies/cat/index.htm.
93. Optional Protocol to the Convention Against Torture and Other Cruel, Inhuman or Degrading Treatment or Punishment, G.A. res. A/RES/57/199, *adopted* Dec. 18, 2002, *reprinted in* 42 I.L.M. 26 (2003)], available at http://www1.umn.edu/humanrts/instree/optprotort.html.
94. Official website of the World Organization Against Torture: http://www.omct.org.
95. Rome Statute of the International Criminal Court, U.N. Doc. 2187 U.N.T.S. 90, *entered into force* July 1, 2002, available at http://www1.umn.edu/humanrts/instree/Rome_Statute_ICC/Rome_ICC_toc.html.
96. Universal Declaration of Human Rights, G.A. res. 217A (III), U.N. Doc

A/810 at 71 (1948), available at http://www1.umn.edu/humanrts/instree/ b1udhr.htm.

97. International Covenant on Civil and Political Rights, G.A. res. 2200A (XXI), 21 U.N. GAOR Supp. (No. 16) at 52, U.N. Doc. A/6316 (1966), 999 U.N.T.S. 171, *entered into force* Mar. 23, 1976, available at http://www1.umn.edu/humanrts/instree/b3ccpr.htm.

98. Official website of the Human Rights Committee: http://www.ohchr.org/english/bodies/hrc/index.htm.

99. Human Rights Committee, General Comment 13, Article 14 (Twenty-first session, 1984), Compilation of General Comments and General Recommendations Adopted by Human Rights Treaty Bodies, U.N. Doc. HRI/GEN/1/Rev.1 at 14 (1994), available at http://www1.umn.edu/humanrts/gencomm/hrcom13.htm.

100. Human Rights Committee, General Comment 29, States of Emergency (article 4), U.N. Doc. CCPR/C/21/Rev.1/Add.11 (2001), available at http://www1.umn.edu/humanrts/gencomm/hrc29.html.

101. *Id.*, para. 16.

102. Convention on the Rights of the Child, G.A. res. 44/25, annex, 44 U.N. GAOR Supp. (No. 49) at 167, U.N. Doc. A/44/49 (1989), *entered into force* Sept. 2 1990, available at http://www1.umn.edu/humanrts/instree/k2crc.htm.

103. Geneva Conventions available at http://www1.umn.edu/humanrts/instree/auoy.htm.

104. Basic Principles on the Independence of the Judiciary, Seventh United Nations Congress on the Prevention of Crime and the Treatment of Offenders, Milan, 26 August to 6 September 1985, U.N. Doc. A/CONF.121/22/Rev.1 at 59 (1985), available at http://www1.umn.edu/humanrts/instree/i5bpij.htm.

105. Basic Principles on the Role of Lawyers, Eighth United Nations Congress on the Prevention of Crime and the Treatment of Offenders, Havana, 27 August to 7 September 1990, U.N. Doc. A/CONF.144/28/Rev.1 at 118 (1990), available at http://www1.umn.edu/humanrts/instree/i3bprl.htm.

106. Basic Principles on the Use of Force and Firearms by Law Enforcement Officials, Eighth United Nations Congress on the Prevention of Crime and the Treatment of Offenders, Havana, 27 August to 7 September 1990, U.N. Doc. A/CONF.144/28/Rev.1 at 112 (1990), available at http://www1.umn.edu/humanrts/instree/i2bpuff.htm.

107. Guidelines on the Role of Prosecutors, Eighth United Nations Congress on the Prevention of Crime and the Treatment of Offenders, Havana, Aug. 27–Sept. 7, 1990, U.N. Doc. A/CONF.144/28/Rev.1 at 189 (1990), available at http://www1.umn.edu/humanrts/instree/i4grp.htm.

108. Principles on the Effective Prevention and Investigation of Extra-Legal, Arbitrary and Summary Executions, E.S.C. res. 1989/65, annex, 1989 U.N. ESCOR Supp. (No. 1) at 52, U.N. Doc. E/1989/89 (1989), available at http://www1.umn.edu/humanrts/instree/i7pepi.htm.

109. Safeguards Guaranteeing Protection of the Rights of Those Facing the Death Penalty, E.S.C. res. 1984/50, annex, 1984 U.N. ESCOR Supp. (No. 1) at 33, U.N. Doc. E/1984/84 (1984), available at http://www1.umn.edu/humanrts/instree/i8sgpr.htm.

110. Universal Declaration of Human Rights, G.A. res. 217A (III), U.N. Doc A/810 at 71 (1948), available at http://www1.umn.edu/humanrts/instree/b1udhr.htm. Covenant on Civil and Political Rights, G.A. res. 2200A (XXI), 21 U.N. GAOR Supp. (No. 16) at 52, U.N. Doc. A/6316 (1966), 999 U.N.T.S. 171,

*entered into force* Mar. 23, 1976, available at http://www1.umn.edu/humanrts/instree/b3ccpr.htm.

111. Convention Against Torture and Other Cruel, Inhuman or Degrading Treatment or Punishment, G.A. res. 39/46, [annex, 39 U.N. GAOR Supp. (No. 51) at 197, U.N. Doc. A/39/51 (1984)], *entered into force* June 26, 1987, available at http://www1.umn.edu/humanrts/instree/h2catoc.htm.

112. Convention on the Rights of the Child, G.A. res. 44/25, annex, 44 U.N. GAOR Supp. (No. 49) at 167, U.N. Doc. A/44/49 (1989), *entered into force* Sept. 2 1990, available at http://www1.umn.edu/humanrts/instree/k2crc.htm.

113. Standard Minimum Rules for the Treatment of Prisoners, adopted Aug. 30, 1955 by the First United Nations Congress on the Prevention of Crime and the Treatment of Offenders, U.N. Doc. A/CONF/611, annex I, E.S.C. res. 663C, 24 U.N. ESCOR Supp. (No. 1) at 11, U.N. Doc. E/3048 (1957), amended E.S.C. res. 2076, 62 U.N. ESCOR Supp. (No. 1) at 35, U.N. Doc. E/5988 (1977), available at http://www1.umn.edu/humanrts/instree/g1smr.htm.

114. Body of Principles for the Protection of All Persons Under Any Form of Detention or Imprisonment, G.A. res. 43/173, annex, 43 U.N. GAOR Supp. (No. 49) at 298, U.N. Doc. A/43/49 (1988), available at http://www1.umn.edu/humanrts/instree/g3bpppdi.htm.

115. Basic Principles for the Treatment of Prisoners, G.A. res. 45/111, annex, 45 U.N. GAOR Supp. (No. 49A) at 200, U.N. Doc. A/45/49 (1990), available at http://www1.umn.edu/humanrts/instree/g2bpt.htm.

116. For example, a period of three days without court review breached article 9(4) ICCPR in *Hammel v. Madagascar*, Communication No. 155/1983,CCPR/C/29/D/155/1983; at paras 18.2 and 20; *see also Torres v. Finland*, Communication No. 291/1988, CCPR/C/38/D/291/1988 at para 7.2 where detention without review for two periods of seven days and one period of five days breached article 9(4) and *Vuolanne v. Finland*, Communication No. 265/1987, CPR/C/35/D/265/1987, where military detention for 10 days without judicial review breached article 9(4). However, in *Portorreal v. Dominican Republic*, Communication No. 188/1984, CCPR/C/31/D/188/1984, detention for a period of fifty hours was found not to breach article 9(4); at para 10.2, although the Committee did find a violation of article 9(2) at para 11.

117. Vienna Convention on Consular Relations, 596 U.N.T.S. 261, *entered into force* Mar. 19, 1967, available at http://www1.umn.edu/humanrts/instree/consularrelations.html.

118. *Avena and Other Mexican Nationals (Mexico v. United States of America)*, 2004 I.C.J. (Judgment); 43 ILM 581 (2004).

119. Standard Minimum Rules for the Treatment of Prisoners, adopted Aug. 30, 1955 by the First United Nations Congress on the Prevention of Crime and the Treatment of Offenders, U.N. Doc. A/CONF/611, annex I, E.S.C. res. 663C, 24 U.N. ESCOR Supp. (No. 1) at 11, U.N. Doc. E/3048 (1957), amended E.S.C. res. 2076, 62 U.N. ESCOR Supp. (No. 1) at 35, U.N. Doc. E/5988 (1977), available at http://www1.umn.edu/humanrts/instree/g1smr.htm.

120. Principles for the Protection of Persons with Mental Illnesses and the Improvement of Mental Health Care, G.A. res. 46/119, 46 U.N. GAOR Supp. (No. 49) at 189, U.N. Doc. A/46/49 (1991), available at http://www1.umn.edu/humanrts/instree/t2pppmii.htm.

121. Geneva Convention relative to the Protection of Civilian Persons in Time of War, 75 U.N.T.S. 287, *entered into force* Oct. 21, 1950, available at http://www1.umn.edu/humanrts/instree/y4gcpcp.htm.

122. *Rasul v. Bush*, 124 S.Ct. 2686 (2004).
123. Official website for the UN Working Group on Arbitrary Detention http://www.ohchr.org/english/issues/detention/index.htm
124. Opinions of the UN Working Group on Arbitrary Detention available at available at http://www1.umn.edu/humanrts/instree/wgad/.
125. *Mourad Benchellali et al. v. United States of America*, Working Group on Arbitrary Detention, U.N. Doc. E/CN.4/2004/3/Add.1 at 33 (2003), available at http://www1.umn.edu/humanrts/wgad/5-2003.html.
126. Universal Declaration of Human Rights, G.A. res. 217A (III), U.N. Doc A/810 at 71 (1948), available at http://www1.umn.edu/humanrts/instree/bludhr.htm.
127. International Covenant on Civil and Political Rights, G.A. res. 2200A (XXI), 21 U.N. GAOR Supp. (No. 16) at 52, U.N. Doc. A/6316 (1966), 999 U.N.T.S. 171, *entered into force* Mar. 23, 1976, available at http://www1.umn.edu/humanrts/instree/b3ccpr.htm.
128. Decisions and views of the Human Rights Committee available at http://www1.umn.edu/humanrts/undocs/undocs-index.html.
129. Human Rights Committee, General Comment 28, Equality of rights between men and women (article 3), U.N. Doc. CCPR/C/21/Rev.1/Add.10 para. 20 (2000), available at http://www1.umn.edu/humanrts/gencomm/hrcom28.htm.
130. Human Rights Committee, General Comment 16 (Twenty-third session, 1988), Compilation of General Comments and General Recommendations Adopted by Human Rights Treaty Bodies, U.N. Doc. HRI/GEN/1/Rev.1 at 21, para. 10 (1994), available at http://www1.umn.edu/humanrts/gencomm/hrcom16.htm.
131. *Toonen v. Australia*, Communication No. 488/1992, U.N. Doc CCPR/C/50/D/488/1992 para. 8.2 (1994), available at http://www1.umn.edu/humanrts/undocs/html/vws488.htm.
132. *Dudgeon v. United Kingdom*, 45 Eur. Ct. H.R. (Ser.A) (1982), 4 Eur. H.R. Rep. 149 (1981).
133. *Lawrence v. Texas*, 123 S. Ct. 2472 (2003).
134. *Coeriel et al. v. The Netherlands*, Communication No. 453/1991, U.N. Doc. CCPR/C/52/D/453/1991 (1994), available at http://www1.umn.edu/humanrts/undocs/html/453-1991.html.
135. Universal Declaration of Human Rights, G.A. res. 217A (III), U.N. Doc A/810 at 71 (1948), available at http://www1.umn.edu/humanrts/instree/bludhr.htm.
136. International Covenant on Civil and Political Rights, G.A. res. 2200A (XXI), 21 U.N. GAOR Supp. (No. 16) at 52, U.N. Doc. A/6316 (1966), 999 U.N.T.S. 171, *entered into force* Mar. 23, 1976, available at http://www1.umn.edu/humanrts/instree/b3ccpr.htm.
137. Protocol No. 4 to the Convention for the Protection of Human Rights and Fundamental Freedoms, E.T.S. No. 46, *entered into force* May 2, 1968, available at http://www1.umn.edu/humanrts/euro/z23prot4.html.
138. American Convention on Human Rights, O.A.S.Treaty Series No. 36, 1144 U.N.T.S. 123 *entered into force* July 18, 1978, *reprinted in* Basic Documents Pertaining to Human Rights in the Inter-American System, OEA/Ser.L.V/II.82 doc.6 rev.1 at 25 (1992), available at http://www1.umn.edu/humanrts/oasinstr/zoas3con.htm.
139. African Charter on Human and Peoples' Rights, *adopted* June 27, 1981,

OAU Doc. CAB/LEG/67/3 rev. 5, 21 I.L.M. 58 (1982), *entered into force* Oct. 21, 1986, available at http://www1.umn.edu/humanrts/instree/z1afchar.htm.

140. Human Rights Committee, General Comment 27, Freedom of movement (Art.12), U.N. Doc CCPR/C/21/Rev.1/Add.9 (1999), available at http://www1.umn.edu/humanrts/gencomm/hrcom27.htm.

141. *Kéténguéré Ackla v. Togo*, Communication No. 505/1992, U.N. Doc. CCPR/C/51/D/505/1992 (1996), available at http://www1.umn.edu/humanrts/undocs/html/VWS50556.htm.

142. Geneva Convention Relative to the Protection of Civilian Persons in Time of War, 75 U.N.T.S. 287, *entered into force* Oct. 21, 1950, available at http://www1.umn.edu/humanrts/instree/y4gcpcp.htm.

143. Protocol Additional to the Geneva Conventions of 12 August 1949, and Relating to the Protection of Victims of Non-International Armed Conflicts (Protocol II), 1125 U.N.T.S. 609, *entered into force* Dec. 7, 1978, available at http://www1.umn.edu/humanrts/instree/y6pagc.htm.

144. Official website for the UN High Commissioner for Refugees (UNHCR): http://www.unhcr.ch/.

145. Official website of the International Committee of the Red Cross (ICRC): http://www.icrc.org/.

146. Official website of the Special Representative of the Secretary-General on internally displaced persons: http://www.ohchr.org/english/issues/idp/index.htm.

147. Guiding Principles on Internal Displacement, U.N. Doc. E/CN.4/1998/53/Add.2 (1998), available at http://www1.umn.edu/humanrts/instree/GuidingPrinciplesonInternalDisplacement.htm.

148. Article 42, Magna Carta (Eng. 1215), available at http://www1.umn.edu/humanrts/education/magnacarta.html.

149. Blackstone's *Commentaries on the Laws of England* (1765–1769), available at http://www.yale.edu/lawweb/avalon/blackstone/blacksto.htm.

150. Treaty of Westphalia, October 24, 1648, available at http://www.yale.edu/lawweb/avalon/westphal.htm.

151. Act of July 27, 1868, c. 249, 15 St. 223; Rev. St. §§ 1999.

152. Human Rights Committee, General Comment 27, Freedom of Movement (Art.12), U.N. Doc CCPR/C/21/Rev.1/Add.9 para. 9 (1999), available at http://www1.umn.edu/humanrts/gencomm/hrcom27.htm.

153. *Id.*, para. 19.

154. The return of refugees' or displaced persons' property, Working paper submitted by Mr. Paulo Sérgio Pinheiro pursuant to Sub-Commission decision 2001/122, U.N. Doc. E/CN.4/Sub.2/2002/17, para. 22 (2002).

155. Universal Declaration of Human Rights, G.A. res. 217A (III), U.N. Doc A/810 at 71 (1948), available at http://www1.umn.edu/humanrts/instree/b1udhr.htm.

156. Convention Relating to the Status of Refugees, 189 U.N.T.S. 150, *entered into force* Apr. 22, 1954, available at http://www1.umn.edu/humanrts/instree/v1crs.htm.

157. Protocol Relating to the Status of Refugees, 606 U.N.T.S. 267, *entered into force* Oct. 4, 1967, available at http://www1.umn.edu/humanrts/instree/v2prsr.htm.

158. *Supra*, note 156.

159. *INS v. Stevic*, 467 U.S. 407 (1984).

160. *INS v. Cardoza-Fonseca*, 480 U.S. 421 (1987).

161. *Ex Parte Sivakumaran*, [1988] AC 958, 992G (HL).

162. UNHCR, Handbook on Procedures and Criteria for Determining Refugee Status under the 1951 Convention and the 1967 Protocol relating to the Status of Refugees, U.N. Doc. HCR/IP/4/ Eng/REV.1 (1992), available at http://www1.umn.edu/humanrts/instree/refugeehandbook.html.

163. James Hathaway, The Law of Refugee Status at 112 (1991). *See also Horvath v. Secretary of State for the Home Department* [2001] 1 AC 489, 495, per Lord Hope of Craighead and *Sepet v. Secretary of State for the Home Department* [2003] 1 WLR 856, 862, para 7, per Lord Bingham of Cornhill.

164. Article 1, International Convention on the Elimination of All Forms of Racial Discrimination, G.A. res. 2106 (XX), Annex, 20 U.N. GAOR Supp. (No. 14) at 47, U.N. Doc. A/6014 (1966), 660 U.N.T.S. 195, *entered into force* Jan. 4, 1969, available at http://www1.umn.edu/humanrts/instree/d1cerd.htm.

165. *Supra* note 162.

166. *Mr. Müümtaz Karakurt v. Austria*, Communication No. 965/2000, U.N. Doc. CCPR/C/74/D/965/2000 (2002), available at http://www1.umn.edu/humanrts/undocs/965-2000.html.

167. *INS v. Elias-Zacarias*, 502 U.S. 478 (1992).

168. *Cordon-Garcia v. INS*, 204 F.3d 985 (9th Cir. 2000).

169. *Hernandez-Montiel v. INS*, 225 F.3d 1084 (9th Cir. 2000).

170. *In re Kasinga*, 21 I. & N. Dec. 357 (BIA 1996).

171. *Abankwah v. INS*, 185 F.3d 18 (2nd Cir. 1999).

172. Immigration and Refugee Board of Canada, Guidelines on Women Refugee Claimants Fearing Gender-Related Persecution (Mar. 1993), *reprinted in* Gender Asylum Law in Different Countries: Decisions and Guidelines 87 (1999); Immigration and Refugee Board of Canada, Guideline 4: Women Refugee Claimants Fearing Gender-Related Persecution: Update (Nov. 13, 1996).

173. *Supra* notes 155 and 156.

174. *Supra* note 155, Article 1, para. F (a).

175. Article 3, Convention Against Torture and Other Cruel, Inhuman or Degrading Treatment or Punishment, G.A. res. 39/46, annex, 39 U.N. GAOR Supp. (No. 51) at 197, U.N. Doc. A/39/51 (1984), *entered into force* June 26, 1987, available at http://www1.umn.edu/humanrts/instree/h2catoc.htm.

176. Article 1, Convention Governing the Specific Aspects of Refugee Problems in Africa, 1001 U.N.T.S. 45, *entered into force* June 20, 1974, available at http://www1.umn.edu/humanrts/instree/z2arcon.htm.

177. *Perez v. Brownell*, 356 U.S. 44, 62 (1958) (Warren, C.J. dissenting).

178. Universal Declaration of Human Rights, G.A. res. 217A (III), U.N. Doc A/810 at 71 (1948), available at http://www1.umn.edu/humanrts/instree/b1udhr.htm.

179. International Covenant on Civil and Political Rights, G.A. res. 2200A (XXI), 21 U.N. GAOR Supp. (No. 16) at 52, U.N. Doc. A/6316 (1966), 999 U.N.T.S. 171, *entered into force* Mar. 23, 1976, available at http://www1.umn.edu/humanrts/instree/b3ccpr.htm.

180. Convention on the Rights of the Child, G.A. res. 44/25, annex, 44 U.N. GAOR Supp. (No. 49) at 167, U.N. Doc. A/44/49 (1989), *entered into force* Sept. 2 1990, available at http://www1.umn.edu/humanrts/instree/k2crc.htm.

181. Convention on the Elimination of All Forms of Discrimination Against Women, G.A. res. 34/180, 34 U.N. GAOR Supp. (No. 46) at 193, U.N. Doc. A/34/46, *entered into force* Sept. 3, 1981, available at http://www1.umn.edu/humanrts/instree/e1cedaw.htm.

182. Convention on the Reduction of Statelessness, 989 U.N.T.S. 175, *entered into force* Dec. 13, 1975, available at http://www1.umn.edu/humanrts/instree/w2crs.htm.

183. Convention Relating to the Status of Stateless Persons, 360 U.N.T.S. 117, *entered into force* June 6, 1960, available at http://www1.umn.edu/humanrts/instree/w3cssp.htm.

184. *Supra* note 179, Article 24.

185. *Supra* note 180, Article 7.

186. *Supra* note 181, Article 9.

187. *Supra* note 182.

188. *Supra* note 183.

189. Hannah Arendt, *Eichmann in Jerusalem* (1963).

190. International Covenant on Economic, Social and Cultural Rights, G.A. res. 2200A (XXI), 21 U.N.GAOR Supp. (No. 16) at 49, U.N. Doc. A/6316 (1966), 993 U.N.T.S. 3, *entered into force* Jan. 3, 1976, available at http://www1.umn.edu/humanrts/instree/b2esc.htm.

191. Clarisa Bencomo and Human Rights Watch, Kuwait, Promises Betrayed: Denial of Rights of Bidun, Women, and Freedom of Expression (2000).

192. *Supra* note 183.

193. *Id.*

194. Article 16, Universal Declaration of Human Rights, G.A. res. 217A (III), U.N. Doc A/810 at 71 (1948), available at http://www1.umn.edu/humanrts/instree/b1udhr.htm.

195. International Covenant on Civil and Political Rights, G.A. res. 2200A (XXI), 21 U.N. GAOR Supp. (No. 16) at 52, U.N. Doc. A/6316 (1966), 999 U.N.T.S. 171, *entered into force* Mar. 23, 1976, available at http://www1.umn.edu/humanrts/instree/b3ccpr.htm.

196. Human Rights Committee, General Comment 19, Article 23 (Thirty-ninth session, 1990), Compilation of General Comments and General Recommendations Adopted by Human Rights Treaty Bodies, U.N. Doc. HRI/GEN/1/Rev.1 at 28, para. 2 (1994), available at http://www1.umn.edu/humanrts/gencomm/hrcom19.htm.

197. *Hendrick Winata and So Lan Li v. Australia*, Communication No. 30/2000, U.N. Doc. CCPR/C/72/D/930/2000 (2001), available at http://www1.umn.edu/humanrts/undocs/930-2000.html.

198. *Id.*, para. 7.3.

199. *Charles E. Stewart v. Canada*, Communication No. 538/1993, U.N. Doc. CCPR/C/58/D/538/1993 (1996), available at http://www1.umn.edu/humanrts/undocs/538-1993.html.

200. *Id.*, para. 9.4.

201. *Id.*, para. 12.10.

202. Convention for the Protection of Human Rights and Fundamental Freedoms, 213 U.N.T.S. 222, *entered into force* Sept. 3, 1953, *as amended by* Protocols Nos. 3, 5, 8, 11, *entered into force* Sept. 21, 1970, Dec. 20, 1971, Jan. 1, 1990, Nov. 1, 1998 respectively, available at http://www1.umn.edu/humanrts/instree/z17euroco.html.

203. *Beldjoudi v. France*, 234 Eur. Ct. H.R. (Ser. A) (1992).

204. *Margaret Buckle v. New Zealand*, Communication No. 858/1999, U.N. Doc. CCPR/C/70/D/858/1999 (2000), available at http://www1.umn.edu/humanrts/undocs/858-1999.html.

205. *Juliet Joslin et al. v. New Zealand*, Communication No. 902/1999, U.N.

Doc. A/57/40 at 214 (2002), available at http://www1.umn.edu/humanrts/undocs/902-1999.html.

206. Article 17, Universal Declaration of Human Rights, G.A. res. 217A (III), U.N. Doc A/810 at 71 (1948), available at http://www1.umn.edu/humanrts/instree/b1udhr.htm.

207. Article 1, International Covenant on Economic, Social and Cultural Rights, G.A. res. 2200A (XXI), 21 U.N.GAOR Supp. (No. 16) at 49, U.N. Doc. A/6316 (1966), 993 U.N.T.S. 3, *entered into force* Jan. 3, 1976, available at http://www1.umn.edu/humanrts/instree/b2esc.htm. Article 1, International Covenant on Economic, Social and Cultural Rights, G.A. res. 2200A (XXI), 21 U.N.GAOR Supp. (No. 16) at 49, U.N. Doc. A/6316 (1966), 993 U.N.T.S. 3, *entered into force* Jan. 3, 1976, available at http://www1.umn.edu/humanrts/instree/b2esc.htm.

208. Permanent Sovereignty over Natural Resources, G.A. res. 1803 (XVII), 17 U.N. GAOR Supp. (No.17) at 15, U.N. Doc. A/5217 (1962), available at http://www1.umn.edu/humanrts/instree/c2psnr.htm.

209. Chorzów Factory Case, 1928 PCIJ (ser. A), No. 17.

210. *J. G. A. Diergaardt (late Captain of the Rehoboth Baster Community) et al. v. Namibia*, Communication No. 760/1997, U.N. Doc. CCPR/C/69/D/760/1997 para. 10.6 (2000), available at http://www1.umn.edu/humanrts/undocs/session69/view760.htm.

211. *Graciela Ato del Avellanal v. Peru*, Communication No. 202/1986, U.N. Doc. Supp. No. 40 (A/44/40) at 196 (1988), available at http://www1.umn.edu/humanrts/undocs/session44/202-1986.htm.

212. Human Rights Committee, General Comment 28, Equality of rights between men and women (article 3), U.N. Doc. CCPR/C/21/Rev.1/Add.10 para. 19 (2000), available at http://www1.umn.edu/humanrts/gencomm/hrcom28.htm.

213. *Ol' Bahamonde v. Equatorial Guinea*, Communication No. 468/1991, U.N. Doc. CCPR/C/49/D/468/1991 para. 11 (1993), available at http://www1.umn.edu/humanrts/undocs/html/vws468.htm.

214. *Supra* note 207, Article 11.

215. Committee on Economic, Social and Cultural Rights, General Comment 4, The right to adequate housing (Sixth session, 1991), U.N. Doc. E/1992/23, annex III at 114 (1991), available at http://www1.umn.edu/humanrts/gencomm/epcomm4.htm.

216. *Supra* note 207, Article 15.

217. Committee on Economic, Social and Cultural Rights, Conclusions and recommendations, Cultural Rights, Czech Republic, U.N. Doc. E/C.12/1/Add.76 para. 10 (2002), available at http://www1.umn.edu/humanrts/esc/czechrepublic2002.html.

218. Article 5, International Convention on the Elimination of All Forms of Racial Discrimination, G.A. res. 2106 (XX), Annex, 20 U.N. GAOR Supp. (No. 14) at 47, U.N. Doc. A/6014 (1966), 660 U.N.T.S. 195, *entered into force* Jan. 4, 1969, available at http://www1.umn.edu/humanrts/instree/d1cerd.htm.

219. Article 16, Convention on the Elimination of All Forms of Discrimination Against Women, G.A. res. 34/180, 34 U.N. GAOR Supp. (No. 46) at 193, U.N. Doc. A/34/46, *entered into force* Sept. 3, 1981, available at http://www1.umn.edu/humanrts/instree/e1cedaw.htm.

220. *Supra* notes 156 and 157.

221. *Supra* note 183.

222. Article 13, Convention concerning Indigenous and Tribal Peoples in Independent Countries (ILO No. 169), 72 ILO Official Bull. 59, *entered into force* Sept. 5, 1991, available at http://www1.umn.edu/humanrts/instree/r1citp.htm.
223. Article 10, Draft Declaration on the Rights of Indigenous Peoples, U.N. Doc. E/CN.4/Sub.2/1994/2/Add.1 (1994), available at http://www1.umn.edu/humanrts/instree/declra.htm.
224. *Maya Indigenous Community of the Toledo District v. Belize*, Case 12.053, Report No. 40/04, Inter-Am. C.H.R. (Oct. 12, 2004).
225. *Id.*
226. Convention for the Protection of Human Rights and Fundamental Freedoms, 213 U.N.T.S. 222, *entered into force* Sept. 3, 1953, *as amended by* Protocols Nos. 3, 5, 8, 11, *entered into force* Sept. 21, 1970, Dec. 20, 1971, Jan. 1, 1990, 1 Nov. 1, 1998 respectively, available at http://www1.umn.edu/humanrts/instree/z17euroco.html.
227. Article 1, Protocol to the Convention for the Protection of Human Rights and Fundamental Freedoms, 213 U.N.T.S. 262, *entered into force* May 18, 1954, available at http://www1.umn.edu/humanrts/euro/z20prot1.html.
228. *Spörrong and Lönnroth* (7151/75), [1982] ECHR 5 (Sept. 23, 1982).
229. Universal Declaration of Human Rights, G.A. res. 217A (III), U.N. Doc A/810 at 71 (1948), available at http://www1.umn.edu/humanrts/instree/b1udhr.htm.
230. International Covenant on Civil and Political Rights, G.A. res. 2200A (XXI), 21 U.N. GAOR Supp. (No. 16) at 52, U.N. Doc. A/6316 (1966), 999 U.N.T.S. 171, *entered into force* Mar. 23, 1976, available at http://www1.umn.edu/humanrts/instree/b3ccpr.htm.
231. Human Rights Committee, General Comment 22, Article 18 (Forty-eighth session, 1993). Compilation of General Comments and General Recommendations Adopted by Human Rights Treaty Bodies, U.N. Doc. HRI/GEN/1/Rev.1 at 35 (1994), available at http://www1.umn.edu/humanrts/gencomm/hrcom22.htm
232. *Id.*, para. 2.
233. *M.A.B., W.A.T. and J.-A.Y.T. v. Canada*, Communication No. 570/1993, U.N. Doc. CCPR/C/50/D/570/1993 (1994), available at http://www1.umn.edu/humanrts/undocs/html/570-1993.html.
234. *Supra* note 231.
235. *Supra* note 231, para. 4.
236. *Clement Boodoo v. Trinidad and Tobago*, Communication No. 721/1996, U.N. Doc. CCPR/C/74/D/721/1996 (2002), available at http://www1.umn.edu/humanrts/undocs/721-1996.html.
237. *Karnel Singh Bhinder v. Canada*, Communication Nos. 208/1986, U.N. Doc. CCPR/C/37/ D/208/1986 (1989), available at http://www1.umn.edu/humanrts/undocs/session37/208-1986.html.
238. *Leyla Şahin v. Turkey*, App. No. 44774/98 (June 29, 2004).
239. *Supra* note 230, para. 11.
240. *J.v.K. and C.M.G.v.K.-S. v. The Netherlands*, Communication No. 483/1991, U.N. Doc. CCPR/C/45/D/483/1991 (1992), available at http://www1.umn.edu/humanrts/undocs/html/483-1991.html.
241. *Supra* note 230, para.9.
242. *Arieh Hollis Waldman v. Canada*, Communication No. 694/1996, U.N. Doc. CCPR/C/67/D/694/1996 (1999), available at http://www1.umn.edu/humanrts/undocs/session67/view694.htm.

388  Notes to Pages 100–106

243. Declaration on the Elimination of All Forms of Intolerance and of Discrimination Based on Religion or Belief, G.A. res. 36/55, 36 U.N. GAOR Supp. (No. 51) at 171, U.N. Doc. A/36/684 (1981), available at http://www1.umn.edu/humanrts/instree/d4deidrb.htm.

244. Official website of the Special Rapporteur on freedom of religion or belief, available at :http://www.ohchr.org/english/issues/religion/index.htm.

245. Universal Declaration of Human Rights, G.A. res. 217A (III), U.N. Doc A/810 at 71 (1948), available at http://www1.umn.edu/humanrts/instree/b1udhr.htm.

246. International Covenant on Civil and Political Rights, G.A. res. 2200A (XXI), 21 U.N. GAOR Supp. (No. 16) at 52, U.N. Doc. A/6316 (1966), 999 U.N.T.S. 171, *entered into force* Mar. 23, 1976, available at http://www1.umn.edu/humanrts/instree/b3ccpr.htm.

247. Human Rights Committee, General Comment 25 (57), General Comments under article 40, paragraph 4, of the International Covenant on Civil and Political Rights, Adopted by the Committee at its 1510th meeting, U.N. Doc. CCPR/C/21/Rev.1/Add.7 (1996), available at http://www1.umn.edu/humanrts/gencomm/hrcom25.htm.

248. *Tae Hoon Park v. Republic of Korea*, Communication No. 628/1995, U.N. Doc. CCPR/C/64/D/628/1995 (1998), available at http://www1.umn.edu/humanrts/undocs/session64/view628.htm.

249. The Johannesburg Principles on National Security, Freedom of Expression and Access to Information, Freedom of Expression and Access to Information, U.N. Doc. E/CN.4/1996/39 (1996), available at http://www1.umn.edu/humanrts/instree/johannesburg.html.

250. *Leo R. Hertzberg, Uit Mansson, Astrid Nikula and Marko and Tuovi Putkonen, represented by SETA (Organization for Sexual Equality) v. Finland*, Communication No. R.14/61, U.N. Doc. Supp. No. 40 (A/37/40) at 161 (1982), available at http://www1.umn.edu/humanrts/undocs/session37/14-61.htm.

251. *The Sunday Times v. The United Kingdom*, 30 Eur. Ct. H.R. (ser. A), 2 E.H.R.R. 245 (1979).

252. Human Rights Committee, General Comment 11, Article 20 (Nineteenth session, 1983), Compilation of General Comments and General Recommendations Adopted by Human Rights Treaty Bodies, U.N. Doc. HRI/GEN/1/Rev.1 at 12 (1994), available at http://www1.umn.edu/humanrts/gencomm/hrcom11.htm.

253. Committee on the Elimination of Racial Discrimination, General Recommendation 15, Measures to eradicate incitement to or acts of discrimination (Forty-second session, 1993), U.N. Doc. A/48/18 at 114 (1994), available at http://www1.umn.edu/humanrts/gencomm/genrxv.htm.

254. *Id.*

255. *Virginia v. Black*, 538 U.S. 343 (2003).

256. *Robert Faurisson v. France*, Communication No. 550/1993, U.N. Doc. CCPR/C/58/D/550/1993 (1996), available at http://www1.umn.edu/humanrts/undocs/html/550-1993.html.

257. *D.I. v. Germany*, App. No. 26551/95, Eur. Comm'n H.R. (June 26, 1996).

258. *Kivenmaa v. Finland*, Communication No. 412/1990, U.N. Doc. CCPR/C/50/D/412/1990 (1994), available at http://www1.umn.edu/humanrts/undocs/html/412-1990.html.

259. *Jong-Kyu Sohn v. Republic of Korea*, Communication No. 518/1992, U.N. Doc. CCPR/C/54/D/518/1992 (1995), available at http://www1.umn.edu/humanrts/undocs/html/vws518.htm.

260. Universal Declaration of Human Rights, G.A. res. 217A (III), U.N. Doc A/810 at 71 (1948), available at http://www1.umn.edu/humanrts/instree/b1udhr.htm.
261. International Covenant on Civil and Political Rights, G.A. res. 2200A (XXI), 21 U.N. GAOR Supp. (No. 16) at 52, U.N. Doc. A/6316 (1966), 999 U.N.T.S. 171, *entered into force* Mar. 23, 1976, available at http://www1.umn.edu/humanrts/instree/b3ccpr.htm.
262. International Covenant on Economic, Social and Cultural Rights, G.A. res. 2200A (XXI), 21 U.N.GAOR Supp. (No. 16) at 49, U.N. Doc. A/6316 (1966), 993 U.N.T.S. 3, *entered into force* Jan. 3, 1976, available at http://www1.umn.edu/humanrts/instree/b2esc.htm.
263. Official website of the ILO: http://www.ilo.org.
264. *Kivenmaa v. Finland*, Communication No. 412/1990, U.N. Doc. CCPR/C/50/D/412/1990 (1994), available at http://www1.umn.edu/humanrts/undocs/html/412-1990.html.
265. *E.C.W. v. The Netherlands*, Communication No. 524/1992, U.N. Doc. CCPR/C/49/D/524/1992 (1993), available at http://www1.umn.edu/humanrts/undocs/html/524-1992.html.
266. *Supra* note 261.
267. *Supra* note 262.
268. *J.B. et al. v. Canada*, Communication No. 118/1982, U.N. Doc. Supp. No. 40 (A/41/40) at 151 (1986), available at http://www1.umn.edu/humanrts/undocs/session41/118-1982.htm.
269. Freedom of Association and Protection of the Right to Organize Convention (ILO No. 87), 68 U.N.T.S. 17, *entered into force* July 4, 1950, available at http://www1.umn.edu/humanrts/instree/m1fapro.htm.
270. Right to Organize and Collective Bargaining Convention (ILO No. 98), 96 U.N.T.S. 257, *entered into force* July 18, 1951, available at http://www1.umn.edu/humanrts/instree/m2rocb.htm.
271. ILO, Freedom of Association, Digest of Decisions and Principles of the Freedom of Association Committee of the Governing Body of the ILO (3d ed. 1985), para. 169.
272. ILO Committee on Freedom of Association, Complaint Against the Government of New Zealand presented by the New Zealand Council of Trade Unions (NZCTU), Report No. 292, Case No. 1698 (1994).
273. ILO Committee on Freedom of Association, Complaint Against the Government of the United States presented by the American Federation of Labor and Congress of Industrial Organizations (AFL-CIO) Report No. 278, Case No. 1543 (1991).
274. ILO Committee on Freedom of Association, Complaint Against the Government of the United Kingdom presented by the National Union of Seamen (NUS) Report No. 277, Case No. 1540 (1991).
275. Universal Declaration of Human Rights, G.A. res. 217A (III), U.N. Doc A/810 at 71 (1948), available at http://www1.umn.edu/humanrts/instree/b1udhr.htm.
276. International Covenant on Civil and Political Rights, G.A. res. 2200A (XXI), 21 U.N. GAOR Supp. (No. 16) at 52, U.N. Doc. A/6316 (1966), 999 U.N.T.S. 171, *entered into force* Mar. 23, 1976, available at http://www1.umn.edu/humanrts/instree/b3ccpr.htm.
277. Human Rights Committee, General Comment 25 (57), General Comments under article 40, paragraph 4, of the International Covenant on Civil and

Political Rights, Adopted by the Committee at its 1510th meeting, U.N. Doc. CCPR/C/21/Rev.1/Add.7 (1996), available at http://www1.umn.edu/humanrts/gencomm/hrcom25.htm.

278. *Id.*

279. *Marshall v. Canada*, Communication No. 205/1986, U.N. Doc. CCPR/C/43/D/205/1986 (1991), available at http://www1.umn.edu/humanrts/undocs/html/dec205.htm.

280. Human Rights Committee, General Comment 23, Article 27 (Fiftieth session, 1994), U.N. Doc. CCPR/C/21/Rev.1/Add.5 (1994), available at http://www1.umn.edu/humanrts/gencomm/hrcom23.htm.

281. *Supra* note 276.

282. *Id.*

283. *Id.*

284. *Id.*

285. International Convention on the Elimination of All Forms of Racial Discrimination, G.A. res. 2106 (XX), Annex, 20 U.N. GAOR Supp. (No. 14) at 47, U.N. Doc. A/6014 (1966), 660 U.N.T.S. 195, *entered into force* Jan. 4, 1969, available at http://www1.umn.edu/humanrts/instree/d1cerd.htm.

286. Conclusions and Recommendations of the Committee on the Elimination of Racial Discrimination, United States of America, U.N. Doc. A/56/18, paras. 380–407 (2001), available at http://www1.umn.edu/humanrts/country/usa2001.html.

287. *Supra* note 277.

288. *Id.*

289. *M.A. v. Italy*, Communication No. 117/1981, U.N. Doc. CCPR/C/OP/2 at 31 (1990), available at http://www1.umn.edu/humanrts/undocs/html/117-1981.htm.

290. Concluding Observations of the Human Rights Committee, India, U.N. Doc. CCPR/C/79/Add.81 (1997), available at http://www1.umn.edu/humanrts/hrcommittee/india1997.html.

291. *Supra* note 286.

292. O.A.S. Charter, Charter of the Organization of American States, 119 U.N.T.S. 3, *entered into force* Dec. 13, 1951; *amended by* Protocol of Buenos Aires, 721 U.N.T.S. 324, O.A.S. Treaty Series, No.1-A, *entered into force* Feb. 27, 1970; *amended by* Protocol of Cartagena, O.A.S. Treaty Series, No. 66, 25 I.L.M. 527, *entered into force* Nov. 16, 1988; *amended by* Protocol of Washington, 1-E Rev. OEA Documentos Oficiales OEA/Ser.A/2 Add. 3 (SEPF), 33 I.L.M. 1005, *entered into force* Sept. 25, 1997; *amended by* Protocol of Managua, 1-F Rev. OEA Documentos Oficiales OEA/Ser.A/2 Add.4 (SEPF), 33 I.L.M. 1009, *entered into force* Jan. 29, 1996, available at http://www1.umn.edu/humanrts/iachr/oascharter.html.

293. American Declaration of the Rights and Duties of Man, O.A.S. Res. XXX, *adopted by* the Ninth International Conference of American States (1948), *reprinted in* Basic Documents Pertaining to Human Rights in the Inter-American System, OEA/Ser.L.V/II.82 doc.6 rev.1 at 17 (1992), available at http://www1.umn.edu/humanrts/oasinstr/zoas2dec.htm.

294. American Convention on Human Rights, O.A.S.Treaty Series No. 36, 1144 U.N.T.S. 123, *entered into force* July 18, 1978, *reprinted in* Basic Documents Pertaining to Human Rights in the Inter-American System, OEA/Ser.L.V/II.82 doc.6 rev.1 at 25 (1992), available at http://www1.umn.edu/humanrts/oasinstr/zoas3con.htm.

295. Organization of American States, Inter-American Democratic Charter, OAS Doc. OEA/SerP/AG/Res.1 (2001); 28th Spec. Sess., OAS Doc. OEA/Ser.P/AG/RES.1 (XXVIII-E/01) (OAS General Assembly) (Sept. 11, 2001), 40 I.L.M. 1289 (2001), available at http://www.oas.org/charter/docs/resolution 1_en_p4.htm.
296. "The Four Freedoms," President Franklin Delano Roosevelt, State of the Union Address [the "Four Freedoms Speech"] (January 6, 1941), 87 Cong. Rec. 44 (1941), available at http://www1.umn.edu/humanrts/education/FDR4freedoms.html.
297. Charter of the United Nations, June 26, 1945, 59 Stat. 1031, T.S. 993, 3 Bevans 1153, *entered into force* Oct. 24, 1945, available at http://www1.umn.edu/humanrts/instree/aunchart.htm.
298. *Id.*
299. Universal Declaration of Human Rights, G.A. res. 217A (III), U.N. Doc A/810 at 71 (1948), available at http://www1.umn.edu/humanrts/instree/b1udhr.htm.
300. *Id.*
301. International Covenant on Economic, Social and Cultural Rights, G.A. res. 2200A (XXI), 21 U.N.GAOR Supp. (No. 16) at 49, U.N. Doc. A/6316 (1966), 993 U.N.T.S. 3, *entered into force* Jan. 3, 1976, available at http://www1.umn.edu/humanrts/instree/b2esc.htm.
302. *Id.*
303. Committee on Economic, Social and Cultural Rights, General Comment 3, The nature of States parties' obligations (Fifth session, 1990), U.N. Doc. E/1991/23, annex III at 86 (1991), *reprinted in* Compilation of General Comments and General Recommendations Adopted by Human Rights Treaty Bodies, U.N. Doc. HRI/GEN/1/Rev.6 at 14 (2003), available at http://www1.umn.edu/humanrts/gencomm/epcomm3.htm.
304. *Id.*
305. Committee on Economic, Social and Cultural Rights, General Comment 9, The Domestic Application of the Covenant (Nineteenth session, 1998), U.N. Doc. E/C.12/1998/24 (1998), *reprinted in* Compilation of General Comments and General Recommendations Adopted by Human Rights Treaty Bodies, U.N. Doc. HRI/GEN/1/Rev.6 at 54 (2003), available at http://www1.umn.edu/humanrts/gencomm/escgencom9.htm.
306. *Id.*
307. *Supra* note 299.
308. *Supra* note 301.
309. International Covenant on Civil and Political Rights, G.A. res. 2200A (XXI), 21 U.N. GAOR Supp. (No. 16) at 52, U.N. Doc. A/6316 (1966), 999 U.N.T.S. 171, *entered into force* Mar. 23, 1976, available at http://www1.umn.edu/humanrts/instree/b3ccpr.htm.
310. See http://www.ilo.org.
311. Employment Policy Convention (ILO No. 122), 569 U.N.T.S. 65, *entered into force* July 9, 1965, available at http://www1.umn.edu/humanrts/instree/n4epc.htm.
312. Convention concerning Basic Aims and Standards of Social Policy (ILO No. 117), *entered into force* Apr. 23, 1964, available at http://www1.umn.edu/humanrts/instree/ilo117.html.
313. *Id.*
314. Available at http://www.ilo.org/dyn/declaris/DECLARATIONWEB.static_jump?var_language=EN&var_pagename=DECLARATIONTEXT.

315. ILO Committee on Freedom of Association, Complaints Against the Government of the United States presented by the American Federation of Labor and the Congress of Industrial Organizations (AFL-CIO) and the Confederation of Mexican Workers (CTM), Report No. 2227, Case No. 332 (2003).

316. African Charter on Human and Peoples' Rights, *adopted* June 27, 1981, OAU Doc. CAB/ LEG/67/3 rev. 5, 21 I.L.M. 58 (1982), *entered into force* Oct. 21, 1986, available at http://www1.umn.edu/humanrts/instree/z1afchar.htm.

317. Charter of the Organization of American States, 119 U.N.T.S. 3, *entered into force* Dec. 13, 1951; *amended by* Protocol of Buenos Aires, 721 U.N.T.S. 324, O.A.S. Treaty Series, No. 1-A, *entered into force* Feb. 27, 1970; *amended by* Protocol of Cartagena, O.A.S. Treaty Series, No. 66, 25 I.L.M. 527, *entered into force* Nov. 16, 1988; *amended by* Protocol of Washington, 1-E Rev. OEA Documentos Oficiales OEA/Ser.A/2 Add. 3 (SEPF), 33 I.L.M. 1005, *entered into force* Sept. 25, 1997; *amended by* Protocol of Managua, 1-F Rev. OEA Documentos Oficiales OEA/Ser.A/2 Add.4 (SEPF), 33 I.L.M. 1009, *entered into force* Jan. 29, 1996. Available http://www1.umn.edu/humanrts/iachr/oascharter.html.

318. American Convention on Human Rights, O.A.S.Treaty Series No. 36, 1144 U.N.T.S. 123, *entered into force* July 18, 1978, *reprinted in* Basic Documents Pertaining to Human Rights in the Inter-American System, OEA/Ser.L.V/II.82 doc.6 rev.1 at 25 (1992), available at http://www1.umn.edu/humanrts/oasinstr/zoas3con.htm.

319. American Declaration of the Rights and Duties of Man, O.A.S. Res. XXX, *adopted by* the Ninth International Conference of American States (1948), *reprinted in* Basic Documents Pertaining to Human Rights in the Inter-American System, OEA/Ser.L.V/II.82 doc.6 rev.1 at 17 (1992), available at http://www1.umn.edu/humanrts/oasinstr/zoas2dec.htm.

320. Additional Protocol to the American Convention on Human Rights in the Area of Economic, Social and Cultural Rights, "Protocol of San Salvador," O.A.S. Treaty Series No. 69 (1988), *entered into force* Nov. 16, 1999, *reprinted in* Basic Documents Pertaining to Human Rights in the Inter-American System, OEA/Ser.L.V/II.82 doc.6 rev.1 at 67 (1992), available at http://www1.umn.edu/humanrts/oasinstr/zoas10pe.htm.

321. *Id.*, Article 6.

322. Juridical Condition and Rights of the Undocumented Migrants, Advisory Opinion OC-18/03, September 17, 2003, Inter-Am. Ct. H.R. (Ser. A) No. 18 (2003), available at http://www1.umn.edu/humanrts/iachr/series_A_OC-18.html.

323. European Convention for the Protection of Human Rights and Fundamental Freedoms, 213 U.N.T.S. 222, *entered into force* Sept. 3, 1953, *as amended by* Protocols Nos. 3, 5, 8, 11, *entered into force* Sept. 21, 1970, Dec. 20, 1971, Jan. 1, 1990, Nov. 1, 1998 respectively, available at http://www1.umn.edu/humanrts/instree/z17euroco.html.

324. European Social Charter, 529 U.N.T.S. 89, *entered into force* Feb. 26, 1965, available at http://www1.umn.edu/humanrts/euro/z31escch.html.

325. *Supra* note 299.

326. *Supra* note 301.

327. Committee on Economic, Social and Cultural Rights, General Comment No. 5, Persons with disabilities (Eleventh session, 1994), U.N. Doc E/1995/22 at 19 (1995), *reprinted in* Compilation of General Comments and General Recommendations Adopted by Human Rights Treaty Bodies, U.N. Doc. HRI/GEN/1/Rev.6 at 24 (2003), available at http://www1.umn.edu/humanrts/gencomm/epcomm5e.htm.

328. Committee on Economic, Social and Cultural Rights, General Comment No. 6, The economic, social and cultural rights of older persons (Thirteenth session, 1995), U.N. Doc. E/1996/22 at 20 (1996), *reprinted in* Compilation of General Comments and General Recommendations Adopted by Human Rights Treaty Bodies, U.N. Doc. HRI/GEN/1/Rev.6 at 34 (2003), available at http://www1.umn.edu/humanrts/gencomm/epcomm6e.htm.
329. *Id.*, para. 30.
330. *Supra* note 309.
331. Human Rights Committee, General Comment 18, Non-Discrimination (Thirty-seventh session, 1989), Compilation of General Comments and General Recommendations Adopted by Human Rights Treaty Bodies, U.N. Doc. HRIGENRev.1 at 26 (1994), available at http://www1.umn.edu/humanrts/gencomm/hrcom18.htm.
332. *S.W.M. Broeks v. The Netherlands*, Communication No. 172/1984, U.N. Doc. CCPR/C/OP/2 at 196 (1990), available at http://www1.umn.edu/humanrts/undocs/newscans/172-1984.html.
333. Human Rights Committee, General Comment 28, Equality of rights between men and women (article 3), U.N. Doc. CCPR/C/21/Rev.1/Add.10 (2000), available at http://www1.umn.edu/humanrts/gencomm/hrcom28.htm.
334. *Ibrahima Gueye et al. v. France*, Communication No. 196/1985, U.N. Doc. CCPR/C/35/D/196/1985 (1989), available at http://www1.umn.edu/humanrts/undocs/session35/196-1985.html.
335. International Convention on the Elimination of All Forms of Racial Discrimination, G.A. res. 2106 (XX), Annex, 20 U.N. GAOR Supp. (No. 14) at 47, U.N. Doc. A/6014 (1966), 660 U.N.T.S. 195, *entered into force* Jan. 4, 1969, available at http://www1.umn.edu/humanrts/instree/d1cerd.htm.
336. Committee on the Elimination of Racial Discrimination, General Recommendation 27, Discrimination Against Roma (Fifty-seventh session, 2000), U.N. Doc. A/55/18, annex V at 154 (2000), available at http://www1.umn.edu/humanrts/gencomm/genrexxvii.htm.
337. Convention on the Elimination of All Forms of Discrimination Against Women, G.A. res. 34/180, 34 U.N. GAOR Supp. (No. 46) at 193, U.N. Doc. A/34/46, *entered into force* Sept. 3, 1981, available at http://www1.umn.edu/humanrts/instree/e1cedaw.htm.
338. *Id.*
339. *Id.*
340. Committee on the Elimination of Discrimination Against Women, General Recommendation 16, Unpaid women workers in rural and urban family enterprises (Tenth session, 1991), U.N. Doc. A/46/38 at 1 (1993), *reprinted in* Compilation of General Comments and General Recommendations Adopted by Human Rights Treaty Bodies, U.N. Doc. HRI/GEN/1/Rev.6 at 241 (2003), available at http://www1.umn.edu/humanrts/gencomm/generl16.htm.
341. Convention on the Rights of the Child, G.A. res. 44/25, annex, 44 U.N. GAOR Supp. (No. 49) at 167, U.N. Doc. A/44/49 (1989), *entered into force* Sept. 2, 1990, available at http://www1.umn.edu/humanrts/instree/k2crc.htm.
342. *Id.*
343. *Id.*
344. Concluding Observations of the Committee on the Rights of the Child, Nigeria, U.N. Doc. CRC/C/15/Add.61 (1996), available at http://www1.umn.edu/humanrts/crc/nigeria1996.html.

345. Concluding Observations of the Committee on the Rights of the Child, Greece, U.N. Doc. CRC/C/15/Add.170 (2002), available at http://www1.umn.edu/humanrts/crc/greece2002.html.

346. Social Security (Minimum Standards) Convention (No. 102), June 28, 1952, 210 U.N.T.S. 131.

347. See http://www1.umn.edu/humanrts/instree/auon.htm and http://www.ilo.org

348. *Supra* note 324.

349. *Schuler-Zgraggen v. Switzerland*, Application No. 14518/89, European Court of Human Rights, June 24, 1983.

350. *Gaygusuz v. Austria*, Application No. 17371/90, European Court of Human Rights, September 16, 1996.

351. *Supra* note 317.

352. *Id.*

353. *Supra* note 299.

354. *Supra* note 301.

355. *Id.*

356. Committee on Economic, Social and Cultural Rights, General Comment 14, The Right to the Highest Attainable Standard of Health (Twenty-second session, 2000), U.N. Doc. E/C.12/2000/4 (2000), *reprinted in* Compilation of General Comments and General Recommendations Adopted by Human Rights Treaty Bodies, U.N. Doc. HRI/GEN/1/Rev.6 at 85 (2003), available at http://www1.umn.edu/humanrts/gencomm/escgencom14.htm.

357. Committee on Economic, Social and Cultural Rights, General Comment 3, The Nature of States Parties' Obligations (Fifth session, 1990), U.N. Doc. E/1991/23, annex III at 86 (1991), *reprinted in* Compilation of General Comments and General Recommendations Adopted by Human Rights Treaty Bodies, U.N. Doc. HRI/GEN/1/Rev.6 at 14 (2003), available at http://www1.umn.edu/humanrts/gencomm/epcomm3.htm.

358. *Supra* note 356.

359. Conclusions and recommendations of the Committee on Economic, Social and Cultural Rights, Finland, U.N. Doc. E/C.12/1/Add.52 (2000), available at http://www1.umn.edu/humanrts/esc/finland2000.html.

360. *Supra* note 335.

361. *Supra* note 337.

362. *Supra* note 341.

363. *Supra* note 309.

364. Principles of Medical Ethics Relevant to the Role of Health Personnel, Particularly Physicians, in the Protection of Prisoners and Detainees Against Torture and Other Cruel, Inhuman or Degrading Treatment or Punishment, G.A. res. 37/194, annex, 37 U.N. GAOR Supp. (No. 51) at 211, U.N. Doc. A/37/51 (1982), available at http://www1.umn.edu/humanrts/instree/h3pmerhp.htm.

365. *Supra* note 316.

366. *Supra* note 319.

367. *Supra* note 320.

368. *Supra* note 324.

369. Constitution of the World Health Organization, WHO Basic Documents, Official Document No. 240 (1991).

370. European Communities—Measures Affecting Meat and Meat Products (Hormones), Report of the Appellate Body, WT/DS26/AB/R & WT/DS48/AB/R (1998).

371. Official website of the Special Rapporteur on the right of everyone to the enjoyment of the highest attainable standard of physical and mental health: http://www.ohchr.org/english/issues/health/right/index.htm.
372. *Minister of Health and Others v. Treatment Action Campaign and Others*, CCT9/02 (2002), 2002 (5) SA 721 (CC); 2002 (10) BCLR 1033 (CC).
373. *Supra* note 299.
374. *Supra* note 301.
375. *Id.*
376. Universal Declaration on the Eradication of Hunger and Malnutrition, adopted by the World Food Conference, Rome, U.N. Doc. E/CONF. 65/20 at 1 (1974).
377. Voluntary Guidelines to Support the Progressive Realization of the Right to Adequate Food in the Context of National Food Security, Report of the 30th Session of the Committee on World Food Security (CFS), Supplement, FAO Doc. CL 127/10-Sup.1, Annex 1 (2004).
378. Committee on Economic, Social and Cultural Rights, General Comment 12, Right to adequate food (Twentieth session, 1999), U.N. Doc. E/C.12/1999/5 (1999), *reprinted in* Compilation of General Comments and General Recommendations Adopted by Human Rights Treaty Bodies, U.N. Doc. HRI/GEN/1/Rev.6 at 62 (2003), available at http://www1.umn.edu/humanrts/gencomm/escgencom12.htm.
379. *Id.*
380. Committee on Economic, Social and Cultural Rights, General Comment 14, The right to the highest attainable standard of health (Twenty-second session, 2000), U.N. Doc. E/C.12/2000/4 (2000), *reprinted in* Compilation of General Comments and General Recommendations Adopted by Human Rights Treaty Bodies, U.N. Doc. HRI/GEN/1/Rev.6 at 85 (2003), available at http://www1.umn.edu/humanrts/gencomm/escgencom14.htm.
381. Concluding Observations of the Human Rights Committee, Democratic People's Republic of Korea, U.N. Doc. CCPR/CO/72/PRK (2001), available at http://www1.umn.edu/humanrts/hrcommittee/korea2001.html.
382. *Supra* note 341.
383. Official website of the Special Rapporteur on the right to food: http://www.ohchr.org/english/issues/food/index.htm.
384. *Supra* note 317.
385. *Supra* note 319.
386. *Supra* note 320.
387. *Id.*
388. *Social and Economic Rights Action Center and the Center for Economic and Social Rights v. Nigeria*, Communication No. 155/96, African Commission on Human and Peoples' Rights (2001), available at http://www1.umn.edu/humanrts/africa/comcases/155-96b.html.
389. *People's Union for Civil Liberties v Union of India & Others* (Supreme Court of India) 2001, Unreported, 2 May 2003.
390. *Supra* note 299.
391. *Supra* note 301.
392. Committee on Economic, Social and Cultural Rights, General Comment 14, The right to the highest attainable standard of health (Twenty-second session, 2000), U.N. Doc. E/C.12/2000/4 (2000), *reprinted in* Compilation of General Comments and General Recommendations Adopted by Human Rights Treaty Bodies, U.N. Doc. HRI/GEN/1/Rev.6 at 85 (2003), available at http://www1.umn.edu/humanrts/gencomm/escgencom14.htm.

393. Committee on Economic, Social and Cultural Rights, General Comment No. 6, The Economic, Social and Cultural Rights of Older Persons (Thirteenth session, 1995), U.N. Doc. E/1996/22 at 20 (1996), *reprinted in* Compilation of General Comments and General Recommendations Adopted by Human Rights Treaty Bodies, U.N. Doc. HRI/GEN/1/Rev.6 at 34 (2003), available at http://www1.umn.edu/humanrts/gencomm/epcomm6e.htm.

394. Committee on Economic, Social and Cultural Rights, General Comment No. 5, Persons with Disabilities (Eleventh session, 1994), U.N. Doc E/1995/22 at 19 (1995), *reprinted in* Compilation of General Comments and General Recommendations Adopted by Human Rights Treaty Bodies, U.N. Doc. HRI/GEN/1/Rev.6 at 24 (2003), available at http://www1.umn.edu/humanrts/gencomm/epcomm5e.htm.

395. Conclusions and Recommendations of the Committee on Economic, Social and Cultural Rights, Canada, U.N. Doc. E/C.12/1/Add.31 (1998), available at http://www1.umn.edu/humanrts/esc/canada1998.html.

396. Conclusions and recommendations of the Committee on Economic, Social and Cultural Rights, Sri Lanka, U.N. Doc. E/C.12/1/Add.24 (1998), available at http://www1.umn.edu/humanrts/esc/srilanka1998.html.

397. *Supra* note 341.
398. See http://www1.umn.edu/humanrts/crc/crc-country.html.
399. *Supra* note 309.
400. *Id.*
401. *Id.*
402. Human Rights Committee, General Comment 22, Compilation of General Comments and General Recommendations Adopted by Human Rights Treaty Bodies, U.N. Doc. HRI/GEN/1/Rev.1 at 35 (1994), available at http://www1.umn.edu/humanrts/gencomm/hrcom22.htm.

403. *Id.*
404. *Supra* note 341.
405. *Id.*
406. *Supra* note 323.
407. Protocol to the Convention for the Protection of Human Rights and Fundamental Freedoms, 213 U.N.T.S. 262, *entered into force* May 18, 1954, available at http://www1.umn.edu/humanrts/euro/z20prot1.html.

408. *Karaduman v. Turkey*, Application No. 16278/90, 74 Eur. Comm'n H.R. Dec. & Rep. 93 (1993).

409. *Dahlab v. Switzerland*, Application No. 42393/98, 2001-V Eur. Ct. H.R. 447.

410. *Leyla Şahin v. Turkey*, Application No. 44774/98, European Court of Human Rights (2004).

411. *Id.*
412. *Id.*
413. *Id.*
414. Elimination of All Forms of Religious Intolerance, Report by the Special Rapporteur of the Commission on Human Rights on Freedom of Religion or Belief, U.N. Doc. A/55/280/Add.1 (2000).

415. *Id.*
416. *Supra* note 299.
417. *Supra* note 301.
418. Committee on Economic, Social and Cultural Rights, General Comment 4, The right to adequate housing (Sixth session, 1991), U.N. Doc. E/1992/23,

annex III at 114 (1991), *reprinted in* Compilation of General Comments and General Recommendations Adopted by Human Rights Treaty Bodies, U.N. Doc. HRI/GEN/1/Rev.6 at 18 (2003), available at http://www1.umn.edu/human rts/gencomm/epcomm4.htm.
    419. *Supra* note 335.
    420. *Supra* note 337.
    421. *Supra* note 341.
    422. *Supra* note 319.
    423. *Supra* note 317.
    424. *Supra* note 418.
    425. Committee on Economic, Social and Cultural Rights, General Comment 7, Forced Evictions, and the Right to Adequate Housing (Sixteenth session, 1997), U.N. Doc. E/1998/22, annex IV at 113 (1997), *reprinted in* Compilation of General Comments and General Recommendations Adopted by Human Rights Treaty Bodies, U.N. Doc. HRI/GEN/1/Rev.6 at 45 (2003), available at http://www1.umn.edu/humanrts/gencomm/escgencom7.htm.
    426. Centre on Housing Rights and Evictions, Forced Evictions: Violations of Human Rights (2003).
    427. Commission on Human Rights, Resolution 1993/77, adopted Mar. 10, 1993.
    428. UN Centre for Human Rights, The Human Right to Adequate Housing: Fact Sheet No. 21 (1996), available at http://www.ohchr.org/english/about/publications/docs/fs21.htm.
    429. Official website of the UN Special Rapporteur on adequate housing: http://www.ohchr.org/english/issues/housing/index.htm.
    430. *Supra* note 317.
    431. *Id.*
    432. *Supra* note 319.
    433. *Supra* note 318.
    434. *Supra* note 320.
    435. *Supra* note 324.
    436. Charter of Fundamental Rights of the European Union, 2000 O.J. (C 364) 1, *entered into force* Dec. 7, 2000, available at http://www1.umn.edu/human rts/instree/europeanunion2.html.
    437. *Government of the Republic of South Africa et al. v. Grootboom,* Constitutional Court of South Africa, Case CCT 11/00, (11) BCLR 1169, Judgment of October 4, 2000).
    438. Committee on Economic, Social and Cultural Rights, General Comment 3, The nature of States parties' obligations (Fifth session, 1990), U.N. Doc. E/1991/23, annex III at 86 (1991), *reprinted in* Compilation of General Comments and General Recommendations Adopted by Human Rights Treaty Bodies, U.N. Doc. HRI/GEN/1/Rev.6 at 14 (2003), available at http://www1.umn.edu/humanrts/gencomm/epcomm3.htm.
    439. *Supra* note 299.
    440. *Supra* note 301.
    441. Committee on Economic, Social and Cultural Rights, General Comment 15, The right to water (Twenty-ninth session, 2003), U.N. Doc. E/C.12/2002/11 (2002), *reprinted in* Compilation of General Comments and General Recommendations Adopted by Human Rights Treaty Bodies, U.N. Doc. HRI/GEN/1/Rev.6 at 105 (2003), available at http://www1.umn.edu/humanrts/gencomm/esc gencom15.htm.

442. *Supra* note 337.
443. *Supra* note 341.
444. Available at http://www1.umn.edu/humanrts/instree/auoy.htm.
445. *Supra* note 438.
446. *Supra* note 337.
447. *Supra* note 341.
448. African Charter on the Rights and Welfare of the Child, OAU Doc. CAB/LEG/24.9/49 (1990), *entered into force* Nov. 29, 1999, available at http://www1.umn.edu/humanrts/africa/afchild.htm.
449. Council of Europe, European Charter on Water Resources, CO-DBP/documents/codbp2001/08e (2001).
450. European Union Directive 2000/60/EC (2000).
451. Conclusions and Recommendations of the Committee on Economic, Social and Cultural Rights, Yemen, U.N. Doc. E/C.12/1/Add.92 (2003), available at http://www1.umn.edu/humanrts/esc/yemen2003.html.
452. Conclusions and Recommendations of the Committee on Economic, Social and Cultural Rights, Ireland, U.N. Doc. E/C.12/1/Add.77 (2002), available at http://www1.umn.edu/humanrts/esc/ireland2002.html.
453. *Social and Economic Rights Action Center and the Center for Economic and Social Rights v. Nigeria*, Communication No. 155/96, African Commission on Human and Peoples' Rights (2001), available at http://www1.umn.edu/humanrts/africa/comcases/155-96b.html.
454. *Delhi Water Supply v. State of Haryana*, 1996 SOL Case No. 556 (1996).
455. Office of the High Commissioner for Human Rights, Human Rights, Trade and Investment, U.N. Doc. E/CN.4/Sub.2/2003 (2003).
456. *Supra* note 299.
457. *Supra* note 301.
458. *Id.*
459. Committee on Economic, Social and Cultural Rights, General Comment 11, Plans of Action for Primary Education (Twentieth session, 1999), U.N. Doc. E/C.12/1999/4 (1999), *reprinted in* Compilation of General Comments and General Recommendations Adopted by Human Rights Treaty Bodies, U.N. Doc. HRI/GEN/1/Rev.6 at 59 (2003), available at http://www1.umn.edu/humanrts/gencomm/escgencom11.htm.
460. *Id.*
461. *Supra* note 297.
462. *Supra* note 299.
463. *Supra* note 341.
464. World Declaration on Education for All, World Conference on Education for All, Jomtien, Thailand, Mar. 5–9, 1990.
465. Vienna Declaration, World Conference on Human Rights, Vienna, June 14–25, 1993, U.N. Doc. A/CONF.157/24 (Part I) at 20 (1993), available at http://www1.umn.edu/humanrts/instree/l1viedec.html.
466. Committee on Economic, Social and Cultural Rights, General Comment 13, The Right to Education (Twenty-first session, 1999), U.N. Doc. E/C.12/1999/10 (1999), *reprinted in* Compilation of General Comments and General Recommendations Adopted by Human Rights Treaty Bodies, U.N. Doc. HRI/GEN/1/Rev.6 at 70 (2003), available at http://www1.umn.edu/humanrts/gencomm/escgencom13.htm.
467. *Id.*
468. *Id.*

469. *Supra* note 335.
470. *Supra* note 337.
471. *Supra* note 341.
472. International Convention on the Protection of the Rights of All Migrant Workers and Members of Their Families, G.A. res. 45/158, annex, 45 U.N. GAOR Supp. (No. 49A) at 262, U.N. Doc. A/45/49 (1990), *entered into force* July 1, 2003, available at http://www1.umn.edu/humanrts/instree/n8icprmw.htm.
473. *Supra* note 317.
474. *Supra* note 318.
475. *Supra* note 319.
476. *Supra* note 320.
477. *Supra* note 316.
478. Protocol to the Convention for the Protection of Human Rights and Fundamental Freedoms, 213 U.N.T.S. 262, *entered into force* May 18, 1954, available at http://www1.umn.edu/humanrts/euro/z20prot1.html.
479. *Supra* note 324.
480. Official website of UNESCO: http://www.unesco.org.
481. Official website of UNICEF: http://www.unicef.org.
482. Official website of the ILO: http://www.ilo.org.
483. See http://www1.umn.edu/humanrts/instree/auon.htm.
484. Official website of the Special Rapporteur on the right to education: http://www.ohchr.org/english/issues/education/rapporteur/index.htm.
485. *Supra* note 299.
486. *Supra* note 301.
487. *Supra* notes 301, 309.
488. *Supra* note 309.
489. Human Rights Committee, General Comment 23, Article 27 (Fiftieth session, 1994), Compilation of General Comments and General Recommendations Adopted by Human Rights Treaty Bodies, U.N. Doc. HRI/GEN/1/Rev.1 at 38 (1994), available at http://www1.umn.edu/humanrts/gencomm/hrcom23.htm.
490. *Supra* note 335.
491. Committee on the Elimination of Racial Discrimination, General Recommendation 23, Rights of indigenous peoples (Fifty-first session, 1997), U.N. Doc. A/52/18, annex V at 122 (1997), *reprinted in* Compilation of General Comments and General Recommendations Adopted by Human Rights Treaty Bodies, U.N. Doc. HRI/GEN/1/Rev.6 at 212 (2003), available at http://www1.umn.edu/humanrts/gencomm/genrexxiii.htm.
492. *Supra* note 341.
493. Universal Declaration on Cultural Diversity, UNESCO Doc. 31C/Res 25, 31st Sess., Annex 1 (2001).
494. *Id.*
495. Mexico City Declaration on Cultural Policies, in the final report of World Conference on Cultural Policies, Mexico City, Jul. 26–Aug. 6, 1982, UNESCO Doc. CLT/MD/1 (1982).
496. *Supra* note 465.
497. *Id.*
498. *Supra* note 316.
499. *Id.*
500. *Id.*
501. *Supra* note 320.

502. Declaration on the Elimination of Violence Against Women, G.A. res. 48/104, 48 U.N. GAOR Supp. (No. 49) at 217, U.N. Doc. A/48/49 (1993), available at http://www1.umn.edu/humanrts/instree/e4devw.htm.

503. *Supra* note 309.

504. *Supra* note 301.

505. UN Sub-Commission on the Promotion and Protection of Human Rights, Intellectual Property and Human Rights, 52nd Sess., 25th mtg., U.N. Doc. E/CN.4/Sub.2/Res/2000/7 (2000).

506. Agreement on Trade-Related Aspects of Intellectual Property Rights, Apr. 15, 1994, Marrakesh Agreement Establishing the World Trade Organization, Annex 1C, Legal Instruments-Results of the Uruguay Round vol. 31, 33 I.L.M. 81 (1994).

507. *Id.*

508. *Id.*

509. Hoggan, Karen, "Neem Tree Patent Revoked," *BBC News Online*, 11 May 2000, available at http://news.bbc.co.uk/1/hi/sci/tech/745028.stm.

510. See http://www1.umn.edu/humanrts/esc/esc-country.htm.

511. Committee on Economic, Social and Cultural Rights, General Comment 17, The Right of Everyone to Benefit from the Protection of the Moral and Material Interests Resulting from any Scientific, Literary or Artistic Production of Which He or She is the Author (article 15, paragraph 1 (c), of the Covenant), U.N. Doc. E/C.12/GC/17 (2006).

512. *Ivan Kitok v. Sweden*, Communication No. 197/1985, U.N. Doc. CCPR/C/33/D/197/1985 (1988), available at http://www1.umn.edu/humanrts/undocs/197-1985.html.

513. *Lansman v. Finland*, Communication No. 671/1995, U.N. Doc. CCPR/C/58/D/671/1995 (1996), available at http://www1.umn.edu/humanrts/undocs/html/671-1995.html.

514. UN Declaration on the Rights of Indigenous Peoples, U.N. ESCOR, Comm. on Human Rights, 11th Sess., Annex 1, U.N. Doc. E/CN.4/Sub.2 (1993), available at http://www1.umn.edu/humanrts/instree/declra.htm.

515. *The Mayagna (Sumo) Awas Tingni Community v. Nicaragua*, Judgment of Aug. 31, 2001, Inter-Am. Ct. H.R. (Ser. C) No. 79 (2001), available at http://www1.umn.edu/humanrts/iachr/AwasTingnicase.html.

516. *Mary and Carrie Dann v. United States*, Case 11.140, Report No. 75/02, Inter-Am. C.H.R., Doc. 5 rev 1 at 860 (2002), available at http://www1.umn.edu/humanrts/cases/75-02a.html.

517. *Supra* note 299.

518. *Supra* notes 301 and 309.

519. Committee on Economic, Social and Cultural Rights, General Comment 14, The Right to the Highest Attainable Standard of Health (Twenty-second session, 2000), U.N. Doc. E/C.12/2000/4 (2000), *reprinted in* Compilation of General Comments and General Recommendations Adopted by Human Rights Treaty Bodies, U.N. Doc. HRI/GEN/1/Rev.6 at 85 (2003), available at http://www1.umn.edu/humanrts/gencomm/escgencom14.htm.

520. *Id.*

521. Committee on Economic, Social and Cultural Rights, General Comment 15, The Right to Water (Twenty-ninth session, 2003), U.N. Doc. E/C.12/2002/11 (2002), *reprinted in* Compilation of General Comments and General Recommendations Adopted by Human Rights Treaty Bodies, U.N. Doc. HRI/GEN/1/Rev.6 at 105 (2003), available at http://www1.umn.edu/humanrts/gencomm/escgencom15.htm.

522. Available at http://www.unep.org/Documents/Default.asp?DocumentID=97&ArticleID=1503.
523. *Id.*
524. Need to Ensure a Healthy Environment for the Well-Being of Individuals, G.A. res. 45/94, U.N. Doc. A/RES/45/94 (1990).
525. Rio Declaration on Environment and Development, Report of the United Nations Conference on Environment and Development, Rio de Janeiro, June 3–14, 1992, chap. I, resolution 1, annex I, A/CONF.151/26 (1992).
526. Draft Principles on Human Rights and the Environment, in Human Rights and the Environment: Final Report Prepared by Mrs. Fatma Zohra Ksentini, Special Rapporteur, UN ESCOR Commission on Human Rights, Sub-Commission on Prevention of Discrimination and Protection of Minorities, U.N. Doc. E/CN.4/Sub.2/1994/9 (1994), annex I.
527. *Id.*
528. Official website of the Special Rapporteur on the adverse effects of the illicit movement and dumping of toxic and dangerous products and wastes on the enjoyment of human rights: http://www.ohchr.org/english/issues/environment/waste/.
529. Adverse effects of the illicit movement and dumping of toxic and dangerous products and wastes on the enjoyment of human rights, Report submitted by the Special Rapporteur, Fatma-Zohra Ouhachi-Vesely, U.N. Doc. E/CN.4/2004/46/Add.1 (2003).
530. Adverse effects of the illicit movement and dumping of toxic and dangerous products and wastes on the enjoyment of human rights, Comm. on Human Rts. res. 2004/17, U.N. Doc. E/CN.4/2004/23 at 70 (2004).
531. *Supra* note 316.
532. *The Social and Economic Rights Action Center and Center for Economic and Social Rights v. Nigeria*, Communication No. 155/96, African Commission on Human and Peoples' Rights, available at http://www1.umn.edu/humanrts/africa/comcases/155-96b.html.
533. Declaration by the European Council on the Environmental Imperative, Bull. Eur. Comm., No. 6, at 17 (1990).
534. *Supra* note 324.
535. *Lopez Ostra v. Spain*, European Court of Human Rights, 20 EHRR 277 (1994).
536. Convention on Access to Information, Public Participation in Decision-making and Access to Justice in Environmental Matters, done at Aarhus, Denmark, June 25, 1998.
537. *Supra* note 320.
538. *M. C. Mehta v. Union of India*, AIR 1987 SC 1086 (1987).
539. *Supra* note 297.
540. Declaration of the UN Conference on Human Environment, U.N. Doc. A/Conf.48/14/Rev. 1 (1973); 11 IL. M 1416 (1972).
541. Declaration on the Right to Development, G.A. res. 41/128, annex, 41 U.N. GAOR Supp. (No. 53) at 186, U.N. Doc. A/41/53 (1986), available at http://www1.umn.edu/humanrts/instree/s3drd.htm.
542. *Id.*
543. Rio Declaration on Environment and Development, Report of the United Nations Conference on Environment and Development, Rio de Janeiro, June 3–14, 1992, chap. I, resolution 1, annex I, A/CONF.151/26 (1992).
544. Agenda 21, Report of the United Nations Conference on Environment

and Development, Rio de Janeiro, June 3–14, 1992, chap. I, resolution 1, annex II, A/CONF.151/26 (1992).

545. Programme for the Further Implementation of Agenda 21, G.A. res. S-19/2, U.N. Doc. A/RES/S-19/2 (1997).

546. United Nations Millennium Declaration, G.A. Res. 55/2, U.N. GAOR, 55th Sess., Supp. No. 49, at 4, U.N. Doc. A/55/49 (2000).

547. Johannesburg Declaration on Sustainable Development, Report of the World Summit on Sustainable Development, Johannesburg, Aug. 26–Sept. 4, 2002, chap. I, resolution 1, annex I, A/CONF.199/20 (2002).

548. Plan of Implementation of the World Summit on Sustainable Development, Report of the World Summit on Sustainable Development, Johannesburg, Aug. 26–Sept. 4, 2002, chap. I, resolution 2, annex I, A/CONF.199/20 (2002).

549. Committee on the Rights of the Child, General Comment No. 1, The Aims of Education, U.N. Doc. CRC/GC/2001/1 (2001), available at http://www1.umn.edu/humanrts/crc/comment1.htm.

550. Committee on the Elimination of Discrimination Against Women, General Recommendation 21, Equality in Marriage and Family Relations (Thirteenth session, 1992), U.N. Doc. A/49/38 at 1 (1994), available at http://www1.umn.edu/humanrts/gencomm/generl21.htm.

551. Conclusions and recommendations of the Committee on Economic, Social and Cultural Rights, Tunisia, U.N. Doc. E/C.12/1/Add.36 (1999), available at http://www1.umn.edu/humanrts/esc/tunisia1999.html.

552. Concluding Observations of the Committee on the Rights of the Child, South Africa, U.N. Doc. CRC/C/15/Add.122 (2000), available at http://www1.umn.edu/humanrts/crc/southafrica2000.html.

553. *The Social and Economic Rights Action Center and Center for Economic and Social Rights v. Nigeria*, Communication No. 155/96, African Commission on Human and Peoples' Rights (2001), available at http://www1.umn.edu/humanrts/africa/comcases/155-96b.html.

554. Protocol to the African Charter on Human and Peoples' Rights on the Rights of Women in Africa, Adopted by the 2nd Ordinary Session of the Assembly of the Union, Maputo, July 11—August 13, 2003, available at http://www1.umn.edu/humanrts/africa/protocol-women2003.html.

555. *Supra* note 297.
556. *Id.*
557. *Id.*
558. *Id.*
559. *Id.*
560. *Id.*

561. Resolution 794 on the Situation in Somalia, adopted by the Security Council at its 3145th meeting, December 3, 1992, U.N. Doc. S/RES/794 (1992).

562. *Supra* note 296.
563. *Id.*

564. An Agenda for Peace: Preventive Diplomacy, Peacemaking and Peace-Keeping, Report of the Secretary-General pursuant to the statement adopted by the Summit Meeting of the Security Council on Jan. 31, 1992, June 17, 1992, U.N. Doc. A/47/277-S/24111 (1992).

565. Advisory Opinion on the Legality of the Threat or Use of Nuclear Weapons, 1996 I.C.J. 226 (1996).

566. Available at http://www1.umn.edu/humanrts/instree/auoy.htm.

567. Available at http://web.amnesty.org/report2004/index-eng.
568. *Supra* note 299.
569. *Supra* notes 91, 301, 309.
570. *Supra* note 335.
571. *Supra* note 308.
572. Human Rights Committee, General Comment 29, States of Emergency (article 4), U.N. Doc. CCPR/C/21/Rev.1/Add.11 (2001), available at http://www1.umn.edu/humanrts/gencomm/hrc29.html.
573. Declaration on the Right of Peoples to Peace, G.A. res. 39/11, Annex, 39 U.N. GAOR Supp. (No. 51) at 22, U.N. Doc. A/39/51 (1984), available at http://www1.umn.edu/humanrts/instree/q3drpp.htm.
574. Available at http://www1.umn.edu/humanrts/instree/auoy.htm.
575. *Id.*
576. Protocol Additional to the Geneva Conventions of 12 August 1949, and Relating to the Protection of Victims of International Armed Conflicts (Protocol I), 1125 U.N.T.S. 3, *entered into force* Dec. 7, 1978, available at http://www1.umn.edu/humanrts/instree/y5pagc.htm.
577. Protocol Additional to the Geneva Conventions of 12 August 1949, and Relating to the Protection of Victims of Non-International Armed Conflicts (Protocol II), 1125 U.N.T.S. 609, *entered into force* Dec. 7, 1978, available at http://www1.umn.edu/humanrts/instree/y6pagc.htm.
578. *Id.*
579. Geneva Convention for the Amelioration of the Condition of the Wounded and Sick in Armed Forces in the Field, 75 U.N.T.S. 31, *entered into force* Oct. 21, 1950, available at http://www1.umn.edu/humanrts/instree/y1gcacws.htm.
580. *Id.*
581. Geneva Convention relative to the Treatment of Prisoners of War, 75 U.N.T.S. 135, *entered into force* Oct. 21, 1950, available at http://www1.umn.edu/humanrts/instree/y3gctpw.htm.
582. Geneva Convention relative to the Protection of Civilian Persons in Time of War, 75 U.N.T.S. 287, *entered into force* Oct. 21, 1950, available at http://www1.umn.edu/humanrts/instree/y4gcpcp.htm.
583. *Id.*
584. *Id.*
585. *Id.*
586. *Supra* note 576.
587. *Id.*
588. *Id.*
589. *Id.*
590. *Id.*
591. *Id.*
592. See http://www1.umn.edu/humanrts/instree/auoy.htm.
593. Charter of the International Military Tribunal, 82 U.N.T.S. 279; 59 Stat. 1544; 3 Bevans 1238 (1945).
594. G.A. res. 96(I), U.N. GAOR, 1st Sess., pt. 2, at 188, U.N. Doc. A/64/Add.1 (1946).
595. Convention on the Prevention and Punishment of the Crime of Genocide, 78 U.N.T.S. 277 *entered into force* Jan. 12, 1951, available at http://www1.umn.edu/humanrts/instree/x1cppcg.htm.
596. *Id.*

597. Statute of the International Tribunal for the Prosecution of Persons Responsible for Serious Violations of International Humanitarian Law Committed in the Territory of the Former Yugoslavia since 1991, SC res. 827, UN SCOR 48th sess., 3217th mtg. at 1–2 (1993); 32 I.L.M. 1159, available at http://www1.umn.edu/humanrts/icty/statute.html.

598. Statute of the International Tribunal for Rwanda, adopted by S.C. Res. 955, U.N. SCOR, 49th Sess., 3453d mtg. at 3, U.N. Doc. S/RES/955 (1994), 33 I.L.M. 1598, 1600 (1994), available at http://www1.umn.edu/humanrts/instree/rwandatrib-statute1994.html.

599. Rome Statute of the International Criminal Court, U.N. Doc. 2187 U.N.T.S. 90, *entered into force* July 1, 2002, available at http://www1.umn.edu/humanrts/instree/Rome_Statute_ICC/Rome_ICC_toc.html.

600. *Prosecutor v. Jelisic*, Case No. IT-95-10 (Trial Chamber), Dec. 14, 1999.

601. *Supra* note 595.

602. *Id.*

603. Official website of the International Criminal Tribunal for the Former Yugoslavia (ICTY): http://www.un.org/icty. See also Application of the Convention on the Prevention and Punishment of the Crime of Genocide (*Bosn. & Herz. v. Yugo. (Serb. & Mont.)*, Judgment, Feb. 26, 2007.

604. Available at http://www.yale.edu/lawweb/avalon/lawofwar/hague02.htm and http://www.yale.edu/lawweb/avalon/lawofwar/hague04.htm.

605. Charter of the International Military Tribunal, 82 U.N.T.S. 279; 59 Stat. 1544; 3 Bevans 1238 (1945).

606. Available at http://www1.umn.edu/humanrts/instree/auoy.htm.

607. *Supra* note 575.

608. *Supra* note 576.

609. *Prosecutor v. Tadic*, Case No. IT-94-1-AR72 (Appellate Chamber), Oct. 2, 1995.

610. *Supra* note 599.

611. *Supra* note 605.

612. Control Council Law No. 10, Punishment of Persons Guilty of War Crimes, Crimes Against Peace and Against Humanity, Dec. 20, 1945, 3 Official Gazette Control Council for Germany 50–55 (1946), available at http://www1.umn.edu/humanrts/instree/ccno10.htm.

613. *Supra* note 597. In March 2005 the UN Security Council referred the crimes against humanity in the Sudan to the ICC for prosecution.

614. Convention on the Non-Applicability of Statutory Limitations to War Crimes and Crimes Against Humanity, G.A. res. 2391 (XXIII), annex, 23 U.N. GAOR Supp. (No. 18) at 40, U.N. Doc. A/7218 (1968), *entered into force* Nov. 11, 1970, available at http://www1.umn.edu/humanrts/instree/x4cnaslw.htm.

615. *Supra* note 593.

616. *Supra* note 597.

617. *Supra* note 599.

618. *Id.*

619. *Id.*

620. *Prosecutor v. Nahimana, Barayagwiza and Ngeze*, Case No. ICTR-99-52-T (Trial Chamber), Dec. 3, 2003.

621. *Prosecutor v. Akayesu*, Case No. ICTR-96-4-T (Appeals Chamber), June 1, 2001.

622. *Prosecutor v. Kunarac, Kovac and Vokovic*, Case No. IT-96-23 and IT-96-23/1 (Appeals Chamber), June 12, 2002.

623. International Convention for the Suppression of the Financing of Terrorism, G.A. Res. 109, U.N. GAOR, 54th Sess., Supp. No. 49, at 408, U.N. Doc. A/54/49 (Vol. I) (1999), *entered into force* Apr. 10, 2002, available at http://www1.umn.edu/humanrts/instree/financingterrorism.html.
624. Available at http://www1.umn.edu/humanrts/instree/terrorismtreaties.html.
625. European Convention on the Suppression of Terrorism, Jan. 27, 1977, 1137 U.N.T.S. 93, Europ. T.S. No. 90, 15 I.L.M. 1272, *entered into force* Aug. 4, 1978, available at http://www1.umn.edu/humanrts/euro/ets90.html.
626. Arab Convention on the Suppression of Terrorism, Apr. 22, 1998, *entered into force* May 7, 1999.
627. Report of the High-Level Panel on Threats, Challenges and Change, A More Secure World: Our Shared Responsibility, U.N. Doc. A/59/565 (2004), available at http://www1.umn.edu/ humanrts/instree/report.pdf.
628. International Cooperation to Combat Threats to Unternational Peace and Security Caused by Terrorist Acts, S.C. Res. 1373, U.N. SCOR, 57th Sess., 4385th mtg., pt. 1, at 291, U.N. Doc. S/INF/57 (2003).
629. Official website of the Counter-Terrorism Committee (CTC): http://www.un.org/Docs/sc/committees/1373/
630. Declaration on the Issue of Combating Terrorism, S.C. Res. 1456, U.N. SCOR, 57th Sess., 4688th mtg., U.N. Doc. S/Res/1456 (2003).
631. Convention for the Suppression of Unlawful Acts Against the Safety of Civil Aviation, Sept. 23, 1971, 974 U.N.T.S. 177, 24 U.S.T. 564, 10 I.L.M. 1151, *entered into force* Jan. 26, 1973, available at http://www1.umn.edu/humanrts/instree/civilaviation.html.
632. *Supra* note 599.
633. *Supra* note 309.
634. Advisory Opinion on the Legality of the Threat or Use of Nuclear Weapons, 1996 I.C.J. 226 (1996).
635. Available at http://www1.umn.edu/humanrts/instree/auoy.htm.
636. International Committee of the Red Cross, Commentary IV, Geneva Convention Relative to the Protection of Civilian Persons in Time of War (Jean S. Pictet ed., Ronald Griffin trans., 1958).
637. Universal Declaration of Human Rights, G.A. res. 217A (III), U.N. Doc A/810 at 71 (1948), available at http://www1.umn.edu/humanrts/instree/b1udhr.htm.
638. *Id.* and International Covenant on Economic, Social and Cultural Rights, G.A. res. 2200A (XXI), 21 U.N.GAOR Supp. (No. 16) at 49, U.N. Doc. A/6316 (1966), 993 U.N.T.S. 3, *entered into force* Jan. 3, 1976, available at http://www1.umn.edu/humanrts/instree/b2esc.htm. International Covenant on Civil and Political Rights, G.A. res. 2200A (XXI), 21 U.N. GAOR Supp. (No. 16) at 52, U.N. Doc. A/6316 (1966), 999 U.N.T.S. 171, *entered into force* Mar. 23, 1976, available at http://www1.umn.edu/humanrts/instree/b3ccpr.htm.
639. *Id.*, Article 5.
640. *Supra* note 299.
641. *Supra* notes 301, 309, Article 1.
642. Convention Concerning Indigenous and Tribal Peoples in Independent Countries (ILO No. 169), 72 ILO Official Bull. 59, *entered into force* Sept. 5, 1991, available at http://www1.umn.edu/humanrts/instree/r1citp.htm
643. Declaration on the Right and Responsibility of Individuals, Groups and

Organs of Society to Promote and Protect Universally Recognized Human Rights and Fundamental Freedoms, G.A. res.53/144, annex, 53 U.N. GAOR Supp., U.N. Doc. U.N. Doc. A/RES/53/144 (1999), available at http://www1.umn.edu/humanrts/instree/Res_53_144.html.

*Part III. Procedures for Implementation of Human Rights*

1. Official website of the UN General Assembly: http://www.un.org/aboutun/mainbodies.htm and http://www.un.org/documents/resga.htm.
2. Charter of the United Nations, June 26, 1945, 59 Stat. 1031, T.S. 993, 3 Bevans 1153, *entered into force* Oct. 24, 1945, available at http://www1.umn.edu/humanrts/instree/aunchart.htm.
3. Official website of the UN Economic and Social Council: http://www.un.org/docs/ecosoc/.
4. Official website of the UN High Commissioner for Human Rights: http://www.ohchr.org.
5. Official website of the UN Security Council: http://www.un.org/Docs/sc/.
6. Official website of the UN Counter-Terrorism Committee: http://www.un.org/Docs/sc/committees/1373/.
7. Official website of the UN Human Rights Commission: http://www.ohchr.org/english/bodies/chr/index.htm.
8. Official website of the UN Sub-Commission on the Promotion and Protection of Human Rights: http://www.ohchr.org/english/bodies/subcom/index.htm.
9. *Supra* note 2.
10. Economic and Social Council res. 1235 (XLII), 42 U.N. ESCOR Supp. (No. 1) at 17, U.N. Doc. E/4393 (1967).
11. South West Africa Cases (Second Phase) (*Eth. v. S. Afr.; Liber. v. S. Afr.*), 1966 I.C.J. 4 (July 18).
12. Committee on the Elimination of Racial Discrimination, General Recommendation 29, Discrimination Based on Descent, (Sixty-first session, 2002), U.N. Doc. A/57/18 at 111 (2002), *reprinted in* Compilation of General Comments and General Recommendations Adopted by Human Rights Treaty Bodies, U.N. Doc. HRI/GEN/1/Rev.6 at 223 (2003), available at http://www1.umn.edu/humanrts/cerd/genrec29.html.
13. Economic and Social Council res. 1503 (XLVIII), 48 U.N. ESCOR (No. 1A) at 8, U.N. Doc. E/4832/Add.1 (1970).
14. See http://www.ohchr.org/english/bodies/chr/complaints.htm.
15. Sub-Commission on Prevention of Discrimination and Protection of Minorities, Resolution 1 (XXIV), U.N. DOC. E/CN.4/1070 at 50–51 (1971), vailable at http://www1.umn.edu/humanrts/demo/1503Resolution1.html.
16. *Id.*
17. *Id.*
18. *Supra* note 13.
19. See http://www.ohchr.org/english/bodies/chr/special/themes.htm.
20. "In Larger Freedom: Towards Development, Security, and Human Rights for All," U.N. Doc. A/59/2005, available at http://www1.umn.edu/humanrts/unreport-largerfreedom.html.
21. Official website of the UN Human Rights Council: http://www.ohchr

.org/english/bodies/hrcouncil/; also see General Assembly res. 60/251, A/RES/60/251 (2006).
22. Official website of the Commission on the Status of Women (CSW): http://www.un.org/womenwatch/daw/csw/.
23. Official website of the UN Commission on Crime Prevention and Criminal Justice: http://www.unodc.org/unodc/en/crime_cicp_commission.html.
24. Official website of the UN Secretary-General: http://www.un.org/News/ossg/sg/.
25. Official website of the UN Department on Political Affairs: http://www.un.org/Depts/dpa/.
26. Official website of the UN Department of Peace-Keeping Operations: http://www.un.org/Depts/dpko/dpko/index.asp.
27. Official website of the UN Development Program: http://www.undp.org/.
28. *Supra* note 4.
29. Official website of the International Court of Justice (ICJ): http://www.icj-cij.org/.
30. Advisory Opinion on Reservations to the Convention on the Prevention and Punishment of the Crime of Genocide, 1951 I.C.J. 15 (May 28).
31. Legal Consequences for States of the Continued Presence of South Africa in Namibia (South West Africa) Notwithstanding Security Council Resolution 276 (1970), 1971 I.C.J. 15 (June 21).
32. *United States Diplomatic and Consular Staff in Tehran (U.S. v. Iran)*, 1980 I.C.J. 3 (May 24).
33. *Case Concerning Military and Paramilitary Activities in and Against Nicaragua (Nicaragua v. United States of America)*, 1986 I.C.J. 14 (June 27).
34. *Id.*
35. Vienna Convention on Consular Relations (*Paraguay v. United States of America*), 1998 I.C.J. 248 (Provisional Measures, Order of 9 Apr.) and 1998 I.C.J. 266 (Apr. 9); 1998 I.C.J. 426 (Nov. 10); 1998 I.C.J. 272 (June 8).
36. *LeGrand Case (Germany v. United States of America)*, 1999 I.C.J. 9 (Provisional Measures, Order of Mar. 3) and 1999 I.C.J. 28 (Mar. 5).
37. *Avena and other Mexican Nationals (Mex. v. U.S.)*, 2003 I.C.J. 2 (Provisional Measures, Order of February 5), 2004 I.C.J. 1 (Judgment), 43 I.L.M. 581. In the case of *Sanchez-Llamas v. Oregon*, 126 S. Ct. 2669 (2006), the U.S. Supreme Court did not challenge the 2003 ruling but refused to mandate application of the exclusionary rule to confessions by a defendants who had not been advised of their rights under the Vienna Convention.
38. *Applicability of Article VI, Section 22, of the Convention on Privileges and Immunities of the United Nations*, 1989 I.C.J. 177 (Dec. 15).
39. Advisory Opinion on the Legality of the Threat or Use of Nuclear Weapons, 1996 I.C.J. 226 (July 8).
40. See http://www1.umn.edu/humanrts/un-orgs.htm.
41. Official website of the UN Human Rights Committee: http://www.ohchr.org/english/bodies/hrc/index.htm; see also http://www1.umn.edu/humanrts/hrcommittee/hrc-page.html.
42. Human Rights Committee, General Comment 7, Article 7 (Sixteenth session, 1982), Compilation of General Comments and General Recommendations Adopted by Human Rights Treaty Bodies, U.N. Doc. HRI/GEN/1/Rev.1 at 7 (1994), available at http://www1.umn.edu/humanrts/gencomm/hrcom7.htm.
43. Optional Protocol to the International Covenant on Civil and Political

Rights, G.A. res. 2200A (XXI), 21 U.N. GAOR Supp. (No. 16) at 59, U.N. Doc. A/6316 (1966), 999 U.N.T.S. 302, *entered into force* Mar. 23, 1976, available at http://www1.umn.edu/humanrts/instree/b4ccprp1.htm.

44. Available at http://www1.umn.edu/humanrts/undocs/undocs-index.html.

45. Official website of the Committee Against Torture: http://www.ohchr.org/english/bodies/cat/index.htm.

46. Optional Protocol to the Convention Against Torture and Other Cruel, Inhuman or Degrading Treatment or Punishment, G.A. res. A/RES/57/199, *adopted* Dec. 18, 2002 [reprinted in 42 I.L.M. 26 (2003)], available at http://www1.umn.edu/humanrts/instree/optprotort.html.

47. Official website of the International Labor Organization (ILO): http://www.ilo.org.

48. ILO Declaration on Fundamental Principles and Rights at Work and Its Follow-Up, *adopted* June 18, 1998, 37 I.L.M. 1233.

49. ILO Constitution available at http://www.ilo.org/public/english/about/iloconst.htm.

50. ILO, Report of the Commission of Inquiry Appointed under Article 26 of the Constitution of the International Labour Organisation to Examine the Observance by Myanmar of the Forced Labour Convention, 1930 (No. 29), 81 Off. Bull., Series B, para. 536 (1998).

51. Official website of UNESCO: http://unesco.org.

52. Official website of the UN High Commissioner for Refugees (UNHCR): http://www.unhcr.ch/cgi-bin/texis/vtx/home.

53. Official website of the International Monetary Fund (IMF): http://www.imf.org/.

54. Official website of the International Bank for Reconstruction and Development (World Bank): http://www.worldbank.org/.

55. Official website of the World Trade Organization (WTO): http://www.wto.org/.

56. Articles of Agreement of the International Monetary Fund, July 22, 1944, 60 Stat. 1401, 2 U.N.T.S. 39, *as amended through* June 28, 1990, available at http://www.imf.org/external/about.htm, *entered into force* Sec. 27, 1945, *amended* Dec. 17, 1945, 16 U.N.T.S. 1942, TIAS No. 5929.

57. Articles of Agreement of the International Bank for Reconstruction and Development, 60 Stat. 1440, TIAS No. 1502, 2 U.N.T.S. 134; *entered into force* Dec. 27, 1945, *amended* Dec. 17, 1945, 16 U.N.T.S 1942, TIAS No. 5929.

58. Marrakesh Agreement Establishing the World Trade Organization, Apr. 15, 1994, 1867 U.N.T.S. 154, 33 I.L.M. 1144 (1994).

59. *Id.*

60. *Supra* note 2.

61. *Id.*

62. International Covenant on Economic, Social and Cultural Rights, G.A. res. 2200A (XXI), 21 U.N.GAOR Supp. (No. 16) at 49, U.N. Doc. A/6316 (1966), 993 U.N.T.S. 3, *entered into force* Jan. 3, 1976, available at http://www1.umn.edu/humanrts/instree/b2esc.htm.

63. Convention on the Rights of the Child, G.A. res. 44/25, annex, 44 U.N. GAOR Supp. (No. 49) at 167, U.N. Doc. A/44/49 (1989), *entered into force* Sept. 2, 1990, available at http://www1.umn.edu/humanrts/instree/k2crc.htm.

64. Joe Oloka-Onyango & Deepika Udagama, Final Report, Globalization and its Impact on the Full Enjoyment of Human Rights, U.N. Doc. E/CN.4/Sub.2/2003/14 (2003).

65. Vienna Convention on the Law of Treaties, 1155 U.N.T.S. 331, 8 I.L.M.

679, *entered into force* Jan. 27, 1980, available at http://www1.umn.edu/human rts/instree/viennaconvention.html.
  66. *Supra* note 2.
  67. *Supra* note 64.
  68. *Id.*
  69. *Id.*
  70. *Id.*
  71. *Id.*
  72. *Id.*
  73. http://www.ilo.org/public/english/dialogue/actrav/publ/strucadj.pdf.
  74. Official website of the Food and Agriculture Organization (FAO): http://www.fao.org/.
  75. Official website of the UN Children's Fund (UNICEF): http://www.unicef.org.
  76. Official website of the World Health Organization (WHO): http://www.who.int.
  77. Proclamation of Teheran, Final Act of the International Conference on Human Rights, Teheran, 22 April to 13 May 1968, U.N. Doc. A/CONF. 32/41 at 3 (1968), available at http://www1.umn.edu/humanrts/instree/l2ptichr.htm.
  78. Vienna Declaration, World Conference on Human Rights, Vienna, 14–25 June 1993, U.N. Doc. A/CONF.157/24 (Part I) at 20 (1993), available at http://www1.umn.edu/humanrts/instree/l1viedec.html.
  79. *Id.*
  80. World Conference Against Racism, Racial Discrimination, Xenophobia and Related Intolerance, Programme of Action, Agenda item 9, adopted Sept. 8, 2001 in Durban South Africa, U.N. Doc. A/CONF.189/5 (2001), available at http://www1.umn.edu/humanrts/instree/wcarprogrammeofaction.html.
  81. *Id.*
  82. Nuremberg Rules, in Agreement for the Prosecution and Punishment of the Major War Criminals of the European Axis, 82 U.N.T.S. 279, *entered into force* Aug. 8, 1945, available at http://www1.umn.edu/humanrts/instree/imt1945.htm.
  83. Control Council Law No. 10, Punishment of Persons Guilty of War Crimes, Crimes Against Peace and Against Humanity, Dec. 20, 1945, 3 Official Gazette Control Council for Germany 50–55 (1946), available at http://www1.umn.edu/humanrts/instree/ccno10.htm.
  84. Statute of the International Tribunal for the Prosecution of Persons Responsible for Serious Violations of International Humanitarian Law Committed in the Territory of the Former Yugoslavia since 1991, U.N. Doc. S/25704 at 36, annex (1993) and S/25704/Add.1 (1993), adopted by Security Council on 25 May 1993, U.N. Doc. S/RES/827 (1993), available at http://www1.umn.edu/humanrts/icty/statute.html.
  85. Official website of the International Criminal Court for the Former Yugoslavia (ICTY): http://www.un.org/icty/.
  86. Official website of the International Criminal Tribunal for Rwanda (ICTR): http://www.ictr.org/.
  87. Security Council Resolution 935, S.C. res. 935, 49 U.N. SCOR at 2, U.N. Doc. S/RES/935 (1994).
  88. Security Council Resolution 955, S.C. res. 955, 49 U.N. SCOR at 1, U.N. Doc. S/RES/955 (1994).
  89. Statute of the International Tribunal for Rwanda, adopted by S.C. Res. 955, U.N. SCOR, 49th Sess., 3453d mtg. at 3, U.N. Doc. S/RES/955 (1994), 33

I.L.M. 1598, 1600 (1994), available at http://www1.umn.edu/humanrts/instree/rwandatrib-statute1994.html.

90. *Prosecutor v. Akayesu*, ICTR-96-4-T (1998), *affirmed by* Appeals Chamber (2001).

91. *Prosecutor v. Karemera*, ICTR-98-44-AR73C) (2006).

92. Official website of the International Criminal Court: http://www.icc-cpi.int/.

93. Rome Statute of the International Criminal Court, 2187 U.N.T.S. 90, *entered into force* July 1, 2002, available at http://www1.umn.edu/humanrts/instree/Rome_Statute_ICC/Rome_ICC_toc.html.

94. Official website of the Special Court for Sierra Leone: http://www.sc-sl.org/.

95. Official website of the UN Transitional Administration in East Timor (UNTAET): http://www.un.org/peace/etimor/etimor.htm.

96. Official website of the UN Mission Interim Administration in Kosovo (UNMIK): http://www.un.org/Depts/dpko/missions/unmik/.

97. *Supra* note 2.

98. Official website of the Council of Europe: http://www.coe.int.

99. Official website of the European Union: http://www.eu.int.

100. Official website of the Organization for Security and Cooperation in Europe: http://www.osce.org.

101. Official website of the European Court of Human Rights: http://www.echr.coe.int/.

102. European Convention for the Protection of Human Rights and Fundamental Freedoms, 213 U.N.T.S. 222, *entered into force* Sept. 3, 1953, as amended by Protocols Nos. 3, 5, 8, 11, *entered into force* Sept. 21, 1970, Dec. 20, 1971, Jan. 1, 1990, Nov. 1, 1998 *respectively*, available at http://www1.umn.edu/humanrts/instree/z17euroco.html.

103. European Social Charter (ETS No. 35) 529 U.N.T.S. 89, *entered into force* Feb. 26, 1965, available at http://www1.umn.edu/humanrts/euro/z31escch.html.

104. Official website of the European Commission Against Racism and Intolerance (ECRI): http://www.coe.int/T/E/human_rights/Ecri/1-ECRI/.

105. Official website of the European Committee for the Prevention of Torture: http://www.cpt.coe.int/en/default.htm.

106. *Supra* note 102.

107. See http://www1.umn.edu/humanrts/euro/eurocon.html.

108. *Supra* note 102.

109. *Id.*

110. Protocol No. 14 to the 1950 European Convention for the Protection of Human Rights and Fundamental Freedoms, (ETS No. 194) *not entered into force*, available at http://www1.umn.edu/humanrts/euro/prot14.html.

111. *Supra* note 102.

112. *Neumeister v. Austria*, 17 Eur. Ct. H.R. (ser. A) (1974).

113. *Engel and Others v. the Netherlands*, 22 Eur. Ct. H.R. (ser. A) (1976).

114. *Stran Greek Refineries and Straits Andreadis v. Greece*, 301 Eur. Ct. H.R. (ser.A) 61 (1994).

115. *Leyla Şahin v. Turkey*, Application No. 44774/98, European Court of Human Rights (2004).

Notes to Pages 316–326    411

116. Convention on Human Rights and Biomedicine (ETS No. 164), *entered into force* Dec. 1, 1999, available at http://www1.umn.edu/humanrts/euro/z37.html.
117. European Social Charter, 529 U.N.T.S. 89, *entered into force* Feb. 26, 1965, available at http://www1.umn.edu/humanrts/euro/z31escch.html.
118. Additional Protocol to the European Social Charter Providing for a System of Collective Complaints (ETS No. 158), *entered into force* Jan. 7, 1998, available at http://www1.umn.edu/humanrts/euro/ets158.html.
119. European Social Charter (revised) (ETS No. 163), *entered into force* Jan. 7, 1999, available at http://www1.umn.edu/humanrts/euro/ets163.html.
120. European Social Charter, List of Complaints and Advancement of the Procedure: http://www.coe.int/t/e/human_rights/esc/4_collective_complaints/List_of_collective_complaints/default.asp#TopOfPage
121. Official website of the Commissioner for Human Rights: http://www.coe.int/T/E/Commissioner_H.R/Communication_Unit/.
122. Treaty Instituting the European Coal and Steel Community, Apr. 18, 1951, 261 U.N.T.S. 140, 143, *entered into force* July 25, 1952.
123. Treaty Establishing the European Economic Community, Mar. 25, 1957, 298 U.N.T.S. 11.
124. Treaty Establishing the European Atomic Energy Community, Mar. 25, 1957, 298 U.N.T.S. 169.
125. Single European Act, O.J. (L 169/1) (1987).
126. Nold v. Commission, Case 4/73, E.C.R. 491 (1974).
127. *Cinéthèque S.A. v. Fédération National des Cinémas Français*, Cases 60 and 61/84, E.C.R. (1985).
128. Charter of Fundamental Rights of the European Union, 2000 O.J. (C364) 1.
129. The Final Act of the Conference on Security and Cooperation in Europe, Aug. 1, 1975, 14 I.L.M. 1292 (Helsinki Declaration).
130. Charter of Paris for a New Europe, Nov. 21, 1990, 30 I.L.M. 193 (1991).
131. CSCE, Declaration and Decisions from Helsinki Summit, July 10, 1992, 31 I.L.M. 1385 (1992).
132. *Id.*
133. Mandate of the OSCE Representative on Freedom of the Media (Nov. 5, 1997), PC Journal No. 137, Decision No. 193, para. 2.
134. Charter of the Organization of American States, 119 U.N.T.S. 3, *entered into force* Dec. 13, 1951; *amended by* Protocol of Buenos Aires, 721 U.N.T.S. 324, O.A.S. Treaty Series, No. 1-A, *entered into force* Feb. 27, 1970; *amended by* Protocol of Cartagena, O.A.S. Treaty Series, No. 66, 25 I.L.M. 527, *entered into force* Nov. 16, 1988; *amended by* Protocol of Washington, 1-E Rev. OEA Documentos Oficiales OEA/Ser.A/2 Add. 3 (SEPF), 33 I.L.M. 1005, *entered into force* Sept. 25, 1997; *amended by* Protocol of Managua, 1-F Rev. OEA Documentos Oficiales OEA/Ser.A/2 Add.4 (SEPF), 33 I.L.M. 1009, *entered into force* Jan. 29, 1996, available at http://www1.umn.edu/humanrts/iachr/oascharter.html.
135. Protocol of Amendment to the Charter of the Organization of American States, Protocol of Buenos Aires," O.A.S. Treaty Series No. 1-A, *entered into force* Mar. 12, 1970, available at http://www1.umn.edu/humanrts/oasinstr/buenos aires.html.
136. Protocol of Amendment to the Charter of the Organization of American States, "Protocol of Cartagena de Indias," O.A.S. Treaty Series No. 66, *entered*

*into force* Nov. 16, 1988, available at http://www1.umn.edu/humanrts/oasinstr/cartagena1988.html.

137. Protocol of Amendment to the Charter of the Organization of American States, "Protocol of Managua," 1-F Rev. OEA Documentos Oficiales OEA/Ser.A/2 Add.4 (SEPF), *entered into force* Jan. 29, 1996.

138. Protocol of Amendment to the Charter of the Organization of American States, "Protocol of Washington," 1-E Rev. OEA Documentos Oficiales OEA/Ser.A/2 Add. 3 (SEPF), *entered into force* Sept. 25, 1997, available at http://www1.umn.edu/humanrts/oasinstr/washington1997.html.

139. *Supra* note 134.

140. American Declaration of the Rights and Duties of Man, O.A.S. Res. XXX, adopted by the Ninth International Conference of American States (1948), *reprinted in* Basic Documents Pertaining to Human Rights in the Inter-American System, OEA/Ser.L.V/II.82 doc.6 rev.1 at 17 (1992), available at http://www1.umn.edu/humanrts/oasinstr/zoas2dec.htm.

141. Interpretation of the American Declaration of the Rights and Duties of Man Within the Framework of Arcticle 64 of the American Convention on Human Rights, Advisory Opinion OC-10/89, July 14, 1989, Inter-Am. Ct. H.R. (Ser. A) No. 10 (1989), available at http://www.umn.edu/humanrts/iachr/b_11_4j.htm.

142. American Convention on Human Rights, O.A.S.Treaty Series No. 36, 1144 U.N.T.S. 123 *entered into force* July 18, 1978, *reprinted in* Basic Documents Pertaining to Human Rights in the Inter-American System, OEA/Ser.L.V/II.82 doc.6 rev.1 at 25 (1992), available at http://www1.umn.edu/humanrts/oasinstr/zoas3con.htm.

143. Additional Protocol to the American Convention on Human Rights in the Area of Economic, Social and Cultural Rights, O.A.S. Treaty Series No. 69 (1988), *signed* Nov. 17, 1988, *reprinted in* Basic Documents Pertaining to Human Rights in the Inter-American System, OEA/Ser.L.V/II.82 doc.6 rev.1 at 67 (1992), available at http://www1.umn.edu/humanrts/oasinstr/zoas10pe.htm.

144. Regulations of the Inter-American Commission on Human Rights, *reprinted in* Basic Documents Pertaining to Human Rights in the Inter-American System, OEA/Ser.L.V/II.82 doc.6 rev.1 at 103 (1992), available at http://www1.umn.edu/humanrts/oasinstr/zoas5cmr.htm.

145. Official website of the Inter-American Commission on Human Rights: http://www.cidh.org/.

146. See http://www1.umn.edu/humanrts/instree/auoz.htm.

147. Official website of the Special Rapporteur for Freedom of Expression: http://www.cidh.oas.org/relatoria/index.asp?lID=1.

148. Official website of the Inter-American Court of Human Rights: http://www.corteidh.or.cr/.

149. *Supra* note 142.

150. *Id.*

151. *Garrido and Baigorria Judgment*, Inter-Am. Ct. H.R. (ser. C) No. 39 (1998).

152. *Velásquez Rodriguez Judgment*, Inter-Am. Ct. H.R. (ser. C) No. 4 (1988).

153. *Godínez Cruz Judgment*, Inter-Am. Ct. H.R. (ser. C) No. 5 (1989).

154. *Fairen and Solis Judgment*, Inter-Am. Ct. H.R. (ser. C) No. 6 (1989).

155. See http://www1.umn.edu/humanrts/iachr/iachr.html.

156. *Velásquez Rodriguez Judgment*, Inter-Am. Ct. H.R. (ser. C) No. 4 at para. 172 (1988).

157. "Other Treaties" Subject to the Advisory Jurisdiction of the Court (art.

64 American Convention on Human Rights), Advisory Opinion OC-1/82, September 24, 1982, Inter-Am. Ct. H.R. (Ser. A) No. 1 (1982), available at http://www1.umn.edu/humanrts/iachr/b_11_4a.htm.

158. *Supra* note 134.

159. Inter-American Democratic Charter, OAS Doc. OEA/SerP/AG/Res.1 (2001); 28th Spec. Sess., OAS Doc. OEA/Ser.P/AG/RES.1 (XXVIII-E/01) (OAS General Assembly) (Sept. 11, 2001), 40 I.L.M. 1289 (2001), available at http://www1.umn.edu/humanrts/oasinstr/demcharter-2001.html.

160. Official website of the African Union: http://www.africa-union.org/.

161. Constitutive Act of the African Union, OAU Doc. CAB/LEG/23.15, *entered into force* May 26, 2001, available at http://www1.umn.edu/humanrts/africa/auconst-act2001.html.

162. African [Banjul] Charter on Human and Peoples' Rights, adopted June 27, 1981, OAU Doc. CAB/LEG/67/3 rev. 5, 21 I.L.M. 58 (1982), *entered into force* Oct. 21, 1986, available at http://www1.umn.edu/humanrts/instree/z1afchar.htm.

163. Protocol to the African Charter on Human and People's Rights on the Establishment of an African Court on Human and People's Rights, June 9, 1998, OAU Doc. OAU/LEG/EXP/AFCHPR/PROT (III), available at http://www1.umn.edu/humanrts/africa/courtprotocol2004.html.

164. Official website of the African Commission on Human and Peoples' Rights: http://www.achpr.org/.

165. *International Pen and Others v. Nigeria*, African Commission on Human and Peoples' Rights, Comm. Nos. 137/94, 139/94, 154/96 and 161/97 (1998), available at http://www1.umn.edu/humanrts/africa/comcases/137-94_139-94_154-96_161-97.html.

166. *The Social and Economic Rights Action Center and Center for Economic and Social Rights v. Nigeria*, Communication No. 155/96, African Commission on Human and Peoples' Rights (2001), available at http://www1.umn.edu/humanrts/africa/comcases/155-96b.html.

167. *Supra* note 163.

168. Richard Bilder, *Rethinking International Human Rights: Some Basic Questions*, 1969 Wis. L. Rev. 171, 178 n.11 (quoting Eleanor Roosevelt, Remarks at a ceremony at the United Nations, New York, Mar. 27, 1958).

169. International Covenant on Civil and Political Rights, G.A. res. 2200A (XXI), 21 U.N. GAOR Supp. (No. 16) at 52, U.N. Doc. A/6316 (1966), 999 U.N.T.S. 171, *entered into force* Mar. 23, 1976, available at http://www1.umn.edu/humanrts/instree/b3ccpr.htm.

170. Available at http://www.congreso.es/funciones/constitucion/indice.htm.

171. UK Human Rights Act, 1998 Chapter 42, available at http://www.hmso.gov.uk/acts/acts1998/19980042.htm.

172. Available at http://www1.umn.edu/humanrts/education/usconstitution.html.

173. [*Murray v. Schooner*] *Charming Betsy*, 6 U.S. (2 Cranch) 34 (1804).

174. *The Paquete Habana*, 175 U.S. 677 (1900).

175. *Atkins v. Virginia*, 536 US 304 (2002).

176. National institutions for the promotion and protection of human rights, G.A. res. 48/134, 48 U.N. GAOR Supp. (No. 49) at 252, U.N. Doc. A/48/49 (1993) ("Paris Principles"), available at http://www1.umn.edu/humanrts/resolutions/48/134GA1993.html.

177. *Supra* note 78.
178. *Supra* note 2

*Part IV. Conclusion*

1. *Doe v. Saravia*, 348 F. Supp. 2d 1112 (E.D. Cal. 2004).
2. *Sosa v. Alvarez-Machain*, 124 S.Ct. 2739 (2004).

# Index of Subjects and Sources

Additional Protocol to the European Social Charter, 318–19. *See also* European Social Charter
Additional Protocol to the European Social Charter Providing for a System of Collective Complaints, 318–19. *See also* European Social Charter
Afghanistan, 159, 204, 219–20, 239–40, 254, 259
African [Banjul] Charter on Human and Peoples' Rights, 34, 39–40, 70, 127, 140, 174, 180, 190, 192–93, 200–201. *See also* African Union; Organization of African Unity
African Charter on the Rights and Welfare of the Child, 166
African Commission on Human and Peoples' Rights, 148, 166, 192–93, 200–201, 334–36. *See also* Organization of African Unity
African Court on Human and Peoples' Rights, 334, 336–38
African Development Bank, 200
African Union, 201, 335–38; Court of Justice, 336–38
Agreement on the Application of Sanitary and Phytosanitary Measures, 141. *See also* World Trade Organization
AIDS/HIV, ix, 11, 35, 137, 141–42, 200, 244, 367–68
Albania, 19, 39, 224, 262, 313, 325
Alfonsín, Raúl, 355
Algeria, 334
Alien Tort Claims Act (ATCA or Alien Tort Statute, ATS), 366–67
Aliens, 15; rights of, 16, 19. *See also* Asylum; Non-citizens; Refugees
Álvarez, Alejandro, 19
American Convention on Human Rights, 160, 326–32; death penalty, 40; economic, social, and cultural rights, 326–27; education, 173; freedom of movement, 70; indigenous rights, 186; labor rights, 127–28; nondiscrimination, 34, 127–28; parties, 326; San Salvador Protocol in the Area of Economic, Social and Cultural Rights, 127, 135, 140, 148, 160, 173–74, 180–81, 190, 194, 330; voting, 116
American Convention on Human Rights to Abolish the Death Penalty, 330
American Declaration of the Rights and Duties of Man, 34, 40, 116, 127, 140, 148, 157, 160, 173, 186, 326–28
American Federation of Labor-Congress of Industrial Organizations (AFL-CIO), 291
Amin, Idi, 353
Amnesty, 354
Amnesty International (AI), 53–54, 209, 225, 255, 306, 337
*Amparo*, 65
Andorra, 313
Angola, 99, 102, 254, 342–43
Annan, Kofi, 236, 264, 301. *See also* Secretary-General, UN
Anti-Slavery Society, 17, 42
*Apartheid*, iv, 284, 356; crime against humanity, 228; UN response, 257. *See also* South Africa
Aquinas, St. Thomas, 15
Arab Charter on Human Rights, 338
Arab Convention on the Suppression of Terrorism, 236
Arbitrary killing, 3. *See also* Summary or arbitrary executions
Argentina: American Convention on Human Rights, 326; ECOSOC resolution 1503, 262; incorporation of treaties into national law, 344; Inter-American Court of Human Rights, 331; structural adjustment, 291; truth and reconcilia-

Argentina (*continued*)
tion, 352, 355–56. *See also* Alien Tort Claims Act; Cruel, inhuman, or degrading treatment; Disappearances; Fact-finding; Inter-American Commission on Human Rights; Working Group on Enforced or Involuntary Disappearances
*Armed Activities in the Territory of the Congo*, 93
Armenians, 224, 313
Asia and Pacific, 338
Asian Development Bank, 200
Asian Human Rights Charter, 338
Assembly, freedom of, 109–12
Association, freedom of (including trade union rights), 109–12, 335
Asylum, 74–81, 244, 322
*Atkins v. Virginia*, 345–46
Aung San Suu Kyi, ix, 366
Australia, 4, 65, 87–88, 273, 282, 304–5, 307; Aboriginals, 185; dualist approach to treaties, 344; private homosexual behavior, 68; Western European and Other Group, 260
Austria, 4, 18, 77, 135, 297, 304, 309, 313, 315–16, 321, 323, 344
Aylwin Azócar, Patricio, 356
Azerbaijan, 313; Karabakh, 32

Bangladesh (formerly East Pakistan), 175
Barbados, 282, 326, 331
Basic Principles for the Treatment of Prisoners, 63
Basic Principles on the Independence of the Judiciary, 61
Basic Principles on the Role of Lawyers, 61
Bechtel Corporation, 167
Belarus, 259, 264
*Beldjoudi v. France*, 89
Belgium, 4, 17, 19, 30, 98, 152, 313, 321
Belize, 94
Benin, 273
Bhutan, 174
Body of Principles for the Protection of All Persons Under Any Form of Detention or Imprisonment, 63
Bolivia, 167, 261, 326, 331, 352
Bosnia-Herzogovina, 10, 30, 74, 219, 224–25, 298, 313, 352; mixed tribunals, 303, 309; national genocide trials, 301; UN peacekeeping with human rights dimension, 254. *See also* Yugoslavia, ICTY

Brazil, 39, 159, 307, 326, 331; child labor, 173; NGO truth commission, 353; visit from Special Rapporteur on adequate housing, 159; visit from Special Rapporteur on toxic waste, 192
British Virgin Islands, 30
*S.W.M. Broeks v. Netherlands*, 132
Buddhism, 14, 224, 305. *See also* Religion
Bulgaria, 18, 189, 313
Burkina Faso, 189, 334
Burma, 366; country-specific rapporteur, 254, 259; forced labor, 47–48, 50–52; Karens, 32. *See also* Aung San Suu Kyi; Business; Forced labor; International Labor Organization
Burundi, 224, 254, 259, 299, 307, 334
Bush, George W., 57
Business, human rights obligations, 11, 146, 192, 256. *See also* Corporations; International Labor Organization; Tort

Cairo Declaration on Human Rights in Islam, 338
Cambodia (also Democratic Kampuchea), 166, 175, 224, 227, 254, 259, 303, 305–6, 309
Cameroon, 19, 174
Canada, 4, 32, 88–89, 97–98, 100, 342, 344; Canadian Immigration and Refugee Board, 78; Committee on Economic, Social and Cultural Rights, 151; First Nations, 185; public participation, 113; Québec, 32; visit from Special Rapporteur on toxic waste, 192; Western European and Other Group, 260
Carson, Rachel, 189
Carter, Jimmy, 117
Carter Center, 117
Central African Republic, 74
Central American Bank for Economic Integration, 200
Central Intelligence Agency (CIA), 239
Centre on House Rights and Evictions (COHRE), 158
Chad, 259, 261, 352
Charter of the Fundamental Rights of the European Union, 322–23
Charter of the Organization of American States (OAS), 116–17, 127, 135, 148, 157, 159–60, 173, 325–27

Index    417

Chechnya, 32, 320. *See also* Russian Federation
Child labor, ix, 284; International Labor Organization, 367. *See also* Convention on the Rights of the Child; International Covenant on Civil and Political Rights; International Covenant on Economic, Social and Cultural Rights; International Programme for the Elimination of Child Labor; UNICEF; United States; World Trade Organization
Child, rights of, 244, 246, 322; sexual exploitation, 11; trafficking in children, 11. *See also* Beijing rules; Child labor; Child soldiers; Convention on the Rights of the Child; Minimum Rules for the Administration of Juvenile Justice; Sale of children
Chile, 326, 331; Constitution, 142, 189; truth and reconciliation commission, 352, 355–56; social security, 135; UN working group on human rights situation, 253. *See also* Pinochet
China, People's Republic of, 237, 265, 305; forced collectivization, 227; Security Council member, 254; visit from special rapporteur on education, 175
Christianity, Christ, 14, 15, 152, 181, 297. *See also* Religion
Churchill, Winston, 22
*Cinéthèque S.A. v. Fédération National des Cinémas Français*, 322
Clothing, right to, 150–56
Code of Conduct for Law Enforcement Officials, 53, 61
Cold War, 121, 254, 297, 312, 323–24
Colombia, 75, 135, 166, 175, 185, 259, 273, 326, 331
Columbus, Christopher, 158
Commission on Crime Prevention and Criminal Justice, UN, 252, 266–67
Commission on Human Rights, UN, 71, 100, 142, 159, 175, 189, 192, 199, 252–53, 255–66, 330, 346; country-specific rapporteurs, 258–59, 298; drafting treaties and other instruments, 25, 192, 255; food, right to, 145, 147–48; forced evictions, 158; indigenous rights, 186; structure and procedures, 255. *See also* Human Rights Council; Sub-Commission; Special Rapporteurs; Thematic procedures

Commission on the Status of Women, UN, 252, 266
Committee Against Torture (CAT), 53–56, 272; communications, 277; Sub-Committee on Prevention, 54, 278. *See also* Convention Against Torture and Other Cruel, Inhuman or Degrading Treatment or Punishment
Committee on Economic, Social and Cultural Rights, 29, 272–73; concluding observations, 93, 166, 199–200, 368; general comments, 121–22, 131, 137–39, 141, 145–47, 151, 157–58, 161, 163–65, 170–72, 190–91, 272. *See also* International Covenant on Economic, Social and Cultural Rights
Committee on the Elimination of Discrimination Against Women (CEDAW), 132–33, 199, 266, 271–72, 277
Committee on the Elimination of Racial Discrimination (CERD), 31, 105, 178, 258, 271, 277
Committee on Enforced Disappearances, 272, 278
Committee on Migrant Workers, 271
Committee on the Rights of the Child (CRC), 133–34, 151, 200, 272. *See also* Convention on the Rights of the Child
Committee on the Rights of Persons with Disabilities, 272, 277–78
Communications: Human Rights Committee, 276–77; Working Group on Communications, 260–61. *See also* Committee Against Torture; ECOSOC resolution 728F; ECOSOC resolution 1235; ECOSOC resolution 1503; Human Rights Committee
Communism, Communists, 222, 312
Comoros, 334
Conference on Security and Cooperation in Europe (CSCE; Helsinki process), 323–24
Confucianism, 14, 15. *See also* Religion
Conscientious objection, 35, 99
Constitutive Act of the African Union, 337
Control Council Law No. 10, 228, 297
Convention Against Discrimination in Education, 284
Convention Against the Taking of Hostages, 235

Convention Against Torture and Other Cruel, Inhuman or Degrading Treatment or Punishment, 9–10, 53–57, 63, 78–79, 276; extradition of Pinochet, 10; Optional Protocol, 54; parties, 54; Preamble, 206. *See also* Committee Against Torture

Convention concerning Indigenous and Tribal Peoples in Independent Countries, 93

Convention for the Protection of Cultural Property in the Event of Armed Conflict, 284

Convention for the Protection of World Cultural and Natural Heritage, 179

Convention for the Suppression of Terrorist Bombings, 235

Convention for the Suppression of Unlawful Acts Against the Safety of Civil Aviation, 235, 237–38

Convention for the Suppression of Unlawful Acts Against the Safety of Maritime Navigation, 235

Convention for the Suppression of Unlawful Seizure of Aircraft, 235

Convention Governing the Specific Aspects of Refugee Problems in Africa, 79

Convention on the Elimination of All Forms of Discrimination Against Women, 36, 163–65; education, 172–73; employment, 132; health, 139; housing, 157; nationality, 82; Optional Protocol, 266; social security, 132. *See also* Committee on the Elimination of Discrimination Against Women; Discrimination (sex)

Convention on Human Rights and Biomedicine, 316

Convention on the Means of Prohibiting and Preventing the Illicit Import, Export and Transfer of Ownership of Cultural Property, 179

Convention on the Non-Applicability of Statutory Limitations to War Crimes and Crimes Against Humanity, 228

Convention on the Physical Protection of Nuclear Material, 235

Convention on the Prevention and Punishment of Crimes Against Internationally Protected Persons, including Diplomatic Agents, 235

Convention on the Prevention and Punishment of the Crime of Genocide, 38, 298, 302; adoption and drafting, 222–23, 257; culture, 179

Convention on the Reduction of Statelessness, 82–83, 85

Convention on the Rights of the Child, 63, 83, 170; Article 4, 288; Article 7, 82; Article 12, 61; Article 14, 154; Article 17, 185; Article 18, 133; Article 20, 133; Article 24, 139; Article 26, 133, 164–65; Article 27, 147, 151–52, 157; Article 28, 173; Article 29, 173, 185, 199; Article 30, 154, 178–79, 185; Article 37, 39, 61; Article 40, 61; Housing, 157; Parties, 39, 82, 212; sale of children, 44

Convention and Protocol Relating to the Status of Refugees, 74, 78–79, 93, 285. *See also* Refugees

Convention Relating to the Status of Stateless Persons, 82–85

*Cordon-Garcia. v. Immigration and Naturalization Service (INS)*, 77

Costa Rica, 307, 326, 331; child labor, 175; visit from special rapporteur on toxic waste, 192

Council of Arab Ministers, 236

Council of Europe, 309, 311–21, 338; Commissioner for Human Rights, 320–21; Committee of Ministers, 166, 312–13, 315, 317–20. *See also* Nongovernmental organizations

Crimes against humanity, 227–29, 236, 302, 304, 306–7. See also *Apartheid*; Control Council Law No. 10; International Criminal Court; International Criminal Tribunal for the Former Yugoslavia; International Criminal Tribunal for Rwanda; International Military Tribunal (Nuremberg)

Criminal sanctions, 9–11, 296–310. *See also* International Criminal Court

Croatia, 30, 224–25, 297–98, 313, 325

Cruel, inhuman, or degrading treatment or punishment (also ill-treatment), 53, 55–57; Iraq, 366; United States, 366. *See also* Convention Against Torture and Other Cruel, Inhuman or Degrading Treatment or Punishment; Declaration on the Protection of All Persons from Being Subjected to Torture and Other

Index    419

Cruel, Inhuman or Degrading Treatment or Punishment; Torture
Cuba, 65, 91, 142, 254, 259, 265, 329–30. *See also* Fact-finding; Guantánamo
Cultural relativism, 7, 152–56, 181–83
Culture, right to, 152–56, 177–88
Customary international law, 6
Cyprus, 259, 313, 316, 321
Czech Republic, Czechoslovakia, 18, 30, 31, 93, 313, 321

*Dahlab v. Switzerland*, 155
Damages, 315, 331, 366–67
*Mary and Carrie Dann v. United States*, 186
Dayton Peace Agreement, 309. *See also* former Yugoslavia; International Criminal Tribunal for the Former Yugoslavia
Death penalty, 38, 345–46, 368
Declaration by the European Council on the Environmental Imperative, 190, 193
Declaration of Principles on International Cultural Cooperation, 179
Declaration of the Rights of Man, 15
Declaration on the Elimination of All Forms of Intolerance and of Discrimination Based on Religion or Belief, 100, 244
Declaration on the Elimination of Violence Against Women, 181
Declaration on the Protection of all Persons from Being Subjected to Torture and Other Cruel, Inhuman or Degrading Treatment or Punishment, 53
Declaration on the Right of Peoples to Peace, 208
Declaration on the Rights of Indigenous Peoples, 32, 93–94, 186, 246, 256, 368. *See also* Indigenous
Declaration on the Rights of Persons Belonging to National or Ethnic, Religious and Linguistic Minorities, 256
Declaration Relative to the Universal Abolition of the Slave Trade, 42
Democracy, 113, 116–17, 317, 333
Democratic Republic of Congo, 10, 39, 225, 238; advisory services, 259; cases before the International Court of Justice, 93; cases before the International Criminal Court, 303; peacekeeping, 204; UN peacekeeping with human rights dimension, 254

Denmark, 10, 17, 32, 78, 313, 316–17, 321
Detention, 63–66, 342; incommunicado, 8.
Development, 288; sustainable, 197–202
*D.I. v. Germany*, 106
Disabled, 244, 322
Disappearances, 330, 365; Argentina, 355–56
Discrimination, 3, 13, 19, 34–37, 178–79, 244, 322, 338; affirmative action, 35–37; economic, social, and cultural rights, 121–22; language, 34–35; racial, 34–37, 114–15, 185; religion, 34–36, 100; sex (gender), 34–37, 132–33
Djibouti, 261
*Doe v. Saravia*, 367
Dominica, 326
Dominican Republic, 158, 326, 329, 331, 368
Draft Declaration of Principles on Human Rights and the Environment, 189, 191–92
Dualist approach to international law, 4–5, 343–45
Dunant, Henri, 17–18

East Timor, 39, 306–8. *See also* Timor-Leste
Economic and Social Council (ECOSOC), UN, 253, 272; role in approving country-specific and thematic procedures, 258; role in regard to slavery, 50
Economic, social, and cultural rights, 120–23, 326–27, 342. *See also* Clothing; Committee on Economic, Social and Cultural Rights; Culture; Education; European Social Charter; Food; Health; Housing; International Covenant on Economic, Social and Cultural Rights; Social security; Water; Work-related rights
ECOSOC resolution 728F, 257
ECOSOC resolution 1235, 257
ECOSOC Resolution 1503 Procedure, 252, 259–62, 266; admissibility standards, 260; Working Group on Communications, 260–61; Working Group on Situations, 261. *See also* Communications
Ecuador, 166, 189, 273, 326, 331, 352
Education, right to, 3, 169–77, 284–85, 322, 338
Egypt, 91, 273, 191

## Index

El Salvador, ix, 326, 331; child labor, 175; Romero, Oscar, ix, 366–67; truth commission, 352–53; UN peacekeeping with human rights dimension, 254
*Engel and Others v. the Netherlands,* 315
Environment, right to healthy, 11, 189–96, 287, 322, 342
Equal protection, 36–37. *See also* Discrimination
Equatorial Guinea, 92, 262
Eritrea, 31, 166
Estonia, 19, 30, 254, 313, 321, 325
Ethiopia, 31, 99, 102, 148, 166, 192, 342–43
European Charter on Water Resources, 166
European Coal and Steel Community Treaty, 321
European Code of Social Security, 134
European Commission Against Racism and Intolerance (ECRI), 312
European Commission of Human Rights, and headscarves, 154–55
European Committee for the Prevention of Torture (CPT), 312
European Committee of Social Rights, 317–20
European Convention for the Prevention of Torture and Inhuman or Degrading Treatment or Punishment, 7–8, 312
European Convention of Human Rights, 5, 7, 128, 134, 312–17, 320–23, 326, 344–45; Article 2, 40; Article 3, 55; Article 5, 315; Article 6, 94; Article 8, 89; Article 9, 154; Article 10, 104; Article 14, 34–35, 135; Article 21, 313; Article 33, 314; Article 41 ("just satisfaction"), 315; Article 46, 317; Article 47, 316–17; Protocol No. 1, 94, 135, 154–56, 174; Protocol No. 2, 316; Protocol No. 4, 70; Protocol No. 6, 40; Protocol No. 11, 313–14; Protocol No. 12, 35; Protocol No. 14, 313–14, 322
European Convention on the Suppression of Terrorism, 235–36
European Court of Human Rights, 55–56, 79, 312–17, 322; advisory jurisdiction, 316–17; damages, 315; environmental pollution, 193; fair trial, 62, 94, 134; headscarves, 155; individual cases, 314–16; interstate cases, 316; "margin of appreciation," 7; property, 94; sexual orientation, 68; social security, 134

European Court of Justice (ECJ), 321–22. *See also* European Union
European Ombudsman, 322
European Parliament, 184, 321, 323. *See also* European Union
European Patent Office (EPO), 184–85
European Social Charter, 128, 134, 140–41, 160, 174, 174, 317–20, 321; revised, 318–20
European Union (EU), 5, 141, 166, 201, 321–23. *See also* Austria; Belgium; Council of the European Union; Cyprus; Czech Republic; Denmark; Estonia; European Commission; European Court of Justice; European Parliament; Finland; France; Germany; Greece; Hungary; Ireland; Italy; Latvia; Lithuania; Luxembourg; Malta; Netherlands; Poland; Portugal; Slovakia; Slovenia; Spain; Sweden; United Kingdom
European Union Agency for Fundamental Rights, 323
Exhaustion of remedies, 260
Expression, freedom of (speech), 102–8, 335, 342
Extradition, 55

Fact-finding, 329–30; Cuba, 329–30; Dominican Republic, 329; Haiti, 329; interviewing, 359; on-site, 359
*Fairen and Solis Judgment,* 332
Fair trial, 3, 59–62, 238, 256, 335, 338, 342
Family, 87–90
*Faurisson v. France,* 105–6
Female Genital Mutilation (FGM), 78, 181
Finland, 19, 103, 106, 109, 139, 185, 313, 319, 321
Food and Agricultural Organization (FAO), 145, 291
Food, right to, 144–50, 183, 287, 291; starvation, 3; Sub-Commission study, 256
Forced evictions, 3, 368. *See also* Housing, right to
Forced labor, 42–52, 280, 282–83, 322
Former Yugoslavia, 46, 74–75, 254, 296, 297–99, 353. *See also* Yugoslavia
France, 4, 16, 17, 19, 30, 72, 74, 84, 89, 91, 98, 105–6, 132, 152–53, 254, 273, 309, 313, 316, 319–20, 321
French Declaration of the Rights of Man and of the Citizen, 17

Index 421

Gabon, 334
Gambia, 166, 334
Gandhi, Mahatma, 20
*Garrido and Baigorria Judgment*, 332
*Gaygusuz v. Austria*, 135
General Agreement on Tarriffs and Trade (GATT), 183. *See also* World Trade Organization
General Assembly, UN, 91, 145, 159, 191, 197–98, 208, 222, 252–54, 263–64, 294, 301–2, 330, 346, 368
Geneva Convention for the Amelioration of the Condition of the Wounded and Sick in Armies in the Field (1864), 18
Geneva Convention Relative to the Protection of Civilian Persons in Time of War (Fourth Convention), 65, 215–17, 239; fair trial, 61; forcible transfer, 71, 216
Geneva Convention Relative to the Treatment of Prisoners of War (Third Convention), 214–16, 239
Geneva Conventions, Additional Protocol I, 61, 212–14, 217–19, 226–27, 239
Geneva Conventions, Additional Protocol II, 61, 71, 212, 214, 227, 239, 304
Geneva Conventions of 1949, 8–10, 53, 56–57, 206, 214 , 235–36, 238–39, 304; Common Article III, 3, 61, 212–13, 219, 239; Criminal sanctions, 9–10, 226, 304, 306; implementation, 298; ratification, 212
Genocide, 222–25. *See also* Convention on the Prevention and Punishment of the Crime of Genocide; Democratic Republic of Congo; Holocaust; International Criminal Tribunal for the Former Yugoslavia; International Criminal Tribunal for Rwanda; Nazi regime; Rwanda
Georgia, 30, 313; Abkhazia, 32; concluding observation of the Committee on the Rights of the Child, 151; Ossetia, 32; UN peacekeeping with human rights dimension, 254
Germany (German), 4, 17, 19, 307, 309, 313, 321, 352; colonies, 19; environment, 189; headscarves, 98, 152–53; visit from special rapporteur on toxic waste, 192; war crimes during World War II, 11, 20–23, 222, 227–29, 231
Ghana, 135, 334, 352–53
Ginsberg, Ruth Bader, 36

Globalization, 184
*Godínez Cruz Judgment*, 332
Golden Rule, 14
W. R. Grace Co., 184
Greece, 14, 16, 18, 74–75, 133–34, 313, 315, 319, 321; environment, 189; European Court of Human Rights, 315–316; UN action, 259–60
Green Party, 184
Greenland, 185
Grenada, 326
Groups at risk, 244–46
Guam, 30
Guantánamo, Cuba, 65–66, 219–20, 239
Guatemala, 77, 116, 174, 185, 254, 326, 331, 352–53
*Gueye et al. v. France*, 132
Guidelines on the Role of Prosecutors, 61
Guiding Principles on Internal Displacement, 71

Habeas corpus, 65
Hague Conventions of 1899 and 1907, 18, 212, 225
Haiti, 142, 151, 252, 254, 259–60, 326, 329, 331, 352
Hammurabi, Code of, 14
*Handbook on Procedures and Criteria for Determining Refugee Status* (UNHCR), 76–77
Hathaway, James, 76
Health, right to, 3, 124–26, 136–44, 189–92, 287, 338. *See also* World Health Organization
*Hertzberg et al. v. Finland*, 103–4
High-Level Panel on Threats, Challenges and Change, 236–37
Hinduism, 14. *See also* Religion
History of international human rights, 3; early development, 14–18; interwar years, 19–20; prior to World War I, 16–18; World War I and League of Nations, 18–19; World War II and beginning of modern movement, 20–26
Holocaust, 11, 14, 21–23, 105–6, 222–23, 230
Homosexuality, 222, 244, 246. *See also* Sexual orientation
Honduras, 39, 261, 326, 331; Environment, 189; Indigenous, 185
Housing, right to adequate (habitat; shelter), ix, 92, 156–63, 256, 291, 368

Human Rights Commission of the League of Arab States, 338
Human Rights Committee, UN, 29, 55–56, 62, 63, 77, 79, 87–89, 97–100, 102–6, 132, 252, 271–77; cases, 54, 185, 273; concluding observations, 147; General Comments, 38, 60–61, 67–68, 70, 72, 92, 97–100, 102, 114–15, 131–32, 153, 207–8, 272, 276; procedure, 273–74; state reports, 273–75. *See also* Communications; International Covenant on Civil and Political Rights
Human Rights Council, UN, 252–53, 255–56, 258–66, 278, 262, 278; indigenous rights, 186, 368; thematic procedures, 39, 71, 142, 175, 192, 246, 262–63
Human Rights Watch, 209, 225
Humanitarian law, 9–11, 212–21; armed conflicts, 212–14. *See also* Geneva Conventions; Hague Conventions; International Military Tribunal (Nuremberg); Tokyo tribunal
Hungary, 18, 135, 142, 309, 313, 321, 325

Iceland, 99, 102, 309, 313, 342–43
*Immigration and Naturalization Service (INS) v. Cardoza-Fonseca*, 75
*Immigration and Naturalization Service (INS) v. Elias-Zacarias*, 77
*Immigration and Naturalization Service (INS) v. Stevic*, 75
*In re Kasinga*, 78
India, 4, 85, 273, 282, 307; caste, 258; child labor, 175; Kashmir, 32, 83; neem tree, 184–85; quota for women in public office, 116; social security, 135; Supreme Court, 148–49, 166–67, 194; water, right to, 166
Indigenous people, ix, 32, 93–94, 185–86, 244, 246; culture, 178–79, 185–86; declaration on rights, 186, 368; ILO, 245; Indians, 185; United States, 185
Indonesia, 87–88, 91, 174–75, 307–8
Intellectual property, 93, 183–85. *See also* Property
Inter-American Commission of Women, 333
Inter-American Commission on Human Rights (IACHR), 5, 252, 327–30; Belize, 94; cases before, 328–29; composition, 327; country studies, 329–30; Cuba, 329–30; Dominican Republic, 329; indigenous rights, 186; individual petition system, 328–29; Proposed American Declaration on the Rights of Indigenous Peoples, 186, 330; Special Rapporteur for Freedom of Expression, 330; Special Rapporteur for Migrant Workers and Their Families, 330
Inter-American Convention Against Terrorism, 236
Inter-American Convention on Forced Disappearance of Persons, 330. *See also* Disappearances
Inter-American Convention on the Granting of Civil Rights to Women, 333
Inter-American Convention on the Granting of Political Rights to Women, 333
Inter-American Convention on the Nationality of Women, 333
Inter-American Convention on the Prevention, Punishment and Eradication of Violence Against Women, 333
Inter-American Convention to Prevent and Punish Torture, 330
Inter-American Court of Human Rights: advisory opinions, 332–33; cases, 331–32; Costa Rica, 331; damages, 331; discrimination, 127–28; indigenous rights, 186; labor rights, 127–28
Inter-American Democratic Charter, 117
Inter-American Development Bank, 200
Intergovernmental organizations, 8–9
Internal Affairs, intervention in, 253
Internally displaced persons, 71, 74, 79, 209, 285
International Bill of Human Rights, 4, 26, 130; discrimination, 185; drafting, 25; interpretation of Articles 5556 of UN Charter, 25. *See also* International Covenants; Universal Declaration of Human Rights
International Center for Transitional Justice, 253
International Centre for the Settlement of Investment Disputes, 167
International Commission of Jurists, 255
International Committee of the Red Cross (ICRC), 212; commentary on Geneva Conventions, 239; internally displaced persons, 71; prison visits, 56, 219–20; role in drafting Geneva Conventions, 8, 18. *See also* Geneva Conventions of 1949

Index 423

International Confederation of Free Trade Unions, 280
International Convention Against Transnational Organized Crime, 45
International Convention for the Suppression of the Financing of Terrorism, 234–36
International Convention on the Elimination of All Forms of Racial Discrimination, 35–36, 76, 93, 139; culture, 178; education 172; hate speech, 104–5; housing, 157; indigenous persons, 185; parties, 3; peaceful relations, 207; states reports, 115; voting, 114–15. *See also* Committee on the Elimination of Racial Discrimination; Discrimination
International Convention on the Protection of All Persons from Enforced Disappearance, 256, 272, 278
International Convention on the Protection of Rights of All Migrant Workers and Members of Their Families, 39, 173, 271
International Convention on the Rights of Persons with Disabilities and Optional Protocol, 272, 277–78
International Court of Justice (ICJ), 252, 268–70; advisory jurisdiction, 206, 269; Article 38, 269; contentious jurisdiction, 269; death penalty, 270; genocide, 225, 269–70; implementing Vienna Convention on Consular Relations, 64, 269–70; Namibia, 269; Permanent Court of International Justice, 268; reservations to treaties, 269; self-determination, 31; South Africa, 269; Statute of the International Court of Justice, 268–69; Threat or use of Nuclear Weapons, 206, 238, 270; U.S. diplomats detained in Iran, 269
International Covenant on Civil and Political Rights, 4, 25, 61, 76, 91–94, 121, 125, 130, 338; Article 1, 29–30, 91, 177, 245; Article 2, 48, 59, 343; Article 4, 60–61, 182, 207–8, 212; Article 5, 245; Article 6, 38, 59, 147, 190–91; Article 7, 45, 53, 55, 59–60, 140, 238; Article 8, 45; Article 9, 46, 59, 63, 238; Article 12, 46 , 48, 70–71; Article 14, 59–61; Article 15, 60; Article 16, 60; Article 17, 67, 87–89; Article 18, 97–99, 153; Article 19, 102–6, 153, 182; Article 20, 104–5; Article 21, 102, 109; Article 22, 102, 109–10, 124, 244; Article 23, 84, 87– 90; Article 24, 82, 87–88, 238; Article 25, 102, 113–14, 116; Article 26, 100, 131–32; Article 27, 92, 99, 153, 178, 185; Article 40, 153; drafting, 257, 359; First Optional Protocol, 9, 25, 54, 276; nondiscrimination, 34–35, 131; part of International Bill of Human Rights, 4; parties, 39; Preamble, 206; ratification, 4; Second Optional Protocol aiming at abolition of death penalty, 38–39, 207. *See also* Human Rights Committee
International Covenant on Economic, Social and Cultural Rights, 4, 25, 76, 91–93, 125, 191, 338; Article 1, 29–30, 91, 151, 177, 245; Article 2, 121, 288; Article 5, 245; Article 6, 124; Article 7, 124; Article 8, 109–10, 124, 244; Article 9, 84, 130; Article 11, 124, 144, 156–57, 190; Article 12, 136–37, 138, 151, 163, 190, 193; Article 13, 169, 171; Article 14, 169–70; Article 15, 177, 183; Article 17, 151; distinguished from civil and political rights, 25; Drafting, 257, 359; Nondiscrimination, 34–35, 12122; part of International Bill of Human Rights, 4; parties, 4; Preamble, 206; ratification, 4. *See also* Committee on Economic, Social and Cultural Rights
International Criminal Court (ICC), 10–11, 238, 296, 301–3; crimes against humanity, 228, 238; definition of genocide, 223–24; history, 229–31; parties, 230–31, 302; rape, 367; Rome Statute, 10, 56, 235; United States, 230–31; war crimes, 227
International Criminal Tribunal for the Former Yugoslavia (ICTY), 10, 61, 225, 229–31, 238, 254–55, 297–99, 303; crimes against humanity, 228; death penalty excluded, 298; definition of genocide, 223; systematic rape, 367; war crimes, 227
International Criminal Tribunal for Rwanda (ICTR), 10, 61, 229–31, 238, 254–55, 299–301, 303, 305; crimes against humanity, 228, 300; genocide, 223, 229; war crimes, 227
International financial institutions, 286–92
International Institute for Democracy and Electoral Assistance (IDEA), 117

International Labor Organization (ILO), 47–52, 109–11, 124–26, 129, 134, 171, 175, 279–84; Burma, 282–83; child labor, 283–84, 367; commission of inquiry, 282–83; Committee of Experts on the Application of Conventions and Recommendations, 281–82; Committee on Freedom of Association, 111–12, 126, 283; Constitution of ILO, 280–83; Convention No. 29, 47–48, 50, 283; Convention No. 81, 125; Convention No. 87, 110–11, 283; Convention No. 95, 49; Convention No. 98, 110–111, 283; Convention No. 102, 134; Convention No. 103, 134; Convention No. 105, 48, 50; Convention No. 110, 125; Convention No. 115, 125; Convention No. 117, 49, 126; Convention No. 118, 134; Convention No. 119, 125; Convention No. 120, 125; Convention No. 121, 134; Convention No. 122, 126; Convention No. 127, 125; Convention No. 128, 134; Convention No. 129, 125; Convention No. 130, 134; Convention No. 131, 48–49; Convention No. 135, 125; Convention No. 136, 125; Convention No. 139, 125; Convention No. 147, 125; Convention No. 148, 125; Convention No. 155, 125; Convention No. 157, 134; Convention No. 161, 125; Convention No. 162, 125; Convention No. 167, 125; Convention No. 168, 134; Convention No. 169, 245–46; Convention No. 170, 125; Convention No. 174, 125; Convention No. 176, 125; Convention No. 182, 49; Convention No. 183, 125; Declaration on Fundamental Principles and Rights at Work, 126, 280; Fact-Finding and Conciliation Commission, 283; Recommendation No. 135, 49; Tripartite Declaration of Principles concerning Multinational Enterprises, 283–84; tripartite structure, 279–80. *See also* Forced labor; International Programme on the Elimination of Child Labor; Labor rights

International Law Commission, 301
International Military Tribunal (Nuremberg), 9, 23, 296–99, 301; war crimes, 227. *See also* London Agreement
International Monetary Fund (IMF), 286–88, 290–91

International Organization of Employers, 280
International Programme for the Elimination of Child Labor (IPEC), 175, 284, 367. *See also* International Labor Organization
International Republican Institute, 117
International Trade Union Confederation (comprised of former International Confederation of Free Trade Unions and World Confederation of Labor), 280
Iran, 91, 135, 152, 159, 189, 254, 264
Iraq, 3, 56–57, 204, 220, 224, 239, 254–55, 297, 366
Ireland, 135, 166, 273, 316, 319, 321
Islam/Islamic law (Muslim), 14, 15, 99, 152–56, 181, 224–25, 231, 294, 297–98, 305. *See also* Religion
Israel, 31, 185, 264
Israeli Occupied Territories, 31
Italy, 15, 17, 22, 116, 309, 313, 316, 319, 321
Ivory Coast (Côte d'Ivoire), 174, 254, 334

Jamaica, 39, 326
Japan, 5, 18, 21–23, 273, 296, 299, 342; caste, 258; expression, 102; religion, 99; sexual slavery ("comfort women"), 22, 46; social security, 135. *See also* Tokyo tribunal
Jehovah's Witnesses, 222
Jews, Judaism (Jewish), 14, 20 B21, 84, 152, 181–82, 222, 294; anti-Semitism, 20, 105–6. *See also* Holocaust; Religion
Johannesburg Principles on National Security, Freedom of Expression and Access to Information, 103
Jordan, 19, 99, 151, 342
Juveniles: executions, 258, 368; international justice standards, 63

*Karaduman v. Turkey*, 154–55
*Karakurt v. Austria*, 77
Kazakhstan, 30, 325
Kenya, 334; child labor, 175; visit from special rapporteur on adequate housing, 159; visit from special rapporteur on toxic waste, 192
*Kitok v. Sweden*, 185
Korea, 22, 46
Korea, Democratic People's Republic of (North Korea), 103, 147–48, 189, 259

Korea, Republic of (South Korea), 103, 106, 352
Kosovo, ix, 32, 39, 303, 308–9; UN peacekeeping with human rights dimension, 254
Kurds, 32, 224
Kuwait, 65, 84, 204, 255, 297
Kyrgyzstan, 30, 325

Labor Rights, ix, 109–12, 245, 279–84, 287, 291, 318; repression of labor organizers, 11; strike, right to, 110–12; sweatshops, 11. *See also* Child labor; European Social Charter; International Labor Organization
Landmines, 209
Language rights, 19
*Lansman v. Finland*, 185
Laos, 166
Latvia, 19, 30, 254, 313, 321, 325
League of Arab States, 338
League of Nations, 18–19, 42–43, 268, 279
League of Nations Slavery, Servitude, Forced Labour and Similar Institutions and Practices Convention, 42–43
Leave, right to, 71–72
Lebanon, 19, 265–66
Lesotho, 334
*Leyla 'ahin v. Turkey*, 155
Liberia, 17, 99, 102, 205, 254, 261, 342, 353–54
Libya, 91, 204, 334
Liechtenstein, 313
Life, right to, 38–41, 147, 335, 338. *See also* Death penalty
Lithuania, 19, 30, 313, 321, 325
Locke, John, 17
London Agreement (Agreement for the Prosecution and Punishment of the Major War Criminals of the European Axis), 23, 222, 225–26, 227–30
*Lopez Ostra v. Spain*, 193
Luxembourg, 4, 313, 321

*M.A. v. Italy*, 116
*M.A.B. et al. v. Canada*, 97
Macedonia, former Yugoslav Republic of, 39, 74, 297–98, 313, 325
Magna Carta, 15, 71
Malawi, 352
Mali, 334
Malta, 313, 321

Mandela, Nelson, ix
Mandelstam, Andre Nicolayevitch, 19
Mao Zedung, 227
Marshall Islands, 264
*Marshall v. Canada*, 113
Masaryk, Jan, 20
Massera, Emilio, 355
Mauritania, 47, 334
Mauritius, 67, 273, 305, 334
*The Mayagna (Sumo) Awas Tingni Community v. Nicaragua*, 186
*M.C. Mehta v. Union of India*, 194
Menem, Carlos, 355
Mexico, 39, 78, 91, 102, 192, 197, 326, 331, 342
Mexico City Declaration on Cultural Policies, 179
Migrant workers, 271
Millennium Declaration, 198
Milošević, Slobodan, 299
Minnesota Advocates for Human Rights, 353–54
Minorities, 15, 16, 18–19, 31, 244–46, 342
*Miranda v. Arizona*, 64
Mixed (international and national) tribunals, 303–10
Moldova, 313, 325
Monaco, 313
Mongolia, 148
Monist approach to international law, 4–5, 343–45
Montenegro, 31, 74
Moreno Ocampo, Luis, 225
Morocco, 174
Mott, Lucretia, 17
Movement, freedom of, 70–73, 322
Mozambique, 142, 151, 189, 254, 334

Namibia, 92, 254, 259
Narcotics trafficking, 301
Nation, 15. *See also* Nationality; Sovereignty
National Democratic Institute, 117
National human rights institutions, 346–51
National security, 207–8, 213–20, 234–43. *See also* Humanitarian law
Nationality, 82–86
Natural law, 3
Nazi Regime, 20–22, 84, 296–97; Adolf Hitler, 20. *See also* Germany; London Agreement; International Military Tribunal; World War II

Nehru, Jawaharlal, 20,
Nepal, 39, 174, 175, 258–59, 352
Netherlands, 18, 84, 91, 167, 204, 313, 315–17, 321, 342, 344; bill of rights, 17; colonial power, 30; constitutional incorporation of treaties, 4, 344; discrimination, 35, 132; environment, 189; International Court of Justice, 268; International Criminal Tribunal for the former Yugoslavia, 229; social security, 135; visit from Special Rapporteur on toxic waste, 192; war crimes trial, 10, 304
*Neumeister v. Austria*, 315
New Caledonia, 30
New Zealand, 4, 89–89, 102, 111, 185, 260, 342–43
Nicaragua, 75, 175, 189, 254, 326, 331
Niger, 334
Nigeria, 133, 148, 166, 193, 200–201, 254, 304, 307, 334–36, 352
No power/no action doctrine, 257–58
*Nold v. Commission*, 322
Non-citizens, 16, 35, 67, 127–28, 256, 322. *See also* Aliens; Nationality
Non-derogable rights, 38, 60–61, 182, 207–8, 334
Nongovernmental organizations (NGOs), 8–9, 249, 314, 319, 338, 359–62, 366; consultative status with ECOSOC, 361; role in drafting treaties and other instruments, 359; role in ECOSOC resolution 1503, 260; role in Human Rights Committee, 274–75; role in preventing torture, 55–55; role in UN, 23–24, 264–65, 360–61; small arms, 209; thematic procedures, 263; truth commission, 353
Non-state actors, 235, 302. *See also* Business
Norms on the Responsibilities of Transnational Corporations and Other Business Enterprises with Regard to Human Rights, 26
Northern Ireland, 353. *See also* United Kingdom
Norway, 17, 185, 313, 316–17

Oloka-Onyango, Joe, 289–90
Oman, 174
Ombudsman, 345, 347
Open Society Institute, 306
Organization for Security and Cooperation in Europe (OSCE), 323–25; Contact Point for Roma and Sinti Issues (CPRSI), 324; Office for Democratic Institutions and Human Rights (ODIHR), 324; Permanent Council, 325; Representative on Freedom of the Media, 325. *See also* Conference on Security and Cooperation in Europe
Organization of African Trade Union Unity, 280
Organization of African Unity (OAU), 334–36. *See also* African Charter on Human and Peoples' Rights; African Court on Human and Peoples' Rights; African Union
Organization of American States (OAS), 116–17, 148, 186, 236, 325–33, 338. *See also* Charter of the Organization of American States
Organization of American States General Assembly, 331–32
OSCE High Commissioner for Minorities, 324–25
Oxfam, 209

Pacific Charter on Human Rights, 338
Pakistan, 82; child labor, 175
Palau, 264
Palestine (Palestinian authority), 19, 31, 32, 39, 159, 253, 259, 265–66, 284
Panama, 166, 326, 331, 352
Papua New Guinea, 307
*The Paquete Habana*, 345
Paraguay, 116, 192, 273, 326, 331
Paris Principles, on national human rights institutions, 346
*Park v. Republic of Korea*, 103
Participation in public affairs, right to, 113–19, 322. *See also* Elections
Peace, 18, 203–11, 222, 229
People's Union for Civil Liberties, 148
Permanent Court of International Justice, 91. *See also* International Court of Justice
Permanent Sovereignty over Natural Resources, General Assembly resolution, 92
Peru, 326, 331, 353; truth and reconciliation commission, 352; visit from special rapporteur on the right to health, 142
Philippines: forced prostitution, 22, 46; truth and reconciliation commission, 352

Philosophy of human rights, ix, 14–15
Pinheiro, Paulo Sérgio, 73
Pinochet, Augusto, 10. *See also* Chile
Pol Pot, 305. *See also* Cambodia
Poland, 18, 102, 313, 321, 342–43
Portugal, 30, 135, 259, 306, 313, 319, 321
Positive law, 3
Principles for the Protection of Persons with Mental Illness and the Improvement of Mental Health Care, 65
Principles of Medical Ethics relevant to the Role of Health Personnel, particularly Physicians, in the Protection of Prisoners and Detainees Against Torture and Other Cruel, Inhuman or Degrading Treatment or Punishment, 140
Principles on the Effective Prevention and Investigation of Extra-Legal, Arbitrary and Summary Executions, 61
Privacy, 67–69
Property, 91–96, 322, 338
Proposed American Declaration on the Rights of Indigenous Peoples, 186, 330
*Prosecutor v. Akayesu*, 231, 301
*Prosecutor v. Jelisic*, 223
*Prosecutor v. Karemera*, 301
*Prosecutor v. Kunarac, Kovac and Vokovic*, 231
*Prosecutor v. Nahimana, Barayagwiza and Ngeze*, 231
*Prosecutor v. Tadic*, 227
Protocol for the Suppression of Unlawful Acts Against the Safety of Fixed Platforms Locating on the Continental Shelf, 235
Protocol of Buenos Aires, 326. *See also* Charter of the Organization of American States
Protocol on the Suppression of Unlawful Acts of Violence at Airports Serving International Civil Aviation, 235
Protocol to the African Charter for the establishment of the African Court on Human and Peoples' Rights, 334, 336–37
Protocol to the African Charter on Human and Peoples' Rights on the Rights of Women in Africa, 201
Protocol to Prevent, Suppress and Punish Trafficking in Persons, especially Women and Children, Supplementing the United Nations Convention Against Transnational Organized Crime, 45
Prussia, 17

Rafael Saravia, Alvaro, 366–67
Rape, 11, 302; as crime against humanity, 367; Democratic Republic of Congo, 225; former Yugoslavia, 231, 367; Rape of Nanking, 21–22. *See also* Violence against women; Women
Ratification of human rights treaties, advantages, 6–7. *See also* International Covenant on Civil and Political Rights; International Covenant on Economic, Social and Cultural Rights; and other treaties
Reagan, Ronald, 116
*Realpolitik*, 6
Recommendation on Safeguarding Traditional and Popular Culture, 179
Refugees, ix, 14, 71, 74–81, 209, 244; number of refugees, 79, 367; UN definition of, 74–77; U.S. definition of, 75–77. *See also* Asylum; Convention and Protocol Relating to the Status of Refugees; Convention Governing the Specific Aspects of Refugee Problems in Africa; Movement, freedom of; UN High Commissioner for Refugees
Regional human rights systems, 311–41. *See also* African Charter of Human and Peoples' Rights; African Commission on Human and Peoples' Rights; African Court of Human Rights; African Union; Council of Europe; European Convention on Human Rights; European Union; Inter-American Commission on Human Rights; Inter-American Court of Human Rights; Organization of African Unity; Organization of American States; Organization for Security and Cooperation in Europe
Religion, 14, 15, 18. *See also* individual religions
Religion, freedom of, ix, 19, 76–77, 97–101, 245, 322, 342; clothing and, 152–56; Declaration, 100. *See also* Religion
Remedies: African Commission on Human and Peoples' Rights, 336; European Court of Human Rights, 315; Inter-

Remedies (*continued*)
American Court of Human Rights, 331–32; truth and reconciliation commissions, 354–55
Republic of China (Taiwan), 21–22, 32, 46
Reservations, 7, 269
Rhodesia, 259. *See also* Zimbabwe
Rights of Athenian Citizens, 14
Roma, 132, 134, 222, 319
Roman Catholic, 152
Romania, 16, 18, 142, 273, 313, 325
Rome Declaration of the World Food Summit, 145–46. *See also* Food and Agriculture Organization
Roosevelt, Eleanor, 342
Roosevelt, Franklin D., Four Freedoms Speech, 22
Rousseau, Jean-Jacques, 17
Russian Federation, Russia, 16, 21, 23, 91, 185, 189, 237, 254, 265, 313–14, 320, 325. *See also* Chechnya; Soviet Union
Rwanda, 19, 105, 238, 296–97, 299–301, 334; killing of Hutus, 224, 231, 299–300; national genocide trials, 301; UN peacekeeping with human rights dimension, 254 . *See also* International Criminal Tribunal for Rwanda

Safeguards Guaranteeing Protection of the Rights of Those Facing the Death Penalty, 61
San Marino, 313
Sanctions, 204
Sankey Declaration (Wells), 20
Sardinia, 17
Saro-Wiwa, Ken, 335
Saudi Arabia, 91, 152, 265
*Schuler-Zgraggen v. Switzerland*, 134–35
Security Council, UN, 203–5, 252–55, 263, 296–98, 300, 303, 308. *See also* United Nations
Self-defense, 206, 240
Self-determination, 15, 19, 26, 29–33, 253; U.S. approach, 29
Self-executing treaties, 5, 345
Sen, Amartya, 148
Senegal, 132, 334
Serbia, 31, 224, 298, 313, 352
Sexual orientation, 35, 78; Human Rights Committee, 68, 89, 90, 103–4
Shintoism, 14. *See also* Religion

Sierra Leone, 10, 254, 259, 303–5, 309, 352–53
Sikh, 152, 182
Singapore, 99, 102, 342
Single European Act (SEA), 321 . *See also* European Union
Slavery, 11, 15, 17, 42–52; sexual, 46, 302
Slovakia, 31, 313, 321, 325
Slovenia, 30, 74, 297, 313, 321
Small Arms Review Conference, 294
Smuts, Jan Christian, 20
*The Social and Economic Rights Action Center and the Center for Economic and Social Rights v. Nigeria*, 192–93, 336
Social security, 129–36
Somalia, 205, 254, 259
*Sosa v. Alvarez-Machain*, 367
South Africa, 273, 334, 342, 344; constitutional socioeconomic rights, 135, 142, 160–62, 166, 367–68; ECOSOC resolution 1503, 259; environment, 200; expression, 102–3; health, right to, 367–68; housing, right to, 160–62; International Labor Organization, 284; Truth and Reconciliation Commission, 352–56; UN peacekeeping with human rights dimension, 254; visit from special rapporteur on toxic waste, 192. *See also Apartheid*; Mandela
Sovereignty or sovereign equality, 15, 17
Soviet Union, 23, 30, 227. *See also* Russian Federation
Spain, 17, 30, 313, 321; Basques, 32; environment, 189; interpretation of constitutional rights, 344; social security, 135
Special Rapporteurs/Representatives/Experts, UN: country rapporteurs, 258–59; mandates, 262–63, 268; on adequate housing, 159; on education, 175, 262; on extreme poverty, 262; on foreign debt, 263; on freedom of expression, 262; on health, 263; on human rights defenders, 263; on human rights and international solidarity, 263; on human rights in countering terrorism, 263; on independence of judges and lawyers, 262; on internally displaced persons, 262; on mercenaries, 262; on migrants, 263; on minority issues, 263; on racism, 262; on religious intolerance, 100, 155–56, 262; on right to develop-

ment, 262; on right to food, 142–48, 263; on sale of children, 262; on summary or arbitrary executions, 39, 262; on torture, 262, 268; on toxic waste, 189, 191, 262; on trafficking in persons, 263; on transnational corporations and other business enterprises, 263; on violence against women, 262. *See also* Afghanistan; Bolivia; Burundi; Cambodia; Chile; Congo; Cuba; El Salvador; Equatorial Guinea; Guatemala; Haiti; Iran; Iraq; Myanmar (Burma); Palestine; Poland; Romania; Rwanda; Somalia; South Africa; Sudan; Togo; Yugoslavia
*Sporrong and Lönnroth*, 94
Sri Lanka, 4, 304; concluding observation of Committee on Economic, Social and Cultural Rights, 151; environment, 189; Tamils, 32, 85; truth and reconciliation commission, 352–53
Stalin, Joseph, 227
Standard Minimum Rules for the Treatment of Prisoners, 63, 64
Stanton, Elizabeth Cady, 17
State of emergency, 256
Stateless, 285. *See also* Nationality
Statutes of limitations (effect on international human rights law), 228
Stevens, John Paul, 345–46
*Stewart v. Canada*, 88–89
Stockholm Declaration of the UN Conference on the Human Environment, 189, 191, 197
*Stran Greek Refineries and Straits Andreadis v. Greece*, 35
Sub-Commission on Promotion and Protection of Human Rights (formerly Sub-Commission on Prevention of Discrimination and Protection of Minorities), UN, 252, 255–58; abolition of death penalty, 39; environment, 189, 191; food, right to, 145; globalization, 184; intellectual property, 183–84; replaced by Advisory Committee, 256; return, right to, 73; water, right to, 166. *See also* Commission on Human Rights; ECOSOC resolution 1235; ECOSOC resolution 1503; Human Rights Council
Sudan, 78; country-specific rapporteur, 259; Darfur, 148, 22–25; International Criminal Court, 10, 238, 303; UN peacekeeping with human rights dimension, 254
*Sunday Times v. United Kingdom*, 104
Supplementary Convention on the Abolition of Slavery, 44, 46, 49
Supreme Court, U.S., 75, 77–78, 345–46; expression, 105; juvenile executions, 258, 368; labor rights, 126; private homosexual behavior, 68
Suriname, 326, 331
Sweden, 17, 94, 185, 273, 313, 316–17, 319, 321, 344, 347
Switzerland, 11, 17–18, 134, 141, 155, 273–74, 313
Syria, 19, 259

Tajikistan, 30
Tanzania, 167, 175, 229, 300, 334. *See also* International Criminal Tribunal for Rwanda
Taylor, Charles, 304
Ten Commandments, 14
Terrorism, 204, 206, 213–20, 234–43, 365
Thailand, 175, 189
Tibet, 32
Timor-Leste, 31, 254, 303, 308–9, 352–53. *See also* UN Transitional Administration in East Timor
Tito, Josip Broz, 297
Togo, 19, 70, 78, 334
Tokyo tribunal, 9, 23, 227–28, 296, 299, 301
Torture, ix 3, 53–58, 306–7, 365; definition, 55; Human Rights Committee General Comment, 276; Inter-American Convention to Prevent and Punish Torture, 330; Iraq, 366. *See also* Convention Against Torture and Other Cruel, Inhuman or Degrading Treatment or Punishment
Trade, 141–42, 183–85. *See also* World Trade Organization
Trade-Related Aspects of Intellectual Property (TRIPS), 183–84
Trafficking in children and other persons, 11, 244, 246
Trafficking in human organs, 11
Treaties, 4; bilateral, 4; interpretation, 345; multilateral, 4, 6; self-executing, 5, 345
Treaty Establishing a Constitution for Europe, 322

Treaty Establishing the European Atomic Energy Community, 321
Treaty Establishing the European Economic Community, 321
Treaty on European Union, 321
Treaty-based procedures, 249, 271–78
Trinidad and Tobago, 98, 301, 326
Trusteeship system, 30–31
Truth and reconciliation commissions, 352–58
Tunisia, 199–200, 237, 273, 291
Turkey, 7–8, 16, 18, 19, 39, 74, 77, 98, 152–56, 175, 189, 297, 309, 313–14, 316
Turkmenistan, 254

Udagama, Deepika, 290
Uganda, 10, 93, 166–67, 175, 238, 303, 334, 352–53
Ukraine, 313, 325
UNICEF. *See* United Nations Children's Emergency Fund
United Kingdom (UK), 15–16, 91, 273, 304, 309; colonial power, 30; common law, 4; dualist, 4–5, 344–45; European Convention, 313, 316, 344; European Union, 321; headscarves, 98; House of Lords, 75–76; Human Rights Act 1998, 5, 344; Joint Parliamentary Committee, 344–45; labor rights, 111; leave, right to, 71–72; role in League of Nations, 18, 19; role in Nuremberg tribunal, 23; role in formation of UN, 23; role in World War II, 21–22; Security Council member, 254; Scotland, 88, 204; slavery, 17; terrorism, 206, 213; visit from special rapporteur on education, 175; visit from special rapporteur on toxic waste, 192
United Nations (UN), 3, 8, 14, 34, 78, 129, 249, 251–71, 295, 352; abolition of slavery, 42, 45; Commission on Sustainable Development, 198–99; Compensation Commission, 255; Conference on Population and Devloment, 166; Counter-Terrorism Committee, 237, 255; Development Programme (UNDP), 200, 291; drafting treaties and instruments, 3, 6, 8, 29; early history, 22–24; members, 38, 253; Secretary-General, 236, 252, 261, 265, 267; Special Rapporteur on the human rights situation in former Yugoslavia, 298; specialized agencies, 279–93; 295; terrorism, 235–38, 240; truth commissions, 353; Water Conference, 165. *See also* Commission on Human Rights; Economic and Social Council; General Assembly; Human Rights Council; International Court of Justice; International Criminal Court; International Criminal Tribunal for the Former Yugoslavia; International Criminal Tribunal for Rwanda; Office of the High Commissioner for Human Rights; Secretary-General; Security Council; Special rapporteurs; Sub-Commission on the Promotion and Protection of Human Rights; Treaty-based procedures; UNHCR
UN Charter, 4, 24–25, 29–30, 34, 206, 208, 249, 252, 311, 335, 365; Article 1, 24–25, 170, 203, 253, 359; Article 2, 170, 203; Article 2(4), 203; Article 2(7), 253; Article 4142, 203–04; Article 51, 205–06, 240; Article 52, 205; Articles 5556, 25, 34–35, 197, 253, 256, 359; Article 68, 25, 255; Article 71, 361; Article 103, 289; Chapter VII, 203–5, 237, 254; Charter-based procedures, 252, 263; creation, 365; parties, 38; Preamble, 24; ratification, 212. *See also* International Court of Justice
UN Children's Fund (UNICEF), 291
UN Conference on Environment and Development (UNCED) (Rio de Janeiro), 189, 191, 197–98, 294
UN Decade for Human Rights Education, 170
UN Economic Commission for Europe Convention on Access to Information, Public Participation in Decision-Making and Access to Justice in Environmental Matters, 190,194
UN Educational, Scientific, Cultural Organization (UNESCO), 171, 174–75, 179, 284–85; Principles on International Cultural Cooperation, 179
UN High Commissioner for Human Rights or Office of the High Commissioner for Human Rights (OHCHR), 167, 252, 260, 267–68, 274, 289, 294
UN High Commissioner for Refugees (UNHCR), 71–72, 74, 76, 79, 85, 255, 285–86, 367. *See also* Refugees

Index    431

UN International Commission of Inquiry on East Timor, 307
UN Mission Interim Administration in Kosovo (UNMIK), 308–9
UN Transitional Administration in East Timor (UNTAET), 307–8
UN Voluntary Fund for Victims of Torture, 53
United States, 273–74, 304–5, 353; African Americans, 32, 114–15; Alien Tort Claims Act, 367; colonial power, 30; death penalty for juvenile offenders, 39, 258, 368; Declaration of Independence, 16; expatriation, 72; federal court, 252; Human Rights Council, 264; Inter-American Commission on Human Rights, 252; international law as guide to interpretation of U.S. law, 345–46; labor rights, 126; national security strategy, 206, 240; opposition to International Criminal Court, 230–31, 301; Report to Committee on the Elimination of Racial Discrimination, 114–15; Security Council member, 254; slavery, 17; terrorism (war on terror), 206, 213–15, 219–20, 234, 239–40, 365; torture and ill-treatment, 56–57; visit from special rapporteur on education, 175; visit from special rapporteur on toxic waste, 192; voting, 114–15; Western European and Other Group, 260. *See also* U.S. Constitution
U.S. Constitution, 342; Article III, 345; Bill of Rights, 17; Eighth Amendment, 345–46, 368; First Amendment, 105; Fourteenth Amendment, 36–37; supremacy clause, 5, 345; Thirteenth Amendment, 49
*United States v. Sanga*, 49
U.S. Virgin Islands, 30
Universal Declaration of Human Rights (UDHR), 3, 4, 10, 24–26, 29, 76, 121, 160, 163, 170, 189, 338, 342, 344; Article 2, 34, 48; Article 3, 38, 189; Article 4, 42, 44–45, 120; Article 5, 53; Article 6, 34; Article 7, 34; Article 8, 59; Article 9, 48, 59; Article 10, 48, 59; Article 11, 48, 59; Article 12, 67; Article 13, 70; Article 14, 74; Article 15, 82; Article 16, 87, 245; Article 17, 91–92; Article 18, 97, 244; Article 19, 48, 102; Article 20, 109–10, 244; Article 21, 113, 116; Article 22, 120–21, 129–30; Article 23, 120–21, 244; Article 24, 120–21, 124; Article 25, 120–21, 129–30, 136, 144, 150, 156, 189; Article 26, 120–21, 169; Article 27, 120–21, 177; Article 28, 245; drafting, 255, 257, 359, 365; economic, social, and cultural rights, 25; interpretation of Articles 55–56 of UN Charter, 25, 365; Part of International Bill of Human Rights, 4, 25, 130; Preamble, 206
Universal Declaration on Cultural Diversity, 179
Universal Declaration on the Eradication of Hunger and Malnutrition, 144. *See also* Food, right to
Universal Declaration on the Human Genome and Human Rights, 284
Universal jurisdiction, 10–11
Uruguay, 326, 331, 352
Uzbekistan, 30, 237, 261–62

*Velásquez Rodriguez Judgment*, 332
Vanatu, 174
Vatican, 4
Venezuela, 91, 116, 166, 264, 326, 331
Videla, Jorge, 355
Vienna Convention on Consular Relations, 64
Vienna Convention on Diplomatic Relations, 93
Vienna Declaration and Programme of Action, 170, 180, 294, 347
Vietnam, 9, 305
Violence against women, 181, 246. *See also* Declaration on the Elimination of Violence Against Women; Female Genital Mutilation; Inter-American Convention on the Prevention, Punishment and Eradication of Violence Against Women; Rape
*Virginia v. Black*, 105
Vote, right to, 113–19. *See also* Democracy; Elections

War crimes, 222, 225–27, 302, 307. *See also* Humanitarian law; International Criminal Court; International Criminal Tribunal for Rwanda; International Criminal Tribunal for the Former Yugoslavia
Warren, Earl, 82
Water, right to, 137, 163–69
Weizmann, Chaim, 20

Wells, H. G., 20
Western Sahara, 30, 32, 254, 259
Westphalia, Treaty of, 14–15, 72
Wiesel, Elie, ix
Wilberforce, Clarkson, 17
Wilson, Woodrow, 18, 29
*Winata v. Australia*, 87–89
Women, 200–201, 244, 246; claims of cultural relativism, 7, 181–82; early history of rights, 15, 17, 34; girl children, 304; Guidelines on Women Refugee Claimants Fearing Gender-Related Persecution, 78; quota for women in public office, 116; social security, 132–33. *See also* Commission on the Status of Women; Committee on the Elimination of Discrimination Against Women; Convention on the Elimination of All Forms of Discrimination Against Women; Convention on the Political Rights of Women; Discrimination; Female Genital Mutilation; Protocol to the African Charter on Human and Peoples' Rights on the Rights of Women in Africa; Violence against women
Work-related rights, 124–29. *See also* Forced labor; International Labor Organization; Labor rights
Working Group on Arbitrary Detention, 65, 262
Working Group on Enforced or Involuntary Disappearances, 262
Working Group on Indigenous Populations, 186

Working Group on people of African descent, 263
World Bank, 286–91
World Conference Against Racism, 294–95
World Conference on Human Rights, 293–94, 347
World Conference on Women, 294
World Declaration on Education for All, 170–71
World Federation of Trade Unions, 280
World Food Conference, 144–145
World Food Summit, 145, 294
World Health Organization (WHO), 141, 147, 166, 181, 291
World Organization Against Torture, 54
World Summit on Social Development, 294
World Summit on Sustainable Development, 159, 197, 199
World Trade Organization (WTO), 141–42, 286–90; dispute settlement mechanism, 141. *See also* Agreement on the Application of Sanitary and Phytosanitary Measures; Intellectual property
World War I, 18, 20–23, 42, 84, 228, 230, 268, 312
World War II, 11, 14, 20–23, 42–43, 46, 74, 228, 230, 286

Yemen, 166, 239
Yugoslavia, 18, 30, 224, 231. *See also* International Criminal Tribunal for the Former Yugoslavia

Zambia, 166, 174, 291
Zimbabwe, 352. *See also* Rhodesia

# Acknowledgments

The authors are grateful for the assistance of Bridget Marks as well as Shervon Cassim, Carlos Castresana, Jovana Davidovic, Mamadou Dieng, Leonardo Filippini, Ilhan Isik, Marina Jovic, Eve Lotter, Daniel O'Donnell, Andrea Park, Jennifer Porter, Michael Rawson, Nick Velde, Sam Walling and Colleen Windler in researching and preparing this book. The authors also wish to thank the John D. and Catherine T. MacArthur Foundation and the University of San Francisco for their support of this project as well as many other individuals, nongovernmental, and intergovernmental organizations for providing useful comments, suggestions, and information, including Michael Dottridge, Sam Garkawe, Alaa Kaoud, Mark P. Lindberg, Fionnuala Ni Aoláin, Tania Penovic, Nigel Rodley, and Kathryn Sikkink. In addition, the authors wish to acknowledge the assistance of Chelsea Haley Nelson and Mary Rumsey in helping with the bibliographical references and of Mary Thacker in performing secretarial services.

www.ingramcontent.com/pod-product-compliance
Lightning Source LLC
LaVergne TN
LVHW040731250326
834688LV00031B/236